Productivity Through People

Productivity Through People

WILLIAM B. WERTHER, JR.
Chair Professor of Executive Management
University of Miami

WILLIAM A. RUCH
Professor of Operations Management
Arizona State University

LYNNE McCLURE
President
McClure Associates

WEST PUBLISHING COMPANY
St. Paul • New York • Los Angeles • San Francisco

Library of Congress Cataloging-in-Publication Data

Werther, Jr., William B.
  Productivity through people.

Copy Editor: Steve Conway
Text Design: Rick Chafian
Cover Design: Taly Design Group
Composition: Rolin Graphics

  Bibliography: p.
  Includes index.
  1. Industrial productivity—Addresses, essays, lectures. 2. Efficiency,
Industrial—Addresses, essays, lectures. I. Ruch, William A. II. McClure, Lynne.
III. Title.
HD56.W47 1986   658.3'14   85-22446
ISBN 0-314-95573-9

Contents

Chapter 11 Productivity and People Development 230

Chapter 12 Productivity and Organization Development 242

List of Readings

Chapter 5   Eugene J. Koprowski, "Cultural Myths: Clues to Effective Management," *Organizational Dynamics* (Autumn 1983):39–51.

J. Sterling Livingston, "Pygmalion in Management," *Harvard Business Review* (July–August 1969):81–89.

Chapter 6   Donald B. Fedor and Gerald R. Ferris, "Integrating OB Mod with Cognitive Approaches to Motivation," *Academy of Management Review* 6, no. 1 (January 1981):115–25.

Chapter 7   Andrew Oldenquist, "On Belonging to Tribes," *Newsweek* (April 5, 1982):9.

Roger D'Aprix, "The Oldest (and Best) Way to Communicate With Employees," *Harvard Business Review* (September–October 1982):31–32.

Chapter 8   D.L. Landen, "The Future of Participative Management," *Productivity Brief* 16 (August 1982):1–8.

Gary P. Latham, Larry L. Cummings, and Terrence R. Mitchell, "Behavioral Strategies to Improve Productivity," *Organizational Dyanamics* (Winter 1981):5–23.

Chapter 9   Lester C. Thurow, "Where Management Fails," *Newsweek* (December 7, 1981):78.

Malcolm S. Knowles, "Releasing the Energy of Others —Making Things Happen," *Journal of Management Development* 2, no. 2 (1983):26–35.

Chapter 10   Richard Pascale, "Fitting New Employees Into the Company Culture," *Fortune* (May 28, 1984):29–40.

Chapter 11   C. Jackson Grayson, Jr., "Training's Crucial Role in the Coming Battle to Restore Productivity," *Training* (October 1980):82.

Andrew S. Grove, "Why Training is the Boss's Job," *Fortune* (January 23, 1984):93–96.

Chapter 12   William Ouchi, "Going from A to Z: The Steps," *Theory Z: How American Business Can Meet the Japanese Challenge* (Reading, Mass.: Addison-Wesley 1981):99–128.

Anthony T. Cobb and Newton Margulies, "Organizational Development: A Political Perspective," *Academy of Management Review* 6, no. 1 (January 1981):49–59.

Chapter 13   William B. Werther, Jr., "Going in Circles with Quality Circles?—Management Development Implications," *Journal of Management Development* 2, no. 1 (1983):3–18.

William B. Werther, Jr., "Productivity Improvement Through People," *Arizona Business* (February 1981):14–19.

Chapter 14   Edward E. Lawler, "Whatever Happened to Incentive Pay?" *New Management* 1, no. 4 (1984):37–41.

Carla O'Dell, "Sharing the Productivity Payoff," *Productivity Brief* 24 (n.d.).

Chapter 15   Glenn H. Felix and James L. Riggs, "Productivity Measurement by Objectives," *National Productivity Review* 2, no. 4 (Autumn 1983):386–93.

Charles E. Craig and R. Clark Harris, "Total Productivity Measurement at the Firm Level," *Sloan Management Review* 14, no. 3 (Spring 1973):13–28.

Chapter 16   Robert B. McKersie and Janice A. Klein, "Productivity: The Industrial Relations Connection," *National Productivity Review* (Winter 1983–84):26–35.

John Hoerr, "Collective Bargaining Is in Danger Without Labor-Law Reform," *Business Week* (July 16, 1984):29.

Chapter 17   Ira Gregerman, "Chapter One—The Rise of the Knowledge Worker," *Knowledge Worker Productivity* (New York: Amacon, 1981):7–18.

William A. Ruch, "The Measurement of White-Collar Productivity," *National Productivity Review* (Autumn 1982):416–26.

Chapter 18   W. Edwards Deming, "Improvement of Quality and Productivity through Action by Management," *National Productivity Review* (Winter 1981–82):12–22.

Frank S. Leonard and W. Earl Sasser, "The Incline of Quality," *Harvard Business Review* (September–October 1982):163–71.

Chapter 19   William A. Ruch and William B. Werther, Jr., "Productivity Strategies at TRW," *National Productivity Review* (Spring 1983):109–25.

Chapter 20   Richard E. Kopelman, "Improving Productivity through Objective Feedback: A Review of the Evidence," *National Productivity Review* (Winter 1982–83):43–55.

States L. Clawson and Carol Ann Meares, "Productivity Information: A Key to Competitiveness," *National Productivity Review* (Winter 1983–84):15–25.

Foreword

Incremental gains in U.S. productivity improvement are inadequate to meet the rigorous test of worldwide competition. We need quantum advances. Yet many of the fifty or more companies I work with each year are reluctant to recognize the need for a major leap forward. Their internal focus of "How do we make U.S. firms *better*?" must be replaced with "How do we make U.S. firms the *best in the world*?"

A key part of the answer is greater attention to productivity improvement. Unfortunately, while office and professional workers constitute as much as eighty percent of the total payroll in some firms, many mangers still view productivity as a manufacturing problem. The result is that productivity efforts are often disjointed, disconnected, short-term programs aimed mainly at symptoms such as absenteeism, overtime, or poor quality work. The real benefits of productivity improvement come from people working together toward organizational objectives. This meshing of hundreds, thousands, and even tens of thousands of employees demands a strategic connection between corporate values, business strategy, and productivity strategies. Only the integration of these variables is likely to lead to long-term success.

The driving force in this integration of values and strategies are innovative chief executive officers (CEOs). These CEOs have a sixth sense that tells them when it's time to look for a new approach. They are not only driven to innovate, but they drive their organizations to find new markets, products, and processes by instilling and supporting the appropriate corporate values. They and their key executives realize that technology, automation, and innovations can fail without a dedicated workforce. But creating a corporate culture that is receptive to employee needs cannot be done by senior managers alone. Employee participation in the decisions that affect them is necessary for the improvement of productivity and quality. Not only does the organization benefit from the employees' unique perspective, but involvement gives the employees a feeling of challenge and ownership in the change process. If employees are part of the process, change is more likely to be supported than resisted.

A people-oriented corporate culture is most likely when leaders create a team structure in which employees can address the problems that affect them. I envision these teams functioning initially under the guidance of a supervisor or senior employee, with problem-solving techniques taught to both supervisors and employees. Problem-solving teams thus become a vehicle for both improved job satisfaction and enhanced productivity.

Team-based employee involvement does not just happen. Ideally, top management supports a comprehensive model that can be followed throughout the organization. Obviously, a natural and appropriate reluctance exists among many CEOs to mandate a particular approach, especially where multiple plants, divisions and subdivisions function autonomously. But a broad model that offers far-flung operations a framework for guidance can be provided.

Whatever framework is used—and many are suggested throughout this book, from traditional organizational development approaches to a modern productivity model we used at TRW, Inc.—it must be customized to the individual organization.

Adapting bits and pieces from other business cultures, particularly from Japan, does little good unless they are truly fitted to the individual organization. A custom-fitted model of productivity improvement—one that involves employees and *at the same time* enables management to encourage and monitor productivity improvement at all levels—allows corporate leaders to achieve short-run benefits with a system that will survive and produce long-term results.

My twenty-five years of installing and managing productivity efforts convince me that long-lasting results require more than just an effective structure. First and foremost, changes in the culture must be modeled and supported by top managers. They too may have to change. A program developed for production workers and installed without senior role models will not have permanence. Second, efforts to motivate employees without including them in the decision-making process will have a short-term effect, if any at all. A balance must exist between a quality of work life (people) orientation and a productivity (task) orientation. Third, performance must be measured and employees must receive feedback. In particular, good performance must be positively reinforced.

For productivity in the United States to meet worldwide competition, we must increase employee awareness of productivity improvement. That awareness can only come by educating managers—from supervisors to CEOs—about the emerging management technologies that are available to enhance productivity through people. This book provides that basic understanding—an understanding every manager must have if we are to achieve the quantum productivity gains necessary for continued prosperity and the preservaiton of our free-enterprise system.

Hank Conn
President, Tarkenton and Company
Atlanta, Georgia

Preface

*The wealth and well-being of any society depends
on the productivity of its people.*
THE AUTHORS

Productivity Through People combines a broad overview of productivity management with the insights of many contributors to explain the role people play in productivity improvement. People—whether workers or managers—are the key resource available to any society that seeks to improve its material well-being. Land, capital, energy, technology, information , and other resources are essential, but *people* ultimately decide how these resources are best used.

Yet, in our teaching—both in academe and industry—no single source offered our students an overview of productivity management and its behavioral implications. Too often, students and managers alike emphasized capital or technology or some other input to the productive process without appreciating the central role of people. We recognized a need for a book that would:

Serve as a foundation for productivity management courses in colleges and universities.

Supplement traditional courses in personnel management, organization behavior and production/operations management with an applied perspective.

Interest non-student readers in the challenging study of productivity management.

Reflect the diversity of issues and perspectives faced by any attempt to improve productivity.

Offer business leaders a single sourcebook through which the reeducation of managers could start.

THEME AND FOCUS

This book is based on the assumptions that productivity is crucial to our efficient use of limited resources and that people truly are the most important resource in organizations. Readers will sense our commitment to helping organizations and people benefit from each other. High productivity requires that both managers and employees satisfy each other's needs within the framework of good business judgment.

The purpose of this book is to pull together the best ideas about management and productivity. It summarizes what the experts have said, comments on the usefulness of these ideas to organizations and gives expert views on specific topics. Our focus is practical, so readers will be able to apply this knowledge to work situations. We have drawn on the ideas of practitioners, behaviorists, economists, and our own writings to maintain a tight focus on the basic elements that impact on organizations' efforts to improve productivity through people.

BALANCED COVERAGE

Our interdisciplinary approach allows us to give the best coverage of a complex topic: how to get the most productivity by meeting people's needs.

Part One, "Productivity Management," introduces the concept of productivity and its effects on management issues. Key productivity models are discussed in terms of how they relate to a systems approach to organizations.

Part Two, "Individual Productivity," presents the ways human needs, perceptions and motivations affect productivity. With this knowledge, readers will understand how to manage in ways that enhance individual productivity and satisfaction.

Part Three, "Organizational Productivity," focuses on group dynamics, decision structures and leadership. Most people work at the group rather than the individual level, so productive management requires an awareness of the ways groups function, make decisions and follow leaders.

Part Four, "Culture and Climate," deals with the dynamics of individuals and groups interacting with the organizational environment. Individuals' values and the development of people and organizations all contribute to the productivity of an organization.

Part Five, "Productivity Frameworks," addresses employee involvement. Quality of work life (QWL) programs, gainsharing plans and measurement methods are key factors in making productivity important to employees.

Part Six, "Organizational Productivity Perspectives," deals with union, white-collar and quality issues. Each segment of the work force has its own objectives and issues. Productive managers must understand how to measure—and get—quality work from employees who may have very different value systems and goals.

Part Seven, "Productivity Systems," discusses ways to apply employee communications and other systems within organizational settings. Both micro-level (systems internal to companies) and macro-level (associations devoted to productivity) considerations are presented.

Selected articles follow each chapter, giving the reader the varied viewpoints of numerous experts. To leave maximum space for the dozens of readings found in the body, the text chapters were kept extremely brief, but they still offer a balanced overview of productivity management.

KEY FEATURES

Productivity Through People incorporates a number of features that add to the usefulness and relevance of the material. Each chapter:

1. Contains a text that provides a succinct overview of the topic's relation to people and productivity.
2. Supports the text with one or more readings from a wide variety of experts in a variety of disciplines.
3. Starts with a brief quotation from a widely recognized expert to reflect one perspective and stimulate interest.
4. Ends with a brief synopsis of the accompanying article and a summary of the text.
5. Offers review questions that help the reader integrate the concepts in the chapter.
6. Includes stimulating articles designed to broaden the reader's understanding of the topics covered.

Additional references—for those who have a special interest in the sub-topics of a given chapter—are provided in an appendix at the back of the book.

ACKNOWLEDGMENTS

Our book is but a stepping stone in a long line of works by scholars and practitioners. We owe a debt to them all.

Our deepest debt is to those closest to us: our families, friends and colleagues. In particular, we would like to thank Dean Jack Borsting of the University of Miami, and Arizona State University Deans Nick Henry and Bill Seidman. (The latter served as cochair of the 1983 White House Conference on Productivity.) Jack Grayson, founder of the American Productivity Center in Houston, also deserves a note of appreciation for further stimulating our interest (and the nation's) in productivity management.

An unpayable debt of gratitude goes to Alec Courtelis for his unself-ish support of higher education.

Although we have worked with many chief productivity officers (CPOs) and other executives throughout North America, we are especially appreciative of our work with Hank Conn, formerly the CPO at TRW, Inc., and now president of Tarkenton and Company, and his able successor at TRW, Ed Stiegerwald. We would also like to express our appreciation to: John Howe of ARCO; Bill Bacigalupo and Betty Nadeau of Combustion Engineering; Mary Rabaut and Dan Yaest of General Motors; Randy Main of Hershey Foods; Doug Borne and Ted Pate of Pennzoil's Duval subsidary; Elias Hebeka of Warner Lambert; David Braunstein of NASA; Jim Bennitt of Western Technologies; Rich Warden of Penton Learning Systems; Chuck Eveland of the Alaskan Medicaid Rate Commission; and Al Davies of the Del E. Webb Corporation.

Although our debt to fellow academics extends back to Adam Smith, we are particularly grateful to our contemporaries: Professors Bob Wright of Pepperdine University, John Kendrick of George Washington University, Don Harvey of Eastern Washington University, Everett Adam of the University of Missouri, Keith Davis, Bob Goyer, and Jim Hershauer of Arizona State University.

Our deep appreciation extends to Dick Fenton of West Publishing. His belief in this book allowed it to be published.

A special note of appreciation is also due to Sue Meador, a partner in the Houston-based consulting firm, The Core Group.

To each of you—and to many others we failed to mention—thank you for the keen insights that have benefited this book. Where we failed to heed your good counsel, the blame rests squarely with us.

PART ONE

Productivity Management

1

Productivity and Management

Progress in improving productivity will come from employees and managers wanting to do things differently and better on a daily basis.

C. JACKSON GRAYSON[1]

Productivity is the ratio of outputs to inputs. Outputs consist of an organization's goods and services—that is, anything of value produced by the organization. Within a department, the output might be a report. For an entire organization, the output is whatever the organization sells in the marketplace. Inputs consist of capital, labor, materials, and energy—the things which are combined to produce the output.[2]

The objective of productivity improvement is to increase the ratio of outputs to inputs. This can be done in five ways:

$\frac{++}{+}$ Most organizations try to improve their outputs (the numerator of the ratio) by adding more inputs (the denominator). They hope that these new additions of labor, capital, materials, and energy will generate proportionate increases in output.

$\frac{-}{--}$ Another way to improve productivity is to reduce outputs more slowly than inputs, an especially common approach when sales are falling. Massive layoffs and plant closures in the auto industry during the 1980s represented the automobile companies' attempts to reduce inputs faster than sales (outputs) were falling, in order to improve productivity.

$\frac{0}{-}$ In some cases, outputs are stagnant (usually because sales are not increasing). In these cases, management can increase productivity by reducing inputs. Often, this is done through an employment freeze, or by selling off unneeded assets, such as surplus land or equipment.

$\frac{+}{0}$ If a firm can increase outputs without increasing inputs, the net effect is also a productivity gain. This approach might be especially useful in slow-growing industries.

$\frac{+}{-}$ In rare circumstances, management may actually be able to increase outputs while reducing inputs. For example, in the forty years since commercial television first became popular, television manufacturers have been able to increase the size and quality (outputs) of their products while actually using fewer human and material resources (inputs).

There is still another way to improve productivity. This one does not involve changing the quantity of outputs or inputs. Instead, the same inputs are used to produce a higher-quality output, thereby improving productivity. Clearly, if the same number of inputs result in a better product, the "output" has increased—even though the number of output units may remain the same.

Organizations that do not improve productivity are destined to fail. If enough firms fail, so does the industry. If enough industries fail, the well-being of society declines and perhaps also fails, as the history of civilization suggests.

THEME AND THESIS: "PRODUCTIVITY THROUGH PEOPLE"

The common element in all productivity improvement is people. It is people who make the ratio bigger; it is people who figure out better ways to use materials; it is people who decide the best way to improve product quality. People are the driving force in any productivity improvement effort.[3] As a slogan in one plant puts it, "Assets make things possible, people make things happen."

But management is paid to *manage* the organization, and management is therefore ultimately responsible for improving productivity.[4] Unfortunately, management faces two major problems here. The first problem is that most employees have a limited understanding of productivity. Many people think productivity improvement means a "speed up." Others feel that improving productivity means making people work harder, often for the same pay and benefits. Another misconception is that improving productivity means increasing profits while reducing jobs, since there appears to be only so much work available, and any effort to get that work done more efficiently must result in fewer jobs.[5]

Management's second problem is that many employees view any effort to improve productivity as "just another program."[6] These employees feel that the "new productivity improvement effort" will fade away and be forgotten, just like previous programs related to safety, quality, and energy conservation. And unfortunately, many times these employees are right. They have seen quality, cost-saving, attendance, safety, and other programs come and go. Why should productivity improvement be any different? Beyond expressing general skepticism, employees may right-fully ask, "What's in it for me?" If management does not identify specific benefits for employees, employees are not likely to increase productivity except through fear of punishment.

Along with employees' misconceptions about productivity, there is an even more fundamental problem: Many managers have only a mini-mum understanding of how productivity is related to behavior. With a more thorough understanding of both employee motivation and produc-tivity improvement techniques, managers (and potential managers) could make productivity improvement a continuous process.

THE PLAN OF THE BOOK

This book is divided into seven parts (twenty chapters). Part I, "Produc-tivity Management," defines productivity and explains its implications for society, organizations and individual workers. The last chapter re-views a variety of productivity models, in order to explain the factors in-fluencing productivity and to show where managers may successfully intervene to boost productivity.

Part II, "Individual Productivity," addresses the human side of pro-ductivity. Part II begins with a look at basic theories about human needs and perceptions, and concludes with a chapter on productivity and human motivation.

Part III, "Organizational Productivity," takes a broader look at human productivity. It examines the roles of group dynamics and decision struc-tures within an organization and shows how they affect productivity and leadership.

Part IV, "Culture and Climate," discusses the role that formal and in-formal values play in helping organizations achieve high productivity and excellence. Special attention is paid to the importance of instilling these values in people through training and development, and to the team-building processes that underlie organization development.

Part V, "Productivity Frameworks," addresses the connections among productivity, quality of work-life, and employee involvement. Discussion then turns to gainsharing and other incentives for improving productivity. The concluding chapter reviews productivity and ways of measuring productivity—an important point for any organization that wants to monitor and reward productivity improvement.

Part VI, "Organizational Productivity Perspectives," points out other groups' views of productivity. It discusses productivity and unions, to il-lustrate some of the opportunities and barriers that confront managers who want to improve productivity in the unionized environment. Subse-quent chapters in Part VI review the effects of productivity on white-collar workers, an increasingly important factor in attempts to enhance productivity. The connection between productivity and quality is also discussed, since improvements in the number of units produced does very little good if quality deteriorates.

Part VII, "Productivity Systems," discusses productivity strategies used by various organizations and shows what an essential role corporate commitment plays in successful efforts to improve productivity. Part VII describes sources of productivity information, both within and outside of the organization.

SUMMARY

Productivity improvement is getting more out of what is put in; in other words, producing more and better goods and services with inputs of labor, capital, materials, and energy. The proper mix of physical resources and effective management is what productivity is all about. Each chapter of this book and each reading addresses one aspect of improving the output-to-input ratio.

SELECTED READINGS OVERVIEW

The first reading is a short essay drawn from the United States Department of Labor's Bureau of Labor Statistics publication entitled, "Productivity and the Economy: A Chart Book." The essay defines labor productivity and describes various ways in which it can serve as an index for measuring productivity improvement.

The second article is entitled, "Managing Our Way to Economic Decline." In this article, Hayes and Abernathy, both professors at Harvard Business School, discuss how modern management principles actually cause, rather than cure, poor economic performance. The authors review some of the commonly cited causes of productivity decline and discuss their implications for productivity improvement.

Next Chapter

The next chapter, "Productivity Implications," examines the ramifications of productivity improvement. Why is productivity improvement so important? What happens if our national productivity does not keep up with that of our trading partners?

Review Questions

1. Define productivity. Why is labor productivity considered to be only a partial measure?
2. Describe the six ways for improving productivity.
3. Who is responsible for productivity improvement? Why?

4. Describe the recommendations found in "Managing Our Way to Economic Decline," by Hayes and Abernathy.

5. Defend or refute the following statement: "Productivity improvement means working harder." Refer to points in the chapter and the readings.

Part I.
Productivity and How It is Measured

Productivity is a concept that expresses the relationship between the quantity of goods and services produced—output—and the quantity of labor, capital, land, energy, and other resources that produced it—input. Productivity can be measured in two ways. One way relates the output of an enterprise, industry, or economic sector to a single input such as labor or capital. The other relates output to a composite of inputs, combined so as to account for their relative importance. The choice of a particular productivity measure depends on the purpose for which it is to be used.

The most generally useful measure of productivity relates output to the input of labor time—output per hour, or its reciprocal, unit labor requirements. This kind of measure is used widely because labor productivity is relevant to most economic analyses, and because labor is the most easily measured input. Relating output to labor input provides a tool not only for analyzing productivity, but also for examining labor costs, real income, and employment trends.

Labor productivity can be measured readily at several levels of aggregation: The business economy, its component sectors, industries, or plants. Nearly all of the productivity measures used in this [book] are measures of output per hour. Depending on the components of the measure used and the con-

text, labor productivity will be called output per hour of all persons engaged in the productive process, output per employee hour, or just output per hour.

The use of labor productivity indexes does not imply that labor is solely or primarily responsible for productivity growth. In a technologically advanced society, labor effort is only one of many sources of productivity improvement. Trends in output per hour also reflect technological innovation, changes in capital stock and capacity utilization, scale of production, materials flow, management skills, and other factors whose contribution often cannot be measured.

The output side of the output per hour ratio refers to the finished product or the amount of real value added in various enterprises, industries, sectors, or the economy as a whole. Few plants or industries produce a single homogeneous commodity that can be measured by simply counting the number of units produced. Consequently, for the purpose of measurement, the various units of a plant's or an industry's output are combined on some common basis—either their unit labor requirements in a base period or their dollar value. When information on the amount of units produced is not available, as is often the case, output must be expressed in terms of the dollar value of production, adjusted for price changes.

Reprinted from: *Productivity and the Economy: A Chart Book* (Washington, D.C.: U.S. Department of Labor, n.d.).

ROBERT H. HAYES
WILLIAM J. ABERNATHY

Managing Our Way to Economic Decline

MODERN MANAGEMENT PRINCIPLES MAY CAUSE RATHER THAN CURE SLUGGISH ECONOMIC PERFORMANCE

How are we to fix responsibility for the current malaise of American business? Most attribute its weakened condition to the virus of inflation, the paralysis brought on by government regulation and tax policy, or the feverish price escalation by OPEC. Not quite right, say the authors. In their judgment, responsibility rests not with general economic forces alone but also with the failure of American managers to keep their companies technologically competitive over the long run. In advancing their controversial diagnosis, the authors draw on their own extensive work in the production field as well as their recent association with Harvard's International Senior Managers Program in Vevey, Switzerland. Having taken a long, hard look from abroad at how American managers operate, they propose some strong medicine for improving the health of American business.

During the past several years American business has experienced a marked deterioration of competitive vigor and a growing unease about its overall economic well-being. This decline in both health and confidence has been attributed by economists and business leaders to such factors as the rapacity of OPEC, deficiencies in government tax and monetary policies, and the proliferation of regulation. We find these explanations inadequate.

They do not explain, for example, why the rate of productivity growth in America has declined both absolutely and relative to that in Europe and Japan. Nor do they explain why in many high-technology as well as ma-

Mr. Hayes is professor of business administration at the Harvard Business School and has served as faculty chairman of the International Senior Managers Program. He is the author of several HBR articles, the most recent being "The Dynamics of Process-Product Life Cycles" (coauthor, Steven C. Wheelwright, March-April 1979). Mr. Abernathy, also professor of business administration at the Harvard Business School, is a leading authority on the automobile industry. He is the author of *The Productivity Dilemma: Roadblock to Innovation in the Automobile Industry* (Johns Hopkins University Press, 1978). This is his second HBR article.

Reprinted from: *Harvard Business Review* (July–August, 1980).

ture industries America has lost its leadership position. Although a host of readily named forces—government regulation, inflation, monetary policy, tax laws, labor costs and constraints, fear of a capital shortage, the price of imported oil—have taken their toll on American business, pressures of this sort affect the economic climate abroad just as they do here.

A German executive, for example, will not be convinced by these explanations. Germany imports 95% of its oil (we import 50%), its government's share of gross domestic product is about 37% (ours is about 30%), and workers must be consulted on most major decisions. Yet Germany's rate of productivity growth has actually increased since 1970 and recently rose to more than four times ours. In France the situation is similar, yet today that country's productivity growth in manufacturing (despite current crises in steel and textiles) more than triples ours. No modern industrial nation is immune to the problems and pressures besetting U.S. business. Why then do we find a disproportionate loss of competitive vigor by U.S. companies?

Our experience suggests that, to an unprecedented degree, success in most industries today requires an organizational commitment to compete in the marketplace on technological grounds—that is, to compete over the long run by offering superior products. Yet, guided by what they took to be the newest and best principles of management, American managers have increasingly directed their attention elsewhere. These new principles, despite their sophistication and widespread usefulness, encourage a preference for (1) analytic detachment rather than the insight that comes from "hands on" experience and (2) short-term cost reduction rather than long-term development of technological competitiveness. It is this new managerial gospel, we feel, that has played a major role in undermining the vigor of American industry.

American management, especially in the two decades after World War II, was universally admired for its strikingly effective performance. But times change. An approach shaped and refined during stable decades may be ill suited to a world characterized by rapid and unpredictable change, scarce energy, global competition for markets, and a constant need for innovation. This is the world of the 1980s and, probably, the rest of this century.

The time is long overdue for earnest, objective self-analysis. What exactly have American managers been doing wrong? What are the critical weaknesses in the ways that they have managed the technological performance of their companies? What is the matter with the long-unquestioned assumptions on which they have based their managerial policies and practices?

A FAILURE OF MANAGEMENT

In the past, American managers earned worldwide respect for their carefully planned yet highly aggressive action across three different time frames:

Short term—using existing assets as efficiently as possible.

Medium term—replacing labor and other scarce resources with capital equipment.

Long term—developing new products and processes that open new markets or restructure old ones.

The first of these time frames demanded toughness, determination, and close attention to detail; the second, capital and the willingness to take sizable financial risks; the third, imagination and a certain amount of technological daring.

Our managers still earn generally high marks for their skill in improving short-term efficiency, but their counterparts in Europe and Japan have started to question America's entrepreneurial imagination and willingness to make risky long-term competitive investments. As one such observer remarked to us: "The U.S. companies in my industry act like banks. All they are interested in is return on investment and getting their money back. Sometimes they act as though they are more interested in buying other companies than they are in selling products to customers."

In fact, this curt diagnosis represents a growing body of opinion that openly charges American managers with competitive myopia: "Somehow or other, American business is losing confidence in itself and especially confidence in its future. Instead of meeting the challenge of the changing world, American business today is making small, short-term adjustments by cutting costs and by turning to the government for temporary relief....Success in trade is the result of patient and meticulous preparations, with a long period of market preparation before the rewards are available....To undertake such commitments is hardly in the interest of a manager who is concerned with his or her next quarterly earnings reports."[1]

More troubling still, American managers themselves often admit the charge with, at most, a rhetorical shrug of their shoulders. In established businesses, notes one senior vice president of research: "We understand how to market, we know the technology, and production problems are not extreme. Why risk money on new businesses when good, profitable low-risk opportunities are on every side?" Says another: "It's much more difficult to come up with a synthetic meat product than a lemon-lime cake mix. But you work on the lemon-lime cake mix because you know exactly what that return is going to be. A synthetic steak is going to take a lot longer, require a much bigger investment, and the risk of failure will be greater."[2]

These managers are not alone; they speak for many. Why, they ask, should they invest dollars that are hard to earn back when it is so easy—and so much less risky—to make

money in other ways? Why ignore a ready-made situation in cake mixes for the deferred and far less certain prospects in synthetic steaks? Why shoulder the competitive risks of making better, more innovative products?

In our judgment, the assumptions underlying these questions are prime evidence of a broad managerial failure—a failure of both vision and leadership—that over time has eroded both the inclination and the capacity of U.S. companies to innovate.

FAMILIAR EXCUSES

About the facts themselves there can be little dispute. *Exhibits I-IV* document our sorry decline. But the explanations and excuses commonly offered invite a good deal of comment.

It is important to recognize, first of all, that the problem is not new. It has been going on for at least 15 years. The rate of productivity growth in the private sector peaked in the mid-1960s. Nor is the problem confined to a few sectors of our economy; with a few exceptions, it permeates our entire economy. Expenditures on R&D by both business and government, as measured in constant (noninflated) dollars, also peaked in the mid-1960s—both in absolute terms and as a percentage of GNP. During the same period the expenditures on R&D by West Germany and Japan have been rising. More important, American spending on R&D as a percentage of sales in such critical research-intensive industries as machinery, professional and scientific instruments, chemicals, and aircraft had dropped by the mid-1970s to about half its level in the early 1960s. These are the very industries on which we now depend for the bulk of our manufactured exports.

Investment in plant and equipment in the United States displays the same disturbing trends. As economist Burton G. Malkiel has pointed out: "From 1948 to 1973 the [net book value of capital equipment] per unit of the labor grew at an annual rate of almost 3%. Since 1973, however, lower rates of private investment have led to a decline in that growth rate to 1.75%. Moreover, the recent composition of investment [in 1978] has been skewed toward equipment and relatively short-term projects and away from structures and relatively long-lived investments. Thus our industrial plant has tended to age..."[3]

Other studies have shown that growth in the incremental capital equipment-to-labor ratio has fallen to about one-third of its value in the early 1960s. By contrast, between 1966 and 1976 capital investment as a percentage of GNP in France and West Germany was more than 20% greater than that in the United States; in Japan the percentage was almost double ours.

To attribute this relative loss of technological vigor to such things as a shortage of capital in the United States is not justified. As Malkiel and others have shown, the return on equity of American business (out of which comes the capital necessary for investment) is about the same today as 20 years ago, *even after adjusting for inflation*. However, investment in both new equipment and R&D, as a percentage of GNP, was significantly higher 20 years ago than today.

The conclusion is painful but must be faced. Responsibility for this competitive listlessness belongs not just to a set of external conditions but also to the attitudes, preoccupations, and practices of American managers. By their preference for servicing existing markets rather than creating new ones and by their devotion to short-term returns and "management by the numbers," many of them have effectively forsworn long-term technological superiority as a competitive weapon. In consequence, they have abdicated their strategic responsibilities.

Exhibit I. Growth in Labor Productivity Since 1960 (United States and Abroad)

	Average annual percent change	
	Manufacturing 1960-1978	All industries 1960-1976
United States	2.8%	1.7%
United Kingdom	2.9	2.2
Canada	4.0	2.1
Germany	5.4	4.2
France	5.5	4.3
Italy	5.9	4.9
Belgium	6.9*	–
Netherlands	6.9*	–
Sweden	5.2	–
Japan	8.2	7.5

*1960-1977.

Source: Council on Wage and Price Stability, *Report on Productivity* (Washington, D.C.: Executive Office of the President, July 1979).

Exhibit II. Growth of Labor Productivity by Sector, 1948-1978

	Growth of labor productivity (annual average percent)		
Time sector	1948-65	1965-73	1973-78
Private business	**3.2%**	**2.3%**	**1.1%**
Agriculture, forestry, and fisheries	5.5	5.3	2.9
Mining	4.2	2.0	-4.0
Construction	2.9	-2.2	-1.8
Manufacturing	3.1	2.4	1.7
Durable goods	2.8	1.9	1.2
Nondurable goods	3.4	3.2	2.4
Transportation	3.3	2.9	0.9
Communication	5.5	4.8	7.1
Electric, gas, and sanitary services	6.2	4.0	0.1
Trade	2.7	3.0	0.4
Wholesale	3.1	3.9	0.2
Retail	2.4	2.3	0.8
Finance, insurance, and real estate	1.0	-0.3	1.4
Services	1.5	1.9	0.5
Government enterprises	-0.8	0.9	-0.7

Source: Bureau of Labor Statistics.

Note: Productivity data for services, construction, finance, insurance, and real estate are unpublished.

Exhibit III. National Expenditures for Performance of R&D as a Percent of GNP by Country, 1961-1978*

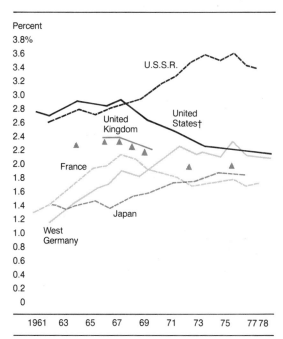

*Gross expenditures for performance of R&D including associated capital expenditures.

†Detailed information on capital expenditures for R&D is not available for the United States. Estimates for the period 1972-1977 show that their inclusion would have an impact of less than one-tenth of 1% for each year.

Source: Science Indicators—1978 (Washington, D.C.:National Science Foundation, 1979), p. 6.

Note: The latest data may be preliminary or estimates.

THE NEW MANAGEMENT ORTHODOXY

We refuse to believe that this managerial failure is the result of a sudden psychological shift among American managers toward a "super-safe, no risk" mind set. No profound sea change in the character of thousands of individuals could have occurred in so organized a fashion or have produced so consistent a pattern of behavior. Instead we believe that during the past two decades American managers have increasingly relied on principles which prize analytical detachment and methodological elegance over insight, based on experience, into the subtleties and complexities of strategic decisions. As a result, maximum short-term financial returns have become the overriding criteria for many companies.

For purposes of discussion, we may divide this *new* management orthodoxy into three general categories: financial control, corporate portfolio management, and market-driven behavior.

Financial Control

As more companies decentralize their organizational structures, they tend to fix on profit centers as the primary unit of managerial responsibility. This development necessitates, in turn, greater dependence on short-term financial measurements like return on investment (ROI) for evaluating the performance of individual managers and management groups. Increasing the structural distance between those entrusted with exploiting actual competitive opportunities and those who must judge the quality of their work virtually guarantees reliance on objectively quantifiable short-term criteria.

Although innovation, the lifeblood of any vital enterprise, is best encouraged by an environment that does not unduly penalize failure, the predictable result of relying too heavily on short-term financial measures—a sort of managerial remote control—is an environment in which no one feels he or she can afford a failure or even a momentary dip in the bottom line.

Corporate Portfolio Management

This preoccupation with control draws support from modern theories of financial portfolio management. Originally developed to help balance the overall risk and return of stock and bond portfolios, these principles have been applied increasingly to the creation and management of corporate portfolios—that is, a cluster of companies and product lines assembled through various modes of diversification under a single corporate umbrella. When applied by a remote group of dispassionate experts primarily concerned with finance and control and lacking hands-on experience, the analytic formulas of portfolio theory push managers even further toward an extreme of caution in allocating resources.

"Especially in large organizations," reports one manager, "we are observing an increase in management behavior which I would regard as excessively cautious, even passive; certainly overanalytical; and, in general, characterized by a studied unwillingness to assume responsibility and even reasonable risk."

Market-Driven Behavior

In the past 20 years, American companies have perhaps learned too well a lesson they had long been inclined to ignore: businesses should be customer oriented rather than product oriented. Henry Ford's famous dictum that the public could have any color automobile it wished as long as the color was black has since given way to its philosophical opposite: "We have got to stop marketing makeable products and learn to make marketable products."

At last, however, the dangers of too much reliance on this philosophy are becoming apparent. As two Canadian researchers have put it: "Inventors, scientists, engineers, and academics, in the normal pursuit of scientific knowledge, gave the world in recent times the laser, xerography, instant photography, and the transistor. In contrast, worshippers of the marketing concept have

Exhibit IV. Industrial R&D Expenditures for Basic Research, Applied Research, and Development, 1960-1978 (in $ millions)

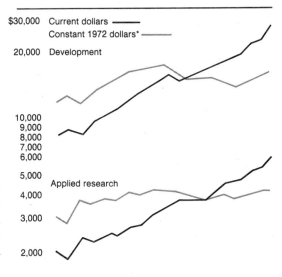

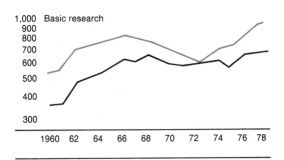

*GNP implicit price deflators used to convert current dollars to constant 1972 dollars.

Source: Science Indicators—1978 p. 87.

Note: Preliminary data are shown for 1977 and estimates for 1978.

bestowed upon mankind such products as new-fangled potato chips, feminine hygiene deodorant, and the pet rock..."[4]

The argument that no new product ought to be introduced without managers undertaking a market analysis is common sense. But the argument that consumer analyses and formal market surveys should dominate other considerations when allocating resources to product development is untenable. It may be useful to remember that the initial market estimate for computers in 1945 projected total worldwide sales of only ten units. Similarly, even the most carefully researched analysis of consumer preferences for gas-guzzling cars in an era of gasoline abundance offers little useful guidance to today's automobile manufacturers in making wise product investment decisions. Customers may know what their needs are, but they often define those needs in terms of existing products, processes, markets, and prices.

Deferring to a market-driven strategy without paying attention to its limitations is, quite possibly, opting for customer satisfaction and lower risk in the short run at the expense of superior products in the future. Satisfied customers are critically important, of course, but not if the strategy for creating them is responsible as well for unnecessary product proliferation, inflated costs, unfocused diversification, and a lagging commitment to new technology and new capital equipment.

THREE MANAGERIAL DECISIONS

These are serious charges to make. But the unpleasant fact of the matter is that, however useful these new principles may have been initially, if carried too far they are bad for U.S. business. Consider, for example, their effect on three major kinds of choices regularly faced by corporate managers: the decision between imitative and innovative product design, the decision to integrate backward, and the decision to invest in process development.

Imitative vs. Innovative Product Design

A market-driven strategy requires new product ideas to flow from detailed market analysis or, at least, to be extensively tested for consumer reaction before actual introduction. It is no secret that these requirements add significant delays and costs to the introduction of new products. It is less well known that they also predispose managers toward developing products for existing markets and toward product designs of an imitative rather than an innovative nature. There is increasing evidence that market-driven strategies tend, over time, to dampen the general level of innovation in new product decisions.

Confronted with the choice between innovation and imitation, managers typically ask whether the marketplace shows any consistent preference for innovative products. If so, the additional funding they require may be economically justified; if not, those funds can more properly go to advertising, promoting, or reducing the prices of less-advanced products. Though the temptation to allocate resources so as to strengthen performance in existing products and markets is often irresistible, recent studies by J. Hugh Davidson and others confirm the strong market attractiveness of innovative products.[5]

Nonetheless, managers having to decide between innovative and imitative product design face a difficult series of marketing-related trade-offs. *Exhibit V* summarizes these trade-offs.

By its very nature, innovative design is, as Joseph Schumpeter observed a long time ago, initially destructive of capital—whether in the form of labor skills, management systems, technological processes, or capital equipment. It tends to make obsolete existing investments in both marketing and manufacturing organizations. For the managers concerned it represents the choice of uncertainty (about economic returns, timing, etc.) over relative predictability, exchanging the reasonable expectation of current income against the promise of high future value. It is the choice of the gambler, the person willing to risk much to gain even more.

Conditioned by a market-driven strategy and held closely to account by a "results now" ROI-oriented control system, American managers have increasingly refused to take the chance on innovative product/ market development. As one of them confesses: "In the last year, on the basis of high capital risk, I turned down new products at a rate at least twice what I did a year ago. But in every case I tell my people to go back and bring me some new product ideas.[6] In truth, they have learned caution so well that many are in danger of forgetting that market-driven, follow-the-leader companies usually end up following the rest of the pack as well.

Backward Integration

Sometimes the problem for managers is not their reluctance to take action and make investments but that, when they do so, their action has the unintended result of reinforcing the status quo. In deciding to integrate backward because of apparent short-term rewards, managers often restrict their ability to strike out in innovative directions in the future.

Consider, for example, the case of a manufacturer who purchases a major component from an outside company. Static analysis of production economies may very well show that backward integration offers rather substantial cost benefits. Eliminating certain purchasing and marketing functions, centralizing overhead, pooling R&D efforts and resources, coordinating design and production of both product and component, reduc-

ing uncertainty over design changes, allowing for the use of more specialized equipment and labor skills—in all these ways and more, backward integration holds out to management the promise of significant short-term increases in ROI.

These efficiencies may be achieved by companies with commoditylike products. In such industries as ferrous and nonferrous metals or petroleum, backward integration toward raw materials and supplies tends to have a strong, positive effect on profits. However, the situation is markedly different for companies in more technologically active industries. Where there is considerable exposure to rapid technological advances, the promised value of backward integration becomes problematic. It may provide a quick, short-term boost to ROI figures in the next annual report, but it may also paralyze the long-term ability of a company to keep on top of technological change.

The real competitive threats to technologically active companies arise less from changes in ultimate consumer preference than from abrupt shifts in component technologies, raw materials, or production processes. Hence those managers whose attention is too firmly directed toward the marketplace and near-term profits may suddenly discover that their decision to make rather than buy important parts has locked their companies into an outdated technology.

Further, as supply channels and manufacturing operations become more systematized, the benefits from attempts to "rationalize" production may well be accompanied by unanticipated side effects. For instance, a company may find itself shut off from the R&D efforts of various independent suppliers by becoming their competitor. Similarly, the commitment of time and resources needed to master technology back up the channel of supply may distract a company from doing its own job well. Such was the fate of Bowmar, the pocket calculator pioneer, whose attempt to integrate backward into semiconductor production so consumed management attention that final assembly of the calculators, its core business, did not get the required resources.

Long-term contracts and long-term relationships with suppliers can achieve many of the same cost benefits as backward integration without calling into question a company's ability to innovate or respond to innovation. European automobile manufacturers, for example, have typically chosen to rely on their suppliers in this way; American companies have followed the path of backward integration. The resulting trade-offs between production efficiencies and innovative flexibility should offer a stern warning to those American managers too easily beguiled by the lure of short-term ROI improvement. A case in point: the U.S. auto industry's huge investment in automating the manufacture of cast-iron brake drums probably delayed by more than five years its transition to disc brakes.

Process Development

In an era of management by the numbers, many American managers—especially in mature industries—are reluctant to invest heavily in the development of new manufacturing processes. When asked to explain their reluctance, they tend to respond in fairly predictable ways. "We can't afford to design new capital equipment for just our own manufacturing needs" is one frequent answer. So is: "The capital equipment producers do a much better job, and they can amortize their development costs over sales to many companies." Perhaps the most common is: "Let the others experiment in manufacturing; we can learn from their mistakes and do it better."

Each of these comments rests on the assumption that essential advances in process technology can be appropriated more easily through equipment purchase than through

Exhibit V.   Trade-Offs Between Imitative and Innovative Design for an Established Product Line

Imitative design	Innovative design
Market demand is relatively well known and predictable.	Potentially large but unpredictable demand; the risk of a flop is also large.
Market recognition and acceptance are rapid.	Market acceptance may be slow initially, but the imitative response of competitors may also be slowed.
Readily adaptable to existing market, sales, and distribution policies.	May require unique, tailored marketing distribution and sales policies to educate customers or because of special repair and warranty problems.
Fits with existing market segmentation and product policies.	Demand may cut across traditional marketing segments, disrupting divisional responsibilities and cannibalizing other products.

in-house equipment design and development. Our extensive conversations with the managers of European (primarily German) technology-based companies have convinced us that this assumption is not as widely shared abroad as in the United States. Virtually across the board, the European managers impressed us with their strong commitment to increasing market share through internal development of advanced process technology—even when their suppliers were highly responsive to technological advances.

By contrast, American managers tend to restrict investments in process development to only those items likely to reduce costs in the short run. Not all are happy with this. As one disgruntled executive told us: "For too long U.S. managers have been taught to set low priorities on mechanization projects, so that eventually divestment appears to be the best way out of manufacturing difficulties. Why?

"The drive for short-term success has prevented managers from looking thoroughly into the matter of special manufacturing equipment, which has to be invented, developed, tested, redesigned, reproduced, improved, and so on. That's a long process, which needs experienced, knowledgeable, and dedicated people who stick to their jobs over a considerable period of time. Merely buying new equipment (even if it is possible) does not often give the company any advantage over competitors."

We agree. Most American managers seem to forget that, even if they produce new products with their existing process technology (the same "cookie cutter" everyone else can buy), their competitors will face a relatively short lead time for introducing similar products. And as Eric von Hipple's studies of industrial innovation show, the innovations on which new industrial equipment is based usually originate with the user of the equipment and not with the equipment producer.[7] In other words, companies can make products more profitable by investing in the development of their own process technology. Proprietary processes are every bit as formidable competitive weapons as proprietary products.

THE AMERICAN MANAGERIAL IDEAL

Two very important questions remain to be asked: (1) Why should so many American managers have shifted so strongly to this new managerial orthodoxy? and (2) Why are they not more deeply bothered by the ill effects of those principles on the long-term technological competitiveness of their companies? To answer the first question, we must take a look at the changing career patterns of American managers during the past quarter century; to answer the second, we must understand the way in which they have come to regard their professional roles and responsibilities as managers.

The Road to the Top

During the past 25 years the American manager's road to the top has changed significantly. No longer does the typical career, threading sinuously up and through a corporation with stops in several functional areas, provide future top executives with intimate hands-on knowledge of the company's technologies, customers, and suppliers.

Exhibit VI summarizes the currently available data on the shift in functional background of newly appointed presidents of the 100 largest U.S. corporations. The immediate significance of these figures is clear. Since the mid-1950s there has been a rather substantial increase in the percentage of new company presidents whose primary interests and expertise lie in the financial and legal areas and not in production. In view of C. Jackson Grayson, president of the American Productivity Center, American management has for 20 years "coasted off the great R&D gains made during World War II, and constantly rewarded executives from the marketing, financial, and legal sides of the business while it ignored the production men. Today [in business schools] courses in the production area are almost non-existent."[8]

In addition, companies are increasingly choosing to fill new top management posts from outside their own ranks. In the opinion of foreign observers, who are still accustomed to long-term careers in the same company or division, "High-level American executives...seem to come and go and switch around as if playing a game of musical chairs at an Alice in Wonderland tea party."

Far more important, however, than any absolute change in numbers is the shift in the general sense of what an aspiring manager has to be "smart about" to make it to the top. More important still is the broad change in attitude such trends both encourage and express. What has developed, in the business community as in academia, is a preoccupation with a false and shallow concept of the professional manager, a "pseudo-professional" really—an individual having no special expertise in any particular industry or technology who nevertheless can step into an unfamiliar company and run it success-fully through strict application of financial controls, portfolio concepts, and a market-driven strategy.

The Gospel of Pseudo-Professionalism

In recent years, this idealization of pseudo-professionalism has taken on something of the quality of a corporate religion. Its first doctrine, appropriately enough, is that nei-ther industry experience nor hands-on tech-nological expertise counts for very much. At one level, of course, this doctrine helps to salve the conscience of those who lack them. At another, more disturbing level it encour-ages the faithful to make decisions about the technological matters simply as if they were adjuncts to finance or marketing decisions. We do not believe that the technological is-sues facing managers today can be meaning-fully addressed without taking into account marketing or financial considerations; on the other hand, neither can they be resolved with the same methodologies applied to these other fields.

Complex modern technology has its own inner logic and developmental imperatives. To treat it as if it were something else—no matter how comfortable one is with that other kind of data—is to base a competitive business on a two-legged stool, which must, no matter how excellent the balancing act, inevitably fall to the ground.

More disturbing still, true believers keep the faith on a day-to-day basis by insisting that as issues rise up the managerial hierar-chy for decision they be progressively dis-tilled into easily quantifiable terms. One European manager, in recounting to us his experiences in a joint venture with an American company, recalled with exaspera-tion that "U.S. mangers want everything to be simple. But sometimes business situa-tions are not simple, and they cannot be di-vided up or looked at in such a way that they become simple. They are messy, and one must try to understand all the facets. This appears to be alien to the American mentality."

The purpose of good organizational de-sign, of course, is to divide responsibilities in such a way that individuals have relatively easy tasks to perform. But then these differ-entiated responsibilities must be pulled to-gether by sophisticated, broadly gauged integrators at the top of the managerial pyra-mid. If these individuals are interested in but one or two aspects of the total competi-tive picture, if their training includes a very narrow exposure to the range of functional specialties, if—worst of all—they are de-voted simplifiers themselves, who will do the necessary integration? Who will attempt to resolve complicated issues rather than try to uncomplicate them artificially? At the strategic level there are no such things as pure production problems, pure financial problems, or pure marketing problems.

Merger Mania

When executive suites are dominated by people with financial and legal skills, it is not surprising that top management should increasingly allocate time and energy to such concerns as cash management and the whole process of corporate acquisitions and mergers. This is indeed what has happened. In 1978 alone there were some 80 mergers involving companies with assets in excess of $100 million each; in 1979 there were almost 100. This represents roughly $20 billion in transfers of large companies from one owner to another—two-thirds of the total amount spent on R&D by American industry.

In 1978 *Business Week* ran a cover story on cash management in which it stated that "the 400 largest U.S. companies together have more than $60 billion in cash—almost triple the amount they had at the beginning

Exhibit VI. Changes in the Professional Origins of Corporate Presidents (percent changes from baseline years [1948-1952] for 100 top U.S. companies)

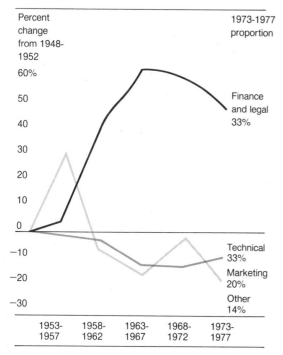

Percent change from 1948-1952

1973-1977 proportion

Finance and legal 33%

Technical 33%

Marketing 20%

Other 14%

Source: Golightly & Co. International (1978).

of the 1970s." The article also described the increasing attention devoted to—and the sophisticated and exotic techniques used for—managing this cash hoard.

There are perfectly good reasons for this flurry of activity. It is entirely natural for financially (or legally) trained managers to concentrate on essentially financial (or legal) activities. It is also natural for managers who subscribe to the portfolio "law of large numbers" to seek to reduce total corporate risk by parceling it out among a sufficiently large number of separate product lines, businesses, or technologies. Under certain conditions it may very well make good economic sense to buy rather than

build new plants or modernize existing ones. Mergers are obviously an exciting game; they tend to produce fairly quick and decisive results, and they offer the kind of public recognition that helps careers along. Who can doubt the appeal of the titles awarded by the financial community; being called a "gunslinger," "white knight," or "raider" can quicken anyone's blood.

Unfortunately, the general American penchant for separating and simplifying has tended to encourage a diversification away from core technologies and markets to a much greater degree than is true in Europe or Japan. U.S. managers appear to have an inordinate faith in the portfolio law of large numbers—that is, by amassing enough product lines, technologies, and businesses, one will be cushioned against the random setbacks that occur in life. This might be true for portfolios of stocks and bonds, where there is considerable evidence that setbacks are random. Businesses, however, are subject not only to random setbacks such as strikes and shortages but also to carefully orchestrated attacks by competitors, who focus all their resources and energies on one set of activities.

Worse, the great bulk of this merger activity appears to have been absolutely wasted in terms of generating economic benefits for stockholders. Acquisition experts do not necessarily make good managers. Nor can they increase the value of their shares by merging two companies any better than their shareholders could do individually by buying shares of the acquired company on the open market (at a price usually below that required for a takeover attempt).

There appears to be a growing recognition of this fact. A number of U.S. companies are now divesting themselves of previously acquired companies; others (for example, W.R. Grace) are proposing to break themselves up into relatively independent entities. The establishment of a strong competitive position through in-house technological superiority is by nature a long, arduous, and often unglamorous task. But it is what keeps a business vigorous and competitive.

THE EUROPEAN EXAMPLE

Gaining competitive success through technological superiority is a skill much valued by the seasoned European (and Japanese) managers with whom we talked. Although we were able to locate few hard statistics on their actual practice, our extensive investigations of more than 20 companies convinced us that European managers do indeed tend to differ significantly from their American counterparts. In fact, we found that many of them were able to articulate these differences quite clearly.

In the first place, European managers think themselves more pointedly concerned with how to survive over the long run under intensely competitive conditions. Few markets, of course, generate price competition as fierce as in the United States, but European companies face the remorseless necessity of exporting to other national markets or perishing.

The figures here are startling: manufactured product exports represent more than 35% of total manufacturing sales in France and Germany and nearly 60% in the Benelux countries, as against not quite 10% in the United States. In these export markets, moreover, European products must hold their own against "world class" competitors, lower-priced products from developing countries, and American products selling at attractive devalued dollar prices. To survive this competitive squeeze, European managers feel they must place central emphasis on producing technologically superior products.

Further, the kinds of pressures from European labor unions and national governments virtually force them to take a consistently long-term view in decision making. German managers, for example, must negotiate major decisions at the plant level with worker-dominated works councils; in turn, these decisions are subject to review by supervisory boards (roughly equivalent to American boards of directors), half of whose membership is worker elected. Together with strict national legislation, the pervasive influence of labor unions makes it extremely difficult to change employment levels or production locations. Not surprisingly, labor costs in Northern Europe have more than doubled in the past decade and are now the highest in the world.

To be successful in this environment of strictly constrained options, European managers feel they must employ a decision-making apparatus that grinds very fine—and very deliberately. They must simply outthink and outmanage their competitors. Now, American managers also have their strategic options hedged about by all kinds of restrictions. But those restrictions have not yet made them as conscious as their European counterparts of the long-term implications of their day-to-day decisions.

As a result, the Europeans see themselves as investing more heavily in cutting-edge technology than the Americans. More often than not, this investment is made to create new product opportunities in advance of consumer demand and not merely in response to market-driven strategy. In case after case, we found the Europeans striving to develop the products and process capabilities with which to lead markets and not simply responding to the current demands of the marketplace. Moreover, in doing this they seem less inclined to integrate backward and more likely to seek maximum leverage from stable, long-term relationships with suppliers.

Having never lost sight of the need to be technologically competitive over the long run, European and Japanese managers are extremely careful to make the necessary arrangements and investments today. And their daily concern with the rather basic issue of long-term survival adds perspective to such matters as short-term ROI or rate of growth. The time line by which they manage is long, and it has made them painstakingly attentive to the means for keeping their companies technologically competitive. Of course they pay attention to the numbers. Their profit margins are usually lower than ours, their debt ratios higher. Every tenth of a percent is critical to them. But they are also aware that tomorrow will be no better unless they constantly try to develop new processes, enter new markets, and offer superior—even unique—products. As one senior German executive phrased it recently, "We look at rates of return, too, but only after we ask 'Is it a good product?' "[9]

CREATING ECONOMIC VALUE

Americans traveling in Europe and Asia soon learn they must often deal with criticism of our country. Being forced to respond to such criticism can be healthy, for it requires rethinking some basic issues of principle and practice.

We have much to be proud about and little to be ashamed of relative to most other countries. But sometimes the criticism of others is uncomfortably close to the mark. The comments of our overseas competitors on American business practices contain enough truth to require our thoughtful consideration. What is behind the decline in competitiveness of U.S. business? Why do U.S. companies have such apparent difficulties competing with foreign producers of established products, many of which originated in the United States?

For example, Japanese televisions dominate some market segments, even though many U.S. producers now enjoy the same low labor cost advantages of offshore pro-

duction. The German machine tool and automotive producers continue their inroads into U.S. domestic markets, even though their labor rates are now higher than those in the United States and the famed German worker in German factories is almost as likely to be Turkish or Italian as German.

The responsibility for these problems may rest in part on the government policies that either overconstrain or undersupport U.S. producers. But if our foreign critics are correct, the long-term solution to America's problems may not be correctable simply by changing our government's tax laws, monetary policies, and regulatory practices. It will also require some fundamental changes in management attitudes and practices.

It would be an oversimplification to assert that the only reason for the decline in competitiveness of U.S. companies is that our managers devote too much attention and energy to using existing resources more efficiently. It would also oversimplify the issue, although possibly to a lesser extent, to say that it is due purely and simply to their tendency to neglect technology as a competitive weapon.

Companies cannot become more innovative simply by increasing R&D investments or by conducting more basic research. Each of the decisions we have described directly affects several functional areas of management, and major conflicts can only be reconciled at senior executive levels. The benefits favoring the more innovative, aggressive option in each case depend more on intangible factors than do their efficiency-oriented alternatives.

Senior managers who are less informed about their industry and its confederation of parts suppliers, equipment suppliers, workers, and customers or who have less time to consider the long-term implications of their interactions are likely to exhibit a noninnovative bias in their choices. Tight financial controls with a short-term emphasis will also bias choices toward the less innovative, less technologically aggressive alternatives.

The key to long-term success—even survival—in business is what it has always been: to invest, to innovate, to lead, to create value where none existed before. Such de-termination, such striving to excel, requires leaders—not *just* controllers, market analysts, and portfolio managers. In our preoccupation with the braking systems and exterior trim, we may have neglected the drive trains of our corporations.

2

Productivity Implications

Many people are simply not willing to make the sacrifices
necessary for economic growth.
HERMAN KAHN[1]

Wealth is a measure of a society's prosperity. The wealthiest nation in the world is the United States—because it is the most productive nation on earth. A more realistic way to measure wealth and productivity is to view them on a per capita basis: When the total wealth or productivity of a nation is divided by the number of people in that nation, the result is per capita wealth (per capita productivity). Although some of the oil-producing nations (Saudi Arabia and Kuwait, for example) produce more per capita wealth than we do, more realistic comparisons are between the United States and other highly industrialized nations, such as Japan, Germany, France, Great Britain, and Italy. When looked at on a per capita basis, these nations are gaining on the United States: Their *rates* of productivity improvement are greater than ours. Admittedly, they are starting from a smaller base, but their faster rate of productivity improvement indicates that most of these nations will achieve parity with the United States on a per capita basis sometime in the 1990s.[2]

Parity by itself is of little concern. Simply stated, parity will mean that our allies are capable of producing outputs with about the same inputs as required by United States firms. In selected industries—automobiles, steel, consumer electronics—some nations have achieved productivity levels that exceed those of the United States; in other industries (for example, agriculture), they lag far behind. As the productivity of these nations approaches that of the United States, competition will become even more rigorous. And if some of these nations can become even more productive than the United States in specific industries, the U.S. will be unable to compete effectively in those industries.[3] By the 1990s, for example, the Japanese intend to leap-frog U.S. computer manufacturers by producing a "fifth generation" computer. To do that, not only must they be innovative in their designs and technology, but they must also become more productive in making the necessary electronic components. If (some would say "when") the Japanese overtake the U.S. electronics/computer industry, that industry will suffer the same fate as steel, shipbuilding, and automobiles: economic decline, with the corresponding plant closings, loss of jobs, and the negative social consequences already witnessed by communities overly dependent upon surpassed industries.[4]

If enough industries are forced into economic decline, the "pie of economic wealth" will cease to expand.[5] Then each claimant (workers, retirees, the poor, national defense, and others) will only be able to get a larger piece of pie if someone else receives a smaller slice. Only through increased productivity can society produce more for all of its constituents. If industries can increase their productivity faster than their foreign competitors can, they will grow and prosper. As they prosper, they will expand the "pie of economic wealth" so there will be more wealth to share among the various claimants. Simply put, productivity improvement creates new national wealth. If the productivity growth rate of the United States remains behind that of its trading partners, the economic significance of the United States will decline. The standard of living its citizens enjoy will grow slowly—and perhaps stagnate or decline. Whether the national standard of living rises or falls depends upon productivity improvement, that is, the way in which we use our resources to create new wealth.

SOURCES OF WEALTH

Wealth is created by the extraction, production, or creation of valued outputs. Nations such as Saudi Arabia and Kuwait, for example, achieve high levels of productivity through the extraction of oil. Their productivity is largely dependent on favorable geological formations and western technology. Likewise, the United States is able to extract wealth from its farms because of favorable soil and climate conditions. Although many of the techniques discussed in this book can be applied to extractive industries, often the key to productivity in such industries is geological luck and technology.[6]

Yet the most significant payoffs in productivity improvement may lie in the industrial and service sectors. The productivity of industrial resources depends on infrastructure and technology. But the most important resource here is people. It is people themselves who productively combine technology, infrastructure, and other resources. While the availability of natural resources significantly affects productivity in extractive industries, people shape productivity in the industrial and service sectors by applying resources in order to achieve valued outputs.[7]

In post-industrial societies, productivity improvement increasingly depends on creating new knowledge and new technologies that become valuable resources in the hands of a rapidly growing white-collar labor force. Here the key to productivity is the creation of this new knowledge and technology, or at least new combinations of knowledge and technology. Whether it is the extraction of natural resources, the production of industrial and service sector resources, or the creation of new knowledge and technology to generate informational resources, the kingpin in the creation of wealth has always been human resources.[8]

THE RISE AND FALL OF INDUSTRIES

Industries move through fairly predictable cycles, and this cyclical movement has significant implications for the creation of wealth for the well-being of human resources. Although some theorists use different terminology, Figure 2-1 provides a basic illustration of an industry life-cycle. The stages of this cycle include introduction, growth, maturity, and decline or renewal. In the introductory phase, productivity is seldom a significant issue; the focus is on extracting, producing, or creating the output, with little regard to the resources required. When the value added by new inputs exceeds the value of the original resources, the industry begins the growth phase, which is characterized by rapid expansion that continues into the third phase, maturity. In a mature industry, a premium is placed on productivity, because the most productive firms within the industry are the ones able to maintain their market share in the face of increasing competition (often resulting from overcapacity). The inevitable result: firms withdraw or combine with other organizations during this mature stage.

During the mature stage, foreign competition often begins to make significant inroads. Foreign competitors are often spared the initial development costs, since they typically enter the market after a product has been developed and proven. They are therefore able to pay lower wage rates, and they have the advantage of newer facilities. With their commitment to expanding their share of the market, new firms in the industry may even forego profits at first. Other firms in the industry must either meet the new competitor's price and watch their profit margins shrink, or attempt to maintain their margins and watch market share decline. Either approach may lead to a decline in profits, which in turn causes the industry to look less attractive as an investment medium. Lower investment in plant and equipment, research and development, and process technology reduces a firm's ability to compete and leads to the decline in it's fortunes. When enough firms are negatively affected by price and other forms of competition in the mature market, the entire industry often begins to decline.

Industries and firms that recognize the onset of decline may choose to renew themselves with injections of capital and other forms of invest-

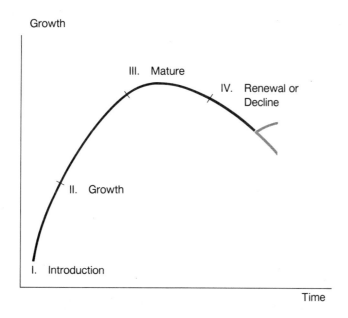

Figure 2-1. Industry/Product Life Cycle

ment aimed at improving productivity. Many Japanese firms in the auto industry, such as Mazda, recognized the industry's maturity and began to substitute automated equipment for employees as a strategy to enhance quality while lowering costs.[9]

On the basis of employment figures alone, systematic work force reductions may appear to signal the decline of a firm or industry. Indeed, work force reductions may come from a natural decline of firms within the industry; but they may also signify attempts to renew these organizations by substituting technology—in the form of new capital, procedures, and energy—for people.

Perhaps the classic example is American agriculture. During the last century-and-a-half, the percentage of the work force devoted to agriculture has declined steadily as labor-saving technology such as cotton gins, McCormick reapers and ever-larger tractors and farm equipment has replaced people. This resource substitution, combined with advances in hybrid seeds, farm chemicals, and improvements in farm management, has resulted in approximately 2.5 percent of the work force remaining in agriculture, down from more than 85 percent a century-and-a-half ago. And yet, total farm production is considerably higher today than at any other time in history. Simply stated, the per capita productivity of the American farmer has increased at an astonishing rate, particularly since the end of World War II.[10]

As Figure 2-2 illustrates, industries typically grow, mature, and are replaced by new emerging industries. Historically, as an industry begins to decline, its demand for resources declines with it. These freed-up human and other resources are then available for newer industries, which absorb them, peak, and subsequently decline. From an employment perspective, the rise and fall in agricultural employment was partially absorbed by the growth industries of railroads and steel in the last half of the 1800s. As the latter industries began to decline, automobiles, consumer appliances, and then aerospace, defense, and microelectronics became the engines of economic growth. And when these industries decline, robotics, bio-genetic engineering, and eventually even space exploration are likely to absorb the resources made available by that decline.

New industries grow and appropriate additional resources as the value these industries create exceeds the value created by older, often declining industries. The more value a new industry can add, the more able it will be to command resources that previously went to other industries.

Competition and productivity play key roles in this process. Competition assures that the process is efficient. When freed of restraints, more efficient firms help to accelerate the decline of other firms within the industry, which explains why many firms in mature industries merge. Large firms are more likely to survive, but only if their growth allows them to outpace the productivity of their competitors.

If, for example, consolidation brings enough financial clout to substitute capital for people, as occurs when automated facilities replace non-automated ones, there may be significant improvement in productivity. If this productivity improvement does not generate a comparable increase in sales, there may be a decline in the number of people who work for the

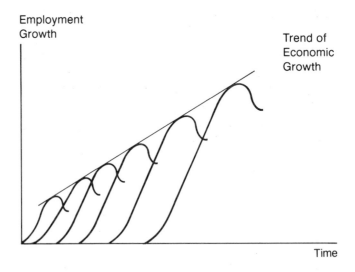

Figure 2–2.   The Rise and Fall of Industries

firm. Thus, the value added by the firm may increase, ensuring survival, but many employees may lose their jobs to machines.

This cause-and-effect relationship between increased productivity and increased layoffs may lead to the false conclusion that increased productivity is entirely detrimental to human resources. Contrariwise, firms and industries which *do not* achieve world-class productivity improvement are likely to see a contraction in their employment levels because the grow less and less able to compete. Those organizations that become more productive and are better able to compete are more likely to survive, assuming that at least some jobs will remain.

THE PRODUCTIVITY GAP

When the productivity growth rate of a nation's industries falls short of that achieved by its trading partners, affected industries must improve their productivity or go into decline. In the absence of improved productivity, the national productivity growth rate actually declines. From the mid-1960s to the early 1980s, the actual productivity growth rate in the United States failed to match the sharp increases of previous periods. Figure 2–3 illustrates this "productivity gap." The straight line in the figure represents the 3.2% annual productivity growth rate that was the norm in the United States from the mid-1940s to the mid-1960s. The difference between it and the other line represents "lost productivity"—goods and services that would have been produced had productivity continued to average 3.2% per year.[11]

As the article at the end of this chapter ("What Can America Do to Solve Its Productivity Crisis?") argues, this slowdown may be attributed to a variety of causes. Economist Milton Friedman places the bulk of the blame on government regulations and other impediments to productivity.

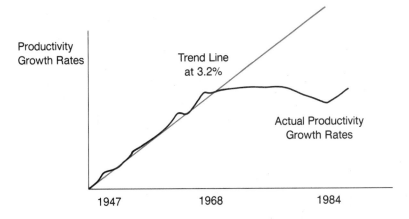

Figure 2–3. Post-World War II Productivity Growth Rates

Friedman and others point to tax laws that fail to create incentives for re-investment and savings, and to unbridled fiscal policies, defense spending, and a wide range of rules and regulations imposed on industry. Other causes frequently mentioned include a decline in research and development investment, a decline in plant and equipment investments, a decline in the quality of education, union work rules and practices, a rapidly growing and inexperienced work force resulting from the baby boom, inappropriate trade restrictions, and higher energy prices.

ORGANIZATION SOLUTIONS TO SURVIVAL

Regardless of the reasons for the productivity gap, the primary creator of wealth is business. When productivity increases are insufficient to hold down price increases, the least productive firms may be forced to raise their prices above competitors' or watch their profit margin shrink. If prices are raised, market share is often lost, which reduces the use of expensive plants and equipment and in turn raises per unit cost. Shrinking profit margins reduce the firm's ability to buy additional resources, which escalates the downward spiral in productivity and cost. Organizations whose productivity improvement is substantially greater than that of their competitors are likely to enjoy larger profit margins or have smaller price increases. The smaller price increases can lead to an expansion of sales and market share, which ensures that workers gain additional experience while companies take advantage of economies of scale, which result from the bulk purchases and effective use of equipment. Even if prices remain unchanged, the larger profit margins allow successful firms to spend additional money on advertising, research and development. These and other sources of innovation lead to increased sales and improved profits, and propel the upward spiral of productivity and profit.

Productivity improvement is essential to organizational survival.[12] Improved productivity can result from many human and non-human sources. Improvements in technology often generate research into product design and manufacturing processes. Better facilities and equipment design can also improve productivity in both the manufacturing and service sectors, particularly if these improvements are accomplished through the use of ergonomics, the science of efficient human/machine interfacing. Improvements in facilities and equipment design may also contribute to improved employee attitudes and morale, which may lead to improvements in productivity beyond those gained from economies of scale. Improvement in work methods and procedures, particularly in job design and layout, may also contribute to productivity improvement. And as mentioned before, the substitution of capital (shovels for hands and bulldozers for shovels) often results in significant, permanent productivity improvement.

In recent years, the productivity of material handling has improved. Through Kanban Systems (which require firms to produce to order, rather than produce for inventory), organizations have attempted to minimize their in-process inventory, often at considerable savings. The energy shock of the 1970s made organizations considerably more aware of their energy costs. As a result, perceptive vendors suggest material and energy-saving alternatives, and smart managers work to minimize scrap and waste of these valuable inputs.

The Human Contribution

Whether productivity improvements result from capital, technology, material substitutions, or other sources, the ultimate driving force is human beings. It is workers and managers who give life to the non-human factors. People are the catalysts that stimulate new productivity.

INDIVIDUAL AWARENESS

People are the cornerstone of productivity. To improve productivity, we must create an awareness of it among the population in general, and among individual workers in particular. Unfortunately, many workers are reluctant to contribute their commitment and ideas to the improvement of productivity. This reluctance does not stem from any inherent shortcoming among workers. Instead, as the rest of this book will discuss in greater detail, willingness to improve productivity and the free flow of employees' ideas depend solely on how human resources are managed. Admittedly, government actions might spur productivity improvement. But the productivity battle will ultimately be won or lost according to how effectively human resources are used in the productive processes. Managers must create awareness of the importance of productivity. To do this, they must first understand the concept of productivity, which the next chapter explains. Subsequent chapters explore the components of individual and organizational productivity.

SUMMARY

The wealth of a society—its standard of living and quality of life—is determined in large measure by the productivity of its people. In a highly competitive international economy, relative rates of productivity growth determine which organizations succeed and which fail.

Within an organization, the productive use of all resources is a prerequisite for survival. The major burden falls on managers, who must use capital, materials, and other resources—including human resources—as efficiently as possible.

SELECTED READINGS OVERVIEW

The articles in this section represent a rather eclectic compilation. The first is from the Society of Chartered Property and Casualty Underwriters, and is entitled "The Restructuring of America in the Decade Ahead." Relying heavily on concepts from the Naisbitt Group, which created the best-seller *Megatrends*, the article discusses significant trends in the United States and the world. These trends hold implications for productivity improvement as firms, industries, and governments attempt to adjust to new realities.

The second reading in this chapter is entitled, "What Can America Do to Solve Its Productivity Crisis?" This piece, taken from an in-house publication of a national accounting firm, is based on interviews with some of the leading thinkers of our time. The perceptions of these renowned economists and industrialists offer some unique insights into the productivity dilemma facing the Western world.

Next Chapter

Productivity improvement is affected by a variety of forces that managers must control. The next chapter presents some frameworks for viewing the overall scope of productivity management. These models highlight the many factors affecting productivity.

Review Questions

1. What is the relationship between national productivity and wealth?
2. What are some of the major reasons why the rate of productivity improvement in the United States has slowed down?
3. What major trends are likely to help increase the rate of productivity improvement? What factors are likely to diminish it?

The Restructuring of America in the Decade Ahead

The general aim of futures research is to recognize changes in familiar trends, the development of new trends, and the emergence of specific events that are imminent or, more often, unexpected. We can look very closely at what is happening in society today and make fairly accurate assessments about the quality of life in the next decade.

The methodology of the Naisbitt Group in developing *The Trend Report* for their clients is to rely almost exclusively on a system of monitoring local events and behavior. Their findings indicate that to an overwhelming degree, America is becoming a bottom-up society and so it is important to note what is going on locally rather than just what is happening in Washington D.C. or New York City. For example, there are five states in the United States where most social invention seems to occur. The other 45 states are, in general, followers. California is the key indicator state; Florida is second, although not too far behind; with the other three trend setter states being Washington, Colorado and Connecticut.

Content studies of major United States newspapers reveal what preoccupations Americans have given up and what preoccupations they have taken up. These have been very useful in establishing trends and predicting the future.

The economic problems we face and the solutions we are beginning to uncover are not occurring in a vacuum. They are occurring in the midst of several powerful trends that are restructuring the economic and social institutions of the United States and most of the industrialized world. There is a tendency to ignore these large trends. We move from one event to another, little noticing the process going on underneath.

There are five broad, powerful trends emerging within which current social and economic events can be understood.

1. The United States is rapidly shifting from a mass industrial society to an information society, and the final impact will be more profound than the 19th Century shift from an agricultural to an industrial society.

2. There is more decentralization than centralization taking place in America —for the first time in the nation's history; the power is shifting from the President to the Congress and from the Congress to the states and localities.

Reprinted from: *CPCU Public Affairs Forum* 3, No. 1 (1982).

3. We are now a truly global economy because of instantaneously shared information, and the world is deeply in a process of redistribution of labor and production. As part of this process all of the developed countries are deindustrializing.

4. The American society is moving in dual directions of high tech/high touch. The introduction of every new technology is accompanied by a compensatory response—or the new technology is rejected.

5. There are the beginnings of a job revolution in America, a basic restructuring of the work environment from top-down to bottom-up. Some companies are experimenting with "bottom-up" quality control systems, based on the premise that workers probably know best what it takes to get the job done right.

INDUSTRIAL TO INFORMATION SOCIETY

The most dramatic way to illustrate how quickly we have shifted to an information society is to look at the changing character of our jobs. In 1950, 65 percent of the U.S. work force was engaged in industrial occupations. Since 1950, that 65 percent has dropped to 27 percent—a dramatic change. In 1950, about 17 percent of the work force was in information jobs (those involved with creating, processing, and distributing information)—today that figure is up to 60 percent—and the projection is that 80 percent of the U.S. work force will be in information jobs by the year 2000!

That group includes people in publishing, in education and the media. It also includes the less obvious—those of us in insurance, banking, the stock market and government. To a large extent, we are what we do. Thus, when most of us work in information jobs, that shapes our society. The strategic resource in the industrial society was capital; the strategic resource in the information society is knowledge, data that is not only renewable but self-generating. That explains the explosion of entrepreneurial activity in the U.S. Since the strategic resource is now in our heads, access to the system is much easier. Not only will we see an impressive increase in the creation of new, small firms, but if large institutions are to survive, they will restructure to encourage entrepreneurial activity within their institutions.

The mass instrumentalities that were created in consonance with the industrial society are out of tune with the times. Just as in 1800 the fact that 90 percent of us in the labor force were farmers dictated the societal arrangements of the day, the fact that most of us were in industrial occupations until recently dictated the arrangements of a mass industrial society—which are now out of tune with the new information society. Organizational and managerial systems that were effective in an industrial setting are no longer appropriate. The dominant skills, attitudes, expectations and motivations of our new work force are not those held by workers we have known as "blue collar."

Three examples are:

1. **Labor unions.** In 1950, with 65 percent of the work force in this country in the industrial sector, more than 30 percent of the workers in the country were members of unions. That's now 19 percent (and only 9 percent of the work force is unionized in the southern and western regions of America—the dynamic population growth areas). There is no way that is going to do anything but continue to go down, as we move more and more into the information society. We are moving toward a union-free society.

2. **Network television.** Network television started down a few years ago, and it is on a long slow, irreversible slide downward. Network television will lose

ground to new options—the incredible array of cable, video disks, and new special interest networks—a Spanish language network, the all-sports network, the all-news network, the children's network, the BBC in America network, etc. By the end of the 1980s, the three big networks (CBS, ABC, NBC) may have fewer than half the viewers they have today.

3. **National political parties.** National political parties, which had their heyday in the industrial society, exist today in theory only. The cross-over in politics came in 1976—a Presidential year—when the number of people contributing to special interest groups exceeded the number of people who contributed to the umbrella Democratic and Republican parties combined. The trend is continuing. The two great American political parties exist in name only. We have a Congress filled with independents. You might say there are 535 political parties in Congress.

Starting just a couple of years ago, the number one occupation in the United States became a clerk, replacing the laborer, and the farmer before that. Farmer, laborer, clerk: a brief history of the United States. (What comes after clerk? Whether it is a soldier or poet depends on how we treat the rest of this century.)

In connection with this shift to an information society it is important to notice a powerful anomaly developing: as we move into a more and more literacy-intensive society, our schools are giving us an increasingly inferior product: this is a powerful mismatch. With the exception of 1981, SAT scores (the tests to qualify for college) have been going down each year for more than a decade. We all experience that our young people are not outstanding when it comes to writing and arithmetic. Consider this: for the first time in the history of the United

States, the generation that is graduating from high school today is less skilled than its parents. Lastly, with the basic restructuring of the society from an industrial to an informational society, the traditional grouping of goods and services won't work anymore. That is why the economists are always wrong. And they will continue to be as long as they rely on the old indices. We need new concepts and new data if we are to understand where we are and where we are going.

CENTRALIZED TO DECENTRALIZED

Trends move in different directions, at different speeds. They have different weights. They have different life cycles. About five years ago, the heft and feel of the movement toward decentralization became greater than the heft and feel of those forces toward continued centralization.

The two great centralizing events in America's history were the Great Depression and World War II, plus the centralizing impact of industrialization. We are now receding from these centralizing influences.

In the 1950s and into the 1960s we began to celebrate ethnic diversity. Polish is beautiful, as well as black is beautiful. We started to celebrate our ethnic restaurants, which of course had been there all the time. An extraordinary thing happened in the late 1960s. We gave up the myth of the melting pot. For years we had taught our children in fourth grade civics that America was a great melting pot, as if we were all put in a giant blender and homogenized into Americans. Now we have given up that myth and recognize that it is our ethnic diversity that has made us such a vital, creative country.

Then a phenomenon of the 1970s was jurisdictional diversity, geographic diversity. We have no national urban policy today because a top-down, master plan, national urban policy is out of tune with the times. The only national urban policy that would be in tune with the times is the national urban policy that would respond to local initiatives. It is an inappropriate question to ask, "Are we going to save our cities?" That's an either/or formulation. It doesn't work in the new multiple option society. The point is, we'll save some of our cities; we'll not save others. We'll save some of our cities a little bit; we'll save others a great deal. We are going to save some parts of cities and not other parts, and it is all going to turn on local initiative.

That's also why we're not getting a national health policy, because you can't do a top-down monolithic kind of policy anymore because of the growing diversity in the United States. We have to look at these things from the bottom up, not the top down.

Now, where we feel centralization continuing most painfully is in government regulations—and that's changing. That is really bending back. More and more, we are going to see the political left and right meeting on this issue of being against big government and against government regulations. And that's part of a larger power shift, too, that's going from the President to the Congress and from the Congress to the states, which means more state regulations.

Proposition 13 has to be understood as having a lot more to do with the initiative trend, or the referendum trend, than it had to do with taxes. We are submitting to the political process questions we never submitted to the political process before. Business has become very involved in those questions where they have had much at stake (like whether or not to build a nuclear plant). And in the process they have helped to legitimize the notion of submitting questions to the political process. There is no end to it. We're going to see more and more of this. It's a part of a larger, "direct democracy." We'll be voting on a great range of new things, at times "leapfrogging" the traditional political process.

In America, the large, general purpose instrumentalities are folding everywhere. An early sign and instructive analogue of this was the demise of *Life*, *Look* and *Post*, the huge circulation, general purpose magazines ten years ago. That same year, 300 special purpose magazines were created, most of which are still being published. There are now more than 4,000 special interest magazines being published in the United States, and no huge circulation, general purpose magazines.

A couple of years ago two big labor unions, the meat cutters and the retail clerks, merged to form a huge union—for survival. That's the dinosaur effect: they get larger just before they go under. There have been over 50 mergers of labor unions in the last ten years.

These kind of "umbrella" organizations are out of tune with the times, just as network television now is becoming. ABC, CBS and NBC will be the *Life*, *Look*, and *Post* of the 1980s and 1990s.

We may see the formation of new political parties, but in tune with the decentralization of the country, they will be local, new political parties—not national. We already have the Right-to-Life party on the ballot in New York State. We will continue to have local special-interest parties developing in the U.S.

The magazine analogue is also instructive in connection with leadership. In the United States, we have all noticed a dearth of leadership. We have no great captains of industry anymore, no great university presidents, no great leaders in the arts, or in civil rights, or in labor, or in politics. It is not because there is any absence of ambition or talent on the part of those who would be leaders. We don't have any great leaders anymore because we followers are not creating them. Followers create leaders—not the reverse—and we followers are not conferring leadership as we did in the past. We are now creating leaders with much more limited mandates: closer to us and on much narrower bands. In the old Taoist model of leadership, "find a parade and get in front of it," we who would be leaders in America are finding much smaller parades—and many more of them.

NATIONAL ECONOMY TO GLOBAL ECONOMY

The other side of relying on less centralized political authority is the growing world economic interdependency. Sir Arthur Clarke said that the two inventions that accounted for America's swift economic growth were the telegraph (later the telephone) and the railroads. Similarly, the two great inventions that are making us a global village are the jet airplane and communication satellite. Marshall McLuhan captured the sense of interdependence when he said, "there are no passengers on spaceship earth. We are all crew."

We are now a truly world economy because of instantaneously shared information. We have wiped out the "information float." The recent successful space shuttle flights have far more to do with this concept of instantaneously shared information than they have to do with space.

We are now deeply in the process of resorting out who is going to make what in this world. As part of this process all of the noncommunist, developed countries are deindustrializing. Even Japan (the most flexible country in the world) is getting out of the steel business and the ship-building business. She knows that in these markets (which are at saturation worldwide), South Korea will outdo her in steel and that Brazil, Poland and Spain will soon be building ships more economically.

The U.S. and the rest of the developed countries are on the way to losing the following industries: steel, automobile, railroad equipment, machinery, apparel, shoe,

textile. The only sector the U.S. is growing in is munitions. By the end of the century, the Third World will make 25 percent of the world's manufactured goods. . . .

We developed nations are probably going to kill ourselves competing over steel and cars, when we should be moving in other new areas as the Third World takes over the old tasks. Consider that in the world automobile market we are reaching saturation; it will soon be a replacement market. There are now 86 countries that have automobile assembly plants. Japan takes 11 manhours to build a car; the U.S. takes 30 manhours. Japan, with the expanding use of robots is moving toward 9 manhours; the U.S. is moving toward 31 manhours. With well over 20 percent of car sales in the U.S., imports have passed Ford and become second only to General Motors. In the bellweather state of California imports were over 50 percent of car sales last year.

Yesterday is over. We must look to the new technological adventures: electronics, bio-industry, alternative sources of energy, mining the seabeds. We have to work out policies (or at least let the marketplace do it) to make the transition from the old to the new. How reliable is the Dow-Jones as a barometer of the economic health of the society or stock market with all those companies from dying industries on its list? Like the economists, they need a new index.

We now have two economies in America, one falling and one rising. We have a group of sunset industries and a group of sunrise industries. We are experiencing a new phenomenon: some sections of the country are in prosperity and other sections are in depression. The economists have averaged them out to spell recession.

FORCED TECHNOLOGY TO HIGH TECH/HIGH TOUCH

Every new technology is followed closely by some "high touch" response on the part of society. With the introduction of television, for example, came the group therapy movement, which, in turn, led to the personal growth movement and the human potential movement.

Similarly, the high technology of the medical field (brain scanners and heart transplants) has led to a new interest in the family doctor and neighborhood clinics. A novel high tech/high touch example is citizen band (CB) radio: people using this technology to get in touch with another human being—anybody! And, in our offices, the high technology of word processing has initiated a revival of hand-written notes and letters. The high technology of chemistry and pharmacology which produced the pill led to a revolution in life styles (away from either/or to multiple-option). Jet airplanes have led to more meetings. A poignant example of high tech/high touch is how the high technology of life-sustaining equipment in hospitals led to a new concern for the quality of death (and to the hospice movement.)

Whenever institutions introduce new technology to customers or employees, they should build in a high touch component; if they don't, people will try to create their own or reject the new technology. We must create compensatory human ballast to go along with sophisticated technological advances.

The high technology of the computer has been somewhat intimidating to many of us, but now see its high touch potential as "computer as liberator." A company with 40,000 employees has always treated those 40,000 the same; it had to because that was the only way it could keep track of them. And that has been unfair, because people are different. Now with the computer to keep track, the company can have a different arrangement with each of its employees as to relation of salary to retirement benefits, work hours, job objective and so forth. And that is the trend: each of us having an individually-tailored contract with our employer. Also, the computer will outmode the hierarchical system of organization (and that is liberating!). We had to have a hierarchy in order to keep track of everybody and what they were up to. Now with the computer to keep track we can restructure to horizontal organization of many small entrepreneurial groups. The pyramid has been outdated by the new technology.

TOP-DOWN TO BOTTOM-UP

Whenever pressing economic trends converge with changing personal values, you get change in a society. That's why we can start to look for revolutionary changes in the workplace. A whole new attitude toward American workers is on the way. And it could result in a revitalization of the spirit of work and America's sagging productivity.

Here's the situation: The productivity growth rate has been on a dismal downswing. At the same time, over the last two decades, personal values have been changing radically; there's a growing demand for more satisfaction from life. Workers feel it, too. Their psychic pain is reflected in their low productivity. They are sick of being treated like machines in the service of increased productivity. Workers refuse to produce and even deliberately sabotage the products they make.

They are no longer content with the traditional remedies offered up by labor unions, such as more pay, four-day weeks, better health benefits. What they really want, like everybody else, is deep human satisfaction from their work.

But industry had no compelling need to give it to them—until now. These dropping productivity figures will finally force industry, in economic desperation, to give more than token attention to the mental health of workers. The workplace is in for a good shaking up. And the American worker is about to be saved by one of the most unlikely forces in society—call it humanization, personal growth, "the human potential movement," participatory management, quality circles, the values of the sixties. Call it whatever, it is about to converge with the economic necessity of the eighties to rescue the American worker from a deadened existence. For one thing, American industry is carefully examining the way Japanese companies are run. As mentioned earlier, it takes Japanese workers 11 manhours to build a car, compared with 30 manhours for American workers.

It's often mistakenly thought that Japanese workers are so productive because they perform like robots, ever subservient to authority. The opposite is true. Unlike American workers, the Japanese are given enormous freedom to both plan and execute their work and solve problems alone without the help or interference of managers. The plants are run not from the "top-down" like ours where managers deliver orders, but from the "bottom-up" where workers make the crucial decisions. Fully 90 percent of Japan's industrial work force is organized in work groups of 8 to 11 people. The whole theory is: the workers know their job better than anyone else, and given a chance, workers will be creative and self-motivated. Interestingly, the Japanese developed some of their management techniques from the theories of our own humanistic psychologists, such as the late Abraham Maslow and Douglas McGregor.

When the Japanese use their techniques on American workers, the changes are astounding. The Japanese Matsushita Company several years ago took over a Motorola plant near Chicago and began to produce Quasar TV sets. The company retained 1000 on-line workers but dismissed half of the 600 supervisors and managers. Within two years, production doubled and the reject rate of sets dropped from 60 percent to 4 percent. Moreover, through good quality control, the company reduced its annual warranty costs from $14 million to $2 million. Just think, too, of the countless customers who were spared the frayed nerves of dealing with defective products. That alone is an important contribution to the nation's sanity.

Our workers are not stupid or lazy. They, like everybody else want a chance for more personal satisfaction. And they are about to get it—even if the trigger is such an eye-glazing event as lower productivity figures. U.S. industry leaders may not understand such a trend as changing personal values, but they do understand dropping productivity.

Because of how economically interlaced the U.S. is with the rest of the world, the only weapon it has against inflation that is in its full control is productivity improvement. As Peter Drucker says in his book *Managing in Turbulent Times*, productivity improvement will be management's most important task for the 1980s. And in this regard, for the 1980s, creative management will be more important than creative technology.

SUMMARY

In America, we are living in a "time of the parenthesis"—a time between eras and that creates turbulence. By definition, turbulence is irregular, non-linear, erratic. But, as Peter Drucker points out, its underlying causes can be analyzed, predicted, managed. An enterprise has to be managed **both** to withstand sudden blows and to avail itself of sudden unexpected opportunities.

The decade ahead will be very exciting and uncertain. We must make uncertainty our friend. It is the only certainty we have. In the decade ahead, we will be restructuring our society.

FROM	TO
an industrial society	an information society
a centralized society	a decentralized society
a national economy	part of an integrated global economy
forced technology	high tech/high touch
top-down society	bottom-up society
North	South
institutional help	self-help
physics	biology
either/or	multiple-option
representative democracy	participatory democracy
economics of scale	appropriate scale
a managerial society	an entrepreneurial society
institutional medicine	personal responsibility
sickness-orientation	wellness-orientation
hierarchies	networking
short term	long term
printing	telecommunications
broadcasting	narrowcasting
department-chain stores	boutiques
family as basic unit	individual as basic unit
party politics	issue politics
non-renewable resources	renewable resources
quantitative information	qualitative knowledge
myth of the melting pot	celebration of cultural diversity
material productivity	knowledge productivity
hired labor	contract labor
left vs. right politics	a politics of the radical center
conquerors of nature	partnership with nature
vertical society	horizontal society

The decade ahead is going to be a very exciting period, a time of great change—and opportunity. The context in which we all operate will continue to change dramatically. Banks, insurance companies and utilities, to name only a few, are in the throes of change. If they try to remain in the business world of the sixties and seventies, they will be out of business.

The Law of the Situation was first postulated by Mary Parker Follett shortly after the turn of this century and is still applicable. . . . It says that when the situation changes, we have to reconceptualize what business we are really in—or what business it would be useful for us to think we are in. Mary Parker Follett went on to identify the following as the tests of a leader:

1. He or she has the power to make purposes understood.

2. He or she has the ability to draw from each person all that there is to achieve the objectives of the organization.

3. He or she has the ability to size up a complex, non-routine situation or series of situations and see it as a whole.

4. He or she has the ability and foresight to see the situations changing.

Something happens—someone perceives it—that person's behavior is predicated upon this perception. The successful individuals in the decade ahead will be the ones who can correctly size up the situation.

During this time between eras we will be a much more complicated society, and the period of working through the structural changes will be painful. But, we will be a more interesting, creative, and nourishing society.

What Can America Do to Solve Its Productivity Crisis?

Business, organized labor and government have all been assigned a share of the blame for recent declines in productivity: business, for focusing more on short-range profit planning than on long-term market planning; labor unions, for stepping up their demands on management; government for imposing tax laws, monetary policies and regulations that stunt economic growth.

It follows that the most urgent piece of business facing the nation today is to reverse the economic and social attitudes that have generated its industrial decline. But how?

To find out, we solicited the opinions of the "best and brightest" on productivity. Our participants—world-class economists, business and labor leaders—were interviewed by World associate editor David Gilman, assisted by special projects editor Eric Ehrmann. "How can America solve its productivity crisis?" we asked them. Herein, their answers.

MILTON FRIEDMAN

Milton Friedman is a senior research fellow at the Hoover Institute of Stanford University. A 1976 Nobel laureate in economics, he spent over 30 years at the University of Chicago, where he rose to the position of Paul Snowden Russell Distinguished Professor of Economics. While there, he stood at the forefront of the Chicago School of monetary economics, which stresses the importance of the quantity of money as an instrument of governmental policy and as a determinant in business cycles and inflation. The author of a variety of books and articles, he collaborated with his wife, economist Rose D. Friedman, on the recent best-selling treatise, Free to Choose. The recipient of six honorary degrees, Friedman served as an economic adviser to Presidential candidate Barry Goldwater, and was an informal adviser to President Richard Nixon.

The productivity problem comes from government measures and it can be solved by eliminating the obstacles that government has placed in the path of productivity

Reprinted from: *World* (Winter 1981).

improvement. The major government measures responsible for the slowdown in productivity are: high marginal tax rates, which discourage productive investments and encourage individuals to accumulate savings in forms that escape tax; inflation, which is partly responsible for the high marginal tax rate and gives individuals an added incentive to put their assets in hedged form rather than in productive form; excessive governmental regulations, ranging over the whole spectrum of industrial activity; the wide uncertainty about future governmental policies with respect to inflation, taxation, and regulation, which makes it difficult for enterprises to plan on long-term horizon.

The solution to these problems is simply to remove these obstacles. We need to have sharply lowered marginal tax rates, we need to conquer inflation, and we need to eliminate the burden of excessive regulations. All of these are measures that only government is in a position to take. In taking them, it is important to emphasize that the real tax on the American people is what the government spends, not the receipts that are called "taxes." The burden of excessive taxation will not be reduced unless government spending is reduced.

It is also important not to go from one extreme to the other. It is counterproductive to impose excessive taxes on savings, and excessive obstacles to investments, but it is just as counterproductive to subsidize savings or investment. What we want is a situation in which consumers, savers and investors are allowed to express their judgements in terms of the real terms that are offered by nature and by public preference. I mention this point because I have found repeatedly in talking with businessmen, a tendency to seek the solution in special subsidies.

Take a very simple example. I believe the failure in corporate taxation to adjust the base for calculating depreciation for infla-

tion, involves taxing capital rather than interest. On the other hand, I believe the investment tax credit is an undesirable measure because it distorts the pattern of investment while hardly adding at all to the aggregate funds available for total investment.

Many have cited a so-called decrease in worker initiative as having contributed to reduced productivity. This is not true at all. Worker initiative is simply a response to the fact that the marginal tax rate on workers is also high. There is nothing wrong with worker initiative, nor with entrepreneurial incentive, that would not be cured by a dose of good government. It is very easy for people to try to find the devil, but the devil is not sluggishness, and the devil is not worker attitudes that shun work. That is nonsense. The working people of this country, the business people of this country, have not changed drastically in the past ten years. What *have* changed drastically are the incentives and conditions under which they operate.

ROBERT B. KURTZ

Robert Kurtz is senior vice president/corporate production and operating services, General Electric. His responsibilities include corporate consulting services, corporate operating services, computer management operation and production resources staff. Kurtz joined GE immediately following his graduation from Lehigh University where he majored in electrical engineering and business, and has held a wide variety of both marketing and manufacturing posts. Outside of the company, he is a member of the Carnegie-Mellon University Business Advisory Council of the Graduate School of Industrial Administration, and associate member of the American Iron and Steel Institute. He is also a member of the Manufacturing Studies Board of the National Research Council Assembly of Engineering, and is chairman of the American National Metric Council.

American industry can improve its productivity performance by helping people work more effectively in two ways: (1) by making sure that things that are fundamental in the plant are done right, and (2) by helping people work "smarter" through new technology. Our government can also help by establishing an industrial policy that will give business a more positive economic environment for growth.

The American business sector must take the initiative by making workers more effective on the front line—the work station—the place where productivity begins. Studies indicated that the average worker in the U.S. today makes a real contribution only about half the time. The other half is wasted on such things as rework, waiting for parts, or problems caused by worn tools—all the result, not of poor workers, but of poor work *management*.

The key to improving productivity on the production line lies with the front-line supervisor. A knowledgeable and inspiring leader will encourage and support a high level of excellence—a standard we sorely need. Today's supervisor must be equipped with the skills to detect work station snags, to hold dialogues with workers about on-site problems, and to gain management's support in assuring that the problems *are* corrected, that the worn tools do get replaced, that parts *do* arrive on time.

The front-line supervisor has the power to regenerate the spirit of productivity that was the hallmark of American industry—to raise the effectiveness of our people to a much higher level. If anyone thinks that's overly ambitious, consider that our industrious grandfathers scored much higher—without the benefit of high technology.

Ironically, the country with the high technology that sent men to the moon is now bogged down with antiquated factories and equipment. But there are encouraging signs which indicate that a revolution in factory technology is now underway. It's a revolution applied to design through interactive computer graphics, and to manufacturing through automation such as robots, which do the repetitive, unpleasant work that people don't want to do.

To accelerate this factory revolution requires an understanding that high technology does not have to be associated with high costs. Right now, U.S. companies can take advantage of different kinds of robots, for example, designed for a range of needs and investment levels—from highly sophisticated models with camera eyes and sensors for complex assembly operations, to lower-cost industrial robots for simpler functions.

So the second thing American industry must do is seize on the new automation—seize on it with the same intense determination as Japan and other nations with which the U.S. competes in world markets.

Now what about the role of government in improving our productivity? Unfortunately, recent policies have encouraged the American people to over-consume and under-invest. These policies have contributed not only to lagging productivity growth, but also inflation, unemployment, trade deficits and less confidence in ourselves and in our world competitiveness.

To restore that competitiveness, we need public policies which stimulate savings and free funds for investment in technology and new plant and equipment.

We do *not* need an industrial policy that has the government picking winners and losers. We *do* need a policy that keeps investment flowing to the young, high-growth industries, while letting *all* industries pass or fail the test of the marketplace—on their own.

PAUL SAMUELSON

Paul Samuelson is an Institute Professor and professor of economics at the Massachusetts Institute

of Technology. A consultant to various federal de-
partments, and former economic adviser to Presi-
dent John F. Kennedy, he won the Nobel Prize for
Economics in 1970. Samuelson also served as
chairman of the President's Task Force on Manag-
ing American Prosperity in 1964. He is an honor-
ary fellow at the London School of Economics.

Part of the productivity problem is external
to us. Much of it is due to the new cost of energy, raw materials, food stuffs and the like.
By and large, it is no reflection on us, for example, that the Chinese had crop failures
and that the Soviet's wheat fields were covered with snow.

Our actual drop in productivity is temporary. It is a worldwide problem, and is the result of two factors: the current recession and
the increase in real OPEC oil prices.

Safety regulation, pollution controls, leisure activities and the like *do* lower productivity as it is conventionally calculated. But
longer lives and purer air are part of what an
affluent society rationally wants. There has
been no quantum step-up in government
regulation in the 1970s, compared with the
1960s, so it's an alibi to blame government
regulations for most of the changed productivity outlook. The truth is that America is
slow investing, and our support for technological and scientific innovation has been
declining. Capital and knowledge are the
prime sources of productivity growth—not
Washington hot air about "supply-side"
economics.

To solve the productivity problem, we
must foster more plentiful capital formation
and garner more support for research and
development. This necessitates austere taxing policies and efficiency in government
and budget surpluses. Monetary policies
must bring down real rates of interest to
clear the market for investments.

We can help the situation by recognizing
today's higher scarcity of energy and making
further adjustments. We must also adopt fiscal measures that favor capital formation as
opposed to consumption. As it stands now,
we have a high-consuming, low-investing
society. We run budget deficits to cure unemployment and stagnation, then we use
tight interest-rate policies to mop up inflation. The result is that consumption is encouraged, while capital formation is
discouraged.

All of this, however, does not add up to a
doomsday picture. But the miracle sprint of
the third quarter of the 20th Century won't
be replicated in the final quarter. Our
growth in the final quarter is more likely to
be 1 or 2 percent.

Consumption has risen, while savings
have declined. The nation's savings has
three components: family saving, corporate
saving and public or governmental saving.
While corporate saving compares favorably
with that abroad, family saving is down
under 5 percent of disposable income. Most
people save through pension plans, and our
social security system makes many feel less
need to save. Finally, the stagnation of real
income, coupled with the rotten real rates of
interest on savings, explains why families
save so little.

GORDON T. WALLIS

Gordon T. Wallis is chairman and chief executive
officer of the Irving Trust Company. He joined Ir-
ving Trust Company in 1940, after graduation
from Columbia College, rising through the ranks
with time out for a stint in the Army Air Corps dur-
ing World War II. Wallis was named chairman and
chief executive officer of Irving Trust Company in
1970. He is a director of General Telephone & Elec-
tronics Corporation, JWT Group, Inc., F.W. Wool-
worth Co., Federal Reserve Bank of New York,
United Way of New York and the Economic Devel-
opment Council of New York. Wallis is also a mem-
ber of the Council on Foreign Relations. He lives in
New York City.

There is an increasing and pervasive awareness that the deterioration of productivity in

recent years is a major national problem, and a remarkable coalescence of opinion that we must do something to reverse this distressing trend. Since half of the solution lies in the recognition of the problem, I find this a particularly encouraging development.

Just about everybody is getting into the act. The academic community has become intensely interested in productivity. Their concern is not a matter of small importance, for few ideas seem to get very far until the academic community is willing to wrap the cloak of intellectual respectability around them.

Nowhere has the shift in concern about productivity been more apparent than among our political leaders. Most of their attention is focused on the problem of capital formation because it is indeed the foundation stone of our economic system. Generation after generation, our system of democratic capitalism has given its workers more tools to work with. There were some major exceptions: two World Wars, the Great Depression, and the most recent development—the Great Inflation of the past decade —have severely undercut capital formation. Our capital stock no longer keeps pace with the growth of our labor force. Since 1969, on average, each new worker has had to make do with fewer, not more, capital resources. This capital shortage has been a key factor in declining productivity growth.

Political leaders of all persuasions have come to appreciate the need for capital. The Reagan campaign strongly emphasized productivity and the whole question of supply-side economics. And there's much talk of tax cuts oriented toward stimulating savings and investment and spurring productivity growth. We should make every effort to ensure that the next tax cut tilts the tax structure away from the stimulation of consumption and toward incentives for investment and productivity.

Saving, of course, is a vitally important aspect of the productivity problem. When most people talk about capital formation they don't give nearly enough attention to where the money is coming from. We tend to forget that we can invest in real terms only if someone provides real savings. In our economy, the corporate executive who makes a decision to invest in plant or equipment may be widely separated from the saver who provides the funds used to make purchases. Thus, a successful national program to stimulate investment must also pay heed to the need to stimulate enough saving to pay for the capital. Otherwise, the shortage of real savings can only be overcome through forced saving in the form of inflation.

Perhaps the most important way to increase saving would be to reduce incentives to spend. President Reagan is committed to streamlining government and limiting or reducing federal spending. The Congress is also more cognizant of the need to hold down government spending and, a necessary adjunct, to stop trying to fine-tune our way out of recessions.

I'm not looking for any sudden miracles. We still need to keep the pressure on our elected representatives to bring government outlays under control, as perhaps the most important policy factor influencing national productivity.

Of course some of the most important factors influencing productivity lie beyond the scope of government taxing and spending and regulation. One important variable is the national state of mind. We'll never match the productivity growth of Germany and Japan until Americans come to look on individual achievement in a more favorable light. We need once again to develop an attitude that tips the hat to success, a society that pats a man on the back when he produces more and thereby adds to the public well-being.

For the first time in many years the majority of our people and the majority of our political leaders understand the need to follow the road of increased saving, investment, and productivity. We have already taken the first tentative steps along that road, and there will be more to come.

HERMAN KAHN

Dr. Herman Kahn, the noted futurist and strategic policy thinker, is the founder of the Hudson Institute in Croton-on-Hudson, New York. Dr. Kahn was instrumental in creating an American awareness of the consequences of nuclear arms proliferation early in the 1960s.

Today's productivity crisis does not stem from a shortage of resources. It's basically a social problem. Many people are simply not willing to make the sacrifices necessary for economic growth.

Right now, we have a group of people—largely upper middle class, worldwide—who are becoming increasingly hostile to productivity. They don't want their economies to grow, or to continue being productive, because, in fact, they, or their families have already made it. Often these people think they are sensitive to the needs of nature, of let's say, the caribou. They feel that they are better than others. They'll ride a bike before driving a car, or they'll take a $50,000 trip around the world and recycle tin cans when they come home. Their self-righteousness is particularly misplaced. Even if we fix the inflation problem, the energy problem, the productivity problem, we will still run into difficulties with those people whose values run counter to productivity.

We talk about the productivity crisis these days because a lot of people are genuinely upset. It's not just another media buzzword.

The Reagan administration is deadly serious about fixing a lot of problem areas. But after those problems are fixed, the roots of the basic troubles will still be found in people's value system. The medicine is going to be strong, and may bring serious social consequences. Whether or not the Reagan administration can cause a genuine change in our national values is the big question.

The Japanese, for example, are quite willing to make sacrifices to help productivity. They are not opposed to shutting their heavy industries down. Their workers will be asked to make an adjustment, to retrain or seek other jobs. In part, the lifetime employment situation in Japan makes this easier. But the Japanese also have a great deal of contract labor that they are laying off. There will be no outcry in Japan. Sacrifice runs deep in the Japanese character.

The Germans, on the other hand, would face extreme social consequences if they shut down. They have much less of a technostructure than Americans or the Japanese. Yet the Germans the the Japanese are slowing down their economic growth. Also, they both compete with us in third markets, which doesn't help us. The only way that competition for third markets helps, ultimately, is that it makes those markets grow more rapidly. I see the United States going along at a steady 3, possibly 3½, percent economic annual growth rate for the next two decades. The rate in Japan and in West Germany should be a bit less, just under 3 percent over the same twenty-year period.

The '60s and '70s saw a great many restrictions on supply, and people seem to be fed up with it. They want to free the system and get it going again. It has been extremely frustrating. We saw the Carter administration trying to help sick industries by allowing labor, management and government to get in bed together. It didn't work. Reagan, on the other hand, believes in deindustrialization—getting rid of the sick industries rather than getting in bed with them. What he wants is a sort of supply side economics that makes sense.

We can gain a great deal of productivity simply by not handicapping and hampering ourselves with regulations. Many people in the business community are talking about how deregulation will help productivity. Actually, I think that it is more important to improve the regulations, to rethink and re-apply them. Once regulations are retooled with productivity in mind, we will be able to throw away the analogy of the "iron trian-gle" of regulatory agencies and their person-nel, staffs of Congress and various pressure groups. These three, working together, as they have often done in the past, are very good at stopping any reform. The Reagan ad-ministration is staffed by a lot of experi-enced people who are savvy about this situation, people who think that regulations can be restructured with productivity in mind, people who think the iron triangle can be busted.

Ultimately, growth in technologies will be our most constant element in winning the productivity crisis. Computers, communica-tions, data processing: that's where the ex-citement is. We will be able to store the entire Library of Congress in something the size of two dictionaries. But though these developments help productivity through their efficiency, they will not make the growth rate go up as rapidly as it has in the past.

LESTER THUROW

Dr. Thurow is professor of economics and manage-ment at the Massachusetts Institute of Technology. An economics consultant for the Los Angeles Times, *and formerly a member of the* New York Times *Editorial Board, he is the author of ten books, including last year's critically acclaimed treatise,* The Zero-Sum Society. *In 1974* Time *magazine named him to its list of "200 Rising Leaders."*

Our productivity problem is akin to death by a thousand cuts. And if you have a thousand cuts, the only cure is a thousand band-aids.

We have literally dozens and dozens of problems that are causing productivity to decline. Taken individually, none of them constitutes a major threat. But together, they signify at the very least that we need multi-ple cures. And that is where it gets difficult, because everyone is looking for this one magical solution.

We certainly need more capital invest-ment. If you believe that we and the Japa-nese are equally smart, and they invest 20 percent of their Gross National Product to our 10 percent, then we can't compete. It simply won't make any difference how hard we work, because they're going to have twice as much capital.

I am strongly in favor of something you might call the national equivalent of a corpo-rate investment committee, designed to pin-point those industries of our economy that show promise and help launch them to greater success. Everyone would agree, for example, that the semiconductor industry was in some sense one of America's "sun-rise" industries. It's my understanding of that industry that it is in the process of shift-ing from a low-capital-intensive technology. Traditionally, the American way of accom-plishing that shift would be to finance it out of retained earnings. The firms borrow a small amount, say 20 or 30 percent of the capital, but basically it's a retained earnings philosophy. The idea is that we will slowly shift to this new technology based on our profits, build these new factories and live happily ever after. The only problem is that the Japanese have an alternative strategy.

In Japan, the strategy is to lend that "sun-rise" industry literally billions of dollars before it ever earns a nickel's worth of profits. They build the factories before we can build them and sell their semiconductors and microprocessors cheaper than we can, running us out of business in the process. Some people contend that they won't be able to do that, but they've done that to both steel and automobiles and they may very well be able to do it to semiconductors. The question is, how do we respond?

Since the private market often identifies companies worthy of investment, but stops short of investing in them itself, we need some sort of committee that is empowered to say, "Hey! This is an American growth area and we will grant them some government loan guarantees." We must bring government into the picture, perhaps in return for nonvoting equities, or even partial ownership so that the public benefits from some of this growth not only in terms of jobs but in terms of rate of return, as well.

You might very well counter that a world where government doesn't get involved is a better world, but that is not the world in which we live. In other countries, governments do get involved, providing the sustained long-term investments that keep firms going before they can generate substantial profits. We must ask ourselves, therefore, "What is the American equivalent?" I submit that it is a national committee which asks of each leading industry. "What do you need to be more successful?" Rather than government telling industry what to do, we'll have industry telling government.

Increasing investment, however, necessitates reducing consumption, and that introduces yet another solution to our productivity problem. We must force people to save by imposing consumption tax increases, needed in any case if we are to regain the revenue lost by investment tax cuts. Let's say we abolish consumer credit. I am not advocating this, but it *would* be one way to

raise savings. If we abolish consumer credit, you can buy a car, for example, only if you have the cash. That necessitates saving all the money ahead of time, which does two things for savings: first, someone else's savings won't have to finance your car and can be used for plant and equipment instead; secondly, business can use your car savings for plant investment and equipment until you save enough to buy your car.

The bad news is that you might have to wait three or four years to buy a car with this method, and if you're not effective in forcing yourself to save it might take even longer than that. But the Japanese and Europeans have been doing it for years. They don't save more money because they love saving and abhor spending; they save more money because they have a system of carrots and sticks that forces them to save. Realistically, since we are not going to abolish consumer credit, we ought to be moving systematically in the direction of making this economic privilege more difficult to obtain.

Increasing our productivity, however, entails more than just cutting consumption and intensifying business investment...it also means knowing how and where to "disinvest" (abandoning "sunset" industries). The Japanese have been much better than us at getting out of dying industries. One of our major problems is that we drag out the whole process of getting out of an industry which is known to be not viable in the United States. Our policy of training workers to move from one industry to another is ineffective, for one thing, and so we end up protecting firms engaged in "sunset" industries. The Japanese, on the other hand, have set up a system where each individual has a vested interest in accepted technical change. With guarantees of lifetime employment, seniority wages, a 50 percent salary bonus and job rotation, they have erased all incentives to resist technological advances. They have organized themselves in such a way that on the worker level there is no conflict between technology and self-advancement. In the U.S., workers resist new technology that might render their functions redundant and lead to their dismissal. The result . . . a decline in productivity.

LLOYD McBRIDE

McBride is the international president of the United Steelworkers of America, a union that represents 1.4 million steelworkers. He started work at the age of fourteen, in a St. Louis metal fabrication plant, and by the time he was 21 had helped the union land its first contract as a member of the first negotiating committee. Three years later he became a career unionist and shortly thereafter, in 1942, was elected president of the Missouri State CIO central body. In 1965 he became director of the district, and twelve years later was elected international president.

In many cases our society is aimed at making sure we spend everything we've got, thereby extracting from the economy far more than we put back. Our failure to reinvest in the most modern equipment and technology shows up in a lagging productivity chart. Workers, after all, are limited as to what they can do by way of contributing to productivity. They work with equipment that is furnished to them by the bosses, in plants that also belong to the bosses.

Still, much has been said about the work ethic and worker attitudes as contributory factors. That attitude is shaped in large measure by employers and employer representatives and, as it is reflected by the relationship on the plant level, is generally adversary in nature. It is not designed by management to be other than adversary. It is a boss-worker relationship that carries with it a certain hostility in which workers are not always overly concerned about the boss's best interests. That relationship reflects itself in productivity.

In all fairness, that attitude tends to prevail when management resists collective bargaining. Those companies that shun the practice of collective bargaining generally view the union as an interloper—an attitude that influences the way in which they relate to their workers. Then, of course, the union reacts, and you've got full-blown hostility on your hands. In such a situation, productivity inevitably suffers.

There are two ways to correct this, and basic to the solution is the involvement of the worker in the decision-making process. Industry must accept the fact that workers quite often are aware of the problems and solutions that would be helpful to the boss, *if* they were included in the process, but with an overall adversary relationship, worker-employer communication is often discouraged. It would be helpful, then, if employers were given to recognize the fact that workers have the brains and the know-how to contribute, and would do so if they only had the opportunity. However, before they can contribute their specialized knowledge that can only be learned on a plant floor, workers must be assured that their job security would not be threatened as a result of the improvements they suggest. Even though their ideas might improve production and cut man hours, they must be assured a continuing role in the scheme of things.

Equipment, however, overrides attitude, and employers must learn that they *must* provide workers with the most modern technology. You can't get productivity with a stone ax. It seems to me that industry in general, and steel in particular, would be well advised to play up the idea that furnishing modern technology is not just desirable, but an integral part of the process. Presidents have historically quarreled with the steel industry with respect to what it charges for its product, and so it seems to me that in order to lower prices by increasing supply we need the most modern equipment we can put our hands on. This is a key factor in achieving our potential in productivity.

If there is going to be hostility towards collective bargaining, it will filter into all of the relationships between the union and management. The labor movement is an intrinsic part of our social structure, and intends to remain that way. We will resist any attempts to fence us out or to diminish our role. I can illustrate, on the other hand, a very cooperative attitude on the part of our own union in many situations where the principle of collective bargaining is accepted as a permanent part of the employer-employee relationship. And where it exists, you will find an attitude of cooperation and a spirit determined to attack the joint problems of the employer and the employees in a very constructive way.

I would personally like to see the Reagan administration enact some labor law reform. I would also like to see the new administration give a spur to collective bargaining which would help ease the adversarial relationship between employers and our union. Only then can we stem the tide of declining productivity.

WILLIAM MILLER

Miller is vice president of labor relations for U.S. Steel. A participant in the last round of steel bargaining as a member of the five-man top negotiating team for the industry, he will also be instrumental in negotiating the new national coal contract as a representative of steel companies that operate their own coal mines. A former head engineer with U.S. Steel who took a law degree and returned for a 20-year stint in labor relations, he is also responsible for safety and environmental health.

Steel is one of this country's basic industries. Our products are fundamental to the needs of this country. It follows, therefore, that productivity improvements in steel would be reflected throughout the entire economy.

The productivity problem is one that in our business is a joint problem between the companies and the steel workers' union, which represents a preponderance of our employees. Increasing productivity can only be accomplished when both management and the union tackle the problem together.

In our 1971 master negotiations with the steelworkers, we negotiated a network of "plant productivity committees," and established one in each of our plants, which runs on anywhere from 4,000 to 12,000 workers. The groups were comprised of three representatives from the plant management and three representatives from the local union representing that plant. We launched those committees and initially they accomplished some worthwhile results. They addressed themselves very much at that time to quality problems as well as to some more traditional productivity problems.

Over the ensuing years, however, we found that the program was not achieving what needed to be achieved. Looking back on what we had done, I am drawn to two conclusions. One is that the committees were established at too high a level. We learned that in a plant of that size, despite the best efforts and best intentions of the six-member committees, they simply did not keep abreast of all the developments in each and every department in that plant. So we decided that we needed to revise our effort in this area by moving those committees down into individual departments. That is one of the changes we made in this latest round of negotiations, and one which we are confident will more effectively identify plant problems, solve them, and raise worker productivity.

The quality of work life on a plant floor is directly related to productivity. Matters such as scheduling, work hours, and the determination of which crews relieve one another—matters which heretofore might have been looked upon too uniformly— should now be regarded with a greater degree of flexibility. "Departmental Participation Teams," which normally discuss the efficiency of operations in their departments, should also be free to talk about some of the matters that bear more on quality of life. Granted, that is reasonably difficult to accomplish in an atmosphere that is already highly structured by a labor agreement.

I do not believe that we can attribute declining productivity to a slackening in worker initiative, as some have done. The make-up of the American worker today has many elements that are competitive and innovative in nature. Instead, we concentrate our effort on what I have mentioned above, as well as on increasing capital investment.

This country currently imports between 17 and 20 million tons of steel a year. Much of that comes from the Japanese, who "dump" their steel here at prices near or even below those that they charge in their home market. The reason—the Japanese produce large quantities of steel very quickly through the process of continuous casting, which allows workers to bypass the time-consuming intermediary step of producing ingots before the final product. We simply do not have the capital monies to purchase and install these continuous casters, which, needless to say, are very expensive. Still, we have recently announced that we are going to build a new continuous caster at the Lorain plant in Ohio, which will enhance our production capability there, as well as our capabilities for producing "rounds"—steel that is later converted into tubular products for the oil and gas industries. We have just announced, as well, that we plan to build a new caster at our Gary, Indiana plant. In short, we are moving as best we can—given the financial restraints—to have more steel made through continuous casting.

Finally, we are attempting to make headway against this critical problem concerning productivity and the quality of work life through the machinery of collective bargaining. Despite what our critics may say, collective bargaining has proven to be a successful instrument in achieving common goals and objectives in the employment relationship between steel labor and steel management. In our collective bargaining sessions every three years, we provide for the filing of local issues by plant-level parties. In the 1980 negotiations alone, U.S. Steel solved some 9,000 local plant-level issues. One of the things I think realized by both sides of the bargaining table this time around was that this matter of local issues and worker grievances has a direct relationship to productivity on the plant floor. Solve the problems, and you increase productivity.

AMITAI ETZIONI

Dr. Etzioni is University Professor at George Washington University. A White House senior adviser from 1979 to 1980, he was a guest scholar at The Brookings Institution for a year prior to that, having served as professor of sociology at Columbia University for 20 years. The author of twelve books on a variety of subjects ranging from political theory to natural science, he is founder of the Center for Policy Research, a not-for-profit corporation dedicated to public policy.

From the 1820s to the 1920s we built a very strong economy, only to have it idle during the Depression. In the '40s, the war effort dominated the economy, followed by 30 years of very high yield. The problem, however, was that we were taking too much out of the economy without plowing back into it sufficiently. Today, after 30 years of overconsumption and under-investment, we are paying the dues.

The number one issue involved in productivity declines concerns the building blocks of our economy. Let's look at them. Our transportation system for goods, as distinct from people, is falling apart. The railroads are falling apart. The highways are deteriorating. The bridges are in terrible shape, and the ports can't handle the coal and the grain. Our transportation system as a whole, while not as bad as that of Panama, is certainly going in that direction.

Energy is another factor. We need cheap, secure energy. Our entire country was built on that, but obviously we are never going to get it again. And so we must make major adaptations to increase energy efficiency and to revise everything from jets to residential homes to conform to our new energy environment.

Basically, we are plowing back about 10 percent of our GNP, compared to 50 percent for the West Germans and 20 percent for the Japanese. It's not that we have to duplicate their numbers. It's just that our numbers are not enough.

We must put our basic productive capacity back in order. We must rebuild the foundations of our economy by shoring up our resources. We need less consumption and more investment. Cutting resources is essential because it represents the best place to free the resources that we need.

Increasing our productivity cannot be accomplished without reversing the recent declines in entrepreneurship, worker initiative and innovation. The best way to get people to work harder is to share with them the fruits of their labor. If workers make an extra effort in the realm of either quality control or productivity, they should be able to share in the gains via a profit-sharing plan. Otherwise, it is difficult for me to see why a worker would put himself out.

It is true that the Japanese offer their workers large salary bonuses, but we can never hope to improve productivity here by trying to take their lead. Many people are prone to look at Japan's productivity and say, "Hah, let's do it the Japanese way!" But theirs is such a vastly divergent system, such a totally different economy and culture. In Japan, people are enslaved to the corporation. The corporation, in turn, is very paternalistic in the way it takes care of them. Consequently, the loyalties there are higher, as are the commitments, and the entire relationship is about as American as a kimono. The best solution is to refer to our own system and devise comparable institutions to deal with our problems. Profit sharing, for example, is a solution we can easily live with.

On the subject of services vis à vis manufacturing, it is true that services are, on average, less productive than the production of hardware, but it would be almost funny to restrict ourselves by saying something like, "Don't eat what you want to eat because it's going to pull the productivity index down." That would be putting the cart before the horse. Instead, what we must do is not blame the service industries exclusively for our woes, but establish our priorities for national investments.

The first line of a nation's investment is its survival. There is no question that you cannot maintain national security unless you invest more in hardware and energy. The second thing we have to worry about is being boycotted and blackmailed by the oil-exporting countries. Our third priority is to put our basic productive capacity in order.

Government can play an important role in helping shore up our productive capacity, but sometimes it hurts more than helps. Bailing out Chrysler, for example, was a terrible mistake...a decision colored completely by the elections. There is a right to fail, just as there is a right to succeed. It is essential for the system to cleanse itself. And there are no exceptions. I don't want to see anything again resembling the Chrysler bailout—ever! It detains the entire process of shedding the unproductive and shoring up the productive.

W. EDWARDS DEMING

W. Edwards Deming is a consultant in statistics to research, industry and government. He is often credited as the statistical mastermind behind the growth of the Japanese economy during the post-war era. He was awarded the Medal of the Sacred Treasure, 2nd Order, by the Emperor of Japan in 1950. The Deming prizes, for advancement of Japanese industrial quality, are awarded annually by the Japanese Union of Scientists and Engineers in his name. Deming received his Ph.D. in mathematical physics from Yale in 1928. A contemporary of Dr. Walter Shewhart, Deming has published and lectured prolifically. He currently lectures at New York University and the George Washington University as well as holding seminars on the management of statistical information around the world. Deming is currently writing a book on productivity and statistics.

Statisticians wish to help management find problems in productivity. That is what they are trained to do. Often, however, management doesn't know that it has problems. Managers know the bottom line doesn't look too good and they read in the papers that productivity is down. But they always look for the problem in the wrong place: blame it on the work force. Management can hold hundreds of hours of meetings and conferences on productivity and just talk. As a statistician, I do something about it.

Statisticians, as experts in the theory of probability, best understand that problems of waste, materials, time and machines require detection and measurement in the first place. Management has no idea where the waste is. The statistician helps him to find it. The simple and important fact is that every fault can be catalogued as belonging either to a specific local condition; the

worker, his machine, something specific he can govern, or, the system.

Problems in the system account for roughly 85 percent of all productivity problems. Yet management traditionally blames the workers for most of the problems. This is false. Statistical methods detect the presence of problems with "special causes," those things the worker can govern, and they only run about 15 percent.

Management is not ordinarily aware that something is wrong with the system. Problems in productivity will only linger and get worse until management identifies and does something about them.

We've always had the statistical knowledge to solve problems in productivity. It's just that we haven't used it. American productivity has been slipping for some time. Other people have been getting ahead. The problem is not a failure to invest in new machinery. It's how we can help people to use what they have and use it efficiently and effectively. Simple statistical analysis will find the waste, and the level of responsibility, for reducing it. Retooling and reindustrializing will only see us fumble around when we try and get to work. Then the problems in productivity will really get worse.

Management has to educate itself to the proper management of statistical information. But they have seminars that waste time discussing things like defectives, quality assurances, process capability and so on. Most managers haven't the faintest ideas of what those words mean. Just a bunch of jawboning. Statisticians, and there are few good ones, have to quantify these terms and know what they are talking about. They can't go around babbling about things like 100 percent quality control, or zero defects.

It has been said that a lot of government regulations are in the way of productivity. The proper management of statistical information by the government can help it become more productive too. But whether government or management, statistical methods give you answers. What problems are "special problems" and which come from the system. Those who don't want to examine the system will have productivity problems forever. Engineers can't find production problems with the naked eye. Computers are generating lots of problems too. And they'll never know it. Through proper use of statistical information you can get the answers on one sheet of paper and not have to deal with piles of printout. That's how you solve the productivity crisis.

Today, top management is showing an increased interest in statistics. Companies are now underwriting seminars and their people are learning about proper management of statistical techniques. But the results will be a long time in coming. Unfortunately, we are starting from negative values.

3

Productivity Models

*I find as impossible to know the parts without
knowing the whole, as to know the whole
without specifically knowing the parts.*
BLAISE PASCAL[1]

Productivity improvement demands a systems approach. Only by understanding the interaction of many organizational variables can a manager
hope to plan and implement a productivity improvement effort that is effective and sustainable. Piecemeal approaches, in which one part of a
problem is attacked or in which one tool or technique is used to excess,
may prevent a coordinated effort throughout the organization. For example, improved productivity in one part of the organization may come at the
expense of reduced productivity in another. Or one factor, such as labor
productivity, may by maximized while other resources are squan-
dered.

The systems approach views the organization as a whole composed of
many interlocking parts. Thus, a single change in one aspect of the organization creates reverberations that affect many other parts. The greater the
manager's understanding of how the parts interact, the more effective the
manager will be in influencing productivity throughout the system.

An essential ingredient in the systems approach is the creation and
use of models. As an abstraction of the real system, a model fosters understanding of complex relationships and provides a framework for analyzing "What if..." questions.

Models and the systems approach are the subjects of this chapter.
First, the need for productivity models will be established. Second, a brief
description of the systems approach will provide the context in which
models can be most effectively used. Finally, modeling will be described,
and different types of models will be discussed. The readings present several productivity models that have proved useful tools for understanding
organizational productivity.

THE NEED FOR PRODUCTIVITY MODELS

Organizations are exceedingly complex phenomena. The sciences of sociology and economics, and the fields of business and political science are devoted almost exclusively to the study of individuals bound together in purposeful organizations. If individuals are complex and difficult to understand, imagine how complex a collection of individuals engaged in a common enterprise can be!

Productivity results from the interaction of people with each other and with the materials, machines, equipment, and other resources of an organization. Although productivity can be defined as a simple output-to-input relationship, the combinations of factors affecting that relationship is almost without limit. Stemming from this complexity are many misconceptions regarding productivity. Some believe, for example, that productivity is a technological factor that can be improved only with faster, more advanced machines and equipment. Others believe it is purely a matter of satisfaction: "The happy worker is the productive worker." These notions—and hundreds of others—are attempts to find "the answer" through a gross abstraction and simplification of reality. Each of these ideas contains an element of truth, but taken as a universal principle, they may cause more incorrect decisions than correct ones.

The list of factors affecting productivity is virtually endless; ultimately almost anything can be included. The *major* factors affecting productivity, however, can be outlined. Ruch and Hershauer, for example, list twelve major factors, many of which have four or more elements.[2] Based upon interviews with a cross-section of managers and workers in a variety of organizations, they distilled this list of factors and framed them into bipolar scales so that a pattern of characteristics could be discerned. This set of "Scales of Measurement" is reproduced as Figure 3–1.

The Scales of Measurement list, define, and identify factors, but provide little insight as to how they might interact. If the factors were independent, then a point on each scale would be seen as "optimal," and a specific pattern would emerge to describe the most productive organization. In fact, when these scales were applied to twelve successful, efficient organizations, such a pattern failed to emerge:

> If there is one broad conclusion that can be drawn from an overview of the scales of measurement for all twelve firms, it must be that commonality among high producing firms can be established only at a gross level of analysis; the more specific the analysis becomes the greater the differences that can be discerned. Most of the firms strongly believe that productivity increases are within the control of the firm; but this apparently common belief is implemented through specific policies, programs, and decisions that are as different among the twelve companies as the products they produce.[3]

SCALES OF MEASUREMENT

1. MANAGEMENT
   A. Leadership Style   participative . . . . autocratic
   B. Selection: PFW   strict PFW . . . . no PFW
   C. Selection Criteria   attitude . . . . skills
   D. Beliefs re Productivity   controllable . . . . uncontrollable

2. SUPERVISION
   A. Leadership Style   participative . . . . autocratic
   B. Selection: PFW   strict PFW . . . . no PFW
   C. Selection Criteria   attitude . . . . skills
   D. Support/Autonomy   maximum . . . . minimum

3. COMMUNICATIONS
   A. Formal   open . . . . closed
   B. Informal   open . . . . closed
   C. Written-Upward   specified . . . . unspecified
   D. Written-Downward   open . . . . closed
   E. Performance Feedback   full . . . . none

4. MONETARY REWARD
   A. Amount of Pay   high . . . . low
   B. Individual Incentive   full . . . . none
   C. System Incentive   full . . . . none

5. NONMONETARY REWARD
   A. Job-Related   high . . . . low
   B. Social Rewards   high . . . . low

6. JOB DESIGN   open . . . . closed

7. WORKING CONDITIONS
   A. Job-Related   maximum . . . . minimum
   B. Not Job-Related   maximum . . . . minimum

8. TECHNOLOGY   leader . . . . anchor

9. LABOR-MANAGEMENT
   CONTENTION   cooperation . . . . belligerence

10. TRAINING   maximum . . . . minimum

11. COMPANY CHARACTERISTICS
    A. Special Programs   dominance . . . . absence
    B. Job Security   maximum . . . . minimum
    C. Reputation   best . . . . worst

12. COMPANY DEMOGRAPHICS
    A. Ownership   unified . . . . diffused
    B. Location   urban . . . . rural
    C. Technological Change   rapid . . . . slow
    D. Worker Representation   unified . . . . diffuses
    E. Labor Market   employer's . . . . employee's

Editor's Note: PFW = promotion from within

Source: William A. Ruch and James C. Hershauer, *Factors Affecting Worker Productivity*
(Tempe, Arizona: Bureau of Business and Economic Research, 1974):50.

Figure 3–1.   Factors Affecting Productivity

The lack of a common pattern indicates that interaction of the factors is as important as the level on the scale. There is a need, therefore, for a model that begins to tie these factors together in ways that foster insight into their interactions. Several of the models in the readings achieve this objective.

THE SYSTEMS APPROACH

A system can be defined, quite simply, as a whole composed of interacting and interdependent parts. A systems approach therefore involves dealing with any complex entity by considering both the parts *and* the way they interact to form a whole.

A bicycle, for example, is a system; the mechanical parts interact to produce movement. If one part is changed—say a larger sprocket is added—some of the other parts will be affected. With a larger sprocket, a longer chain would be required. In addition, the bicycle would now require more effort to pump (input), although it would produce higher speed (output).

The field of general systems theory offers concepts and constructs useful to all who deal with systems.[4] It is one of the "mother disciplines" for fields as diverse as medical science, mechanical engineering, and business administration. The physician must take a systems approach to the treatment of disease, by recognizing that the various subsystems of the body interact, often in subtle ways. A medication prescribed to cure one ailment may create side effects that are even worse.

The emphasis here, of course, is to focus the systems approach on business and governmental organizations, where many of the same principles apply. A manager may implement an incentive pay program, for example, with little planning and no thought to possible side effects. The immediate objective of higher production may be achieved, but quality could suffer greatly. If the measurement system on which the incentive is based is not adequate, subsequent pay inequities could result in a severe drop in morale. In total, then, the treatment could prove to be worse than the disease.

Schoderbek, Schoderbek, and Kefalas indicate that the systems approach for the manager begins by building awareness in a series of three steps:

1. viewing the organization as a system;
2. building a model;
3. using information technology as a tool, both for model building and for experimentation with the model (i.e., simulation).[5]

They point out that this way of thinking is contrary to all that the manager has learned. From the fragmented college curriculum of specialized subjects to the departmentalized organization in which the manager works, the emphasis is on the parts, not on the whole. Reward systems are designed to encourage specialization and analysis, not compromise, coordination, and synthesis.

Systems thinking is a way of culling orderly intelligence from experience. In becoming aware of the interactions in an organization, the manager learns to recognize that it cannot be understood or managed simply by dealing with the parts and adding them together—the whole may be greater, or less than, the sum of the parts. The manager can understand the organization only by studying the impact of the parts and subsystems on each other and the net influence of the parts on the whole organization. "In simple terms, it [systems thinking] enables the manager to get the 'big picture' in its proper perspective, rather than requiring him to devote attention to relatively minor aspects of the total system."[6]

MODELS

A model is an abstraction of reality; it contains some, but not all, of the real thing being modeled. Generally, it is a simplification of reality that permits the study of systems too complex to be understood by any other means. Models permit experimentation when it would be impossible or too costly to experiment with the real thing.

Models come in many types. Most of us are familiar with scale-model airplanes and architects' models of planned buildings. These are examples of concrete models. Abstract models, on the other hand, may use words, symbols, equations, or other abstractions to represent reality.

Models can be quantitative or qualitative. Sets of equations used for inventory reordering or project scheduling form a quantitative model, while organization charts, drawings, and verbal models are qualitative in nature.

Normative models tell what *should* be done; they prescribe or recommend. Descriptive models, by contrast, attempt to explain what *is* and what *can be*. They describe relationships among variables without necessarily proposing a solution.

"Models have always been with us, an awareness that models have existed has been with us for several hundred years, but the recognition of model properties is just yesterday's achievement."[7] Increasingly, managers are using models to guide decision making and systems design. The use of computers to aid in complex calculations or to run in simulation models has given model building a major thrust. The process of model building, however, is not just simplifying reality and dealing with the resulting simplicity. Figure 3–2 illustrates how the manager begins with the real world and forms a conceptual model, less complex but more understandable. From this is born a scientific model, more orderly than the conceptualization, but still less complex than reality itself. From the model, the manager gains the insight needed to help design a system to deal with reality. The system is not a model; it is a reality, with all the complexity of a reality.

The Real World, the Model, and the System

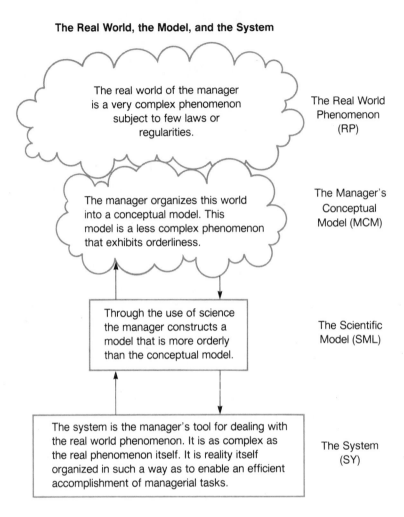

The real world of the manager is a very complex phenomenon subject to few laws or regularities.

The Real World Phenomenon (RP)

The manager organizes this world into a conceptual model. This model is a less complex phenomenon that exhibits orderliness.

The Manager's Conceptual Model (MCM)

Through the use of science the manager constructs a model that is more orderly than the conceptual model.

The Scientific Model (SML)

The system is the manager's tool for dealing with the real world phenomenon. It is as complex as the real phenomenon itself. It is reality itself organized in such a way as to enable an efficient accomplishment of managerial tasks.

The System (SY)

Figure 3–2.   The Manager's Use of Models

In concrete terms, an architect observes the real site, conceptualizes a building, and constructs a series of models, such as drawings, models of stress analysis, and scale models. Using these as a guide for analysis and as a basis for communication with others, the architect supervises the construction of the building—reality.

Management systems are generally more abstract, but the process is the same. The manager observes reality and forms a conceptual model of how best to manage the organization. Drawing on a variety of scientific models, such as behavioral theories, compensation plans, and the like, the manager designs the real system to be implemented.

AN INPUT-OUTPUT MODEL
OF THE FIRM

One example of a conceptual managerial model is the input-output model developed by Ruch and Hershauer.[8] The purpose of this elementary model of the firm (Figure 3–3) is to emphasize that productivity, at the company level, is a function of all of the various inputs to the production function and that, in turn, the firm's productivity is a major determinant of those inputs, because it creates the product or service that generates revenues to pay or otherwise reward the input factors. Viewed in this way, productivity is the pivotal point around which the firm, as a system, revolves.

This model focuses on productivity and enlarges it in relation to the other factors in the system. It distorts the importance of productivity only if one accepts the narrow definition of productivity as the output of direct operative labor. The broader definition of productivity at the firm level—the rate of conversion of inputs into all outputs—is faithfully represented and properly emphasized in this model of the firm.

Peter Drucker recently said that to be concerned exclusively with the productivity of the production worker is to look at only one factor. This leads to suboptimization—raising the productivity of the worker at the cost of reducing the productivity of capital, land, and physical resources. What is needed is a systems approach that includes all factors.[9] This model is designed to focus attention on all of the inputs to the firm's

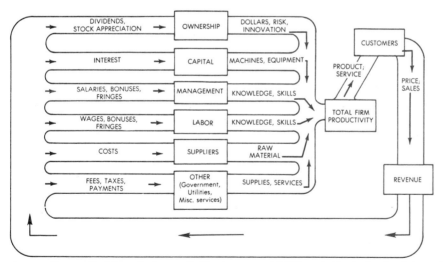

Source: Everett E. Adam, Jr., James C. Hershauer, and William A. Ruch, *Productivity and Quality: Measurement as a Basis for Improvement.* Copyright Everett E. Adam, Jr. 1984. p. 120.

Figure 3–3.   An Input-Output Model of the Firm

productivity, in order to encourage a systems approach to thinking about productivity.

The model identifies six sources of inputs and illustrates the general nature of each. These factors of production are combined in some way within the box labeled "Total Firm Productivity." No attempt is made in this model to indicate *how* these inputs are converted into goods and services. The model's purpose is to emphasize that output is a function of all of these factors, and that productivity is a function of both the level of the inputs and the way in which they are combined.

The output of the firm flows to the customer, where it is converted into dollars of revenue for the firm as determined by price and demand. The revenue then becomes a payment for each of the inputs to the firm, and the process recycles.

When the firm changes the absolute or relative level of the input factors, it changes the level of output, even though the efficiency of combining those inputs has not changed. For example, a new piece of capital equipment may be installed (perhaps combined with a reduction in labor) to cause an increase in output. If demand permits, this will result in a revenue increase sufficient to cover the cost of the additional capital. The change, it is hoped, will also generate enough revenue to increase the flow of funds to the owners of the firm. If labor is reduced as a part of the change, payment to this human factor is correspondingly reduced.

Sometimes changes occur that are outside the control of the firm. For example, an increase in the interest rates on capital will make capital more expensive in relation to labor. This should indicate a change toward a more labor-intensive process in an effort to return the system to equilibrium. It should be noted, however, that the ownership factor is often residual, in the sense that it seldom has the power to demand higher payment for its inputs; it must accept what remains after all other inputs are covered.

Changing the absolute or relative level of the inputs is only one way to return the system to equilibrium. A second way is adjusting the price of the output. If demand permits, an increase in the cost of some input, say, in the cost of raw materials, can be passed along to the customer through an increase in price. Thus, if the model is viewed as a hydraulic network, price can be interpreted as an adjustment valve to balance the flow of output and dollars, just as each input has an adjusting valve to control the flow of that input into the system.

Another major adjusting valve—one that is often overlooked—is productivity. If the cost of an input increases and demand in the marketplace does not permit adjustment of the "price valve," the firm may have to "work smarter" if it is to avoid a decrease in payments to its ownership. Working smarter means adopting a better, more efficient way of combining inputs, in order to create more output with the same, or even fewer, inputs. In other words, working smarter means attempting to increase productivity.

If productivity is increased in direct response to cost pressures from some input, the additional funds generated may be directed exclusively to that input. But, the real world is seldom that simple. Many changes are taking place simultaneously, and the system is generally in a state of "dynamic disequilibrium," attempting to make adjustments in an effort to achieve a better balance. Thus, when a productivity gain is achieved, it is sometimes difficult to isolate the direct cause of the change or to recompense one input factor. Of the input groups, ownership and labor are both likely to claim credit for the productivity gain and feel that they deserve the benefits from it.

This issue—the equitable division of the benefits of productivity gains among owners, management, and labor—is at the heart of many labor disputes and has formed the basis for many profit-sharing plans now in existence. This model will not solve that dispute, but it may serve to clarify the nature of the dispute by diagramming the part that each factor plays in the productivity of the firm and by establishing that each has a legitimate claim to the returns from productivity gains. (For a discussion of gainsharing, see Chapter 14.)

Although this model provides some insights into productivity as an integral part of an input-output analysis of the firm, it leaves a great deal unsaid by representing productivity as a "black box." Other models, such as the servosystem model in the readings for this chapter, look into that "black box" and examine how various individual and organizational factors affect worker productivity.

SUMMARY

Because productivity is such a complex set of interrelated variables, a systems approach is needed to recognize the interaction of the parts and their effect on the whole organizational system. The systems approach involves, in part, modeling complex phenomena in order to create greater understanding, and better results, in the planning, design, and implementation of productivity improvement efforts.

Compared to most disciplines, productivity modeling is in its infancy. Detailed mathematical simulations of productivity systems do not yet exist. The models created to date, however, are useful conceptualizations of the factors affecting productivity and their interaction.

SELECTED READINGS OVERVIEW

The Productivity Focus Model described by John Belcher was developed at the American Productivity Center, based upon the experience of many organizations in productivity improvement efforts. Its simplicity belies the complex relationships involved, but it has proven to be useful as a starting point for diagnosing organizational weaknesses and planning to overcome them.

The second reading describes "A Worker Productivity Model and Its Use at Lincoln Electric." The model, which Ruch and Hershauer developed under a research grant, was used in Lincoln Electric as part of a training program for supervisors, but in this case the supervisors were asked to study the model and explain it to the rest of the class.

Next Chapter

"Models" could also be an appropriate title for the next chapter. While examining productivity and human needs, the chapter describes a number of conceptual models, including Maslow's Hierarchy of Needs and Herzberg's Model of Motivation. Behavioral models help us to understand the role of human needs in the operation of the organization. These "models" look primarily at only one part of a system, however—the human part. By designing systems that take individual needs into consideration, managers can develop more productive organization.

Review Questions

1. If you were the project manager for a "greenfield" project (building a new plant from the ground up), list and describe several types of models you would need to build the plant, do the layout, and design the human systems that would operate this new facility.

2. Consider the solar system as a system. Describe the parts, or subsystems, and how they interact. Include in your description some of the physical laws that apply. Then describe the educational system of your community in the same way.

3. Using the input-output model by Adam, Hershauer, and Ruch, suppose that the wage rate of labor suddenly increased by ten percent. Trace that change through the network and describe several ways that you, as a manager, could restore the system to equilibrium.

4. Of the seven factors Belcher describes in the Productivity Focus Model, which one is the most important? Which one must be done first, second, . . . last?

5. An age-old question concerns the relationship of performance to satisfaction. In the Servosystem Model of Worker Productivity, does satisfaction lead to higher performance, or does high performance lead to satisfaction?

JOHN BELCHER
Staff Vice President, American Productivity Center

Productivity Focus: A Structure for Organizational Diagnosis and Planning

An important early step (and later an on-going part) of any productivity improvement effort is opportunity assessment or the identification of tactical approaches to increase productivity. Through the assessment process, an organization identifies the best opportunities for productivity improvement so that it can focus its scarce resources.

All managers do assessment to one degree or another, but more often than not, assessment is an informal process and does not receive the time and attention that it warrants.

In addition, the assessment that does take place is typically narrow in scope, focusing on technical or capital-related opportunities. And all too often, assessment is strictly a management endeavor with no involvement from the vast majority of the workforce. The result of these shortcomings is limited ideas, inadequate evaluation and insufficient employee support for the improvement effort designed to follow the assessment.

EFFECTIVE ASSESSMENT APPROACHES

To be effective, assessment should be a required, formalized process, multi-disciplinary in nature, involving as many employees as possible. It should be comprehensive—examining the potential for improvements in labor, capital, materials and energy deployment. It should not consider just technical approaches to improvement but should also examine human resource management and quality of work life improvement opportunities.

The assessment approach chosen will depend largely upon situational issues like size and geographic proximity of work units, types of employees, time and budget constraints, etc. It might take the form of audits, structured diagnostics, functional analyses, surveys, informal observations, interviews, operations analyses, structured brainstorming or a combination of techniques.

PUTTING THE FINDINGS IN FOCUS

Once an organization begins asking its employees "What could make you more productive in your job?" the floodgates open and the opportunities for productivity improvement seemingly pour forth. The resulting list of barriers and potentials may at first appear random and divergent.

Reprinted from: *Manager's Notebook* 1, No. 2 (1984).

What is needed following any assessment process is a means of bringing some focus to the findings. Since most successful productivity efforts have a number of principal elements in common, it is only logical to design the assessment mechanism and to sort out the issues raised in the assessment process according to the same elements.

The Productivity Focus framework can serve as a model for this process. Essentially, the model organizes opportunities and barriers into seven key areas—assets, goals, rewards and recognition, communication, measurement and analysis, employee participation and organization and leadership.

Productivity Focus

Productivity Focus is a structure and process for organizational diagnosis and planning. It serves as the basis for systematically examining the seven key areas of organizational functioning specifically with respect to their impact on productivity and quality of work life.

ASSETS

If the assessment turns up problems regarding outmoded equipment, poor workflow or lack of job knowledge, the organization may want to examine its use of assets (including labor, capital and material resources) as a means of improving overall productivity.

The assets component is the broadest of the seven, encompassing those opportunities for improving the utilization of the organization's resources. The more traditional approaches to productivity improvement reside here: revised plant layout or workflow, improved production scheduling practices, reduction in equipment downtime, skills training, job redesign, etc. The common denominator of these approaches is that they are designed to improve the effectiveness of the organization's utilization of its labor, capital or material assets.

GOALS

What goals appear to be driving employees' behavior? How have these goals been established and communicated? Do informal or personal goals appear to be overriding the formal ones?

Goals establish expectations and direct individuals' efforts toward a desired end. This component of the assessment model analyzes the impact of the operative goals, both formal and informal, of the organization. Opportunities may exist through the establishment of more explicit operating goals, through better communication of existing goals, through the provision of a better balance between goals (such as volume/quality goals) or through wider involvement in the establishment of goals.

REWARDS AND RECOGNITION

What are people rewarded for? Do they receive recognition for doing a good job? Are the criteria for promotion clearly understood by the work force? Do employees see a clear link between performance and rewards?

The impact of the reward system, both financial and non-financial, is examined in this component. It is often concluded that the system of financial rewards is not encouraging the kind of behavior desired, and that performance evaluation and merit increase practices are not providing effective incentives. Promotional criteria may not be clear to the organization, with the result that employees are demotivated. Perceived inequities in the reward system may be a source of resentment and a barrier to employee commitment. Recognition, a powerful motivator and a quality of work life element, is often not an operative tool.

COMMUNICATION

If the assessment process reveals confusion among employees as to what is expected of them or widespread distrust of management's decisions, communication may be an important improvement opportunity.

Generally one of the most fertile fields for productivity improvement, communication is examined from all points of view—top down, bottom up and sideways. Communication may be a serious barrier to performance, as when employees lack the information to perform their jobs effectively. Ineffective communication between departments may be a hinderance to productivity improvement. Communication also has important quality of work life implications; when employees are informed about organizational performance and the reasons behind decisions, their level of satisfaction and commitment is raised.

MEASUREMENT AND ANALYSIS

The development and use of reliable productivity measures covering all major in-

puts may seem to be an obvious opportunity, but this component encompasses more than productivity measurement. It addresses the organization's entire information system and its use of analytical data to study and solve problems. In many cases, adequate data to define problem causes and facilitate solutions are lacking.

An organization may, for example, be concerned about a high rate of turnover but lack information regarding the reasons behind employee resignations. Not knowing whether the turnover resulted primarily from dissatisfaction with wages, benefits, working conditions, career opportunities, conflicts with management or some other cause, it would be difficult for management to come to grips with the problem.

EMPLOYEE PARTICIPATION

In this component of our model, the organization evaluates the degree to which employees have an opportunity to input ideas and influence decisions. Are there formalized programs to encourage employee involvement? If so, how well are they working? Which involvement techniques would be most appropriate for this organization?

Prior to the assessment process, of course, management should have made a commitment to quality of work life and employee involvement as integral elements of the productivity management process and should have attended to the broader, more strategic issues surrounding productivity and quality of work life: visible management commitment, reinforcement, etc. During the assessment phase of the effort, management would be concerned with the design of specific employee involvement structures, taking into consideration the existing environment for participation and the degree of management experience in involving employees.

ORGANIZATION AND LEADERSHIP

What does the assessment process reveal about the predominant management style? Does the organization structure get in the way of organizational effectiveness? Are there major turf issues between functional groups?

The hub of the assessment model, the organization and leadership component addresses management practices and capabilities. Management accountabilities, delegation practices and organization structures are all appropriate subjects for examination here. The leadership capabilities of first-line supervisors should be evaluated as a possible improvement opportunity. Inter-department cooperation and collaboration often surface as an issue in this component. A thorough diagnosis may reveal any number of management practices that are inhibitors to productivity improvement.

CONCLUSION

The Focus model is a useful tool for diagnosing any organization—manufacturing or service, blue collar or white collar, business or government. The contemplation of its seven components broadens one's thinking about productivity and the possible routes to productivity improvement.

The effective execution of the assessment process clearly requires a multi-disciplinary team, with technical, human resource and financial skills represented. Another requisite is broad organizational participation; attempting to assess improvement opportunities by gathering information only from management is a prescription for biased, narrow results.

JAMES C. HERSHAUER
Arizona State University
WILLIAM A. RUCH
Arizona State University

A Worker Productivity Model and Its Use at Lincoln Electric*

ABSTRACT

A worker productivity model was developed to illustrate the manner in which factors interact to yield productivity. Thirteen individual factors and fourteen organizational factors are combined as a servosystem using procedures similar to those of industrial dynamics. Use of the model in training supervisors at the Lincoln Electric Company is reported.

INTRODUCTION

The Lincoln family has always been vitally interested in the productivity of their business enterprises and the well-being of their employees. John C. Lincoln established a company at the turn of the century, and began to apply and refine his "win-win-win" philosophy. The prime tenet of this philosophy is simply that all parties in a business venture can win: stockholders, employees, suppliers, and customers. More than just a "style of management," this philosophy has been applied to a variety of business ventures by other members of the Lincoln family. David C. Lincoln, a nephew of John C.,

has several business ventures in Arizona. As he is interested in making these even more productive for all concerned, he offered a research grant to Arizona State University to study the factors affecting worker productivity.

To carry out this research, we first had to develop a definition of productivity that cut through the maze of confusing and conflicting definitions in the literature. We then began a search for worker productivity models that had already been developed. Our findings: they do not exist. With the exception of a model by Sutermeister [19], we could find no comprehensive conceptual frameworks of worker productivity. Consequently, we set out to develop our own. We developed the initial framework for the model and then set out to visit seventeen organizations of varying size and type to help us further develop and refine our model.

Recognizing that Lincoln Electric was setting records in productivity, we wrote to Mr. William Irrgang, Chairman of the Board, and Mr. George E. Willis, President of Lincoln Electric. They agreed to let us tour the plant

*Based on research funded by the David C. Lincoln Foundation. An earlier version of this paper was presented in the Session on System Dynamics, National ORSA/TIMS Joint Meeting, Las Vegas, Nevada, 1975.

Reprinted from: *Interfaces* 8, no. 3 © 1978, The Institute of Management Sciences, 290 Westminster Street, Providence, RI 02903.

69

and talk to key people in the organization. Their input proved to be quite valuable in making our model more realistic and workable.

The completed model has been well received and is becoming well used. Lincoln Electric, for one, uses the worker productivity model outlined in this article as a training tool for front-line supervisors. They felt that the model properly described their operating philosophy and, thus, should be understood by all supervisors. One supervisor, in each of three departments, was given the model to study. At the next supervisor's meeting, this individual was asked to present and explain his analysis of the model to his peers. Hearing the presentation from a fellow supervisor, rather than from a top manager, ensured more effective communication of the ideas in the model and enhanced its chances for acceptance and implementation.

George E. Willis, President of Lincoln Electric, informed us of the following results, based upon their use of the model:

1. When the supervisors presented the model to their peers, it was obvious that they had attained a better understanding of the complexity of their jobs, and the interrelationships and tradeoffs that lead to higher productivity.

2. It has, according to Mr. Willis, significantly improved interactions with employees and peers for two of the three supervisors who studied and presented the model. (The third supervisor, who is nearing retirement, showed no appreciable change.)

The use of this model at Lincoln Electric, and in other contexts such as executive seminars, indicates that it has some value in explaining the complexity of productivity. It is appropriate, therefore, that we share this model with others.

THE IMPORTANCE OF PRODUCTIVITY

Productivity is one of the most popular topics of discussion today. Labor leaders, managers, stockholders, and consumers are all talking about it. But, is anyone really doing anything about it?

It is apparent that much more is said about productivity than is known about it. Sound research and theory are badly needed. Perhaps the primary reason we are not doing a better job of increasing productivity is confusion about defining and measuring the concept. Few concepts have so many different definitions and interpretations as the concept termed *productivity*; yet few terms are so often used as if a precise definition existed. Some persons assume "productivity" means using more capital and less labor, while others mean working harder, faster, or smarter. Some would say "productivity" means more output, while others mean the same output produced with fewer resources. If the speaker and the listener have different definitions, then communication will be difficult, if not impossible.

DEFINING PRODUCTIVITY

Productivity, in its most general sense, refers to a ratio of outputs to inputs. It *should* refer to the ratio of *all* outputs of an organizational entity to *all* of the inputs employed [6], [8]. The obvious difficulties of defining and measuring either the numerator or the denominator of that ratio, however, prevent utilization of this ratio for anything except the most general statements. These difficulties stem from three related problems:

1. problems of partiality;
2. problems of measurement;
3. problems of scale.

Most operational definitions of productivity are really partials of the basic input/

output ratio. Labor productivity, for example, is defined as output (measured in dollar value or in units), divided by man-hours of labor (usually, though not always, direct labor) [4]. This definition forces the user of the statistic to make some assumptions regarding changes, if any, in the capital equipment employed. Similarly, "capital productivity" usually means output per dollar of capital employed, but it is seldom clear what assumption is being made regarding changes in other inputs.

Measurement problems exist with even the simplest of partial definitions of productivity [9]. The search for a common unit almost invariably leads to dollars, yet the dollar value of both inputs and outputs may reflect inflationary trends, social changes, market considerations, and many other factors not directly related to the productivity changes to be measured.

Problems of scale arise from the fact that "productivity" can refer to a single worker, a group, plant, company, industry, or even nations. At different levels of aggregation, the definition of productivity changes. The productivity of a company is not the sum of the productivity measures of its elements (labor and capital) [13]. National productivity is yet a third concept—related but significantly different from individual or company productivity [22].

With such problems, it is clear that the development of a general operational definition of productivity is not a simple task [13]. Consequently, for a point of reference, the following definition of productivity is advanced. *Productivity relates input to output through a conversion process.*

The "Servosystem Model of Worker Productivity", depicted in Figure 1, represents this conversion process for workers. It is based upon inputs from an extensive review of the literature [8], [16], [20], [21] and from the information gathered during visits with several productivity-conscious organizations [15]. The models by Lawler [11] and Sutermeister [19] were particularly useful in forming the model. In addition, the modeling procedures of industrial dynamics, as developed by Forrester [7], guided the form used.

STRUCTURE OF THE MODEL

The model depicted in Figure 1 has been kept at a level of detail that, hopefully, maintains both conceptual meaning and practical utility. Individual worker performance is shown as the focal point of the model; organizational and individual factors either directly or indirectly impact this performance. Any factor shown in the model can be traced through the model as an input to worker performance. In fact, many factors also can be traced to performance as an output. Because of this feedback effect and the time delay characteristics, the model has been labelled a "servosystem", i.e. a dynamic feedback system. As stated by Nancy Roberts [14], "A dynamic feedback system is an ongoing set of relationships in which the output of an action taken by one person or group eventually has an effect again on that person or group."

Factors are indicated in the model in several different ways. First, individually-controlled factors are distinguished from organizationally-controlled factors by differently shaped figures. Second, factors that may be changed significantly only in the long run are identified separately by dotted-line figures. Third, some factors serve to control the rate of transfer of one or more of the other variables. Fourth, the model includes time as an implicit factor, since the feedback would take place over time. The time factor is also explicitly included by the time delays shown at a variety of places in the model. These delays indicate that changes in the factors to which they relate will affect performance gradually over time.

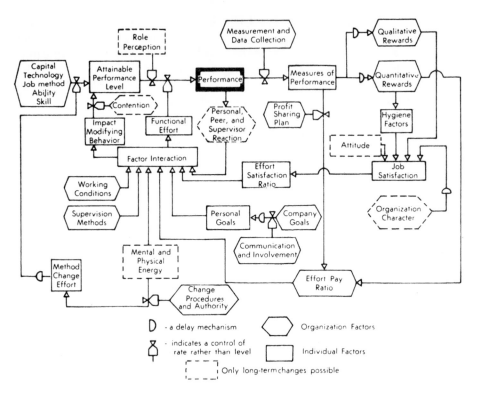

Figure 1.   Servosystem Model of Worker Productivity

Fifth, the "factor interaction" block indicates that "functional effort" of individuals is a complex phenomenon that is more than a simple addition of the levels of the factors that are direct inputs of the individual.

A detailed description of each of the significant portions of the "Servosystem Model of Worker Productivity" is included in the Appendix to this article.

MODEL LIMITATIONS AND POTENTIAL

The primary difficulty in practical usage of the model, as well as its extension to simulation analysis, is that it is not currently possible to measure the behavioral and managerial factors quantitatively. Thus, the abil-

ity to predict or evaluate absolute levels of performance is beyond theoretical development. However, it is possible to evaluate the direction and relative impact of factor changes in an organization by combining: (1) the model; (2) hypothesized behavioral relationships; and (3) partial quantification of organizational factors. This can be accomplished by the use of Likert-type [12] scales.

A major obstacle to extensive and ready use of the model is validation. Because there are no standard performance measures, it is impossible to make empirical comparisons across organizations. Although longitudinal comparisons within specific organizations are more feasible, the length of time involved and the fact that only a few organizations can be sampled, make such research unattractive to most academicians and organizations.

Perhaps the greatest potential of the model is its use as a diagnostic model. The model makes it possible to determine the implied relationships of existing conditions and to trace the expected impact of various predicted relationships.

To the reader who may be discouraged by the stated limitations, we offer the following quote:

> As science develops more and more measures, it also requires new kinds of qualitative judgements...Quantification at any stage depends on qualification. What is qualified at one stage may be quantified at another; but at any stage some qualitative judgements are required. Consequently, progress in science is a function not only of an increased capacity to quantify efficiently (i.e. to measure) but also of an increased capacity to qualify efficiently [1].

CONCLUSION

We believe that we have qualified worker productivity effectively, that is, we have shown relationships correctly at a proper level of complexity and aggregation. We suggest that the "Servosystem Model of Worker Productivity" provides a level of qualitative analysis needed to define, comprehend, and improve productivity. It forces managers and researchers alike out of the "partial measure" trap; it focuses concerns about measurement of productivity by demonstrating desired organizational goals and points of resource consumption; and it draws attention to the major factors which must be considered in developing productivity improvement programs.

APPENDIX

Model Description

In the figures that follow, each significant portion of the model is explained separately.

It is important to note that these are only parts of the total model; they do not stand on their own. Once understood, they must be integrated into the total model depicted in Figure 1.

Figure 2 indicates that there are basically two ways to obtain "performance." First, a potential for each job exists as an "attainable performance level." Second, the functional effort exerted by an individual determines what portion of the attainable is achieved.

Figure 2 also concentrates on one factor influencing functional effort: "personal, peer, and supervisor reaction." Worker performance leads to some reaction from both peers and supervisors and also leads to an internal reaction by the worker himself in the form of pride, shame, indifference, or some other feeling. These reactions become a part of the factor interaction which results in functional effort. A common example of this phenomenon is the problem with rate busting that exists in many organizations. Standard performance set by the company may not be achieved because workers have decided, within informal groups, that the standard is unfair. They can set their own lower standard and are able to enforce conformity through the creative use of peer

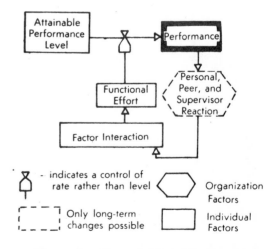

Figure 2. Central Model Factors

pressure on the new employee who attempts to reach the organizational goal.

Figure 3 centers on the "mental and physical energy" of the worker and how this energy is employed in the organization. Typically, most of the worker's energy flows through the factor interaction to become functional effort directed toward performance.

In some organizations, however, emphasis is placed on working smarter rather than working harder. This occurs when an explicit program exists that encourages changes in the methods and procedures for performing the work. Thus, a worker may devote some fraction of his mental and physical energy to "method change effort" which should help to determine a better way to perform the job rather than simply using that time and energy to produce a few more units. This allows the resources of the organization to be employed more efficiently and effectively and raises the attainable performance level for the task. Thus, organizations may control attainable performance levels through "change procedures and authority" as well as through the normal investments in "capital, technology, job method, ability, and skill."

An individual variable that intercedes between attainable performance level and functional effort is also shown in Figure 3. An improper "role perception" on the part of an individual worker may cause his functional effort to be devoted toward an improper objective and result in poor performance regarding desired objectives.

In Figure 4 we address performance. True performance leads to "measures of performance"—measures that are as accurate or as inaccurate as the "measurement and data collection" system employed. Measures of performance, in turn, lead to "qualitative (nonmonetary) rewards" and "quantitative (monetary) rewards." Both types of rewards have important influences on the individual's "job satisfaction".

Job satisfaction leads to an individual factor, the "effort/satisfaction ratio." This factor represents the amount of effort an individual is willing to expend for different levels of satisfaction. Different individuals, of course, could have vastly different effort/satisfaction ratios. In addition to being a determinant of job satisfaction, quantitative rewards also lead to the "effort/pay ratio." This organizational factor indicates the amount of pay the organization considers commensurate with a given level of effort— a concept reflecting the notion of a fair day's work for a fair day's pay.

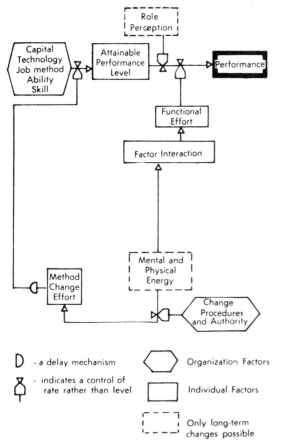

Figure 3.   Worker Energy and Technology

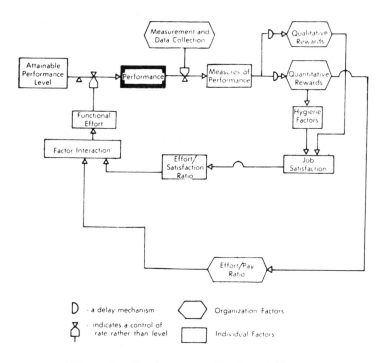

Figure 4.   Performance Feedback Factors

Both of these effort ratios lead to the critical factor interaction box. Here the effort ratios interact with the other factors in some complex way to yield the functional effort of the individual at his job. If that functional effort is normal, then the attainable performance level will be achieved in actual performance. If effort is less than normal, actual performance will fall short of what is possible. At this point, we have come full circle and the feedback cycle is ready to begin again.

Figure 5 is used to highlight those variables whose impact on functional effort is fed back through the effort/satisfaction and effort/pay ratios.

Measures of performance lead to the effort/pay ratio in two ways. First, monetary payment is reflected in quantitative rewards through programs regarding salary, hourly rate, direct bonus for above-standard per-formance, pay increments reflecting performance relative to others, and price incentives. Second, there is a direct link whose rate of transfer is controlled by the "profit sharing plan" used by the organization. The concept of profit sharing is to have all employees share in any improvements in organizational savings or profits immediately and directly in a known manner. The effort/pay ratio is controlled by the organization. However, employees are quick to discover any discrepancies, inequalities, or inadequacies that exist in the ratio structure.

Effort/satisfaction is a more nebulous and complex ratio controlled by the individual worker based upon his job satisfaction. Job satisfaction level is strongly influenced in the long run by the "attitude" of the individual and the "organization character." In the short run, "hygiene factors" that the individual can purchase with quantitative rewards provided and motivation created by qualitative rewards received can cause fluctuations in an individual's job satisfaction.

In most of the previous partial diagrams the factor interaction block has been an integral part. Figure 6 highlights the factors comprising this interaction and its immediate results.

There is strong evidence for linking each of the interacting factors shown to worker performance; however, the synergistic effect of combining them in a specific mix is not well understood. Typically, each factor is studied, analyzed, and changed separately with additive combinatorial effects being assumed. This model makes no simplistic assumption, but neither does its propose the specific nature of the interactions.

In addition to previously discussed variables, two others—"working conditions" and "personal goals"—have a direct bearing on the functional effort of the individual. Personal goals will relate back to "company goals" to the extent that "communication and involvement" characterize management philosophy. The congruence of personal and company goals largely determines the functional nature of personal effort, whereas the other six variables entering the factor interaction block primarily determine level of effort.

The result of the factor interaction may be functional effort—effort expended on the task in organizationally acceptable ways. An alternative, however, is for the worker to engage in some "impact-modifying behavior" (often to relieve the boredom of a routine or

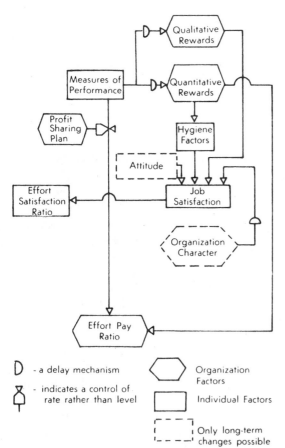

Figure 5. Effort Ratios

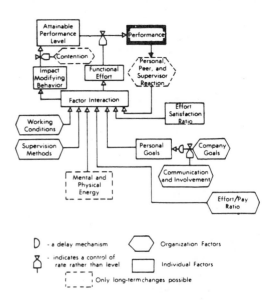

Figure 6. Factor Interaction Variables

distasteful job) and engage in nonproductive or even antiproductive acts. This impact-modifying behavior, controlled partly by the degree of "contention" between labor and management, may reduce the attainable performance level by disrupting the flow of work, destroying company resources, losing time, or a host of other variations.

When the five partial diagrams are combined, the result is the integrated model presented as Figure 1. The complexity of the model is necessary. Anything less would omit significant variables or relationships and would thus cloud the understanding of worker productivity.

PART TWO

Individual Productivity

4

Productivity and
Human Needs

*The problem of management (in any organization or society)
can then be approached in a new way: how to set up social
conditions in any organization so that the goals of the
individual merge with the goals of the organization.*

ABRAHAM H. MASLOW[1]

PRODUCTIVITY AND INDIVIDUALS

The productivity models covered in Chapter 3 help define "productivity."
At the heart of these models are the people—managers and employees—
who make it all happen. People make a difference at work.

This chapter looks at the needs of people and suggests answers to the
following questions: Why are people better workers at one time than at
another, or in one organization than in another? Why are some people better workers than others? Why are people better at some jobs than at others? The reasons for these differences are explained, in part, by various
theories.

Some Theories About Individuals

Several theories attempt to explain differences in work performance.
While theories have different points of view, they all assume that needs
affect the way individuals work.

Maslow's hierarchy of needs

Based on early needs theorists such as H.A. Murray,[2] Abraham Maslow[3] says human needs fall into five categories, in this order: physiological, safety, love, esteem and self-actualization. He also says these categories build on each other. Physiological needs, such as hunger and thirst, must be largely met before the next level, safety, can become important to a person. And personal safety needs must be met before feelings of love or belonging can matter. Once the need to belong, to feel "loved," is met, esteem needs for recognition, growth and accomplishment become activated. The building process goes on until a person reaches the need for self-fulfillment or self-actualization, as Maslow calls the fifth and final level in his hierarchy of needs.

Maslow's theory also says that once each level of needs is met, those needs no longer motivate the person. New needs emerge from the next level up, and it is these new needs the person will try to fill. Although needs may temporarily be suppressed, lower-level needs cannot go unsatisfied for long while someone pursues the higher level needs.

How does Maslow's hierarchy of needs theory apply to work? It says that to motivate an employee, a manager must learn which needs are unmet in that employee. Then, the manager must assign work and give rewards in ways that meet those needs. For example, a person whose physiological needs are not met may take any job that pays enough money to buy food. But if the physiological, safety and love needs are met, the employee will need work that is interesting and challenging enough to add to his or her self-esteem. For this employee, a reward such as praise may mean more than a pay increase.

Alderfer's ERG model

C.P. Alderfer[4] reduces Maslow's five levels to three. In Alderfer's ERG model, "existence" includes physiological and safety needs, "relatedness" covers love, and "growth" includes esteem and self-actualization needs.

Research does not support the idea that needs always follow the described order.[5] A useful point of both Maslow's and Alderfer's theories, though, is that only unmet needs can motivate a person. After a point, more of the same reward may have a diminishing value.

Herzberg's motivation-hygiene theory

F. Herzberg[6] says two types of factors affect how people feel about their jobs. The first factor is called "satisfiers." It includes everything that makes people feel good about work and makes them want to do a good job. These satisfiers include achievement, recognition, work itself, responsibility, advancement and growth. Because the satisfiers make people feel good about work, they also are motivators—elements that motivate employees to improve job performance.

The second factor is called "dissatisfiers." It includes things that can make employees feel unhappy at worst, but only neutral at best. Company policy, working conditions, supervision, salary, relationships with the boss and with peers, status, security and personal life all make up this factor. Herzberg calls them "hygiene" factors, because they are part of the environment. Like garbage collection in a town, they can cause problems if they are not taken care of, but if they are done well, no one will notice. When minimized, the most a hygiene factor can do is prevent dissatisfaction. It takes satisfiers, like those listed above, to motivate employees.

Controversy surrounds the motivation-hygiene theory. Some critics say that a hygiene factor for one group may be a motivator for other groups.[7] Others say that by blaming bad feelings on the environment and taking personal credit for good feelings, the theory allows for a lot of excuses.[8] A useful point of Herzberg's theory, though, is that managers must find ways to help employees go beyond neutral and feel motivated. A safe environment and equitable policies, for example, only meet employee's expectations. Other rewards are needed to elicit superior performance.

Achievement- affiliation- and power-motive theory

This theory asserts that three needs—achievement, affiliation and power—motivate people and affect how they act.

David McClelland[9] argues that people with a high need for achievement take personal responsibility for solving problems, set moderate goals, take calculated risks and want concrete feedback on how well they are doing. They tend to be more effective than others in high-level or entrepreneurial jobs[10] and feel dissatisfied when jobs lack challenge, feedback or recognition.[11]

People with a high need for affiliation, however, put more value on being with others and having others like them. They tend to do well in jobs that involve coordinating, mediating and selling.[12] One problem for managers with high needs to be liked is that often they have trouble making decisions.[13] They may be afraid that someone will not like a decision they have made.

This theory also deals with two forms of power.[14] "Personal" power, in which one wants to control others, often causes negative reactions. Effective managers tend to use "social" or "institutional" power, emphasizing employees' abilities to set and reach goals. Institutional power means the ability of institutions—such as social customs or laws—to get people to behave in certain ways. For example, traffic laws keep most drivers from speeding.

The achievement- affiliation- power-motive theory suggests that managers should match individuals' needs with the tasks of a specific job. For example, an employee with a high need for achievement may do well planning a budget, while a person with a high need for affiliation may do well running a committee.

What the Theories Have In Common

These theories share some points that are useful to managers. First, individuals are alike in that we all have certain needs, but we also are different in the ways we value and act on each need. Effective managers learn the different needs of their employees. Second, unmet needs motivate people. Managers should design work in a way that gives employees a chance to fulfill some of their unmet needs. Third, good working conditions and other hygiene factors prevent dissatisfaction, but they do not inspire anyone. Managers need to use growth, work itself and other satisfiers to motivate employees, while minimizing the dysfunctional results of dissatisfiers.

The theories also imply that there is a link between performance and personal satisfaction, although causality never has been established. People do something because, at least in part, they receive some benefit. Likewise, organizations benefit too. Each depends on the other. This duality of benefits exists because organizations and individuals have needs.

ORGANIZATIONS AND INDIVIDUAL NEEDS

Organizations and individuals help each other in many ways. Organizations receive effort, ideas, creativity, and results from individuals. Although organizations need a variety of resources, their success depends on individual members—their skills, talents, ideas, goals, and ability to work together.

Individuals get a lot out of their relationship with the organization, too. The pay received is the primary way that physiological and security needs are met in developed nations. Besides a steady paycheck, work provides a social context for people, many friendships, and reference groups. Task forces, committees and the natural flow of work give employees a chance to get to know people in many departments. Company teams, picnics and get-togethers add to the social aspect of work.

Work also gives people a chance to reach new goals, meeting the esteem needs for growth, recognition and achievement. Changes in the work force—more older people, more women, more minorities—mean new challenges for both employees and their managers. New goals could include learning new skills, dealing with people from different cultures, adjusting to a new environment or taking jobs previously reserved for the opposite sex. By setting and reaching new goals, people have a chance to grow.

The exchange between individuals and organizations does not always go as smoothly as it could. Sometimes, employees feel that the organization's leaders are indifferent to personal needs or that individual efforts do not bring as much from the organization as they put into it. The organization's leaders may feel they are not getting all they are paying for from individuals. What is wrong?

One possibility is that employees' needs are not being met. Anger, frustration, boredom, or other negative feelings lead to poor job performance. Who is responsible for this situation? At least two people are—the employee and the manager. Employees must know and express what they need. The manager must attempt to identify and meet employee needs while pursuing organization objectives. This is seldom easy for either party. Employees may fail to recognize or express their needs. Even if they do, the manager may be unable to respond because of situational constraints.

SUMMARY

Organizations and employees have needs. Successful managers try to satisfy both sets of needs at the same time. This is not always possible. Still, it is a manager's responsibility to try to find ways to meet employee needs in the context of organization objectives.

SELECTED READINGS OVERVIEW

The first article, "Why Job Security Is More Important Than Income Security," is by John Hoerr. When management is committed to job security, employees can contribute more freely to major changes at work that improve productivity. However, "unemployment benefits are so enticing that some workers would rather close a plant than save it."

The second article is "Employee Performance and Employee Need Satisfaction: Which Comes First?" by Robert A. Sutermeister. While some authors claim that satisfaction contributes to improved productivity, others say good performance leads to satisfaction of needs. In this article, Sutermeister shows that the relationship between performance and satisfaction is circular.

Next Chapter

The next chapter discusses individual differences, perception and learning. The differences are important, because they require managers to treat people according to individual needs. By understanding the ways people learn and perceive the world, managers can work more effectively with their employees.

Review Questions

1. What is the difference between "job security" and "income security"?
2. What is meant by the "circular" relationship between performance and satisfaction?
3. Why is it important for managers to know their employees' needs?
4. How do employee needs relate to organization needs?

JOHN HOERR

Why Job Security Is More Important Than Income Security

The first law of American business, as an auto executive puts it, is, "You get into trouble, you lay off people." That has been the barrier preventing unions from obtaining "job security" for their members. Instead, labor has usually accepted "income security" provisions, such as unemployment benefits and early pensions. But the costs—to both the companies and the economy—of paying people for not working are becoming so huge that the argument for avoiding layoffs and providing real job security to workers is overwhelming.

Income-security programs provided a safety net for millions of unemployed workers in the last recession. But they had, and still have, unintended effects. Jobless benefits provided by the government and supplemented by private industry tend to increase the duration of unemployment. In steel and autos, union-negotiated benefits related to plant shutdowns are so enticing that in some instances workers have preferred to close the plant rather than grant concessions that might have saved jobs. Moreover, it is easy for workers to construe income-security programs as payoffs rather than as incentives to help make their company more competitive and thus strengthen job security.

IN A CORNER

These consequences have renewed labor and management interest in providing some type of job or employment guarantees, especially in the heavily unionized basic manufacturing industries. Some experiments are under way in the steel, autos, aluminum, and can-manufacturing industries as well as at American Telephone & Telegraph Co. and the Bell System. Moreover, no-layoff programs that combine retraining, job transfers, and a diligent management effort to avoid furloughs have long been successful at a few nonunion companies such as International Business Machines Corp. and Lincoln Electric Co.

"We may have backed ourselves into a corner by settling for income security rather than dealing with the immense complexities of fashioning job security arrangements," says Ben Fischer, director of Carnegie Mellon University's Center for Labor Studies. At a recent CMU conference, labor and management officials in the auto and metals industries indicated cautious support for emphasizing job security over income security. "Where companies have shown a concern for the security of workers, they get paid back several times over in increased efficiency," says Donald E. Ephlin, a vice-president of the United Auto Workers.

Work in America Institute Inc. has set up a national advisory committee of labor, management, and government representatives to study "employment security." The institute uses this term, which is broader than job security, to emphasize the need for companies to find outside jobs, if necessary, for laid-off workers. Robert Zager, an institute vice-president, says that "when we have a management commitment of employment, workers are able to cooperate much more freely in major changes in the workplace to improve productivity and product quality."

The debate over the ill effects of income security is not new. At the national level, some economists have long argued that the size and duration of unemployment insurance (UI) benefits tend to delay the search for new jobs. But the permanent loss of hundreds of thousands of jobs in basic industries has brought the debate down to the company level. Provisions that were originally meant only to maintain income during occasional layoffs and to alleviate the effects of isolated plant closings have not been able to cope with massive dislocations in steel and autos.

In these and other metals industries, unions first won supplemental unemployment benefits (SUB) in 1955, at a time of fast economic growth. "The whole thrust of our program then," Ephlin says, "was to try to make management keep everybody at work. Never have we aimed at getting people time off with pay for doing nothing." But that is what SUB becomes in a slow-growth economy.

Steel, aluminum, and canmaking have more extensive "lifetime employment" programs than the Japanese, but they have turned out to be income-maintenance, rather than employment-maintenance, programs. Workers with 20 years of service are guaranteed SUB payments for two years of layoff, even if the SUB funds are dried up. If the company cannot then offer "suitable employment," workers who are at least 45 years old can collect regular pensions, plus $400 monthly supplements until Social Security kicks in.

"BENEFIT BATTERY"

Some income maintenance is essential when workers lose their jobs permanently, but these programs are draining staggering amounts of cash from hard-pressed steel companies and jeopardizing jobs that remain. J. Bruce Johnston, executive vice-president for employee relations at U.S. Steel Corp., notes that younger workers with no income guarantees have lost jobs when older employees collected benefits instead of renegotiating a union contract. In some cases, U.S. Steel has decided against calling long-term employees back to work for short periods, because this would "recharge the benefit battery for up to two years," Johnston says.

Retraining must be a key element of an employment-guarantee program. Under their 1982 contracts with the UAW, Ford Motor Co. and General Motors Corp. are retraining laid-off workers for outside jobs if none are available in the auto plants. For example, workers at a Buick plant in Flint, Mich., are guaranteed training if their jobs are eliminated through productivity-improvement ideas offered by workers. Sixty workers are undergoing full-time training at a center set up by management and UAW Local 599. In the past, says Local 599 President Al Christner, "it was hard for the union to take any position that could result in somebody getting laid off." But with the employment guarantee, he adds, "we can intelligently go in and work with the membership in order to improve things and get competitive."

ROBERT A. SUTERMEISTER

Employee Performance and Employee Need Satisfaction: Which Comes First?

Assuming Maslow's hierarchy of needs theory is correct.[1]

What is the cause and effect relationship between employee performance and need satisfaction?

Does high performance result in satisfaction of needs?

Does satisfaction of needs result in improved performance?

Or is there a circular relationship, each contributing to the other and each being affected by the other?

These are difficult questions. Brayfield and Crockett established in 1955 that "satisfaction with one's position in a network of relationships need not imply strong motivation to outstanding performance within that system."[2] Roberts et al. conclude there is no present technique for determining cause and effect of performance and satisfaction.[3] Porter and Lawler state that the greatest future research need is for data to provide evidence

on the direction of causality in their model relating performance and satisfaction (see Figure 1.)[4]

A number of authors state or imply that satisfaction contributes to improved performance and productivity. Herzberg et al. examined studies in which the effect of job attitudes on productivity was measured. They found "that in 54 percent of the reported surveys high morale was associated with high productivity" although the correlations in many of these studies were low; they concluded there was "frequent evidence for the often suggested opinion that positive job attitudes are favorable to increased productivity."[5] Sorcher and Meyer in a study of factory employees found that giving more meaning to routine jobs, making them more satisfying, and meeting some of the human needs of workers resulted in greater productive motivation and higher quality workmanship.[6] Pigors and Myers state a working hypothesis that job satisfaction of a certain kind and at a given level

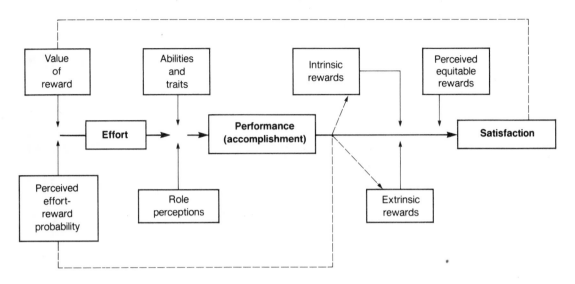

Figure 1.   Porter-Lawler Theoretical Model

may have a positive relationship to individual productivity.[7] And Sutermeister proposes a generalization for individuals who have strong egoistic needs: that the chances of motivating good employee performance are greater if the egoistic needs are fairly well satisfied on a continuing basis or if the employees feel that their present activities will lead to such satisfaction in the future.[8] The suggestion is that satisfaction (now or anticipated) of needs (especially egoistic) leads to improved performance.

Other authors state or imply a different point of view: that outstanding performance leads to greater satisfaction of needs. Miles, Porter, and Craft state that work satisfaction may improve as a by-product of subordinates' making full use of their resources: that satisfaction is intrinsic in the work; that subordinates get a major portion of their rewards merely from their own feelings of accomplishment and doing the job well.[9]

THE PORTER AND LAWLER MODEL

Porter and Lawler devised perhaps the most complete model of a satisfaction-perform-

ance relationship in their study of managerial attitudes and performance. Their model *predicts* that satisfaction results from performance itself, the rewards for performance, and the perceived equitability of those rewards.[10] (Ideally rewards come as a result of performance, but actually people can and often do receive rewards unrelated to performance.) However, they are careful to point out that the direction of causality the model predicts remains to be validated in future research.

In the Porter and Lawler model, if an individual is attracted by the value of the reward he envisions for a higher level of performance, and if he perceives as highly probable that increased effort will lead to that reward, he will increase his effort. And, if he has the required abilities and accurate role perceptions, his performance or accomplishment will improve. If the intrinsic and extrinsic rewards he receives from improved performance are perceived as equitable, then satisfaction will result, satisfaction being the difference between perceived equitable and actual rewards. In short, the model predicts that performance leads to satisfaction rather than satisfaction to improved performance.

THE CYCLE CONCEPT

It may be useful to think of the performance-satisfaction relationship in terms of a series of cycles. The Porter-Lawler study did not collect data to predict how "changes in level of need satisfaction affect the future values of certain rewards." This is a major area well worth further study and research.

Since psychologists seem agreed that a satisfied need is no motivator, one could hypothesize that if an individual's needs are met and satisfaction has been achieved, he would not be motivated to improve his performance. Such an hypothesis overlooks the possibility that higher level needs may become activated, and the individual may now be motivated to satisfy them. It may be helpful to view satisfaction in the Porter and Lawler model as the end of one cycle and as the beginning of another.

It is difficult, of course, to pinpoint the end of one cycle and the start of another. In general it might be said one cycle ends when the individual receives his rewards, whether intrinsic, extrinsic, or both. Some people whose satisfaction depends mostly on pay (as an extrinsic reward) receive their rewards annually at pay increase time. Other people whose satisfaction depends mostly on intrinsic rewards may receive their rewards in the form of recognition and accomplishment at annual performance review time (which may be different from pay increase time). For others, who view their most important rewards as meeting challenges and self-fulfillment through utilization of their highest capacities, the rewards may be self-bestowed and come at any time. Thus various individuals are likely to have different times for ending one performance-reward cycle and starting the next.

LIFE CYCLE AND ASPIRATION LEVEL

In addition to considering a performance-satisfaction cycle, it is convenient to consider a "life cycle" through which each person passes.

The young man getting out of school and embarking on his career is likely to be eager and enthusiastic and his aspiration level high. The role which he plays during these early years in his career may be quite different from the roles he plays later on. Money may be an important incentive as he tries to carve out his niche among his peers. On the other hand, some individuals are more interested in the opportunities a job offers than in its immediate financial reward. If they feel the job is "leading to something," represents a path to a goal they have set for themselves, the money may be of secondary importance.

A man's turning point often comes in the middle of his career. Here he may find a definite fork in the road. If he has accumulated a string of successes in achieving his goals, he may follow one fork and set his cap for a higher goal: or if he has become thwarted in achieving his goals, he may follow the other fork and resign himself to something less than he had started out to achieve. This is a critical period in which the "climber" may change into the "conserver," when reality may replace idealism and one may compromise or settle for less than earlier goals.[11] The level of aspiration a person now adopts will depend on whether he has achieved his previously set levels of aspiration or whether he has failed to reach them and now therefore lowers his aspirations.

In his late career a man is even more likely to become a conserver and hold on to what he has. He may feel that insufficient years remain for him to achieve the high-level goals sought in his youth, so he may be tempted to ride out his career until retirement at 65.

This description of a life cycle represents, of course, a general pattern. Specific individuals vary widely from the described scheme. Many men are going strong at 65 and have distinguished careers into their

80's and 90's. Others become conservers and "retire" at 30. The important point is not that there is a single pattern the same for everyone, but rather that the position one occupies in his life cycle is likely to have a great bearing on his level of aspirations.

LEVEL OF NEEDS

At the end of a cycle, and referring only to needs activated on the job, have the individual's needs been fully met or are they unfulfilled? Has the fulfillment of certain egoistic needs been followed by activation of higher-level needs? For some individuals higher-level needs are never completely satisfied. Fulfillment of one need simply activates a higher-level need in a never-ending striving for complete self-fulfillment.

ALTERNATIVES FOR THE UNSATISFIED

Let's assume for the moment that at the end of a cycle the individual's needs are not satisfied (see Figure 2). Whether he begins a search for a way to satisfy them depends upon his level of aspiration, which in turn is affected by his position in his life cycle.

A person late in his life cycle may have become a conserver or a backslider and have lowered his level of aspiration; or,

Even if he is a climber in his life cycle, his failure to satisfy his needs in the previous cycle could lower his level of aspiration in the new cycle; or

He may have a high level of aspiration and intensify his need-satisfaction search.

He may do this by seeking a different job in the same firm or in a new firm. He may do this by exerting greater effort on his present job, provided, in accordance with the Porter-Lawler model, the value of the reward he anticipates in the next cycle is high enough,

and the effort-reward probability strong enough.

If he becomes convinced that his chances of satisfying his needs are not good or are not worth the effort, he may give up his search. Thus his actual behavior will be strongly influenced by his level of aspiration, which in turn is affected by what happened in the previous performance-satisfaction cycle and by his place in his life cycle.

ALTERNATIVES FOR THE SATISFIED

Now let's assume that when the individual receives his reward he perceives it as equitable and is satisfied (see Figure 3). He now has to plan his behavior for the next cycle.

Will his effort drop to a lower level?

Will he maintain it at the present level?

Will he try to improve it?

If a satisfied need is no motivator, his initial reaction may be to reduce his effort. His decision again will depend on a number of factors.

What is the individual's level of aspiration as influenced by his position in his life cycle?

Have higher-level needs been activated?

If so, is the anticipated value of the reward in the next cycle satisfactory?

And, is the effort-reward probability perceived as satisfactory?

For some individuals higher-level needs may become activated. They may be in a climbing period in their life cycles, or for other reasons have high aspiration levels; and if the value of reward and perceived effort-reward probability are satisfactory, they may be motivated to greater effort and improved performance. (A unionized worker may find his higher level needs activated. But if his rewards come from higher

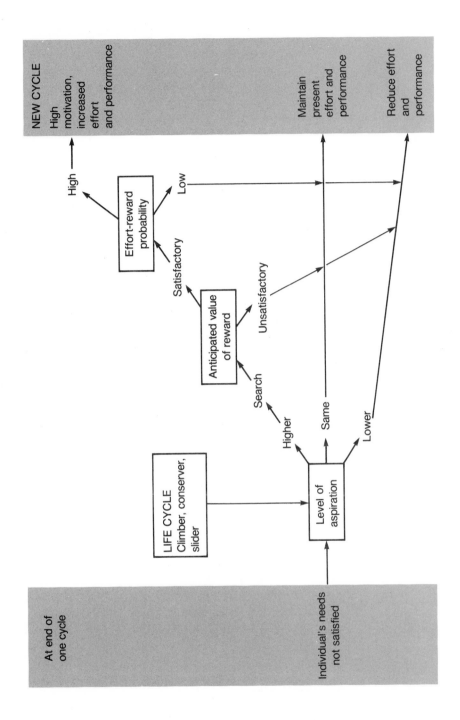

Figure 2.   Alternatives for the Individual Whose Needs Are Not Satisfied at End of a Performance-Satisfaction Cycle

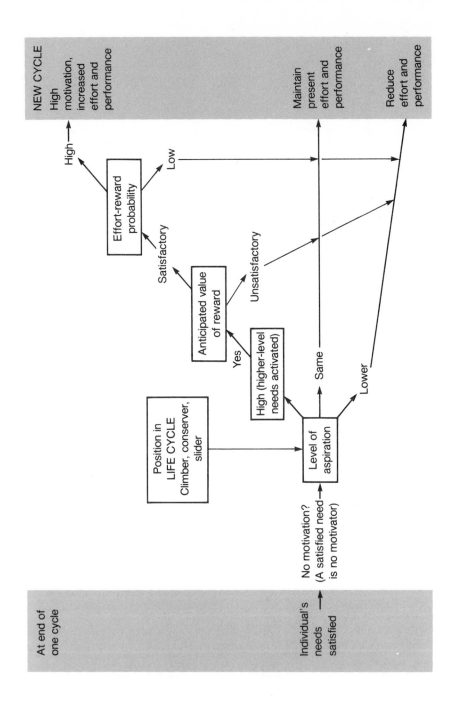

Figure 3.   Diagram Representing Individual Whose Needs Are
Satisfied at End of a Performance-Satisfaction Cycle

pay, and pay is determined through union negotiations and not through personal effort, there is low probability of effort leading to reward. In the new cycle, then, his effort and performance are not likely to be high.)[12]

A second group of individuals may decide that they would like only to continue enjoying their present satisfaction. They may be in the middle of their life cycles, and have become conservers, wishing merely to retain their present level of power, prestige, and income. Their needs are satisfied, but this does not mean that they have no motivation. Rather they are motivated to continue their efforts at a level which will retain the rewards they now enjoy, provided, of course, the value of the reward and the perceived effort-reward probability remain the same.

A third group of individuals may decide to lower their levels of aspiration. Perhaps they are far along in their life cycles and desire to ease up on their efforts and be satisfied with a lower reward. In this case the value of the reward and the perceived effort-reward probability, even if high, are of little concern.

CONCLUSION

The degree of satisfaction at the end of one performance-satisfaction cycle and the individual's position in his life cycle will affect his level of aspiration in the new performance-satisfaction cycle. If his level of aspiration is raised, and if the value of the reward and the perceived effort-reward probability appear satisfactory to him, he will be motivated to improve his effort and performance in the new cycle. If his level of aspiration remains the same, and value of reward and perceived effort-reward probability remain the same, he will be motivated to continue his previous level of effort in the new cycle. And if his level of aspiration is lowered, he will reduce his effort in the new cycle regardless of the value of reward and perceived effort-reward probability.

We may theorize, then, that effort and performance affect satisfaction, and that satisfaction by its influence on level of aspiration affects subsequent effort and performance. Thus it would seem as if the satisfaction-productivity relationship is circular, as the final figure [Figure 4] shows.

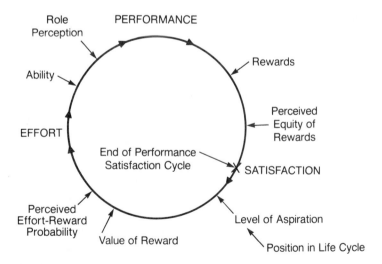

Figure 4. Satisfaction-Productivity Relationship

5

Productivity and Human Perceptions

Let us remember: We never deal with reality per se, but rather with images of reality.
PAUL WATZLAWICK[1]

INDIVIDUAL PERCEPTIONS

Individuals emphasize and express their needs differently, as Chapter 4 discusses. In fact, individuals experience the world differently, too.

What Affects Perception?

Every person perceives things differently and responds to those perceptions in different ways. Because of differences in perceptions, the "reality" each person faces may differ. The following paragraphs discuss some of the major factors that shape our perceptions.

Selective perception

Selective perception is the process by which unimportant cues from the world around us are filtered. Sensitivity to some stimuli and not to others is what makes one's perception selective. For example, someone who values relationships may notice people's interactions during a meeting, while someone who is more concerned about money may pay more attention to facts and figures reported during the meeting.

Stereotypes

According to Festinger, stereotypes identify potential allies in situations where we feel out of control.[2] Assumptions based on a person's looks, dress, accent, or other traits facilitate quick decisions based on our own internal version of reality. By using stereotypes to filter perceptions, we further distort reality.

Closure

The need for closure causes people to reach conclusions even when information is limited or absent. Later, information that conflicts with the "conclusion" may be rejected, according to Kohler,[3] because a decision (or closure) already has occurred. People's perceptions may be limited after they make up their minds.

Halo effect

What Nisbett and Wilson call the "halo effect" means that a *general* feeling about someone or something tends to dominate (and distort) *specific* observations about that person or object.[4] Someone's positive halo often causes others to overlook that person's less acceptable behaviors.

Life position

We even perceive ourselves differently from the way others perceive us and themselves. People decide on a "life position."[5] A life position is someone's perception of where he or she "stands" in the world. This position tells people who they are, what they should do, and how they relate to other people. It also affects what and how we perceive, and what we screen out.

Self-image

One's self-image affects perception, and perception affects one's self-image. People tend to perceive information that reinforces their beliefs about themselves and others.

Combinations

Many things affect individual perceptions. Selective perceptions, stereotypes and other sources of distortion combine with the individual's present needs, concerns and personal background. Because of this mix, no two people perceive in exactly the same way.[6]

THEORIES ABOUT PERCEPTION

Beyond the factors that make individual perceptions unique, there are certain factors we all have in common. Several theories help to explain the way we all perceive things. By applying these theories, a manager can help create a more productive environment.

Cognitive Dissonance Theory

Festinger[7] says that "cognitive dissonance" means that contradictory ideas exist at the same time in a person's mind. For example, some people might know they are intelligent, but also know that they keep failing. The knowledge of these contradictory facts creates cognitive dissonance.

According to Festinger, cognitive dissonance causes a person to take action to reduce the gap between reality and perceptions. To do this, the person will try to change one of the cognitions. Using the previous example, people might decide that they are not really intelligent, or that previous outcomes were not really failures. This theory says that people change their perceptions to match their beliefs.

The cognitive dissonance theory applies to work in several ways. Employees' self-images may be higher—or lower—than their perceptions of how their company treats them. Job descriptions may not match the job's day-to-day duties, which is why some employers give potential workers realistic job previews. By showing the potential new hire what the job is really like, the cognitive dissonance between expectations and the actual job are likely to be less. Job satisfaction is apt to be higher and subsequent employee turnover among new hires is likely to be lower.

If employees perceive that the rewards are too small for an important task, they will change their cognition either of the rewards or of the task. They might perceive the task as less important than it really is; or they may perceive the rewards as larger than they really are. Managers can help prevent cognitive dissonance in several ways. They can describe such things as jobs and rewards as accurately as possible. They can find out how employees perceive work. They can be consistent in their behaviors.

Equity Theory

"Equity" is a sense of fairness. It applies to one's sense of how appropriate rewards are, compared to rewards others receive and to the work required to earn the rewards. When employees perceive inequities, satisfaction and motivation may decline. Productivity declines as a result. If employees do not feel that they get a fair amount of recognition, pay or other rewards, their negative feelings may lead to poor performance. Employees feel that overpayment is as unfair as underpayment, according to research by Adams and Jacobsen.[8]

How does a manager make sure employees get fair rewards? One way is to make clear, in advance, the relationship between efforts and rewards. The manager must then make sure to apply that relationship even-handedly to all employees. Another method is to ask employees which rewards fulfill their needs, as discussed in the previous chapter.

Expectancy Theory

Steers and Porter[9] describe the expectancy theory this way: The strength of a person's motivation to perform comes from (1) a belief that the performance will lead to a reward, and (2) the perceived value of the reward. For example, some students may want to earn an A in a class, while others will be happy with a C. If both groups of students believe that lots of studying will lead to an A, the first requirement is met—students believe that performance (studying) will produce a reward (an A grade). The students who want As will be motivated to study, because they value the rewards. But the students who are happy with Cs will not be as motivated, because they do not value the reward as highly. The valence, or weighted value, of a reward may change within people over time. Managers should recognize this dynamic side of rewards.

The expectancy theory presents some useful insights for managers. First, clear goals are important. They give both managers and employees a way to measure performance. Second, employees ultimately determine which rewards will be valued, not the manager. Some employees may prefer money, while others want time off, added responsibilities or recognition. Because the value of rewards keeps changing, managers should know their employees well enough to tell which rewards will motivate them at any given time. Third, managers must convince employees that good performance leads to desired rewards. Managers should define "good performance" in terms of the specific behaviors and outcomes they want from employees. The more specific these terms are, the more agreement there will be about how well they were fulfilled.

Self-image plays a role here. An employee may believe that a certain performance will lead to a reward, and he or she may value the reward. But the employee also has to believe he or she *can perform* as needed. A low self-image may stop an employee from doing a good job. Managers can help build employees' self-images by praising each step that leads towards the desired goal.

Managers' treatment of employees can become part of the reward system, whether intended or not. Employees may gain a sense of self-satisfaction from their performance, but the manager may confuse them by giving a token raise several months later and making no comments. While the employees will enjoy the self-satisfaction, they may not know how to interpret the raise. Why? Because it came too late to be seen as a reward for the specific work that was done. And the manager's silence could lead to misunderstandings. It could mean that the manager did not notice the work, did not think it was good, or whatever else the employees "fill in." The manager's behavior, in this case, leaves lots of room for misunderstanding.

Social Learning Theory

According to Bandura's social learning theory,[10] behavior, environment and individuals affect each other in a circular way. Some theories say that people act in certain ways because of inner needs and drives. Other theories say people act the way they do because of their environment. The social learning theory says people, their actions and the setting are all interrelated. Changes in *any* of the three factors will bring about changes in the others. The interaction among people, behavior and environment is an ongoing process.

Modeling is a key part of social learning theory. Modeling means that people learn how to act from what they hear and see around them. Notice how important perception is: Two people may learn different behaviors from the same models. In families, for example, even twins may behave very differently from each other. Each person's perception plays an active role in modeling. Modeled behaviors serve as guides for proper actions. Much social learning comes from casually noticed everyday events.

At work, people learn behaviors from each other. These behaviors form part of the company's culture. Behaviors may differ among firms, and also among departments within a firm. Managers and co-workers act as models for employees. This means that managers should behave as they want their employees to behave. That is, managers should lead by example. It also means that employees will notice—consciously or not—which actions managers reward. The rewards may take the form of attention, recognition, money, laughter, or other responses. Managers should realize which behaviors they reward and which ones go unrewarded. Rewards convey powerful messages.

Based on the social learning theory, managers' actions—and the actions they reward—will serve as models for employees. Managers should emphasize productive behaviors and lead by example.

CHANGES IN THE WORK SETTING

How people perceive changes in the work setting affects how they respond to them. In turn, their responses affect productivity.

Changes in the work setting are affected by values and each generation has its own values. Years ago, men spent entire careers at one firm. If women worked, it was usually only to bring in "extra" money. Company transfers determined where the family lived. Family needs and society's needs were second to the organization's needs. In the 1970s and early 1980s, values changed. Family life, individual creativity, social issues, political interests, and other areas of life became increasingly important. For many women, careers became as important as their other roles, especially since many were heads of households. Both men and women wanted to become more complete people, with a new balance between work and other aspects of life. Individuality and leisure have begun to affect the older work ethic. For some people this represents a decline in our society. Others see it as a chance to have broader and richer life experiences. Money, for example, may not motivate some employees as much as others. Managers have to recognize these differences, to prevent possible misunderstandings and to motivate workers toward higher productivity.

Aging Work Force

More older people work today than ever before. Just as families may suffer from generation gaps, so may companies. Older workers may have different values than younger workers. Viewing work as an end in itself is more common among older workers. Younger workers may be more prone to see work as a means to other ends. Differences in upbringing, schooling and experience create different views of work, even among those in the same age group.[11]

Women

Women have always worked. But it was not until the 1970s that great numbers of women sought career-oriented positions. Women's traditional roles had kept them in supportive, helping positions, not leadership positions. In addition, many women were raised to be "cooperative" rather than assertive. Affirmative action pressures to hire women put many women in a double-bind: While they wanted a chance at a career, history and their personal backgrounds had not always prepared them for leadership positions at work.

Many women have succeeded at work, too. They hold management positions, serve as role models for other women and balance their careers, families, politics, and other activities just like any strong individual. Sometimes, these successful women have a different kind of problem. Some co-workers, employees and even managers perceive them as threatening, for several reasons: These women may not match others' stereotypes of what women "should" do; they may increase the competition for good jobs; or their abilities may trigger others' personal insecurities.

At work today, women still must deal with traditional stereotypes. Managers—many of them women—can help by being aware of the problems and focusing on behaviors, rather than gender or personality, at work.

Minorities

Like women, members of minority groups must battle against history, tradition and stereotypes. And like some women, minority members may have been hired to meet affirmative action requirements and pushed into jobs for which they were ill-prepared. Yet, training, experience, education and the media have helped minority groups—and their images—to become better accepted by the majority culture. Managers, including those belonging to minority groups, must be alert to these problems and must focus on individual performance and skills, not on stereotypical perceptions.

Technology

Technological changes at work are frequent enough to be taken for granted. But change is not easy for anyone, and many people react negatively to technological change. When the word-processor replaced the typewriter, for example, many people felt resentful, afraid and unwilling to learn. Sometimes, people even sabotaged the new equipment.

New technology means that people have to learn new skills. They may perceive that they have become outdated or useless. They may fear that they are "too old to learn." They may simply want to keep old habits and routines. Unless a company is willing to invest time and money in retraining, and sometimes in counseling, employees may lose their jobs when new equipment requires new skills.

SUMMARY

People perceive things differently from each other. Their perceptions affect their productivity. Managers can help employees by recognizing these differences and treating employees accordingly. Increased productivity will follow because employees perform better when their individual needs are met.

SELECTED READINGS OVERVIEW

The first reading is "Cultural Myths: Clues to Effective Management," by Eugene J. Koprowski. Every culture has its myths. The myths are powerful because they can lead to action. This article shows how myths have affected women's roles at work, the emulation of Japanese management techniques, and leadership roles for managers.

The second article is "Pygmalion in Management," by J. Sterling Livingston. What managers expect from their employees helps determine how well employees do. Even when managers are not aware of it, their actions tell employees what the managers think of them. Managers have the opportunity and the responsibility to help their employees develop, both as workers and as people.

Next Chapter

The next chapter draws on previous discussions of needs and perceptions, and applies these principles to human motivation. Motivation plays a key role in improved productivity. Managers must understand the bases of motivation in order to get the best from their employees.

Review Questions

1. How do managers influence employees' self-images?
2. In what ways can managers become modern-day cultural heroes?
3. How does perception affect productivity?
4. How can managers help employees perceive rewards as equitable?
5. In what ways do managers act as models?

EUGENE J. KOPROWSKI

Cultural Myths: Clues to Effective Management

Mythology, which lies at the heart of culture, can provide managers with clues on how to tackle such modern challenges as the increasing role of women in the workplace, the feasibility of applying Japanese management techniques to American industry, and the leadership role of managers themselves.

Our "left-brained" society, which values logic and rationality, seems to have little concern for the myth as a legitimate vehicle for understanding ourselves and our social institutions. This is unfortunate because the great myths of history contain unique elements of truth that elude rational thought and categorization. Among these are our hopes, fears, dreams and aspirations. To dismiss these from conscious consideration is to try to understand the human condition with only half of our faculties.

The stunning accomplishments of science leave little room for what many consider prescientific folklore—for science can point with just pride to advances in the control of disease and increased longevity among many segments of the population. Equally impressive has been the exploration of space and the harnessing of electric technology.

Gene Koprowski is professor of management at the University of Colorado's College of Business and Administration. His management experience includes serving as manager of personnel and labor relations for National Farmers Union Insurances, management consultant for The McMurry Company in San Francisco, and corporate director of manpower planning and development for Kaiser Aluminum & Chemical Corporation. He also served as associate dean for the College of Business at the University of Colorado's Denver Campus. Dr. Koprowski has published two books and numerous articles on management topics. He consults with a wide range of organizations in the private and public sectors.

Test tube babies, pills that control psychic moods, aircraft that fly faster than the speed of sound, microcomputers, sophisticated telecommunications systems, and robotics all testify to the increasing power of science.

So who needs myths? Apparently we do. Closely paralleling advances in science and technology are our burgeoning interests in religion, art, music, the occult, extrasensory perception, unidentified flying objects, space heroes and, yes, even extraterrestrials. This parallel development of two seemingly opposite views of reality is no accident. For the more we master and are mastered by science and technology, the more we yearn for escape and for meaning. It is at this point that myths attempt to satisfy needs that cannot be satisfied by other means. Carl Jung puts it in slightly different terms by suggesting that the myth is mental therapy for the sufferings and anxiety of mankind.

Furthermore, history suggests that myths are more than primitive forms of thought that will eventually be replaced by science and logic. Just as Mr. Spock's logic and Commander Kirk's humanity are necessary to run the Starship Enterprise, so are science and mythology necessary to run a sane and human society. If this is true on a societal level, surely there are important implications for managers and the management process.

With a subject as broad as mythology, shifting from generalities to specifics presents obvious difficulties. Volumes have been written on both mythology and management but to my knowledge few, if any, linkages have been made between the two. In this article I will focus on three important contemporary management challenges and demonstrate how an understanding of cultural myths can help managers deal more effectively with them. The challenges are:

The changing role of women in the workforce.

Japanese management.

Managers as heroes.

Because I will not offer scientific proof for the speculations that follow, I do want to establish early in this article that I have drawn heavily on the works of Joseph Campbell and Carl Jung. While excellent descriptive accounts of various myths may be found in Larousse's *World Mythology* and in Edith Hamilton's classic, *Mythology*, both Campbell and Jung take us one step beyond in providing interpretive insights into the meaning of myths to our society.

WOMEN AND MANAGEMENT

With the twentieth century drawing to a close, there is a plethora of new books and articles on the future of management. Typical of this genre is an article by Richard B. Freeman that appeared in *Work in America: The Decade Ahead*. In it the author points out that the most important change in the post-World War II labor force was the extraordinary increase in the number of women. The percentage of eligible women who work jumped from 28 percent in 1947 to 45 percent in 1976, and the percentage continues to grow.

These same writers point out, and justly so, that the recent influx of women into the workforce calls for such new approaches to management as more flexible work hours, day-care centers, and more equitable pay and promotion policies. I do not argue with these observations, but contend that they only scratch the surface in terms of the subtle and complex problems managers will face in the future because of the changing role of women in our society and in our work organizations.

These emerging problems may be viewed from several different perspectives. The first, and most immediate, concern to managers is the increase of conflict among men and women as they compete for top jobs.

The second involves social equity. Despite conspicuous pockets of progress, women continue to earn roughly one-third less than men for comparable jobs. The third, and most critical in the long run, is the disintegration of the nuclear family. For as more women gain their primary sense of self-worth outside of their traditional roles as mothers and wives, the family as we know it today will be required to undergo major adaptive changes. It is in the family that attitudes toward authority and work are first developed.

Embedded in these problems is an interesting question for the thoughtful manager: Why must we be concerned about conflict and equity between men and women when our country was founded on the notion of "liberty and justice for all"? To answer this question, it is necessary to go beyond rationality and logic. Cultural myths can provide useful clues in explaining why, despite all the stated good intentions, women must struggle for that which should be their birthright. Myths can also provide important insights about how we are most likely to resolve these problems in the future.

Three major mythological traditions will be examined and applied to the challenge of the changing role of women in the workplace. These are the historical stature of women in myths, their symbolic value, and the duality of human nature.

Stature of Women in Myths

An examination of both Occidental and Oriental myths reveal that women have historically held a secondary place to men. The supreme deities in most mythological systems are masculine. Examples include the Olympian Zeus, the Egyptian Ra, the Babylonian Anu, the Indian Brahma, the Chinese P'an-Ku, and the Japanese Izanagi. These dominant male deities suggest that the current plight of women is nothing new.

Joseph Campbell concluded that until the beginning of the Neolithic period of history, roughly 5500 B.C., women served basically as drudges in a male-dominated hunting society. With the beginning of systematized agriculture, the role of women was somewhat enhanced. Campbell suggests, "She participated—perhaps even predominated—in the planting and reaping of the crops, and, as the mother of life and nourisher of life, was thought to assist the earth symbolically in its production. It seems that for this brief moment, before recorded history, matriarchy was the order of the day. It was a time when the Great Goddess was feared and worshipped in her many forms in Sumer, Egypt, and Crete."

We can conclude that the prestige of women was historically linked to those activities that were required for the survival of the culture. When survival was based on hunting skills, men predominated. With the advent of agriculture, the role of women was greatly enhanced. When it became necessary to protect the land and crops from wild beasts and from invading tribes, the male warrior hero predominated. This is where we seem to be fixated today despite all of our scientific and technological progress. Our basic hero remains the male warrior hero. In American he is epitomized in the cowboy and his high-tech replicas who zing around outer space in our sci-fi fantasies.

Women as Symbols

While the status of women in myths suggests they have historically held a secondary role, the symbolic value of women in myths suggests that they have been historically feared as well as desired and possessed by men. Jung, who spent much of his professional career studying the psychological meaning of symbols and myths, suggests that women through the ages have come to symbolize the following: maternal solicitude and sympathy; magic authority; wisdom and spiritual exaltation that transcends reason; and helpful instinct or impulse; all that is benign; all that cherishes and sustains; all that fosters growth and fertility; magic transformation and rebirth; the underworld and its inhabitants; anything that is secret, hidden, dark; the abyss; the world of the dead; anything that devours, seduces, and poisons or that is terrifying and inescapable like fate or death.

If Jung is correct, men react to women not only as people, but also as symbols. This means men will be attracted to women because of their sexual and nurturing qualities, but will fear women because they symbolize all that is irrational and mysterious.

Beyond this, women represent what Jung calls the Mother archetype. As such, they are a source of great ambivalence. For we wish to be nourished, nurtured, and protected by Mother, but we also need to free ourselves from Her to become individuals in our own right. This further confounds the relationship of men and women in our society.

The Duality in Human Nature

Oriental mythology has dealt with the relationship between men and women in a healthier fashion. In the Chinese creation myth, all things (including people of both sexes) were formed out of chaos through the conflicting and complementary interaction of two primal forces called the Yin and the Yang, and all things have some characteristics of both. Yin represents the dark, feminine, passive, cold, moist, malignant, and negative aspects of reality. Yang represents the light, masculine, active, hot, dry, beneficent, positive aspects of reality.

In Occidental myths, the dual aspect of human nature has been dealt with by creating distinctly masculine and feminine roles for each sex. Thus it is considered abnormal for an individual to display characteristics of the opposite sex. In Western cultures, this serves to enhance the positive symbolic value of men and the negative symbolic value of women because Yang traits are more highly valued than Yin traits. The net result is the creation of formidable obstacles that inhibit the full exploration and development of our dual natures and that exacerbate the potential for conflict between the sexes.

Implications for Management

In a recent book, *The Coming Matriarchy*, Elizabeth Nickles and Laura Ashcraft suggest that there are powerful forces at work in our society that will eventually turn the balance of power over to women. This, they say, will happen because:

1. Women will soon outnumber men in the workforce.

2. Women's natural leadership styles are more appropriate to modern society than men's.

3. A new breed of "pacesetter" women will lead the way for others.

4. Women will eventually reshape those social institutions that are not geared to meet the changing role of women.

If there is any validity to the idea that myths represent a culture's hopes, fears, dreams, and aspirations, it seems unlikely that the Nickles and Ashcraft scenario presents a realistic vision of the future. It is more probable that the stuttering progress of women will continue within a framework of sophisticated tokenism perpetuated by a male-dominated society that is not about to abdicate its power.

This latter scenario is suggested by the fact that, historically, men have developed very ambivalent feelings toward women and the powerful elements in nature that they symbolize. Men currently hold the upper hand in terms of power in our society, and they are not likely to relinquish that power to women without a struggle. Myths further suggest that the basis for man's dominance comes from the fact that the male warrior hero is still necessary to protect our tribe from outside invaders. Until the world learns to live in peace and until rationality and logic replace lust, greed, and the quest for power, it is doubtful that any of us will see the "coming matriarchy."

The practical implications for managers are that powerful social forces have been set in motion that are likely to escalate conflict between men and women in work organizations. It is especially important to recognize that conflicts of this nature have both rational and emotional components. The rational struggle between men and women in work organizations involves social equity. The emotional struggle involves men's fear and ambivalence toward women and what they symbolically represent.

For these reasons, it is a bit naive for us to assume that the ideal of social equity for women in the workplace will be implemented without considerable conscious or unconscious foot dragging and resistance on the part of the male power structure. The recent defeat of the Equal Rights Amendment and the general erosion of the legal enforcement of human rights legislation reinforces this conclusion.

Managers must realize, however, that social equity for women is more than ideological struggle. It has practical implications. To optimize creative productivity in any work organization, it is important for all members to feel they are being fairly treated. As the proportion of women in the workforce continues to increase, so will their potential contributions to organizational productivity. How they feel about equity will play a major role in how much they are willing to contribute.

The emotional components of this struggle must also be addressed if the ideal of social equity is to be achieved. Here, the Oriental concept of the duality of human nature provides a blueprint for progress. For if all things are a composite of feminine and masculine elements embodied in the Yin and the Yang, so are all people. Thus if men could accept the feminine aspects of their personalities and women the masculine aspects of their personalities, the we/they elements of the conflict would be greatly reduced.

The practical question is how to make this happen in a macho, male-dominated society. To date, the most promising strategies seem to be education and the restructuring of social roles. In terms of education, books like June Singer's *Androgyny* provide fresh new insights into the subject. A growing number of consultants are also beginning to explore these issues and are designing workshops to demonstrate how human growth is enhanced through a realization of the duality of human nature.

Even more promising is the expanded range of social roles that are considered "acceptable" for men and women. For example, an increasing number of women have become active in sports that were once considered the exclusive domain of men, and an increasing number of men have become housefathers while their wives play breadwinner.

Although managers have little control over who plays broad social roles, they do control the matter of who occupies "masculine jobs" and "feminine jobs" in their organizations. A conscious policy of increasing the number of women in traditionally masculine jobs and vice versa would go a long way toward changing attitudes. So would a job rotation program in which male executives, as part of their development program, would be required to spend one month as a secretary or in some other traditionally female occupational role.

To summarize, an examination of cultural myths suggests that the roots of man/woman conflict go deep. Even though most of us agree with social equity for women in an abstract sense, there is much foot dragging because men do not want to share power and because men fear what women symbolically represent. Through strict enforcement of human rights legislation, education, and restructuring of social roles, it is possible that we can minimize fear, suspicion, and destructive conflict between men and women in our work organizations. The balance of power, however, is not likely to shift in the favor of women until that day when the male warrior hero, in all of his modern forms, is no longer required to protect the tribe against hostile invaders.

JAPANESE MANAGEMENT

Current management literature abounds with articles about what Americans can learn from the Japanese. William Ouchi's book, *Theory Z: How American Business Can Meet the Japanese Challenge*, had the rare distinction of spending months on the nonfiction best sellers list, which is rare for a book on management. American firms of every size and shape are holding special seminars on how they can utilize Japanese managerial techniques to improve their lagging productivity.

Despite its current vogue, many American managers remain wary about importing Japanese group-style management to this country. They have a vague feeling that there is something almost un-American about the paternalistic, womb-to-tomb, participative approaches of our oriental competitor. There is equal suspicion of the subtleties and ceremonial aspects of the decision-making process that characterizes the Japanese style. Many of these unconvinced American managers appropriately ask, "Will it work here?"

A comparative analysis of mythology can help answer that question. For if human nature, as revealed through myths, is the same the world over, management theories and practices from one culture should work reasonably well in another. But is human nature the same the world over? The answer to that question is an equivocal yes and no.

Myths the world over contain certain universal themes. Joseph Campbell, after extensive scholarly research, concluded that a universal vision of human nature is indeed implicit in these themes. He suggests that this is perceptively captured in the world view of ancient Indian writers who stated that all people strive for three ends, and three ends only. These are love and pleasure, power and success, and lawful order and moral virtue. The first two categories represent individual appetites and inclinations, and the third category grows out of the collective imperative. For without lawful order or moral codes, modern society could not exist.

While these three elements represent the basic building blocks of human nature, there are infinite local variations on these themes. These variations tend to cluster into two broad historical traditions, the Occidental and the Oriental. An understanding of differences between these two can shed considerable light on the cross-cultural application of management theories and practices.

The Split

Until roughly 2500 B.C., both Occidental and Oriental mythology were strikingly similar. They both proceeded through a period of animism during which god or spirit existed in all things. As agriculture replaced hunting as the primary means for human survival, primitive animism was replaced in most major cultures by the Goddess Mother of the universe who encompassed all things—including gods, men, plants, animals, and even inanimate objects. This was a time when, in both Occidental and Oriental cultures, there was no distinction between gods and men. They were all part of the same cosmic, organic whole.

Then the common trunk of human experience began to branch in two different directions: one distinctly Occidental and the other distinctly Oriental. This occurred in the Near East during the period of the first Semitic kings. Gradually, the matriarchal myths of the Goddess Mother gave way to myths depicting thunder-hurling warrior gods who by 1500 B.C. had become the dominant divinities in that part of the world.

Concurrent with the patriarchal vision was the gradual separation of the spheres of god and man. The king was no longer god but the servant of God. In the centuries that followed, this separation created the need for new myths that built bridges between Occidental people and the God that stood above them. This was accomplished in two ways: first by endowing God with human characteristics and second by creating the "road to salvation."

Zoroaster, the Persian who lived about the same time as Buddha and Confucius, played a key role in this Occidental formulation of human beings' place in the universe. He is credited with three radical innovations that set the Western view of human nature apart from the Eastern view. The first was the notion that life is not the endless cycle depicted in Oriental mythology but, instead, a cosmic battle between good and evil that had a specific beginning and will have a specific end with the eventual triumph of good. The second innovation is the proposition that each individual has a free will and may decide to follow the path of either good or evil. The final contribution is the contention that the way to conquer the forces of evil is through engagement rather than through disengagement.

It was within this context that Western society's respect for the individual human personality was born. It is also the context that shaped Olympian and Roman mythology and later the Christian, Jewish and Islamic traditions. It permeates every Western social institution, from the family to the work organization, and can be seen in the motivational theories of Abraham Maslow, Frederick Herzberg, and many others.

During this period, there were also refinements in the Eastern mythologies that helped shape an appreciably different view of human nature. In all of this, India played a seminal role. Many of the mythologies that had their origin there were transported to China and later to Japan.

Because of its geographic isolation, Japan is a relative latecomer on the vast stage of Oriental mythology. Its late-developing mythologies stem from two major influences, one indigenous and the other imported. The indigenous tradition is Shinto, which is difficult for the Western mind to grasp. In his book on Oriental mythology, Campbell tells the story of a Western sociologist who, after visiting numerous Shinto shrines and observing many ceremonies, confronted a Shinto priest by saying he still didn't understand Shinto theology. After thoughtful consideration, the Shinto priest replied, "We do not have theology. We dance." Which is to say, Shinto is not the following of abstract moral codes, but living in gratitude and awe amid the mystery of things. Beyond this is a great zeal for purity in all forms, from the clean house to the clean heart, and also the unwavering conviction that nature cannot be evil.

Superimposed on the Shinto tradition is Buddhism, which came to Japan via Korea in 552 A.D. Without going into a lengthy summary of the major Eastern movement, I will focus on those elements that serve as a foundation for Japanese management.

To begin with, Buddhism does not emphasize the cosmic struggle between good and evil but concentrates on ways of alleviating human suffering here on earth. Because the cause of suffering is human craving and selfish desire, the way to alleviate it is through the elimination of these cravings and desires. This is accomplished by practicing what Buddha called the Middle Way (moderation in all things) and by pursuing the Noble Eightfold Path. The ultimate goal for the Buddhists is not eternal life or Heaven, but rather Nirvana, the ultimate reality that is reached when, through meditation and good works, one is able to disassociate one's self from one's personal ego.

From these Occidental and Oriental traditions, it is possible to delineate two very different world views and conceptions of human nature. It is out of these traditions that Western and Eastern approaches to management developed. To assume that we can transplant specific managerial practices from Japan to America without taking into account these cultural differences is unrealistic.

Our review of Occidental and Oriental mythological systems reveal basic similarities in our fundamental strivings, but profound differences in the specific local forms those strivings take. These distinctions help explain the differences between Japanese and American management set forth by

Ouchi. (For characteristics of both, see Figure 1.)

It is easy to see that Japanese management is firmly based on the Oriental world view that stresses the organic unity of all things—in which individuality is an illusion in the endless cycle of life. On the other hand, American management is firmly based on the Occidental world view that stresses the perfection of the individual personality in the quest for salvation.

Americans are in a hurry not so much because they have greater needs for power and success, but because the Occidental world view is time-bound. There was a beginning, and there will be an end. This is true of individual lives, and it is true for the general course of human beings here on earth. This is one of the reasons that rapid evaluations and promotions are so important to Americans.

Americans also epitomize the individualism so highly valued in the Occidental tradition. Although we can't boast of knights of the Round Table who individually go off to seek the Holy Grail, we do have our cowboys who, through their mythical transformation in print and on film, have projected the American brand of rugged individualism to the rest of the world. Cowboys are not con-

Japanese	American
Lifetime employment	Short-term employment
Slow promotions and evaluations	Rapid promotions and evaluations
Nonspecific career paths	Specific career paths
Implicit control systems	Explicit control systems
Collective decision making and responsibility	Individual decision making and responsibility
Wholistic concern	Segmented concern

Figure 1.
Characteristics of Japanese and American Management

cerned with lifetime employment. They go where their mood suits them. Security doesn't concern them because a good cowboy—one who has mastered his trade and shows good character—can get a job almost anywhere.

The contemporary American cowboy doesn't wear a gun. He carries a pocket computer, and his trade is modern technology. When he joins a firm, he wants to know where he's going and how to get there. He doesn't like groups and committees because they're too slow. Furthermore, if the group is successful no one knows who should receive the individual credit—and if it fails, no one knows who should get the individual blame.

Implications for Management

Certainly, there have been examples in which Japanese-style management has been imported into this country and has thus far worked effectively. But these experiments are in a minority, and there is reason to suspect the Hawthorne effect at work in some of these success stories. It is also probable that for every success story in transplanting Japanese management to this country, there have been at least an equal number of failures.

Does this mean that the differences between East and West are so great that we are doomed to ultimate failure in trying to import Japanese approaches to management? Not necessarily. Review of mythology does suggest, however, that the following be considered. First, certain Japanese management practices are less likely to work in this country than in others. For example, the Japanese practice of slow promotions and evaluations is contrary to the Western need to prove one's individual self-worth. Similarly, the practice of nonspecific career paths robs the individual of an important vehicle for self-

perfection. Going back to my analogy, the cowboy's sense of freedom and self-worth comes from mastering his trade.

Second, it may be necessary to modify certain promising Japanese practices to make them compatible with our American cowboy mentality. Participative decision making is a prime example. In Japan the ritualized practice of *ringi* seems to work just fine. Everyone in the firm affected by a decision must sign a proposal before it is put into effect. In this country the hybrid practice of consultative decision making is much more consistent with the Occidental view of human nature.

This is quite different from ceremonial *ringi* or pure consensus decision making. Consultative decision making calls for the manager to make the final decision after carefully considering the inputs from his or her subordinates. It also requires that everyone knows the name of the game up front. In this way there is involvement, but in a sense that is consistent with the Western view that it is the manager's individual responsibility to make major decisions—a responsibility that those in the Western world feel cannot be abdicated to the group.

Modifications may also be necessary to make quality circles work in this country. Again drawing heavily on Occidental mythical themes, this strategy is most likely to be successful in American when:

1. The formal supervisor is also the QC leader.
2. Differential individual contributions are recognized and rewarded.
3. Profits from savings are shared with workers.

Third, certain types of people in certain types of organizations are more likely to respond favorably to Japanese practices than are others. Central to this proposition is the Oriental concept of Yin and Yang. In general,

Japanese management has a decidedly Yin flavor, whereas American management has a decidedly Yang flavor. This is also true of Japanese workers and American workers. And there are specific American industries that are much more Yang than Yin. For example, Big Steel is decidedly a Yang industry. As a result, Japanese forms of management are not likely to work in it even though there are examples of small steel companies that have imported Japanese management approaches. Mining, automobile manufacturing, and oil are also examples of Yang industries. Health care, retailing, and any other industry employing large numbers of women or engaged in helping or nurturing activities may be considered Yin organizations. It is in these Yin industries that Japanese management has the best chance of success.

There are also Yin and Yang occupations. Engineering, accounting, and law enforcement are examples of Yang occupations while psychology, medicine, and teaching are examples of Yin occupations. Once again, people in these specific occupations would tend to be differentially predisposed to Japanese management.

Finally, age, sex, and personality play a role. Young people who have had greater exposure to cross-cultural influences are more predisposed to Yin management practices than those who had less. In general, women should respond better than men to Japanese management although personality makeup plays a mediating role. Obviously, there are many men who have feminine makeups and many women with masculine makeups. Therefore, personality makeup is more critical than sex per se.

To summarize, this review of Occidental and Oriental mythology suggests some rather divergent views of human nature and reality. Because all management practices are based on assumptions about human nature and reality, it is important to consider these differences in our current attempt to import Japanese or other management approaches to this country. It follows that those practices that do not violate our core values and beliefs will have a greater chance for success that those that do. It is also likely that even those practices that show promise will require modification, or "Americanization." Finally, the ultimate success of Japanese management in this country will depend on matching those practices to industries, occupations, and individuals who have a propensity to the Yin aspects of life.

MANAGERS AS CULTURAL HEROES

The influx of women into the workforce and the mounting pressures of foreign competition will force managers to reappraise their roles. Within this context, the hero myth is of particular importance for several reasons. First, it is the most common and best-known myth in the world, and it is found in both primitive and contemporary cultures. Second, it embodies those values that are held most highly by a given civilization. And third, hero myths symbolically represent those stages of growth that are required for mature functioning in any given society.

In a very real sense, managers are one variant of the contemporary culture hero. They are expected by society to provide leadership. It follows that an essential element of that leadership is some sense of vision that embodies the expressed or vaguely sensed values of those being led. Unfortunately, this vision will not be found in textbooks or workshops on leadership. Despite hundreds of books and thousands of articles on the subject, few if any deal with the importance of vision and other important heroic qualities necessary for leading.

The hero myth provides a rich source of insight into these important issues. These insights will be explored in terms of universal themes, their symbolic value, and implications for managers.

Universal Themes

Regardless of where we encounter the hero myth, we find that these exemplary individuals usually have humble but often miraculous beginnings. Hercules, for example, came from the questionable mating of Zeus with the mortal woman, Amphitryon. Most heroes also encounter mentors early in their lives who teach them the ways of the world and the sources of special power. King Arthur's mentor, Merlin the magician, is a classic medieval variation of this universal theme.

Heroes prove themselves early in life by notable feats of superhuman strength that are required to appease the gods or to save the tribe. These feats change in complexion as civilizations face new challenges. The most primitive heroes conquer dragons or other wild beasts. More modern heroes conquer other men or forces within themselves. Prototypes of such heroes are the Greek Perseus, who slew the Minotaur; Achilles the warrior-hero of Homeric Greece; and Buddha, the metaphysical hero of Oriental mythology.

It is interesting to note that very often a beautiful woman is involved in the hero's quest. Although this theme appears in early Greek mythology, it reaches its most elaborate development in the myths surrounding King Arthur and the knights of the Round Table. Launcelot, Galahad, and Percival, in particular, spent a good deal of their time saving beautiful and virtuous women in distress. The power of this theme is still very evident in the exploits of such modern heroes as Superman, Luke Skywalker of *Star Wars*, and Indiana Jones of *Raiders of the Lost Ark*.

Despite all of their incredible achievements, most mythological heroes have one glaring weakness—the sin of pride. Sooner or later they take themselves too seriously, overstep their bounds, and incur the wrath of the gods and the loss of respect from other members of their tribe. A classic case in point is the Greek Titan Prometheus, whose pride and boldness prompted him to steal fire from the gods. His punishment, ordered by Zeus, was to be chained to a rock where an eagle was sent nightly to tear out his liver.

Finally, heroes are often called upon to redeem their fall from grace by one final act of supreme self-sacrifice that culminates in the hero's giving his life for the greater good of all.

Symbolic Value

The hero myth is important not only because it demonstrates what various societies expect and fear from their heroes, but also because it formulates a symbolic model for human growth and development. Jung provides rich insights into symbolic meaning of the hero myth. He suggests that it represents each individual's struggle from self-centered infantilism to mature, self-sacrificing adulthood. Within his framework of speculation, fighting dragons, saving beautiful women, and learning from mentors have special symbolic value.

Accordingly, to become a mature adult, each of us must first conquer the powerful primitive forces within us. Our narcissistic, childish impulses that demand immediate gratification represent the dragon that must be conquered for the good of society. Our symbolic "lady in distress" is the complementary aspect of our dual nature that is being held captive. For men, this is the feminine side of their nature and, for women, the masculine side. Thus saving the beautiful maiden is gaining access to the total personality.

To help us with this painful growth process, we need mentors who can show us the way. Symbolically, these mentors are not necessarily individuals, but represent the culture's laws, mores, and folkways. It is important to note that mentors "are not forever." When mythological heroes reach a certain point in their development, they instinctively know when to disassociate themselves from their mentors and when to strike out on their own.

Implications for Managers

Recurring themes from the hero myth highlight those qualities that have remained most valued by both Occidental and Oriental civilizations. These are courage, strength, self-sacrifice and humility.

In a recent article in *Time* magazine, Japanese success in the world marketplace was linked to the exposure of their executives to the writings of Miyamoto Musashi. Musashi was a courageous samurai warrior who in the 17th century reportedly killed over 60 opponents in hand-to-hand combat. These exploits were followed by a period of contemplation and writing. The product was *A Book of Five Rings*. In it, Musashi emphasizes the importance of courage and provides prescriptions on how to kill your opponent before he kills you.

The value of courage also lives on in the exploits of Ted Turner, who recently made the cover of *Time* for his courage and resourcefulness in taking on the major networks with his all-news cable TV network. The lesson for management is clear: Whether courage is displayed in taking a chance with an innovative product or process, in fighting for scarce organizational resources, or in defending your subordinates, it is a quality followers look for and respond to in their leaders.

Strength is the second quality that characterizes the mythological hero. Since there are no longer any dragons to slay, the importance of physical strength has diminished in most societies. Still, other forms of strength are necessary for survival. In work organizations, strength is equated with power that comes from three major sources: control of scarce resources, technical expertise, and character. Of these three, character is the most elusive. In the hero myth, strength of character is equated with knowing where you are going and how to get there, and with knowing right from wrong and knowing how to respond to each.

In any society, many people have courage and strength but never become heroes. This is because a third element, self-sacrifice, is also necessary. Self-sacrifice is the bridge between personal pleasure and the collective good. This means that effective managers will exercise courage and strength for the greater good of the organization rather than for personal gain and aggrandizement.

Finally, heroic myths indicate cultural ambivalence toward their heroes. This may be gleaned from two major themes: humble birth and the sin of pride. Humble birth is important because it demonstrates the need for heroes to have close touch with the common people. The sin of pride is important because it demonstrates the fallibility of all individuals, no matter how great. Managers who get the message will make special efforts to be accessible to their subordinates and will work hard at not taking themselves too seriously.

Beyond what can be learned from universal themes are lessons to be found in the symbolic meaning of the hero myth. These lessons deal with individual growth and development and occur on two different levels. The first lesson has to do with the manager's learning to deal with his or her primitive need for power and self-aggrandizement. Until this need for power can be put to work for the collective good of the organization, the manager will not realize his or her full potential as a leader.

The second lesson has to do with the manager's dual nature, which is both masculine and feminine. In most people, regardless of their sex, one of the two predominates and shapes the personality. To become a whole person, it is necessary to gain access to one's "other half." Elsewhere in this article I have suggested how this might be done.

SUMMARY

Managers represent one form of the modern-day hero. As such, they are expected to extoll those virtues that have permeated the heroic myths of the past. Among these virtues are courage, strength, self-sacrifice, and humility. Before these noble qualities can be put to work for the collective good, it is necessary for the manager to reach full emotional maturity by slaying two formidable dragons that reside within the psyche: self-serving narcissism and the fear of one's complementary nature, whether it be masculine or feminine.

In concluding this article, I would like to leave the reader with a thought expressed by Joseph Campbell in his *The Masks of God: Primitive Mythology*: "Clearly, mythology is no toy for children. Nor is it a matter of archaic, merely scholarly concern, of no moment to modern men of action. For its symbols touch and release the deepest centers of motivation, moving literate and illiterate alike, moving mobs, moving civilizations."

J. STERLING LIVINGSTON

Pygmalion in Management

A MANAGER'S EXPECTATIONS ARE THE KEY TO A SUBORDINATE'S PERFORMANCE AND DEVELOPMENT

Pygmalion was a sculptor in Greek mythology who carved a statue of a beautiful woman that subsequently was brought to life. George Bernard Shaw's play, Pygmalion (the basis for the musical hit, "My Fair Lady"), has a somewhat similar theme; the essence is that one person, by self effort and will, can transform another person. And in the world of management, many executives play Pygmalion-like roles in developing able subordinates and in stimulating their performance. What is the secret of their success? How are they different from managers who fail to develop top-notch subordinates? And what are the implications of all this for the problem of excessive turnover and disillusionment among talented young people in business? Such are the questions discussed here. The title of the article was inspired by Pygmalion in the Classroom, a book by Robert Rosenthal and Leonore Jacobson that describes the effect of expectations on the intellectual development of children.

In George Bernard Shaw's *Pygmalion*, Eliza Doolittle explains:

"You see, really and truly, apart from the things anyone can pick up (the dressing and the proper way of speaking, and so on), the difference between a lady and a flower girl is not how she behaves, but how she's treated. I shall always be a flower girl to Professor

Mr. Livingston is professor of business administration at the Harvard Business School, where he is studying the early careers in business of college graduates. In addition to his observation of management in many companies, he draws on extensive personal experience as an executive. He is president of Sterling Institute, which he founded; he was also the founder of Management Systems Corporation and for many years was its president. Other organizations he has served as chief executive are Peat, Marwick Livingston & Co., Logistics Management Institute, Technology Fund of Puerto Rico, Harbridge House, Inc., and Tamarind Reef Corporation.

Reprinted from *Harvard Business Review* (July–August 1969).

117

Higgins, because he always treats me as a flower girl, and always will; but I know I can be a lady to you, because you always treat me as a lady, and always will."

Some managers always treat their subordinates in a way that leads to superior performance. But most managers, like Professor Higgins, unintentionally treat their subordinates in a way that leads to lower performance than they are capable of achieving. The way managers treat their subordinates is subtly influenced by what they expect of them. If managers' expectations are high, productivity is likely to be excellent. If their expectations are low, productivity is likely to be poor. It is as though there were a law that caused subordinates' performance to rise or fall to meet managers' expectations.

The powerful influence of one person's expectations on another's behavior has long been recognized by physicians and behavioral scientists and, more recently, by teachers. But heretofore the importance of managerial expectations for individual and group performance has not been widely understood. I have documented this phenomenon in a number of case studies prepared during the past decade for major industrial concerns. These cases and other evidence available from scientific research now reveal:

What managers expect of their subordinates and the way they treat them largely determine their performance and career progress.

A unique characteristic of superior managers is their ability to create high performance expectations that subordinates fulfill.

Less effective managers fail to develop similar expectations, and, as a consequence, the productivity of their subordinates suffers.

Subordinates, more often than not, appear to do what they believe they are expected to do.

IMPACT ON PRODUCTIVITY

One of the more comprehensive illustrations of the effect of managerial expectations on productivity is recorded in studies of the organizational experiment undertaken in 1961 by Alfred Oberlander, manager of the Rockaway District Office of the Metropolitan Life Insurance Company.[1] He had observed that outstanding insurance agencies grew faster than average or poor agencies and that new insurance agents performed better in outstanding agencies than in average or poor agencies, regardless of their sales aptitude. He decided, therefore, to group his superior agents in one unit to stimulate their performance and to provide a challenging environment in which to introduce new salespeople.

Accordingly, Oberlander assigned his six best agents to work with his best assistant manager, an equal number of average producers to work with an average assistant manager, and the remaining low producers to work with the least able manager. He then asked the superior group to produce two thirds of the premium volume achieved by the entire agency the previous year. He described the results as follows:

"Shortly after this selection had been made, the men in the agency began referring to this select group as a 'super-staff' since, due to the fact that we were operating this group as a unit, their esprit de corps was very high. Their production efforts over the first 12 weeks far surpassed our most optimistic expectations... proving that groups of men of sound ability can be motivated beyond their apparently normal productive capacities when the problems created by the poor producer are eliminated from the operation.

"Thanks to this fine result, over-all agency performance improved 40 percent and stayed at this figure.

"In the beginning of 1962 when, through expansion, we appointed another assistant manager and assigned him a staff, we again utilized this same concept, arranging the men once more according to their productive capacity.

"The assistant managers were assigned ...according to their ability, with the most capable assistant manager receiving the best group, thus playing strength to strength. Our agency over-all production again improved by about 25-30 percent, and so this staff arrangement was continued until the end of the year.

"Now in this year of 1963, we found upon analysis that there were so many men... with a potential of half a million dollars or more that only one staff remained of those men in the agency who were not considered to have any chance of reaching the half-million-dollar mark."[2]

Although the productivity of the "super-staff" improved dramatically, it should be pointed out that the productivity of those in the lowest unit, "who were not considered to have any chance of reaching the half-million-dollar mark," actually declined and that attrition among them increased. The performance of the superior agents rose to meet their manager's expectations, while that of the weaker ones declined as predicted.

Self-Fulfilling Prophesies

However, the "average" unit proved to be an anomaly. Although the district manager expected only average performance from this group, its productivity increased significantly. This was because the assistant manager in charge of the group refused to believe that he was less capable than the manager of the "super-staff" or that the agents in the top group had any greater ability than the agents in his group. He insisted in discussions with his agents that every person in the middle group had greater potential than those in the "super-staff," lacking only their years of experience in selling insurance. He stimulated

his agents to accept the challenge of out-performing the "super-staff." As a result, in each year the middle group increased its productivity by a higher percentage than the "super-staff" did (although it never attained the dollar volume of the top group).

It is of special interest that the self-image of the manager of the "average" unit did not permit him to accept others' treatment of him as an "average" manager, just as Eliza Doolittle's image of herself as a lady did not permit her to accept others' treatment of her as a flower girl. The assistant manager transmitted his own strong feelings of efficacy to his agents, created mutual expectancy of high performance, and greatly stimulated productivity.

Comparable results occurred when a similar experiment was made at another office of the company. Further confirmation comes from a study of the early managerial success of 49 college graduates who were management-level employees of an operating company of the American Telephone and Telegraph Company. David E. Berlew and Douglas T. Hall of the Massachusetts Institute of Technology examined the career progress of these managers over a period of five years and discovered that their relative success, as measured by salary increases and the company's estimate of each one's performance and potential, depended largely on the company's expectations of them.[3]

The influence of one person's expectations on another's behavior is by no means a business discovery. More than half a century ago, Albert Moll concluded from this clinical experience that subjects behaved as they believed they were expected to.[4] The phenomenon he observed, in which "the prophecy causes its own fulfillment," has recently become a subject of considerable scientific interest. For example:

In a series of scientific experiments, Robert Rosenthal of Harvard University has demonstrated that a "teacher's expectation for her pupils' intellectual competence can come to serve as an education self-fulfilling prophecy."[5]

An experiment in a summer Headstart program for 60 preschoolers compared the performance of pupils under (a) teachers who had been led to expect relatively slow learning by their children, and (b) teachers who had been lead to believe their children had excellent intellectual ability and learning capacity. Pupils of the second group of teachers learned much faster.[6]

Moreover, the healing professions have long recognized that a physician's or psychiatrist's expectations can have a formidable influence on a patient's physical or mental health. What takes place in the minds of the patients and the healers, particularly when they have congruent expectations, may determine the outcome. For instance, the havoc of a doctor's pessimistic prognosis has often been observed. Again, it is well known that the efficacy of a new drug or a new treatment can be greatly influenced by the physician's expectations—a result referred to by the medical profession as a "placebo effect."

Pattern of Failure

When salespersons are treated by their managers as superpeople, as the "super-staff" was at Metropolitan Rockaway District Office, they try to live up to that image and do what they know supersalespersons are expected to do. But when the agents with poor productivity records are treated by their managers as *not* having "any chance" of success, as the low producers at Rockaway were, this negative expectation also becomes a managerial self-fulfilling prophecy.

Unsuccessful salespersons have great difficulty maintaining their self-image and self-esteem. In response to low managerial expectations, they typically attempt to prevent additional damage to their egos by avoiding situations that might lead to greater failure. They either reduce the number of sales calls they make or avoid trying to "close" sales when that might result in further painful rejection, or both. Low expectations and damaged egos lead them to behave in a manner that increases the probability of failure, thereby fulfilling their managers' expectations. Let me illustrate:

Not long ago I studied the effectiveness of branch bank managers at a West Coast bank with over 500 branches. The managers who had had their lending authority reduced because of high rates of loss became progressively less effective. To prevent further loss of authority, they turned to making only "safe" loans. This action resulted in losses of business to competing banks and a relative decline in both deposits and profits at their branches. Then, to reverse that decline in deposits and earnings, they often "reached" for loans and became almost irrational in their acceptance of questionable credit risks. Their actions were not so much a matter of poor judgment as an expression of their willingness to take desperate risks in the hope of being able to avoid further damage to their egos and to their careers.

Thus, in response to the low expectations of their supervisors, who had reduced their lending authority, they behaved in a manner that led to larger credit losses. They appeared to do what they believed they were expected to do, and their supervisors' expectations became self-fulfilling prophecies.

POWER OF EXPECTATIONS

Managers cannot avoid the depressing cycle of events that flow from low expectations merely by hiding their feelings from subordinates. If managers believe subordinates will perform poorly, it is virtually impossible for them to mask their expectations, because the message usually is communicated unintentionally, without conscious action on their part.

Indeed, managers often communicate most when they believe they are communicating least. For instance, when they say nothing—become "cold" and "uncommunicative"—it usually is a sign that they are displeased by a subordinate or believe that he or she is "hopeless." The silent treatment communicates negative feelings even more effectively, at times, than a tongue-lashing does. What seems to be critical in the communication of expectations is not what the boss says, so much as the *way he or she behaves*. Indifferent and noncommittal treatment, more often than not, is the kind of treatment that communicates low expectations and leads to poor performance.

Common Illusions

Managers are more effective in communicating low expectations to their subordinates than in communicating high expectations to them, even though most managers believe exactly the opposite. It usually is astonishingly difficult for them to recognize the clarity with which they transmit negative feelings. To illustrate again:

The Rockaway district manager vigorously denied that he had communicated low expectations to the agents in the poorest group who, he believed, did not have "any chance" of becoming high producers. Yet the message was clearly received by those agents. A typical case was that of an agent who resigned from the low unit. When the district manager told the agent that he was sorry he was leaving, the agent replied, "No, you're not; you're glad." Although the district manager previously had said nothing to the man, he had unintentionally communicated his low expectations to his agents through his indifferent manner. Subsequently, the agents who were assigned to the lowest unit interpreted the assignment as

equivalent to a request for their resignation.

One of the company's agency managers established superior, average, and low units, even though he was convinced that he had no superior or outstanding subordinates. "All my assistant managers and agents are either average or incompetent," he explained to the Rockaway district manager. Although he tried to duplicate the Rockaway results, his low opinions of his agents were communicated—not so subtly—to them. As a result, the experiment failed.

Positive feelings, on the other hand, often do not come through clearly enough. For example:

Another insurance agency manager copied the organization changes made at the Rockaway District Office, grouping the sales people he rated highly with the best manager, the average salespeople with an average manager, and so on. However, improvement did not result from the move. The Rockaway district manager therefore investigated the situation. He discovered that the assistant manager in charge of the high-performance unit was unaware that his manager considered him to be the best. In fact, he and the other agents doubted that the agency manager really believed there was any difference in their abilities. This agency manager was a stolid, phlegmatic, unemotional man who treated his agents in a rather pedestrian way. Since high expectations had not been communicated to them, they did not understand the reason for the new organization and could not see any point in it. Clearly, the way a manager *treats* his or her subordinates, not the way he organizes them, is the key to high expectations and high productivity.

Impossible Dreams

Managerial expectations must pass the test of reality before they can be translated into performance. To become self-fulfilling prophecies, expectations must be made of sterner stuff than the power of positive thinking or generalized confidence in one's subordinates—helpful as these concepts may be for some other purposes. Subordinates will not be motivated to reach high levels of productivity unless they consider the boss's high expectations realistic and achievable. If they are encouraged to strive for unattainable goals, they eventually give up trying and settle for results that are lower than they are capable of achieving. The experience of a large electrical manufacturing company demonstrates this; the company discovered that production actually declined if production quotas were set too high, because the workers simply stopped trying to meet them. In other words, the practice of "dangling the carrot just beyond the donkey's reach," endorsed by many managers, is not a good motivational device.

Scientific research by David C. McClelland of Harvard University and John W. Atkinson of the University of Michigan[7] has demonstrated that the relationship of motivation to expectancy varies in the form of a bell-shaped curve [as in Figure 1]. The degree of motivation and effort rises until the expectancy of success reaches 50%, then begins to fall even though the expectancy of success continues to increase. No motivation or response is aroused when the goal is perceived as being either virtually certain or virtually impossible to attain.

Morever, as Berlew and Hall have pointed out, if a subordinate fails to meet performance expectations that are close to his or her own level of aspirations, he or she will lower personal performance goals and standards, performance will tend to drop off, and negative attitudes will develop toward the task activity or job[8]. It is therefore not surprising that failure of subordinates to meet the unrealistically high expectations of their managers leads to high rates of attrition either voluntary or involuntary.

Secret of Superiority

Something takes place in the minds of superior managers that does not occur in the minds of those who are less effective. While superior managers are consistently able to create high performance expectations that their subordinates fulfill, weaker managers are not successful in obtaining a similar response. What accounts for the difference?

The answer, in part, seems to be that superior managers have greater confidence than other managers in their own ability to develop the talents of their subordinates. Contrary to what might be assumed, the high expectations of superior managers are based primarily on what they think about themselves—about their own ability to select, train, and motivate their subordinates. What managers believe about themselves subtly influences what they believe about their subordinates, what they expect of them, and how they treat them. If they have confidence in their ability to develop and stimulate them to high levels of performance, they will expect much of them and will treat them with confidence that their expecta-

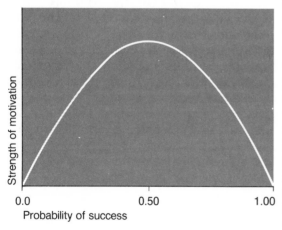

Figure 1

tions will be met. But if they have doubts about their ability to stimulate them, they will expect less of them and will treat them with less confidence.

Stated in another way, the superior managers' record of success and their confidence in their ability give their high expectations credibility. As a consequence, their subordinates accept these expectations as realistic and try hard to achieve them.

The importance of what a manager believes about his or her training and motivational ability is illustrated by "Sweeney's Miracle,"[9] a managerial and educational self-fulfilling prophecy:

James Sweeney taught industrial management and psychiatry at Tulane University, and he also was responsible for the operation of the Biomedical Computer Center there. Sweeney believed that he could teach even a poorly educated man to be a capable computer operator. George Johnson, a black man who was a former hospital porter, became janitor at the computer center; he was chosen by Sweeney to prove his conviction. In the morning, George Johnson performed his janitorial duties, and in the afternoon Sweeney taught him about computers.

Johnson was learning a great deal about computers when someone at the university concluded that, to be a computer operator, one had to have a certain I.Q. score. Johnson was tested, and his I.Q. indicated that he would not be able to learn to type, much less operate a computer.

But Sweeney was not convinced. He threatened to quit unless Johnson was permitted to learn to program and operate the computer. Sweeney prevailed, and he is still running the computer center. Johnson is now in charge of the main computer room and is responsible for training new employees to program and operate the computer.

Sweeney's expectations were based on what he believed about his own teaching ability, not on Johnson's learning credentials. What a manager believes about his or her ability to train and motivate subordinates clearly is the foundation on which realistically high managerial expectations are built.

THE CRITICAL EARLY YEARS

Managerial expectations have their most magical influence on young people. As subordinates mature and gain experience, their self-image gradually hardens, and they begin to see themselves as their career records imply. Their own aspirations, and the expectations of their superiors, become increasingly controlled by the "reality" of their past performance. It becomes more and more difficult for them, and for their managers, to generate mutually high expectations unless they have outstanding records.

Incidentally, the same pattern occurs in school. Rosenthal's experiments with educational self-fulfilling prophecies consistently demonstrate that teachers' expectations are more effective in influencing intellectual growth in younger children than in older children. In the lower grade levels, particularly in the first and second grades, the effects of teachers' expectations are dramatic.[10] In the upper grade levels, teachers' prophecies seem to have little effect on children's intellectual growth, although they do affect their motivation and attitude toward school. While the declining influence of teachers' expectations cannot be completely explained, it is reasonable to conclude that younger children are more malleable, have fewer fixed notions about their abilities, and have less well-established reputations in the schools. As they grow, particularly if they are assigned to "tracks" on the basis of their records, as is now often done in public schools, their beliefs about their intellectual ability and their teachers' expectations of them begin to harden and become more resistant to influence by others.

Key To Future Performance

The early years in a business organization, when young people can be strongly influenced by managerial expectations, are critical in determining their future performance and career progress. This is shown by a study at American Telephone and Telegraph Company:

Berlew and Hall found that what the company initially expected of 49 college graduates who were management-level employees was the most critical factor in their subsequent performance and success. The researchers concluded that the correlation between how much a company expects of an employee in the first year and how much that employee contributes during the next five years was "too compelling to be ignored."[11]

Subsequently, the two men studied the career records of 18 college graduates who were hired as management trainees in another of the American Telephone and Telegraph Company's operating companies. Again they found that both expectations and performance in the first year correlated consistently with later performance and success.[12]

Berlew and Hall summarized their research by stating:

"Something important is happening in the first year...Meeting high company expectations in the critical first year leads to the internalization of positive job attitudes and high standards; these attitudes and standards, in turn, would first lead to and be reinforced by strong performance and success in later years. It should also follow that a new manager who meets the challenge of one highly demanding job will be given subsequently a more demanding job, and his level of contribution will rise as he responds to the company's growing expectations of him. The key...is the concept of the first year as a *critical period of learning*, a time when the trainee is uniquely ready to de-velop or change in the direction of the company's expectations."[13]

Most Influential Boss

A young person's first manager is likely to be the most influential person in his or her career. If this manager is unable or unwilling to develop the skills the young employee needs to perform effectively, the latter will set lower personal standards than he or she is capable of achieving, that person's self-image will be impaired, and he or she will develop negative attitudes toward the job, the employer, and—in all probability—his or her career in business. Since the chances of building a successful career with the employer will decline rapidly, he or she will leave, if that person has high aspirations, in hope of finding a better opportunity. If, on the other hand, the manager helps the employee to achieve maximum potential, he or she will build the foundation for a successful career. To illustrate:

With few exceptions, the most effective branch managers at a large West Coast bank were mature people in their forties and fifties. The bank's executives explained that it took considerable time for a person to gain the knowledge, experience, and judgment required to handle properly credit risks, customer relations, and employee relations.

However, one branch manager, ranked in the top 10% of the managers in terms of effectiveness (which included branch profit growth, deposit growth, scores on administrative audits, and subjective rankings by superiors), was only 27 years old. This young person had been made a branch manager at 25, and in two years had improved not only the performance of the branch substantially but also developed a younger assistant manager so that the assistant, in turn, was made a branch manager at 25.

The assistant had had only average grades in college, but, in just four years at the bank had been assigned to work with two branch managers who were remarkably effective teachers. The first boss, who was recognized throughout the bank for unusual skill in developing young people, did not believe that it took years to gain the knowledge and skill needed to become an effective banker. After two years, the young person was made assistant manager at a branch headed by another executive, who also was an effective developer of subordinates. Thus it was that the young person, when promoted to head a branch, confidently followed the model of two previous superiors in operating the branch, quickly established a record of outstanding performance, and trained as assistant to assume responsibility early.

Contrasting Records. For confirming evidence of the crucial role played by a person's first bosses, let us turn to selling, since performance in this area is more easily measured than in most managerial areas. Consider the following investigations:

In a study of the careers of 100 insurance salesmen who began work with either highly competent or less-than-competent agency managers, the Life Insurance Agency Management Association found that men with average sales aptitude test scores were nearly five times as likely to succeed under managers with good performance records as under managers with poor records; and men with superior sales aptitude scores were found to be twice as likely to succeed under high-performing managers as under low-performing managers.[14]

The Metropolitan Life Insurance Company determined in 1960 that differences in the productivity of new insurance agents who had equal sales aptitudes could be accounted for only by differences in the ability of managers in the offices to which they were assigned. Men whose productivity was high in relation to their aptitude test scores invariably were employed in offices that had production records among the top third

in the company. Conversely, men whose productivity was low in relation to their test scores typically were in the least successful offices. After analyzing all the factors that might have accounted for these variations, the company concluded that differences in the performance of new men were due primarily to differences in the "proficiency in sales training and direction" of the local managers.[15]

A study I conducted of the performance of automobile salesmen in Ford dealerships in New England revealed that superior salesmen were concentrated in a few outstanding dealerships. For instance, 10 of the top 15 salesmen in New England were in 3 (out of approximately 200) of the dealerships in this region; and 5 of the top 15 men were in one highly successful dealership; yet 4 of these men previously had worked for other dealers without achieving outstanding sales records. There seemed to be little doubt that the training and motivational skills of managers in the outstanding dealerships were the critical factor.

Astute Selection

While success in business sometimes appears to depend on the "luck of the draw," more than luck is involved when a young person is selected by a superior manager. Successful managers do not pick their subordinates at random or by the toss of a coin. They are careful to select only those who they "know" will succeed. As Metropolitan's Rockaway district manager, Alfred Oberlander, insisted: "Every man who starts with us is going to be a top-notch life insurance man, or he would not have received an invitation to join the team."[16]

When pressed to explain how they "know" whether a person will be successful, superior managers usually end up by saying something like, "The qualities are intangible, but I know them when I see them." They have difficulty being explicit because their selection process is intuitive and is based on interpersonal intelligence that is difficult to describe. The key seems to be that they are able to identify subordinates with whom they can probably work effectively—people with whom they are compatible and whose body chemistry agrees with their own. They make mistakes, of course. But they "give up" on a subordinate slowly because that means "giving up" on themselves—on their judgment and ability in selecting, training, and motivating people. Less effective managers select subordinates more quickly and give up on them more easily, believing that the inadequacy is that of the subordinate, not of themselves.

DEVELOPING YOUNG PEOPLE

Observing that his company's research indicates that "initial corporate expectations for performance (with real responsibility) mold subsequent expectations and behavior," R.W. Walters, Jr., director of college employment at the American Telephone and Telegraph Company, contends that: "Initial bosses of new college hires must be the best in the organization."[17] Unfortunately, however, most companies practice exactly the opposite.

Rarely do new graduates work closely with experienced middle managers or upper-level executives. Normally, they are bossed by first-line managers who tend to be the least experienced and least effective in the organization. While there are exceptions, first-line managers generally are either "old pros" who have been judged as lacking competence for higher levels of responsibility, or they are younger people who are making the transition from "doing" to "managing." Often, these managers lack the knowledge and skill required to develop the productive capabilities of their subordinates. As a consequence, many college grad-

uates begin their careers in business under the worst possible circumstances. Since they know their abilities are not being developed or used, they quite naturally soon become negative toward their jobs, employers, and business careers.

Although most top executives have not yet diagnosed the problem, industry's greatest challenge by far is the underdevelopment, underutilization, and ineffective management and use of its most valuable resource—its young managerial and professional talent.

Disillusion and Turnover

The problem posed to corporate management is underscored by the sharply rising rates of attrition among young managerial and professional personnel. Turnover among managers one to five years out of college is almost twice as high now as it was a decade ago, and five times as high as two decades ago. Three out of five companies surveyed by *Fortune* magazine in the fall of 1968 reported that turnover rates among young managers and professionals were higher than five years ago.[18] While the high level of economic activity and the shortage of skilled personnel have made job-hopping easier, the underlying causes of high attrition, I am convinced, are underdevelopment and underutilization of a work force that has high career aspirations.

The problem can be seen in its extreme form in the excessive attrition rates of college and university graduates who begin their careers in sales positions. Whereas the average company loses about 50% of its new college and university graduates within three to five years, attrition rates as high as 40% in the *first* year are common among college graduates who accept sales positions in the average company. This attrition stems primarily, in my opinion, from the failure of first-line managers to teach new college recruits what they need to know to be effective sales representatives.

As we have seen, young people who begin their careers working for less-than-competent sales managers are likely to have records of low productivity. When rebuffed by their customers and considered by their managers to have little potential for success, the young people naturally have great difficulty in maintaining their self-esteem. Soon they find little personal satisfaction in their jobs and, to avoid further loss of self-respect, leave their employers for jobs that look more promising. Moreover, as reports about the high turnover and disillusionment of those who embarked on sales careers filter back to college campuses, new graduates become increasingly reluctant to take jobs in sales.

Thus ineffective first-line sales management sets off a sequence of events that ends with college and university graduates avoiding careers in selling. To a lesser extent, the same pattern is duplicated in other functions of business, as evidenced by the growing trend of college graduates to pursue careers in "more meaningful" occupations, such as teaching and government service.

A serious "generation gap" between bosses and subordinates is another significant cause of breakdown. Many managers resent the abstract, academic language and narrow rationalization typically used by recent graduates. As one manager expressed it to me: "For God's sake, you need a lexicon even to talk with these kids." Noncollege managers often are particularly resentful, perhaps because they feel threatened by the bright young people with book-learned knowledge that they do not understand.

For whatever reason, the "generation gap" in many companies is eroding managerial expectations of new college graduates. For instance, I know of a survey of management attitudes in one of the nation's largest companies which revealed that 54% of its first-line and second-line managers believed that new college recruits were "not as good as they were five years ago." Since what managers expect of subordinates influences the way they treat them, it is understandable that new graduates often develop negative attitudes toward their jobs and their employers. Clearly, low managerial expectations and hostile attitudes are not the basis for effective management of new people entering business.

CONCLUSION

Industry has not developed effective first-line managers fast enough to meet its needs. As a consequence, many companies are underdeveloping their most valuable resource—talented young men and women. They are incurring heavy attrition costs and contributing to the negative attitudes young people often have about careers in business.

For top executives in industry who are concerned with the productivity of their organizations and the careers of young employees, the challenge is clear: it is to speed the development of managers who will treat their subordinates in ways that lead to high performance and career satisfaction. Managers shape not only the expectations and productivity of their subordinates, but also influence their attitudes toward their jobs and themselves. If managers are unskilled, they leave scars on the careers of the young people, cut deeply into their self-esteem, and distort their image of themselves as human beings. But if they are skillful and have high expectations of their subordinates, their self-confidence will grow, their capabilities will develop, and their productivity will be high. More often than one realizes, the manager is Pygmalion.

O the despair of Pygmalion, who might have created
a statue and only made a woman!
ALFRED JARRY, 1873-1907
L'Amour Absolu

6

Productivity and Human Motivation

Behavior is shaped and maintained by its consequences.
B.F. SKINNER[1]

"How do you motivate employees?" The problem of understanding motivation begins with this question. It assumes that there *is* a way to motivate employees. More likely, the employee is motivated from within. A manager attempts to match knowledge of the employee with knowledge about human motivation, in hope of finding the right combination to induce the employee to behave in the desired way. The manager who simply applies a "standard motivational formula" fails to consider the unique needs of each employee. This failure to adapt motivational concepts to the unique characteristics of the individual worker leads to a supervised decline in employee productivity and job satisfaction.

Effective managers seek a broad-based understanding of motivation theory to maximize their options for dealing with individual employees. This understanding is helped by mainstream motivation theory, which has two primary branches: cognitive and behavioral theories. This chapter will discuss both and attempt to unify them around a single model.

COGNITIVE THEORIES

Cognitive theories assume that behavior is purposeful and rational. Each of the cognitive theorists suggests certain underlying assumptions from which rationally motivated behavior emerges.[2]

For simplicity of discussion, the cognitive theorists can be subdivided into two broad, and admittedly overlapping, groups. One group bases theories on understanding human needs. As explained in more detail in Chapter 4, theorists such as Maslow, Alderfer, Herzberg, Murray, and McClelland look at the individual employee and hypothesize about the individual's internal needs structure. Simply put, these theorists argue that individuals are motivated to satisfy their needs. The manager's job is to identify which needs are most likely to be strongest and then "motivate" the employee by promising to satisfy those needs.

The needs these theorists ascribe to workers hold a surface validity and an intuitive appeal. Maslow, for example, suggests that employees have a hierarchy of needs that begins with the physiological and then proceeds through the security, social and esteem needs, which may then culminate in self-actualization (see Chapter 4).[3] Alderfer's existence-relatedness-growth needs closely parallel the concepts laid down by Maslow.[4] Herzberg's two-factor model argues that hygiene factors (or dissatisfiers) include such elements as company policy and administration, supervision, relationship with supervisor, working conditions, and other variables that may lead to strong dissatisfaction.[5] Even when properly handled, these hygiene factors *do not* produce motivation; instead, Herzberg suggests, the motivation comes from goals such as achievement, recognition, work itself, responsibility, advancement, and growth in the job setting. Increasing the motivators (or the higher-level needs in Maslow or Alderfer) is the key to motivation. Certainly, the needs these theorists describe are felt by the vast majority of workers.

Another group of cognitive theorists have a slightly different viewpoint. They say that motivation is significantly influenced by the individual's perceptions. Included in these perceptions is one's own self-image. As Chapter 5 explains in more detail, Festinger suggests that people are motivated to reduce dissonance between their expectations and reality.[6] Perhaps the most sophisticated of the cognitive theories center around expectancy theory. Expectancy theory rests on the assumption that people develop subjective probability estimates about the amount of effort needed to achieve some level of work performance and the relationship between that level of work performance and a desired outcome.[7] The higher the subjective probability that the effort will lead to the desired performance and that the desired performance will lead to the valued outcome, the higher one's motivation. Again, surface validity exists, since we all make subjective probability estimates about work-related outcomes from time to time.

The intuitive appeal of cognitive theories is that they presuppose a rational human being who exercises free will. The rational appeal of these theories is furthered by their ability to ascribe motives to human behavior. It is difficult to prove their accuracy, even through rigorous scientific research, because it is difficult to measure individual needs. Nevertheless, to the extent that these theories are correct, the manager can tap the internal wellspring of motivation when an employee's expectations of a desired outcome are high. More specifically, the manager should attempt to understand what needs or outcomes are valued highly by the employee. Then, by constructing a work environment and job that allow the employee to fulfill these needs and achieve these desired outcomes, the manager may produce high levels of motivation.

BEHAVIOR THEORY

The law of effect states that "behavior is a function of the consequences." This concept forms the cornerstone of operant psychology. When applied to organization settings, it is called organizational behavior modification, or "OB Mod."[8] Regardless of the name applied, behavior theory suggests that behaviors which have positive consequences are more likely to be repeated. It also says that antecedents, or cues, are more likely to trigger the desired behavior when the person knows that the outcome of the behavior will be positive.

Figure 6–1 illustrates the relationships between behavior, consequences, and antecedents. As can be seen from the figure, the antecedents that trigger or cue the behavior are influenced by the consequences of that behavior. If these consequences are positive, the person has a positive predisposition, which becomes one of the antecedents of the behavior. The more favorable the consequences, the more favorable the predisposition toward behavior; the more favorable the predisposition toward behavior, the more likely the behavior is to occur.[9]

Reinforcement Schedules

How, and how often, must a behavior be reinforced to increase the likelihood that it will be repeated? Continuous reinforcement means that each desired behavior meets with a positive consequence. But desired behaviors need not be rewarded each time they occur. Behavior may receive reinforcement according to one of the four schedules described below:

> *Variable Interval.* Reinforcement occurs after a varied or random number of time periods.

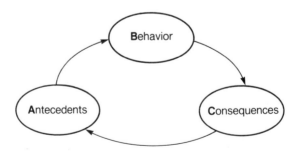

Figure 6–1.   The A-B-C Model of OB Mod

Fixed Interval. Reinforcement occurs after a certain time period, such as hourly, daily or weekly.

Variable ratio. Reinforcement occurs after a varied or random number of instances of the behavior.

Fixed ratio. Reinforcement occurs after a specific number of instances of the behavior.[10]

Research shows that variable-ratio reinforcement is the most powerful motivator among the four choices. A classic example of variable ratio is slot machines. They pay on a variable ratio schedule. Since the payoff is totally unpredictable, players are often reluctant to leave a machine without "one more try."

Managerial Intervention and Implications

With cognitive theory, it is difficult for the manager to know the needs, expectations and objectives of every employee at all times. Behavior theory, however, focuses on behavior, which can be observed and measured. It largely ignores one's internal needs and is sometimes seen as manipulative because it attempts to control the worker's environment. An example of OB Mod interventions is a performance audit in a work situation. In the audit, the manager attempts to identify specific behaviors that are to be positively reinforced with praise, recognition or other rewards. Interventions focus on giving employees praise for specific behaviors that are seen as desirable. The purpose of the positive reinforcement is to increase the probability that the desired behaviors will occur. The interventions often begin with extensive feedback that usually diminishes through time. Studies conducted at Emery Air Freight suggest attitudinal and other improvements are possible if they revolve around carefully designed OB Mod interventions.[11] While desirable behavior is reinforced, undesirable behavior is allowed to disappear by withholding reinforcement, not through punishment. In fact, it may be that the elimination of punishment contributes to the positive attitudes often reported in connection with OB Mod intervention.

AN INTEGRATED VIEWPOINT

The dilemma for managers and researchers is that both cognitive and behavioral theories show evidence of validity. Both cannot be right unless they are parts of a larger picture. This difficulty in explaining behavior in organizations is probably best summarized by Fedor and Ferris:

> ...behavioral scientists traditionally have conceptualized motivational processes and phenomena in either cognitive or behaviorist frameworks. While such attempts to maintain the differentiation of perspectives are regarded as advancing our understanding of behavioral outcomes, it appears that a related

purpose is to set off the more widely accepted cognitive theories from the less popular behaviorist approaches. Such differentiation, regardless of intent, has served to deprive us of a
potentially richer understanding of motivation and organizational behavior. Particularly for the practitioner that attempts
to translate organizational theories in the usual prescriptions,
confusion abounds.[12]

Workers do think. They do have needs. They think about these
needs. Clearly, the cognitive theorists are supported by statements of this
kind. At the same time, however, behaviors that have favorable consequences are more likely to reoccur; thus, support for the behaviorists also
exists. Assuming both sides are correct, at least in part, we can construct
a circular model that incorporates many concepts from both approaches.
Figure 6–2 depicts how various theories may contribute to a more fundamental understanding of motivation.

As Figure 6–2 suggests, results that are met with rewards or reinforcements, and thereby fulfill employee needs, enhance the employee's self-
image. The employee's self-image as a worker leads to certain
self-expectations. In turn, these expectations fuel efforts which lead to
results. Results must be approximately congruent with self-image, or a
dissonance sets in. According to Festinger, employees will strive to avoid
dissonance and, therefore, results will be consistent with the self-image.
If results consistently fall below the self-image, then expectations will
have to be adjusted accordingly.

At the same time, rewards may influence self-expectations. In cases
where rewards are highly valued and the connection between effort and

Figure 6–2.   An Integrated Model of Motivation

reward is clear, expectancy theory seems to work well. That is, if efforts are seen as likely to produce acceptable results, and results are likely to lead to desired rewards, then expectancy theory predicts that the individual will be highly motivated.

The needs theorists also argue that effort is related to unsatisfied needs. The more important (or the less satisfied) these needs are, the more effort will occur. Again, there is a balance between needs and effort. We have all known workers, for example, who were not very motivated because the rewards offered did not meet their needs. As a result, their efforts were less than they could have been.

The model even supports diminished use of punishment, as associated with organizational behavior modification. Discipline, even when properly administered, may very well result in lowering the employee's self-image. A lowered self-image reduces expectations, effort and subsequent results. This reduced performance reduces rewards and reinforcements, satisfying fewer of the employee's needs and thus contributing to a further reduction of the self-image.

When a manager improves an employee's self-image through positive reinforcement, the employee's expectations rise, pushing effort and results to higher levels. The self-image therefore becomes the wellspring of motivation. The manager doesn't really "motivate" the employee; instead, the manager attempts to arrange the work environment so that desired behavior is reinforced and individual employees' needs and expectations are met when the desired performance occurs.

Unfortunately, many managers strictly apply the "exception principle": Only behavior that significantly deviates from expectations is noticed. Only negative behavior elicits a reaction, in the form of discipline. Results are as follows: The *antecedent* of poor employee performance results in a managerial *behavior*—discipline—which leads to positive *consequences* for the manager. This completes the cycle. The manager learns that discipline works (and it usually does in the short run). If the manager applies the exception principle, disciplining poor performance without positively reinforcing good behavior, the result is an employee who receives considerable discipline and little praise.

Figure 6–3 illustrates the likely outcome of this managerial behavior. Variances in employee performance go largely unnoticed unless the employee falls below some minimum accepted level of performance. At that point, discipline is applied. To avoid the discipline, the employee's performance begins to exceed the minimal level consistently. At the same time, the previous peaks of performance that have gone unrewarded begin to disappear. The result is a "steady performer." When an organization has acquired enough steady performers, it has become a bureaucracy that performs above the minimal level, but contains people who are not very self-motivated to achieve higher and higher levels of productivity.

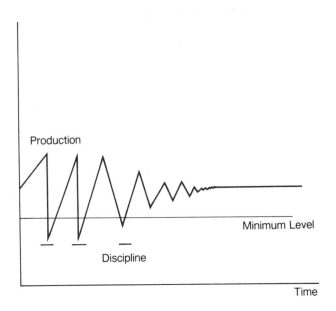

Figure 6–3. The Effects of Punishment without Positive Reinforcement

SUMMARY

Motivation is one of the keys to high productivity in people. Cognitive theories say that people can be motivated to satisfy real and perceived needs. Behavioral theories, however, suggest that people are motivated to behave in ways that have yielded rewards in the past. Both of these theoretical approaches are integrated here into a practical model of motivation for productivity.

SELECTED READINGS OVERVIEW

The reading for this chapter is one by Donald B. Fedor and Gerald R. Ferris, entitled "Integrating OB Mod with Cognitive Approaches to Motivation." This article examines underlying assumptions related to organization behavior modification and to the cognitive theories. It suggests potential benefits for both techniques and discusses some of the frontiers in our understanding of cognitive and behaviorial approaches to motivation.

Next Chapter

Employee motivation does not take place in a vacuum. It is strongly influenced by peer pressure and other aspects of group dynamics. A group's characteristics, values, norms, structure, roles, and cohesion all affect individual motivation. The next chapter reviews these topics and their relationship to productivity.

Review Questions

1. What are the basic differences between the cognitive and behavior views of motivation theory?

2. Compare and contrast Maslow and Alderfer's views of need theory.

3. Herzberg's model of motivation rests upon two sets of factors. Describe them.

4. Define the law of effect. Describe the various reinforcement schedules associated with organizational behavior modification.

5. Diagram and explain the Integrated Model of Motivation.

DONALD B. FEDOR
University of Illinois—Urbana

GERALD R. FERRIS
University of Illinois—Urbana

Integrating OB Mod with Cognitive Approaches to Motivation[1]

Cognitive and behaviorist theories of work behavior typically have been discussed separately and conceptualized as sharing little, if anything, in common. While this may not be a particularly disconcerting state of affairs for the theoretician, it can be for the practitioner who is attempting to bring behavioral science research and theory to bear on organizational problems. Our purpose here is to provide an integration of divergent perspectives and to develop a supportive rationale and legitimization for organizational behavior modification (OB Mod). In the process, by pointing out new avenues for organizational research, we intend to provide the practitioner with practical tools that can be applied in organizational settings.

In efforts to explain behavior in organizations, behavioral scientists traditionally have conceptualized motivational processes and phenomena in either cognitive or behaviorist frameworks. While such attempts to maintain the differentiation of perspectives are regarded as advancing our understanding of behavioral outcomes, it appears that a related purpose is to set off the more widely accepted cognitive theories from the less popular behaviorist approaches. Such differentiation, regardless of intent, has served to deprive us of a potentially richer understanding of motivation and organizational behavior. Particularly for the practitioner who attempts to translate organization theories into useful prescriptions, confusion abounds. With this in mind, our purpose with this paper is to take an eclectic

Donald B. Fedor and Gerald R. Ferris are doctoral candidates in organizational behavior at the University of Illinois, Urbana-Champaign.

Reprinted from: *Academy of Management Review* 6, No. 1 (1981): 115–125. © 1981 by the Academy of Management 0363-7425.

approach, providing specific suggestions for blending the divergent perspectives that offer prescriptive methods for maximizing worker motivation. Our focus is on bringing this blending of perspectives to bear on the legitimization and utility of what has come to be known as organizational behavior modification (OB Mod), in an attempt to address the controversy that has recently emerged in this area [Grey, 1979; Locke, 1977, 1979; Parmerlee & Schwenk, 1979].

UNDERLYING ASSUMPTIONS

The principal cognitive motivation theories in the organization literature are need-satisfaction models [Maslow, 1965], expectancy/valence theory [Vroom, 1964], and goal-setting theory [Locke, 1968]. Clearly, the cognitive component, focusing on rational behavior, is the common thread linking all three theories. Needs have been equated with the concept of "drive," a purely behavioral, non-cognitive notion in the experimental psychology literature [e.g., Hull, 1943]; the organizational literature extends the need concept to cognitive elements such as self-actualization. The notion that individuals exhibit needs for growth and development traditionally has enjoyed considerable acceptance by practitioners, presumably owing to the intuitive appeal and face validity of the arguments.

The assumption that individuals are composed of complex internal mechanisms that determine their behavior is perpetuated in the expectancy/valence theory of motivation [Vroom, 1964]. This theory and subsequent elaborations [e.g., Porter & Lawler, 1968] assume that individuals formulate subjective probability estimates of the extent to which a given level of effort leads to work performance (expectancies), and the extent to which a given performance level leads to certain valued outcomes (instrumentalities). Presumably, the greater the certainty in these two links, the stronger the

predictability of work motivation or effort expected.

The work-design literature [e.g., Hackman & Oldham, 1980] perhaps represents a blend of the need-satisfaction and expectancy/ valence theories of motivation. The approach is explicit in specifying that work itself should be designed to maximize the rewarding properties and facilitate the psychological growth of the individual.

The other work-motivation theory reflecting a cognitive orientation is the goal-setting formulation [Locke, 1968]. Sharing the idea, with expectancy/valance theory, that behavior is intentional or purposive [Tolman, 1932], this theory makes the assumption that motivation and performance are functions of goal accomplishment. While sharing certain ideas, goal setting differs from expectancy/ valence theory in contextual prediction. That is, motivation is believed to be highest, in the expectancy/valence framework, when effort-to-performance and performance-to-outcome links are well defined and certain, leading to more informed subjective probability estimates structuring behavior. Alternatively, in the goal-setting framework, motivation is believed to be highest when the goals set are difficult. The inconsistency between prediction using expectance/valance and goal-setting theories is evident. Goals perceived as difficult would be translated into low effort-to-performance probabilities, which would result in lower motivation according to expectancy/valence theory.

The alternative perspective concerning motivation in work organizations is behavioristic in nature, and is exemplified by OB Mod. OB Mod is based on the assumption that individual behavior is a function of its consequences [e.g., Luthans & Kreitner, 1975]. By definition, the antecedents of behavior are found in the environment, not embodied in an internal state, such as personality or mind. This view differs from the cognitive one of individuals actively seeking their destiny through independent, self-determined action, and instead represents a view of behavior as a function of past and present reinforcement contingencies. This view, of course, has its roots in principles of operant conditioning, which has existed in the experimental literature for quite some time [Skinner, 1953]. Much of the present antagonism toward the application of operant conditioning principles to explaining behavior in organizations derives from reactions against the issues of determinism and control, perhaps first exemplified in a popular novel on behavioral control in society [Skinner, 1948]. This also has resulted in charges of manipulative control and Machiavellianism, which have contributed to the less-than-favorable image of OB Mod, since many are reluctant to accept the belief that behavior is determined totally by the environment.

To date, no truly eclectic approach has emerged to functionally integrate aspects of OB Mod with the cognitive orientation of widely espoused management philosophies. Thus the practitioner has been dependent on intutitive guidance to make implementation choices.

Nord [1969] took the first step toward merging these different orientations by examining the frameworks of behaviorism and Theory X and Y assumptions detailed by McGregor [1960]. He believed that "the importance of environmental factors in determining behavior is the crucial and dominant similarity between Skinner and McGregor" [p. 377]. In this integrative attempt, Nord demonstrated, theoretically, not only the strong congruence between these supposedly competing approaches, but also the manner in which concepts of reinforcement contingency contribute to organizational effectiveness, even under the guise of a more cognitive framework. Additionally, he noted that factors of the job can be analyzed as reinforcers, whether they are considered to be intrinsic or extrinsic.

Luthans and Kreitner [1975] took the next step by demonstrating how an understanding of OB Mod techniques can facilitate the design of job enrichment, management-by-objectives programs, and organizational development interventions. These authors argue that job enrichment could profit by contingently enriching the worker's task, based on performance. Therefore, the more enriching job components would serve as naturally occurring rewards for good performance. This would be expected to eliminate the problems of reinforcing poor performance (i.e., enriching the job of the below-standards worker) or changing the job against the worker's will. Management-by-objectives is also a popular management technique that should profit from OB Mod principles. Luthans and Kreitner propose that many management-by-objectives programs are failing because employees are not adequately reinforced for achieving performance objectives. Finally, they believe that OB Mod can legitimately play a role in organizational development interventions, because theoretically these programs are intended to facilitate or stimulate reward processes in organizations. The techniques employed typically focus on interpersonal relationships while disregarding environmental factors. Although their suggestions are appealing, there has been a virtual absence of empirical investigations directed toward testing these ideas.

Proceeding further in reducing the distance between these divergent orientations necessitates identifying specific opportunities where framework boundaries have created an absence of concrete data. Overlapping studies must be used to assess the relative merits of the different management approaches. The attempts to integrate and differentiate these motivational schemes to date have focused on paradigm or rightful domain implications [Grey, 1979; Locke, 1979; Parmerlee & Schwenk, 1979]. This confrontation over primarily theoretical issues is not serving the development of a motivational system that will contribute to individual and organizational effectiveness. We hope to cast this conflict in a somewhat different light, proposing new areas of investigation that will benefit the practitioner.

We will borrow from the eclectic approach recommended by Peters [1960], who argued that no single theory of motivation could explain all behavior. In essence, he proposed combining portions of a number of contributing approaches to account for all relevant factors within a construct as complex as human motivation. This advice seems particularly appropriate in that management must be concerned with both worker performance and satisfaction, neither of which has been reduced to a simple cause/effect relationship. According to some theory and research, performance and satisfaction are dependent on different variables [e.g., Lawler, 1973]. Even within the performance area, both cognitive and behavioral aspects appear relevant. Campbell and Stanley [1966] claimed that when competent researchers are strongly split over an issue, both sides are likely to be examining a different but valid portion of the complete answer.

Perhaps one of the most notable and effective attempts at integrating the cognitive and behavioral perspectives with respect to motivation is social learning theory [Bandura, 1977]. Social learning theory purportedly overemphasizes neither internal forces nor environmental factors in explaining behavior. Rather, individual functioning is seen as a continuous interaction among cognitive, behavioral, and environmental factors. Social learning theory has received attention primarily in experimental and clinical settings, but recently a concerted attempt has been made to apply it directly to explaining behavior in organizations [Davis & Luthans, 1980]. This effort focuses attention on observable behavior in "organization member-behavior-environment interaction" [p. 287].

Additionally, principles of social learning theory have been incorporated in training and development techniques. Goldstein and Sorcher [1974] incorporated the principles of social learning in their behavior modeling program for supervisors, intended to instill functional work-related behaviors. Extending this idea, it has been demonstrated that social learning theory can explain the development of supervisory styles [Weiss, 1977] and the adoption of work values in organizations [Weiss, 1978]. Most recently, Latham and Saari [1979] applied principles of the theory in another training program for supervisors through behavior modeling.

An extensive review of OB Mod applications in business organizations revealed that research of this sort has assumed a narrow and perhaps defensive position, owing perhaps to its somewhat controversial nature. Integration of this area with others must be preceded by systematic research that begins to address some of the questions regarding the behavioral perspective. A principle question of our paper is whether the results of field studies using OB Mod methods in work organizations are providing the necessary data for effective application and integration. We have identified a number of artificial boundaries being perpetuated in research designs that are counter-productive to the potential contributions of OB Mod.

Field studies in business organizations have taken a very myopic view of the factors considered as dependent variables. Most of the current OB Mod research is conducted and interpreted as if it were an isolated discipline [Petrock & Gamboa, 1976]. Advocates of OB Mod seek to demonstrate that the method works as predicted. Luthans and Kreitner [1975] argue that changing research environments does not alter rules for behavior control. Support for the operant approach in organizational settings has been provided by several studies [At Emery Air Freight, 1973; McCarthy, 1978; Nord, 1970; Pedalino & Gamboa, 1974; Runnion, Johnson, & McWhorten, 1978; Runnion, Watson, & McWhorten, 1978]. However, despite the semblance of success, the research being conducted is not adequately addressing fundamental issues that will continue to plague OB Mod regardless of the level of sophistication in either statistical analysis or the environmental control of variables. Previous analyses of field studies by Kazdin [1973] and Andrasik [1979] are primarily concerned with whether behavior change can be attributed to the intervention as it is designed and reported. Although some commentary is valuable, this alone will not earn OB Mod a place of respect. A broadening of the research scope, as discussed later, must address the multifaceted criticisms raised by cognitively oriented behavioral scientists such as Fry [1974], Argyris [1971], and Hackman [1979]. Before detailing the areas for future investigation, we will discuss the potential benefits and costs of utilizing OB Mod.

POTENTIAL BENEFITS AND COSTS OF OB MOD

OB Mod is behavior- or performance-oriented. Unlike the case with need- and expectancy-based theories, managers focus on performance-related behaviors of workers, not on underlying psychological states as a means of achieving performance goals. Thus, the manager is not forced into the position of playing the role of clinician. Management based on worker needs or expectancies

necessitates a considerable degree of subjective evaluation and, perhaps, periodic professional assessment. With OB Mod, however, it is incumbent upon management to determine and communicate specific performance objectives and definitive plans of action. The reduction in management's flexibility and room for arbitrary action could be cause for resisting the use of such a system. Despite this requirement, Cummings and Molloy in their discussion of OB Mod conclude that "one of its major contributions . . . is to show how qualitative aspects of performance can be quantified" [1977, p. 185].

Luthans and Kreitner [1975] emphasize that managers using OB Mod do not directly manage the individual. Instead, an environment is created that reinforces desired behavior. The implication is that the operant approach turns control of supervision over to workers, since supervisory behavior is directly contingent on subordinate actions. In the typical OB Mod intervention utilizing positive verbal reinforcement, the manager is trained to wait for the appropriate response from the worker. So while the worker's reinforcement is contingent on his own behavior, the manager's behavior becomes directly dependent on it. Interestingly, this appears to be a refinement of what naturally occurs between subordinates and their superiors. There is some empirical support in the leadership literature for the claim that subordinate performance causes leader behavior [e.g., Barrows, 1976; Lowin & Craig, 1968]. An additional perspective on this issue is presented by Luthans and Davis [1979]. They discuss how the individual can use structuring of the environment and planning of consequences to enhance behavioral self-control.

In conjunction with a performance orientation, OB Mod strongly de-emphasizes the use of punishment in organizational settings. Laboratory research results support the belief that desirable behavior should be reinforced and that undesirable behavior should be allowed to extinguish through the withholding of reinforcement. Lack of punishment in work settings can be important for employee relations and the general working climate. One reason is that the worker may associate the punishment with the supervision instead of the punished act. An additional cost of punishment is increased employee stress, which can result in retaliation or withdrawal from work [Gupta & Beehr, 1979]. It may be worthwhile to consider the predominance of punitive control in light of the current pervasiveness of worker alienation [Walton, 1980].

Reese [1966] believes that punishment may be the dominant method of behavior control because of its innate capacity to immediately halt undesired behavior. Presumably, an immediate halt would convey to management a feeling of greater accomplishment and control. However, punishment does not ensure or even direct proper performance, as OB Mod purports to do. The benefit of using punishment is that its effects require less diligence and patience than operant techniques. So while positive reinforcement can be viewed as beneficial to human relations and employee training, it does appear to necessitate additional time and effort that must be absorbed by management during the initial conditioning phases.

It should be noted that management is expected to fully analyze the tasks assigned to its workers. The implementation of an OB Mod program is typically preceded by a "performance audit." Management cannot justifiably base recommendations for performance improvement intervention solely on work-group attitude. In our own experience in supervisor training, we have observed that different behavioral components become aggregated along with the inferences concerning individual attitudes. The charge against the worker then is escalated from mere poor performance to an assumed personality flaw as well. Typically there is little attempt to separate the components of performance, to zero-in on those aspects in need of improvement. The supervisor's reaction to the worker will then be based on the image held of that individual as a poor worker, troublemaker, and so forth, virtually ignoring observable behaviors in many cases. In contrast, the performance audit provides a systematic framework within which to make such behavioral determinations. It sets a base line that can be compared to the objective the organization has established. In some cases, the audit identifies unforseen discrepancies [At Emery Air Freight, 1973].

OB Mod's measurement bias reflects its behaviorist heritage. It is a scientifically based theory that allows managers and supervisors to accurately assess program progress. Changes in quantifiable variables are recorded and used instead of attitudinal measures. The inclusion of psychological states currently confounds the motivation issue for practitioners. Therefore, the ability of management to generate and analyze its own data, after appropriate training, adjusts the intervention to the practioner's level of sophistication. As Nord states, "the Skinnerian approach leads to rational planning in order to control outcomes previously viewed as spontaneous consequences. This approach could expand the area of planning and rational action in administration" [1969, p. 401].

Most applications of behavior modification in work organizations include positive verbal feedback or objective feedback as a reinforcer to effect performance changes. The belief that feedback is a major factor in the OB Mod intervention is not at all unusual. Feedback is a core dimension of contemporary measures of job characteristics [Hackman & Oldham, 1975; Sims, Szilagyi, & Keller, 1976] and is consistent with performance appraisal systems objectives to let workers know where they stand [Haynes, 1980], and with the philosophy implicit in the quality of working life movements. OB Mod takes a substantially different approach by formalizing both the types and the timing of reinforcement, regardless of whether the focus is on feedback, pay, or other valued rewards. Although the question of whether rewards must be immediately contingent on behavior/performance will likely remain a debatable issue for some time, OB Mod utilizes a schedule of reinforcement stressing timing as an issue in the development of a supportive environment that will elicit and reinforce desired behavior. Such a prescriptive strategy may offend practitioners and theorists who emphasize individual needs and differences, but it does ensure that the worker will be provided with feedback concerning correct behavior. This is essential for practical application where the prescription "more feedback" is found lacking in specificity.

OB Mod interventions often begin with a great deal of verbal reinforcement and then gradually lessen the frequency of this external feedback. The expectation is that the direct performance feedback from the task will naturally take over the reinforcer role. So, over the course of an OB Mod program, there is a shift in emphasis from supervision to aspects of the job itself. For individuals beginning a new job, the OB Mod prescription is consistent with results presented by Katz [1978]. He found that during the initial stages of an individual's job, task feedback is strongly desired. Following the usual OB Mod schedule of reinforcement, early frequent feedback tapers off to later permit greater autonomy.

In summary, OB Mod provides a definitive framework from which to implement and test an intervention by taking into account the types and timing of reinforcement that supports or punishes job behaviors. It is ob-

vious that we have a positive view of OB Mod; we believe that this approach has an orientation and associated techniques that are useful and complementary to popular motivation schemes. The next step is to begin collecting organizational data that will test the fit between OB Mod and other orientations. This necessitates expanding the parameters considered appropriate by behaviorist researchers. The following topics represent a partial list of issues OB Mod researchers need to consider more directly.

THE ROLE OF PARTICIPATION

Participation in decision making has become a popular issue during this decade, owing largely to its convergence with individual growth, job involvement, and job enrichment. OB Mod, on the other hand, has been viewed typically as a top-down approach that is applied to the employee with virtually no concern for individual development [Hackman, 1979]. In theory, these orientations are in clear opposition. The role of participation in operant conditioning can be viewed in a number of ways. Since people presumably react to their environment based on reinforcement history, feelings of involvement and individual growth could be considered irrelevant. Participation might be perceived as a confounding factor in the intervention if it causes changes in the experimental design or in the reinforcers. Conversely, getting the participants to assist in developing the OB Mod program, such as determining the proper reinforcers, designating the "best" behaviors to accomplish the stated objectives, and discovering the reinforcers utilized by the informal organization could eliminate some of the problems. The feeling of involvement itself may be an effective reinforcer.

Komaki, Waddell, and Pearce [1977] were forced to use a participative approach in order to secure the cooperation of the participants in conducting their experiment. Although this was mentioned, it was not cited as a relevant factor in interpreting the reported success of the experiment. Nord [1970] suggests using worker ideas about the type of program and rewards as valuable input with which to modify and redefine the OB Mod project. In this way, the positive verbal reinforcement is seen as a way to enhance communication between managers and workers.

In each of these cases, as in most OB Mod interventions, there is a conspicuous attempt to account for those factors that cannot be controlled directly. It is interesting that researchers concerned with the generalizability of their experimental designs feel justified in ignoring the facilitative function of a cognitive factor as potentially persuasive as participation. Unfortunately, no research reviewed to date has compared the efficacy of OB Mod interventions for groups with and without participant involvement. A comparative research design would address the question of the extent to which these theoretically divergent orientations are, in fact, complementary.

OB MOD AND GOAL SETTING

We believe that OB Mod and goal setting are complementary techniques originating from divergent perspectives. Both orientations focus on goal attainment, but traditionally have selected different factors for experimentation. For this reason, the distinction between OB Mod and goal setting can be blurred in an applied setting. As previously noted, the objective of most OB Mod interventions is to have the standards and feedback from the task eventually take over the reinforcement role [At Emery Air Freight, 1973]. The individual presumably is performing at a higher level, owing to greater goal difficulty [Locke, 1968]. Many of the goal-setting investigations have been concerned with the effect of incentives on performance and the extent to which they affect performance through goal level [Locke, 1968; Pritchard & Curtis, 1973; Terborg, 1976]. The overlap of these two orientations is apparent, but it is virtually always ignored. None of the organization-based OB Mod studies we reviewed discussed differential target levels of performance. The relevant factors for behaviorists doing field research seem to be the following: to determine the correct or desirable behavior, to select the appropriate reinforcement(s) and the schedule of application, and to test the level of goal attainment within an appropriate experimental design. Our argument is that OB Mod and goal setting focus on different aspects of the same issue. The information concerning differential goal setting should be tested in conjunction with OB Mod.

We find it interesting that the goal-setting literature [e.g., Latham & Yukl, 1975, 1976] has focused on the relationship between assigned goals and those set participatively. Operant conditioning techniques traditionally have relied on unilaterally set target behaviors and standards of performance. This adds further support to the belief that OB Mod ignores individual perceptions and expectations. The gain or loss caused by assigning objectives also has not been explored adequately to date.

WORKER AND MANAGER RESPONSES TO BEHAVIOR MODIFICATION

OB Mod has been criticized severely for being dehumanizing and ignoring individual cognitive processes [e.g., Fry, 1974]. Even though findings from current research do not support the belief that satisfaction is consistently related to productivity [Locke, 1976], worker responses to their jobs can have an impact on labor relations, absenteeism, tardiness, and turnover—areas of particular concern to management. Typically, OB Mod field experiments measure the effects of an intervention on, for example, absenteeism, with the issue of morale addressed only briefly in the conclusion. Cummings and Molloy [1977] cite the lack of attitudinal references in their review of OB Mod research. Only Adams [1975] has examined the relationship between positive reinforcement and attitudes about product quality. His results, however, were inconclusive.

A related issue has to do with management's reaction to workers when positive verbal reinforcement is used as part of an OB Mod program. Adams noted that one supervisor adopted a less autocratic style of management as a result of the forced interaction with subordinates. Nord [1970] suggested using the increased level of supervisory response as a method for involving the individual in the job. In addition, the negative sanctions used by management (i.e., punishment) are greatly reduced, because managers are forced to relate to their subordinates on a positive basis. Presumably, this experience should precipitate some attitudinal change in managers, but such potential benefits have not been evaluated to date. So, although the application of operant conditioning techniques is less Machiavellian than the underlying theory might suggest, research has not shown any sustained interest in dispelling this negative image. Regardless of the behaviorist bias against attitudinal measures, the worker's response to any intervention is an important factor for managers. Therefore, assessing these attitudes should be equally relevant to the research and should be incorporated in future OB Mod designs.

OB MOD AND WORK DESIGN

When viewing work design within a systems framework, one must account for the worker, the work itself, and the work context (pay, co-workers, supervision, etc.). Corresponding to the above factors and their interaction, a number of salient issues arise for practitioners interested in a pragmatic approach to work design. These issues can be classified under three headings: individual differences, locus of control, and trade-offs between different design alternatives.

Traditional work design theorists deal with both individual differences and the work context by measuring growth-need strength (GNS) and satisfaction with specific contextual variables (see Hackman & Oldham [1980] for a review). Essentially, if the focal individual has a sufficient level of GNS and demonstrates satisfaction with the job context, then the work design process is intended to create an enriching task [Oldham, Hackman, & Pearce, 1976]. This entails designing the task to provide such things as increased skill variety, autonomy, and feedback. The implication is that the locus of control should reside with the individual worker. Factors typically of concern in traditional work design research are those intrinsic to the task. These factors occur through the process of performing the task, and are therefore mediated by the worker and not by other organizational agents or mechanisms external to the individual. This orientation suggests that work design fits neatly into a managerial framework where the worker is granted greater latitude within which to function. Deci's [1975] research on internal motivation indicates that for tasks which are intrinsically enriched, extrinsic variables, which supposedly alter the locus of control from internal to external, cause a decrease in internal motivation. As a result, at the managerial end of the job spectrum, where tasks exhibit more design flexibility, the traditional job design method seems appropriate and possible to implement.

OB Mod again poses a divergent orientation. Individual differences are literally ig-

nored and the notion of determining individual satisfaction with compensation and work context, as advocated by Oldham, Hackman, and Pearce [1976] and equity theory research [Adams, 1965], does not fit its behaviorist framework. The reinforcers, in an OB Mod intervention, generally are mediated externally—despite Nord's [1969] argument that, owing to the contingent nature of the reinforcement, the individual retains ultimate control. For tasks that cannot be sufficiently enriched, OB Mod offers an attractive alternative. This may be one reason why this motivational technique has been predominantly applied to blue-collar positions. Presumably it is better to provide external feedback when the task itself does not than to simply ignore the deficiency.

From the above approaches to work design, it is easy to conceptualize a number of potential alternatives available to the organization designer when tasks fall somewhere between the extremes of "impossible" and "easily enriched." For example, an organization could expend its resources to redesign a task, building in greater skill variety, or use the same resources to provide the job holder with a greater variety of reinforcers external to the task. Cummings and Molloy [1977] identify such alternatives as the choice within the organization. In situations where different action levels represent realistic alternatives, the incongruity between these orientations becomes extremely confusing. Despite Nord's [1969] belief that reinforcers are the common denominators, there are different costs and benefits to these available choices. Perceptual differences may not directly affect motivation or performance, but these factors could be important to other organizational elements, such as the climate and the attractiveness of the organization.

An additional consideration is that jobs are sometimes designed or redesigned to correct for anticipated problems in worker motivation or satisfaction. Management may desire to act before predicted behavioral changes take place. Therefore, the responses workers have to different job components are sometimes used as behavioral predictors. For example, if the research suggesting that absenteeism is not an effective indicator of future turnover is correct, there may be no behavioral antecedents to identify a worker's propensity to leave the organization. In other words, if "behavioral units" of job tenure cannot be identified, then it may not be possible to determine the efficacy of current reinforcement until it fails to produce the desired results. In this case, valued employees could be lost before the necessity for a design change would be realized. So despite the inexact and unstable nature of internal states [Salancik & Pfeffer, 1977], assessing worker attitudes may, in some instances, be the only available indicator of future difficulties.

The focal problem here is a paucity of comparative studies between behaviorist and nonbehaviorist methods. Apparently, only Cummings and Molloy [1977] have reviewed and compared different orientations within the framework of the quality of working life and productivity to determine the different action levers relied on and the types of outcomes achieved in research interventions. More detailed studies are necessary to determine the immediate outcomes and the more indirect implications of selecting different approaches. To date, there are no available data on whether the choice of an intervention should be influenced by the individual(s) being targeted, the type of task, or the climate of the organization. Work design theorists sensitive to the locus-of-control issue presumably would argue that substituting OB Mod techniques for intrinsic components will never be a satisfying tradeoff for the worker. Nord [1969], Luthans and Kreitner [1975], and others would likely counter with the argument that if reinforcement is designed properly, there should be no qualitative differences. At this point consultants and practitioners must rely on their own intuition in the absence of concrete evidence.

COMPLEXITY AND CREATIVITY

As previously noted, most of the jobs used to generate test data for OB Mod could be classified as blue-collar positions. The environment is usually stable and the worker's function can be dissected into reinforceable behavioral events. Two related issues emerge from these factors, concerning complexity and creativity. One question is: How is OB Mod adapted to *complex managerial positions* that do not have clearly defined tasks? In spite of the case cited by Luthans and Kreitner [1975] suggesting that complex behaviors, such as initiative, can be effectively reinforced, OB Mod may, in fact, be more applicable to lower-level organizational positions. From anecdotal accounts such as those presented by Kerr [1975], it is evident that we must not merely reinforce the components of the job that are quantifiable. If the entire job is not reinforced, employee responses will center on activities that consistently gain positive feedback. The remaining functions of the job will be allowed to extinguish along with the inappropriate behaviors.

To our knowledge, no comparative studies exist demonstrating the efficiency of OB Mod in relation to other motivational techniques. Andrasik confirms this conclusion in stating that "none of the [interventions reviewed] consisted of comparisons with alternative, non-behavioral approaches" [1979, p. 99]. In the absence of quantifiable data, how is the manager in charge of the OB Mod intervention to deal with qualitative information? Needless to say, behavioral researchers

must begin to report and analyze interventions involving all levels of the organizational hierarchy.

The more important question, however, deals with *creativity*. If the individual's job is broken down into behavioral units, will this not drastically reduce worker flexibility in making behavioral (qualitative) adjustments? The incentive to search for more efficient work patterns would be greatly decreased unless reinforcement for creativity were built into the program. Unfortunately, this idea was not tested in any of the experiments reviewed. This potential problem coincides with the discussion concerning participation. Involving employees in project design and maintenance may circumvent the problems of selecting the most effective behavior, determining appropriate reinforcement for creative activities, or encouraging feedback with which to change ineffective or inappropriate elements of the OB Mod program. However, with no evidence available at present, such a hypothesis awaits empirical examination.

CONCLUSION

OB Mod is a behavior- or performance-oriented management technique. Quantitative output data are used to design a reinforcing environment for appropriate work behavior. This offers management a straightforward method for analyzing the effect of supervision and other reinforcers, such as pay, on worker conduct. As a perspective divergent from more intuitively appealing and generally accepted cognitive motivation theories, OB Mod has been cast as a separate discipline and forced to justify its existence and defend its viability. Possibly because of this ostracism, OB Mod proponents have narrowed their research focus to charting behavioral changes while ignoring implications of their interventions, such as the participants' attitudinal responses resulting from the intervention.

We have sought to illuminate the differences between the two orientations on the issue of employee motivation. Our emphasis has been on suggesting further research that may necessitate a reconceptualization of the purpose of OB Mod assessments in business organizations. Instead of escalating this conflict over paradigm definition and justification as others have done [e.g., Parmerlee & Schwenk, 1979], we have tried to take a pragmatic view of the linkages between these now competing perspectives.

We hope this paper will encourage the functional incorporation of effective motivational techniques, whether currently labeled cognitive or behaviorist. The current state of the art is generating considerable confusion for those interested in applying social science research findings to real problems of creating work environments that are motivating and satisfying.

PART THREE

Organizational Productivity

7

Productivity and Group Dynamics

Many of the best companies really do view themselves as an extended family.
THOMAS J. PETERS AND ROBERT H. WATERMAN, JR.[1]

PURPOSES OF GROUPS

Motivation, as discussed in the last chapter, has to do with individuals. Yet individuals work in groups. A familiar saying tells us, "The whole is more than the sum of its parts." The same point applies to work groups— they are made up of individuals, but they are more than just a collection of individuals. To understand what makes a work group productive, we need to examine the inner workings of group dynamics.

Definitions

A group exists when two or more people join together for a purpose. The purpose may be to do a task, to take part in an activity, to be with other people, or to reach a common goal.[2]

Subgroups

Large groups have smaller subgroups. A company's subgroups may be its departments, such as accounting or advertising. Subgroups also consist of professions or trades within the firm, such as the salespeople, the lawyers or the ironworkers. Subgroups may contain smaller groups formed on the basis of similar jobs or friendships. Sometimes, subgroups span organization boundaries and divide members' loyalties. Accountants, for example, deal with many departments and may feel conflict between the goals of the accounting department, the department they are helping and the larger organization.

Time

Some groups are more permanent than others. "Permanent" is a relative term. It means individual members may change, but the group keeps its identity. A firm and its departments are examples of permanent groups. At the opposite extreme are groups that exist only as long as it takes to do a specific task. Task forces and committees generally are temporary groups.

Formal and informal

Some groups, such as companies and clubs, are formal. They have written goals and policies, specific chains of command and official rules that potential members must observe. Informal groups have "unwritten" rules. These rules are just as real as those of formal groups, but they are not as clear-cut. In some organizations, the informal system supports the formal one; in other organizations, it contradicts the formal one. Only a supportive informal system can help increase an organization's productivity.

CHARACTERISTICS OF GROUPS

People belong to groups for many reasons. The value of belonging to a group, of remaining in it, and of participating in its activities is closely related to the benefits members feel they receive from the group.[3] People are attracted to groups that offer prestige,[4] cooperation,[5] friendly interaction[6] and success.[7] People also like groups that are relatively small.[8] Fear sometimes draws people to groups.[9] In return for the benefits, members are expected to conform to group norms and values.

Norms

Norms are group rules about how members should act.[10] They are unwritten and informal. Group members take norms so much for granted, they often think they are acting naturally and not following any "rules."

The strange or "outsider" feeling when one joins a group often comes from lack of knowledge about the group's norms. It takes time to learn the group's style of dress, gestures, expressions, mannerisms, and other expectations of its members. Even within the larger group called the "organization," employees in one department may look, talk and act very differently from those in another department. Finance specialists, for example, often differ from a firm's sales people.

Values

Groups also have their own values, beliefs and assumptions. They are the basis of "the way we do things around here."

Some firms value education. These firms hire people who have degrees, send employees to seminars and pay employees' college tuition. The belief here may be that educated employees give more to the company. The firm assumes it will be paid back, in the long run, for investing in its employees.

SOCIALIZATION PROCESSES

How do new people become like the rest of the group? To some extent, they may look, act or think like group members before they join. But groups also pressure members to conform to group norms. The pressure works because of internal needs and external forces.

Internal Needs

We may not be aware of internal needs that make us seek out groups, but research shows we need to resolve ambiguity and gauge social expectations. Groups help meet these internal needs.

Many problems have more than one possible answer, and sometimes issues are unclear. In these cases, people tend to follow the group's opinion, even if it conflicts with their own.[11] Our need to resolve ambiguity means we often let groups determine much of what we perceive, a phenomenon sometimes called "groupthink." We also use groups as a standard by which we judge our abilities and opinions.[12] The group's norms create a social reality for individuals.

External Forces

Groups want members to conform, to maintain the group and to achieve its goals. Group maintenance means that the group stays together. Groups will develop whatever norms appear to maintain the group. These may include relatively harmless acts such as waiting until all members arrive before starting, or pressuring members to attend meetings. They may also include such behaviors as ignoring tensions or problems. While this norm may please members in the short run, it can lead to bigger problems later on.

To achieve group goals, members may have to conform to specific behaviors or procedures. Standard forms for taking orders and standard procedures for building a house are good examples.

Forms of Socialization

Socialization is the process by which a person internalizes a group's norms. Conformity occurs when a member acts like others in the group—

looking and talking like them, for example. While the pressure to conform is there, it is generally indirect. The decision comes from inside the person. Pressure to conform tends to increase as groups get larger,[13] as the member likes the group more,[14] and as conforming behavior is encouraged.[15] Sometimes, group pressures to conform may conflict with organization goals. An example of this is rate-busting, where a group of employees pressures members to produce at a slower rate, so as not to make the others look slow. The group may have goals—such as recognition, higher pay, pleasant atmosphere, no conflict, job security, or an easy pace—that conflict with the organization's goal of greater output at lower cost.

Pressures to comply are more direct than pressures to conform. In compliance, someone asks you to do something. Some people find it hard to refuse, and others find it easy. To avoid resistance, a group may do favors for a member, so that the individual is left owing the group a favor.[16] Cults often use a "foot-in-the-door" method, starting with small requests and asking for more as the person agrees,[17] while holding out the possibility of rejection should the group "requests" be denied.

In obedience, group pressures are even stronger. The group has some kind of power over a person. Formal organizational sanctions include discipline, criticism and demotions. Informal sanctions may include ostracism or, in some cases, violence. Research shows that some people obey authority figures against their own moral judgment,[18] but that if even a few people resist, others will follow.[19]

People are most likely to accept a group's norms under certain conditions. The first condition is that they want to remain members of the group. If so, they will behave so as to fit in.[20] Another condition that promotes compliance is identification with the group. When members identify with the group, they want their actions to reflect well on the group. A third condition is fear of punishment for not going along with the group. A fourth condition is cohesiveness, or how attractive the group is to its members. Highly cohesive groups often have greater conformity.[21]

GROUPS AT WORK

We deal with groups all the time at work, although it is sometimes easy to overlook this fact. At work, we tend to focus on the job to be done or the problem to be solved, not on the group processes that take place. Nevertheless, all work-related activity in organizations is influenced by formal and informal groups.

Formal and Informal Groups

The formal groups at work include command groups (people with a common boss) and task groups (people with a common goal or task). Managers and employees at each level also make up formal groups. Committees, too, are formal groups; they exist until they reach their goals.

The purpose of formal groups is to support the chain of command in reaching company goals. For example, the manager of one department cannot, formally, assign work to an employee from another department. According to the authorized chain of command, employees get work only from their own managers. Assignments from other managers would confuse everyone. But informal groups thrive within the formal organization structure. They are based on friendships, common interests and other personal issues. Informal groups may cut across formal lines to include people from diverse areas and levels of the organization.

ROLES WITHIN GROUPS

Formal and informal groups require people to play different roles. Formal roles are official, such as that of manager. Informal roles are unofficial and more fluid. In addition, the same person may play different roles at different times.

Roles fall into three categories: group task roles, group building and maintaining roles, and individual roles. The lists below, all from the same source, identify behaviors that fit each role.[22]

Task Roles

Task roles help the group to identify and solve problems related to its goals. Some of the more common group task roles are:

Initiator-contributor: brings new ideas to the group.

Information-seeker: wants issues clarified.

Opinion-seeker: wants to know the values behind people's ideas.

Information-giver: offers facts or opinions based on experience.

Opinion-giver: states beliefs or opinions based on values.

Elaborator: suggests possible outcomes of each alternative.

Coordinator: ties together different ideas and various efforts within the group.

Orienter: compares ongoing work and outcomes to group's original goals; helps set direction of group.

Evaluator-critic: compares work so far with a group value, such as "practicality" or "logic."

Energizer: helps keep group active.

Procedural technician: takes care of the group's practical needs, such as meeting rooms and equipment.

Recorder: keeps a written record of suggestions, decisions and other group outcomes.

Building and Maintenance Roles

Building and maintenance roles help the group to function and maintain itself. They include roles such as the following:

Encourager: praises and accepts members' contributions and expresses warmth toward members.

Harmonizer: tries to ease tension among members and to lessen differences within the group.

Compromiser: gives up part of his or her stance when there is conflict.

Gate-keeper and expediter: tries to keep communication open by getting input from everyone.

Standard-setter: suggests values toward which the group should aim.

Group-observer: keeps track of group processes and of the group's evaluation of itself.

Follower: passively goes along with group decisions.

Individual Roles

Individual roles involve needs which do not help the group to maintain itself or to reach its goals. These behaviors are more individual-centered than group-centered:

Aggressor: acts destructively toward other members' ideas and goals.

Blocker: stubbornly and unreasonably disagrees with suggestions and brings up issues already rejected by the group.

Recognition-seeker: inappropriately tries to draw attention to himself or herself.

Self-confessor: uses the group as an audience for feelings and insights not related to group issues.

Dominator: manipulates the group through excess authority.

Help-seeker: tries to get sympathy from other members.

Special-interest pleader: hides biases by claiming to speak for the sake of certain groups.

GROUP PRODUCTIVITY

Content and Process

Groups function in two ways—content and process. Content refers to what the group does: its goals and outcomes. Process refers to how the group does these things: how the members set goals, divide the work and relate to each other. Productive groups pay attention to both the content and process of their work.

Cohesion

As mentioned above, "cohesion" means the degree of attraction members feel toward the group. Cohesiveness can make a group more productive.[23] Members who feel accepted and supported are more likely to cooperate. But cohesiveness can also hurt group productivity. Members may want agreement more than accuracy, and thereby ruin the quality of their decisions.[24] In this case, members' liking for each other becomes a trap.

A productive group wants cohesiveness without the trap. Gordon Lippitt[25] suggests five ways in which groups can keep this balance. First, they can make goals and purposes clear, instead of assuming members know what they are. Second, they can be aware of processes going on in the group. Third, they can bring out members' talents and skills, instead of limiting members to certain roles. Fourth, groups can set up ways to evaluate both their processes and content. Fifth, groups can create new tasks and subgroups as goals change.

Open Versus Closed Systems

Lippitt's suggestions for productive groups describe an open system. A system consists of multiple parts which contribute to the same goal. When a system is influenced by the environment, the system is open. A group is an example of an open system. Its members form parts of the system and the group is affected by its environment. As an open system, a group makes changes based on feedback from its members and its environment. The changes are the system's way of adapting to the members' and the environment's needs. When a company updates its logo or offers new products, it adapts to new needs.

A group which follows Lippitt's suggestions is more open than closed because its members give input and help decide how the group functions. Open systems are productive because they can change. They are more likely to identify the need for change and to make the necessary changes.

Problems and Opportunities

Groups help us do more than we can do alone. But groups also create problems. This book discusses ways for turning the problems into opportunities. Group members share responsibilities. This sometimes means that no one feels or acts committed to the work, because members also share the credit. Conflict also is common in groups. It can help lead to better decisions, if the group handles it well. Cooperation is necessary, too, as long as members value quality as much as agreement.

The specialist helps a group by giving expert ideas on a subject. But his or her vision may be too narrow. The generalist helps by giving a broader view of possibilities, although he or she may not know enough about a certain topic. Groups need input from both specialists and generalists.

SUMMARY

People work in groups. Group characteristics and processes affect productivity. Managers can improve employee productivity by helping work groups become more open, more aware of their processes and more willing to change. Group activities can fulfill the needs of both group members and the organizations to which they belong.

SELECTED READINGS OVERVIEW

The first article is "On Belonging to Tribes," by Andrew Oldenquist. We need to identify with something larger than ourselves and to feel that the groups to which we belong are *ours*. Certain activities can help win people's loyalty and commitment to society.

The second reading is "The Oldest (and Best) Way to Communicate with Employees," by Roger D'Aprix. The best way a manager can communicate is through face-to-face conversations with employees, D'Aprix argues, adding that too many managers overlook the value of these conversations.

Next Chapter

The next chapter discusses decision-making, an important process in organizations. Different methods of decision-making have different effects on groups and on productivity.

Review Questions

1. How can managers help employees feel that they "belong" to the group?
2. Why are managers often reluctant to have face-to-face conversations with their employees?
3. What can employees do to create a "family feeling" for each other?
4. How do people take on certain roles in groups?

ANDREW OLDENQUIST

On Belonging to Tribes

What makes some people sacrifice time and effort trying to save Laker Airlines, and what makes others stay drunk on auto-assembly lines and weld Coke bottles into the rocker panels? "Some people have a sense of group loyalty and others are alienated." But *why*?

Laker Airlines was just a company, after all. But perhaps people are such social animals that if our official communities and tribes don't generate in us a deep enough sense of belonging, we invent new ones. Saying we are social animals means we evolved to feel a need to belong to something larger than ourselves (because that is where our security lay), and that we are wretched and "incomplete" if we feel we belong to nothing.

Think of parents rallying to save a mediocre school from closing, neighbors uniting to save a park that they scarcely noticed before, English workers marching together to save Freddie Laker's airline. They are moved by loyalties they did not even know they had, before some ancient call for tribal defense stirred deep within them. If this is so and we are by nature tribal creatures who crave to share with others a common good, then we are group egoists, collectivists as well as individualists.

When I think of what makes me a dedicated member of a social group I realize that burdens and crises are more effective than benefits. Perceived threats to the common good stir us to work and sacrifice to a degree that appeals to self-interest never can. This behavior in turn reinforces our sense that the "tribe" we sacrifice for is *our* tribe.

WISDOM

Thus schools that make students shovel snow and bloodthirsty dictators who hold their citizens' loyalty by provoking international crises share a common wisdom. Cause a person to believe there is something larger than himself which is *his*, a social unit in terms of which he partly defines himself and moreover which *needs* him, and his group egoism will triumph over his personal egoism every time.

This line of reasoning tells us that to make students loyal to their school, require them to do chores, make minor repairs, participate

Oldenquist teaches philosophy at Ohio State University

in school ceremonies and "adopt" younger schoolmates. To make young people see their neighborhood as theirs, require them through the schools to visit shut-ins and help local needy and handicapped people. In this way age segregation is diminished and the elderly again become part of one's tribe. To attack and rob the elderly would be unthinkable for youth who live with or regularly help the aged. (In the movie "On Golden Pond," try to imagine the adolescent who spends a month with Henry Fonda and Katharine Hepburn saying nothing if his friends were to propose mugging an 80-year-old.)

We help produce national loyalty by expecting immigrants (and their children) to learn English. It is a primary badge of tribal membership. It would be unthinkable for an immigrant to France or Mexico not to be expected to learn French or Spanish.

A year of compulsory national service for *everyone* at 18, with very low pay, would, like a tribal rite of passage, tell young men and women that they belonged and were needed. It would, at the same time, virtually eliminate youth unemployment, provide an opportunity to teach skills to the unskilled, and each year cycle perhaps 20 percent of these 18-year-olds through military training. The defense budget would be reduced and the quality of those who choose the military would improve.

I don't think I am unusual in sensing that if, and only if, I perceive a thing as *mine*, will I be proud when it prospers, ashamed when it deteriorates and indignant when it is threatened. I don't feel this way about, say, an iceberg: I can be neither proud nor ashamed of an iceberg unless some clever fellow persuades me that it is my iceberg and hence a possible object of loyalty. If I am persuaded it is mine I will be unlikely to burgle or vandalize it.

American educators, juvenile-justice professionals, urban planners and social think-ers in general appear not to know what causes group loyalty; they also appear to fear it. They may think that because sense of community creates "insiders" and "outsiders" it inevitably leads to intolerance and war. These individualists do not seem to realize that the greater problem facing American society today is not the competition of group loyalties but their absence—alienation and not giving a damn.

RULES

What seems probable, and also hard for us Americans to grasp—especially during the '60s and '70s when individualism went mad—is that young people are social animals who need the socialization process itself to complete their natures. Just being given the security and benefits of society is not enough. For example, we know that criminals tend to come from families that both didn't accept them and didn't set firm rules and limits on behavior. These are two essential functions of a tribe, our families being mini-tribes; actually, they are a single function, since if a social group does not impose its rules on me and hold me responsible to it, I know it does not accept me as a member. It is also worth noting that here is something we know affects criminal behavior which has nothing to do with money.

Perhaps human beings are born genetically primed to be socialized, just as we are born genetically primed to learn a language. We are born ready and receptive to be limited and molded by rules, ethics, ritual, manners and tradition, and we go bad when our society—our tribe—neglects to limit and mold us in these ways. We go bad because this is a form of rejection. We are rejected as surely when we are not held accountable, not expected to dance to the drums or walk with the others on the red hot coals, as when we are denied food or shelter.

On this view we can understand "mindless" violence that serves no rational interest—frenzied vandalism, refusing to be taken alive for a traffic citation, pushing strangers in front of subways—as rage at tribal exclusion. It is the revenge of an innately tribal creature for not being initiated into society and treated as a member. To be a social animal means subjection to rules and being held personally answerable to them in ways in which a mad dog or a virus is not.

ROGER D'APRIX

The Oldest (and Best) Way to Communicate with Employees

In most organizations employee communication is a bastard function. Either no one is willing to acknowledge parentage and advocate the function's right to life or it is embroiled in a halfhearted (though in some cases heated) custody fight—with public relations claiming the tasks and personnel claiming the charter. Whichever way this peculiar conflict is resolved, custody battles do the function no good. Through the years it has suffered from lack of definition, inadequate budgets, limited professional staffing, and nearsighted vision.

But out of necessity the tide may finally turn. Corporate management is beginning to face the fact that you can't take your people for granted, that domestic indifference soon leads to domestic trouble. Thus the longtime orphan function may get a chance to establish its place in the family.

Why the sudden desire to do better? There are two major reasons: first, companies are dealing with a different kind of employee than heretofore—an employee who is looking for job satisfaction, who believes in personal options, and who wants meaningful work. But, you may protest, this has been the case for at least a decade. That's correct. Yet when this first reason is coupled with the success of the Japanese—who regard their workers highly and who are evidently having great success in human resource management (as well as in international markets)—companies face powerful indicators for self-examination.

However, even when it spends considerable time trying to improve the flow of communications, management largely ignores the importance of the human transmitter. The result is overemphasis on expensive, often ineffective, equipment and one-way communication to an audience that is demanding an opportunity for dialogue.

Mr. D'Aprix heads his own consulting firm, Organizational Communication Services, in Rochester, New York. Formerly he was manager of employee communication for Xerox Corporation. He is the author of Communicating for Productivity (Harper & Row, 1982), from which this article is adapted.

Reprinted from: Harvard Business Review (September-October 1982).

THE THREATENING CORRIDOR

Management consultant Scott Myers tells a story that shows how simple yet complex the communication function is. He was called in by a client to suggest ways management might communicate better with its work force. The company, always run along traditional lines, was trying to update itself and its communication practices. Before retaining Myers, management had decided to stress the traditional media methods—more articles in the company paper on corporate objectives and employee benefits, improvement of bulletin board displays, and a new monthly letter from the president.

In his initial talk with the president, Myers learned that the company was about to spend almost $300,000 to install what it saw as the most effective and up-to-date way to transmit messages to employees: closed-circuit television monitors scattered throughout the premises. Myers, dismayed by this news, asked for a short delay of the order until he could size up the situation and make some recommendations. The president reluctantly agreed.

In the course of examining the organization's communication efforts, Myers discovered an interesting practice. For some years employees had had a common coffee break during which all coffee machines were programmed to dispense the beverage free. At the same time, a cart carrying free pastries for everyone was wheeled into each area.

Watching the proceedings one morning, Myers recognized an opportunity. At his next meeting with the president, Myers suggested that he join his people out in the corridor at a coffee bar. The president smiled patiently and said that he couldn't do that. Asked why not, he replied that "it simply wasn't done." Top officers all had their coffee in their own offices dispensed from a mahogany cart. They never mingled with other employees during breaks. It would have

been bad form and might even constitute an intrusion.

Myers persisted, however, and reluctantly the president agreed to try the radical idea. His first attempt was an abysmal failure. He didn't even know how to work the coffee machine. A bystander, seeing him fumble with coins, walked over and told him the coffee was free. Red-faced, he took the cup in hand and looked for someone to begin a conversation with. No one approached him; employees were clustered in little groups quietly discussing their various concerns and glancing curiously at him. He drank his coffee and walked back into his office.

To Myers he pronounced the experiment a flop—they wouldn't talk to him. Myers told him that the problem was twofold. He made his appearance too formal; instead of wearing his suit coat, he should have gone out in his shirt sleeves. Moreover, the workers weren't used to seeing him in their area. To make this a fair test, Myers urged, he must go back tomorrow. At first the president was emphatic in his refusal to subject himself again to such humiliation. Eventually he agreed to try it one more time, but with his coat off.

This time he got his coffee without incident and screwed up the courage to break into the perimeter of a small gathering. After some conversation about the weather, he asked how things were going and heard some pleasantries from the group indicating that everything was fine.

The following morning, after doing some homework on a current concern of the work force (the opening of a plant in Europe), he raised the subject with a coffee-break group and explained the logic behind the decision. He was surprised to find himself in the middle of an animated discussion about the plant.

The next day and the next the president went out to the corridor for his morning coffee. In time he found himself holding forth on all kinds of company issues with employees, who now felt comfortable enough to air their concerns. The kaffee-klatsches were working so well that he asked his senior staff to begin mingling with their people at coffee time. He also canceled the TV equipment in favor of the simpler and more effective technique of firsthand, face-to-face communication.

THE IMPERSONAL MEDIA

What has employee communication comprised in most companies? Its history is practically one and the same with the history of the company house organ. And that's too bad: organization communication is much bigger than the mere process of producing publications—even good publications. But we have deluded ourselves for years into believing that the existence of such material is evidence that the organization is doing something about its communication problem.

In fact, publications can be counterproductive. In too many cases the world they portray is idealized and is a contradiction of the real world employees work and try to survive in. Employee distrust, breakdown of credibility, and a sense of disbelief bordering on schizophrenia are the result.

Appearances count for a good deal here. A profusion of positive pronouncements may give the impression of communication even when the words don't say much of anything. Messages from the president on mundane and insignificant subjects in the company paper, announcements giving full coverage to employee activities but excluding business issues, and bulletin boards overflowing with activity-oriented and "inspirational" posters are typical of what passes for employee communication in many companies.

To be sure, there are many enlightened organizations that go beyond the simplistic and give thoughtful attention to the mission of communication. Even so, they often fall short of a comprehensive view of the function. They tend to see it as having three objectives:

Explaining in factual terms the organization's progress, plus introducing new programs with a bit of salesmanship.

Answering employees' complaints and criticisms—usually by restating the rationale of the program in question.

Defending the status quo and the wisdom of top management.

Even sophisticated organizations take mostly an impersonal approach. Whether the approach is embodied in a house organ or in a medium as advanced as closed-circuit television, it is merely a symbol on a sheet of paper or an electronic signal on a screen.

Rarely if ever is the managerial hierarchy itself entrusted to carry important messages. Senior executives feel ill at ease delivering such messages, or they fear distortion of their meaning at the hands of humans.

NOT EXTRACURRICULAR

In large modern organizations, executives have isolated themselves to protect their time and their schedules. In so doing they have forgotten that true leadership can never take place in a vacuum. Leaders must see and feel what their followers are experiencing; otherwise they become literally out of touch.

Executives (and that word obviously means more than just the CEO) should see face-to-face communication not as a burden —as an activity that interrupts their real work—but as a critical element of their jobs. The seemingly dramatic medium of closed-circuit television that Myers's client wished to use when he had something important to announce would only have increased the distance between him and the work force.

Moreover, this approach smacks of Big Brother and *1984*.

Status and trappings, which in most corporations are part of officers' perks, combine with the physical barrier of executive suites and executive dining rooms to make face-to-face communication with employees difficult unless senior executives decide it should be a regular part of their activities.

Too many managers at all levels see employee communication as a lip-service activity. If they acknowledge its importance in managing people, they may add with evident sincerity, "If I ever get the time, I'll do better." They see the communication process as extracurricular—something to be attended to when all the meetings are over and all the memos and phone calls have been answered. This failure to understand that management *is* communication and that face-to-face discussion with workers is vital at all levels is costing America dearly in efficiency, productivity, and the will to compete.

8

Productivity and Decision Structures

The system must be free to evolve its own definitions of how one work group will interact with another, how the work groups will relate to the organization, and how the organization operates in relation to other divisions as a corporation.
DUTCH L. LANDEN[1]

Earlier in this century, Max Weber said that the ideal organization had a "bureaucratic" structure. Weber meant "bureaucratic" in a complimentary way. The ideal bureaucratic organization was one where a well-defined hierarchy used a division of labor along functional lines, such as production, finance, and marketing departments. A system of rules and procedures defined the roles of job incumbents and set forth guidelines for work situations. Each job was crisply defined, and people were recruited to fill those very specific jobs on the basis of technical competence. This "mechanistic" view of organizations was designed to ensure impersonality and high degrees of efficiency.[2] And as long as the organization's objectives and environment remained relatively stable, the well-defined structure of a bureaucratic organization proved to be efficient. The effectiveness suffered, however, when the organization had to deal with change. Burns and Stalker suggest, and subsequent research indicates, that organic, or free-form, organizations tend to respond to changing objectives and environments more readily than the rigid structure of bureaucratic organizations.[3]

ORGANIZATION ASSUMPTIONS

Organizations develop their own cultures and personalities.[4] Embedded in the foundations of an organization's culture are the assumptions managers make about the people in the organization. Some organizations are built upon the assumptions underlying McGregor's Theory X.[5] Namely, the organization is designed to accommodate employees who are unmotivated, uncommitted to organization goals, and who lack initiative. The well-defined jobs and organization relationships of a highly structured bureaucratic organization assure that poor performance will be detected.

On the other hand, if the organization assumes that employees are self-motivated, committed to organization goals, and have initiative, the need for rigid job descriptions and relationships is lessened. These Theory Y assumptions allow the designers of organizations to assume that employees have good judgment.[6]

Assumptions about employees strongly influence the shape of organization. To control unmotivated workers, Theory X organizations tend to be tall and to have narrow spans of control. Each supervisor manages only a limited number of employees to ensure close supervision, and extensive levels of supervision replace individual employee motivation. Close supervision ensures that each employee's efforts are aimed at the desired goal. Likewise, multiple layers of organizational hierarchy serve to review the actions of lower-level supervisors. But these vertical organizations, with their narrow spans of control, are typically unable to respond quickly to changes in the competitive environment or changes in the overall organization's direction. Multiple layers must approve even the most minor changes, and these multiple levels of approval obviously delay the decision-making process. Communications, both up and down the organization hierarchy, are also delayed and, many times, filtered or distorted.

These underlying assumptions about employees also affect human resource development. When employees are seen as largely unworthy, human resource development efforts tend to be minimal. The development of managerial and personal skills tends to lag or become nonexistent. Even informal and experiential approaches to developing managers lag, because the narrow spans of control allow the individual employees very little decision-making latitude. The employee is unable to develop the judgment and decision-making skills that are at the heart of all human development.

Limited decision-making discretion results from a Theory X tendency to centralize the decision-making process at very high levels in the organization. Although the centralization of decision-making ensures uniformity, it often results in slow decisions that may not be responsive to the unique situations faced by lower levels of management.

When the underlying organizational assumptions include a belief that employees are self-motivated and committed to organizational goals, the design in the decision-making process becomes much different. Since employees are self-motivated, spans of control tend to be wider, leading to a flatter organization. Flatter organizations have fewer levels of management between the worker and top executive, so communications tend to be quicker and less distorted. The broader span of control also limits the amount of time a manager can spend with any one person. This flat organization contributes to a greater decentralization of the decision-making process. And, although the manager may have less time to spend developing any one employee, workers are given broader responsibilities and corresponding authority.

MANAGERIAL ASSUMPTIONS

Beyond the organizational assumptions that become ingrained in the organization's culture, individual managers also make assumptions. For example, many managers assume their job is to make decisions. That assumption leads them to keep as much decision-making discretion to themselves as possible. Restated, individual managers often are reluctant to share their decision-making authority with others in a participative fashion. This reluctance is understandable, considering the managers' assumptions about whose job it is to make decisions. Some managers, however, have a clearer vision of their job. They see their role as getting decisions made, not necessarily making decisions themselves.

Although that difference may seem slight, it's important. Managers who perceive their role as getting decisions made also recognize that the manner in which decisions are made is important. For these managers, *who* makes the decisions is a valid concern. As discussed in greater detail in Chapter 13 ("Productivity, QWL and Employee Involvement"), employees do not resist their own ideas. Managers who assume that their job is to get decisions made, and that employees are self-motivated, are much more likely to develop a participative approach to decision-making.[7]

DECISION-MAKING PROCESS

Regardless of managerial or organizational assumptions, all decisions pass through standard steps. Although different researchers would use different terminology and might even vary the number of steps, decision-making must take the following course:

Step 1: Recognition and formulation of the problem

Step 2: Creation of alternatives

Step 3: Selection of alternatives

Step 4: Implementation

Step 5: Evaluation/follow-up

In centralized organizations, these steps take place at higher organizational levels. In decentralized organizations, this decision-making process occurs at lower levels. If the organization is decentralized and the manager assumes the job is to get decisions made (rather than to make the decisions), the manager will probably follow the sequence on the right-hand side of Figure 8–1. Managers who think their job is to make decisions are more likely to follow the left-hand side of Figure 8–1. As the figure indicates, both managers go through the same steps in the same sequence. Yet the more participative manager involves his or her employees in the early stages of the decision-making process, and this involvement takes longer. The process of getting agreement on the nature of the problem, jointly generating alternatives, and cooperatively selecting the best alternative is more time-consuming than if the manager unilaterally generates and picks the "best" alternative.[8]

On the surface, therefore, the participative approach is less efficient in these early stages. This approach has some outstanding benefits, however. First of all, when more people are involved in the decision-making process, the formulation of the specific problem is likely to be more accurate. Rather than echoing the manager's perspective, the participative approach to decision-making is likely to produce a description of the problem that represents various viewpoints and a high level of agreement. Employee involvement also leads to more creative alternatives. And when employees are allowed to help assess these alternatives, the final choice is often a better one.

The real benefit of employee involvement in the decision-making process, however, comes when the decision is implemented. The "manager-centered" approach to decision-making generally encounters considerable resistance to change.[9] Employees are expected to imple-

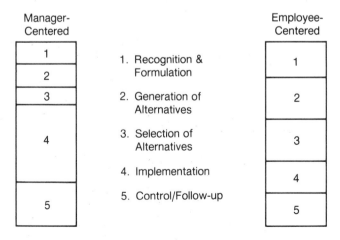

Figure 8–1. Steps in the Decision-Making Process

ment the manager's ideas, not their own. In the more participative approach, employees are implementing their own ideas. It is axiomatic that employees "do not resist their own ideas." Less resistance to change also implies less need for control or follow-up after the decision is implemented.

The "funnel" view of decision-making that appears in Figure 8–2 underlines the importance of early employee involvement in the decision-making process. If the decision-making process is viewed as a funnel, the first step is the most crucial. The problem must be defined if the proposed solution is to solve the problem. Whether a manager-centered or employee-centered approach to decision-making is used, the first step in the decision-making process may only define the symptom of the problem. When this happens, the ultimate outcome of the decision-making process is unlikely to solve the problem; all that managers can hope for is symptomatic relief.

At the same time, if the early stages of the decision-making process define the issue as a problem, rather than as an opportunity, management's goals will be different. In problem-solving, management generally seeks to regain the level it would have achieved had the problem not occurred. That is, problem-solving merely seeks to reduce barriers that prevent the attainment of desired performance. But if the issue at hand is truly an opportunity, then management and employees may attain results beyond their original goals by exploiting the new opportunity. Opportunities, simply put, open the door to previously unhoped-for levels of performance. (Problem-solving usually seeks to achieve the same goals that existed before the problem arose.)

Finally, employee involvement in the decision-making process creates a sense of ownership. When employees help generate the solutions, they have a vested interest in them.

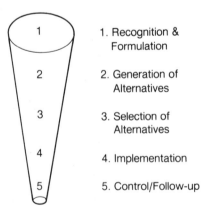

Figure 8–2.   The "Funnel" View of Decision Making

DEFEATING BUREAUCRACY

Extensive behavioral research over the last fifty years indicates that employees seek jobs with autonomy, task variety, task significance, and feedback.[10] One seldom sees an article entitled, "How Do We Motivate Our Executives?" Even the title is absurd. Motivation among executives is seldom a problem because their jobs contain motivating characteristics. But when the manager makes decisions alone, many enriching elements of the job are withheld from employees. Without a meaningful voice in the decision-making process, employees often lack the sense of achievement, accomplishment, growth, and recognition that are necessary for satisfaction and motivation. As a result, little within the job excites these employees. Apathy reigns.

If organizations are to defeat the "bureaucratic syndrome" of poor performance, poor quality and slow rates of response to changing environments, employees must actively take part in the decision-making process. Unfortunately, this transition is unlikely to occur among managers who see themselves as sole decision-makers. To share the decision-making process with employees is at best threatening, and at worst, a usurpation of the manager's right to make decisions. But once again, it is not the manager's "right" to make decisions—it is simply the manager's "responsibility" to get the right decisions made.[11]

SUMMARY

Decision-making is a process that can help win employee commitment—if managers are willing to include employees in the process. In productive organizations, managers realize that their responsibility is not to make decisions, but to assure that decisions are made. Under most circumstances, a more participative style of decision-making pays dividends in higher long-term productivity improvement.

SELECTED READINGS OVERVIEW

The first of the two articles in this section, by Dutch Landen, is entitled "The Future of Participative Management." Landen, a former vice president in charge of organization development at General Motors, begins with a discussion of the conditions that seem necessary for the success of participatory management. He talks about how participatory, organization and managerial principles represent an alternative to more bureaucratic and autocratic structures. In fact, he goes so far as to argue that participative management may be the major force to revitalize American industry. One important conclusion he reaches, based on research at General Motors, is that plants with a higher quality of work life also have a higher product quality, customer satisfaction, and better morale.

The title of the other article in this chapter aptly describes the authors' purpose: "Behavioral Strategies to Improve Productivity." Latham, Cummings and Mitchell discuss how managers should evaluate performance outcomes, rather than continuing to focus on personality traits. By identifying discrepancies between goals and achievement within organization units across time, managers today are better able to identify the causes of poor performance. After identifying the causes, managers can make decisions—such as jointly setting realistic goals with their employees—that lead to constructive performance improvement on the part of the employees.

Next Chapter

How managers make decisions is closely connected to their overall leadership style. Different managers make decisions and lead in different ways. The next chapter examines various leadership styles and the implications these styles hold for organizations and their productivity.

Review Questions

1. Describe the features of a bureaucracy as Max Weber envisioned it.
2. How does a manager's assumptions about employees affect the design of an organization? The decision-making process?
3. What is the significance of the "funnel" view of decision-making?
4. How does participative management contribute to organizational productivity?

D. L. LANDEN
Distinguished Fellow, American Productivity Center

The Future of Participative Management

INTRODUCTION

At a recent conference on QWL an executive from a large multi-national corporation stated, "QWL is being treated as just another fad. I wouldn't be surprised that in 10 years we would be attending conferences on the values of authoritarian management."

An interesting point of view. But one that I do not share.

At an in-house conference on quality circles, the president of a major U.S. electronics corporation spoke about QWL and participative management. The guts of the first three-quarters of the speech were on the need for new organizational participatory concepts and the importance of getting everyone in-volved in problem identification and problem solving.

The last quarter of the speech stressed the necessity for management to maintain discipline, "We can't lose control of the organization. We can't lose our sense of direction. We can't sacrifice our profit goals."

I thought I had fallen asleep only to wake up a "decade later." I couldn't belief that it was the same speaker. I'm sure he felt he was being consistent. I thought he was being schizophrenic.

At yet another conference on QWL sponsored by the president of another major U.S. corporation, Donald Ephlin, vice president, United Auto Workers, was asked about the union's position on participative manage-

Dr. D.L. "Dutch" Landen has long been involved in the activities and development of the American Productivity Center.

Landen, who recently retired as director of organizational research and development at the General Motors Corporation, has spent more than 25 years in the field of organizational change and employee involvement. He is widely recognized for his work at General Motors particularly in the development of the corporation's joint quality of work life effort with the United Auto Workers.

In addition to bachelor and master's degrees from Wayne State University, Landen holds a Ph.D. in industrial psychology earned at Ohio State University.

As a Center Distinguished Fellow, Landen will continue in his role as an advisor and will participate in productivity and quality of work life efforts and research projects.

Reprinted from: *Productivity Brief* 16 (August 1982).

ment. He responded to the question by stating, "Participative management should not be seen as the union participating with management. Rather, it should be seen as management participating with workers."

Another manager once stated how strongly he practiced participation. "I give an order, my subordinates pass on my directions to their subordinates, who do the same with theirs, and so on. Everyone participates in the process!"

I suppose he could have also added that "if anyone can't handle that form of participation, we will help him exit the company."

One final point of view. A high level executive of a Fortune 500 multinational company once defined QWL as, "getting better quality with less cost while not losing control of our right to run the business."

It is obvious that we lack consensus as to precisely what is meant by the term *participative management*.

WHAT PARTICIPATIVE MANAGEMENT IS AND IS NOT

Participative management is not soft. It is not undisciplined, not uncontrolled, not undirected and certainly not permissive!

Participative management is perhaps the most difficult form of management. It is highly disciplined, controlled and goal-oriented.

One fundamental distinction between authoritarian and participative management is *who* exercises control, discipline and directionality. One underlying rationale of any participatory process is that everyone in the organization is capable of and willing to help guide and direct the organization (or the sub-unit of which they are a part) toward agreed upon goals and objectives.

More fundamentally, participative management is an organized set of ideas about *how* to manage a modern and progressive business enterprise.

Participative management is a set of concepts predicated on a philosophical conviction that the vast majority of employees can make significant contributions to business, human and social objectives if they are provided the opportunity, knowledge, support and reinforcement to do so.

Given this philosophy, the term "management" must be treated as a set of concepts, not as a group of people. Such concepts as planning, coordination, control and decision-making can be utilized and applied by every employee. Indeed one of the greatest weaknesses in American corporations today is that too few people are allowed to practice management techniques. Hence, organizations have become over-staffed, over-regulated, overly-rigid, overly-inefficient, and basically ineffective.

What Determines the Future of Any Form of Management?

There are six conditions that seemingly determine whether or not managerial forms are sustained.

1. Is the prevailing form effective?
2. Is there an alternative form (or forms) known to be more effective?
3. Are there any pressures (from society, unions, workers, legislation, etc.) to substitute a new form of management for the existing one?
4. Are the educational resources available to enable people to learn a new form of management?
5. Will the business environment reward new forms of behavior?
6. Is a "critical mass" developing that has the force to bring about a shift from the prevailing form to another more effective form? (e.g., an international "worker democracy movement" whether it is called codetermination, self-management, workplace design, spirit of Wa, or quality of work life.)

What is presently known as "traditional management" is by no means the form which has always existed. It has been shaped to one degree or another by each of these six pressures.

The early form of modern-day management was highly individualistic. The entrepreneurial spirit is what created most contemporary business institutions. The Carnegies, Fords, Mellons, Rockefellers, Durants, Watsons were all very much their own men. They had a vision about what they wanted to create and a strong will to make it happen. Men of this type are not, however, generally remembered for their managerial acumen nor their statesmanship.

In fact, it is not unusual for men who create successful businesses to demonstrate a complete inability to manage them. Both Henry Ford and William Durant, creator of General Motors, were notoriously poor managers. The Ford Motor Company ultimately had to be bailed out by Henry Ford II and the "Whiz Kids." Willy Durant was rescued by the Duponts and Alfred P. Sloan.

A new breed of managers replaced the entrepreneurs because of economic necessity. The skills that were required to create Ford Motor Company and General Motors were not sufficient to sustain them.

Professional management was spawned out of the same crucible that gave birth to scientific management. The old spirit of "damn the torpedos, full speed ahead" gave way to "the god of efficiency."

A new ideology replaced an old one. Success was measured in short increments of profitability. The rallying cry became "What's the bottom line?" If an investment, a decision, an action was judged to be good for short-term profitability, it had the unwavering support of the professional manager, since his primary reward was based on "What did he accomplish last year?"

For the professional manager, the goal became maximum production with minimum labor. The manufacturing organization was measured on how much it produced with the least amount of labor—i.e., labor efficiency. This goal became the compelling justification to simplify work into its most basic elements.

Scientific management was, and is, predicated on the belief that the best way, if not the only way, to achieve maximum efficiency is to simplify work, create stationary work stations and have the product to be worked on move on a conveyor system whereby simple repetitive tasks can be endlessly repeated by workers who require a minimum amount of skill, intelligence and training.

The principles of scientific management were, and are

1. "scientifically" design the job;
2. "scientifically" select workers to match the job requirements;
3. "scientifically" train the workers to perform the job as instructed.

As Irving Bluestone, retired vice president of International UAW, has remarked on several occasions, "Scientific management is neither science nor management."

Bluestone's remark is both profound and prophetic. Even Frederick Winslow Taylor, the father of "scientific management," asserted a fourth principle that rarely gets mentioned by his devotees and advocates. "The other principles, if they are to work, must be done in a *spirit of cooperation.*" (Emphasis added.)

The era of scientific management has hardly been one of cooperation. Quite the contrary. The major labor problems of industrial history are attributable to the concepts of scientific management coupled with authoritarianism.

The fact that authoritarianism as a philosophy of scientific management and scientific management as a theory of job design should co-exist should not surprise anyone. They are based on the same rationale:

The purpose of organization is to accomplish work. The purpose of work is to produce goods and services. The purpose of goods and services is to supply market demand. The product of this equation is profitability.

Since the equation is simple and straightforward, the organizational and managerial processes should be simple and straightforward. An elite group of people called managers will execute all managerial functions. Another group of people called workers will execute, as directed, the elements of the work that they are assigned.

A simple concept for simple times.

But as times became more complex, the organizational system based upon this simple concept began to break down. Workers began to rebel against the indiscriminate use of managerial authority. Managers attempted to mollify workers by employing yet another overly simplistic set of managerial principles called human relations.

While the *principles* of human relations management emerged out of the Hawthorne Studies at the Western Electric Plant outside of Chicago, the *techniques* of human relations emerged out of the managerial training programs. "Treat people nicely and they will behave nicely." How do you do that? Communications! Learn about people's hobbies, their family, their interests. Call them by their names instead of their clock numbers. Say "good morning" to them. Wish them a happy birthday. Talk to them at least once a day whether they need it or not.

Simple ideas for simple people. But people are not that simple. They never were. And so another management theory began to flounder.

Before floundering, both scientific management and human relations did for a period of years accompany the growth and success of many business institutions.

It would be false to conclude from this correlation that the success of many American businesses was a direct function of their managerial concepts, skills and techniques. If the current plight of many American corporations is not testimony enough to the inappropriateness of outdated management concepts, it would be difficult to conjure up many other valid explanations.

Managerial Styles Alone Are Not the Culprit

One of the strong arguments for participative management is that, because the business environment is vastly more turbulent and unpredictable, organizations need to be able to respond more quickly. The bureaucracy is built on a tradition of stability.

The hierarchy is designed under the assumption that only a limited number of people at the top of the organization are required to guide and direct large enterprises. Recent experience provides evidence to the contrary. It is becoming increasingly apparent that greater flexibility can be achieved when plans are made and problems are identified and solved at the lowest reasonable level.

Many contemporary business structures are predicated on the same principle that governed the organization of work under "scientific management." They are simplified by functions (called functional differentiation or line and staff), fractionated by levels (called echelons), directed by "magic" ratios of supervisors to subordinates (called span or control), and governed by use of military jargon (called rank and file, chain of command, unity of command and esprit de corps).

Are these concepts and labels appropriate to a democratic society? Do these structures and these designations speak to the heart of a participatory social, economic and political paradigm? Neither the language nor the structures nor the processes nor the concepts on which they are based are in harmony with democratic values and participatory processes.

Participatory organizational and managerial principles do represent clear alternatives to scientific/authoritarian management. The old systems are not working. The new ones have demonstrated their value. Now comes the slow and agonizing process of re-educating an old generation of managers and workers and providing a supportive environment to them and to a new breed of working people.

What Is the Future of Participative Management?

Participative management may be the major force to revitalize American industry.

Productivity improvement has become a national pursuit. And rightfully so. The U.S. economy is inexorably linked to the productivity of our nation's businesses and industries. But whether we are advocates of "macro" national monetary and legislative solutions or company-based solutions focusing on better utilization of capital, technology, energy and human resources, the ultimate test will be how well people understand and manipulate the complex and dynamic interplay between all these variables and others not cited.

The key to improved productivity appears to be the creation of broadly conceived organizational improvement programs that are grounded both in short-term pragmatic goals and long-term visionary strategies.

Sustained productivity improvement can only be achieved by management systems that are founded on a blend of incremental steps and profound transformation stages. The goal must be to produce quantum-like innovations in the organizational forces that mobilize and energize organizations—goals, strategies, plans, resources and leadership.

William Abernathy of the Harvard Business School speaks of the "productivity di-

lemma." He asserts that because of the push for cost savings and greater manufacturing efficiency industries became overly standardized and more rigid. The gains from economies of scale came at the expense of innovation and technological competitiveness. Abernathy states, "To compete, American manufacturers must move from an era in which there was little change in production systems to a time of greater turbulence in equipment, employee skills and organization—elements that run counter to a belief in standardization." (New York Times, May 30, p. F 21).

The assertion that participative management not only has a future, but is the only viable future form of management is the inherent bond between leadership and participation.

Participatory management, the inverse of scientific management, is grounded in the value premise that all people possess leadership ability—the capacity to influence the attitudes and behavior of others towards the accomplishment of common goals and objectives.

The greatest contribution that participatory organizations can make to American institutions and to American society is to provide the opportunity and support for every worker to become directly involved in creating and managing more competitive enterprises.

Among the characteristics of the "high performing systems" identified by Peter Vaill[1] are human systems that internalize society's prevailing culture, have a distinct style or flair, are able to accomplish things other organizations can't achieve (frequently with fewer resources) and are able to sustain their achievements over extended periods of time.

Systems that perform so superbly cannot be built around personalities or operated as political fiefdoms. They are organizations that have clearly articulated philosophies, which embrace the society's values, and are structured so as to engage the competencies of all people who are empowered to make things happen, to get things done and *to make the system perform to its maximum capabilities.*

Therein lies the essence of participatory organizations. These are not human systems where people are mere executors of work but instead systems where people are the organization's architects and engineers. They help design work systems, and having designed them, make them perform.

Making Participatory Systems Work

Every human system needs people who have a vision about what the system should be and can be. Every human system needs a plan, a *process,* for transforming the system from its present state of effectiveness to qualitatively and quantitatively higher states of effectiveness.

In authoritarian systems, only a limited number of people are permitted to engage in this process.

In participatory systems, every employee is encouraged to be creatively involved to the limits of his or her interests and capabilities.

Various labels are applied to this process. Some call it quality of work life (QWL). Some call it employee involvement (EI). Others call it workplace innovations. Still others call it workplace democracy or industrial democracy.

The term "participatory organizations" is meant to encompass all of these terms and their underlying principles and values.

As we seek to create higher performing human systems, or "higher commitment organizations," to use Richard Walton's[2] preferred term, participatory processes are essential.

In unionized organizations this mandates a joint working relationship between union leaders and company managers. Over the last decade a number of joint QWL/EI efforts have been initiated. Many of the most significant efforts in this country have been propelled through the rubric of national negotiated agreements such as exist in the auto, steel and communications industries.

In other cases the motivating force was a realization that productivity improvements are frequently a by-product of effective QWL/EI efforts.

Research in General Motors conducted over the last two decades clearly supports this conclusion. One study involving 23 assembly plants showed that those plants have the highest quality of work life, as measured by GM's QWL survey, also have higher product quality, higher customer satisfaction ratings, lower absenteeism, fewer grievances, less discipline, and the lowest labor costs.

The same findings were found in a similar study that involved different types of plants —manufacturing and fabricating, assembly.

An independent study conducted by two university professors and a graduate student demonstrated the same statistical relationship.[3] Their analysis showed that such industrial relations variables as absenteeism, grievances, discipline rates, number of local contract demands in 1979 negotiations and the length of time required to reach a contract settlement are statistically interrelated at high levels of statistical consistency.

Moreover, they found that the 18 or so plants involved in the study with the highest QWL survey scores also exhibited the most consistently effective performance on all of the industrial relations variables over a span of 10 years.

And if further evidence is needed in support of QWL, those plants that demonstrated the best industrial relations performances over the decade of the '70s also had the highest product quality and most efficient operations.

CONCLUSION

Perhaps in the final analysis it will take evidence like this to convince some American managers that participatory principles are not only in the best interest of American workers but are in the best interest of American industry.

Participatory management did not come into being because it was "right" or "nice." It came into existence because of accumulating evidence that such processes will help to create more *productive* organizations.

It will continue to flourish for the same reasons.

But let us not be deluded into believing it is easy or quick or simple or free.

Like any good organizational system, high performing, high commitment systems require initiative, leadership and risk-taking, as well as knowledge of what the future must be and of the strategies and resources for achieving new, more effective organizations. Compounding the challenge even more is the fact that the future state is a moving target, changing with shifting market trends and the overall business environment. The transformation process must be flexible to accommodate the market and other social and economic requirements.

Creating and maintaining highly adaptive complex organizations cannot be effectively achieved without the full support of all employees. One of today's organizational axioms is that "people support what they help create."

If support, commitment, high performance and adaptability are what is critical in today's highly volatile and competitive environment, then participatory organizations are the best means of achieving these qualities.

Once organizations realize that their own destiny is in the hands of all the people, and once people experience the challenge and the satisfaction of helping to make organizations perform more effectively, the importance of participative management will grow in intensity and in achievement.

GARY P. LATHAM

LARRY L. CUMMINGS

TERENCE R. MITCHELL

Behavioral Strategies to
Improve Productivity

*Selecting the appropriate strategy for improving productivity through
the utilization of human resources requires a systematic appraisal
of the causes of good and bad performance.*

Gary P. Latham is a research professor in the
Department of Management and Organization, School
of Business Administration, at the University of
Washington, Seattle. Previously he was manager of
Human Resources Research at the Weyerhaeuser
Company in Tacoma. He received his Ph.D. in
Industrial Psychology from the University of Akron,
his M.S. from the Georgia Institute of Technology, and
his B.A. from Dalhousie University, Nova Scotia. Dr.
Latham is a member of the Canadian Psychological
Association and the Academy of Management. He is a
Fellow of the American Psychological Association. He
has published more than 100 articles and technical
reports including a book, *Increasing Productivity
Through Performance Appraisal*.

Larry L. Cummings is a Slichter Research Professor,
an H.I. Romnes Faculty Fellow, and director of the
Center for the Study of Organizational Performance
in the Graduate School of Business, University of
Wisconsin–Madison. He has served as associate dean
(Social Sciences) of the Graduate School and is the
author, co-author, or editor of nine books, including
*Readings in Organizational Behavior and Human
Performance* (Richard D. Irwin Inc., 1969, 1973, third
edition in press); *Introduction to Organizational
Behavior: Text and Readings* (Richard D. Irwin, Inc.,
1980); and *Bargaining Behavior: An International
Study* (Dame Publications, 1980). Dr. Cummings has
also had more than seventy-five articles published in
a variety of scholarly journals, including the
Academy of Management Journal and the *Journal of
Applied Psychology*. He serves as an associate editor
of *Decision Sciences*. He has also served as one of the
vice-presidents of the American Institute for Decision
Sciences and has served as editor of the *Academy of
Management Journal*. Dr. Cummings is a fellow of the
American Psychological Association, the Academy of
Management, and the American Institute for Decision
Sciences. He has also served as one of the
vice-presidents of the American Institute for Decision
Sciences and as vice-president and program chair of
the Academy of Management; he is currently
president of the latter. He is a consulting editor in
Management and the Behavioral Sciences for Richard
D. Irwin. Inc.

Reprinted, by permission of the publisher, from *Organizational Dynamics* (Winter 1981).

Terence R. Mitchell is professor of Management and Organization at the Graduate School of Business, University of Washington. He has an advanced diploma in Public Administration from the University of Exeter and an M.A. and a Ph.D. in social psychology from the University of Illinois. Dr. Mitchell's interests are in the areas of organizational behavior, leadership, and motivation. He has recently published articles on these topics in *Organizational Behavior and Human Performance*, *The Academy of Management Review*, the *Academy of Management Journal*, and the *Journal of Applied Phycology*. He is the author of *People in Organizations* (McGraw-Hill, 1978) and is a joint author with William G. Scott of *Organization Theory: A Structural and Behavioral Analysis* (Irwin-Dorsey, 1976). He is currently working on research projects and studying leadership and subordinate motivation in several organizational settings.

America is in trouble. The competitive spirit has caught on around the world, and we no longer lead in productivity gains—indeed, some people argue that we are dangerously close to being out of the game. According to statistics from the Bureau of Labor Statistics, the United States ranked sixth among seven leading industrial nations in productivity increases from 1968 to 1978. The rankings from the study appear in Table 1.

Top decision-making executives are beginning to recognize the importance of using the organization's human resources to improve productivity. The many approaches to developing human resources range from improving work methods to improving quality of work life. Before selecting a particular tactic, a systematic appraisal of the causes of good and poor performance is necessary. The three stages in our proposed process for improving productivity through the utilization of human resources are: strategies for *identifying* poor performance, strategies for *deciding* what causes poor performance, and strategies for *coping* with poor performance.

IDENTIFYING POOR PERFORMANCE

How should managers go about identifying problems? How do they do so? The answers to these two questions may not be the same. Basically, an ideal approach to identifying problems can be called a rational approach. By contrast, we can describe the way managers actually do identify performance problems as a conditionally rational approach that is subject to the limitation of managers as information processors and decision makers. Emerging evidence indicates that the

Productivity Increases of the Top Seven Countries (1968–1978)

Rank	1968–1978 Productivity Increases
1. The Netherlands	93.7%
2. Japan	89.1
3. West Germany	63.8
4. France	61.8
5. Italy	60.1
6. United States	23.6
7. United Kingdom	21.6

Source: Bureau of Labor Statistics, United States Department of Labor, 1979.

processes actually used by managers in identifying and formulating performance problems are not always completely rational. Hopefully, a better understanding of what managers actually do can lead to the development and implementation of strategies that will bring them closer to what they should do.

TYPICAL EVALUATION PROCEDURES

This section describes the two most prevalent criteria for evaluating performance in today's organizations—performance outcomes and personality traits. We then describe (1) the judgment processes underlying the use of rational procedures in identifying performance problems and (2) several limitations involved in using these rational processes.

Performance Outcomes

Senior-level management, stockholders, and consumers are generally concerned with performance outcomes, or results, as measures of an individual's or organization's productivity level. That is, they are concerned with such cost-related measures as profits, costs, product quantity and quality, returns on investment, and so forth. The person who scores well on these measures is presumed to be highly motivated toward performance improvement. The person who has received adequate resources (including training) to do the job, but who performs poorly on these measures, is presumed to be poorly motivated.

Performance outcomes may be an excellent gauge of an organization's health or effectiveness, but they are generally inadequate, by themselves, in measuring an individual employee's job effectiveness. Indeed, they can even be demotivating, if not de-

structive, for both employee and employer. Here's why:

First, cost-related measures are often affected by factors over which an individual has little or no control. One individual's performance is often affected by the performance of others. It not only is unfair, but may be illegal, to distribute organizational rewards and punishments (for example, promotions, transfers, demotions, dismissals, or bonuses) on the basis of measures over which an employee has minimal control.

Second, these measures often fall short because they omit important aspects of a person's job. When a superintendent in one district, for example, lends equipment to a superintendent in another district, profits may increase for the company while costs increase for the superintendent who lent the equipment. A superior's poor memory and an incomplete accounting system that merely "keeps score" may identify a "winner" and a "loser" rather than two team players who contributed to the company's overall profits.

Third, these measures can encourage a results-at-all-costs mentality that can run counter to corporate ethics or policies—not to mention legal requirements. Moreover, a results-at-all-costs mentality can run counter to the organization's overall productivity. In the above example, lending equipment hurt the lender's monthly cost sheet, but it significantly increased the organization's profits. The reverse might have been true if the lender had adhered to a "my own results at all costs" philosophy.

Fourth, it is difficult to formulate cost-related measures for most white-collar jobs. Such measure of a log-cutter's effectiveness, for example, might be the number of trees cut divided by the number of hours worked. But what cost-related measures exist for the jobs of an engineer or a newspaper reporter?

Finally, and most important from a performance-improvement standpoint, economic measures or performance outcomes fail to give the employee information about what he or she needs to do to maintain or increase productivity. Telling a baseball player that he just struck out, for example, will not come as a surprise to him. What the player needs to know is what he must *do* to get to first base or possibly hit a home run.

Personality Traits

For one or more of the above reasons, 90 percent of today's organizations measure an employee's effectiveness—at least lower levels—primarily in terms of traits or distinguishing human qualities that those in the organizational hierarchy believe are desirable, not in terms of cost-related outcomes. These trait measures generally include commitment, creativity, loyalty, initiative, and the like. The problem with traits, from a productivity standpoint, is twofold. First, telling a person to "be a better listener" or to "show more initiative" may be excellent advice, but it doesn't tell the person what to do to implement this advice. Before such discussions can motivate the employee to behave appropriately, traits must be defined explicitly.

Second, trait measures are looked upon unfavorably by the courts when decisions based on them adversely impact people in a protected class. This is because, in the words of one court decision, traits are susceptible to partiality and to the personal taste, whim, or fancy of the evaluator. [*Wade v. Mississippi Cooperative Extension Service*, 372 F. Suppl. 126 (1974), 7EDP 9186.]

Rationally Identifying Performance Problems

These two approaches to assessing performance represent the most popular techniques currently used in industry. Notice that both tell the subordinate very little about what he or she has done wrong and how to correct it. Also, evaluations in terms of cost or traits are far removed from what the employee actually does.

In this section we will describe some less frequently used procedures that are based on more rational models. They represent attempts to describe more specifically what the subordinate is doing incorrectly. The heart of these rational approaches is to base evaluations on comparisons. Three different types of comparison can be used to detect performance problems and establish ways to assess or identify such performance problems. The key is to discover a performance gap. The three approaches differ on what components they compare to discover the gap.

Discrepancy Between Goals and Achievement

Identifying a performance problem may require comparing a goal with actual performance. For example, one could compare the number of cars sold by a salesperson in a given month with the agreed-upon goal for cars to be sold that month. When fewer are sold than planned, a performance gap exists. This approach, of course, is the one taken by performance improvement programs such as management by objectives (MBO), work planning and review, and other results-oriented management strategies. As an approach to identifying performance problems, it works best when several important conditions are present:

1. Performance goals can be defined in measurable terms.

2. The goals are not contradictory; that is, one performance goal is not attained at the expense of another (for example, increasing quantity of performance at the expense of quality).

3. The employee's performance can be measured in units identical to the way in which the goal is expressed (for example, number of cars sold versus number of cars that were supposed to be sold).

In many cases these three conditions cannot be met. For example, a salesperson being urged to develop sustained, long-term relationships with customers may actually be compensated for short-term, quarterly sales results. When performance is multidimensional, as it is in most if not all complex jobs, identifying gaps between performance goals and actual performance may lead to the identification of performance areas that are being emphasized to the detriment of other, equally important areas.

Finally, while it may be feasible to establish quantifiable goals, it may not be possible to measure an individual's performance in relation to these goals. For example, while it may be necessary to reduce scrap by 15 percent, scrap may be affected in many ways by one or more groups as well as by people within a group. Thus documenting an individual's performance on the basis of performance outcomes can prove difficult.

Comparisons Among People, Units, or Organizations

Perhaps because of this difficulty, managers often compare individuals, divisions, or organizations with one another. This can be achieved without setting specific, measurable performance goals for any individual, division, or organization. Because the comparison is made on the basis of performance relative to others, those who rank lowest are identified as those who have performance problems.

However, combining different dimensions of job performance and measuring achievement on each dimension frequently poses a problem. For example, even though two managers may agree that individuals X and Y are "poor" supervisors relative to others, such comparisons are not particularly helpful in diagnosing the causes of poor performance. As we shall note later, these two managers may well attribute high or low performance to quite different causes even though they agree on the overall performance ranking. And this is unfortunate, because such attributions can be crucial in deciding what to do to sustain high performance and/or improve low performance.

Comparisons Across Time

Single individuals, units, or organizations can be compared with themselves across time. This type of comparison implies that the definition of poor performance is declining performance (and increasing performance is good). As long as the same dimensions of performance are compared across time this approach avoids both problems identified earlier. Of course, performance still must be measurable in units that are meaningful and understandable to the employee in question. But managers' agreement on goals and performance ranking is not necessary with this approach.

However, this approach is susceptible to naïve application and gross myopia. Frequently, increasing performance may not indicate success or even survival (for example, when the competition is improving even more rapidly). It is also possible that decreasing performance may not be dysfunctional (for example, when an individual's performance decrement is necessary to prevent overload and possible detrimental stress). Actually, a short-term performance decline may even be necessary to ensure long-run survival and continued productivity.

In summary, each of these three approaches to identifying performance problems assumes that performance is measurable. Each assumes that some standard for assessment exists or can be derived. In the first case, the standard consists of well-defined quantifiable goals. In the second, the standard is the performance of another individual, unit, or organization. In the third, the standard is previous performance.

However, there are problems with these procedures. A manager may have biased or inadequate information or the information processing may require technical assistance. In addition, there are human limitations to the efficient use of these procedures. We need to know what these are and how to overcome them before we can discuss the practical implications of determining and coping with the causes of poor performance.

Human Limitations

Personal characteristics of the evaluator and/or the subject may influence the diagnosis in such a way that it becomes less rational and systematic and more intuitive. The personal characteristics that might influence evaluations include these:

First, managers are frequently willing to accept the first satisfactory identification of a performance problem rather than pursue the best possible and most accurate identification because a long pursuit may not be cost effective. A completely rational analysis may not even be humanly possible when managers are confronted with many performance symptoms and a wide array of possible causes for poor performance. Also, because the managerial world involves frequent interruptions, rapid reordering of priorities, political subtleties, and considerable time pressures, the complex comparison processes may not be feasible in day-to-day managerial situations.

Second, goals and the assessment of performance problems are not always the impetus for managerial action. In fact, they frequently become "after the fact" rationalizations or justifications for what has already occurred. This displacement of goals and performance definitions is common when mangers justify a salary increase or promotion decision (which has already been made on other than performance grounds) by appealing to selective cases of high performance that were not carefully documented or defined beforehand. In other words, goals and definitions of desirable performance are derived from observations of performance rather than being established prior to instruction, guidance, and other managerial actions aimed at producing high performance.

Third, performance problems and performance goals and definitions are subject to varying interpretations on the basis of managers' values, beliefs, and experiences. Seldom does an organization allow a single manager with a single goal to define a problem solely from his or her perspective. Rather, managers with varying and possibly conflicting values and objectives use political, bargaining, and negotiating skills to evolve performance definitions. With these forces set in motion, the analytical, systematic, and logical processes of comparison required by the three rational perspectives become less feasible. At a minimum, the realities of multiple parties with multiple objectives result in more diffuse and less certain definitions of performance and performance problems.

Fourth, performance goals and problems are not static, frozen, or rigid; they tend to shift, to be unstable and dynamic. In growing organizations, particularly at the top, expected performance dimensions shift over time, occasionally in unpredictable ways. This instability and dynamism mean that rational approaches would require continuous comparisons that adjust for changing environmental inputs. Such a requirement is clearly unfeasible and unrealistically costly. To fixate on single, static performance measures can embed a manager in a quagmire of rigidity and frozen action. In order to maintain needed flexibility, wise managers usually resist complete rationality and thorough systematization.

When we combine these all-too-human characteristics, an effective manager seems to be a person who is flexible, dynamic, possessed of limited information-processing capacity, and willing to compromise and bargain—but who, most of all, is subject to major constraints in identifying performance gaps and establishing performance goals. Does this mean that careful analysis of performance problems is impossible? That systematic approaches to enhancing performance are impossible? That meaningful goals cannot be set? That there is little to help managers correct performance deficiencies? Clearly, the answer to these questions is an emphatic "no!" It is equally clear, however, that if normative, purely rational comparative perspectives on identifying performance problems are to be helpful, we must understand and account for the underlying realities of decision making on performance problems.

Thus we now move to a discussion of several new findings about how managers go about the difficult and complex task of deciding what causes a performance problem once it has been identified. The point is, of course, to do something about it—a move that logically arises from assumptions about its presumed cause. However, causes and assumptions about causes are not obvious in the world of performance appraisal.

DECISIONS ON CAUSES OF POOR PERFORMANCE

What happens when a manager or supervisor observes or is informed about a subordinate's poor performance? That is, given the manager's knowledge of the problem, how does he or she proceed to remedy it?

Until recently, the literature on this question has been rather sparse and tends to be descriptive or based on personal experience. There seems to be agreement that certain violations merit an immediate punitive response. For example, theft, falsification of records, fighting with the supervisor, or flagrant insubordination usually result in severe reprimands, probation, and/or termination. This kind of response is often dictated by company policy, leaving the supervisor very little discretion about how to respond.

However, most cases of performance deficiencies are not so clear-cut. What usually happens is that a subordinate misses a deadline, is tardy or absent occasionally, won't work overtime when needed, engages in horseplay, does sloppy work, or commits some other, less extreme violation of expected behavior. The supervisor or manager's task is more complex in these situations because there are few clear prescriptions or rules on how to proceed.

When there's no clear policy, the supervisor probably first tries to determine why the behavior occurred—soliciting information from a variety of sources, including the person involved. Then the information must be processed, sorted, and evaluated, and eventually some cause or causes ascribed. The poor performance might, for example, be attributed to a low skill level, a lack of motivation, poor instruction, or insufficient support services.

After the cause is determined, the supervisor usually selects some course of action aimed at the perceived cause. If, for example, the subordinate's poor performance is perceived to stem from low motivation, the supervisor might resort to the formal discipline procedure or orally reprimand the employee. If, on the other hand, the reason is seen as insufficient information or support, the supervisor might institute changes in the work setting; if low-level ability is seen as the cause, training might be instituted.

Two key points about this process need to be highlighted. First, it is a two-stage process encompassing a diagnostic phase in which the supervisor determines the cause of poor performance and a decision phase in which a response is selected from a set of alternatives. Second, we must recognize that the process entails active information processing by the supervisor. Therefore, simply having good performance appraisal instruments or prescribed disciplinary procedures is not enough. To understand what is happening and how poor performance can be handled more effectively, we must understand this evaluation process more fully.

A Model for Diagnosing and Responding to Poor Performance

We have designed a model to represent the two-stage process described above. The foundation for its development comes from a variety of sources and more detailed discussions can be found elsewhere. However, we must emphasize that the assumptions and hypotheses built into the model were largely generated by social psychological research on attribution theory rather than from literature on industrial discipline or performance appraisal. A brief review of attribution theory and its relevance to performance appraisal issues will contribute to a better understanding of the following material.

Attribution theory is essentially a theory about people's naïve assumptions about the causes of their own and others' behavior. All of us try to figure out why we did things and/or why other people did what they did. The process of determining the causes of behavior is called an attribution process—we attribute our behavior or other people's behavior to various causes. Engaging in this process gives order and understanding to our prediction of our own and others' actions.

The contributions of attribution theory to the problem of performance evaluation are threefold. First, research on the attributional process has shown that people are fairly systematic in their diagnoses of behavior. We know a fair amount about what sort of information is processed and how it is processed. Second, we have learned that a number of both rational and less rational activities go on. Some of these "errors" in the attributional process are built into our model. Third, one major, exceptionally helpful distinction has been the idea that causes of behavior fall into two major classes—internal and external. Internal causes concern people—their abilities, effort, personality, and mood. External causes concern the setting—task difficulty, available information, interpersonal pressures. Obviously, whether a supervisor makes an internal or external attribution about the causes of poor performance is critical to understanding what response will be selected.

The model is presented in Figure 1. The two main stages are labeled links 1 and 2. Link 1 refers to the process of making an attribution, and link 2 refers to the process of choosing an appropriate response. At both stages there are some rational factors and some biases that affect the supervisor's judgments. The rest of this section briefly describes these "moderators" in more detail.

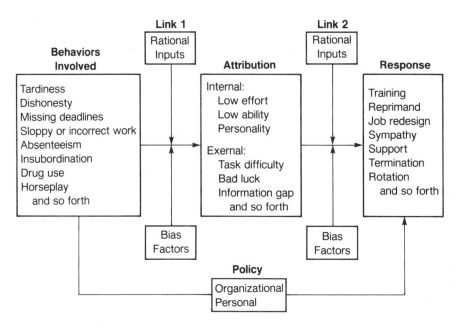

Figure 1.   A Model of Supervisory Responses to Poorly
Performing Subordinates

Attribution Factors

The most obvious rational factors on which attributions are based are distinctiveness, consistency, and consensus. *Distinctiveness* refers to the extent to which a subordinate has performed poorly on other tasks. The less distinctive the performance, the more likely the attribution is external. *Consistency* refers to the extent to which the employee has previously performed poorly on this particular task. The greater the consistency, the more internal the attribution. Finally, *consensus* refers to the extent to which other subordinates perform this task poorly. The lower the consensus, the more internal the attribution.

Let's take an example. Suppose a subordinate fails to turn in a budget report on time. The supervisor recalls that (1) this subordinate is always tardy in submitting any report, (2) he/she is always late with financial reports, and (3) none of the other subordinates are late. Therefore, the supervisor is likely to attribute this poor performance to something about the subordinate (for example, ability or motivation). If, on the other hand, (1) the subordinate has never before missed a deadline for any task, (2) he or she has always submitted financial reports on time, and (3) everybody had trouble getting their reports in this particular month, then an external attribution—that is, something about the financial situation this month (or perhaps too much work)—is probable.

In addition to these rational informational cues, other factors can affect attribution—many of which introduce bias into the process. First, and probably the most important, is the actor/observer bias. It has been well documented that people think their own behavior stems from external forces while others' behavior stems from internal factors.

That is, someone else's behavior is salient to the outside observer, but the environment is salient to the actor. Therefore, the subordinate (actor) is likely to blame external events for his or her behavior, while the supervisor (observer) is likely to blame internal factors. The same result arises from self-serving biases that lead people to attribute successes to themselves and failures to forces beyond their control. The difference in attributions is likely to lead to conflict, disagreement, and hard feelings.

Other sources of error in this attribution phase are possible. Anything that increases the distance (psychologically and physically) between the supervisor and the subordinate is likely to increase actor/observer and self-serving errors. For example, the less the supervisor likes the subordinate, the less experience the supervisor has with the subordinate's job and the more power the supervisor has, the more likely the supervisor is to make internal attributions for poor performance.

Decision and Response

The second link in the model is the decision phase—the supervisor must select a response. Obviously, if an internal attribution has been made, the response is likely to be directed at the subordinate (reprimand, for example, or training), but if an external attribution is made, a response directed at the task would be more appropriate (provide more support, for example, or change the task). Again, some rational and some less rational factors affect this response.

On the rational side is the fact that supervisors at this point usually do some sort of cost/benefit analysis. That is, they weigh the pros and cons of various responses. They consider the probability that a given response will change the subordinate's behavior, have a positive or negative impact on other employees, make the supervisor feel good, adhere to company policy, and so on. These considerations are clearly important to the decision.

But less obvious factors may enter in. For example, there's considerable evidence that the consequences of the poor performance affect the supervisor's response. If the missed deadline for the financial report results in a lost contract, the supervisor is much more likely to be vindictive and punitive than if nothing negative occurs, even though the subordinate may have had no control over the outcome.

Another source of bias might be the subordinate's apologies, excuses, and external explanations. Even though the supervisor has accurately diagnosed that a subordinate performed poorly because of low motivation, he or she is less likely to be punitive and severe if the subordinate apologizes and promises it will never happen again.

A final source of bias springs partly from the actor/observer error. Supervisors are less likely to look for ways in which a task can be changed than for ways in which the person can change; it is somehow easier to tell someone to "be different" than to try to change the environment.

If one summarizes the implications of these two phases, the following conclusions emerge. First, supervisors are likely to see subordinates' poor performance as internally caused. Second, there is likely to be disagreement about that attribution. Third, there are forces that combine with the internal attribution to push the supervisor toward a personal, punitive response. However, apologies and social or organizational constraints may make it difficult to actually use such responses. Thus we are faced with a situation in which a supervisor may unknowingly make some errors in judgment about the causes of poor performance, and then feel frustrated because of certain social or organizational prohibitions about the responses he or she feels are required.

One final point needs to be mentioned. The attributional process is not used when there's a personal or organizational policy to deal with the specific type of poor performance (for example, three unexcused absences in a month requires a written reprimand). We have represented this situation in our model by a line that goes directly from the behavior to the response.

This model has a number of implications for both theory and practice. But perhaps the most important point to recognize is that the supervisor is an active processor of information and that a variety of both relevant (for example, past performance) and nonrelevant (for example, similarity) cues affect his or her judgment about a subordinate. Thus there are rational and nonrational components in (1) the definition of poor performance, (2) the manager's interpretation of its cause, and (3) the response made to it. Before turning to a discussion of ways to improve the process, we will briefly describe the process from the subordinate's perspective.

COPING WITH POOR PERFORMANCE: THE SUBORDINATE'S PERSPECTIVE

What happens when an employee is confronted with data indicating a serious performance problem? Frequently a sequence of psychological and behavioral events occur—so that the employee will:

Deny it. In many cases the first reaction is a cognitive adjustment of denial. The facts are disputed, the actuality or reality is denied or interpreted in a more favorable light, or a different mission than the one intended by the evaluator is claimed. People resort to this defense mechanism quickly and frequently because it protects them, at least momentarily, from loss of esteem, confidence, and face. Moreover, if others accept the denial (which may be backed by equivocal evidence and ambiguous goals), the performer does not need to spend time and energy in actually correcting or improving his or her performance. On the surface, denial appears to be a reasonable, first-shot strategy for coping with a performance problem. It is a subordinate's natural reaction. Managers should expect it, be prepared to confront it, and encourage movement beyond this stage of coping.

Hide it. If denial doesn't work, many problem performers will move from a cognitive adjustment to explicit behavior aimed at hiding, covering, or burying observable symptoms of the substandard performance. Such behavior may be aimed at shielding the symptoms from the boss's view; in professional occupations, considerable effort may be exerted to hide poor performance from other evaluators —for example, peers, public regulators, or agency inspectors. Unfortunately, such a response is not infrequent in publicly sensitive professions, such as nuclear inspection, medical practice, public accounting, and even presidential affairs. This coping strategy represents a recognition that denial is either not possible (that is, there is too much evidence that confirms poor performance) or too risky (that is, if the evidence were public, previous denial would appear dishonest and stupid).

Justify it. Let's elevate the coping process one more step. If the performance problem cannot be denied (it *did* happen) and cannot be hidden (the boss knows or perhaps peers and even the public know), then *what?* Typically, at this stage, the problem performer will attempt to justify or rationalize behavior. Most frequently he or she will try to diminish the significance of the performance problem. Phillip Caldwell, Ford Motor Company chairman, when confronted by a *Wall Street Journal* reporter who compared Ford's recent financial losses to Chrysler Corporation's evolving collapse, reportedly responded, "Ford is a strong company and intends to remain a secure leader in the world of automotive production and technology." [*The Wall Street Journal*, April 16, 1980] In other words, it could be worse. When compared with Chrysler, Ford's performance problems appear minuscule. Caldwell *could* well have said, "Ford intends to survive on its own, and that's better than Chrysler." Of course, the art of justification in the face of declining performance depends on the creative and selective use of comparisons. Ford looks quite different when compared with the Toyota Motor Company or Nissan Motor Company.

Allocate it. The plot thickens. What happens if denial is denied the poor performer? If substandard performance is public knowledge? If comparisons with even poorer performers are impossible or unbelievable? Frequently, individuals and organizations will then allocate responsibility for the poor performance to someone else or to an external agent (for example, a competitor engaging in unfair acts, the government, or an unpredictable, adverse twist of nature)—that is, an external attribution. This stage involves aggressive fault-finding and emotional assertions of blame.

Why These Strategies?

Why are these reactions to performance problems so prevalent? Our analysis suggests at least two fundamental reasons. The first focuses on the nature of performance environments and the way in which performance goals are typically articulated. The second is that, until recently, managerial and behavioral science knowledge had not produced a valid and realistic technology for changing and improving human performance—that is, one supported by theory,

evidence, and experience. But more on this later.

These four coping strategies are most likely to occur and to undermine the supervisor's ability to deal with poor performance when one or more of the following three conditions exist:

1. When statements of desired performance are ambiguous.
2. When public admission of poor performance is punished (for example, is politically dangerous).
3. When commitments to specific performance goals are avoided in order to maintain future flexibility and accessibility to opportunism.

Our final selection suggests some ways to deal with these processes.

COPING THROUGH CONSTRUCTIVE PERFORMANCE IMPROVEMENT

Coping with the poor performer involves at least four basic steps. First, what are the critical elements of the job that the worker must perform effectively? As noted earlier, some methods of identifying poor performance also lead to definitions of desired performance. But some do not. So in order to improve performance, we must go beyond merely identifying undesirable performance to specify what is better performance. In the process we can also reduce uncertainty and ambiguity. The second step is to make sure that managers are able to recognize effective performance when they see it. Rating errors must be recognized and reduced; inaccurate appraisals lead to employees' discouragement and apathy. Third, one must set specific goals for the employee. It has repeatedly been shown that specific goals that are difficult but attainable lead to effective outcomes. Finally, one must ensure that the consequences of goal attainment are positive for the employee, or the goals will not be accepted. What we are suggesting is that (1) a clearer, better definition of performance can be made, (2) rating errors and biases can be recognized and reduced, (3) goals can be set in behavioral or other terms that are fair, agreed upon, and assessable, and (4) commitment to these goals can be attained.

Defining Effectiveness

To motivate someone to improve productivity, it is first necessary to specify what the person must start doing, stop doing, or continue doing. That is, productivity must be defined in terms of what an individual employee is to do on the job. Traditionally, performance outcomes or personality traits have been used to evaluate performance; we have already evaluated the shortcomings of those measures. Recent literature places the emphasis on defining effectiveness on the basis of behavior, and we feel this procedure has promise.

Behavioral Measures

Measures of performance based on behavior can be related more directly to what the employee actually does, and they are more likely to minimize irrelevant factors that are not under the control of the employee than are cost-related measures or personality traits. Behavioral measures developed from a systematic job analysis can serve as indicators of such performance outcomes as units produced/work hours, attendance, accidents, and so forth. Great performance outcomes, such as high profits, do not come about through osmosis; someone must do something to create them. Behavioral measures based on a thorough job analysis indicate precisely what is being done by an employee to warrant recognition, discipline,

transfer, promotion, demotion, or termination. Thus behavioral measures not only define personality traits (for example, initiative) explicitly, but also encompass performance-related outcomes. For example, reducing costs by 10 percent, selling 52 cars in a month, and turning in a report on time are observable behaviors. What makes behavioral measures desirable from a productivity standpoint is that they measure the individual on things over which he or she has control and, most important, specify what the person must do or not do to attain these outcomes.

Developing accurate behavioral measures of performance begins with a thorough job analysis that identifies the strategies that one must take to impact an organization's bottom line. One of the most frequently used and straightforward job analysis procedures for developing behavioral measures is the critical incident technique (CIT). The CIT involves interviewing people who are aware of the aims and objectives of the job in question, who frequently observe job incumbents on the job, and who are capable of differentiating between competent and incompetent performance. The interviewees are asked to describe examples of effective and ineffective behavior that they observed in the past 12 months—behavior that was critical to doing the job effectively. The emphasis on the past 12 months ensures that the information obtained is applicable to the organization's current needs. For example, some behaviors that were effective for an engineer in the 1960s may no longer be effective in the 1980s.

In describing effective/ineffective incidents, an interviewee is asked to explain the circumstances surrounding a specific incident in which the behavior was demonstrated, exactly what was done, and how the behavior was effective or ineffective. Critical incidents that are similar, if not identical, are grouped together to form one behavioral item. For example, incidents in which a supervisor encouraged subordinates to work effectively with one another were used to develop the item: "Orally praises a subordinate for voluntarily helping another employee on any aspect of the job." Behavioral items that are similar are grouped together to form one criterion or yardstick for defining and measuring an employee's effectiveness. For example, items dealing with supervisory involvement with employees might be called "Interactions with Subordinates." Each behavioral item is rated on a scale of five points—with a particular rating dependent upon the frequency with which an employee engages in a behavior. Such scales are referred to as behavior observation scales (BOS). These scales possess several important advantages for improving performance. First, substantial input from employees goes into their development. Thus employees usually understand and are committed to the measures.

Second, BOS explicitly spell out behaviors an employee needs to perform a given job. As a job description, BOS can also be used as a realistic preview for job candidates by showing them what they will be expected to do on the job. Such previews are an effective means of reducing turnover because they give candidates enough knowledge to ascertain whether they would have the desire and ability to satisfactorily perform the job duties on a regular basis.

Third, the BOS facilitate fair appraisals because they let both supervisor and employee know what will be observed on the job. Through the job analysis, the BOS contain a representative sampling of the behaviors that are critical to performing effectively in the organization.

Finally, BOS facilitate explicit performance feedback because they encourage meaningful discussions between supervisor and employee about the latter's strengths and weaknesses. Generalities are avoided in favor of specific overt behaviors that the employee is encouraged to demonstrate on the job or for which he or she is praised. Explicit feedback using BOS combined with the setting of specific goals (to be discussed shortly) has repeatedly been shown to be effective in bringing about and/or maintaining positive behavior change.

However, while BOS are a preferred strategy for assessing performance, they are subject to human errors both in their development and in their administration. It is important to minimize these errors. What strategies are available?

Minimizing Rating Errors

Human judgment enters into every criterion of employee effectiveness, regardless of whether the criterion is an economic, trait, or behavioral measure. If feedback based on the measures is to serve as a motivator rather than a demotivator, careful observation is necessary. Unfortunately, most organizations assume that the careful construction of performance measures obviates the need to train supervisors how to observe, record, and evaluate objectively what they have seen. Because observers are usually unaware of their own rating errors, training is necessary or employees may be erroneously promoted, demoted, transferred, or terminated. Common rating errors may be based on contrast effects, halo, similar-to-me, leniency, and attributional biases.

The *contrast effects* error results from a rater's tendency to evaluate an employee in relation to others rather than on the job requirements. A typical outcome of this error occurred recently in an organization where an "average" manager in an exceptionally good department was laid off. An equally "average" manager who was doing exactly the same job, but in a poor department, was given additional responsibility and was subsequently promoted. Thus even though these two individuals had comparable job performances, one benefited from the mediocrity of peers, while the other suffered because of outstanding peers.

Halo error involves an overgeneralization from one aspect of a person's job performance to all aspects of the person's performance. For example, a person who is outstanding at inventory control may be rated inaccurately as outstanding in credit management, customer relations, and other aspects of the job in which performance is less than outstanding.

The *similar-to-me* error involves the tendency to judge those people who are similar to the rater in attitudes and background more favorably than those who are dissimilar, regardless of whether the similarity is job-related.

Raters who rate everyone at the high or the low end of the scale are guilty of *leniency* errors.

Finally, as we mentioned before, there are a number of judgment errors based on *attributional biases*. Supervisors tend to see the causes of poor performance as internal and to blame subordinates for failure to see this. Supervisors also tend to be biased by apologies or other irrelevant information (for example, outcomes).

What makes these errors insidious is that they appear to be well-developed rating habits resistant to change. People may continue to make them even after receiving lectures and warning on why the errors must be avoided. They continue to make them after receiving information on how to spot potential rating errors (for example, when one person is rated favorably on everything or when one evaluator rates everyone at the low end of an appraisal scale).

The only training program that is effective in minimizing rating error is one that incor-

porates three learning principles basic to bringing about a relatively permanent behavior change—that is, active participation, knowledge of results, and practice.

This means, first, that an effective program that reduces rating errors must allow trainees to rate individuals during the training process. (Simply giving a lecture or showing a film on how to serve a tennis ball is unlikely to increase the skill level of a novice tennis player.)

Second, the training program must provide immediate feedback on the accuracy of the trainee's rating. Discussion can then focus on what the trainee did correctly or incorrectly.

Finally, the training program must allow sufficient time for the trainee to practice the correct behavior. The literature tells of many unsuccessful five-minute to one-hour training programs that increased managers' observation skills only temporarily.

The probability of stimulating the employee's productivity is greatly decreased, and the probability of a discrimination charge is significantly increased if supervisory observations are inadequate, biased, or reported inaccurately.

One training program that is effective in reducing rating errors and increasing observer accuracy allows the trainees to view job applicants on videotape. They rate a job applicant on the basis of a job description distributed before they observe the applicant. The trainer then tells the trainees the correct rating. The discussion that follows focuses on (1) what the applicant was observed doing in the film to justify the rating, (2) examples of where each trainee has seen a given rating error in both on-the-job and off-the-job settings, and (3) ways to minimize the occurrence of each rating error.

Goal Setting

Once effective or ineffective performance can be described and defined and supervisors have been trained to recognize and record it accurately, the issue of improving performance can be addressed directly. Most current theories of performance motivation incorporate setting goals or specifying exactly what the individual should do on the job.

Goal setting is effective because it clarifies exactly what is expected of an individual. As several engineers have commented to us, "by receiving a specific goal from the supervisor we are able to determine for the first time what that *@?% really expects from us." Moreover, the process of working against an explicit goal injects interest into the task. It gives challenge and meaning to a job. When they attain their goals, people experience feelings of accomplishment and recognition (from self and/or supervisors and others).

When goals are set, the following points should be taken into account:

1. Setting specific goals leads to higher performance than adopting an attitude of "do your best." A specific score on each BOS should be specified as well as the key behavior or behaviors that the employee needs to work on to improve or maintain the score.

2. Employee participation in setting goals generally leads to higher goals than when the goal is unilaterally set by a supervisor.

3. The higher the goal, the higher the performance.

4. Performance feedback is critical to maintaining employee interest in the job, revision goals, and prolonging effort to attain them. Feedback reinforces goal setting.

5. If employees are evaluated on performance rather than goal attainment, they will continue to set high goals whether the goals are attained or not. High goals lead to higher performance levels than

do easy goals. If employees are evaluated on goal attainment rather than actual performance, they are likely to set low goals or reject higher goals imposed by supervisors.

6. The employee must have some latitude in influencing performance. Where performance is rigidly controlled by technology or work flow, as on the typical assembly line, goal setting is likely to have little effect.

7. Workers must not feel threatened by the prospect of job cuts—affecting their own jobs or the jobs of others—resulting from their increased performance under the goal-setting procedure. Most people are careful to avoid putting themselves or others out of work by being too productive.

These principles are basic to most management by objectives (MBO) programs. The primary difference between what we are saying here and what has been advocated by MBO enthusiasts is that the latter often emphasize the use of cost-related measures (for example, number of sales); we are arguing for the use of behavioral measures for *counseling/development/motivational purposes*. We have no objection to the use of MBO as a vehicle for planning where the organization, department, or individual should focus attention and efforts over the next three months, year, or five years. Nor do we have any objection to the inclusion of these objectives with behavioral measures. Cost-related objectives can clarify the context or situation in which the employee's behavior will be appraised. But it should not be surprising if the two sets of measures lead to different conclusions. As pointed out previously, environmental factors or organizational constraints beyond the employee's control may be preventing him or her from attaining satisfactory cost-related outcomes. BOS are helpful here because they alert the manager to look for organization-related obstacles if the employee is doing everything correctly. In instances where the cost-related outcomes are satisfactory despite unsatisfactory employee behavior, the satisfactory cost-related outcomes may be short-lived because other employees, subordinates, and/or clients may respond adversely to this behavior. After all, cost-related outcomes occur because people in the organization—virtually always more than one person—"did something." Accounting for what each person *did* is one of the purposes of developing behavioral measures. Finally, cost-related and behavioral measures may not correlate with each other because of recording errors on the part of the appraiser. This is why the training of rates is so important.

Insuring Goal Acceptance

A straightforward aid in understanding why an employee does or does not accept a goal is to draw up lists showing the good and bad consequences of desirable and undesirable behavior.

Head the first list "desirable behaviors." In a column to the right of that, list all positive consequences the employee gains from engaging in each desirable behavior and in a third column list all the negative consequences for each. One desirable behavior for a mechanic, for example, might be working ten hours instead of six. A positive consequence for him would be earning two additional hours of straight-time pay and two hours of overtime pay. Undesirable consequences of this behavior might be fatigue or arriving home later for dinner.

Head another list "undesirable behaviors" and repeat the process of showing positive and negative consequences of undesirable behavior. The results can provide the basis for an in-depth analysis of the consequences when you discuss them with the employees in question. This approach can provide a ra-

tional way to gain insight and develop hypotheses about why people behave the way they do. More important, it gives you the information you need to motivate subordinates to do what you want them to do by pointing up what consequences need to be changed in order to change their behavior. The approach is straightforward and costs little; however, the cost of changing the consequences sometimes exceeds the benefits of changing the behavior, in which case a change may not be advisable. The advantage of this approach is that one can estimate the costs knowing, with a high degree of certainty, that if the consequences are changed, the behavior involved will change accordingly.

Emery Air Freight successfully used this approach. The company was losing nearly $1 million annually because people on airport loading docks were shipping small packages separately rather than placing those with the same destination in one container that would be carried at lower rates by air carriers. Management found containers were being used 45 percent of the time when they should have been used 90 percent of the time. Instead of setting up a training program, management examined the positive consequences employees would enjoy if they loaded shipments properly. This analysis revealed that such behavior had no consequences of any kind (either positive or negative) at the time. Moreover, most employees believed they were performing efficiently.

The program required each employee to fill out a behavioral checklist similar in concept to BOS. Goals were set for each job—for example, to ship small packages with the same destination in a single container. All improvements in employee performance were reinforced by supervisory praise regardless of whether company goals were attained. Failure to attain a goal was assuaged by praise for honesty in reporting that failure. Thus was behavior shaped toward desired goals through praise, a positive consequence.

It is important to note that the positive consequences of engaging in a given behavior must be perceived immediately by the employee. If the consequences aren't immediate, their effectiveness decreases because the employee doesn't clearly see the connection between the consequences and the behavior. Even worse, delayed positive consequences may inadvertently reinforce inappropriate behaviors. For example, a new division manager in a start-up operation may initially perform at a high level. The organization may want to reward the manager with a salary increase. Unfortunately, final approval of salary increase may take months. By that time the manager's high level of performance may have diminished as a result of numerous frustrations, including the lack of reward. When the salary increase finally comes through, the manager is, in effect, being reinforced for mediocre performance.

In summary, a straightforward approach to coping with poor performance and enhancing productivity includes these four steps:

1. *Define performance behaviorally.* The manager must identify and define specific behavior or behaviors required of the employee on the job. The behavior must be pinpointed so that it can be reliably observed and recorded. Thus "Showing initiative" is not pinpointed— but "Calling on a customer without being asked by anyone" is. The ability to specify behavior in observable terms is the first skill managers must acquire before they can change or maintain an employee's performance.

2. *Train managers to reduce rating errors.* Rating errors are observers' errors in judgment that occur in a systematic

manner. These errors are insidious because observers are usually unaware that they are making them. And even if they are aware of the error, they are frequently unable to correct themselves. The end result can be an employee who is erroneously promoted, demoted, transferred, or terminated.

3. *Set specific goals.* Involving the employee in goal setting has two advantages: First, it increases an employee's understanding of what the job must accomplish, and second, it can lead to the setting of higher goals than those the supervisor would set unilaterally. The higher the goal, the higher the performance.

4. *Establish positive consequences for goal attainment.* If goals are to be accepted, the employee must perceive that goal attainment will lead to positive consequences.

CONCLUSION

What prescriptions flow from our analysis of reducing performance gaps and improving productivity? The process depicted here suggests several guidelines for managerial action:

1. Adopt a flexible posture toward identifying performance problems. At times, any one of the three comparisons we have described may be appropriate but, where possible, clear and specific behavioral goals can be used for comparisons across both people and time. Beyond the comparison processes, the limitations of people as information processors and decision makers must be recognized and accommodated when attempting to spot performance gaps.

2. Understand and use the knowledge of how people identify *causes* of poor per-

formance. Paying attention to attributional processes will make it easier to focus on ways to improve problem diagnosis and the problem-solving process.

3. Do not expect that people will always attack performance problems with constructive, proactive steps aimed at productivity improvement. It may be necessary to assist managers through the usual coping strategies that so frequently hinder direct confrontation and improvement of substandard performance. That is, pushing beyond denial, cover-up, and blame allocation for performance gaps may be necessary before performance problems can be confronted and solved.

4. Follow the steps toward constructive performance improvement; define desired outcomes behaviorally, set goals carefully, implement evaluation training to reduce assessment errors, encourage feedback, and make positive rewards for performance improvement.

Clearly, our analysis and prescriptions go well beyond the components of traditional performance appraisal systems and techniques. It is our belief that performance definition, diagnosis, appraisal, and improvement needs to be firmly anchored in what is currently known about people as observers of performance, as evaluators, and as facilitators of change. Such an orientation provides the best opportunity for advancing beyond generally unproductive and unrealistic techniques and strategies for improving productivity by developing an organization's human resources.

9

Productivity
and Leadership

Like a housewife's, a manager's work is never done.
ANDREW S. GROVE[1]

DEFINITIONS OF LEADERSHIP

Productivity requires good leadership. Leadership styles, and theories about them, vary. The question of what makes a good leader intrigues managers and scholars today as much as ever. Even the definition of "leadership" varies with the theory. Some theories say leaders are born with traits that make them different from the rest of us. Others say leadership comes with the position in an organization, not with the person. Still others say leadership depends on the situation. Some theories say people's behaviors, not traits, make them leaders.

LEADERSHIP THEORIES

No one really knows where leadership comes from. The question is an important one, though, because leadership affects an organization's productivity, and because managers have to choose "leadership styles" that will work for them. Familiarity with major theories about leadership can help managers to make that choice wisely.

Tannenbaum and Schmidt's Leadership Continuum

Tannenbaum and Schmidt[2] suggest that there is a continuum of seven leadership styles.

Leadership styles

The styles range from manager-centered to employee-centered leadership (see Figure 9–1). In the first style, the manager makes all the decisions and simply tells employees what these decision are. In the second style, the manager "sells" these decisions to the employees. The third style is a little more open, because the manager presents decisions to employees and invites questions, but still retains decision-making authority. In the fourth style, the manager presents tentative decisions and asks for employee input. This input may affect the manager's tentative decision. The fifth style is the first in which the manager's decision has not been made in advance. Here, the manager presents the problem to employees, gets their input and then makes the decision. In the sixth style, the manager defines the problem and the limits of its solution, but the whole group, of which the manager is a member, makes the decision. In the seventh style, the group shares authority equally with the manager, helping both to define and to solve the problem.

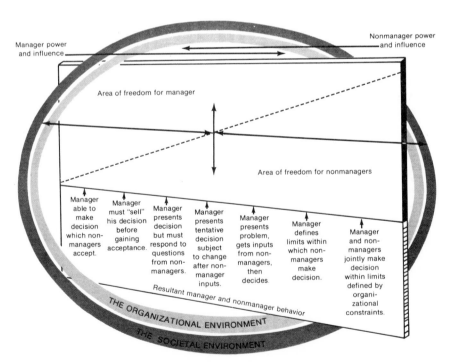

Figure 9–1. Continuum of Manager-Nonmanager Behavior

Forces

In choosing the "best" style, three forces must be considered: those within the manager, those within the employees, and those within the situation.

Forces within the manager are personal values, confidence in employees, leadership preferences, and the ability to deal with uncertainty. These forces determine the style which best suits the manager. For example, a manager who has a lot of confidence in employees will give them more decision-making power than a manager who has little confidence in employees.

Forces within the employees are their needs for independence and responsibility, tolerance for ambiguity, interest in the problem, knowledge base for solving it, identification with company goals, and interest in decision-making. This combination of forces determines which style best suits employees. If, for example, employees are very interested in a problem and are able to solve it, their input is more likely to be helpful than if they are neither interested nor qualified.

Forces within the situation are the type of organization, group effectiveness, the nature of the problem, and time pressures. These forces determine which style best fits the organization. For example, authoritative decision-making may be appropriate when time is short, as in an emergency, whereas longer timeframes allow for participative decision-making.

According to the Tannenbaum/Schmidt Leadership Continuum, the "best" of the seven leadership styles is the one that most effectively combines all three sets of forces at any given time.

Blake and Mouton's Managerial Grid

Blake and Mouton measure leadership styles on a two-dimensional Managerial Grid.[3] The horizontal dimension represents concern for people, and the vertical dimension represents concern for production. Each dimension is divided into nine units, or points.

A manager who scores "2" on production does not emphasize tasks as strongly as one who scores "8." The same applies to scores on concern for people. According to Blake and Mouton, a "9,9" style is most effective. This manager has high concern for both people and production. Other extreme points on the grid represent ineffective styles. A "9,1" manager has high concern for people but none for productivity. A "1,9" manager has high concern for productivity but none for people. A "1,1" manager does not care about either productivity or people.

While the "9,9" style is the ideal, time and other constraints force many managers to use a "5,5" style. This is a compromise in which concern for both people and productivity are reasonably high and nearly equal. Concern for both productivity and people leads to increased productivity.

Likert Systems 1–4

Likert's study of organizations[4] places leadership styles on a continuum ranging from "job-centered" to "employee-centered" behavior. He groups the range into four systems.

System 1

System 1 is exploitive-authoritative behavior. The manager tells employees what to do, assumes they are neither capable nor interested in doing good work and focuses on the finished product.

System 2

System 2 is benevolent-authoritative behavior. The manager still makes all the decisions, but pays more attention to employees' suggestions.

System 3

System 3 is consultative behavior. The manager consults with employees and seeks their ideas about decisions.

System 4

System 4 is participative-group behavior. The manager and employees jointly make decisions.

Likert says System 4 is the best leadership style in most situations. It calls for employees' involvement and results in employee satisfaction. His idea of the "best" leadership style does not change with individuals or situations.

Fiedler's Contingency Model

Fiedler's theory[5] measures leadership effectiveness in terms of group productivity. Satisfaction is a by-product, not a cause, of productivity. In Fiedler's model, two factors—type of leader and situation—determine the appropriate leadership style.

Type of leader

The first factor in Fiedler's model is the type of leader. A task-motivated leader values accomplishment. Satisfaction comes from the work itself and from knowing the manager did a good job. This leader may also value employees' feelings, but the task comes first. Relationship-motivated leaders, on the other hand, value employees' feelings. They are more prone to share decision-making responsibilities with employees and to want good relationships with them. These leaders seek admiration and support. Their focus on the task usually is secondary to relationships. Both task- and relationship-oriented leaders can be productive, but because of their orientations, their styles differ.

Situation

The other factor which affects leadership style in Fiedler's model is the situation.[6] When he says "situation," Fiedler means whether it is easy or hard for the manager to influence the group. Fiedler's research says task-oriented leaders generally are most effective in situations that are either strongly favorable or strongly unfavorable to the leader. Situations of intermediate favorableness call for a more human-relations orientation. The favorableness of the situation depends primarily on three conditions. The first is leader-employee relations, which can be extremely good, bad or somewhere in between. The second condition is task structure, and the third condition is the leader's position power. Structure refers to how well defined the job is, and position power refers to how much authority the manager has.

SOURCES OF LEADERSHIP POWER

The theories we have just discussed (and others) deal with factors affecting leadership styles. But style is only one side of the issue. The other is the group's willingness to accept someone as their leader. How do leaders get this power?

Formal Versus Informal Leadership

Chapter 7 talks about formal and informal roles. The same distinction applies to leadership. Formal leadership comes with the position on the organization chart. The *position* of manager means that the person in it has more decision-making authority than employees in lower spots—no matter who the manager is, or how effective the manager is. In a formal sense, all positions at the same level on the chart are equal.

But *informal* leadership is just the opposite. It resides in the person, not the position. Two managers may be on the same level of the organization chart, but one may have more power than the other. Or, an employee may be below a manager on the chart but, in day-to-day issues, have more power than the manager.

Forms of Power

What makes some people more powerful than others? There are several kinds of power.

Legitimate power

Legitimate power is the formal power discussed above. The position gives the person certain authority. And because a person occupies that position, subordinates respect the person's right to make certain decisions.[7]

Reward power

The ability to give rewards is closely tied to legitimate power, because it means the giver has access to valued resources. Rewards vary with people and situations. Some people may want more money as a reward, while others want more recognition or more choice assignments. If people do not value the rewards managers can give, managers have no power over them.

Coercive power

This is the converse of reward power. Coercive power means the ability to take away something a person values, or to give the person something negative. A manager may threaten to fire an employee. More subtly, the manager may assign the employee boring work, an inconvenient shift or an unattractive location.

Expert power

A person may know a lot about a subject. This knowledge gives that person power, if others believe that knowledge means ability.[8]

For example, when a company first gets computers, many young employees use them better than their managers. The employees' expertise—and the fact that the managers depend on it—gives them power to make decisions beyond the scope of their formal jobs.

Charisma

Charismatic power is the opposite of formal power. Instead of position, it depends on the leader's personality and the followers' needs.[9] The circumstances are also very important. The same personality, under different circumstances, may not be a leader at all.

Referent power

Referent power means that people want to be like the leader.[10] Charisma may be the cause, but so may specific qualities such as intelligence, helpfulness or status.

Leadership power takes several forms and comes from different sources. Most leaders have more than one source of power. Managers who have informal as well as formal power are very fortunate, because employees enjoy having them in charge—and voluntary support from employees means greater productivity.

LEADERSHIP ROLES

Leadership is fun, but certain responsibilities come with the job.

Organization and Group Goals

One of managers' main responsibilities is to make organization and group goals fit together. This is not as easy as it sounds. Organization goals may be too long-term or too vague for employees to understand. Yet employees need to understand organization goals if certain parts of their own jobs are to make sense.

Sometimes organization goals conflict with group goals. Suppose a manager spends $3,000 less on travel than was budgeted for the year. The savings helps organization profits, but it might mean the manager will get $3,000 less for next year's travel. This could hurt the group. Whose goals should the manager try to reach? Part of a manager's job is to coordinate company and group goals.

Constructive Feedback

Managers must tell each employee about job performance. Does the employee's work meet department goals? What is the quality of the work? What does the employee do well? Where does the employee need help?

Feedback can be tricky. It can improve employees' motivation and performance if it involves specific goals.[11] A manager may say, "Let's aim for you making three more units a day. Start with one more a day this week, go to two more next week, and see if you can make three more a day by the third week."

But feedback can also bring resentment. Managers sometimes feel uncomfortable about giving it. They may give it at the wrong time or turn it into criticism.[12] Effective feedback is constructive. It focuses on behaviors done well, new behaviors the employees should learn and ways in which they can learn these behaviors.

Employee Input

Good managers get ideas from their employees. To do this, a manager must be open and approachable. Employees have to feel comfortable about a manager before they can make suggestions.

Inspiration

Good leaders inspire their followers. Managers act as role models and set the example for employees. They also have access to many sources of power. Employees' needs, managers' access to resources, and leadership style all affect how much a manager inspires employees.

SUMMARY

Managers have many ways to become good leaders. But if they match their style with their group's needs, the result is always greater productivity.

SELECTED READINGS OVERVIEW

In the first reading, "Where Management Fails," Lester C. Thurow says that promotions and bonuses must be based on long-term, not short-term, profits if organizations want to gain employee loyalty and increase productivity. Under a short-term reward system, good decisions for individuals lead to poor decisions for society.

The second reading is "Releasing the Energy of Others—Making Things Happen." Here Malcolm S. Knowles argues that organizations are systems of human energy. Creative leaders release this energy more effectively than leaders who control. Eight behaviors characterize creative, "releasing" leaders.

Next Chapter

The next chapter deals with people's values and the relationship between values and behavior. Managers must recognize their own values and understand how values affect their leadership styles.

Review Questions

1. Why does productivity require long-term, rather than short-term, goals?
2. What behaviors fit Knowles's description of a "releasing" manager?
3. How does informal leadership affect formal leadership?
4. How can managers help themselves and their employees feel more comfortable about feedback?

LESTER C. THUROW

Where Management Fails

When American industries first started to fall behind their foreign competitors, the phenomenon was dismissed as isolated cases of bad luck. The American steel industry just happened to be slow in shifting to oxygen furnaces and continuous casting. Consumer electronics just happened to miss the significance of the transistor.

But as the list of industries—textiles, consumer electronics, steel, autos—that have been conquered or need government protection to survive has grown, it has become increasingly obvious that something is systematically wrong with American management. Not so long ago General Motors was commonly referred to as the "best-managed firm in America." Why couldn't the best-managed firm in American see the Japanese challenge coming and defeat it? *Fortune* magazine's current candidate for the best-managed firm in America, General Electric, has essentially become a marketer of foreign products in its consumer-electronics division. Why can't the best-managed firm in America compete with American-made products?

AMERICAN FAILURES

The foreign successes spring from two American failures. American managers have been unable to generate an environ-ment where the labor force takes a direct interest in raising productivity, and they have let their time horizons—the time over which projects must pay for themselves—become so short that they will not undertake the basic research and development, make the necessary investments, or build the service networks necessary for long-run survival.

Other factors, such as education and work attitudes, play a role, but a high-quality, well-motivated work force interested in raising productivity is ultimately a management responsibility. New labor-saving machines that lead to improvements in productivity typically mean layoffs in most American firms. Who is going to work to raise productivity if it means that they or their friends are going to be fired? In 1980 labor-force turnover averaged 4 percent per month in American manufacturing. Who can build a high-quality work force interested in the long-run prosperity of the firm when almost 50 percent of the labor force either quits or is laid off every year?

Whatever Americans decide about more or less government in the economy, government is not going to solve the productivity problem. Tax laws and other regulations can be improved, but foreign tax laws are always going to be just about as good as those in the United States. If American managers cannot generate a work force as interested in increasing productivity levels as those abroad, American industry will simply continue to get beaten. Productivity problems will be solved on the shop or office floor, or they will not be solved.

Management time horizons are short not because Americans are impatient or stupid, but because we have created an environment where it is individually rational for everyone to have a short time horizon. The chief executive officer (CEO) of every firm is worried about quarterly profits lest the financial markets saddle him with a low stock-market value and a hostile takeover bid aimed at eliminating his job. CEO's also typically get a bonus, based on current profits, that will end up being a substantial fraction of their own lifetime income, but they are typically CEO's for only five or six years. What short-term CEO will take a long-run view when it lowers his own income? Only a saint, and there aren't very many saints.

In many corporations middle-level managers have been set up as independent profit centers and promoted or demoted based on quarterly profits. Is it any surprise that middle management has a short time horizon?

INDIVIDUAL INCENTIVES

The net result is an economic environment where everyone is rationally responding to individual incentives, but the sum total of those individually smart decisions is social stupidity.

There is an obvious place, however, to begin attacking the problem. Those charged with the long-run survival of the firm, boards of directors, should stop giving chief executive officers a bonus based on current profits. If CEO's are to get a bonus based on profits, it should be a bonus based on the earnings of the firm in the ten years after they cease being CEO's. If CEO's, including those at financial firms, were paid based on the long-run profits of the firms they manage, the internal structure of the firms would soon change to lengthen the time horizons of both middle management and the financial markets.

MALCOLM S. KNOWLES

Emeritus Professor, North Carolina State University

Releasing the Energy of Others—Making Things Happen

Several years ago I began an intellectual adventure that has paid high dividends in terms of understanding the role of leadership and in selecting more effective leadership strategies. The adventure consisted of seeing what would happen if one conceptualized a social system (family, group, organization, agency, corporation, school, college, community, state, nation, or world) as a system of human energy.

All at once a set of questions very different from those typically asked by leaders started coming to mind: What is the sum total of the human energy available in the system? What proportion of this energy is now being used? Where is the unused energy located? Why is it not being tapped? What kinds of energy (physical, intellectual, psychic, moral, artistic, technical, social) are represented? What might be done to release this energy for accomplishing greater goals for the system and the individuals in it?

By virtue of simply asking these kinds of questions I began to have to think differently about the role of leadership. Having been raised in the era of Frederick Taylor's "scientific management," I had perceived the role of leadership to consist primarily of *controlling* followers or subordinates. Effective leaders, I had been taught, were those who were able to get people to follow their orders. The consequence of this doctrine was, of course, that the output of the system was limited to the vision and ability of the leader, and when I realized this fact I started rethinking the function of leadership. It gradually came to me that the highest function of leadership is *releasing* the energy of the people in the system and managing the processes for giving that energy direction toward mutually beneficial goals.

Perhaps a better way of saying this is that *creative leadership* is that form of leadership which releases the creative energy of the people being led.

In the intervening years since this way of thinking emerged in my mind I have been trying to understand it—and test its validity—in two ways. First, I have been observing leaders of various sorts (teachers, business executives, educational administrators, and organizational and political leaders) through this frame of reference. I have wanted to see if I could identify charac-

Reprinted from: *Journal of Management Development* 2, no. 2 (n.d.).

teristics that "releasing leaders" possess that "controlling leaders" don't have. Secondly, I have reexamined the research literature on human behavior, organizational dynamics, and leadership to find out what support it contains for this way of viewing the concept of leadership. I would like to share with you the results of this bifocal inquiry in the form of the following propositions regarding the behavioral characteristics of creative leaders.

1. *Creative leaders make a different set of assumptions—essentially positive—about human nature from the assumptions—essentially negative—made by controlling leaders.* It has been my observation that creative leaders have faith in people, offer them challenging opportunities, and delegate responsibility to them. Two of the clearest presentations of these contrasting assumptions in the literature are reproduced in Table I: by Douglas McGregor in the case of assumptions by managers and by Carl Rogers in the case of assumptions by educators.

    The validity of the positive set of assumptions is supported by research which indicates that when people perceive the locus of control to reside within themselves they are more creative and productive (Lefcourt, 1976) and that the more they feel their unique potential is being utilized the greater their achievement (Herzberg, 1966; Maslow, 1970).

2. *Creative leaders accept as a law of human nature that people feel a commitment to a decision in proportion to the extent that they feel they have participated in making it.* Creative leaders, therefore, involve their clients, workers, or students in every step of the planning process—assessing needs, formulating goals, designing lines of action, carrying

out activities, and evaluating results (except, perhaps, in emergencies). The validity of this proposition is supported by locus of control studies (Lefcourt, 1976) and by research on organizational change (Bennis, Benne, and Chin, 1968; Greiner, 1971; Lippitt, 1969; Martorana, 1975), administration (Baldridge, 1978; Dykes, 1968; Getzels, Lipham, and Campbell, 1968; Likert, 1967; McGregor, 1967), decision-making (Marrow, Bowers, and Seashore, 1968; Millet, 1968; Simon, 1961), and organizational dynamics (Argyris, 1962; Etzioni, 1961; Schein, 1965; Zander, 1977).

3. *Creative leaders believe in and use the power of self-fulfilling prophesy.* They understand that people tend to come up to other people's expectations for them. The creative coach conveys to his team that he knows they are capable of winning; the good supervisor's employees know that he or she has faith that they will do superior work; the good teacher's students are the best students in school. The classic study demonstrating this principle, Rosenthal and Jacobson's *Pygmalion in the Classroom* (1968), showed that the students of teachers who were told that they were superior students *were* superior students whereas the students of teachers who were told that they were inferior *were* inferior students. And, of course, there was no difference in the natural ability of the two groups of students. The relationship between positive self-concept and superior performance has been demonstrated in studies of students (Chickering, 1976; Felker, 1974; Rogers, 1969; Tough, 1979) and in general life achievement (Adams-Webber, 1979; Coan, 1974; Gale, 1974; Kelly, 1955; Loevinger, 1976; McClelland, 1975).

4. *Creative leaders highly value individuality.* They sense that people perform at a

Table I.   A Comparison of Assumptions About Human Nature
and Behaviour by Leaders in Management and Education

Theory X Assumptions about Human Nature (McGregor)* *(Controlling)*	*Assumptions Implicit in Current Education (Rogers)*** *(Controlling)*
The average human being inherently dislikes work and will avoid it if he can.	The student cannot be trusted to pursue his own learning.
Because of this characteristically human dislike of work, most people must be coerced, controlled, threatened in the interest of organizational objectives.	Presentation equals learning.
	The aim of education is to accumulate brick upon brick of factual knowledge.
	The truth is known.
The average human being prefers to be directed, wishes to avoid responsibility, has relatively little ambition, wants security above all.	Creative citizens develop from passive learners.
	Evaluation is education and education is evaluation.

Theory Y Assumptions about Human Nature *(Releasing)*	*Assumptions Relevant to Significant Experiential Learning* *(Releasing)*
The expenditure of physical and mental efforts is as natural as play or rest.	Human beings have a natural potentiality for learning.
External control and threat of punishment are not the only means for bringing about effort toward organizational objectives. Man will exercise self-direction and self-control in the service of objectives to which he is committed.	Significant learning takes place when the subject matter is perceived by the student as relevant to his own purposes.
	Much significant learning is acquired through doing.
Commitment to objectives is a function of the rewards associated with their achievement.	Learning is facilitated by student's responsible participation in the learning process.
The average human being learns, under proper conditions, not only to accept but to seek responsibility.	Self-initiated learning involving the whole person—feelings as well as intellect—is the most pervasive and lasting.
A high capacity for imagination, ingenuity, and creativity in solving organizational problems is widely, not narrowly distributed in the population.	Creativity in learning is best facilitated when self-criticism and self-evaluation are primary, and evaluation by others is of secondary importance.
Under the conditions of modern industrial life, the intellectual potential of the average human being is only partially utilized.	The most socially useful thing to learning in the modern world is the process of learning, a continuing openness to experience, and incorporation into oneself of the process of change.

*Adapted from McGregor (1960) pp. 33-34 and 47-48 in Knowles (1978) p. 102.
**Adapted from Rogers (1972) pp. 272-279 in Knowles (1978) p. 102.

higher level when they are operating on the basis of their unique strengths, talents, interests, and goals than when they are trying to conform to some imposed stereotype. They are comfortable with a pluralistic culture and tend to be bored with one that is monolithic. As managers they encourage a team arrangement in which each member works at what he or she does best and enjoys most; as teachers they strive to tailor the learning strategies to fit the individual learning styles, paces, starting points, needs, and interests of all the students. This proposition is widely supported in the research literature (Combs and Snygg, 1959; Csikzentmihaly, 1975; Erikson, 1974; Goldstein and Blackman, 1978; Gowan, et al, 1967; Kagan, 1967; Maslow, 1971; Messick, et al, 1976; Moustakas, 1974; Tyler, 1978).

We should add another dimension to this proposition—more of a philosophical note than a behavioral observation. It is that creative leaders probably have a different sense of the purpose of life from that of the controlling leaders. They see the purpose of all life activities—work, learning, recreation, civic participation, worship—to be to enable each individual to achieve his or her full and unique potential. They seek to help each person become what Maslow (1970) calls a self-actualizing person, whereas the controlling leader's mission is to produce conforming persons.

5. *Creative leaders stimulate and reward creativity.* They understand that in a world of accelerating change creativity is a basic requirement for the survival of individuals, organizations, and societies. They exemplify creativity in their own behaviour and provide an environment that encourages and rewards innovation in others. They make it legitimate for people to experiment, and treat failures as opportunities to learn rather

than as acts to be punished. (Baron, 1963; Bennis, 1966; Cross, 1976; Davis and Scott, 1971; Gardner, 1963; Gowan, et al, 1967; Herzberg, 1966; Ingalls, 1976; Kagan, 1967; Schon, 1971; Toffler, 1974; Zahn, 1966).

6. *Creative leaders are committed to a process of continuous change and are skillful in managing change.* They understand the difference between static and innovative organizations as portrayed in Table II, and aspire to make their organizations the latter. They are well grounded in the theory of change and skillful in selecting the most effective strategies for bringing about change (Arends and Arends, 1977; Baldridge and Deal, 1975; Bennis, Benne, and Chin, 1968; Goodlad, 1975; Greiner, 1971; Hefferlin, 1969; Hornstein, et al, 1971; Lippitt, 1973; Mangham, 1978; Martorana and Kuhns, 1975; Schein and Bennis, 1965; Tedeschi, 1972; Zurcher, 1977).

7. *Creative leaders emphasize internal motivators over external motivators.* They understand the distinction revealed in Herzberg's (1959) research between satisfiers (motivators)—such as achievement, recognition, fulfilling work, responsibility, advancement, and growth—and dissatisfiers (hygienic factors), such as organizational policy and administration, supervision, working conditions, interpersonal relations, salary, status, job security, and personal life. They take steps to minimize the dissatisfiers but concentrate their energy on optimizing the satisfiers. This position is strongly supported by subsequent research (Levinson, Price, et al, 1963; Likert, 1967; Lippitt, 1973).

8. *Creative leaders encourage people to be self-directing.* They sense intuitively what researchers have been telling us for some time—that a universal charac-

Table II. Some Characteristics of Static vs. Innovative Organizations

DIMENSIONS	CHARACTERISTICS	
	Static Organizations	*Innovative Organizations*
Structure	Rigid—much energy given to maintaining permanent departments, committees; reverence for tradition, constitution & by laws.	Flexible—much use of temporary task forces; easy shifting of departmental lines; readiness to change constitution, depart from tradition.
	Hierarchical—adherence to chair of command.	Multiple linkages based on functional collaboration.
	Roles defined narrowly.	Roles defined broadly.
	Property-bound.	Property-mobile.
Atmosphere	Task-centered, impersonal.	People-centered, caring.
	Cold, formal, reserved.	Warm, informal, intimate.
	Suspicious.	Trusting.
Management Philosophy and Attitudes	Function of management is to control personnel through coercive power.	Function of management is to release the energy of personnel; power is used supportively.
	Cautious—low risk-taking.	Experimental—high risk-taking.
	Attitude toward errors: to be avoided.	Attitude toward errors: to be learned from.
	Emphasis on personnel selection.	Emphasis on personal development.
	Self-sufficiency—closed system regarding sharing resources.	Interdependency—open system regarding sharing resources.
	Low tolerance for ambiguity.	High tolerance for ambiguity.
Decision-Making and Policy-Making	High participation at top, low at bottom.	Relevant participation by all those affected.
	Clear distinction between policy-making and policy-execution.	Collaborative policy-making and policy-execution.
	Decision-making by legal mechanisms.	Decision-making by problem-solving.
	Decisions treated as final.	Decisions treated as hypotheses to be tested.
Communication	Restricted flow—constipated.	Open flow—easy access.
	One-way—downward.	Multidirectional—up, down, sideways.
	Feelings repressed or hidden.	Feelings expressed.

teristic of the maturation process is movement from a state of dependency toward states of increasing self-directedness (Baltes, 1978; Erikson, 1950, 1959, 1964, 1974; Goulet and Baltes, 1970; Gubrium and Buckholdt, 1977; Havighurst, 1970; Kagan and Moss, 1962; Loevinger, 1976; Rogers, 1961).

They realize that because of previous conditioning as dependent learners in their school experience, adults need initial help in learning to be self-directing and look to leaders for this kind of help (Kidd, 1973; Knowles, 1975, 1978, 1980; Tough, 1967, 1979). And to provide this kind of help, they have developed their skills as facilitators and consultants to a high level (Bell and Nadler, 1979; Blake and Mouton, 1976; Bullmer, 1975; Carkhuff, 1969; Combs, et al, 1978; Lippitt and Lippitt, 1978; Laughary and Ripley, 1979; Pollack, 1976; Schein, 1969; Schlossberg, et al, 1978).

No doubt additional propositions and behavioral characteristics could be identified, but these are the ones than stand out in my observation of creative leaders and review of the literature as being most central. And I have seen wonderful things happen when they have been put into practice. I have seen low-achieving students become high-achieving students when they discovered the excitement of self-directed learning

under the influence of a creative teacher. I have seen bench workers in a factory increase their productivity and get a new sense of personal pride and fulfillment under a creative supervisor. I have seen an entire college faculty become creative facilitators of learning and content resource consultants through the stimulation of a creative administration. And I have observed several instances in which the line managers of major corporations moved from controlling managers to releasing managers when their management-development programs were geared to these propositions.

Perhaps we are on the verge of beginning to understand how to optimize the release of the enormous pent-up energy in our human energy systems.

PART FOUR

Culture and Climate

10

Productivity and Values

[An organization's] purpose is defined more nearly by the aggregate of action taken than by any formulation in words.

CHESTER BARNARD[1]

PEOPLE AND VALUES[1]

Good leaders relate well to their followers. One reason may be that they know what matters to people—what their values are. People do not carry around lists of values. People do not always know what they believe in until they have to make a choice or solve a problem. By serving as benchmarks, values affect how people perceive each other.[2] They also affect what people take for granted and how they act. Whether people work productively depends in large measure on individual and organization values.

CULTURAL VALUES

Values form the heart of a culture. Society consists of many subcultures, based on age, profession, ethnic background, educational level, relationships, personal interests, religion, geography, and other common bonds.

Herzberg's "Immigrants"

Each subculture has its own values. According to Herzberg, today's work force has three groups of "immigrants" whose values conflict with each other's.[3] "External" immigrants value hard work, material rewards and

217

traditional male and female roles. "Organization man" immigrants value efficiency, "one-upsmanship" and the chance to become "president of something." "Internal" immigrants—women and minorities—value personal significance and the right to hold certain positions at work. Because members of all three groups believe their values are "right," many conflicts may result when they try to work together.

Massey's Generations

Massey[4] says values vary with generations. "Traditionalists," born in the 1920s and 1930s, value close families, traditional roles, financial security stability, and the work ethic. "Rejectionists," born in the 1950s, value individuality, sensual experience and equality based on performance. The values of "in-betweeners," born in the 1940s, can go either way. "Synthesizers," born in the 1960s and later, combine values from many different areas. They are in the work force now, with their own unique values. For managers, the challenge is how to get people with different values to work together productively.

Companies

Like other subcultures, organizations have their own values. Managers' day-to-day actions tell employees what these values are.[5] Managers may *say* they value new ideas and creativity, but instead may *reward* ideas that fit "the way we've always done things here." Employees learn quickly what behaviors managers reward. In this example, employees would keep new ideas to themselves and make suggestions that supported the status quo.

VALUES IN ORGANIZATIONS

Chapter 7 discusses the interaction among individuals' norms, values and productivity in work groups. The same interaction takes place, on a larger scale, at the organization level.

In a firm, top management's personal values help determine corporate strategy.[6] A manager's values come from family, education and experience. Actions, and choices about what behaviors to reward, come in turn from these values.

Formal

When values are formalized, they are called "policies." An example is Sears' emphasis on customer satisfaction. This policy—satisfaction or your money back—means that the firm will resolve customer complaints even at the expense of profits. Company policy is a framework for making decisions. One firm may have a policy of promoting from within, while another's policy may be to hire new managers from outside. When openings occur, each company's managers already "know" where to look for people.

Companies do not claim policies are "right" or "wrong." In the example above, the firms' managers have different values about employees, promotions and rewards. Company policies are official, formal expressions of these values.

Informal

Values filter down to other managers and employees. In the process, though, they change. Often there is room, within company policy, for people to make judgments based on their own values. For example, company policy may say to promote from within, but managers may still use their own standards to choose the best employee.

Conflict

Sometimes personal values conflict with those of the company. When this happens, should people try to impose their values on the firm, or should they give up their own values? The kinds of compromises people make depend on many things—how strongly they hold their values, how politically powerful they are, whom they know, how important the issue is, and what the consequences are.

Certain practices may not match company policy. Managers and employees find shortcuts, unofficial channels and other informal ways to do their work. Informal practices may override official policy on a day-do-day basis, just as informal leadership may override formal leadership. But, as with leadership, company policy takes over whenever problems or crises occur.

Change

Over time, values change because of informal processes. People with different values form coalitions, and the coalitions change over time. Outside pressures may affect top management's values. Power shifts among groups. At any point in time, some people are happier than others about current values.[7]

VALUES AND BEHAVIOR

Values affect people's decisions and actions. Although people already have their own personal values by the time they take a job, their work may influence these values.

Managers

According the Guth and Tagiuri,[8] managers fall into six categories, based on their values. The first is the theoretical manager, whose values emphasize truth and knowledge. This manager may want even more information than is needed to make decisions, because decisions represent truth and knowledge.

The second category is the economic manager, who values whatever is useful. This manager may get information from many sources or may overlook material that is interesting but not useful.

The third manager is political and values power. This manager chooses information and associates on the basis of how much power they provide.

The fourth type is the aesthetic manager, who values form and harmony. To this manager, appearances and cooperation may be more important than "best" answers.

The fifth category is the social manager, who values people. This manager may put people's feelings ahead of work output.

The religious manager is the sixth type. This manager values unity in the universe, and may believe very strongly in personal convictions. Managers' decisions and behaviors depend on their orientations.

Employees

Employees' values affect how they work. If their values match management's, productivity can be high. Part of management's job is to know employees' values and try to make the work match these values.

As employees become more educated and, on the average, older, their expectations of work change. In the past, job enrichment—in which employees had more to say about their job duties—helped to humanize work. Nowadays, *employment* enrichment includes flexible work schedules, dynamic rather than rigid policies, employee enrichment programs, and optional benefits packages.[9]

Values as Guides

Managers reward employees in many ways. Company policy may define the range of pay increases, promotions, vacations, educational opportunities and other rewards. But managers still determine who gets these rewards. They are also free to use praise, recognition, work schedules, and job assignments as rewards.

Who gets the rewards? Company values serve as guidelines here. Company values help managers define "good" performance. Managers' personal values also affect their decisions, but people who have become managers are likely to have values similar to those of the firm.

If people's values are so complex, and if there are so many different value systems today, how can managers increase employee productivity?

Sinetar says management's challenge is to give employees a chance to find self-actualization through work.[10] Herzberg says one value applies to everyone:

> . . . the basic need of human beings to be needed. People want to be responsible and efficient when they can perceive that their work serves a meaningful purpose.[11]

SUMMARY

Managers must coordinate their own, their firm's and their employees' values. At work, values determine behavior and affect productivity. Effective managers get productive work from employees with diverse sets of values, by recognizing different values and adjusting rewards accordingly. Values and behavior have a complex relationship.

SELECTED READING OVERVIEW

This chapter's reading is "Fitting New Employees Into the Company Culture," by Richard Pascale. It deals with the issue of socialization, the process through which new employees "learn the ropes" about a firm. Few companies talk about this process, and many may be unaware of how it takes place. At the same time, American tradition resists "manipulation of individuals for organizational purposes." Everyone would benefit from more explicit descriptions of what behaviors companies want from them.

Next Chapter

The next chapter deals with the development of people within organizations. Through this development, companies increase the personal satisfaction of employees and the productivity of the firm.

Review Questions

1. Why is it important for new employees to be "socialized" in terms of company values?
2. How do values affect people's behavior at work?
3. Identify several values of your own generation, and explain how you would deal with them if you were a manager.

RICHARD PASCALE

Fitting New Employees Into the Company Culture

Many of the best-managed companies in America are particularly skillful at getting recruits to adopt the corporate collection of shared values, beliefs, and practices as their own. Here's how they do it, and why indoctrination need not mean brainwashing.

What corporate strategy was in the 1970s, corporate culture is becoming in the 1980s. Companies worry about whether theirs is right for them, consultants hawk advice on the subject, executives wonder if there's anything in it that can help them manage better. A strong culture—a set of shared values, norms, and beliefs that get everybody heading in the same direction—is common to all the companies held up as paragons in the best-seller *In Search of Excellence*.

There is, however, one aspect of culture that nobody seems to want to talk about. This is the process by which newly hired employees are made part of a company's culture. It may be called learning the ropes, being taught "the way we do things here at XYZ Corp.," or simply training. Almost no

Richard Pascale is a consultant, a lecturer at the Stanford Business School, and the co-author of *The Art of Japanese Management*.

one calls it by its precise social-science name—socialization.

To American ears, attuned by Constitution and conviction to the full expression of individuality, socialization tends to sound alien and vaguely sinister. Some equate it with the propagation of socialism—which it isn't—but even when it is correctly understood as the development of social conformity, the prospect makes most of us cringe. How many companies caught up in the corporate culture fad will be quite as enthusiastic when they finally grasp that "creating a strong culture" is a nice way of saying that employees have to be more comprehensively socialized?

The tradition at most American corporations is to err in the other direction, to be culturally permissive, to let employees do their own thing to a remarkable degree. We are guided by a philosophy, initially articulated by John Locke, Thomas Hobbes, and

Adam Smith, that says that individuals free to choose make the most efficient decisions. The independence of the parts makes for a greater sum. Trendy campaigns to build a strong corporate culture run into trouble when employees are asked to give up some of their individuality for the common good.

The crux of the dilemma is this: We are opposed to the manipulation of individuals for organizational purposes. At the same time we increasingly realize that a degree of social uniformity enables organizations to work better. One need not look to Japan to see the benefits of it. Many of the great American companies that thrive from one generation to the next—IBM, Procter & Gamble, Morgan Guaranty Trust—are organizations that have perfected their processes of socialization. Virtually none talk explicitly about socialization; they may not even be conscious of precisely what they are doing. Moreover, when one examines any particular aspect of their policy toward people—how they recruit or train or compensate—little stands out as unusual. But when the pieces are assembled, what emerges is an awesome internal consistency that powerfully shapes behavior.

It's time to take socialization out of the closet. If some degree of it is necessary for organizations to be effective, then the challenge for managers is to reconcile this necessity with traditional American independence.

Probably the best guide available on how to socialize people properly is what the IBMs and the P&Gs actually do. Looking at the winners company by company, one finds that, with slight variations, they all put new employees through what might be called the seven steps of socialization:

Step one. The company subjects candidates for employment to a selection process so rigorous that it often seems designed to discourage individuals rather than encourage them to take the job. By grilling the applicant, telling him or her the bad side as well as the good, and making sure not to oversell, strong-culture companies prod the job applicant to take himself out of contention if he, who presumably knows more about himself than any recruiter, thinks the organization won't fit his style and values.

Consider the way Proctor & Gamble hires people for entry level positions in brand management. The first person who interviews the applicant is drawn not from the human resources department, but from an elite cadre of line managers who have been trained with lectures, videotapes, films, practice interviews, and role playing. These interviewers use what they've learned to probe each applicant for such qualities as the ability to "turn out high volumes of excellent work," to "identify and understand problems," and to "reach thoroughly substantiated and well-reasoned conclusions that lead to action." Initially, each candidate undergoes at least two interviews and takes a test of his general knowledge. If he passes, he's flown to P&G headquarters in Cincinnati, where he goes through a day of one-on-one interviews and a group interview over lunch.

The New York investment banking house of Morgan Stanley encourages people it is thinking of hiring to discuss the demands of the job with their spouses, girlfriends, or boyfriends—new recruits sometimes work 100 hours a week. The firm's managing directors and their wives take promising candidates and their spouses or companions out to dinner to bring home to them what they will face. The point is to get a person who will not be happy within Morgan's culture because of the way his family feels to eliminate himself from the consideration for a job there.

This kind of rigorous screening might seem an invitation to hire only people who fit the mold of present employees. In fact, it often *is* harder for companies with strong cultures to accept individuals different from the prevailing type.

Step two.   The company subjects the newly hired individual to experiences calculated to induce humility and to make him question his prior behavior, beliefs, and values. By lessening the recruit's comfort with himself, the company hopes to promote openness toward its own norms and values.

This may sound like brainwashing or boot camp, but it usually just takes the form of pouring on more work than the newcomer can possibly do. IBM and Morgan Guaranty socialize with training programs in which, to quote one participant, "You work every night until 2 A.M. on your own material, and then help others." Procter & Gamble achieves the same result with what might be called upending experiences—requiring a recent college graduate to color in a map of sales territories, for example. The message is clear: while you may be accomplished in many respects, you are in kindergarten as far as what you know about this organization.

Humility isn't the only feeling brought on by long hours of intense work that carry the individual close to his or her limit. When everybody's vulnerability runs high, one also tends to become close to one's colleagues. Companies sometimes intensify this cohesiveness by not letting trainees out of the pressure cooker for very long—everyone has so much work to do that he doesn't have time to see people outside the company or reestablish a more normal social distance from his co-workers.

Morgan Stanley, for instance, expects newly hired associates to work 12- to 14-hour days and most weekends. Their lunches are not the Lucullan repasts that MBAs fantasize about, but are typically confined to 30 minutes in the unprepossessing cafeteria. One can observe similar patterns —long hours, exhausting travel schedules, and almost total immersion in casework—at law firms and consulting outfits. Do recruits chafe under such discipline? Not that much, apparently. Socialization is a bit like exercise—it's probably easier to reconcile yourself to it while you're young.

Step three.   Companies send the newly humble recruits into the trenches, pushing them to master one of the disciplines at the core of the company's business. The newcomer's promotions are tied to how he does in that discipline.

In the course of the individual's first few months with the company, his universe of experience has increasingly narrowed down to the organization's culture. The company, having got him to open his mind to its way of doing business, now cements that orientation by putting him in the field and giving him lots of carefully monitored experience. It rewards his progress with promotions at predictable intervals.

While IBM hires some MBAs and a few older professionals with prior work experience, almost all of them start at the same level as recruits from college and go through the same training programs. It takes about 15 years, for example, to become a financial controller. At Morgan Stanley and consulting firms like McKinsey, new associates must similarly work their way up through the ranks. There is almost never a quick way to jump a few rungs on the ladder.

The gains from this approach are cumulative. For starters, when all trainees understand there is just one step-by-step career path, it reduces politicking. Since they are being evaluated on how they do over the long haul, they are less tempted to cut corners or go for short-term victories. By the time they reach senior positions they understand the business not as a financial abstraction, but as a reality of people they know and skills they've learned. They can communicate with people in the lowest ranks in the shorthand of shared experience.

Step four. At every stage of the new manager's career, the company measures the operating results he has achieved and rewards him accordingly. It does this with systems that are comprehensive and consistent. These systems focus particularly on those aspects of the business that make for competitive success and for the perpetuation of the corporation's values.

Procter & Gamble, for instance, measures managers on three factors it deems critical to a brand's success: building volume, building profit, and conducting planned change—altering a product to make it more effective or more satisfying to the customer in some other way. Information from the outside world—market-share figures, say—is used in the measuring along with financial data. Performance appraisals focus on these criteria as well as on general managerial skill.

IBM uses similar interlocking systems to track adherence to one of its major values, respect for the dignity of the individual. The company monitors this with surveys of employee morale; "Speak Up," a confidential suggestion box; a widely proclaimed policy of having the boss's door open to any subordinates who want to talk; so-called skip-level interviews, in which a subordinate can skip over a couple of organizational levels to discuss a grievance with senior management; and informal social contacts between senior managers and lower level employees. Management moves quickly when any of these systems turns up a problem.

The IBM culture includes a mechanism for disciplining someone who has violated one of the corporate norms—handling his subordinates too harshly, say, or being overzealous against the competition. The malefactor will be assigned to what is called the penalty box—typically, a fairly meaningless job at the same level, sometimes in a less desirable location. A branch manager in Chicago might be moved to a nebulous staff position at headquarters. To the outsider, penalty box assignments look like just an-other job rotation, but insiders know that the benched manager is out of the game temporarily.

The penalty box provides a place to hold a manager while the mistakes he's made and the hard feelings they've engendered are gradually forgotten. The mechanism lends substance to the belief, widespread among IBM employees, that the company won't fire anybody capriciously. The penalty box's existence says, in effect, that in the career of strong, effective managers there are times when one steps on toes. The penalty box lets someone who has stepped too hard contemplate his error and return to play another day.

Step five. All along the way, the company promotes adherence to its transcendent values, those overarching purposes that rise way above the day-to-day imperative to make a buck. At the AT&T of yore, for example, the transcendent value was guaranteeing phone service to customers through any emergency. Identification with such a value enables the employee to accept the personal sacrifices the company asks of him.

Placing oneself at the service of an organization entails real costs. There are long hours of work, weekends apart from one's family, bosses one has to endure, criticism that seems unfair, job assignments that are inconvenient or undesirable. The countervailing force making for commitment to the company in these circumstances is the organization's set of transcendent values that connect its purpose to human values of a higher order than just those of the marketplace—values such as serving mankind, providing a first-class product for society, or helping people learn and grow.

Someone going to work for Delta Air Lines will be told again and again about the "Delta family feeling." Everything that's said makes the point that Delta's values sometimes require sacrifices—management takes pay cuts during lean times, senior flight attendants and pilots voluntarily work fewer hours per week so the company won't have to lay off more-junior employees. Candidates who accept employment with Delta tend to buy into this quid pro quo, agreeing in effect that keeping the Delta family healthy justifies the sacrifices that the family exacts.

Step six.   The company constantly harps on watershed events in the organization's history that reaffirm the importance of the firm's culture. Folklore reinforces a code of conduct—how we do things around here.

All companies have their stories, but at corporations that socialize well the morals of these stories all tend to point in the same direction. In the old Bell System, story after story extolled Bell employees who made heroic sacrifices to keep the phones working. The Bell folklore was so powerful that when natural disaster struck, all elements of a one-million-member organization were able to pull together, cut corners, violate normal procedures, even do things that would not look good when measured by usual job performance criteria—all in the interest of restoring phone service. Folklore, when well understood, can legitimize special channels for moving an organization in a hurry.

Step seven.   The company supplies promising individuals with role models. These models are consistent—each exemplary manager displays the same traits.

Nothing communicates more powerfully to younger professionals within an organization than the example of peers or superiors who are recognized as winners and who also share common qualities. The protégé watches the role model make presentations, handle conflict, and write memos, then tries to duplicate the traits that seem to work most effectively.

Strong-culture firms regard role models as constituting the most powerful long-term

training program available. Because other elements of the culture are consistent, the people who emerge as role models are consis-
tent. P&G's brand managers, for example, exhibit extraordinary consistency in several traits—they're almost all analytical, energetic, and adept at motivating others. Unfortunately most firms leave the emergence of role models to chance. Some on the fast track seem to be whizzes at analysis, others are skilled at leading people, others seem astute at politics: the result for those below is confusion as to what it *really* takes to succeed. For example, the companies that formerly made up the Bell System have a strong need to become more market oriented and aggressive. Yet the Bell culture continues to discriminate against potential fast-trackers who, judged by the values of the older monopoly culture, are too aggressive.

Many companies can point to certain organizational practices that look like one or two of the seven steps, but rarely are all seven managed in a well-coordinated effort. It is *consistency* across all seven steps of the socialization process that results in a strongly cohesive culture that endures.

When one understands the seven steps, one can better appreciate the case for socialization. All organizations require a degree of order and consistency. They can achieve this through explicit procedures and formal control or through implicit social controls. American companies, on the whole, tend to rely more on formal controls. The result is that management often appears rigid, bureaucratic, and given to oversteering. A United Technologies executive laments, "I came from the Bell system. Compared with AT&T, this is a weak culture and there is little socialization. But of course there is still need for controls. So they put handcuffs on you, shackle you to every nickel, track every item of inventory, monitor every movement in production and head count. They control you by the balance sheet."

At most American companies, an inordinate amount of energy gets used up on fighting "the system." But when an organization can come up with a strong, consistent set of implicit understandings, it has effectively established for itself a body of common law to supplement its formal rules. This enables it to use formal systems as they are supposed to be used—as tools rather than straitjackets. An IBM manager, conversant with the concept of socialization, puts it this way: "Socialization acts as a fine-tuning device; it helps us make sense out of the procedures and quantitative measures. Any number of times I've been faced with a situation where the right thing for the measurement system was X and the right thing for IBM was Y. I've always been counseled to tilt toward what was right for IBM in the long term and what was right for our people. They pay us a lot to do that. Formal controls, without coherent values and culture, are too crude a compass to steer by."

Organizations that socialize effectively use their cultures to manage ambiguity, ever present in such trick matters as business politics and personal relationships. This tends to free up time and energy. More goes toward getting the job done and focusing on external considerations like the competition and the customer. "At IBM you spend 50% of your time managing the internal context," states a former IBMer, now at ITT. "At most companies it's more like 75%." A marketing manager who worked at Atari before it got new management recalls: "You can't imagine how much time and energy around here went into politics. You had to determine who was on first base this month in order to figure out how to obtain what you needed to get the job done. There were no rules. There were no clear values. Two of the men at the top stood for diametrically opposite things.

Your bosses were constantly changing. All this meant that you never had time to develop a routine way for getting things done at the interface between your job and the next guy's. Without rules for working with one another, a lot of people got hurt, got burned out, and were never taught the 'Atari way' of doing things because there wasn't an Atari way."

The absence of cultural guidelines makes organizational life capricious. This is so because success as a manager requires managing not only the substance of the business but also, increasingly, managing one's role and relationships. When social roles are unclear, no one is speaking the same language; communication and trust break down. A person's power to get things done in a company seldom depends on his title and formal authority alone. In great measure it rests on his track record, reputation, knowledge, and network of relationships. In effect, the power to implement change and execute business strategies depends heavily on what might be called one's social currency—as in money—something a person accumulates over time. Strong-culture firms empower employees, helping them build this currency by supplying continuity and clarity.

Continuity and clarity also help reduce the anxiety people feel about their careers. Mixed signals about rewards, promotions, career paths, criteria for being on the "fast track" or a candidate for termination inevitably generate a lot of gossip, game playing, and unproductive expenditure of energy. Only the naive think that these matters can be entirely resolved by provisions in a policy manual. The reality is that many criteria of success for middle- and senior-level positions can't be articulated in writing. The rules tend to be communicated and enforced via relatively subtle cues. When the socialization process is weak, the cues tend to be poorly or inconsistently communicated.

Look carefully at career patterns in most companies. Ambitious professionals strive to learn the ropes, but there are as many "ropes" as there are individuals who have made their way to the top. So the aspirant picks an approach, and if it happens to coincide with how his superiors do things, he's on the fast track. Commonly, though, the approach that works with one superior is offensive to another. "As a younger manager, I was always taught to touch bases and solicit input before moving ahead," a manager at a Santa Clara, California, electronics firm says, "and it always worked. But at a higher level, with a different boss, my base-touching was equated with being political. The organization doesn't forewarn you when it changes signals. A lot of good people leave owing to misunderstandings of this kind." The human cost of the failure to socialize tends to go largely unrecognized.

What about the cost of conformity? A senior vice president of IBM asserts: "Conformity among IBM employees has often been described as stultifying in terms of dress, behavior, and lifestyle. There is, in fact, strong pressure to adhere to certain norms of superficial behavior, and much more intensely to the three tenets of the company philosophy —respect for the dignity of the individual, first-rate customer service, and excellence. These are the benchmarks. Between them there is a wide latitude for divergence in opinions and behavior."

A P&G executive echoes this thought: "There is a great deal of consistency around here in how certain things are done, and these are rather critical to our sustained success. Beyond that, there are very few hard and fast rules. People on the outside might portray our culture as imposing lock-step uniformity. It doesn't feel rigid when you're inside. It feels like it accommodates you. And best of all, you know the game you're in—you know whether you're playing soccer or football; you can find out very clearly

what it takes to succeed and you can bank your career on that."

It is useful to distinguish here between norms that are central to the business's success and social conventions that signal commitment and belonging. The former are essential in that they ensure consistency in executing the company's strategy. The latter are the organizational equivalent of shaking hands. They are social conventions that make it easier for people to be comfortable with one another. One need not observe all of them, but one wants to reassure the organization that one is on the team. An important aspect of this second set of social values is that, like a handshake, they are usually not experienced as oppressive. Partly this is because adherence doesn't require much thought or deliberation, just as most people don't worry much about their individuality being compromised by the custom of shaking hands.

The aim of socialization is to establish a base of shared attitudes, habits, and values that foster cooperation, integrity, and communication. But without the natural rough-and-tumble friction between competing coworkers, some might argue, there will be little innovation. The record does not bear this out. Consider 3M or Bell Labs. Both are highly innovative institutions—and both remain so by fostering social rules that reward innovation. Socialization does not necessarily discourage competition between employees. Employees compete hard at IBM, P&G, major consulting firms, law firms, and outstanding financial institutions like Morgan Guaranty and Morgan Stanley.

There is, of course, the danger of strong-culture firms becoming incestuous and myopic—what came to be known in the early days of the Japanese auto invasion as the General Motors syndrome. Most opponents of socialization rally around this argument. But what one learns from observing the likes of IBM and P&G is that their cultures keep them constantly facing outward. Most companies like this tend to guard against the danger of complacency by having as one element of their culture an *obsession* with some facet of their performance in the marketplace. For example, McDonald's has an obsessive concern for quality control, IBM for customer service, 3M for innovation. These obsessions make for a lot of fire drills. But they also serve as the organizational equivalent of calisthenics, keeping people fit for the day when the emergency is real. When, on the other hand, the central cultural concern points inward rather than outward—as seems to be the case, say, with Delta Air Lines' focus on "family feeling"—

the strong-culture company may be riding for a fall.

Revolutions begin with an assault on awareness. It is time to be more candid and clear-minded about socialization. Between our espoused individualism and the reality of most companies lies a zone where organizational and individual interests overlap. If we can manage our ambivalence about socialization, we can make our organizations more effective. Equally important, we can reduce the human costs that arise today as individuals stumble along in careers with companies that fail to articulate ends and means coherently and understandably for all employees.

11

Productivity and People Development

What Third Wave employers increasingly need . . . are men
and women who accept responsibility, who understand how
their work dovetails with that of others, who can handle ever
larger tasks, who adapt swiftly to changed circumstances, and
who are sensitively tuned into the people around them.
ALVIN TOFFLER[1]

DEVELOPMENT OF PEOPLE

Productive companies focus on the development of their people, who ultimately determine the organization's productivity. "Development" means bringing out people's potential,[2] which includes work skills and personal qualities. Well-developed people know their own feelings, express themselves, enjoy working toward goals, and have creative ideas.[3] Individuals help shape the environment that, in turn, shapes them. Managers and employees share the responsibility for developing people. But what causes people to develop? One group of researchers offers the following explanation:

> Paradoxically, we believe that through more effective team interaction, most individuals find a heightened sense of individuality and enhanced ability to influence others. No longer are individuals as much subject to the prevailing unit or organizational culture. They are now more active agents in shaping that culture.[4]

230

Individuals are responsible for their own development. When people are curious, eager to learn and ready to try new ideas, they grow. Companies may offer workshops, courses and tuition reimbursements—but it is up to employees to benefit by taking part in them.

Managers

Managers help determine whether employees grow. Managers decide how much money goes into development and who gets which opportunities. Because of managers' positions of authority, their feedback affects employees' self-images. These, and other factors, influence the degree to which employees are able to develop.

Peters and Waterman note an important behavior on the part of managers in successful companies:

> Treat people as adults. Treat them as partners; treat them with respect. Treat them—not capital spending and automation—as the primary source of productivity gains. These are the fundamental lessons from the excellent companies research.... They turn the average Joe and the average Jane into winners. They let, even insist that, people stick out.[5]

When employees become "winners," they increase their productivity as well as their self-esteem. One of management's responsibilities is to help employees develop.

DEVELOPMENT REFLECTS VALUES

Managers who help develop their people are part of a move away from game-playing, status-chasing, distrust, withdrawal, and competition—a move toward authentic behavior, trust, confrontation, risk-taking, and collaboration. Tannenbaum and Davis have this to say:

> We place a strong emphasis on increasing the sanity of the individuals in the organization and of the organization itself. By this we mean putting the individuals and the organization more in touch with the realities existing within themselves and around them. With respect to the individual, this involves his understanding the consequences of his behavior. How do people feel about him? How do they react to him? Do they trust him?[6]

Managers who act out these values instill them in their employees. For example, suppose an employee is not sure how to do part of the assigned work. In a company where distrust and competition are the rule, the employee would be afraid to ask for help, and productivity would suffer. But if respect and collaboration were the rule, help would replace the need to hide mistakes. Everyone benefits from a humanistic environment.

TRAINING AND DEVELOPMENT METHODS

Many methods help people develop. In large companies, separate training departments are staffed by professionals who specialize in employee development. These professionals may be trainers, counselors or psychologists. Smaller firms may send their employees to outside experts or use consultants who provide these services to organizations of all sizes. Managers play an important role in both the development and training of their people.

Training

Training means improving people's job skills. These skills relate to the jobs people hold now, and the ones they may hold in the future. Whether training departments, outside consultants or department managers are teaching the skills, according to Ribler they follow six general steps:

Conduct needs assessment. Consists of comparing employees' skills to job requirements; training fills any gaps between them.

Develop course objectives. Specific behaviors, and ways to measure them, become the objectives for courses.

Develop practice and test items. These items serve as examples during the course and as test questions.

Define strategy. Strategy includes methods of teaching, class size, use of audio-visual equipment and related items.

Prepare training manuals. Trainers' manuals give instructions for teaching the course; trainees' manuals have materials which allow trainees to practice new skills.

Evaluate course. New courses may be tested on "pilot groups" who have the needed skills and can give feedback about the value of the course; actual trainees' skills can be measured after a course, and on the job, to determine whether the course was effective.[7]

Managers can be good trainers, because they know their employees' needs and departments' goals. But sometimes managers do not have the time, the skills or the desire to conduct training. Whoever does the training must work closely with the managers in such cases, to make sure the work setting reinforces new skills employees learn.

Development

Employee and management development go beyond specific skills training. Development deals with the ways people change through learning.[8] Often, a firm's human resource development department is formally responsible for staff development. In a practical sense, development takes several forms.

New employees learn official and formal aspects of the company culture—such as policies and rules—through employee orientation sessions. Depending on their jobs and levels of responsibility, they also may learn about company needs, problems and goals. Many firms offer human relations training for employees. Beyond job skills, people at all levels need help in communicating, making decisions, resolving conflicts, and other aspects of human relations.

Newly-promoted managers and executives need to develop philosophies, as well as skills, that match their responsibilities within the firm. Management and executive development programs help in this area. Employees at all levels need help to identify potential promotions, the skills needed for those promotions and ways to learn those skills. Career development programs provide employees with this information. Sometimes, upward career paths do not exist for employees. A company's growth rate may slow down, people in higher positions may choose not to retire, or other factors may block promotions. When this happens, employees may need help adjusting their attitudes toward, and expectations of, work.

When people from different backgrounds work together, misunderstandings often become major problems. Employees at all levels need to learn how to work with people from different cultures. Personal problems also affect employees' work. Sometimes managers can deal with these problems. For example, an employee whose father dies may need time off to deal with the grief. Often, though, the problems require more skill or time than managers can give. Drug and alcohol abuse and other self-destructive behaviors, for example, are too widespread, complex and dangerous to deal with casually. Trained professionals, such as counselors and psychologists, are more effective than managers in solving these problems.

By sending them to counselors when appropriate, managers show that they support and believe in their employees. They see employees as whole persons, beyond their functions at work. Carl Rogers describes the counseling relationship as one in which

> . . . warmth of acceptance and absence of any coercion or personal pressure on the part of the counselor permits the maximum expression of feelings, attitudes, and problems. . . . The relationship is a well-structured one, with limits of time, of dependence, and of aggressive action which apply particularly to the client, and limits of responsibility and of affection which

the counselor imposes on himself. In this unique experience of complete emotional freedom within a well-defined frame-work, the client is free to recognize and understand his impulses and patterns, positive and negative, as in no other relationship.[9]

Managers' roles

Whether they do the work themselves or send employees to other professionals, managers must be active in development and training. They can show interest in their employees' needs and progress. They can help other professionals work with their employees. They can ask employees how they feel about new programs. And they, too, can continue to grow.

DEVELOPMENT AND SOCIETY

How is development related to a productive society? Individuals make up organizations. As Beer says:

> When the organization cannot harness enough of its members' energy and direct them toward organizational goals, it may not be able to deliver its product or service at a competitive price. Individuals who work in organizations that cannot compete, will not long be able to achieve their personal goals through the organization.
> The well being of society is dependent on effective exchanges between (1) individuals and their organization, and (2) between organizations and their environment.[10]

Society depends on organizations, which in turn depend on their individual members—that is, the *development* of their individual members.

SUMMARY

Effective managers contribute to organizations and society by helping to develop individual employees. Individual growth leads to increased productivity as well as personal satisfaction. Individuals, businesses and society benefit from the development of people.

SELECTED READINGS OVERVIEW

In the first reading, "Training's Crucial Role in the Coming Battle to Restore Productivity," C. Jackson Grayson, Jr., points out seven ways that in-house trainers can increase productivity.

The second reading is "Why Training Is the Boss's Job," by Andrew S. Grove, president of Intel. Grove says good training is crucial to a firm's success, and managers are best qualified to teach employees.

Next Chapter

The next chapter presents ways in which entire organizations can be developed. The purpose of organization development (OD) is to improve the effectiveness and productivity of organizations.

Review Questions

1. What does Grayson mean when he says trainers face a "thankless task"?
2. Why does Grove think that training is the boss's job?
3. What factors help determine an employee's ability to develop?
4. What can managers do to help employees develop?
5. How does employee development contribute to society?

C. JACKSON GRAYSON, JR.

Training's Crucial Role in the Coming Battle to Restore Productivity

America's seriously declining productivity at last is receiving the broad attention and concern it deserves. Labor, business and government leaders have become convinced that without improved productivity our country as we now know it will not survive. But recognition alone is not enough where a problem of this magnitude exists. We are like a giant ship in the open seas. Once a decision is made to change course, it is many miles and minutes before any results become apparent.

I have studied productivity intensely for more than two decades, comparing our efforts with those of other countries and assessing the potential value of their approaches in America. It has become staggeringly clear that extensive changes are needed in labor, business and government, as well as in our historical ways of interfacing between each of these sectors. Rather

C. Jackson Grayson, Jr., is founder and chairman of The American Productivity Center, Houston, TX.

than expound on these vast needs, let it suffice to say that a common denominator does exist. This is the point at which the ship actually begins to change course after the captain has issued the orders. That common denominator is the trainer.

During the time I have been engaged with specific study of productivity, I have seen several major evolutions occur in companies. Two of them bear special attention by the trainer:

Major colleges have dropped productivity related courses from their studies.

Corporate CEO slots have gone to financial or marketing executives, rather than to those with production backgrounds as in the past.

The emphasis now is cycling back toward the supply side of the supply/demand equation. Companies are directing their attention toward productivity within their own organizations (getting more out of their slice of the pie), rather than penetrating new markets or expanding market share (building a bigger pie). Certainly that is not applied absolutely. Companies are continuing to expand and penetrate new markets. The difference is that while doing so, they are making the most of their current resources.

As the cycle nears completion, management and scholars are directing their efforts toward improving productivity and improving productivity improvement skills, respectively. Until their efforts begin to change our cumbersome economic course, trainers very likely will provide the transition. They may do so by directing their programs toward productivity improvement skills. It would seem prudent, then, for trainers to ensure their competence in productivity improvement. We at The American Productivity Center already are seeing positive responses by trainers. Many are visiting the Center to learn all they can about productivity, then applying these principles to their own organizations.

By scaling our national efforts at the Center to your own organization, you—the trainer—may come up with the following suggested list of initial steps toward changing our economic course:

Create awareness. Use your company communications of all sorts, from newsletters to bulletin boards, to make your fellow workers aware of the problem of declining productivity.

Research. Learn all you can about the subject. Seek to separate reality from myth about productivity, to identify sources of productivity and obstacles.

Measurement. Learn how to measure productivity as a total factor. The Center's Total Factor Productivity Index recently was inaugurated to help companies assess their productivity in light of industry averages.

Appraisal. Learn how to appraise the productivity potential of a firm or industry so as to identify strengths and weaknesses.

Take action. Devise formal programs to enable your organization to work constructively toward positive productivity goals.

Promote cooperation. Help allay fears and concerns between labor and management so the very real rewards of increased productivity are mutually realized.

Provide support. Find and make available tools, methods, ideas and experiences that may help people become more productive.

The road to productivity improvement is strewn with obstacles in the form of fear, misunderstanding, suspicion and adversarial relationships. Those of you at the vanguard very likely will face a thankless task, a role most trainers tell me is not unfamiliar. But this time, for sure, the stakes make the effort well worthwhile.

ANDREW S. GROVE

Why Training Is the Boss's Job

Recently my wife and I decided to go out to dinner. The woman who took reservations over the phone seemed flustered and then volunteered that she was new and didn't know all the ropes. No matter, we were booked. When we showed up for dinner, we quickly learned that the restaurant had lost its liquor license and that its patrons were expected to bring their own wine if they wanted any. As the maitre d' rubbed his hands, he asked, "Weren't you told this on the phone when you made your reservations?" As we went through our dinner without wine, I listened to him go through the same routine with every party he seated. I don't know for sure, but it's probably fair to assume that nobody instructed the woman taking calls to tell potential guests what the situation was. Instead, the maitre d' had to go through an inept apology time and time again, and nobody had wine—all because one employee was not properly trained.

The consequences of an employee being insufficiently trained can be much more serious. In an instance at Intel, for example, one of our sophisticated pieces of production machinery in a silicon fabrication plant—a machine called an ion implanter—drifted slightly out of tune. The machine operator, like the woman at the restaurant, was relatively new. While she was trained in the basic skills needed to operate the machine, she hadn't been taught to recognize the signs of an out-of-tune condition. So she continued to operate the machine, subjecting nearly a day's worth of almost completely processed silicon wafers to the wrong machine conditions. By the time the situation was discovered, material worth more than $1 million had passed through the machine —and had to be scrapped. Because it takes over two weeks to make up such a loss with fresh material, deliveries to our customers slipped, compounding the problem.

Situations like these occur all too frequently in business life. Insufficiently trained employees, in spite of their best intentions, produce inefficiencies, excess costs, unhappy customers, and sometimes even dangerous situations. The importance of training rapidly becomes obvious to the manager who runs into these problems.

For the already overscheduled manager, the trickier issue may be who should do the training. Most managers seem to feel that training employees is a job that should be

Andrew S. Grove is president of Intel Corp., the renowned Santa Clara, California, maker of microprocessors and computer memory devices. He describes this article as the chapter he inadvertently left out of his recent book *High Output Management*.

left to others, perhaps to training specialists. I, on the other hand, strongly believe that the manager should do it himself.

Let me explain why, beginning with what I believe is the most basic definition of what managers are supposed to produce. In my view a manager's output is the output of his organization—no more, no less. A manager's own productivity thus depends on eliciting more output from his team.

A manager generally has two ways to raise the level of individual performance of his subordinates: by increasing motivation, the desire of each person to do his job well, and by increasing individual capability, which is where training comes in. It is generally accepted that motivating employees is a key task of all managers, one that can't be delegated to someone else. Why shouldn't the same be true for the other principal means at a manager's disposal for increasing output?

Training is, quite simply, one of the highest-leverage activities a manager can perform. Consider for a moment the possibility of your putting on a series of four lectures for members of your department. Let's count on three hours of preparation for each hour of course time—12 hours of work in total. Say that you have ten students in your class. Next year they will work a total of about 20,000 hours for your organization. If your training efforts result in a 1% improvement in your subordinates' performance, your company will gain the equivalent of 200 hours of work as the result of the expenditure of your 12 hours.

This assumes, of course, that the training will accurately address what students need to know to do their jobs better. This isn't always so—particularly with respect to "canned courses" taught by someone from outside. For training to be effective, it has to be closely tied to how things are actually done in your organization.

Recently some outside consultants taught a course on career development at Intel.

Their approach was highly structured and academic—and very different from anything practiced at the company. While they advocated career plans that looked ahead several years, together with carefully coordinated job rotations based on them, our tradition has been more like a free market; our employees are informed of job opportunities within the company and are expected to apply for desirable openings on their own initiative. Troubled by the disparity between what was taught in the course and what was practiced, the participants got a bit demoralized.

For training to be effective, it also has to maintain a reliable, consistent presence. Employees should be able to count on something systematic and scheduled, not a rescue effort summoned to solve the problem of the moment. In other words, training should be a process, not an event.

If you accept that training, along with motivation, is the way to improve the performance of your subordinates, and that what you teach must be closely tied to what you practice, and that training needs to be a continuing process rather than a one-time event, it is clear that the *who* of the training is *you*, the manager. You yourself should instruct your direct subordinates and perhaps the next few ranks below them. Your subordinates should do the same thing, and the supervisors at every level below them as well.

There is another reason that you and only you can fill the role of the teacher to your subordinates. Training must be done by a person who represents a suitable role model. Proxies, no matter how well versed they might be in the subject matter, cannot assume that role. The person standing in front of the class should be seen as a believable, practicing authority on the subject taught.

We at Intel believe that conducting training is a worthwhile activity for everyone from the firstline supervisor to the chief executive officer. Some 2% to 4% of our employees' time is spent in classroom learning, and almost all the instruction is given by our own managerial staff.

We have a "university catalogue" that lists over 50 different classes. The courses range from proper telephone manners to quite complicated production courses—like one on how to operate the ion implanter, which requires nearly 200 hours of on-the-job training to learn to use correctly, almost five times the hours of training needed to get a private pilot's license. We train our managers in disciplines such as strategic planning as well as in the art of constructive confrontation, a problem-solving approach we favor at Intel.

My own training repertoire includes a course on preparing and delivering performance reviews, on conducting productive meetings, and a three-hour-long introduction to Intel, in which I describe our history, objectives, organization, and management practices. Over the years I have given the latter to almost all of our 5,000 professional employees. I have also been recruited to pinch-hit in other management courses. (To my regret, I have become far too obsolete to teach technical material.)

At Intel we distinguish between two different training tasks. The first task is teaching new members of our organization the skills needed to perform their jobs. The second task is teaching new ideas, principles, or skills to the present members of our organization.

The distinction between new-employee and new-skill training is important because the magnitude of the tasks are very different. The size of the job of delivering a new-employee course is set by the number of new people joining the organization. For instance, a department that has 10% annual turnover and grows 10% per year has to teach 20% of its staff the basics of their work

each year. Training even 20% of your employees can be a huge undertaking.

Teaching new principles or skills to an entire department is an even bigger job. If we want to train all of our staff within a year, the task will be five times as large as the annual task of training the 20% who represent new members. Recently I looked at the cost of delivering a new one-day course to our middle-management staff. The cost of the students' time alone was over $1 million. Obviously such a task should not be entered into lightly.

So what should you do if you embrace the gospel of training? For starters, make a list of the things you feel your subordinates or the members of your department should be trained in. Don't limit the scope of your list. Items should range from what seems simple (training the person who takes calls at the restaurant) to loftier and more general things like the objectives and value systems of your department, your plant, and your company. Ask the people working for you what they feel they need. They are likely to surprise you by telling you of needs you never knew existed.

Having done this, take an inventory of the manager-teachers and instructional materials available to help deliver training on items on your list. Then assign priorities among these items.

Especially if you haven't done this sort of thing before, start very unambitiously—like developing one short course (three to four lectures) on the most urgent subject. You will find that skills that you have had for years—things that you could do in your sleep, as it were—are much harder to explain than to practice. You may find that in your attempt to explain things, you'll be tempted to go into more and more background until this begins to obscure the original objective of your course.

To avoid letting yourself bog down in the difficult task of course preparation, set a schedule for your course, with deadlines, and commit yourself to it. Create an outline for the whole course, develop just the first lecture, and go.

Develop the second lecture after you have given the first. Regard the first time you teach the course as a throw-away—it won't be great, because no matter how hard you try, you'll have to go through one version that won't be. Rather than agonize over it, accept the inevitability of the first time being unsatisfactory and consider it the path to a more satisfactory second round. To make sure that your first attempt causes no damage, teach this course to the more knowledgeable of your subordinates who won't be confused by it, but who will help you perfect the course through interaction and critique.

With your second attempt in the offing, ask yourself one final question: will you be able to teach all members of your organization yourself? Will you be able to cover everybody in one or two courses, or will it require ten or 20? If your organization is large enough to require many repetitions of your course before different audiences, then set yourself up to train a few instructors with your first set of lectures.

After you've given the course, ask for anonymous critiques from the employees in your class. Prompt them with a form that asks for numerical ratings but that also poses some open-ended questions. Study and consider the responses, but understand that you will never be able to please all members of your class: typical feedback will be that the course was too detailed, too superficial, and just right, in about equal balance. Your ultimate aim should be to satisfy yourself that you are accomplishing what you set out to do.

If this is your first time teaching, you'll discover a few interesting things:

Training is hard work. Preparing lectures and getting yourself ready to handle all the questions thrown at you is difficult. Even if you have been doing your job for a long time and even if you have done your subordinates' jobs in great detail before, you'll be amazed at how much you don't know. Don't be discouraged—this is typical. Much deeper knowledge of a task is required to teach that task than simply to do it. If you don't believe me, try explaining to someone over the phone how to drive a stick-shift car.

Guess who will have learned most from the course? You. The crispness that developing it gave to your understanding of your own work is likely in itself to have made the effort extremely worthwhile.

You will find that when the training process goes well, it is nothing short of exhilarating. And even this exhilaration is dwarfed by the warm feeling you'll get when you see a subordinate practice something you have taught him. Relish the exhilaration and warmth—it'll help you to arm yourself for tackling the second course.

12

Productivity and Organization Development

They are methods which give an onlooker
the impression of magic if he be not himself initiated or
equally skilled in the mechanism.
H. VAIHINGER[1]

DEFINITIONS OF ORGANIZATION DEVELOPMENT

Individual development leads to more productivity in both personal and professional ways. When this process involves groups, it is called organization development (OD). OD is the management of change. Its purpose is to "increase organization effectiveness and health."[2] The philosophies and practices of OD vary to some degree with each practitioner and scholar. Yet OD practitioners share common values and methods.

Shared Values and Methods

Laboratory training

OD began with the laboratory training movement of the mid-1940s. Through small discussion groups, participants learned about their own interactions with people. They used this knowledge to help make changes in behavior at work. Kurt Lewin was the key leader of this movement.[3]

Survey research and feedback method

OD's second root is the survey research and feedback method, also developed by Lewin in the mid-1940s. This technique relies on attitude surveys to identify employees' feelings about the workplace and their jobs. Results are discussed in data feedback workshops. Baumgartel compares this method to more traditional techniques used in the 1940s:

> . . . [Lewin's method] deals with the system of human relationships as a whole (superior and subordinate can change together) and it deals with each manager, supervisor, and employee in the context of his own job, his own problems, and his own work relationships.[4]

Following Lewin, such people as Marian Radke, Leon Festinger, John R.P. French, Jr., Floyd Mann, and Rensis Likert further developed the survey research and feedback method. Together with the laboratory training movement, the survey research and feedback method evolved into OD.

The Process of Change

OD starts with some assumptions about change: (1) it is a natural process; (2) it cannot be stopped; (3) people tend to resist it; (4) it can be managed; and (5) it can therefore be made acceptable to people. By planning, instead of just reacting to what happens, managers make change more predictable and less haphazard. According to Beckhard, OD is a *"planned change effort"*:

> An OD program involves a systematic diagnosis of the organization, the development of a strategic plan for improvement, and the mobilization of resources to carry out the effort.[5]

Chapter 5 of the present work discusses group norms. In some organizations, the norm may be to focus on work content—*what* gets done—and to ignore process—*how* it gets done. Social processes include how employees or departments work together, how (and whether) people resolve conflicts, how much input employees have, and related issues. Through OD, organizations begin to take process issues as seriously as content issues. OD also involves certain *kinds* of change. Burke and Hornstein describe OD's goals:

> . . . [the] change of an organization's culture from one which avoids an examination of social processes . . . to one which institutionalizes and legitimizes this examination.[6]

Value Systems

OD values true teamwork. It begins with a culture based on sharing. Collaboration and group ownership of the culture lead to more effective management than traditional top-down approaches.[7]

Tannenbaum and Davis note that OD marks a shift in attitudes toward people.[8] One change is from the assumption that people are essentially bad to the assumption that they are basically good. Another change is from avoiding or reacting negatively to people, to confirming their worth as human beings. Closely related is a change from seeing individuals as "fixed" to seeing them "in process," a view that allows for growth. Another change is the acceptance of, rather than resistance to, individual differences. A natural outcome of this change is a shift from game-playing towards more authentic behavior. All of these changes represent a shift from distrusting people to trusting them. OD practitioners believe behaviors based on these assumptions increase productivity.

OD deals with the whole system, not with separate parts. OD is based on a systems view of organizations. OD practitioners realize that events, needs, activities, outcomes, goals, and relationships interact with each other. They do not exist in vacuums. Lewin emphasizes the need to deal with the "field as a whole," rather than with isolated parts.[9]

Because they deal with whole systems, effective OD programs require commitment from organizations' top managers. Argyris says top management's commitment to learning and change must be strong, to allow the organization to internalize OD.[10] Beckhard indicates that the OD effort itself must start with top management.[11]

THE ORGANIZATION DEVELOPMENT PROCESS

Based on these values and assumptions, OD methods take the form of *interventions*. Argyris defines "interventions" in this way:

> To intervene is to enter into an ongoing system of relationships, to come between or among persons, groups, or objects for the purpose of helping them. There is an important implicit assumption...: the system exists independently of the intervenor.[12]

Outside consultants, or change agents, usually help intervene. As outsiders, their view may be system-wide. Ultimately, however, client organizations absorb the activities the consultant starts.

Diagnosis

OD begins with diagnosis. A diagnosis measures the present state of a system and identifies underlying conditions or forces leading to that state.[13]

The diagnosis helps to determine an appropriate intervention. Just as a medical diagnosis must be correct before the physician can help a patient, the OD specialist must make an accurate diagnosis of the organization. Issues to consider at the diagnostic stage include the following:

Timing. When should data-gathering begin and end?

Extent of participation. How many levels, and which individuals, should be included in the data-gathering process?

Confidentiality. Should the process be open or anonymous?

Structure. Should data be gathered about pre-selected topics, or should problems emerge through open-ended questions?

Strategy. Are the data-gathering and analysis part of an organization's long-term strategy, or are they isolated events?

Target. What is the nature of the target group?

Technique. Would questionnaires be more effective than interviews? Should people meet individually or in groups?

Depth. How deeply should the diagnosis go?[14]

Similar questions are asked about interventions. The appropriateness of an intervention depends on the nature of the problem, the depth required, time constraints, the size and complexity of the client organization, and other issues.

Process Interventions

Schein describes "process interventions" as activities aimed at helping individuals and groups to examine and change their behavior and relationships.[19] These interventions focus on the *way* people work together.

Team-building

According to Beer, team-building, or group development, is

> ...a process by which members of a group diagnose how they work together and plan changes which will improve their effectiveness. ...It is critically important that managers understand that group development is an activity in a broader plan for [OD].[15]

Team-building sessions may have three purposes. The first is to set individual and group goals. Sometimes, goal-setting means that the group must work through conflicts, increase personal motivation or better understand how they relate to other groups in the organization. Groups often become more effective when members clarify their goals.[16]

The second purpose of team-building is to improve interpersonal skills within groups. According to Argyris, groups become more effective as the members improve their skills at interpersonal relationships.[17] Team-building efforts help members to share feelings, ideas and perceptions in non-judgmental ways.

Team-building's third purpose is to help members clarify their roles. Katz and Kahn define a "role" as a set of behaviors which a person expects—and is expected by others—to perform, based on the person's job.[18] Problems may occur when people's expectations conflict, when roles are not clear, or when roles do not match people's values. Team-building processes help clarify perceptions of roles. Effective team-building sessions focus on one major purpose. At the same time, the sessions also may serve the other two purposes to some degree.

Meeting processing

Managers spend more than half their time in meetings.[20] OD practitioners assume that the productivity of meetings depends on the processes which take place, whether participants understand and share goals, the degree to which members are open to each other, how much and what kinds of control the leaders have. OD consultants may analyze processes that go on in meetings. By giving feedback to the group, the consultant helps the group to recognize and improve its behaviors.

Intergroup laboratory

Groups within organizations often conflict because their values and behaviors differ. For example, manufacturing may organize for stability (assign the same worker to the same task each day) while sales organizes to please customers (require sales persons to know about many aspects of the customer's needs). Conflict worsens without an intervention.[21] In intergroup laboratories, an outside consultant develops trust with both of the conflicting groups. The consultant then brings them together for an off-site meeting. At the meeting, both groups share perceptions of each other. The groups separate to identify problems and meet again to share diagnoses. The purpose is to improve communication and understanding between the groups.

Interpersonal peace-making

Two individuals may conflict over power, resources, status or recognition. Their behaviors may hurt the organization. Again, an outside consultant must win trust from both parties. The consultant then structures a meeting, which aims at helping both people give and take feedback from each other and agree to make certain changes.

OD traditionally focuses on process interventions, which Leavitt calls the "people approaches" to change.[22] However, as a system-wide approach, OD also deals with organization structures.

Structural Interventions

Structural interventions deal with organization design, job design, reward systems, performance management systems, and control systems.[23]

Organization design

A company's organization design affects its productivity. Managers may choose from several designs, such as functional, decentralized or matrix. The choice depends on the degree of uncertainty in the environment, organization strategy and the firm's capacity for sharing resources and for processing information. OD change agents may help managers choose a more productive design. If a firm changes its design, OD specialists ease the transition through process interventions.

Job design

Sometimes job designs also need to change, because of new technology, increases in employee skills or changes in the organization.

Changes in job design bring new problems. Some employees may like the new design, while others may not. If the change means that employees will make more decisions than in the past, some managers may feel threatened. Sometimes, the company culture resists needed changes. OD practitioners help organizations to deal with these kinds of problems.

Reward systems

According to Lawler, a company's reward system must meet both employee and organization needs.[24] To be productive, employees must perceive pay and promotions as fair. Rewards should attract employees, encourage attendance, motivate employees, and reinforce the company's management style. OD practitioners help managers identify and implement effective reward systems.

Performance management systems

To increase productivity, companies need system-wide evaluation and development systems. New forms and procedures are not enough. When organization culture works against management methods for effective performance, OD may help bring change to the culture.

Control systems

According to Lawler and Rhode, accounting and other control systems often fail to consider the human element.[25] For example, a control system may give information that is not useful to the managers who make decisions. Or emphasis on the "bottom line" may reward inappropriate behaviors. OD helps managers to identify needed changes in the control system.

By creating new environments, these structural changes may lead to more productive behaviors. The OD process helps managers to identify and implement necessary changes.

Individual Interventions

Process and structural interventions deal with organizations on the group level. As these changes occur, managers and employees often need help adjusting to them. Individual interventions deal with change on a personal level.

Counseling and coaching

Employees and managers sometimes need help adjusting to change. Do they fit into the changing organization? Must they change certain attitudes or behaviors to fit in? Do they want to make these changes? What new skills do they need? This self-knowledge helps people to grow and learn, and it leads to greater productivity at work.

Change agents help employees learn about themselves. They begin with open-ended questions. They restate the employee's comments without judgment. They give appropriate feedback. Once the employee understands the real situation—which includes feelings and goals—the change agent helps the employee develop an action plan. Coaching and counseling help employees to recognize and deal with new realities at work.

SUMMARY

OD is a humanistic way to manage change. Through process, structural and individual interventions, it helps people recognize and improve *how* they work together. OD leads to increased productivity in organizations.

SELECTED READINGS OVERVIEW

In the first reading, "Going from A to Z: The Steps," from *Theory Z*, William Ouchi outlines the best characteristics of both Japanese and American companies. By functioning in certain ways, effective firms secure employee cooperation and commitment.

"Organization Development: A Political Perspective," by Anthony T. Cobb and Newton Margulies, is the second reading. The authors discuss an aspect of OD that often goes unrecognized: the political side. They note the need for political involvement and the problems that go along with politics.

Next Chapter

The next chapter deals with productivity through employee involvement. Effective managers help win employee commitment to work by using employees' ideas and involving them in decisions that affect work.

Review Questions

1. What does Ouchi mean by "Theory Z"?
2. Why do Cobb and Margulies think politics are important in OD?
3. How is team-building related to productivity?
4. How is OD related to productivity?

WILLIAM OUCHI

Going From *A* to *Z*:
The Steps

STEP ONE: UNDERSTAND
THE TYPE Z ORGANIZATION
AND YOUR ROLE

To begin, ask each of the managers involved to do some reading so that all are familiar with the underlying ideas of Theory Z represented here. The bibliography at the end of the book will suggest additional sources. Some people whom you ask to join in the reading will be skeptical of these ideas, just as others will embrace them. It is important at this and at later stages to present the reading and the ideas in a manner that invites the open display of skepticism. Invite discussion of ideas. Resist interpreting skepticism as foot-dragging, lack of cooperation, or the like; if you do, the skeptics will conceal their doubts and thus never go beyond them. And because in most companies the skeptics outnumber the true believers, their reservations must be openly debated for change to occur.

A second and more fundamental reason to invite skepticism has to do with the development of trust. Trust consists of the understanding that you and I share fundamentally compatible goals in the long run, and thus we have reason to trust one another. In the process of organizational change, the nature of these goals becomes ambiguous. The skeptic who is being asked to abandon his old managerial objectives does not know whether or not, in fact, he does share goals that are compatible with the new ideas. In such a case, a specific form of trust cannot be achieved, but a more generalized form of trust can. This is the trust that comes from knowing that, fundamentally, you and I desire a more effective working relationship together and that neither desires to harm the other. But how to believably establish this basis of trust? In my experience, the clearest evidence is complete openness and candor in a relationship. One who seeks to conceal nothing from me is one who, in all likelihood, does not seek to harm me. How is this best done?

Of the many ways in which openness can be encouraged, the only one that really matters is by setting an example. The leader who frankly disagrees with others and who goes out of his way to create an atmosphere where differing opinions are welcomed will produce change. Of course, this process will lead naturally to a key issue that emerges in all such developmental efforts—performance evaluation. Openness does not mean hostility, nor does it mean sweetness and light. Openness values a realistic appraisal of both problems and achievements. Ultimately subordinates will demand performance appraisal before they willingly attempt more cooperation and less self-protection. When a boss calls for frankness, the openness that subordinates care about most is forthrightness in discussing their performance, their pay, and their future prospects. This most basic form of candor precedes all others.

In this initial process of reading and discussion, the substance of the ideas of Type Z organization is important, but the *process* through which the discussion takes place is equally important. This process must reflect the egalitarianism, the openness, and the participativeness that are the ultimate objectives of the change. The leader, if the company has been largely of Type A, will have become accustomed to an authoritarian relationship to an extent that he is not likely to appreciate fully. Although the leader may perceive his own behavior as being quite open and egalitarian, research shows consistently that the subordinates will perceive him to be far less so. If you are taking this leadership role, be prepared for frank criticisms of your non-participative lapses. More important than criticism is your response to it. A consistently open and egalitarian response will begin to develop the underlying generalized trust.

STEP TWO: AUDIT YOUR COMPANY'S PHILOSOPHY

A statement of your company's objectives—its philosophy—gives people a sense of values to work and to live by. It suggests ways to behave in the organization and a way for the organization to behave in response to its people, its clients, and the community it serves. A philosophy can provide answers to such questions as "Is this the right way to carry out a deal?" or "Am I doing x because profits are of paramount concern to the company—or are ideals of company image much more important?" If it seems unusual that a business should depend upon a philosophy of all things, reconsider: A philosophy clearly sets forth the company's motivating spirit for all to understand. Whether directly or indirectly, that philosophy determines how insiders and outsiders alike appraise, trust, and value the company and its products.

Though I describe in detail how companies construct such a philosophy in Chapter 6, I want to portray here some notion of when this step should occur in the process of going from A to Z. Usually it comes second, though it is a step of the first importance. Your group of managers must take stock of your company's current, actual, operating philosophy. Ask yourself, what is our business strategy, our goals in the marketplace, and the kind of value we place in people? The point here is not to define what your organization *should be*, but what it *is*. The reasons for this "audit" are many.

First, it is not possible to develop a philosophy out of thin air. It is necessary to understand your company's culture by analyzing the four or five key decisions the company has made in the past. Which have worked well? Which have failed? Where are the inconsistencies and omissions? Hold a series of meetings to identify these decisions and to discover what principles were consistently applied across many of those decisions. From this, the basis of a desired philosophy will begin to emerge.

The second reason a philosophy is important is that every organization develops inconsistencies over time between what is officially declared to be desirable by top managers and what those top managers actually do. Those inconsistencies between word and deed will be revealed through an audit, and the very openness and candor with which past inconsistencies are treated will be an important signal of the openness to be generally promoted. I would venture to guess that many of the inconsistencies of the greatest importance will have to do with decisions in promotion and hiring. A promotional decision is typically so complex that a distant observer can attribute any cause to explain it. An open discussion of the basis for specific key promotions in the past will help clarify the underlying basis on which individual performance is valued, provide openness, and promote the development of trust.

Third, the audit will reveal the connections between business strategy and management philosophy. Every company has a business strategy statement of some sort. Often, this statement refers purely to financial goals such as market share, sales growth, and measures of cost or of profitability. Other times, the strategy refers to development of technology, of managerial competence, and to other such broader objectives. Rarely are these statements of objectives linked explicitly to an understanding of the organization. The connection, however, is both critical and intimate.

Many different techniques can be used to carry out this audit. One firm may choose to employ an outside consultant, while another holds a series of discussions among a team drawn from within. One may circulate a simple questionnaire to managers, soliciting their written views on the above questions, while another may prefer personal interviews. Depending upon the particulars of the situation, each of these approaches is viable.

Again, this process of identifying the current and future statements of philosophy is discussed in greater detail in Chapter 6. This step is one that should ordinarily be taken early on in the process of change, perhaps in the first month, but soon after a tentative decision to proceed with a general process of organizational analysis has been taken.

STEP THREE: DEFINE THE DESIRED MANAGEMENT PHILOSOPHY AND INVOLVE THE COMPANY LEADER

Once a clear understanding of the prevailing practices is achieved, it usually becomes obvious which of the current beliefs are inappropriate, which are at odds with other practices, and where there are omissions. Precisely at this stage is the role of the formal leader or chief executive most critical.

Ultimately, a process of organizational change cannot succeed without the direct and personal support of the top person in the hierarchy. That individual cannot be expected to support a statement of managerial philosophy which he or she finds to be wanting. At one company, the process of discussing Theory Z had developed an overwhelming sense of the importance of egalitarian participation. As a result, it became quite awkward for the top person to express disapproval of some key elements of the statement, since others had already reached a consensus on those elements. Sometimes this occurs when the group of managers is expected to disagree openly with the top executive. If such a group, with the encouragement of their leader, undertakes a participative approach to an audit, they will be just beginning to practice a new-to-them egalitarian relationship. The leader may be afraid of upsetting their tentative moves at confrontation and thus may withhold personal views on key issues. Consequently, the group discussing the issue will often reach a consensus, assuming the leader has given tacit consent. Unfortunately, the result will be public commitment to a position not personally supported, and that will produce a half-hearted and ultimately unsuccessful attempt at change.

On the other hand, say the person in charge does not want to share all decisions participatively with subordinates. Leaders may fear that a partial move to participation will result in inconsistent behavior that will be interpreted as an uncertain commitment to egalitarianism, causing the whole effort to fail. A few experts believe that subordinates will not be upset with sharing only some rather than all decisions, since sharing in some decisions most often represents an improvement over the current situation. The impression of inconsistency can be avoided if the most senior person involved in the process openly expresses, in advance, the intent to do just that. Certain decisions will be submitted to a fully consensual process of decision making, others partially by seeking information or suggestions while reserving the final decision to management. Finally, other decisions will be made privately, with others informed only after the fact.

Of course, the more fully the superior trusts the others to share this point of view, and the more completely it is in the best interests of all, the larger will be the fraction of all decisions that he can share with them. The more decisions that are shared, the greater will be the benefits of cooperation produced in the management team. Thus, the top manager has an incentive to develop, over time, a trusting relationship that permits a sharing of the decision-making authority with subordinates. Early on, however, no one expects that to happen, and an open recognition of that fact will permit the top person to intervene in the process of establishing the desired future statement of philosophy in a manner that is not disruptive.

STEP FOUR: IMPLEMENT THE PHILOSOPHY BY CREATING BOTH STRUCTURES AND INCENTIVES

In a sense a company's formal reporting relationships—its system of who reports to whom—are crutches to prop up the occasional lapses in information and in cooperativeness that befall humans. My ideal of a completely efficient and perfectly integrated organization is one that has no organizational chart, no divisions, no visible structure at all. In a sense, a basketball team that plays well together fits this description, although on a small scale. The problem facing a basketball team is huge in its complexity, and the speed with which problems occur is great. Yet an effective team solves these problems with no formal reporting relationships and a minimum of specialization of positions and of tasks. Each person understands his task and its relationship to other tasks so well that the coordination is unspoken. In a less cooperative team, however, the players attempt to hog the ball, to take as many shots for themselves as possible, and in these attempts frequently move out of their defensive positions. The coach responds to this human frailty by asserting the hierarchical right to monitor each player closely, forcing them to stick to their job descriptions, to demur to authority, and to carry out bureaucractically prescribed plays and moves. Such a team can never perform with the same grace, the same satisfaction, nor the same productivity as can the one that operates as a clan.

Most organizations, though, need structure to guide them towards cooperation and subtlety, towards the long view when other conditions dictate the opposite. It is no disgrace for a group of twelve managers, each of whom earns more than $70,000 a year, to admit their frailties and to erect formal committees, reporting relationships and divisions of people and tasks that will support their long-run desire to learn how to work together.

STEP FIVE: DEVELOP INTERPERSONAL SKILLS

Skills that involve dealing with clients, customers, even family, are the kinds of skills that people must learn to adapt to colleagues and co-workers. Interpersonal skills are central to the Z way of doing business, because working cooperatively and considerately is not just a means for soothing egos or getting your way. The stakes are much larger. Let me show you what I mean.

In a sense, a Type Z organization succeeds through the flexibility to modify its form as its needs change. Like the basketball team that speedily moves from one formation to another, a Type Z organization can rapidly meet the changing needs of customers and of technology. Formal reporting relationships are ambiguous in a Type Z, making varied responses possible. A job assignment is often unclear, how much authority over people or things is unclear, and the division between one department and another is also unclear. But because of the easily understood management philosophy, Z organizations have the capacity for the subtle and the complex. In such a setting, the number of corporate stripes on a manager's sleeve do not necessarily signal who is in charge. When a special committee meets Z-style to solve a problem, included will be four persons of equal official rank, three of subordinate rank who know more about the problem, and three of ambiguous rank and authority, who may be superior, equal or subordinate, but no one knows exactly. In most cases, when rank is clearly specified, then everyone falls into well-understood patterns of interaction. Everyone knows when to defer, when to assert, and how to deal with disagreements. Of course, in that situation, the

person who knows most may be ignored because of rank, but conflict is concealed and social intercourse appears to be smooth. In a Z company the complete opposite holds true.

Often, the skillful leader does more listening than talking. What matters most is the skill of observing the pattern of interaction in the group and knowing when to intervene. One case that I recall involved the skillful use of silence by the manager. Allowing a period of quiet every now and then instead of filling up space with talk enabled the real issue, which commonly lies just below the surface, to become apparent. Too often managers will talk around an issue, particularly in fledgling Z companies, just for the sake of filling that uncomfortable silence. "Letting the silence sit there until it's become so compelling it allows the real issue or conflict to surface," is the key, as one manager described it.

Nor does straight probing of co-workers suffice as an inter-personal skill. It does no good to ask employees to learn how to reach decisions and how to handle conflict in unstructured, non-hierarchical groups if the problems that matter most are not solvable. Once those primary steps to solving them have been taken, however, then formal training in participative decision making should begin. There exists a large number of competent consultants, professors, and counselors who are experienced at teaching these skills. The skills may be thought of as being of basically two types.

The first skill to be learned is the skill of *recognizing patterns of interaction* in decision-making and problem-solving groups. Just as one can learn in medical school to interpret an X ray meaningless to the untrained eye, so one can learn to "see" group interaction in quite a different way than that of the layperson. Learning to see when a group moves too quickly to a solution in order to avoid discussing the real problem, learning to observe how some members interfere in subtle ways with an open discussion, learning to note when the group drifts off course—all of these are acquired skills. One way to develop them is to try role playing outside of the context of a formal meeting. All participants need do is to exchange the roles: subordinates "play" supervisor, and vice versa, in order to develop an appreciation for the ways other people feel in different roles. Another possibility is the fish bowl exercise. One group observes behavior, takes notes, and then feeds back to the discussants their observations of who led, in what style, who interrupted, who contributed little, and so on. This gives everyone a clear idea of who needs to contribute more or in some cases less in order to achieve an egalitarian group balance. During a meeting, the same result can be achieved if everyone were asked to stop every forty-five minutes or hour and take five minutes to discuss the *process* taking place at the meeting, rather than its substance.

After learning to recognize patterns of group interaction, the second skill, of course, is learning to provide leadership in such a group, so that the group can quickly identify the important issues, get to the bottom of conflicts, and arrive at high-quality, creative solutions that have everyone's support. With practice, this skill can also be learned.

If the goal of these structural variations is to produce cooperation, then their form must force individuals to work together to share information, resources, and plans. One such typical structure is the committee composed of the seven or eight individuals who represent various departments involved, say, in planning a new product. If each of these individuals is a respected and influential member of his or her own department and can simultaneously continue to work in both the department *and* on the committee, then the committee will possess the information, the influence, and the energy to support a cooperative venture. Of course, the committee could also degenerate into a bickering focus of conflict. Which results occur depends on the general atmosphere of the firm. If these committees are presented as one part of a more general attempt to create cooperation, if changes in incentives, career paths, and evaluations are simultaneously taking place, then these structural crutches will be helpful. When a committee or a quality control circle is an isolated attempt at cooperation, it may become nothing more than the arena for multiple contests fought to no avail.

In addition to the subtle cultural influences, the explicit incentives facing each person must be designed. Incentives are the key for each manager and class of employee in the organization. What, in terms of the current philosophy, do you personally have to do to be a success? What does the manufacturing manager have to do? The sales manager? If short-term incentives spur you and co-workers on, then perhaps the sales manager can succeed only by maximizing sales volume today. This may mean demanding frequent changes in production runs for rush orders to a new customer, and, not incidentally, causing factory costs to rise and productivity to decline. The manufacturing manager, conversely, may be able to succeed only by minimizing per unit cost, causing a fight against all requests for changing the production schedule even when it would mean winning an important new customer. How about the director of research, the foreman, the secretaries and the clerks? At each step, the real incentives that currently face employees should be systematically assessed.

STEP SIX: TEST YOURSELF AND THE SYSTEM

I have always found it difficult to convince managers of the utility of the scientific method. When an organization innovation is implemented, there must be some test to reveal whether it had the expected effect or not. The test need not be elaborate nor terribly expensive but must be capable of helping to convince the skeptic that his or her concerns were unfounded. On the other hand, the test serves to cool the enthusiasm of a true believer who is blind to the weaknesses of personal attempts at change. Before the top level of managers implement Theory Z management at lower levels, they must first test themselves to determine how much of the philosophy has taken hold.

The only form of testing inappropriate at the immediate outset is self-testing. A manager who has worked hard at being more cooperative and participative, who has intellectually embraced a new approach, is hardly a reliable first judge of personal progress. Instead, the initial process of testing might involve a brief questionnaire sent by each manager to direct subordinates who are asked to evaluate this person for participativeness, egalitarianism, and other changes that involve either personal managerial skills or changes in policy and structure. Of course, such an evaluation will be useful only if it contains candid reactions. An outside consultant or an obviously secure internal process of questionnaire distribution and collection will protect the anonymity of the respondents and insure honest responses.

Another form of testing invites someone not involved in the attempted change to visit the operation, interview some of the managers and their subordinates, and to write down impressions of the organizations. Preferably this "auditor" should not be informed about the extent or nature of the process until after the report is written. Knowing what has been attempted will necessarily color impressions.

Later, and in addition to these relatively formal tests, each manager can apply a personal test that I have found to be quite reliable. When the change to Type Z organization takes hold, each manager should begin to feel less harried and less pleased. Less harried because there should be fewer occasions where subordinates need help resolving disputes, fewer new projects that get into trouble through lack of information, fewer demands to create a specific policy or rule to decide an issue. In short, the managers end up having more time to plan, to wander around, to reflect. Their jobs are not being passed down the line to subordinates who are busier and busier; rather, the time formerly consumed by fixing some lack of coordination and in settling disputes is now only partially filled by committees and meetings. The remainder of the time is available for going beyond remedial management to the building of a more effective organization.

STEP SEVEN: INVOLVE THE UNION

At some point, preferably well before any substantive changes in working conditions such as stabilizing employment (Step 8) or introducing slow evaluation and promotion (Step 9) are discussed, the new Type Z company will have to involve the union in its plans. Any company that has some or all of its employees represented by a collective bargaining unit, or union, will approach its union with great care. Dealing with the union is among the most emotionally-charged elements in a process of organizational development. "The union" has become among managers a code word representing poor quality, low productivity, worker apathy, absenteeism, work stoppages, and even employee theft. Sometimes, it seems as though unions invented these problems, to hear managers talk about them. Often, managers have fused into a single complaint their frustrations over inadequate employee relations and the existence of the union. Only if the management arrives at a clear understanding of how to distinguish these two realities and formulate a systematic philosophy of employee relations will it safely navigate the issue of working with a union.

Professor Richard Walton of Harvard University has crystallized this important issue: Unions do not necessarily stand for poor employee relations. Many United States unions grew up protecting the interests of employees who were being systematically abused by managements and have thus developed a contentious relationship with management. But Japanese companies are unionized with no apparent ill effect, although those unions constantly battle against attempted infiltration by the Communist party. Recent research such as Professors James Medoff of Harvard and Kathryn Abraham of M.I.T. have done indicates that, on the whole, unionized companies in the United States have had higher productivity than have nonunionized companies. Everyone is against poor productivity and poor employee relations, but everyone need not be against unions.

Remember that the Type Z organization relies to a great extent upon an egalitarian distribution of power for its success. One way to achieve this is through the creation of workers' councils as is done in West Germany, France, and Sweden. A second method provides systems of employee influence through Scanlon Plans or Type Z organization as outlined in the final stage (Step 13) below. Yet a third method creates distributed centers of power through the formation of unions. If the principles of egalitarianism and of equity are acceptable, then the principle of unionism must also be acceptable.

In many companies, however, the union has been forced into an adversarial position by an unfair and irresponsible management. Having no trust in the company, the union has resorted to extremes of bureaucracy. The union insists on detailed work rules to specify which classes of workers operate the machines, which repair the machines, and so on. This extensive rule-making protects employees from unfair demands by managers. The unintended consequence of this practice is a loss of flexibility. It is as though the players on the basketball team were told that one player may only take set shots, another must always bring the ball down the court, and two others may only rebound. Although the actual distribution of tasks roughly does correspond to this kind of specialization on a basketball team, the effect on productivity would be disastrous if the shooter could never rebound, even if the ball fell into his hands. Our form of unionization has brought great costs in productivity. To counteract this, many Japanese companies opening manufacturing plants in the United States always first secure the best labor law firm available. Japanese companies already located here systematically warn others that the one thing in the United States that can ruin a company's productivity is an inflexible union contract. If that is so, then we can readily understand why our businesses, most of which must contend with these restrictive work agreements, have difficulty competing with the Japanese.

When the motives of the management conflict with a hostile union, the company can counteract to weaken the union. An increase in employee fringe benefits may work. Management may even try to decertify unionized plants, thereby throwing the union out. But in the long run, these approaches must fail.

A company that changes from an autocratic to a democratic style of management will and should win the trust of its employees who will have less need for union protection. Instead of sabotaging the union, a patient management will discover that the union eventually recognizes the need for more flexibility in work rules in order to provide higher productivity and job security. Indeed, in a healthy setting, the union provides the company with a ready-made conduit through which to communicate with employees, to organize them and explain benefits plans, and to integrate educational, social, and recreational activities. Winning over the employees *and* the union is necessary because in a Type A company where hourly employees mistrust the management, the attempt to push the union out will be perceived as a sign of bad faith. If the company believes in more worker participation, the employees will ask, then why not participate through the union? Or do they want to get rid of the union to take advantage of us in the future? On the other hand, the company, recalling past abuses, remembers local union officers elected in each plant who have specialized in baiting the management, fighting the management, and where possible, humiliating the management. In a sense, these union heads with specialized skills and narrow incentives stand for all that's inimical to a Type Z company. Given these veterans of wars past, the company argues, the hope of creating a new tie with employees is slim. Still, any attempt to drive out the union gives employees further proof of the duplicity of management.

For a workable situation with the union or any industrial relations specialists, both management and employees must be convinced of the value of different incentives broader than just protecting and fighting one another—incentives to sustain a productive working relationship. After all, unions and companies who fail to work for these changes lower productivity and otherwise bring about failure. These bureaucratized unions and companies will go out of business.

These provocative issues may prompt dissent. I do not expect all readers, whatever their persuasion, to entirely agree with me. The union-management relationship, complex to the point of confusion, is difficult to sort out since the issue is emotionally laden. Numerous discussions will be necessary within the company, within the union, and between the two.

STEP EIGHT: STABILIZE EMPLOYMENT

Stability of employment comes in part as a direct outcome of policy. A great deal of voluntary termination by employees who have better alternatives can be overcome by providing them with a work environment that offers equity, challenge, and participation in decisions about their work. In Japan, where low unemployment makes finding workers quite difficult, firms have adopted the practice of widespread part-time employment. The Sony plant in Ichinomiya outside Tokyo, for example, operates shifts of four, six and eight hours, with varying starting times to fit schedules of women with young children who want to work while their children are at school. These variable shifts carry some scheduling costs, but such costs may be more than offset by an experienced and dedicated set of employees who stay with the firm for thirty or forty years.

Involuntary termination, or mass layoff and specific firing of employees, is largely a matter of company policy. Some companies will argue that layoffs are forced on them when the economy weakens and sales decline. To a basically noncompetitive company that is going out of business, layoffs become standard procedure when the economy declines. However, a company or economy suffering from short-run decline can avoid layoffs through a sharing of the misfortune. Shareholders can share in the loss by accepting less profits or even moderate losses for one year. In exchange, a highly committed and experienced team of employees will repay them in future years with large profits. Similarly, employees at all levels can share the burden by accepting shortened work weeks and paychecks, foregoing perquisites, and temporarily performing tasks they find distasteful. Twice in recent times, Hewlett-Packard has adopted the nine-day fortnight along with a hiring freeze, a travel freeze, and the elimination of perquisites. Each time, these steps kept employees on while other companies in the industry had layoffs. The result at Hewlett-Packard has been the lowest voluntary turnover rate, the most experienced workforce in the industry, and one of the highest rates of growth and profitability.

In a more basic sense, the fate of most firms ties into employment security. A company that enters frequently into unfamiliar technologies knowingly risks its investment in research, plants, and equipment. However, it also assumes a greater risk of failure almost never recognized. In entering this new business, a company typically moves some old employees into the new effort and hires from the outside as well, in order to bring expertise to this area. If the effort should fail, then the employees associated with the venture, except for a lucky few, are commonly turned out into the street. The cost of this layoff to the firm shows up in greater difficulty in hiring the most talented employees in the future, in the higher cost of voluntary turnover, and in the lower commitment of the employees who stay. If actual costs of these ventures were added up, fewer firms would undertake them. Should such a shift occur, the rate of innovation would not slow down, rather new ventures would be undertaken only by companies who already have some knowledge of the field.

A pivotal factor in stabilizing employment is slow evaluation and promotion.

STEP NINE: DECIDE ON A SYSTEM FOR SLOW EVALUATION AND PROMOTION

Motion is relative. Young people are impatient. Despite the constancy of these two facts of life, slowing down the process of evaluation and promotion is vital to underscore to employees the importance of long-run performance. They they will forget about the short run and instead do what basically makes sense for the short or long run—right?

That approach overlooks that the best people always have the most outside options and that impatient, young people may irrationally leave a more promising career with a Type Z company to join a Type A company. The solution to the problem is simple: promote them rapidly compared to the competition so that they won't leave, but promote them slowly compared to their peers so that they will develop a long-run view. Of course, there is a catch. This solution requires that a whole cohort of new bankers, managers, etc., who entered together (roughly during the same six months, usually in the spring) all be promoted rapidly. The best of them have no incentive to leave, since all are being promoted at the same rate internally. If everyone is going to be promoted, to evaluate any of them is unnecessary, except for your personal amusement. Over the long run, the high performers will emerge and will take the positions of greater responsibility while developing long-term values and cooperative attitudes. That is a considerable gain, perhaps worth the cost of having to relatively overpay the low performers in the group during the early years. A modified and perhaps superior overall method is to promote the entire cohort at a faster rate than the average person in the class merits, but not quite as fast as the most talented person deserves. In this case, fewer people will be overpaid during the early years, but a few will be underpaid and may leave for their better options. The overall result may be preferable.

No doubt someone who performs at a high level without recognition will, justifiably, feel frustrated and leave. But superior performance need not be acknowledged with higher pay during the early years in a career.

People aged twenty-one who know they are above average in ability regularly enter a long period of below-average income in order to become physicians. Aha, you say, but they look on those early years as an investment in their future income that will more than offset their current loss. Indeed, that is so as it is among young lawyers, accountants, and managers in Japan. What is critical is that this young person realize that his or her superior performance is recognized and will indeed be well compensated for in the long run. In order to induce young employees to accept a slower process of formal evaluation and promotion, a system of non-monetary forms of evaluation, such as frequent involvement with superiors on projects, including close instruction and guidance, must be provided. They communicate the expectation of greater income in the future without creating short-run incentives. In an extensive and thorough process of performance reviews set up by an organization, employees can receive feedback from more than one superior on their effectiveness during the past six months or year.

The slowing down of promotion will also be aided, at this point, by some of the other Type Z innovations that have been put in place. For one thing, as turnover declines and managers young and old move from assignment to assignment, each young person will develop quickly a wide circle of more experienced acquaintances. Some will naturally develop a mentoring relationship with that young person and will provide the kind of specific and believable feedback needed. The cooperative atmosphere provides many opportunities for new employees to participate in challenging and important assignments where senior managers can be observed in action. This kind of challenge comes only with promotion in a Type A company. After a few years, the more senior managers will specifically ask for the young

person's help in one or another project that cuts across departmental lines, and these requests will serve to further bolster confidence in future rewards. Indeed, in a Type Z organization, the employees do not receive less information about performance and prospects; they receive more. At the same time, however, they know that the fundamental granting of hierarchical position and of future large differences in pay are based upon performance over a long run.

STEP TEN: BROADEN CAREER PATH DEVELOPMENT

Recently, as it has become increasingly clear that the United States' economy was entering a sustained period of slow growth, research has increasingly focused on the middle-aged, middle-level professional or manager who has limited prospects for further advancement. The results to date suggest that managers who continue to circulate across jobs within a company, but without hierarchical promotion, retain their enthusiasm, their effectiveness, and their satisfaction at a level almost as high as that of the "stars" who continue to move both around and up. By comparison, those who remain in the same position without vertical or horizontal movement quickly lose their interest, their enthusiasm, and their commitment. A number of large United States firms have, therefore, begun to develop systematic programs of job movement for all managerial, professional, and white-collar employees as a consequence of this research, much of it conducted at the schools of business at Columbia University, M.I.T., and the University of Southern California.

The approach to developing non-specialized career paths will vary widely by industry and to some extent by firm. In the insurance industry or the retail industry, the nature of jobs does not change radically from one year to the next. Such industries can develop a systematic process of advertising new positions widely and encourage employees to transfer to related jobs that permit them to learn something new. In rapidly-growing companies, this process occurs naturally: As new stores, offices, or factories open up, jobs must be filled by people who understand the company, and the best candidate comes from a related but not identical job.

In order to have the process of career circulation succeed, top level of managers need to set an example. If the top managers rotate every three to five years between jobs, so that the vice-president of personnel takes over international sales, and the vice-president of international sales takes over domestic manufacturing, then each of them will, over time, bring along managers at the next level down whose skills they need. Those managers will, in turn, want to bring along some that they know, and the process will naturally trickle down through the organization.

The most difficult move in this direction is the first one, especially in a company with a firm tradition of specialization throughout a career. Typically, the people in the computer department will argue, "You can bring a plant scheduler in here, and inside of one day our whole system will be down. They can barely add, let alone understand our computer system." The marketing people, in turn, will say, "If you let one of those computer jocks get close to any of our customers, we'll be out of business in a year." I can only say that in my experience firms tend to overestimate the value of specialization in many cases and to underestimate the importance of having people in each department who understand the other departments. When such a change is implemented after conditions of cooperation have been established to some extent, they lead to superior performance. New product introductions go off on schedule and without mishap, because design, manufacturing, and marketing are better coordinated. New information systems are introduced more rapidly and effectively when systems understand the plants and vice versa. After all, it's not as though the plant scheduler has never seen a computer print-out. Not only doesn't he need retraining in computers, he's been on the receiving end of the technology for years—and has been complaining about its failings. He will, hopefully, be able to make suggestions about how to improve the print-out for other schedulers—things the computer specialists wouldn't understand. Encouraging a better blend of related expertises benefits everyone.

A successful program of career circulation is based on a cadre of managers widely informed about the skills available in departments other than their own. Working together they can make appointments to benefit not only their department but the departments with whom they must coordinate. With the properties of the Type Z organization in place, this information will be widely distributed, and the incentive to cooperate emerges. Each of the elements of the Type Z organization relates to the others. In isolation, none will accomplish much. Together, they constitute a cooperative system.

STEP ELEVEN: PREPARING FOR IMPLEMENTATION AT THE FIRST LEVEL

All the stages of implementation to this point have focused on managerial and professional employees. Many suggestions will prompt managers to deal with first-level supervisors and with hourly or production and clerical employees in new ways, but the target group so far has been the middle and upper employee. Traditionally most United States firms have introduced changes in the lower ranks. But Theory Z advocates the opposite approach that has been taken by Japanese companies as well as some United States firms such as General Motors.

The reasons for starting at the top boil down to one central issue: A lower level employee or manager cannot participate unless those above provide the invitation to do so. If an organization begins by being rigidly hierarchical, evolutionary change must begin at the top of that hierarchy. The only change that can begin at the bottom in such an organization is revolution, and revolution was the solution that brought on the United States labor union movement in its currently antagonistic form.

The steps outlined above will typically take one to two years to achieve, and they will produce notable results of their own. The improved integration of efforts and willingness to cooperate will yield greater efficiency and productivity. Managers will less often be forced to respond to short-run objectives and disrupt the activities of plants and offices. First-level supervisors will less often be caught in contests for power and resources between competing middle managers. All of these improvements will be felt by the sales clerk, the machinist, the stewardess. Only after these results have begun to emerge should implementation at the first level of employees be contemplated.

The hourly employee and the first-line supervisor live a world apart from the professional and the manager in most organizations. The hospital orderly is as distant from the surgeon as the bank teller is from the commercial lending officer. In most American organizations, those employees who determine the basic productivity and quality of the products and services know little about the future plans or current performance of the company. Rarely are they asked for opinions. They receive different benefits packages, are paid hourly rather than monthly and, not surprisingly, don't stay for very long. As a consequence, these employees have little understanding of the

company, little trust in the management, and little tolerance for a confused attempt to make a fundamental shift in the management style.

The first-line supervisor has, in many ways, the most difficult task of all. This supervisor must maintain enough goodwill among workers of short experience and low trust and commitment to meet his production quotas while at the same time keep sufficient credibility with superiors to exert influence in favor of the employees when needed. Both workers and managers expect the foreman to represent their interests to the other side, and both suspect the foreman of having sold out to the other side. As long as management and workers take opposing sides, the foreman will be in the middle. Until the management has developed some confidence in its own ability to achieve cooperation and trust, it cannot support the magnitude of change that will take place in the plant and office.

If employees at the bottom of the corporate pyramid are to be included in a cooperative and trusting relationship that departs sharply from their current state, they will have to overcome the deepest sort of skepticism. This skepticism can be overcome only through great effort and only with the most consistent signals from above. The workers in the plants and in the field do not rub shoulders with the decision makers, do not look them in the eye. They can gauge their true intent only dimly, through the decisions and the policies handed down from afar. Although a more direct approach to communication with employees will help, there are simply never enough top managers to provide first-hand evidence of commitment to change to all of the workers. Instead, the policies and decisions affecting the hourly employee must consistently express openness, trust, and emphasis on the long run.

STEP TWELVE: SEEK OUT AREAS TO IMPLEMENT PARTICIPATION

If equitable reward, job stability, and inter-departmental coordination have been achieved, then the commitment and the productivity of hourly employees will already have begun to rise. Although I know of no systematic way to test the proposition, I would guess that most of the poor productivity attributed by managers to workers in fact is the result of inputs not received, machinery not repaired, and designs poorly coordinated by uncooperative managers who are competing against one another. Nonetheless, significant gains in productivity have been achieved by companies such as Procter & Gamble, Herman Miller, and General Motors, through the application of participative approaches at the office or shop floor level. Solicit suggestions from workers as a group rather than from a few anonymous suggestions boxes. And don't be fearful of implementing them. In one office, orders taken from customers were passed on to the distribution part of the company. These customers, however, consistently called at the busiest part of these office workers' day. Management's attitude had traditionally been grin-and-bear-it. But, under a Type Z approach, the employees decided to contact those customers, explain their problem, and try to understand the customers' needs. A system was arranged whereby the bottleneck of calls was soon avoided—all through employees', not management's, ideas.

STEP THIRTEEN: PERMIT THE DEVELOPMENT OF WHOLISTIC RELATIONSHIPS

Wholistic relationships are a consequence rather than a cause of organizational integration. In part, they help to maintain the egalitarian nature of the organization by bringing superiors and subordinates together as temporary equals and thus demonstrate that the distance between them is neither great nor impassable. However, it would be a mistake for an organization to expect to attain the benefits of productivity and of social integration by dressing employees in uniforms, commissioning the writing of a company song, and sponsoring bowling leagues and picnics. These are the kinds of expressions of solidarity, of cohesiveness, that emerge from a group of employees who enjoy working together and who enjoy sharing their feelings of belonging. Any organization blessed with such an atmosphere will have a difficult time keeping it under wraps.

A wholistic relationship cannot be developed, but once the Z changes are underway, it has a chance to grow. Regular question and answer sessions among hourly employees will help. Talk to employees about how the company is working against competitors, about its successes and problems. Be prepared to ask as well as answer some tough questions. These work-related issues hold the key to wholistic relations and keep them free of any company paternalism.

ANTHONY T. COBB
NEWTON MARGULIES

Organization Development: A Political Perspective

During the last several years the area of organizational politics (OP) has attracted the interest of social scientists and practitioners alike. In the field of organization development (OD), interest has focused on the use of OP in intervention programs. It is now generally recognized that such programs inevitably affect organizational politics and are affected by them (Bennis, 1969; Cobb, 1977; Pettigrew, 1975).

Despite this knowledge, the movement of OD into the study and use of OP has been cautious and conservative. At present, the interest OD displays in OP remains largely peripheral to what can be called its clinical or process orientation: one that relies on a relatively intimate client/consultant relationship to facilitate self-discovery, help, and renewal (Margulies & Raia, 1978, pp. 110-11). There are a number of views regarding this level of OP interest. One extreme holds that any political orientation will necessarily divert attention from OD's clinical mission and inevitably subvert it. Another extreme view holds that OD consultants ought to assume a political activist role to ensure that program objectives are implemented. Both views maintain that OD has been devoid of any political orientation. The former maintains that this is how it should be, the latter that it must no longer remain so.

Our purposes in this article are two: First, we assert that, while OD is not politically sophisticated, neither is it devoid of a political orientation. OD has developed an unrecognized political orientation in many of its values and some aspects of its most frequently used technology. Although this political orientation is restricted in scope, it has proved useful in supporting OD's clinical objectives. We believe that the effectiveness of OD can be enhanced when professionals recognize, accept, and use this existing political orientation in the service of organizational change.

Our second purpose is to explore some of the ramifications of a greater level of political involvement in intervention programs. Although increased political involvement can aid the OD consultant and the host organization, so too can it do harm, particularly when it moves to the extreme of political activism.

To address these issues properly, a political perspective is developed first to view OD's past and its alternative political futures. This perspective provides focus for subsequent discussions.

Reprinted from: *Academy of Management Review* (January 1981).

A POLITICAL PERSPECTIVE

A political perspective with sufficient range to deal with the issues raised here can be developed by briefly addressing two topics. First, a definition of the term *organizational politics* is provided and, second, what can be called the "political subsystem" is described.

The Meaning of Organizational Politics

The literature provides many definitions of OD developed from a variety of perspectives. Mayes and Allen (1977) provide an adequate survey of these. In terms relevant to OD, organizational politics can be defined as *the use of power to modify or protect an organization's exchange structure.* An exchange structure is composed of an organization's resource distribution system and those who have formal authority to decide to what purposes resources will be used. An exchange structure in equilibrium represents the status quo and is "legitimate." Efforts to change the status quo, then, involve political action both on the part of those who challenge and those who seek to maintain it.

As seen in this light, OP per se is neither good nor bad. Actually, OP can either help or hinder the organization, depending on the processes used and the objectives sought. Even though it is easy for the OD consultant to become involved in politics, it is entirely another matter to have the sophistication to manage the use of OP productively.

The Political Subsystem

For convenience, the notion of a social subsystem (Guest, Hersey, & Blanchard, 1977) is used here to denote the subsystem about which the OD consultant is expert and in which he or she operates. This subsystem coexists with many others, one of which can be labeled the political subsystem.

The political subsystem is composed of the sources, locations, and flow of power through the organization. The basic criterion of effectiveness within the subsystem is the extent to which sufficient power can be accumulated and transferred to those locations (i.e., individuals) in the organization to maintain productive operations, solve problems, and implement solutions. A political subsystem is efficient to the extent that power can be accumulated and transferred quickly and with precision.

A tenet of general systems theory is that subsystems interact with one another. Therefore, changes in either the social or political subsystem will produce changes in the other. The interactive relationship poses at least two basic problems to OD consultants concerned with organizational politics. The first is determining how support can be generated within the political subsystem to aid work within the social subsystem. The second is knowing what changes are necessary in the social subsystem to facilitate the development of an effective and efficient political subsystem.

Political Orientations in Organization Development

Because there is interaction between the social subsystem and the political subsystem, successful change in the former requires complementary and supportive changes in the latter. It is because OD is well aware of such subsystem interaction (Benne & Bernbaum, 1969; Leavitt, 1965) that there has been recent concern that OD consultants should become more politically sophisticated and active in order to increase intervention success (Burke, 1976; Pettigrew, 1975). Yet, historically speaking, OD interventions on the whole have enjoyed a great deal of success. Given that OD consultants have traditionally displayed, at most, a minimal interest in OP, the issue must be raised of how they are able to survive at all, much less be successful. One reason may be just good fortune. Another may be that clients themselves come to see that political cooperation is necessary to protect their own self-interests. We will argue that there is still a third reason: OD has developed a largely unrecognized political orientation in addition to its clinical one and this political orientation complements the clinical one in producing successful interventions.

Where in OD does this political orientation lie? Even now, organization development does not appear to be an easily defined field or profession. For the purposes here, OD can be viewed as a profession built on a foundation composed of three basic interactive elements: its values, its technology, and its knowledge of the human side of organizations. If there is a political orientation in OD that helps guide the political behavior of consultants, then, it should reside in one or more of these elements.

The knowledge base of OD incorporates clinical concepts relevant to power, models of power, and even sources of power available to consultants for work in interventions (Huse, 1980, pp. 143-148). Properly viewed, such concepts of power *can* form a foundation on which to build political theory and intervention strategy. Yet, even today the knowledge base of OD remains essentially lacking in political theory and models to help *guide* the consultant in terms of political intervention strategies (Beer, 1976; Bennis, 1969). Therefore, if political assistance is given to the consultant, it must come from the value or technological base of the field. It is our view that it comes from both.

Political Support in the Value Base

For the purposes here, the value component of OD is viewed in structural terms. At its base lie fundamental philosophical or value orientations. These would include rationalism, pragmatism, existentialism (Fried-lander, 1976), humanism, and democracy (Friedlander & Brown, 1974). These basic orientations, then, provide the context for the development of more specific values: values concerning intervention concepts, means, and end-states. Valued clinical *aims*, or end-states of intervention, include individual growth and increased organizational effectiveness with the capability of self-renewal (French, Bell, & Zawacki, 1978). Valued *means* for reaching this end-state include confrontation, honesty, open communications, the movement toward power equalization, and collaboration. Concepts that support these valued means include beliefs in the goodness of people, Theory Y assumptions, and the potential and desire for growth by organizational members. Such historically entrenched values of OD, then, provide the general context here for discussion.

The OD consultant is an expert in creating a social environment within which the client system can achieve full utilization of its own human resources to solve its problems (French et al., 1978). Basic to the full utilization of human resources are such necessary processes as collaboration and participation. Collaboration, however, requires that power be exchanged, shared, and pooled. Participation in decision making requires a "franchise" that comes only with the power to make inputs. Thus, if the consultant is to achieve collaboration and participation in the social subsystem, supportive changes must occur within the political subsystem to allow it. Some of these changes include the general reduction of power differentials between organizational members, the transfer of power to those who are to participate in decision making, and the removal of structural obstacles to the flow of power in the organization generally and between levels of authority in particular. The consultant is guided in these tasks by many of the values OD has developed.

The belief that power equalization should be used in interventions is a central concept in OD (Leavitt, 1965). Strauss (1963, p.41) stated, for example, that "the main thrust of the human relations movement over the last 20 years has been toward. . .'power equalization.'" In the nearly twenty years since Strauss's observation, this general orientation has become valued in its own right and is reflected in a number of other values that focus on more specific political problems. This can be demonstrated by examining specific values oriented to the individual, superior/subordinate relations, and organization structures paralleling the micro, intermediate, and macro perspectives of the organization.

The Individual's Political Position. Participation raises the basic political issue of who should be given the right, and thus the power, to participate in decision making. On the level of the nation or state, for example, the extent of citizen participation is justified and supported by the assumptions made regarding the capabilities and traits of the polity (i.e., citizens).

The political position of organizational members is justified and supported as well by basic assumptions regarding workers. McGregor (1960) has articulated some of these assumptions. Theory X assumptions support a political structure in which power is centralized and participation removed from the rank and file. Theory Y assumptions support a political structure in which power is decentralized, justifying a wide base of participation. The clinical side of Theory Y assumptions focuses on the individual as a potential resource in problem solving. Theory Y also justifies the political necessity of transferring some measure of participatory power to the worker. Thus, although OD consultants may not recognize it, when they promote a clinical value orienta-

tion, coinciding with Theory Y, they are establishing as well some of the political subsystem changes needed to support their clinical aims.

Superior/Subordinate Relations. Historically, one of OD's principal concerns has been with leadership style. In its clinical context, OD has tied leadership style to interactions among subordinates, satisfaction, and productivity (Lewin, Lippitt, & White, 1939). In terms of organizational change, OD has recognized that changes on one level require "complementary and reinforcing changes in organizational levels above and below that level" (Benne & Bernbaum, 1969, p.331). It is not surprising, therefore, to see that OD has developed a value orientation to leader/subordinate relations that supports the power exchange required for collaboration and interlevel adjustments between subordinates and superiors. Authoritarian leadership removes power from subordinates, thereby suppressing participation, collaboration, and the upward flow of influence, whereas democratic leadership facilitates them. The fact that OD values democratic leadership produces changes not only in the social subsystem, but complementary and reinforcing changes in the political subsystem as well.

The Organization Structure. In accordance with general systems theory, the structural subsystem (Guest et al., 1977) will affect the political subsystem. Although they did not address the political subsystem specifically, Burns and Stalker (1961) recognized this interactive effect. They noted that the rigid power structure of mechanistic organizations tends to hamper the power flow necessary for broad organizational problem solving. Organic organizations, on the other hand, facilitate problem solving by allowing an easier flow of power through the political subsystem to wherever it is needed.

The behavioral administrative structures articulated by Likert (1961, 1967) are relevant to this discussion. System 1 tends to impede, but System 4 tends to facilitate the flow of power through the political subsystem. As a result, System 4 facilitates broad organizational collaboration, participation, and communication in the establishment of goals and resource distribution.

Organization development values an organic System 4 administrative structure for a number of clinical reasons. When such a structure is adopted by the client, however, it promotes changes within the political subsystem. These political changes, in turn, facilitate work within the social subsystem.

The Practical and Political Utility of Values. Fundamentally, OD values a democratic workplace and the power equalization inherent in it. It was demonstrated above that this value orientation is manifest whether one takes a micro, intermediate, or macro perspective of the organization. Part of the reason OD may hold these values is that they are generally accepted in our society. Clinically speaking, they are valued because OD believes that they promote effective organizational performance and personal growth. One should not ignore, however, the political utility these values have in terms of the consultant's clinical objectives.

Consider the problems typically faced by the consultant and client system. They tend to be unstructured, complex, novel, and complicated. Evidence indicates that these types of problems are best solved by a broad-based participatory effort utilizing the resources of those best able to attend to them regardless of formal power position (Burns & Stalker, 1961; MacCrimmon & Taylor, 1976).

Such collaborative and participative efforts, however, require commensurate political subsystem support. Many OD values, some of which have been presented here, can be seen as helpful in promoting political support for clinical objectives.

Political Support in the Technological Base

The technological base of OD can be divided into two interdependent components. One includes the tools and techniques the consultant can use in intervention. The second includes the roles assumed by the consultant (e.g., facilitator, interviewer) and the operational know-how, expertise, or knowledge to use the tools, techniques, and roles available to the consultant. Political supports can be found in both components.

Tools and Techniques. The value OD gives to power equalization finds expression in some of its techniques as well. Laboratory training, for example, promotes a commitment to open and honest communications regarding interpersonal relations, organizational life, and diagnosis. But such a commitment "does inevitably imply some democratization [that]...may indeed undermine formal authority to a considerable degree" (E. Schein, 1972, p. 93). Intervention techniques that include such components as these, then, serve to operationalize the political as well as clinical side of the democratic values held by OD consultants.

Other techniques appear to play a political part in integrating vested interests by facilitating actual change in the exchange structure. Techniques oriented toward roles provide a case in point. Organizational roles prescribe occupant behavior, areas of decision making, character of reporting relationships, legitimate power, and the like. In short, roles contain many components of the status quo exchange structure. Many role techniques, therefore, have a political side in that they intervene "directly in the relationship of power, authority, and influence" of role occupants and reciprocals (Harrison, 1978, p. 159). When OD consultants facilitate change in such role components, then, they are working within both the social and political subsystems to accomplish their aims.

The political subsystem is also affected by a number of techniques oriented to "structural" or "work engineering." The negotiation of resource exchanges and integration of vested interests, for example, is a political subsystem change that occurs along with the institution of a management-by-objectives system. The clinical objectives of job enrichment include ownership of the task, increases in perceived task importance, and the like. To accomplish these objectives, however, "vertical loading" is required, whereby previous supervisory perogatives are given to the subordinate.

Consultant Roles and Operational Knowledge. Consultants are called on to play a variety of roles when using their knowledge and techniques. The literature describes many of these roles; our focus here is on a distinctly political role that cuts across many others and is often ignored: the diplomatic role. The purpose of this role is to communicate the vested interests of one party to another in a language that can be fully understood. The diplomat then seeks to integrate these vested interests when possible and, when not, to reduce the friction caused by competition by negotiations, tradeoffs, and the like.

In order to support the clinical objectives of intervention, the consultant often assumes one of at least two diplomatic roles. One might be called the "enfranchiser" role. The socio-organizational distance between higher- and lower-level participants is often large. So, too, is the power differential within the political subsystem. In order to communicate and facilitate the integration of vested interests, the consultant often becomes a "communications channel" between the parties. For lower-level participants, consultants become surrogate participants in decision making; for higher-level decision makers they are representatives of the organizational citizenry.

The consultant often plays a diplomatic role horizontally in the organization as well. The consultant is frequently called on to mediate between organizational groups that are interdependent but have different vested interests, values, perceptions, and beliefs. Like Lawrence and Lorsch's integrator (1967), the consultant facilitates communication between parties by serving as a communications channel or by facilitating face-to-face interaction. By working with and between both groups, the consultant aids in the integration of their vested interests while focusing on their interaction process.

Whether moving vertically, horizontally, or obliquely in the organization, the OD consultant is in a unique position to carry the interests of one party to another. The parties can speak openly to the consultant, without fear of repercussions, and can be confident that the consultant is concerned about them as well as about the general welfare of the organization. This promotes the power generation and transfer necessary for effective political subsystem operation. Thus, the consultant plays the clinical role of communications channel and the political role of power channel at the same time for the same purpose: beneficial change in the social subsystem.

The Political Side of Organization Development

The more one explores OD, the more one can see its political side. It is true, however, that OD's clinical orientation remains paramount and that the political side plays a mostly unrecognized, supportive role. Evaluations made by Bennis (1969), Beer (1976), and Burke (1976) hold true today. Organization development has not come to fully appreciate the impact that OP has on change programs. Nor has OD developed the models, knowledge, and facts that represent a sophisticated political orientation.

Nevertheless, OD's brand of "political pacifism" should not be ignored. It needs to be further explored for at least three reasons. The first is to see if the direction it provides is appropriate for the various situations OD consultants encounter. Second, if OD is determined to become more politically active, a foundation for such growth may be found not only in the values and technology of OD but its knowledge base as well. Third, OD's present political orientation can serve as a reference point. As such, it is useful for exploring those issues involved in assuming a greater political role.

POLITICAL INVOLVEMENT: CONSIDERATIONS FOR ORGANIZATION DEVELOPMENT

The OD profession has been urged to become more politically oriented and active (Bennis, 1969; Burke, 1976; Pettigrew, 1975). In this regard at least two questions need to be raised. First, what would be the utility of increased political intervention? Second, what would be the consequences in terms of OD's ethical/value base? Before these questions can be answered, just what is meant by "increased political involvement" needs to be explored.

A Continuum of Political Involvement

It is possible to describe the extent and character of OP involvement along a continuum. At the extremes lie "political pacifism" and "political activism." The midrange is represented by the "political moderate" position.

Political Pacifism. Political pacifism has been represented above. It includes a fundamental commitment to clinical rather than political intervention. While a political element does exist, it is minimal, generally unrecognized, and oriented to clinical support rather than being used as a means of change in its own right.

Political Moderation. The political moderate advocates the development of knowledge, models, and strategies to overcome political blindspots (Bennis, 1969; Harrison, 1978; Pettigrew, 1975). The use of these, however, remains subordinate to, and strictly supportive of, work within the social subsystem. The political role played by the consultant is at most one of a "political facilitator" who seeks to establish a political climate supportive of clinically oriented change. Honesty, truth, collaboration, participation, and the like are still pursued. Political facilitation works to overcome the political impediments to these components of change. The clients operating within this climate work toward the establishment of a new status quo, *one chosen by them.*

Political Activism. Political activism advocates deep involvement in the political subsystem—at least as much as, if not more than, in the social subsystem. Here the consultant adopts the role of "political activist," of someone who has some vision of what the client system's condition ought to be. This vision is realized by politically overcoming resistance to it. In this sense, then, the political activist maintains that "the ends justify the means" and advocates such strategies as limiting and channeling communication for political purposes, the use of covert or hidden agendas, and the political use of intervention research (V. Schein, 1977). Coercive politics may also be used. Damaging information gained in intervention, for example, might be used against those who stand in the way of the consultant (Pettigrew, 1975).

The Utility of Increased Political Involvement

It has been argued that increased political involvement will lead to greater chances of intervention success than that provided by the current approach of political pacifism. Because these arguments have been directly and indirectly stated in the literature (Bennis, 1969; Harrison, 1978; Pettigrew, 1975; V. Schein, 1977), they are only briefly reviewed here.

The moderate position takes due note of the evidence that supports the existence of OP and the political subsystem, and their effect on any change program (Bennis, 1969; Cyert & March, 1964; March, 1962; March & Simon, 1958; Thompson, 1967). Ignoring this evidence creates a significant gap in the operational knowledge of OD and its approach to change. Furthermore, this knowledge gap makes it impossible to develop appropriate reactive and proactive strategies to support the clinical aims of the intervention program. Evidence can be cited demonstrating that once this gap is filled, political tools, techniques, and strategies can be developed to serve the clinical ends of the OD consultant (Harrison, 1978, Selznick, 1949). Although individual studies are subject to criticism, the corpus of evidence represents a systematic approach with generally positive results across applications. As a whole, then, the evidence lends support to the moderate position.

Political activism builds on the arguments provided by the moderate position. Activists assume that not only are politics a fact of organizational life but that some powerful and sophisticated members of the client system use politics to protect and extend their own selfish interests. These are formidable "opponents." Political activism, say the activists, is the best way to deal with them, and they cite evidence indicating that activist techniques (e.g., political manipulation of communication, research information) have successfully overcome such opponents (Pet-

tigrew, 1975; V. Schein, 1977). Unfortunately, most of this evidence is anecdotal and lacking in empirical validation. Much more empirical work needs to be done to support the activist position.

Some Caveats Regarding Increased Political Involvement

With all the arguments made for increased political involvement on the part of the OD consultants, there is a surprising lack of attention given to some of the problems that may emerge. These potential problems deserve attention.

Political Success Requires Political Sophistication. Consultants in OD are probably more politically sophisticated than they realize or may be willing to admit. Nevertheless, OD consultants are clinicians, not politicians. Their training may have prepared them for political pacifism but not activism. To urge political pacifists to use techniques employed by activists can invite disaster. Recently, a broader base of political training and knowledge has been offered to OD consultants (Huse, 1980, pp. 143–148; NTL Institute, 1980). Though consultants now have the opportunity to develop greater political sophistication, the cautious and conservative progress of OD into OP may well be justified on utilitarian grounds. Little, if any, sophistication is required to enter the political arena, but a great deal is required to work productively within it.

Political Reaction in the Client System. Largely ignored in arguments favoring political involvement are considerations of how the client system may react. Activists maintain, for example, that organizational "opponents" should be politically overcome. It must be remembered, however, that what is home ground to the opponent is foreign territory to the consultant. If opponents have any political sophistication, they will have identified and marshalled sources of power, formed long-standing alliances, and developed political strategies that have proven value in that particular system. One can expect such opponents to use their power and strategies when they perceive that their vested interests are attacked.

In addition, one needs to consider how the client system itself will react to political confrontation. It is one thing to be able to win a political confrontation; it is quite another to keep such confrontations from adversely affecting the political subsystem. Political pacifism seems to have evolved to minimize the danger of disruption. Political moderates, and activists in particular, need to carefully consider this aspect of political subsystem reactivity.

Reaction to the OD Profession.   Perhaps the biggest concern related to increased political activity, particularly political activism, is how clients will react to OD itself. Since its beginning, OD has developed an image of being close to what Charles Perrow (1977) called "the forces of light." This image derives from the emphasis on such fundamental values as honesty, openness, collaboration, and a steadfast concern for everyone in the client system. This image has utilitarian value. OD technology, for example, requires cooperation, trust, and client confidence in the consultant. The OD image supports these qualities, and the consultant depends on this image.

The success that political activists have enjoyed may be partly based on this image as well. Limiting and channeling communication for political purposes, the use of hidden or covert agendas, and the political manipulation of intervention research strategies may be successful partly because clients don't expect OD consultants to behave in this manner. Thus, using the element of surprise, the activist can catch the opponents unprepared to effectively resist.

Images can change. As the reputation of the activist consultant grows, clients will no longer be caught by surprise. They can be expected, rather, to take the initiative and attack the consultant first. At the very least, the activist will no longer enjoy the trust and cooperation of clients who are preparing for political confrontation.

This would be a relatively minor concern for OD as a profession if clients could be counted on *not* to generalize their perceptions of activist consultants—an unrealistic hope. If the OD profession suffers an image change reflecting political activism, the chances of success even for political pacifists are reduced.

Consider the following example: A nationally known consultant company conducted management audits for a major governmental unit in the Pacific Southwest. Following the audits, high-ranking officials were fired, in light of evidence gained in some of the audits. Word quickly spread that these audits were political covers with the hidden agenda of marshalling evidence to do away with preselected officials. Whether or not this rumor was correct, from that point forward the audits created a great deal of political turmoil. Perhaps the activist is prepared for this type of reaction. The issue, however, is whether OD as a profession can accept this type of image change.

Facilitation versus Activism.   Political moderates remain committed to the traditional clinical orientation of organization development. They argue that political facilitation of social change is not only compatible with this orientation but will increase chances of intervention success as well. They conclude, therefore, that OD ought to promote such political involvement on the part of its practitioners. Although there is evidence to support this position, a number of caveats must be kept in mind. First, OD must take care to see that consultants are properly prepared to assume the role of a political facilitator. Second, political facilitation must be exercised with due caution lest the client system overreact. Third, OD must recognize that it is all too easy to slip from the facilitator role into the activist role. The boundaries between them are often difficult to define, particularly in the hour-to-hour and day-to-day operation of an intervention program.

Political activists maintain that political facilitation is not enough to achieve intervention success in the face of undetermined political resistance. Greater rates of success can, however, be expected if the consultant uses whatever power politics are required to confront and remove such resistance. Political activism, however, carries with it not only the problems of negative client-system reaction, but also the problems of a negative image change for the OD profession as a whole.

On utilitarian grounds alone, OD is well advised to increase political involvement only with extreme caution and due deliberation. Beyond utilitarian considerations, OD consultants and the field as a whole should address as well the issue of how political involvement affects the value base of the profession.

Value Considerations

Political involvement, particularly as it approaches political activism, has consequences for the values of organization development. There has been a general lack of discussion regarding what these consequences may be, yet this is an important topic, because the distinctive character and practice of OD, as with any professional field, is based as much on its values as on its technology and knowledge (Margulies & Raia, 1978). The value base plays an important role in the image of OD, the use of its technology, and in providing the context and

objectives for intervention itself. The value base reflects the nature of the relationship between client and consultant and what constitutes acceptable consultant behavior. Clients depend on the value base of OD just as they do in any professional relationship. It has been argued above that consultants depend on it as well.

Political activism provides a good context for discussion. The sharp contrast between the values inherent in political activism and the traditional values of OD produces issues more easily discerned than when lesser levels of political involvement are addressed. At the same time, the issues raised by these contrasts provide some points of departure for addressing the more subtle issues of lesser forms of political involvement. The assertion that the ends justify the means, whether explicitly advocated (V. Schein, 1977) or implicitly assumed, provides the focus for value considerations.

Can the Means and Ends Be Separated?   In theory, it may be possible to separate one's objectives and the means used to achieve them. In practice, and particularly in OD, the means used appear more often than not to affect the ends attained. From a value perspective, an OD intervention program is successful if the organizational health of a client system is improved and if it has achieved or expanded its capacity for self-renewal (French et al., 1978). These goals, in turn, are dependent on, and evolve from, the achievement of a host of other clinical objectives. Such objectives may well be displaced in an intervention program using the philosophy and techniques of political activism.

The displacement of clinical objectives can occur for a number of reasons. First, intense political activity often leads to the compromise of objectives for political expediency. One must consider the point at which such compromise becomes failure from a clinical perspective. Second, political activism, by its nature, fosters political activity in the client system of a similar character. Such activity can itself displace clinical goals. Moreover, the aftermath of political activism, with its tendency to produce win/lose conflict, can leave strains and tensions in the client system that drain energy from productive uses and future renewal. Finally, the capacity for self-renewal requires that the consultant teach those in the client system the concepts, methods, and values that will allow them to solve future as well as present problems (French et al., 1978). One must consider, then, whether political activism teaches the client methods of self-renewal, or suspicion, distrust, and the fine art of political warfare.

Presuming the Ends that Justify the Means. Political activism is literally presumptuous: the activist presumes to know the good ends that justify the means used to achieve them. Traditionally, however, the OD consultant leaves the configuration of the ends (i.e., desired condition) to the decision making of the clients. In fact, the end traditionally pursued by OD consultants is to help establish the means by which the client can effectively and efficiently pursue a new status quo. Thus, within OD the means and ends are often the same.

The political-moderate position recognizes this. It seeks to work within the political subsystem to help establish the climate necessary to support such traditional change elements as honesty, openness, collaboration, and participation. There is no doubt that these elements are value laden. To the extent that political activism replaces these traditional elements with a conscious restriction of openness and a limitation of both collaboration and participation, it is replacing the valued ends of OD for the means to reach some other set of objectives. Thus OD must consider, for example, if political re-

sistance is a form of participation to be confronted and worked through or confronted and wiped out for some vision of what ought to be. In so considering, OD must consider as well whether it will still value the welfare of individuals, even those frightened enough to resist.

On the Value of Conserving OD Values. If OD itself is to remain dynamic, the profession must constantly undergo changes to meet the challenges it faces. To the extent that OD values have promoted political naiveté within the profession, they may need to change to guide action in the political arena. It should be recognized, however, that the value base has served OD well in the past. If some values are to change, perhaps this would be best accomplished conservatively with the objective of *guiding* political involvement to reach *clinical ends.* Certainly traditional values should not be casually tossed aside to allow for politically expedient behaviors.

CONCLUDING REMARKS

We have focused on an important aspect of the growing field of organization development—its movement into the study and use of organizational politics. The present political orientations in the field, largely operationalized by OD consultants themselves, have been generally ignored and in some cases rejected. One purpose of the foregoing discussion has been to establish, as clearly as possible, the existence of these orientations. Broader recognition of OD's political orientations and the further development of political knowledge and skills can aid both the OD consultant and the field.

Political involvement is not, however, without its problems, and our second purpose has been to explore some of the utilitarian and value problems that can arise from increased political intervention. By exploring OD's present political orientation and its future political alternatives, we obtain a more complete understanding of the roles, skills, and strategies available to the OD consultant. This understanding, in turn, can only enhance the field.

PART FIVE

Productivity Frameworks

13

Productivity, QWL and Employee Involvement

Today, more and more individuals view their work life as one part of a broader life experience which involves not only job, but family, community, social responsibilities, and the concern for political and economic issues.

ROBERT A . SUTERMEISTER[1]

What is quality of work life? Quality of work life (QWL) is one's perceptions of the work experience. Since individual perceptions vary, the true meaning of quality of work life is unique to each individual. In general, however, high quality of work life exists when people have jobs that offer autonomy, variety and the feeling of making a meaningful contribution to the organization's effectiveness. The significance of a job is based on the feedback an employee receives. When feedback gives employees a sense of accomplishment and growth, the employees report high quality of work life.[2] High quality of work life is based on the assumption that individual employees are willing and able to contribute to the organization's success. Effective QWL efforts structure the work environment and the job on the basis of this assumption.[3]

QWL has grown in importance for several reasons. As society becomes more affluent, a growing percentage of the work force shifts its expectations from merely wanting a job to wanting a meaningful and satisfying career.[4] At the same time, an affluent society offers workers a safety net in the form of health care, welfare, unemployment insurance, and other social services designed to guarantee subsistence. Workers of two generations ago may have been content to have any job at all, because they were keenly aware of what it meant not to have one during the Great Depression. But for their grandchildren, who don't remember the Depression, having a job seems to be a right, rather than a privilege.

Social changes, in other words, create pressures for a better QWL. The success of such companies as General Motors, Ford, IBM and Hewlett-Packard suggest that high QWL also may be necessary to sustain high levels of productivity.

THE PRODUCTIVITY TRADE-OFF

For many centuries, the only large organizations in the western world were the military and the Catholic Church. Within both of these organizations, unswerving loyalty to superiors was the norm. The emphasis in these and many subsequent organizations was on task orientation; that is, the objectives of the organization were of paramount importance. Humanistic organizations also existed, but even their primary focus was on achieving organizational objectives (as it is in most organizations today).

When the emphasis is exclusively on achieving tasks, with no consideration for the quality of work life, productivity is apt to be low. On the other hand, total concern for the welfare of employees with no pressure to meet production or delivery schedules also would result in low productivity. Somewhere between the "sweat shop" and the "country club" is an optimal balance of emphasis between organizational objectives and employee needs that will result in the highest productivity for the organization (illustrated as point B in Figure 13–1).

Although most organizations seek this balance, they often give first priority to the organization's objectives with less emphasis on employee needs. Most U.S. companies are operating around point A, where productivity is less than it could be. Increasingly, major corporations are realizing that productivity gains are possible by achieving a better balance between the objectives of the organization and the needs of the people. In fact, an optimal leadership style might well be defined as one that concurrently meets both the needs of the people and the objectives of the organization. Admittedly, trade-offs of time, resources and ability make it difficult to realize this definition of leadership. Still, the closer an organization can move to the optimal balance, the higher its productivity will be.[5]

Unfortunately, some managers consider it a waste of time to discuss quality of work life. These managers may think QWL means being nice to people at the expense of production. Or they may think of QWL in relation to high wages and good benefits. Or they may define it as pleasant work conditions or good supervision. Obviously, good quality of work life includes all of these elements. To argue that employees have good quality of work life on the basis of one element alone is unrealistic and ineffective.

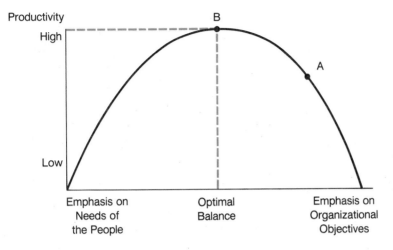

Figure 13-1.   The Productivity and QWL Trade-off

Employees often associate the following characteristics with the "best" organization they have ever worked for:

Clear objectives

Trust

Good communications

Meaningful work with challenge and variety

Chance for recognition, growth, achievement and autonomy

Sufficient feedback

Considerate leadership

A successful organization

QWL THROUGH EMPLOYEE INVOLVEMENT

Employee involvement means allowing employees to participate in decisions that affect them. This does not mean anarchy, where management abdicates its decision-making roles and responsibilities. Instead, it means that management's responsibilities in decision-making are shared with employees. Through the process of sharing the decision-making process (as discussed in Chapter 8), a sense of trust between management and workers develops. Traditional assumptions about employees' unwillingness to be self-motivated and committed to the organization's goals begin to fade as employees show their enthusiasm and commitment to problems they are attempting to solve.[7] Besides increasing trust and commitment, employee involvement can improve employee communications and attitudes. Involved employees are more likely to produce ideas, since the involvement process conveys management's interest in hearing these ideas. Through employee involvement, employees achieve a higher quality of work life. In turn, a higher quality of work life tends to generate higher levels of commitment to the organization's objectives and higher pro ductivity.

COMMON APPROACHES TO EMPLOYEE INVOLVEMENT

Employee involvement can occur in any part of the organization. It may be an organization-wide attempt to improve productivity, or it may be limited to a single department or division. Successful employee involvement efforts, however, are not viewed as discrete programs or projects. Instead, they are seen as long-term, ongoing elements of the organization's culture. That is, these are not short-term solutions to specific productivity problems, but long-term approaches to managing.[8]

Communications Efforts

The cornerstone of any long-term employee improvement effort is good communications. Attempts to improve communications focus first on the flow of information from the organization to individual employees. In many cases, employees are woefully uninformed about the organization, its strategy, goals, profit margins, key customers, vendors, and other aspects of the business. In fact, the inability of most organizations to communicate this information to employees may contribute to employee indifference about the organization. "If they don't want to tell us about the organization, we won't worry about it."[9]

Many employees also get limited information about their performance on the job. Poor performance is brought to the employee's attention. Very often, though, employees are not given ongoing feedback about their performance, particularly when it is acceptable or good. Employees need positive reinforcement; ideally, they should receive feedback whenever they do well. With little feedback about the organization's business activities or their own productivity, employees may become less motivated. Even if they remain motivated, they cannot modify their behavior in constructive ways without feedback.

A second aspect of employee communications is "bottom-up" communications. Most organizations are able to communicate information *down* the organization hierarchy with reasonable speed and accuracy. The major communications breakdown occurs in the flow of employee ideas and suggestions *up* through the organization. In many cases, employee ideas are actively discouraged by first-line supervisors. The supervisors may see employee ideas as implicit criticism, or they may see following up on employee ideas as time-consuming. Even when follow-up is not time-consuming, many supervisors are reluctant to go to their bosses with new ideas, fearing criticism or the additional effort that a detailed justification may require. Nevertheless, without bottom-up input, management has less information with which to guide the organization.

Attitude Survey Feedback

Closely tied to communications issues is the use of attitude survey feedback. Companies such as General Motors and Bendix systematically collect information about employee attitudes on a variety of organizational issues. Questions may be about the physical work environment, the quality of supervision, compensation and benefits, or other aspects of organizational life. Information about these issues is collected through a detailed questionnaire, analyzed, summarized, and fed back to the employees. That is, aggregate responses are averaged, and these averages are shared with employees.

After sharing the attitude survey information, management attempts to draw from the employees examples of what the figures mean. The next step is to develop a specific action plan that addresses the most unacceptable aspects of the work environment. Through this process of data collection, feedback and action plans, the organization is better able to address specific employee concerns. The goal is to improve employees' quality of work life.

Suggestion Systems

Good quality of work life and employee involvement programs assume that employees have good ideas and that it is management's responsibility to tap those ideas. Suggestion systems offer one systematic way of collecting ideas from employees. Although not a new concept (NCR and Kodak both had suggestion systems operating in the 1890s), this approach remains highly effective.

Most modern suggestion systems have done away with the "suggestion box." Instead, an employee gives the immediate supervisor the suggestion. After receiving comments from the supervisor, the employee rewrites the suggestion and resubmits it to the supervisor for final review.[10] The idea is then forwarded to the suggestion system office, where it is recorded and sent to people in the firm who can best evaluate the idea. Once the evaluation process is complete, a recommendation is made to the suggestion system office. Feedback to the employee then follows. If the idea is accepted, the employee normally receives recognition and some monetary remuneration—commonly ten percent of the first year's savings.

Many suggestion systems exist in name only; they are not actively used by employees because of several pitfalls. One pitfall is the long evaluation period—typically 80 days, according to the National Association of Suggestion Systems. In practice, long evaluations are necessary to determine in detail what the exact savings will be. Some organizations have sidestepped this problem by simply paying the employee a flat or token amount for each idea, without regard to the amount of savings. The result is that the evaluation can be made on a simple "use it/don't use it" basis, without the need for a detailed estimate of the annual savings.

Equally damaging is management's failure to implement employee's ideas. Some companies are capable of evaluating an idea promptly and paying the employee a suggestion system bonus in a fairly short time. But, if the idea is not subsequently used, the employee may conclude that the suggestion system is a charade that doesn't really lead to the implementation of ideas. And without implementation, the organization cannot hope to increase productivity with the suggestion system. Without implementation, employees may withdraw their support for the suggestion system.

The success of any suggestion system depends on a strong commitment from top management. That commitment must be evident in speeches, public pronouncements, letters to employees, company newspaper articles, attendance at award functions, and, most important, in subsequent implementations. If the supervisor views employee suggestions as implicit criticism of his or her ability to manage, or if each employee suggestion creates a mountain of paperwork and red tape for the supervisor, new ideas will not be encouraged. Such implicit and explicit penalties for supervisors should be eliminated if they are expected to solicit, endorse and promote employee suggestions. Ideally, the organization will create an environment in which every idea is respected and appreciated, whether or not it is useable.

Team Building and Quality Circles

During the last twenty years, many efforts have been made to increase the sense of teamwork within an organization. As Chapter 12 discusses in more detail, a variety of organization development techniques have been applied in pursuit of this goal. Perhaps one of the newest teamwork techniques has been quality circles.[11]

Quality circles, originally developed in Japan as a result of research done in the United States, consist of small groups of employees that meet periodically with their immediate supervisors to identify and resolve workplace problems. Generally, problems are limited to those which specifically affect the circle members' jobs.

Circles originate when a member of management makes a presentation to a group of supervisors to explain quality circles. Supervisors who are interested may volunteer. Next, an overview presentation is made to these supervisors and their employees, to see if the employees are also interested. If the employees volunteer to form quality circles, training begins. Training for supervisors usually lasts two or three days and involves not only quality circle concepts, but also such areas as leadership and group dynamics. Following the supervisory training, employees are trained, generally for one day. Employee training focuses on decision-making skills. Employees learn about brainstorming, data collection techniques, and other methods of analyzing information and making decisions. After the training is over, the circles generally meet one hour per week on company time to work on problems.

Members of the group identify specific workplace problems they wish to resolve and, by consensus, develop a list of problem priorities. Data are then collected by the members about the specific problem at hand, and weekly meetings are used to analyze and discuss these data. Once a consensus solution is reached, the group often makes a presentation to higher levels of management who have the authority to approve the recommendations of the circle.

To assist the typically eight to twelve members of the circle and their supervisor, most companies have full-time quality circle administrators or facilitators. These staff personnel train supervisors and members and also serve as in-house consultants to the quality circles. In addition, they advise the steering committee, which usually consists of senior management at the site location and the people who report directly to them. It is the steering committee that decides the scope of the quality circle effort and authorizes budgets for the growth of the program.

SUMMARY

Quality of work life efforts assume that employees will add to a company's success if they feel that their contributions are meaningful and important. Rather than using specific short-term programs, effective companies secure employee involvement through improved communication, ongoing survey feedback processes, suggestion systems, team building, and quality circles.

SELECTED READINGS OVERVIEW

The first article, "Productivity Improvement Through People" was written by William B. Werther, Jr., one of the authors of this text. His article briefly reviews the typical causes of slow productivity growth and their relation to employee involvement. Werther then identifies many of the key issues surrounding improvements of productivity through employee involvement. The article concludes with a brief discussion of some of the more common employee involvement approaches to QWL.

The second article in this chapter, also by Werther, is entitled "Going in Circles with Quality Circles?—Management Development Implications." Here Werther takes a closer look at quality circles, their purpose, structure, origins, and the opportunities they present.

Next Chapter

The importance of employee involvement is that it taps employee ideas while building a greater sense of trust among workers and management. But when employees are asked to contribute their ideas, instead of simply doing their jobs, they often wonder "What's in it for me?" Gainsharing recognizes and rewards the extra contribution of employees by sharing with them the gains achieved through their contribution. The next chapter describes gainsharing and its connection to productivity improvement.

Review Questions

1. Explain what quality of work life is and why it is important in improving productivity.
2. Describe the trade-off between meeting employee needs and organizational objectives.
3. What objections are sometimes raised by managers to installing a QWL program?

WILLIAM B. WERTHER, JR.

Productivity Improvement Through People

An important question facing business today is, What can individual managers and employees do about the productivity crisis? Since low productivity growth rates are a national problem, many people conclude that solutions must be national in scope. A review of the causes of the productivity dilemma listed in Table 1 appears to reinforce the idea that no one individual manager or employee can alter the course of current productivity trends. Each factor in the table seems to require government action or fundamental changes in our culture. Since these requirements are outside the scope of any one individual, managers and workers often feel absolved of any need for action.

Table 1.
Common Causes of Slow
Productivity Growth

- Government regulations, taxes and high interest rates
- Few businesses and individual incentives
- Slow capital formation and outdated industrial base
- Insufficient research and development expenditures
- Poor attitudes toward work in the workforce
- Adversary labor-management attitudes and values
- Improper mix of skills among workers
- Large and growing service and government sectors
- Resource shortages and high energy prices
- Inflation
- Foreign competition

Source: Developed by the author.

Reprinted from *Arizona Business* (February 1981). All rights reserved.

Nevertheless, ongoing productivity gains have been achieved by individual workers, managers, firms, and industries in the United States. These gains represent only partial solutions to our national crisis, but the cumulative effect of these gains—if extended to more organizations—can alter the productivity of the nation.

Through employee involvement, companies such as Texas Instruments, IBM, Lockheed, Northrup, Control Data, Tektronics, General Motors, Beech Aircraft, Champion International, Solar Turbines, Bendix, and others have achieved substantial productivity gains.[1] Each of these companies has reported returns of 200, 300, and 400 percent from their investments involving employees in workplace decisions.

EMPLOYEE INVOLVEMENT: THE CONCEPT

The key to successful employee involvement is allowing nonmanagement employees to solve problems that affect their job performance, job setting, and the job itself. Although management retains the authority to decide if employee ideas will be used, management challenges workers to uncover problems and make recommendations for improvement. The challenge may be focused on lowering costs, reducing defects, improving safety, increasing output; or it may be unfocused with the object of challenging the workers to find easier ways to do their job.

The challenge usually is delivered to the workers through training programs that teach employees how to be problem solvers. Training includes topics ranging from data collection and analysis techniques, to problem solving and presentation skills. Since employees are taught the need for analytical solutions that are justified by facts not feelings, recommendations to management are accompanied by businesslike justifications. Interestingly, demands for wage and benefit increases or other cost increases seldom arise from these groups unless accompanied by documentation and justification. Instead, solutions usually recommend changes that contribute to improved job performance.

As part of employee involvement, management usually allows employees time during work hours to apply these concepts—individually or in groups—to elements of the job and job setting that need improvement. Although management may suggest areas of consideration, employees are usually free to select the issues that interest them. When employees are free to select the work-related problems that concern them, they appear more interested in finding solutions. Since their solutions are achieved participatively, their commitment is higher and their resistance to the change is lower.

Problems with Involvement

If employee involvement benefits employers and workers, why has it not been used by more companies? Although the problem is very complex, the answer to this question lies partly in some fundamental assumptions and perspectives of many American managers.

Too often managers view their employees as less educated, less motivated, and less dedicated than themselves. Many managers assume their workers are apathetic and treat them accordingly. Feedback is often limited to discipline with too little recognition for good performance. Management reports are seldom widely shared with employees, and sometimes, not even with first level supervisors. Glossy stockholder reports go to investors who may be far removed from the workplace, but employees may not know last week's productivity performance in their department. High scrap rates, absenteeism, and defective units are produced partly because many workers are not educated by management to be businessmen and businesswomen.

Another problem is the short perspective found among many managers and chief executive officers (CEOs). Unrelenting pressure is applied to achieve short-term goals, which for managers means meeting budgets, and for CEOs means ever increasing quarterly earnings per share growth. Short-run expedience is substituted for sound business judgment in such cases. A simple example illustrates the point: No manager would consider spending $12,000 for a word processor without training the operator how to run the machine. Yet, even some supposedly well-managed firms promote workers into supervision without a single minute of supervisory training. A hearty handshake, a pat on the back, and on offer of help if needed constitute the typical orientation and training program for the elated, but often bewildered, new supervisor. Yet, this supervisor may manage a payroll of hundreds of thousands of dollars and workers who actually produce the firm's products or services.

An extension of the apathetic assumption and the short-run perspective also affects employee involvement efforts. Many top and middle managers are reluctant to make the necessary "investment" in supervisory and employee training programs that should precede a major employee involvement effort. For example, Solar Turbine, Inc. (a San Diego based subsidiary of International Harvester, Inc.) invested $79,000 in its involvement program during the first eighteen months. This type of up-front investment is less clearly measured, however, than investments in plant, equipment, advertising, or other claimants on organizational budgets. Even when the "investment" in people is made, the rate of return is difficult to measure and is easily curtailed in times of high interest rates and limited budgets.

When top management is committed to employee involvement, concern is often expressed over the voluntary aspects of involvement programs. Voluntarism is another concept foreign to operating managers who believe their job is to solve problems and make decisions. Allowing employees the autonomy to select problems they wish to solve may be seen by managers as an abdication of their responsibility or even a threat to their authority. Often supervisors and middle managers require training to understand their role in the organization, which is not so much to make decisions or to solve problems, but to get decisions made and problems solved.

Once managers accept their role as managers, not doers, the feelings of abdication and threat subside. They are then better able to turn their attention to the planning, organizing, directing, staffing, and controlling that are the core functions of management. In the managerial capacity, they remain responsible for meeting objectives. When pressing problems arise that employees do not wish to tackle or are unable to solve, managers must then intervene through delegation or hands-on activities. Although employee involvement means extensive participation by employees in problem-solving areas traditionally reserved for management, it does not mean an abdication of management's responsibility for results. Instead, it means sharing the need-satisfying aspects of work.

PRODUCTIVITY AND QUALITY OF WORK LIFE

Perhaps the major problem with employee involvement is that many managers do not see the connection between productivity and quality of work life. Yet, the main effect of employee involvement is to improve the employees' quality of work life; it makes the job and the employment relationship more satisfying. In turn, employee-initiated workplace improvements lead to increased productivity through increased commitment to the organization and its objectives.

The clearest connection between employee involvement and quality of work life is shown in the features of the ideal organization. Table 2 lists characteristics commonly identified by people when asked to describe an ideal organization. Firms that lack most or all of these characteristics do not provide a high quality of work life. People are frustrated, uncertain of what is expected. Outstanding performance is treated in a manner similar to acceptable performance. Top management may have motives for improvement, but employees see few reasons for improving their performance and productivity. Productivity gains, if any, come from new equipment, technological advances, or favorable economic circumstances. Even when productivity gains do accrue to the firm, they often are less than gains that might be expected from employees who experience high quality of work life and the commitment it implies.

Through increased employee involvement, however, employees are given opportunities to clarify objectives and role expectations. The process of participation leads to opportunities for recognition, autonomy, growth, achievement, and feedback. Involvement presents employees with new challenges that add variety to daily tasks. Improved communications lead to better rapport with management, which provides additional insights into leadership styles and performance expectations. People become more open and willing to find better ways of doing their jobs.

Japanese vs. American Approaches

Perhaps nowhere is the impact of employee involvement and quality of work life more evident than in the gains made by Japanese firms. The approach of major Japanese firms to employee involvement offers a useful contrast with American management practices. Some of the more noteworthy comparisons are highlighted in Table 3. These differences certainly are not the only reasons for Japan's post-World War II success.

Table 2.
Characteristics of
the Ideal Corporation

- Clear objectives
- Good communications and feelings of trust
- Meaningful work with challenge and variety
- Known role expectations
- Opportunities for recognition, autonomy, growth, and achievement
- Ample feedback on performance
- Capable leadership
- Fair treatment (including discipline and compensation)
- Success at meeting organizational objectives and employee needs

Source: Developed by the author based upon the in-class responses of more than 1,000 seminar participants.

However, they do contribute to the well publicized work ethic of Japanese workers.[2]

Lifetime employment. Not all Japanese workers have lifetime employment. Most women, workers over 55, and employees of small firms lack this level of employment security. However, the major Japanese employers—particularly those successful firms with which United States industry must compete—usually offer employment for life to their core work force of Japanese males.[3]

While American managers fear indolent workers as the result of lifetime employment, Japanese managers get high commitment and performance. Poor performers in Japan are subject to discipline by management and peer pressure. But those who wish to perform have the freedom to be creative. If production workers or supervisors can eliminate their job, the prospect is recognition, not the unemployment line. Job security is assured if the firm survives. This realization causes Japanese employees to see their personal success as intertwined with their employer's success. Perhaps this relationship is best illustrated by the observa-

tion of Kyonosuke Ibe, Chairman of Sumitomo Bank.

> In Japan, when a worker is asked what he does for a living, he generally tells you he works for Sumitomo or Mitsubishi or Matsushita. It takes a second question to find out that he is a chauffeur, or engineer, or chemist, which, in my experience, is the first answer you get from an American.[4]

Although a policy of lifetime employment sounds abhorrent to most American managers, it is often an unstated but common reality. Few firms ever lay off workers with more than five years' seniority. Growth companies, like IBM, boast of not laying off a worker in over thirty-five years.[5] Even the disastrous 1980 production year in the American automobile industry saw the vast majority of American automobile workers escaping layoffs. Perhaps a greater commitment to employee job security by American firms might be reciprocated by a stronger commitment of employees to the organization and its objectives.

Orientation.   Most American employee orientation programs are postemployment sessions of a few hours to half a day. Then, too

Table 3.
Japanese and American Approaches
to Employee Relations

Japan	*United States*
1. "Lifetime employment"	No employment guarantees
2. Extensive pre-employment and post-employment orientation	Minimal new-employee orientation
3. Seek employee suggestions	Resist employee ideas
4. Emphasis on quality	Emphasis on costs
5. Decision making through participation and consensus	Decision making through reliance on authority

Source: Developed by the author.

often, the employee is left exposed to sink or swim. Many Japanese firms, however, provide extensive preemployment education. These efforts go beyond even the use of job previews found in some American firms. The Japanese approach may involve several posthire, preemployment trips to the firm's facilities. Extensive company literature is given the worker before employment begins. Materials range from detailed accounts of the company's history to procedures manuals.[6] When the employee does report for work, it is often marked by an entrance ceremony followed by extensive orientation and training that continue throughout the worker's career.

Quality vs. Costs.   The emphasis on quality gives many Japanese firms a core value that serves as a template against which even low level decisions are evaluated.[7] Although American firms seek quality too, their emphasis is often on cost effectiveness. The subtle communication received by workers from their supervisors is that cost effectiveness is the main concern. By contrast, Japanese managers expect the worker to be concerned with quality and not leave it to some distant quality control department. Often, each worker is expected to check the quality of previous steps in the production process. At Toyota, for example, production workers are allowed to halt the assembly line when defects are uncovered.

Employee Suggestions.   Since Japanese workers often identify closely with the employer, they often feel obligated to provide ideas and suggestions. Against the backdrop of employment security, ideas have little chance of creating a loss of job or status.[8] Moreover, this ethic of seeking employee ideas is seen as a key part of the supervisor's role.

The contrast with American supervisors is often one of perspective. American managers evaluate new ideas in terms of net benefits to the organization. From the expected gains of the idea, the costs (financial and psychological) of the change are subtracted. The Oriental perspective is different. Japanese supervisors often take the view that all employee ideas should be implemented unless an obvious harm would result. Although many ideas have little or no benefit, the implementation of even marginal ideas reinforces the employee's desire to provide other suggestions, which may lead to substantial improvements in productivity.

Consensus Management.   Beyond merely seeking employee suggestions, Japanese managers appear to value consensus among those affected by a decision.[9] From a Western perspective, Japanese managers may appear indecisive and slow to make decisions. More accurately, these managers devote considerable time to participatively formulating a statement of the problem and exploring the alternatives. Although the process is initially time consuming, the result is a consensus among those affected by the decision. When the decision is made, its implementation encounters comparatively little resistance.

By contrast, American management styles seem to favor unilateral decision making—often in the name of accountability. While the formulation of the problem and exploration of alternatives move quickly, these managers usually expend considerable time and effort overcoming subsequent resistance to the change caused by the decision.

Whether the Japanese or American styles result in better or faster decisions is unclear. What is clear, however, is that employee commitment to decisions is apt to be higher under the Japanese approach. Furthermore, feelings of employee satisfaction, quality of work life, recognition, achievement, growth, and organizational loyalty are all likely to be higher.

The Cultural Barrier Myth

American managers often dismiss cross-cultural comparisons of management style as not appropriate in the United States work environment. They reason that the cultures and people are so vastly different that the use of Japanese techniques on American workers would be folly. Although systematic studies are unavailable, limited case evidence suggests that Japanese-inspired leadership styles are successful with American workers.

Sony, Sanyo, Honda, and Quasar have reported excellent results with their American facilities. In some cases, quality, productivity, costs, and employee satisfaction have been improved simultaneously, as happened at Quasar.

Although limited case evidence does not validate the universal applicability of Japanese approaches, their methods are compatible with the description of the ideal organization. Their techniques provide employees with high levels of security to meet basic needs; participation through employee involvement contributes to social need satisfactions; and the involvement creates opportunities for recognition, personal growth, achievement, and other potential motivators.

INVOLVEMENT TECHNIQUES: AN OVERVIEW

With a population approximately one-half of the United States, on a land mass the size of Montana, and with few natural resources, the Japanese leaders during the post-World War II era recognized the need for export earnings. To survive in the export markets they saw the need for high quality products. With human resources as the only apparent abundant commodity, this small island nation recognized the crucial role that people would (in fact, must) play in rebuilding Japan.

Quality Control Circles

Out of the necessities of their condition, Japanese firms developed internal cultures that prize cooperation, teamwork, and employee participation. Although many involvement techniques are used in Japan, the most common formal approach is quality control circles.

Quality control circles are workplace teams composed of the immediate supervisor and subordinates. Circles are created voluntarily. Only if the supervisor wants to create one, and only if the employees agree to join, do circles occur in Japanese plants.

When a supervisor elects to form one, the supervisor receives training in group dynamics, meeting skills, and decision making. Employees also receive training in problem-solving and decision-making skills. Training usually includes explanations of brainstorming, *Pareto* analysis, cause and effect diagrams, check sheets, and other data gathering and analyzing tools.

Once the initial training phase is completed, employees and their supervisors meet for one hour per week on company time. During this meeting, the group (not management) identifies and selects work-related problems that it wishes to solve. Members use brainstorming, data gathering, and other techniques to uncover the causes of the problem objectively. Recommended solutions are presented to management, which retains the authority to decide on implementation. Then the group selects another problem and the process continues.

This approach, or variations of it, has been applied successfully in the United States. Companies such as Lockheed, General Motors, Northrup, Solar Turbines, RCA, Control Data, and others often report returns of 200, 300, and even 400 percent on their investments in quality circle programs. More striking than the financial benefits are the perceptions of managers and workers about improvements in absenteeism, employee turnover, satisfaction, attitude, and production.

Other Involvement Techniques

Even where quality circles are inappropriate or unwanted by management, other involvement techniques have proved helpful in improving both productivity and the quality of work life.

Team-building approaches that do not follow the rigid pattern of quality circles may achieve similar benefits. These approaches may vary the training content, structure, or voluntary nature of the group, when compared with quality circles, but the key similarity is a team spirit built through group training and problem-solving sessions.

Even suggestion systems have proved to be a useful involvement technique. Successful systems usually omit the "suggestion box" and instead mandate employees and supervisors to discuss the suggestions of the employee. This discussion serves as an opportunity for improved communications (particularly feedback about the idea), involvement in refining the idea, growth, and recognition. American companies like Allen-Bradley, IBM, Beech Aircraft, Honeywell, and Phillips Petroleum are just a few of the firms that have effective suggestion programs.

PROGRAMS VERSUS
A WAY OF LIFE

Interestingly, many employee involvement efforts are implemented for reasons other than improving productivity. Safety, employee satisfaction, and communication improvements are other common goals. But a common thread seems to run among the long-established and more successful employee involvement efforts. Most of the administrators avoid thinking of their approaches as programs. Instead, they view employee involvement activities as an ongoing way of life that seeks a high quality of working life for all employees.

This view moves these managers away from thinking in terms of a short duration quick fix to employee satisfaction. Instead, they seek to build a work force committed to the organization and an organization committed to a high quality work life.

Although these managers seldom discuss profitability or productivity, they often view these gains as by-products of a high quality work life. They realize that the path to their productivity goal is a cohesive and goal-oriented worker even though short-run profits can be maximized through autocratic approaches, pressure for performance, forceful discipline, and fear. But like their Japanese counterparts, they prefer to build a high quality of work life environment, which leads to improved productivity and profitability in the long run.

PRODUCTIVITY AND
MANAGERS: THE CONCLUSIONS

Productivity improvement—the increase of outputs relative to inputs—is the basis for improving the success of our organizations and the well-being of our society. As our once abundant resources are consumed, the ability of our nation's organizations to deliver more products and services will depend on how well our resource inputs can be converted to outputs that satisfy the needs of our nation and its people.

Like the Japanese after World War II, our most bountiful and important resource is the skill and creativity of our people—all our people. The United States can no longer afford to leave the challenge and creativity of work to management alone. Even the most competent and capable managers must seek the good ideas of their employees. Not only must managers make use of their employees' creativity, but they must also make work challenging if this country is to tap the potential wellspring of productivity every employee offers. What can individual managers do to improve the productivity of our nation? They can and must involve all their human resources in problem-solving and decision-making processes.

WILLIAM B. WERTHER, JR.

Going in Circles with Quality Circles?—Management Development Implications

IBM, General Motors, RCA, Westinghouse, Control Data, Union Carbide, Tektronics, Lockheed, Northrup Aircraft, Babcock and Wilcox, Waters Associates, Solar Turbines, and American Express are operating effective quality circle efforts. Companies like Motorola, Champion International, TRW, and others use different forms of team building that are closely related to the quality circle concept. As a result, the print and electronic media are creating waves of favourable publicity about the idea. These "success stories" are leading a number of executives to consider quality circles for their company. Unfortunately, publicity releases and press reports seldom alert top management to potential problems.

The pitfalls that are emerging from corporate programmes do not mark the demise of quality circles. Their success establishes them as a useful management tool. Quality circles work; they are unlikely to be a fad. The problems discussed here are not fatal flaws in the concept but may be fatal to company programmes that ignore them. Certainly, for those who seek reasons to avoid quality circles, ample ammunition follows.

However, a variety of businesses operate successful quality circle efforts—and these efforts may be a path through the productivity crisis that faces other companies.

HOW QUALITY CIRCLES OPERATE

Exhibit I outlines the most common aspect of quality circles (QC). It defines quality circles and indicates their organisation, training, and process requirements. Although each user may vary the specifics of the reporting relationships, the composition of the steering committee, or the training content, all programmes make extensive use of facilitators and training.

Perhaps the most important feature of quality circles is their potential impact. When fully deployed throughout a plant or company, circles may transform the organisation's culture into one which facilitates constructive change. The circle process identifies and evaluates areas of needed change. Employee ideas are encouraged. Success with the process moves the organisation toward more open communications,

Reprinted from the *Journal of Management Development* 2, no. 1 (1983). All rights reserved.

Exhibit I.   An Overview of Quality Circles: Their
Organisation, Training and Process

QC Definition
A quality circle is a group of workers and their supervisor who voluntarily meet to identify and solve job-related problems.

QC Organisation
Quality circle efforts rely extensively on the existing line structure in the organisation. To train and support the quality circle teams, a coordinator (or facilitator) position is established. This full-time person usually reports to a high level line manager, such as a plant, division, manufacturing, or other executive officer. The facilitator's role includes the design of the programme and training materials, introduction of the concept to potential circle members, training of members, liaison among the circles and other departments, coaching circles, and keeping the steering committee informed of circle activities.

The steering committee is composed of representatives from groups affected by circle actions. The committee members are usually the heads of the staff and line departments at the location where the programme is operating. Thus, a plant-wide programme finds the committee members consist of the plant manager's direct reports. If the programme is on a divisional or corporate basis, the committee will include the direct reports of the divisional or corporate executive.

QC Training
1. *Employees*—although each firm adjusts its training according to the needs of circle members, most companies give workers eight hours of training, usually in one session. The training includes an explanation of quality circles and decision making techniques. Normally the techniques taught are brainstorming, cause-and-effect (or "fishbone") diagrams, graphing approaches including Pareto analysis, basic quality control sampling and charting methods, and presentation skills.

2. *Supervisors*—again, the training varies from firm to firm, but usually includes all the topics taught to employees. In addition, the supervisors receive training about group dynamics, human behaviour, leadership, quality of work life, and committee skills. This training usually lasts two days.

3. *Facilitators*—training for facilitators includes the same materials taught to supervisors. Topics such as individual behaviour, group dynamics, committee skills, leadership, and quality of work life, however, are covered in more detail. Facilitators also receive training in teaching skills since they usually serve as in-house trainers. Training programmes for facilitators by the American Productivity Center of the International Association of Quality Circles last five days.

Exhibit I.   An Overview of Quality Circles: Their
Organisation, Training and Process (continued)

---

4. *Steering Committee*—members of the steering committee are often given a one-half to full-day seminar. The seminar describes quality circles, their structure, and their training needs. The seminar also explains the benefits and commitments associated with quality circles.

The Quality Circle Process
Once managers, supervisors and employees are trained, the process usually begins with a brainstorming session to identify likely problems the group can address. Through discussion a consensus is reached by the members as to which problem should be tackled. The problem is defined. Likely causes are then identified, usually through a cause-and-effect diagram. Data may be needed to identify specific causes. This information is obtained though the workers' use of observation and check sheets or by securing needed data from the facilitator. Data are arrayed usually graphically in a Pareto Chart to isolate most common causes.

Once a solution is agreed upon, the members present their analysis and recommendations to the appropriate manager or the steering committee. Feedback is received from management, and another problem is identified and the process repeats.

Usually meetings are in company time and last one hour per week. When continuous process production or other demands preclude meeting during regular hours, workers meet on an overtime basis before or after work.

---

trust, and involvement of employees in the decision making process. At first glance, quality circles appear to demand an instant transformation of the corporate culture. However, implementation generally proceeds slowly so that the organisation can evolve gradually into the new culture.

Although substantial research into the benefits of quality circles is lacking, extensive case studies reveal important advantages of this management tool. Of these gains, executives and productivity administrators emphasise a few as being most significant. Access to employee ideas usually heads the list.

For an organisation to more fully reap the benefits of its employees' ideas requires the development of a highly trained cadre of managers—managers who are self-confident enough to seek and use the good ideas of employees. Managers, who by their day-to-day behaviour encourage those around them to share in the excitement of meaningful accomplishments, however measured.

Quality circles, by themselves, will not transform an organisation's culture into this ideal state. However, the training in group dynamics, consultation skills, and decision making help develop circle participants. Ongoing coaching from the facilitator furthers the developmental process. And, the voluntary nature of circles serves as a check on autocratic excesses by supervisors or managers, since members can resign if the circle process is not satisfying to them. If the process is initially successful and top management continues its *active* interest and support, the benefits in Exhibit II spread through the organisation. In time, these attitudinal changes are reflected in the behaviour of management and non-management employees. Continued long enough in the presence of a far sighted top management, the very culture of the organisation evolves to one more conducive to high productivity and quality of work life. How long circles serve up these benefits parallels the length of management's on-going commitment to developing its people. When top management forgets circles are primarily a development tool, it courts "cost savings reports" and detailed productivity measures that may communicate only limited interest in the development of human resources. Interest by all is then likely to wane.

Quality circles yield well-reasoned and substantiated ideas. It is from employee ideas that the benefits of quality circles accrue to the employer and workers. By design, these ideas are aimed at workplace obstacles that prevent higher productivity and lower the employees' quality of work life. Often these ideas initially seem trivial. For example, employees on the F-5 assembly line at Northrup Aircraft had long complained of dull drill bits. The usual response was, "Get a new bit." When one of the circles studied this problem, they found that some bits would break before drilling one hole, while other bits efficiently drilled hundreds of holes before they needed to be reworked. Circle members recommended tightening rework tolerances on used bits and management agreed. The result was several thousand dollars saved in that one department, increased productivity per hour, and improved quality of work life for employees. What often surprises management is not just the dollar savings but the sophistication and thoroughness of the employees' analysis.

Another frequently mentioned benefit is the "carry-over effect." Employees usually spend one hour per week in circle meetings, but their effort does not stop there. Employees often are overheard discussing the problem on breaks or seen working on displays during lunch hours. This carry-over effect also extends to employee-supervisory cooperation outside the circle meeting. Supervisors are seen as more receptive to employees which leads to improved communications, satisfaction, organisational loyalty, teamwork, and an air of mutual respect. The result is a free-flow of productivity improvement ideas.

Observation of circle meetings and presentations also helps management identify potential leaders. Self-confidence, communication skills, and other leadership traits stand out during circle activities. In fact, many Japanese managers consider the development and identification of potential leaders to be a major benefit of quality circles.

Dollar savings are another obvious benefit. However, for a variety of reasons, many companies deliberately do not trace the total costs and financial returns on quality circle efforts. As a result, the dollar returns are seldom quantified—although facilitators and executives usually estimate direct returns in the 200 to 400 per cent range. One exception is Solar Turbines. When its programme began, it was a subsidiary of International Harvester and it tracked financial costs and benefits closely. During the 18 month start-up period, its total outlays were $79,000. At the end of that period, circle ideas had contributed $90,000 in first year savings! These figures understate the true return to Solar in several ways. The $79,000 figure included all start-up costs, facilitator salaries, and costs of developing training materials. The $90,000 figure was the *first year's net savings*, after the costs of implementing the ideas were subtracted. Since many of those ideas will generate savings in subsequent years, the actual discount cash savings from those ideas is undoubtedly two or three times higher. Finally, the savings do not include any estimate of the carry-over effects, such as improved communications, loyalty, absenteeism, turnover, or morale. After the start-up period, Solar has consistently posted a return on its quality circle programme of 400 per cent, which is in line with similar programmes at other firms. On the other hand, those companies that use circles primarily to emphasise quality of work life seldom trace the return on their quality circle investment.

Although many other benefits are discussed in Exhibit II, the most important gains may be intangible. Circles create a more open atmosphere in the organisation. Innovation is encouraged. Participation in problem solving enhances feelings of teamwork and satisfaction. Progress is part of everyone's job, not something imposed from on high.

Since most companies have been successful without quality circles, many top managers do not sense an urgent need to use this management tool. Their reasoning is often a variant of the following: "We have been successful with our traditional 'top-down' approach. Why risk future success on a relatively new technique?" Perhaps the best way to respond to this reasoning is to review the origins of quality circles.

Origins of Quality Circles

Following World War II, the Japanese faced staggering problems. With half the population of the United States living in an area about the size of Montana, Japanese leaders quickly realised that national prosperity rested with exporting. To export successfully, resource-poor Japan had to import natural resources, add value, and export quality products. But in the immediate postwar era, "made in Japan" meant "cheap junk." To avoid becoming an economic colony of the United States and to overcome their image of poor quality, Japanese industry focused on producing quality products.

Quality circles were born out of necessity. The only significant resource the Japanese had was an educated and diligent workforce. Japanese management provided workers with training in quality control and decision making concepts. Then company time was allowed for workplace meetings to solve quality problems. Today, eight million Japanese workers are in circles formally registered with the Japanese Union of Scientists and Engineers.

When non-registered circles and variations on this concept are considered, estimates range to more than 25 million circle participants—or about half of the Japanese workforce.

OPPORTUNITIES AND ROADBLOCKS

To tap this nearly limitless resource, more and more companies are turning to quality circles or other variations of employee involvement. However, this emerging trend—limited mostly to multi-billion corporations—is a major undertaking. It demands new management attitudes and behaviours, which change slowly and with great difficulty. Those managements that adhere to traditional attitudes and behaviours may find themselves unable to respond to competitors who have gained greater employee dedication to productivity and quality.

The following pages outline the fundamental changes required to make quality

---

Exhibit II.   Some Benefits of Quality Circles

Awareness
- Increases management's awareness of employee ideas
- Increases employee awareness of management's desire for ideas
- Increases employee awareness of the need for innovation

Commitment
- Creates an employee commitment to the organisation, its product/service quality, and co-workers
- Creates a commitment by the organisation to employee ideas

Communications
- Improves supervisory/employee communication
- Facilitates upward communications

Competitiveness
- Allows the firm to become more competitive through improved costs, quality, and/or commitment to QWL
- Improves recruiting and retention of quality employees that enhances competitiveness

Development
- Develops supervisors into better leaders and decision makers by providing them with new tools
- Develops employees to think as managers and gives them new decision making tools

Innovation
- Encourages innovation through receptivity to employee ideas

Respect
- Shows management's respect of employees
- Allows the supervisor to earn the respect of employees

Satisfaction
- Enhances employee satisfaction through participation in decision making
- Enhances supervisory satisfaction by improving communication
- Reduces employee and supervisory dissatisfaction caused by resistance to change

Teamwork
- Requires teamwork for successful QC meetings
- Furthers teamwork outside the QC meetings

---

circles work. Where these changes do not occur, problems with quality circles will arise. How top management deals with these challenges to past attitudes and behaviours will determine the success of individual quality circle efforts. For, in the final analysis, quality circles are not merely the application of a new technique, but a basic change in how management manages.

Top-Down Commitment

Quality circles change the culture of the organisation. To succeed, management must be receptive to the ideas of employees—particularly at the hourly and supervisory level. In the circle meetings, supervisors serve as discussion leaders. If they seek to impose their will on the group, the selection of problems and solutions is not arrived at by consensus. Since the employees do not feel a sense of ownership in the process or its outcomes, resistance to change is likely to remain and the effectiveness of the quality circle process is severely damaged. In extreme cases of supervisory dominance, the group disbands since membership is voluntary.

Although supervisory training helps avoid this pitfall, no amount of training makes supervisors receptive to the process without a strong commitment from upper management. For example, supervisors are usually under pressure to produce results—whether those results are higher production or fast solutions to workplace problems. If middle management expresses disdain for the circle process or if they express contempt for the "slow pace" of decision making, the supervisor may dominate circle meetings.

The implications for top management are twofold: First, quality circles must be explained even to middle managers who are not directly involved in conducting meetings. It is unreasonable to expect middle management support when these managers do not understand the process. Second, the top manager and other members of the steering committee must exhibit their commitment to quality circles. Speeches, directives, and articles in the house organ help. Attendance at circle meetings helps even more. But top management must evaluate middle managers on the effectiveness of the circles under their jurisdiction. If middle managers are rated on the success of quality circles, they are more likely to understand and support the concept.

A final note of caution about commitment concerns top management's view of quality circles. If they are seen as merely a quick-fix or a programme to be layered on top of the existing organisation culture, management's commitment is actually little more than permission—permission for someone to try circles in some remote enclave of the organisation. Facilitators, middle managers, supervisors, and employees will sense this low level of commitment. When production problems or other pet programmes conflict with circle activities, the circles will likely get "back-burner" treatment. Some circles may survive, but long-term and widespread successes are unlikely. The lack of commitment is most common when a new middle or plant manager begins to supervise those with circles. Circles are seen as someone else's programme; the need for patience and meeting time is not understood. Support is withdrawn and the circles fade away. Lockheed's pioneering effort in quality circles met this fate when key managers were changed.

Bottom-Up Receptivity

Most Western organisations rely on downward communications. New ideas are initiated by managers and "imposed" on the organisation from the top. This approach has several flaws. It assumes that those further down the hierarchy have little to contribute other than their labour. However, productivity improvement starts with those actually creating the company's products or services; they are the true experts.

The top-down communication of ideas is damaging in other ways. When a new idea is imposed on a work group, they have little invested in its success or failure. It's not their idea. Resistance to change is likely. Resistance is even more likely when employees have other ideas they deem to be better. Fundamentally, the top-down approach is resented by those upon whom management relies for success because it does not acknowledge that employees have good ideas, too.

Many managers react to these observations with defensive statements like: "But, we want and use the good ideas of employees." Yet, most attitude surveys in those same firms show hourly employees find little opportunity for creativity. Why the disparity?

The disparity between management's desire for ideas and the paucity of creativity in most hourly-paid jobs arises from low levels of receptivity to employee ideas. What really happens when a new employee has a usable idea? The employee discusses it with the supervisor. The experienced supervisor knows the middle manager will look for flaws in the idea. To ensure that the idea is practical, the supervisor will likely grill the employee, who often has not thoroughly thought through the idea. Some flaw usually is uncovered and the idea dies. It dies because every idea carries the potential for disruption if not failure. To implement the idea is to risk disruption or error. What incentive does the supervisor have to try the idea? The safest course of action is to kill the idea in its infancy. After one or two more tries with other ideas, the employee soon learns that management (in the form of the supervisor) does not want new ideas. The flow of ideas from hourly workers slows. Since new ideas are necessary for productivity improvement and organisational survival, they must come from the top with all its attendant problems and resistance.

Resistance to employee ideas stems from an informal cost/benefit analysis. The supervisor (and higher levels of management) evaluates the cost of employee ideas. The costs include not only the direct expenses but also the indirect ones such as lost-time to sell the idea, overcoming the boss's resistance to change, new controls, and the resulting disruption to present production. Since many of these costs cannot be quantified, they loom large in the eyes of decision makers. As a result, many ideas are rejected. (Of course, those ideas that originate further up the hierarchy may not factor in these

costs so more of these ideas seem feasible to their originators.)

More employee ideas would be implemented if supervisors and their managers adopted a "no harm/implement philosophy." This approach assumes all employee ideas are sound and are to be implemented unless a demonstrated harm is shown. Here, the burden is on experienced managers to use employee ideas. Of course, ideas that are illegal, impair the quality of work life of others, or have direct costs that exceed benefits are rejected. If management cannot point to specific shortcomings, the idea is implemented. Even when ideas only break even financially, benefits accrue. The employee learns that management genuinely wants ideas. The next time an employee has an idea, it is more likely to be presented to management. Even when ideas are rejected under the no harm/implement philosophy, the employee is given specific reasons for rejection, not broad platitudes about infeasibility or company policy. Ideas that are rejected for cause are less likely to dam the flow of new ideas than the grilling and disinterest many workers now encounter.

Quality circles help get employee ideas accepted. Not only does management expect ideas as the return on its investment in a quality circles undertaking, but the process assures that ideas are researched and cost/benefit justified. When the process is truly a consensus, decision makers sense the group's commitment to successful implementation. This commitment lessens management's fears of intangible costs such as work disruption and resistance to change. As a result, most companies implement over 80 per cent of quality circle ideas.

For circles to succeed, they must occur in a setting receptive to employee ideas. The receptive setting should precede the implementation of circles. Managers who think a mandated circle effort will automatically change the corporate culture are likely to find quality circles do not work well. If implementation is not accompanied by top management's *active commitment*—rather than mere permission—quality circles are not likely to work at all.

Purpose, Name and Location

What is the purpose of the company's quality circle programme? Is it to improve quality? Productivity? Quality of work life? Profits? Costs? All of these? The answer to these questions will establish a theme and direction for the programme.

No one approach is inherently superior. If the major impediment to organisational success is product quality, worker commitment, costs, or the like, the company's purpose for quality circles is clear. For example, the Japanese recognised that their firms had a poor quality image in the 1950s and 1960s. Circles were started specifically to address product quality. As quality became less of an issue, the theme in many Japanese programmes became costs. Today many Japanese managers view circles as a quality of work life and employee/supervisory development programme.

Nevertheless, the initial theme selected by top management does hold significant implications. At Control Data, for example, quality circles are viewed as a vehicle for quality of work life improvement. As a result of that perspective, Control Data does not maintain detailed records or perform detailed audits of savings that result from team suggestions. Cost savings and quality improvement are by-products of their programme. At Solar Turbines, the focus was quality. Their customers are more concerned with quality and reliability of turbine powered compressors and power generation platforms than cost. As a result, Solar's programme seeks quality improvements and cost reduction; quality of work life improvements are a by-product of their circles.

The purpose of the circle effort carries implications for the name of the programme and its organisational location. At Solar Turbines and in most Japanese companies, for example, the quality circle name is used. Since quality was their primary focus, the term, quality circles, was appropriate. At Control Data, Tektronics, and Union Carbide's Y-12 plant, different themes led to different names: Control Data has *Involvement Teams*; Tektronics has *Tekcircles*; and Union Carbide has *Employee Pride Circles*, which stands for *Productivity through Recognition, Involvement and Development of Employees*. These companies and many others sought to avoid the term quality circles because they did not want the connotation that circles were aimed solely or primarily at quality.

Another implication of the programme's purpose is the reporting relationship for the chief facilitator or administrator. Little agreement has emerged as to whom the circle effort should report. Many programmes are located in the manufacturing hierarchy with the administrator reporting to the plant, divisional, or corporate manufacturing director. Tektronics and Control Data are examples. Plant-wide programmes often report to the plant manager or the steering committee. A few programmes are housed in the human resource department, as is done at the western regional offices of American Express. Although all of these approaches work, they have a common element: Each administrator reports to an executive (or group of executives) with clout. Access to top management indicates their commitment and earns the administrator the attention of middle managers.

Speed, Consultants and Failure

Once committed to the quality circle concept, top management seeks action—often quickly. But, beginning too quickly may spell failure. Quality circles usually represent a change in the culture of the organisation. Changing the corporate culture is analogous to changing an individual's personality: It can be done but only slowly and with great effort. Virtually every successful circle programme has six months to a year of staff work behind it *before* the first group of workers is trained. Time is needed to find and train a facilitator, design training materials, educate the steering committee, and solicit interest from supervisors and workers.

Consultants can help speed up implementation. Many have packages of training material that can be painlessly adapted to the company's needs. They may be able to help recruit, evaluate, and train facilitators. And, they can help top management understand and evaluate the quality circle process. However, the risk is that the programme becomes dependent upon the consultant's availability. It is the "consultant's" programme, not top management's. The presence of the consultant may lull management into a low level of commitment. Many successful programmes at companies like Tektronics, Union Carbide, and American Express used consultants in the planning and design phases. However, these firms and others quickly shift responsibility to inhouse staff to make the programme succeed.

Growth and Success

Not only do successful circle approaches require careful planning, they grow slowly. The most common start-up involves two to five circles, usually started at the rate of one per month.

During the planning phase, the facilitator learns which middle managers are likely to be supportive. In conversations with these managers, the facilitator seeks to identify the best first-line supervisors. "Best" is defined as supervisors who have a good rapport with their employees, who are open to

employee ideas, and who are participative in their approach to leadership. Also, these supervisors usually are selected from line departments that are already successful. Line departments often are selected because productivity measures are likely to be available. Since the programme starts small and uses line departments, productivity and quality of work life improvements can be compared with groups that were not involved with circles. These comparisons, along with the measured savings from the circles' ideas, give top management data on the effectiveness of the quality circle process.

Once preparations are complete and middle managers advised of the circle process, likely supervisors are identified. These supervisors then are invited to a brief in-house presentation that describes the quality circle concept. Volunteers are sought, since participation is voluntary for all involved. A meeting with these supervisors and their employees is held to explain the concept and seek volunteers among the supervisors' employees. Supervisory and employee training follows—usually in a one-day, off-site session for employees after the supervisors receive their two days of training.

The pilot circles often operate for three months to a year. If an assessment of the programme is positive, additional circles are usually added at the rate of one or two per month thereafter. Here again, top management's zeal may cause damage. Once favourable results are achieved, top management may seek a very rapid expansion of the quality circle effort. "If a few circles are good, many more circles would be better" seems to be the logic. This logic, however, fails for several reasons. The initial circles were "hand selected." Other circles may not have the same high-quality leadership. Another problem is that existing circles must be serviced. A facilitator does not merely train people, attend the first couple of sessions, and abandon the circle to start more of them. Advice, assistance, information, and other demands are made on the facilitator's time by existing circles. As one facilitator commented, "It is easier to start circles than to service them." When circles are still in their first year, a facilitator can handle about ten of them. After the circles gain a year's experience, the facilitator can seldom assist more than twenty circles.

These mathematics lead to the problem of insufficient facilitators, which serves as a brake on the growth of circles. Most facilitators come from within the organization since there are few to be found by recruiting. As a result, in-house facilitators must be trained—usually through a process of external training programmes and internal apprenticeships.

Admittedly, some companies have started scores of quality circles within the first year. But companies like Tektronics and Reynolds Metals Company are exceptions. Tektronics added over 250 circles in a little more than a year. But it already had made extensive use of the workplace teams before starting quality circles. Furthermore, the culture of the organisation was receptive to quality circles and experienced facilitators were available. Reynolds' approach to rapid growth relies on decentralisation. A corporate team—after considerable planning—began installing circle programmes on a plant-by-plant basis. The local plant management and facilitators then were responsible for the growth at their site. In Reynolds' case, their strategy was to start multiple circle programmes rather than using a circle-by-circle approach.

Grass Roots Fanfare and Expectations

As with many new programmes, there is an almost irresistible urge for fanfare. The tendency is to have kick-off articles in the company newspaper, mass meetings with speeches from top management, posters, banners, and other hoopla. All this is done in the name of "communicating with the employees."

The problem with fanfare is the expectations it creates among workers. Even a quick expansion of circles throughout the company is unlikely to involve more than a small fraction of the employees during the first year. At Tektronics, for example, less than 3,000 employees were in circles after the first 18 months. Although an impressive number, that still leaves 19,000 employees not in circles. What happens to the expectations of those not reached by quality circles? If corporate-wide fanfare is used, many (if not most) employees will view circles as another "programme-of-the-month."

Virtually every successful circle effort begins quietly. A small group of supervisors and workers are involved after their middle management people are briefed on it. When other employees see members leave their job for a meeting, curiosity and the grapevine will publicise what is happening. Interest of non-members will be a function of employee comments—a more powerful endorsement than meetings, banners, or speeches would ever generate. However, since the effort is both experimental at first and completely voluntary, the grapevine should produce few anxieties. A supervisor whose employees express interest is more likely to be receptive to circles because employee eagerness is substituted for resistance. In fact, the most common problem with the use of grass roots fanfare is that facilitators often find more interest for new circles than they can accommodate.

Long-Term Viability

Experience in Japan suggests that circles continue in a supportive environment for as long as workplace problems exist. Although U.S. firms do not have the length of experience of the Japanese, circles have been in continuous use in some companies for six years.

Besides a drop in management's commitment to circles, several other factors can destroy the on-going success of circles. The most obvious is a lack of employment stability within the circle. High turnover among circle members can ruin the group's cohesion. It matters little whether this turnover is caused by layoffs, transfers, quits, promotion, or reorganisations. Particularly damaging is to replace the supervisor—especially with someone who is not familiar with the circle process. Companies like Control Data try to train supervisors and employees who transfer into a work group whose members are in an active circle.

Another potentially damaging problem is non-joiners. Since circle membership is voluntary, some employees may not join. Most companies train these employees along with those who elect to join so at least non-joiners understand the process. Tektronics goes a step further and posts minutes of circle meetings in the work area for all to review.

Since circles are usually limited to ten employees, several strategies have been developed when more than that number want to join. If the supervisor has a broad span of control, two circles may be formed with each group working on different problems. When two circles are not used, participants are usually rotated. After each problem is solved, some members are rotated out of the circle to make room for others. Usually half or less of the members are affected in any one rotation in order to provide continuity.

Risk and Failure

Many managers are more comfortable buying a new piece of technology or even acquiring another company than beginning quality circles. Purchases of equipment are subject to detailed analysis with estimatable payoffs. Quality circles—like most other human resource undertakings—are not precisely predictable nor measurable. Even for human resource managers to propose quality circles carries high risks. Success or failure of quality circles is largely outside the control of those who are responsible for their implementation. A distrustful organisational culture, lack of commitment by any level of management, budget cutbacks, or other changes can seal the fate of even a well-conceived circle effort.

Thus, why have so many companies committed themselves to this idea? The answer seems to be in two parts: Competition and benefits. As more and more competitors benefit from innovative approaches to management, laggards risk losing key employees and even their competitive position. Although attributing Japan's success solely to quality circles would be a crass exaggeration, few can doubt that circles have helped them build a productive and committed workforce. Corporate benefits are another consideration since successful quality circles repeatedly yield returns of 200, 300, or even 400 per cent. Few companies face investment opportunities even one-fourth as attractive. And the *major* corporate benefits may come from improved employee commitment to their jobs and productivity in ways that are not measurable as a return on investment.

Even if the quality circles fail, what has been lost? Virtually every dollar spent on circles is directed at training people to be better leaders and decision makers. Although dividends from training are difficult to measure, the monies spent on employees are never totally lost.

Moving beyond competition and benefits, one comes to humanitarian considerations. What makes a job enjoyable? For many management and staff people, it is being involved in decisions that matter. It is being where the action is! The people in hourly jobs are no different—in any fundamental way—from top managers. They may lack degrees, experience, mentors, and luck. But, they too seek satisfaction from their jobs. They too seek to be involved in the decisions that directly affect them. Technology and efficiency may dictate repetitive, mundane work. But, to deprive hourly workers of the opportunity to use their creativity, deprives them of job satisfaction and commitment to their employer. From a bottom-line perspective, it deprives the company of the good ideas that employees can offer. Simply put, quality circles offer hourly paid employees a chance to use their creativity—a chance to improve their jobs and the company's productivity.

TOWARD BETTER ORGANISATIONS

Quality circles are not an academic pipe dream. They have worked in Japan for decades and have been successful in the United States for several years. From the experiences of executives, facilitators, and consultants in these organisations, a pattern for success is emerging. Although there is no one best way to make a quality circle effort work, there is growing agreement among these experienced people about the most common problems and pitfalls.

Avoiding the danger points outlined here does not guarantee success; other roadblocks exist that are unique to individual organisations. The biggest danger, however, is a long-standing reluctance to form a partnership between management and workers that allows participation in the decision making process. In the name of efficient decision making and accountability, employee participation is limited. This limitation on involvement creates a more damaging barrier to corporate success: Resistance to change by the very people who produce the company's goods and services.

There is little question that quality circles work. In less than a decade, a sprinkling of leading corporations have begun successful efforts. These pioneers stand as proof of both the feasibility and usefulness of quality circles. Too many of these companies find significant benefits from quality circles to dismiss this idea as either fad or folly. What remains to be seen is whether the widespread use of quality circles in these companies will lead to decisive, competitive advantages. If improvements in quality of work life and productivity yield a significant advantage, those without quality circles may be unable to apply this "people technology" fast enough to catch up. If they launch quality circles on a crash basis, failure is likely because of the need for a radical change in corporate culture. If they wait too long to begin a circle effort, a methodical introduction may be too little, too late. In the final analysis, the major challenge confronting executives in coming years may be the need for organisations that tap the creativity of all their people.

In the long run, the major pitfall may simply be the initial success of quality circles. Many productivity administrators suffer a nagging concern that once a circle effort is established and no longer a novelty, top management will lose interest. As one vice president commented in reference to his company's president, "I wonder if quality circles can survive their own success or economic prosperity?" The verdict is still out. However, if top management's attention begins to focus on summary reports about the number of solutions implemented quarterly or the firm's annual return on its "investment" in quality circles, other levels of management will forget that. Quality circles are primarily a management development programme. Neglect by top management is likely to be an early clue to declining interest by middle and lower level managers. The programme will wane. Task forces will be appointed to revitalise circles and management will be "going in circles with quality circles."

14

Productivity and Gainsharing

No doubt other patterns of relationship will be found which yield results comparable with or superior to the Scanlon Plan. . . However, I will venture the prediction that we will succeed in increasing our utilization of the human potential in organizational settings only as we succeed in creating conditions which generate a meaningful way of life.

DOUGLAS McGREGOR[1]

All members of an organization contribute to its success or failure and all should benefit or suffer accordingly. This concept has led to the idea of "gainsharing": All who contribute to the organization's success should share equitably in the benefits. When carried out successfully, gainsharing produces a feeling of common destiny or common fate, a feeling that "we are all in this together." The Scanlon Plan, mentioned in the quote that opens this chapter, is just one of a number of specific plans designed to create this feeling of common fate by sharing the benefits of improved productivity.

This chapter builds a bridge from the theoretical concepts of common fate, worker values, individual motivation, and the like to the practical applications of sharing productivity gains. Gainsharing is not just a giveaway; it fosters communications and cooperation and results in a more productive organization. The purpose of this chapter is not to "sell" any particular technique, but to present a number of highly successful approaches to managing with incentives. The resurgence of interest in gainsharing during the 1980s suggests that additional approaches will be developed for business and industry.

THE CONCEPT OF COMMON FATE

"The real task of management," McGregor argued, "is to create conditions which result in genuine collaboration throughout the organization."[2] Too often, the design of an organization—its systems and procedures—has fostered an adversarial relationship between labor and management, and feelings of distrust, competition and animosity between the individual worker and the organization. If the worker is treated as a disposable resource to be hired, used and fired at will, it is not surprising that some organizations have difficulty instilling loyalty and motivation. Workers protect their self interests—pay, benefits, job security, and working conditions, for example—by bargaining for favorable work rules, threatening work stoppages and exhibiting other aggressive behaviors.

Enlightened managers in many organizations, such as Lincoln Electric, Donnelly Mirrors and Hewlett-Packard, recognize that the organization's performance is a direct function of the combined efforts of all of its members. Management can direct the behavior of workers to some extent, but complete control is impossible. The margin of success comes from replacing the adversarial relationship with cooperation and collaboration, so that workers feel they have a stake in the business and a responsibility for making a productive contribution.

The concept of common fate is clear to the sailor in a naval battle. If the ship sinks, it matters not who was at fault. The failure of one individual, whether the captain or the cabin boy, may lead to disaster for all.

Common fate in business is not as direct or clear-cut, but the concept is the same: Any failure to do a job properly—by the CEO or the custodian—can cause all members of the organization to be less successful than they might otherwise be. Stated more positively, the combined contributions of each and every employee are necessary to create a successful organization. And only successful organizations can provide workers with what they want: increased pay, fringe benefits, better working conditions, job security, and so on.

The Lincoln Electric Company can serve as an example. Some years ago, a custodian came up with a method for reclaiming scrap materials—a method that saved the company tens of thousands of dollars per year. In this highly productive company, the possibility of reclaiming scrap from one machine at a time had been studied extensively, but deemed too expensive to be practical. From his unique perspective, however, the custodian saw a way to segregate the "trash" and combine the scrap from several machines in a way that yielded significant savings. Under the Lincoln Electric profit-sharing plan, increased profit was returned to all employees as part of their bonus. The custodian had a stake in the business. He benefited slightly from his own suggestion, but he also benefited from everyone else's suggestions and efforts. He was proud of his contribution, because it helped to "pay back" those from whom he had benefited.[3] He felt a sense of common fate.

According to Carla O'Dell, common fate is a dimension of the culture of the organization. "This point of view stresses the importance of employees as valued members of the firm. As such, all employees should share in the gains or losses that affect their company whether these changes are the result of market factors or their own internal productivity performance."[4] The worker who says "It's not my job" or "I don't get paid to do that" is not operating from a sense of common fate, but under a contractual relationship with an organization which pays for a certain level of performance at an agreed-upon rate.

A FRAMEWORK FOR INCENTIVES

Before exploring the link between common fate and gainsharing, we should examine a framework for incentive systems. This will help us later to compare gainsharing with other forms of rewards for performance.[5]

Many people define "incentives" as cash payments for superior individual performance; actually, the term can be much broader than that. The framework in Figure 14–1 first divides incentives on the basis of their form: financial, non-cash financial and nonfinancial. The other dimension separates incentives based on individual performance from those based on the performance of a work group, department or entire firm.

	Individual	Group
Cash Financial	Piece rates Commissions Time payments Well pay Tuition refund	Profit sharing Scanlon Plan Rucker Plan Improshare
Non-Cash Financial	Flexible benefits Seniority benefits Awards	Group benefits Group awards
Nonfinancial	Earned time Flexitime Job enrichment Perquisites	Quality circles Communication programs Quality of work life Team building

Figure 14–1. A Framework for Incentives

Which are more effective, cash financial, non-cash financial, or non-financial incentives? Opinions and research findings vary widely on this point. All of these forms have been successfully used in a variety of firms, yet most of them have failed in at least some specific applications. The general rule is that no one approach is best for all circumstances; each must fit the culture of the organization, the technology of the process and other organizational conditions. The motivation theories discussed in Chapters 4 and 6 give some insight into the complexity of money as a motivator and the need to match total reward systems with employee needs and the organization's goals. The article by Lawler at the end of this chapter gives additional critical opinions on the role and effectiveness of incentive pay.

Are individual incentives more desirable or more powerful than incentives for group performance? Again, no simple answer is possible; each can be effective, and each has its place. Individual incentives tend to foster competition. Commissions, for example, are effective partly because they result in higher income, but also because they are a way of "keeping score"—the highest commission for the month "wins." Sometimes the prize is overt: The individual with the best performance gets the trip to Hawaii. At other times, the only prize is the implicit satisfaction of "winning" and being the number one performer.

Group incentives, on the other hand, foster cooperation. If one member of the group falls behind, other members are likely to take up the slack in order to assure that the group receives its reward. The group develops an internal structure, complete with support systems and discipline procedures. It behaves as a team, rather than as a collection of independent individuals.

But that explanation only begs the question: Which is best, competition or cooperation? Effective managers know that each is desirable under different circumstances. They know that incentive systems cannot be designed in a vacuum. They must fit the organization's goals, the type of process and the characteristics and needs of the employees. Because so much has been written about this subject and so many organizational situations exist, it is impossible (and irresponsible) to give simplistic rules for applying each type of incentive. It would be appropriate, however, to explain each type briefly and illustrate it with an example.

Individual Incentives

Cash financial

There is evidence that this type of incentive existed in a formal compensation system as early as 604 B.C. in Babylonia. It is still prevalent today.[6] Yet some new versions of this category have been developed in the last few years. While piece rates and sales commissions have existed for centuries, tuition refunds are more recent in origin. So are "well pay" schemes, which discourage employees from abusing sick leave, but do not encourage ill employees to come to work. Well pay plans often compensate the worker for part of the sick leave days not used. Preliminary results indicate that some well pay plans are more cost-effective than others, but as a technique, well pay plans look promising.

Non-cash financial

This type of incentive generally costs the organization something, but the employee receives a benefit or award other than cash. Flexible benefits programs, for example, allow employees to choose the mix of fringe benefits (within limits) that best fits their individual circumstances and goals. Older workers, for example, can increase their contribution to retirement programs while dropping maternity benefits. Although seldom tied directly to individual performance, these incentives recognize the individual needs of employees and thus may elicit more loyalty and higher performance than a traditional benefits package.

Individual awards range from "employee of the month" to testimonial dinners, jeweled logo pins and certificates of performance. Several firms provide a preferred parking place as an award; some even provide a free company car for the duration of the award period. One bank holding company, Central Bancshares of the South, has a "Rose Program" for clerical employees. Workers recognized for any service above the expected level will find a fresh rose on their desk the next morning. It is an effective way to say "thank you, we appreciate your performance."

Nonfinancial

Nonfinancial incentive programs are more recent in origin. Earned time off and "flexitime" are just two of the methods that offer time, rather than money, as an incentive. Earned time off gives employees additional time off when they meet some objective. They may get a day off with pay as a reward for their superior performance during the month, for example. As worker values and needs change (see Chapter 4), leisure time may become as powerful a motivator as money.

Programs in this category may differ considerably in their relationship to work performance. With earned time off, for example, the outcome is direct and concrete. With flexitime or job enrichment, however, the incentive aims to increase loyalty, improve attitudes and build desirable work behaviors. The payoff is in sustained, long-term performance, but the link between the incentive and the outcome is sometimes difficult to demonstrate.

Group Incentives

Cash financial

Although the term "gainsharing" may refer to almost any form of incentive, a more precise definition would include only incentives in this category. Since productivity is an organizational effort and all employees contribute to it in some way, the logic of gainsharing dictates that all should share in the benefits by receiving a cash bonus. Various plans and formulas, some recent and some very old, are used to calculate each employee's share of the gain from productivity improvement. Several of these plans and their underlying philosophies are explained in the next section.

Non-cash financial

Like non-cash financial incentives for individuals, incentives in this category may provide either direct or indirect rewards, depending on the nature of the plan. The form of the reward is limited only by the creativity of its originator.

One interesting but unusual example involved a Massachusetts company, Data Terminal Systems, and a trip to Europe.[7] Over three hundred employees worked together and more than doubled sales and earnings in one year. The owner closed down the plant for a week and took all of the employees and their families on a trip to Rome as a reward for a job well done. Obviously, not every company could use this program, but the effect on Data Terminal Systems was lasting and profound.

Nonfinancial

"Group," in this framework, may refer to a work team of a few individuals, an entire corporation or a group of any size between these two extremes. Generally, the reward is tied to the performance of the group, although performance may be affected by conditions beyond their control, such as sales, market conditions or resource price levels. All members of the designated group share in the reward.

Quality circles or employee participation groups are examples of this type of incentive. As explained in Chapter 13, quality circles often build a sense of cohesion as well as pride in work. The reward is the recognition for contributing to improvements in the organization. Communications programs, quality of work life efforts, and a host of other programs may also fit into this category.

GAINSHARING PLANS

One writer offers this succinct definition of gainsharing plans:

> Programs designed to involve employees in improving productivity through more effective use of labor, capital, and raw materials. Both employees and the company share the financial gains according to a predetermined formula that reflects improved productivity and profitability. The emphasis is on group plans as opposed to individual incentives.[8]

Debates over the effectiveness of gainsharing plans, in relation to other incentive schemes, often involve as much emotion as logic. People who believe strongly in the value of one approach tend to discount the value of the other. Evidence indicates, however, that no one approach or plan is best in all circumstances. The choice is a matter of personal preference and suitability for the organization in question.

A U.S. General Accounting Office report sums up the rationale for gainsharing:

> Although group sharing—including profit sharing—has been in existence for many years, especially in the higher managerial levels, only recently has it attracted considerable interest as a total organization incentive system. . . . Many managers believe that if group plans can help obtain and keep competent managers, they can have the same effect with other employees.[9]

Of the many gainsharing plans and variations that have been developed over the years, four are most prevalent: profit sharing, the Scanlon Plan, the Rucker Plan, and Improshare.

Profit Sharing

Profit sharing, the oldest form of gainsharing, began as a way of rewarding top managers for the improved performance of the firm. Today, some plans still follow this model, but many others have expanded it to include all employees. According to one estimate, more than 350,000 companies have some type of profit sharing; and in some sectors, such as banking and manufacturing, the profit sharing occurs in twenty-five to fifty percent of the firms.[10]

Profit sharing can take many forms. Some involve only selected executives; others cover all managers or all employees. In some profit sharing plans, the payout is deferred and becomes available to employees only upon termination or retirement. Many plans pay an annual bonus, but others may pay quarterly, monthly, or at every pay period. Generally, the share of profit is included in a separate check to differentiate it from regular pay.

The most striking example of a profit sharing plan is the one instituted by Lincoln Electric Company. In addition to incentive pay, such as piece rates, the owners of Lincoln Electric share virtually all of the company's profit with all employees. After deducting an amount for reinvestment and for a "fair" dividend to stockholders, the owners distribute the remainder of the profit to employees on the basis of their salary levels and performance ratings. The result is a very loyal and productive workforce who earn approximately twice the industry average in salary and bonus.[11]

Scanlon Plan

In 1935, Joseph Scanlon, president of the local steelworkers union at Empire Steel and Tin Plate Company, devised a plan to save the struggling company from impending failure. His philosophy was that labor and management should cooperate to form a productive environment in which all could prosper. This meant that all should share in the prosperity through job security and by earning a share of the financial rewards. Scanlon professed the belief, not particularly popular in the 1930s, that workers want to contribute their energy, skills, talents, and ideas for improvement whenever there is an opportunity and incentive to do so.

The plan Scanlon developed encourages employees to identify problems in the workplace and submit suggestions for improvement to a departmental or plant-wide screening committee for evaluation and possible implementation. Many of the suggestions reduce the labor cost of the product, and the company agrees to share these cost savings with employees.

Suppose sales for the month (adjusted for inventory change) were $80,000 (see Figure 14–2), and labor cost historically associated with this level of sales was $50,000. If employee efforts and cost-saving suggestions produce the same level of sales with only $40,000 of payroll costs, the $10,000 savings is shared with employees, with workers receiving the larger share (75%).

The Scanlon Plan (and variations of it) has operated successfully in some companies for as much as fifty years. It has become a fundamental way of managing, if not a way of life. Although the Scanlon Plan has had its failures, there is currently a resurgence of interest in it, and efforts are underway to see if the plan's philosophy and calculations can be adapted to non-manufacturing applications.[12]

Sales value of production		$80,000
Expected payroll	$ 50,000	
Actual payroll	40,000	
Bonus pool	$ 10,000	
25% reserve*	2,500	
Available for distribution	$ 7,500	
Company share (25%)	1,857	
Employee share (75%)	$ 5,625	
Bonus percent of payroll	14.1%	

*The reserve is a contingency for possible negative results in future periods. Reserves are distributed at year end.

Figure 14–2.   Sample Scanlon Plan Calculation

Rucker Plan

At about the same time as the Scanlon Plan emerged, Alan Rucker, an economist, developed the plan that bears his name. Similar in philosophy and operation, it differs from the Scanlon Plan mainly in the way in which the benefits are calculated and the ratio according to which they are distributed.

The Rucker Plan begins with the "value added," which is calculated by subtracting the costs of raw material and purchased services from sales revenue. Once it has been determined, the value added is used to calculate the Rucker standard, an historical ratio of variable payroll costs to value added. Stated more simply, the Rucker standard is the percentage of value added that is normally attributable to payroll costs. Figure 14–3 shows the typical series of calculations for a Rucker Plan.

In any given month, the value of goods and services produced is multiplied by the Rucker standard to determine the expected or allowed payroll. If actual payroll is less, the difference is shared equally between the company and all employees.[13]

Sales value of production		$1,000,000
Less: Raw material and purchased services		250,000
Production value		$ 750,000
Variable payroll	300,000	
Rucker standard*	$\dfrac{300,000}{750,000} = 0.40$	

*Note: This is an historical standard based upon several years of data.

Current month's sales	$ 100,000
Less: Raw material and purchased services	20,000
Current production value	$ 80,000
Times: Rucker standard	.40
Allowed payroll	$ 32,000
Actual payroll	28,000
Bonus available	$ 4,000
Company share (50%)	2,000
Employee share (50%)	$ 2,000
Contingency reserve (20%)	400
Bonus paid	$ 1,600
Bonus percent of payroll	5.7%

Figure 14–3.   Sample Rucker Plan Calculation

Improshare

Individual production bonuses are typically based on how much the individual produces above some standard amounts. Mitchell Fein, an industrial engineer, has applied that concept to the total work group—production and non-production employees—in a plan called Improshare (Improved Productivity through Sharing).

In Improshare (see Figure 14–4), base period figures are used to establish labor standards for products and to calculate a Base Productivity Factor. The Base Productivity Factor (BPF) makes it possible to include non-production or indirect employees who also contribute to the productivity of the firm. In the example illustrated in Figure 14–4, the BPF of 1.8 means that each hour of a production worker's time is normally supported by an additional 0.8 hours of an indirect employee's time.

The bonus is determined in any month by calculating the difference between the standard (Improshare hours) and actual hours and dividing this figure by the actual hours. One half of the savings goes to the employees; the other half stays with the company.

Unlike the Scanlon and Rucker plans, Improshare is not steeped in philosophy and participative management style. It is basically a straightforward program to reward employees as a group for performance above the standard, regardless of how the savings occurred. While Improshare promotes increased interaction between employees and management, its major benefit is in creating a cooperative, supportive atmosphere, one that encourages employees to make the most effective contribution possible.

SUMMARY

Incentive plans come in many forms and types, and no one system is best in all circumstances. Evidence exists for the effectiveness of both monetary and non-monetary rewards, and undoubtedly both will continue to be used. Incentives based on individual performance foster a competitive atmosphere which can be effective or counterproductive, depending upon the circumstances. Group incentives, on the other hand, generate a cooperative atmosphere and are especially appropriate for work processes requiring a sense of teamwork.

Gainsharing, in its common definition, refers to systems of monetary rewards for group performance. The plans reviewed here—profit sharing, the Scanlon Plan, the Rucker Plan, and Improshare—vary in their history and applications. All have significant track records, yet none can claim success in every application.

With the increased concern for productivity, and with the shifting values of workers today, gainsharing plans are experiencing a resurgence in popularity. It is likely that additional applications will be found and that new variations will be developed in the future.

BASE PERIOD

Ten employees worked forty hours each to produce 1000 units of product A.

Work hour standard (product A): $\dfrac{10 \times 40}{1000} = 0.4$

Fifteen employees worked forty hours each to produce 500 units of product B.

Work hour standard (product B): $\dfrac{15 \times 40}{500} = 1.2$

Total standard value hours:

$$
\begin{array}{llll}
\text{Product A} & 0.4 \times 1000 = & 400 \\
\text{Product B} & 1.2 \times \ \ 500 = & \underline{600} \\
& \text{Total} & 1000
\end{array}
$$

Twenty non-production employees worked forty hours each (800 hours).

Base Productivity Factor (BPF):

$$\dfrac{\text{Total production and non-production hours}}{\text{Total standard value hours}}$$

$$= \dfrac{(10 \times 40) + (15 \times 40) + (20 \times 40)}{1000} = 1.8$$

BONUS CALCULATION

Current month

Product A = 0.4 hrs. $\times$ 900 units $\times$ 1.8 BPF =   648

Product B = 1.2 hrs. $\times$ 600 units $\times$ 1.8 BPF = $\underline{1296}$

Improshare hours   1944

Actual hours (current month) $\underline{1600}$

Gained hours   344

Employee bonus:

$$\dfrac{\text{½ gained hours}}{\text{actual hours}} = \dfrac{172}{1600} = 10.75\%$$

Figure 14–4. Sample Improshare Calculation

SELECTED READINGS OVERVIEW

Edward E. Lawler asks—and answers—the provocative question, "Whatever Happened to Incentive Pay?" in the first reading of this chapter. Lawler explains how some forms of incentive pay have lost popularity because of problems of implementation and maintenance of the systems, but he makes a good case for the overall value of gainsharing plans for today's businesses.

In "Sharing the Productivity Payoff," Carla O'Dell gives a concise overview of the characteristics of gainsharing plans and the reasons for their effectiveness.

Next Chapter

Rewards, in whatever form, are based on employee performance. A sound measurement system is therefore necessary for evaluating productivity and structuring reward systems and other management decisions. Accounting data give some indication of an organization's performance, but productivity measures—in the form of output/input ratios separate from prices and costs—are needed to help management effectively utilize the firm's output.

Review Questions

1. List advantages and disadvantages of both individual and group incentives for a particular application. Which appears to be the best choice?

2. "Employees get paid a fair day's pay for a fair day's work. Additional pay is unnecessary." Do you agree or disagree?

3. Strong emphasis is placed today on non-monetary incentives. If you had to design an incentive program for truck drivers making local deliveries to retailers, list several (eight to ten) non-cash rewards that could be used and explain how they would be awarded.

4. According to Lawler, incentive pay can sometimes create nonproductive or counterproductive behavior. Explain how this is possible and give specific examples.

5. After reading the O'Dell article, what advice would you give to a small manufacturing firm thinking about implementing a gainsharing program. Should the firm have one? Which one?

EDWARD E. LAWLER

Whatever Happened to Incentive Pay?

Historically, the popularity of incentive pay has gone hand-in-hand with the scientific management approach to work design. The 1920s and 1930s saw a tremendous growth in the installation of piece-rate and other individual incentive plans. For the last several decades, however, the popularity of incentive plans has been in steady decline. Fewer and fewer new ones have been adopted, and many of those that are in place are being eliminated. The impact of this trend has appeared in the attitudes of the American workforce: A 1983 study by the Public Agenda Foundation found that only 22% of American workers say there is a direct link between how hard they work and how much they are paid.

The movement away from incentive pay has had its costs, for there is considerable evidence that pay can be a particularly pow-

Edward E. Lawler is Research Professor of Management and Organization at USC. Author of over 100 articles and nine books, his interests include organizational development, motivation and pay systems, and the quality of work life. He is currently Director of USC's Center for Effective Organizations and a member of the Board of Editors of *New Management*.

erful incentive. Research shows productivity increases of between 15% and 35% when incentive pay systems are put into place. And there is some evidence that the absence of such pay is a *disincentive*. The Public Agenda Foundation survey reports that 73% of American workers attribute their *decreased* job efforts to a lack of incentive pay. Given such effectiveness, the declining popularity of incentive pay systems is, at first glance, hard to understand. After all, there is a desperate need for management approaches that will increase productivity. So why not return to pay for performance?

There are important reasons for the decline of certain kinds of incentive pay—in particular, piece rates—that need to be considered before we turn to what can be done to make better use of pay as an incentive.

PROBLEMS WITH PIECE-RATE PAY

The literature on incentive plans is full of vivid descriptions of the counterproductive behavior that piece-rate incentives produce. In many respects, this is caused not so much by the inherent nature of these incentives in themselves, but by the way they have been utilized in organizations. Nevertheless, it is difficult to separate the problems of implementation from the general nature of incentive pay. Here is a brief review of the major problems with piece-rate incentive plans:

Beating the System

Numerous studies have shown that, when piece-rate plans are put into place, an adversarial relationship develops between the designers of the system and the workers who participate in the plans. Employees play all sorts of games in order to get rates set in such a way that they can maximize their financial gains relative to the amount of work they do: They work at slow rates in order to mislead time study experts who come to set production standards; and they hide new work methods or productive procedures from the time study experts so that standards will not be changed. Additionally, informal norms tend to develop concerning how productive workers should be. In effect, workers set informal limits on their production, and anyone who goes beyond the limit may be socially ostracized (and sometimes even physically abused). Unfortunately for the organization, the informal standard is usually set far below what the workers are capable of producing.

Other games include:

producing at extremely low levels (when employees consider the official standards too difficult to reach), and

using union grievance procedures to eliminate rates that are too difficult.

Finally, in order to gain leverage in negotiating piece-rates, employees may even organize unions so that they can deal from a more powerful base.

Often, unions are able to negotiate rates that allow workers to perform below standards—while being paid at a rate that represents their previous high level of performance. Thus, organizations end up with the undesirable combination of high pay and low performance.

Divided Work Force

Since many staff and non-production jobs do not lend themselves to production standards, an organization often ends up with part of its workforce on incentive pay and part of the workforce not on it. This leads to a we/they split in the workforce that can be counterproductive, and it leads to noncooperative work relationships. This split is not a management/worker split, but a worker/worker split. In its most severe form, this gulf can lead to conflict between the production people on incentives and those who are not—the people in materials handling, maintenance, and other support functions on whom production workers depend. This split can also lead to dysfunctions in the kind of career paths people choose—individuals may bid for, and stay on, incentive jobs even though these don't fit their skills or interests. The higher pay of incentive jobs also causes individuals to be inflexible when asked to change jobs temporarily, and causes them to resist new technology that might require a rate change.

Maintenance Costs

Because incentive plans are relatively complicated and need to be constantly updated, a significant investment needs to be made in the people whose job it is to maintain them. This maintenance problem is further complicated by the adversarial relationship that develops between employees and management. Since employees try to hide new work methods and to avoid changes in their rates (unless, of course, their rates are being raised), management needs to be extremely vigilant in determining when new rates are needed. In addition, every time a technological change is made, or a new product introduced, rates need to be adjusted.

Finally, there is the ongoing cost of computing wages relative to the amount and kind of work employees do. All this activity requires the efforts of engineers, accountants, and payroll clerks. Added together, the support costs of a piece-rate incentive system are thus significantly greater than those associated with alternative systems.

Organization Culture

The effect of dividing the workforce into those who are and those who are not on incentive pay—combined with the adversarial process of rate setting—can create a negative organizational climate. It produces a culture characterized by low trust, lack of information sharing, poor support for joint problem solving, inflexibility due to individuals protecting their rates, and the absence of commitment to organizational objectives.

In short, incentive pay is, at best, a mixed blessing. Although it may improve work performance, the counterproductive behavior that it generates, the maintenance costs, the splitting of the workforce, and the poor climate that it creates, may make it a poor investment. Hence, many organizations have dropped incentive pay (or decided not to adopt it) because they feel the negative effects outweigh potential productivity advantages. The decreasing popularity of incentive pay, however, cannot be understood solely from this perspective. Some important societal changes have taken place since Frederick Winslow Taylor first wrote about scientific management. These changes have also led to the declining popularity of piece-rate pay.

SOCIETAL CHANGES

The United States has changed dramatically since the first installations of incentive pay. The society, workers, and nature of the work itself have all changed. Let us see how these changes relate to the decline in incentive pay:

Nature of the Work

In the early 1900s many manufacturing jobs involved the production of relatively simple, high-volume products. Today, the United States is moving rapidly toward a service-knowledge-information-high technology-based economy. Many of the simple, repetitive jobs in manufacturing have been automated (or exported to less-developed countries). Instead of the traditional simple, stand-alone jobs that one individual could do, many jobs today involve the operation of complex machines, continuous process technologies, or the delivering of services which require the integrated work of many individuals.

Work in the United States today, therefore, is less amenable to individual measurement and to the specification of a "normal level" of individual production than it was in the past. Instead, performance can only be measured reliably and validly when a group of workers or an entire plant is analyzed. In many knowledge-based jobs, it is even difficult to specify what the desired product is until it has been produced. Work of this nature simply does not lend itself to incentive pay. Moreover, many jobs in services as well as manufacturing are subject to rapid technological change. This change conflicts directly with incentive pay because stability is needed to set rates and to justify start-up costs.

Finally, even in those situations where there might be simple, repetitive, stable jobs that would lend themselves to piece-rate pay, corporations are making these jobs more complex and creating conditions in which employees will be intrinsically motivated to perform them well. For example, in many companies, self-managing teams are being given responsibility for large chunks of work. Thus, the process of enriching jobs has made them less likely candidates for incentive pay because, first, a different kind of motivation is present and, second, the enrichment process has made the simple, measurable, repetitive, and individual nature of the jobs disappear. All told, then, the nature of jobs in the United States is less and less amenable to individual incentive pay.

Nature of the Workforce

When incentive pay was introduced in the United States, the manufacturing workforce was primarily composed of poorly-educated, immigrant workers who were entering factories for the first time. Today, workers are more highly educated and there is evidence to indicate that they have different values and different orientations toward their jobs than did their parents. For example, over 20% of today's workers have a college education and this, combined with a number of other social changes, has produced workers who are interested in influencing workplace decisions, who desire challenging work, and who seek to develop their skills and abilities. Piece-work pay plans tend not to fit the desires and interests of such workers.

Nature of the Society

During the last ten years, the United States has seen an expansion in employee rights, employee entitlements, and the kinds of legal avenues that are open to employees when they feel unfairly treated in the workplace. This has made incentive pay plans subject to grievances and to legal challenges which make them difficult and expensive to maintain.

In addition, the nation has seen increased international competition and the export of jobs to other countries. The consequent fear of job loss can lead to production restriction: Employees reduce production because they are afraid that, if they produce too much, they will work themselves or their co-workers out of a job. Hence, the long-term, macro need to be productive for purposes of international competitiveness gets lost in the short-term, individual struggle to maintain jobs.

CURRENT SITUATION

The net effect of these changes seems to have been to push the society toward pay practices that are more egalitarian and in which there is a smaller percentage of pay "at risk," that is, based on individual performance. Overall, the United States has become a society in which the profits of *companies* are at risk as a function of performance, but the pay of *individuals* is affected only at the extremes of performance. An employee only loses when the company is in such poor shape that it has to lay him or her off, and the employee only gains when growth is such that the employee has the opportunity to be promoted. The society seems to have evolved to where employees consider that they are *entitled* to a fair wage and extensive fringe benefits simply because they are employed. This kind of thinking is represented in union contracts that have eliminated piece-rate pay, and in companies that have offered high base wages to all employees in order to stay nonunion.

FUTURE DEVELOPMENT

Looking to the future, there are no indications of social or workplace changes in the offing that are likely to tip the scales in favor of incentive pay. Indeed, if anything, the trends that have led to the abandonment of incentives seem to be continuing. There is, however, one important trend which seems to call for the increased use of pay as a motivator—the lack of growth in national productivity and worsening international competitive situation.

Given the international situation, it would seem foolish to abandon such a potentially powerful incentive as pay for performance. Just this point was made by the 1983 White House Conference on Productivity at which the increased use of pay as a motivator was recommended. The Public Agenda Foundation study also supports pay for performance: It found that 61% of workers surveyed want their pay tied to performance. Yet, my analysis so far has suggested that piece-rate and similar forms of incentive pay may be inappropriate. Moreover, the typical merit increase plan also has many drawbacks and is seldom an adequate motivator (because it fails to effectively tie significant amounts of pay to performance). What, then, is the answer?

There probably is no *single* answer, but for some companies a good strategy is to use some combination of profit sharing, gain-sharing, and stock ownership. In proper combination, these approaches can dramatically increase the motivation of everyone in the organization. Not surprisingly, the use of these plans is showing a dramatic increase, and every indication is that they will continue to grow in popularity. Let us look at each of these three promising methods:

Gain-Sharing Plans

The Scanlon Plan is the oldest and best known gain-sharing plan. More recently, a number of companies have adopted the Improshare plan and others have developed their own plans. The idea behind them all is

to define a business unit—typically a plant or a major department—and to relate pay to the overall performance of that unit. Monthly bonuses are paid to all employees in a unit based on a pre-determined formula.

Typically, bonuses are paid when there is a measurable decrease in such costs as labor, materials, and supplies.

The Scanlon Plan was formulated by Joe Scanlon, a union leader in the 1930s, and has been a place in some companies for over 30 years. Until recently, it was used primarily in small, family-owned manufacturing organizations. During the 1970s, however, an interesting and important trend developed: Such large companies as General Electric, Motorola, TRW, Dana, and Owens-Illinois began Scanlon-like gain-sharing in some of their manufacturing plants. This tendency of large corporations to subdivide into smaller units, each with its own bonus plan, seems to be spreading. The reasons for this are many and relate directly to the kinds of changes in the work force and the society discussed above. Gain-sharing plans seem to fit current conditions better than piece-rate plans for five reasons:

First, gain-sharing does not rely on individual performance measurement. This is important in workplaces where performance can only be measured objectively at the group or plantwide level, and where technology does not lend itself to the identification of individual output.

Second, gain-sharing is typically developed and administered in a participative fashion. That is, employees have a say in the design of the plan and are able to participate in its ongoing maintenance and administration. This tends to significantly decrease the adversarial relationship between employees and management, and to fit better with a society in which workers want to be involved in business decisions.

Third, gain-sharing affects everyone in the work force: managers, production employees, and support people. Thus, it encourages the cooperation and teamwork that tends to produce an increase in overall organizational performance. The ability to include everyone in a plan can be an important advantage in almost all workplaces—since it means that the performance of the many can be increased, and not just the performance of a few.

Fourth, gain-sharing meets the needs of organizations for increased productivity. Gain-sharing can positively affect organizational productivity because it creates a good fit between organizational performance and the payout to the individual—that is, situations are unlikely to develop where a bonus is paid and the organization performs poorly. Because the connection between individual performance and reward is less direct in gain-sharing, it may be a less powerful motivator than *individual* piece-rate incentives; nonetheless, in those workplaces where *cooperation* is the key to performance (e.g., where process production techniques are used), gain-sharing often leads to higher productivity.

Fifth, gain-sharing requires less administrative support than individual piece-rate plans. While it still requires some administration, it does not require the setting of individual standards for each job, nor the calculation of pay for individual workers based upon their performance.

Thus far, gain-sharing has largely been limited to manufacturing organizations, but recently a few service organizations (such as banks and hospitals) have begun to experiment with it. My guess is that over the next five to ten years there will be increased use of gain-sharing plans, although a great deal remains to be learned about how they should be installed in nonmanufacturing environments.

Profit Sharing and Stock Ownership

Profit sharing and employee stock ownership are better known, older, and more widely-practiced than gain-sharing. However, by themselves, they typically are less effective as motivators. This is particularly true in large organizations where the link between individual performance and corporate performance is poor, and the connection between individual performance and stock price is virtually nonexistent. Thus, particularly in large organizations, these pay systems are desirable primarily because of their symbolic value. Such approaches effectively tell all workers that they are part of a single organization and that their joint efforts are needed. Stock ownership, in particular, can emphasize the importance of long-term organizational performance (and, in very small organizations, they make gain-sharing plans unnecessary because they have the same effect). In most organizations, however, these two system should be thought of as symbolic and as balancing supplements to gain-sharing. The one exception is with top managers. For them, profit sharing and stock ownership plans should be thought of as the *major* motivators of performance.

MULTIPLE SYSTEMS

Installing *multiple* pay systems that reward performance is potentially the most effective approach to improving organizational productivity and profitability. Yet, it is surprising how slow most organizations have been to use multiple bonus plans. Particularly in large organizations, many workers have lost a sense of the business and of their involvement in ongoing operations. As a result, they often become mere bureaucrats routinely carrying out tasks with little appreciation or concern for how their performance relates to the overall success of the business. Indeed, this type of relationship between individuals and organizations has contributed to both the stagnation in national productivity growth and, in many cases, to the manufacture of poor quality products.

Gain-sharing, profit sharing, and stock ownership are financial ways of getting people involved in their organizations. Such managerial approaches as quality circles, self-managing work teams, and individual job enrichment can also do this. But experience shows that the two tracks work best when they run parallel. Everything that is known about incentives clearly points out that motivation is greatest when people have both a psychological stake *and* a financial stake in the organization's success. The absence of a relationship between the success of the organization and the pay of the employee causes an important part of the business experience to be missed for the individual worker. Organizations that are "shot through with" a variety of participative and managerial systems produce this necessary link.

CARLA O'DELL
Consultant

Sharing the Productivity Payoff

A GAINSHARING PRIMER

INTRODUCTION

Productivity gainsharing and its companion concept profit sharing have been the subject of interest and experimentation since their inception in the 1930s. Devised initially during the Depression to link wage increases to the company's fate, gainsharing approaches eventually fell from favor as both labor and management looked increasingly to long

Carla O'Dell is a consultant and a specialist in human resource strategies, cooperative labor/management relations, gainsharing and employee involvement approaches to productivity improvement and organizational effectiveness.

O'Dell served as senior advisor and consultant with the American Productivity Center for four years and continues to work closely with the Center. She has developed and managed Center projects and workshops including one on productivity gainsharing and approaches to employee involvement.

She frequently participates in productivity and quality of work life conferences as a trainer and speaker. Currently O'Dell is serving as moderator of the Center's computer teleconference discussions of reward systems and will prepare comments for the White House Conference on Productivity later in 1983.

Reprinted by permission from *Productivity Brief* 24 (Houston, Tex.: American Productivity Center, n.d.).

term wage agreements and cost-of-living adjustments during the prosperous fifties and sixties.

But the turbulent decade of the seventies brought a renewed interest and there are now over 500 American plants with gainsharing plans and thousands of other firms with some version of profit sharing. More and more companies are asking their employees to link part of their compensation to the productivity of their work group or the fortunes of their firms.

Observers have long argued that the compensation practices of American firms respond too slowly to changes in business conditions. High salaries and wages are granted when productivity and profits are growing, but there is no way to cut back in hard times except to lay people off.

During the inflationary seventies, compensation far outstripped real productivity growth, but companies could pass through their payroll costs in the form of higher prices. No longer able to do so, they are looking for means of reducing labor costs to compete in the international marketplace. They notice that the major Japanese firms are able to vary their labor costs to reflect the current market conditions by paying 10 to 50 percent of their compensation to lifetime employees in the form of semiannual bonuses. The Japanese model is one factor setting the stage for gainsharing.

In addition, employees are more willing to link their pay to productivity, which they now see as an urgent national issue. In a recent Harris survey, 63 percent of the American people and their leaders in business, labor and government agreed that sharing the gains of productivity improvements would have a significant positive impact on the problem. In another survey, a *Business Week* poll of executives found 83 percent would be willing to share the gains in productivity improvement with employees in return for wage and work rule concessions.

It is against this backdrop that the current experiments with gainsharing are being played out. While the general economic conditions set the stage, the reasons firms actually adopt gainsharing are far more specific to their particular situations.

A BASIC DEFINITION

Gainsharing—Any of several programs designed to involve employees in improving the productivity of their work group through better use of labor, capital, materials and energy. Gains resulting from "working smarter" are shared between the company and the employees according to a predetermined formula that reflects progress toward productivity and profitability.

Gainsharing plans are designed to share the value of improvements in productivity or financial performance over historical levels between a company and a group of employees (a department, a plant or the whole firm). In order to be considered gainsharing, the gains in improvement are shared in *cash*,

and they are based on group performance. Individual incentive plans, such as piece rates or commissions, may be appropriate and effective reward systems, but they are not gainsharing. Individual rewards tend to put worker output ahead of plant or group output and lack a focus on overall productivity gains. Variations in which merchandise or time off with pay are the rewards may also be valid and effective, but they too are outside the mainstream of gainsharing.

There are four major gainsharing plans to use: Scanlon, Rucker, Improshare and profit sharing. Some companies have created their own approaches which tend to be hybrids of the four common plans. Though generally cited as a group incentive, profit sharing straddles the gainsharing fence since the payout from many such plans is a contribution to a pension fund and not cash.

Beyond their emphasis on cash payouts for group performance, gainsharing plans have several other dimensions in common.

All must be built upon some *historical base period*. In order to reward for improvement, some baseline measure of performance has to be established. Usually, the formula reflects average performance over a representative time frame of one to five years. When this level of performance is exceeded, a bonus is earned.

The company and employees *share the gains* according to a *predetermined agreement* about what is an equitable split. The ratio varies with each plan. Improshare, which rewards for improvements in units per labor hour, splits the gains 50/50 with employees. Typically, Scanlon plans give 75 percent to employees. The Rucker split is based on the historical ratio of labor costs to value-added. Profit sharing splits are variable and reflect a perceived level of fair ROI or ROA before payout. Regardless of the split, the principle is always the same—it should be fair and acceptable to the company and the employees.

Time periods vary, but every gainsharing plan involves *paying a periodic bonus.* The bonus is calculated and paid weekly (Improshare), monthly (Scanlon and Rucker) or quarterly to annually (profit sharing). With each of these there are tradeoffs. The more frequently a bonus is paid, the more likely people are to see a relationship between the bonus and their performance. However, the short-term focus may not be in the best long-term interests of the operation as a whole. Companies often try to create a balance of long-term and short-term rewards. Figure 1 illustrates different gainsharing plans and other reward systems in terms of two dimensions—the performance factors on which rewards are based and the time frame in which they tend to be calculated.

A fourth characteristic of gainsharing plans is that bonus distribution is based on *group performance.* If a 10 percent bonus is earned by a group of employees, then every employee gets additional compensation (a bonus) during the bonus period amounting to 10 percent of his or her salary and wages. Most companies pay in a separate check so that there is no confusion between regular pay and bonus.

In Scanlon, Rucker and Improshare plans, some percentage (usually 25 to 30 percent) of the employee share of the bonus is held back each bonus period in a *deficit reserve.* This serves as a cushion for those periods when performance falls below historical levels. At the end of the year, any money in reserve is distributed to employees in a lump sum,

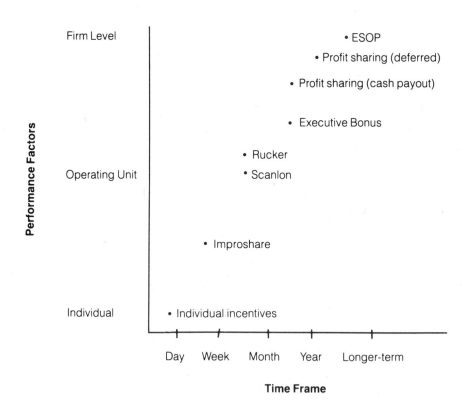

Figure 1.   Factors Affecting Payout

which can be substantial if the company and employees have had a good year.

Most companies with Scanlon, Rucker or Improshare plans try to *define the work group* to include everyone at a particular location in the gainsharing pool. The purpose is to increase *esprit de corps* and overcome some of the handicaps of the territorial boundaries that form between departments, management and blue and white collar employees. For profit-sharing plans the group can be the entire firm, spanning many locations.

VARIATIONS ON A THEME

Beyond these common features, gainsharing plans differ along two dimensions: 1) their formula and 2) the degree of formal employee involvement that accompanies the reward system.

Every company considering gainsharing must develop its own formula. It must decide whether measures of performance will be financial or physical and whether the measures will include labor-only inputs or other inputs such as material, energy and capital (Figure 2).

Financial formulas, such as Scanlon, Rucker and profit sharing, have the virtue of reflecting market factors, so that employee earnings vary with changes in business performance, as well as the contribution of employees. But these formulas can also be distorted by inflation and shifts in pricing and costs. Many financial factors are beyond

Financial Measures   **Physical Measures**

Output/Labor

Scanlon

$$\frac{\text{Sales value of production}}{\text{Payroll costs}}$$

Improshare

$$\frac{\text{Number of units produced}}{\text{Labor hours}}$$

Allowed Labor

Allowed labor/unit - Actual labor/unit

Output/Multiple Inputs

Rucker (Value-added)

$$\frac{\text{Sales value - materials and outside purchases}}{\text{Payroll costs}}$$

Profit Sharing (multi-cost)

$$\frac{\text{Sales}}{\text{All costs}}$$

Total Factor

$$\frac{\text{Total outputs}}{\text{All inputs}}$$

Figure 2. Types of Gainsharing Formulas

the direct control of people in the operation segment of the company—sales, pricing, marketing strategies, materials and supply costs. For this formula to work, employees need to understand how these financial factors affect performance.

Gainsharing formulas based on physical measures of labor productivity, such as Improshare and allowed labor, are not influenced by changes in base wages/salary or selling price of the product, but they are very volume sensitive. As orders for product decline, few companies reduce direct and indirect labor at the same rate; the result is often reduced labor productivity. It is also possible to be paying a bonus based on improved labor-per-unit ratios while the company is losing money because of market pressure to reduce selling price. Generally, physical performance formulas provide stronger motivation to production employees than office, technical and support functions.

There is no "perfect" gainsharing formula —all reflect trade-offs and points of emphasis. Consequently, each company should give consideration to developing its own unique formula to reflect its business and philosophy. Though the process requires more planning on the front end than does adopting someone else's formula, the results will have a long-term payoff in employee support and increased productivity. (See Box 1.)

Formula issues tend to get the most attention when managers are exploring gainsharing options. However, the form and extent of *employee involvement* are probably a better determinant of a gainsharing program's ability to achieve productivity and quality of work life improvement. Employee involvement is the engine that drives gainsharing. It is the vehicle through which employees make the innovations on a daily basis that lead to long-term improvements in productivity.

Box 1.   Favorable Conditions for Employee Involvement and Gainsharing

- A skilled, interested workforce
- Fair and equitable pay rates
- Perceived job security
- Employees who want to develop themselves
- Work that requires a high degree of cooperation
- A belief that rewards are based on performance
- Willingness to create a more open management climate
- Willingness to listen and use employee ideas—and a formal process for doing so
- Ability to set up management systems for sharing information and tracking performance
- Workable labor relations
- Effective production control and accounting procedures
- Willingness to give supervisors a key role in the process
- Willingness to involve the union in the design of the program
- Relatively stable product lines or an ability to develop a stable formula
- Consistency between the reward system and the basic management philosophy

The degree of involvement varies from plan to plan, and often evolves as gainsharing becomes a part of the organizational fiber.

Scanlon plan companies place great emphasis on employee involvement systems and participative management. Most start with a suggestion committee review structure, and then expand later to more sophisticated communication and decision-making systems.

Rucker plans are usually implemented with plant-level Rucker committees that review employee suggestions. But many expand later into small group participation activities, such as quality circles or labor-management teams.

One company which has expanded the involvement factor of its Rucker plan is Morse Borg-Warner in Denver. Managers there describe the gainsharing plans as a "Rucker plan with a Scanlon philosophy." They are referring to the strong formal and informal emphasis on involving employees in identifying and solving productivity related problems in their operation. For them, as for many other gainsharing companies, there are many intangible benefits to involvement and the formula is a way to "keep score and reward people for playing the game."

Companies often embark on Improshare without much attention to developing employee involvement systems for handling ideas. Often suggestion systems will evolve out of necessity after the plan is implemented. Columbus Auto Parts is one company that started with Improshare and has added quality circles to the approach.

Experience has shown that gainsharing plans without some mechanism for responding to employee ideas and sharing relevant information with them are unlikely to produce lasting changes in the workplace or to be sustainable during poor business conditions. Once employees are given the opportunity to share in improvements, they expect management to listen to some of their ideas. As one manager at Phillips Petroleum (which has several gainsharing plans) said, "Management must be willing and able to suddenly have a lot of partners in their business." Plans that start up without adequate preparation to respond to employee ideas create a frustrated and uncooperative workforce and an overloaded maintenance and engineering function and reinforce employee perceptions that management is not really interested in making them "partners in productivity."

During an economic downturn, most well-designed gainsharing plans will stop paying a bonus. Without an involvement system, the plan itself is effectively inoperative. With a strongly supported involvement system, companies needn't rely on the bonus alone to drive productivity improvement. Their plans work as well or better during downturns because employees are even more motivated to keep coming up with cost reducing and productivity enhancing ideas.

Variations on both formulas and employee involvement approaches are infinite. Choosing the most effective system is an important decision. That decision must be closely linked to the organization's reasons for embarking upon gainsharing and the philosophy underlying the plan.

The reasons tend to fall into some major categories: 1) a financial, competitive or labor relations crisis, 2) a belief in the power of financial incentives, 3) the need to replace or supplement an individual incentive, and 4) a desire to extend participation and teamwork into the reward system.

CRISIS AS CATALYST

A financial, competitive or labor relations crisis is often the catalyst that sends a firm searching for solutions they would never have considered in less trying circumstances. For example, many gainsharing plans are being born at the bargaining table. One that seems to have the ingredients for success is the Ford/UAW agreement on profit sharing which went into effect on January 1, 1983. In exchange for giving up their annual three percent improvement factor, Ford workers will share in the gains when Ford's annual before-tax profits exceed 2.3 percent of domestic sales. Just as importantly, Ford and the UAW are committed to employee involvement at every location, a "mutual growth forum" for addressing issues of common concern, and intensive skill training programs. Ford employees may be more willing to accept a stake in the company's future if they feel they have some influence in shaping it.

While a contractual agreement often leads to gainsharing, it does not assure the gainsharing plan's success. It is becoming apparent that gainsharing cannot survive a breakdown in cooperation. Corry Jamestown Furniture Company had a labor management cooperation program and Improshare from 1974 until recently. A breakdown in labor relations has severely jeopardized the gainsharing program.

Gainsharing alone is not enough to create committed employees and improved labor relations. Other aspects of the day-to-day relationships between employees and managers have to change as well. Companies have to change the way they manage. For many, that is more than they "bargained for."

BELIEF IN POWER
OF INCENTIVES

When managers talk about gainsharing, their comments often echo the following statements:

"The only way to get people to work more is to pay them more."

"All these people care about is their paycheck."

"The first thing people ask when we talk about productivity improvement is, 'What's in it for me?'"

"They won't believe we are serious about productivity unless we put some money behind it."

To managers who, accurately or not, believe in the power of financial incentives, gainsharing provides a seemingly low risk, low cost way to give people more money in return for productivity improvement without being locked into permanent increases in compensation.

These managers are partially correct. People are concerned about their personal welfare and compensation; they do think that they should get a fair share of gains they help create. The danger lies in the tendency of these mangers to ignore the other reasons people might be concerned about their productivity—job security, their own development, control over their jobs, etc. A commitment to sharing the gains will not, by itself, address those issues.

REPLACEMENT FOR
INDIVIDUAL INCENTIVES

Many companies in the manufacturing sector have individual incentive plans that are costly to administer, reflect standards that are difficult to maintain, and create endless friction and bickering between management, industrial engineering and employees. Many indirect employees are not covered by these plans, which contributes to a lack of cooperation between departments and difficulty transferring people between jobs.

Nonetheless, the incentive culture dies hard. Gainsharing is an acceptable alternative to scrapping incentives altogether. Instead of focusing on the output of an individual worker, gainsharing shifts the emphasis to the overall productivity of the work group—that is, the production of the finished products. Consequently, workers are more likely to appreciate the entire production process. Instead of every employee being a business unto himself or herself, there is now an incentive for cooperation.

Atwood Vacuum shifted their 1,900 employees from an individual incentive plan to Scanlon. Their plan covers four separate locations, making it easier to transfer people within the company. They have averaged a 13 percent bonus over the years with some years much higher.

PHILOSOPHICAL UNDERPINNINGS

These three reasons for beginning gainsharing all arise from the organization's need to solve a particular problem—a financial or labor crisis, worker resistance to productivity efforts or friction caused by individual incentives.

"COMMON FATE"

But companies are now embracing gainsharing for other non-crisis reasons as well. As a part of their overall productivity and quality of work life strategies a small but growing number of companies view gainsharing as a means of extending participation and teamwork into the reward system. They see gainsharing as a move toward a "common fate" culture. This point of view stresses the importance of employees as valued members of the firm. As such, all employees should share in the gains and losses that affect their company (or operating unit) whether these changes are the result of market factors or their own internal productivity performance. (See Box 2.)

This philosophy is in contrast to the contractual point of view traditionally held by American manufacturing—a belief that the company "contracts" with employees to produce a particular level of performance, with clear job descriptions and clear lines of authority and influence. Rewards in such companies tend to be based on factors over which workers have immediate influence—labor hours, product quality and reduced waste. Because of this narrowed focus, the companies see little need to share financial and business information nor do they tend to encourage a high degree of involvement in decision making or problem solving.

The responsibilities of employees are far broader and less clearly defined in a common fate culture. The emphasis is on creativity, cooperation, occasional self-sacrifice, a high degree of job security and ongoing employee development.

Companies who have or are developing the common fate—or "we're all in this together"—philosophy, tend to create formulas that are more comprehensive than a labor-only calculation. The formula often includes "bottom line" business factors—financial performance will determine the long-term ability of the company to maintain jobs and grow through increased investment.

Consequently, employees need to understand the financial factors affecting performance and need to become more knowledgeable about the business as a whole. A management that hesitates to share financial information with employees—especially in organized settings—will find it has nearly insurmountable problems in implementing this philosophy.

CONCLUSION

Armed with an understanding of the basic concepts and philosophies underlying gainsharing, any organization can strengthen the link between productivity performance and rewards within the organization. From the experiences of companies that have successfully implemented gainsharing programs emerges the following advice.

First, design your own formula, based on the key leverage point in the organization and on a desire to build a common fate rather than contractual culture. Make the design process a model for what you want the organization to be; that is, involve key people from all departments, get early union

Box 2.   Characteristics of Philosophical Positions

	COMMON FATE	CONTRACTUAL
Philosophy	Shared responsibility, commitment, rewards	Fair day's work for a fair day's pay
Objectives	Increased productivity, profitability, quality, satisfaction and loyalty	Increased productivity, quality, profitability—focus on labor
Major Constituencies	All employees, customers, stockholders	Managers, stockholders, customers, employees
Employee Involvement	Extensive, within and between levels and functions; "way of life"	Programs—quality circles, etc.; employees; usually no formal system
Education & Training	Economic education; multiple skill training; problem solving and group process	OJT; feedback on job performance
Gainsharing Structure	Designed and administered by management-employee committee; formal, early union involvement	Management designed and administered
Job Security	Formal commitment; a key consideration in all decisions	Labor as variable cost; layoffs common during business downturn
Information Sharing	Open books—share broad information; profits, productivity, quality, costs, capital spending plans	Limited to information in bonus computation
Types of Formulas	Single/split ratio (Scanlon); Value-added (Rucker); Multi-cost; Profit sharing	Improshare; allowed labor; production bonus

involvement in the exploration, build commitment and understanding through involvement rather than trying to sell the program later. Don't underestimate the time or energy involved in designing and implementing the formula.

Second, begin with the basic premise that employee involvement will be an integral

part of gainsharing. Start with employee involvement if that makes sense in your organization, or initiate gainsharing and involvement together—but do them both. Involvement has implications for behaviors across the organization. Management will have to change toward a more responsive and cooperative mode. Engineering and maintenance as well as other critical management systems will find themselves under scrutiny from people who will turn to them to help implement solutions. Be prepared to get rid of internal barriers.

Third, even though barriers are overcome, it will take time for improvements to build up to produce major changes, so temper people's expectations. The best way to do that is through education and communication about how the formula works and about operating numbers and data. This communication cannot be limited just to the start-up phase of the effort but must be sustained and designed to incorporate new employees. They will need to be oriented to understand that this common fate culture is different from any situation they may have ever worked in before.

Fourth, sustaining the program will require a degree of organizational stability. Be sensitive to the need for stable management —don't transfer the location manager, who has championed gainsharing, to another site six months into the program. Provide supervisors and managers with the skills they need as the involvement program evolves.

Finally, never assume that the gainsharing effort has been perfected and can be cast in concrete. Conduct a formal annual review of the program to see how it is working, what problems have arisen and where it needs to be changed. Then get consensus around those changes.

15

Productivity Measurement

Faced with the impossibility of exact answers to questions
that we would clearly like to answer, we have three options:
we can forget about it, we can willfully force the answers and
try to use our authority to make them stick, or we can devise
an acceptable and believable process for generating answers,
even if the answers themselves are known to be imperfect.
DANIEL H. GRAY[1]

Productivity measurement is not an end in itself: It is a means for communicating work performance results to those who can do something about them. In any team sport, an overall score is maintained to indicate the success or failure of the team as a whole, but individual players on the team also measure their performance to monitor their contribution to the overall team score. So it is with any measures of business activity. Overall "scores" are kept on profit, sales and other global factors, but they are supported by thousands of detailed measures that tell individuals and groups within the organization what is expected of them and how they are doing.

Productivity measures are part of the total measurement system of the organization. Financial and cost measures are important controls, but they are not sufficient. Decision-makers also must be aware of the ratios of physical outputs to physical inputs, for these ratios indicate the efficiency and effectiveness of resource utilization in the firm. Without measures of productivity it would be difficult, if not impossible, to set goals and define expectations, control resource utilization rates, and plan for future activity levels.

Good productivity measures help define the concept of "productivity" for workers and help guide workers' behavior toward goals. For example, suppose waiters and waitresses are hired for a new restaurant.

338

They are paid no salary, wages or tips; just a very large (or very small) bonus based on their productivity on the job. Not knowing how productivity was to be measured would be very frustrating to them. Would they be better off (more productive) serving many customers short orders, or a few customers full meals? In this situation, there might be hundreds of different productivity measures, and each would lead the workers to act in a different way. Here are just a few of the possible measures of productivity:

1. Number of customers served per shift
2. Number of meals served per shift
3. Number of tables served per shift
4. Number of checks per shift
5. Dollar amount of food served per shift

If their bonus is based on the dollar amount of food served per shift, the waiters and waitresses quickly become salespersons. They encourage customers to have appetizers, side dishes, desserts, and more expensive entrees. Whether that behavior is good or bad for the restaurant depends on the type of facility and the specific goals and objectives involved. It might be fine for a fast-food chain but entirely inappropriate for an exclusive restaurant that depends on return customers. In any case, the waiters and waitresses are working on the basis of the measure that was set up and on the basis of their own self-interest, as they should.

Bad productivity measures also direct behavior, but they direct it in the wrong way. Suppose, in this example, the bonus was based on the number of checks turned in at the end of the shift. The workers' bonuses would be maximized if they wrote a separate check for each person at a table, and each time an item was ordered. They would probably spend more time writing checks than they would serving customers, and this would lead to terrible problems for the customers, and for other employees in the restaurant: Paying checks, recordkeeping and controlling the operation would all become difficult. This example clearly illustrates a "bad" productivity measure. Measures should lead to activity that satisfies organization objectives and benefits employees.

MEASUREMENT, BEHAVIOR AND ORGANIZATIONAL GOALS

The elements of this example can be tied together in a model of measurement, behavior and organizational goals to explain how the three interact with work incentives. (See Figure 15-1.)

Notice first that productivity is defined by the way in which it is measured. In the restaurant example the input in the productivity ratio was always one eight-hour workshift, but the output could be defined in a

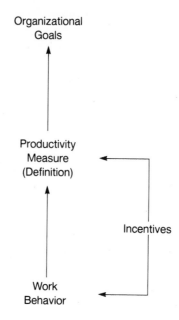

Figure 15–1. Goals, Measurement and Behavior Model

number of different ways. Without a clear definition, employer and employee could be operating on two entirely different sets of expectations.

Second, notice that the measure used for productivity determines work behavior. If the measure is number of customers per shift, the resulting behavior is to serve people quickly and efficiently, so more customers can be handled in a shorter time. On the other hand, if the measure is dollar value served, more time will be taken to sell more food to each customer.

Third, the aim of the organization is to align work behavior with organizational goals. It is the responsibility of management, therefore, to develop measures that will elicit organizationally desirable behaviors. For example, if the restaurant is a deli in the downtown district, specializing in business lunches, the primary goal may be speedy service to keep customers satisfied. The appropriate measure would then be number of customers served per time period. Provided that quality and other standards are maintained, a fast employee would be more valuable to the organization. Of course, in a different type of restaurant with different goals and objectives, emphasis on quickness could be detrimental.

Finally, our model shows that employees tend to work on the basis of the measure in any circumstances. If there is a net incentive for high performance, the link between behavior and the measure will be stronger. The greater the incentive, the stronger the relationship between the two.

The term "net incentive" is used to indicate that many incentives may operate in a given set of circumstances. Peer pressure to avoid "rate busting," the inherent desire for an easy job, and the tendency to socialize at work interact with financial incentives, opportunity for promotion, sanctions for poor performance, and many other variables. As discussed in Chapters 4 and 6, worker motivation is a complex issue. Taking all of that complexity into consideration, our model suggests that the net incentive must be positive. It must also be tied to performance. Otherwise, the work behavior will never begin to approach the productivity measure or the ultimate goals of the organization.

PRINCIPLES OF PRODUCTIVITY MEASUREMENT

Productivity Ratios

True productivity measures are ratios of outputs to inputs in physical, rather than financial, terms. Profit margins, earnings per share, return on investment, and liquidity ratios are examples of financial measures necessary for control of the firm, but they are not true measures of productivity. Tons shipped per employee, customers served per labor hour, gallons of gasoline produced per barrel of crude oil, pieces delivered per truck mile, units produced per kilowatt hour, and units sold per square foot of store space are examples of productivity measures.

Output consists of the products and services produced by the firm. These may be measured in units, tons, customers served, or a variety of other ways. Inputs, as explained in Chapter 1, can be categorized as labor, capital, material, or energy. The examples given above include some measures in each category.

Global measures, such as units produced per employee (i.e., total units produced in a period divided by the number of full-time equivalent employees during this period), generate a gross measure of labor utilization for the entire organization. More detailed measures are needed, however, to rate the productivity of departments, work groups and individual employees. If the employees are involved in direct manufacturing, measures are relatively straightforward: units per hour, for example. The output of indirect or staff departments, however, may simply be their contribution to the primary activity of the firm. The productivity of a purchasing department, for example, may be measured by the amount of material purchased or the number of purchase orders written (this is what IBM does). A personnel department may be rated by the number of employees it hires or trains.

Partial versus Total Measures

A partial measure is a ratio of output to just one of the input factors. Units per hour, for example, measures only the labor component of productivity; gallons of gasoline per barrel of crude oil measures only the raw material component. Partial measures are by far the most common measures, and they are quite useful if properly applied. The major misuse of partial measures is undue emphasis on one factor of production, without recognition of the trade-offs involved. If labor productivity were the only issue, a totally automated facility (factory, bank or barber shop) would be ideal; but with present technology, it would probably not be cost-effective. Intelligent use of partial measures balances the cost, availability and effectiveness of all four resource categories: labor, capital, materials, and energy.

A total productivity measure, as the name implies, is a ratio of output to all four resources. A total productivity measure is desirable because, in theory at least, it incorporates trade-offs of resources. From a practical point of view, however, it is difficult to add together dissimilar units of different resources. Some total productivity measurement systems do exist, but they are generally complex and require relatively sophisticated accounting and information systems.[2]

Output Unit of Measure

The output of a firm can be measured in a variety of ways. Sometimes the output measure is obvious: for example, the number of cars produced, the number of transactions processed or the number of haircuts given. Often, however, a firm produces a variety of dissimilar products and services with no common unit. In these cases, several solutions are possible.

Dollar measures

Sales dollars, or value of production, can be used if figures are appropriately adjusted for the impact of inflation. Sales per employee, for example, is a useful measure and easy to obtain; but if sales per employee go up by ten percent, has productivity increased? The ten percent change could be due either to an increase in productivity, or to an increase in the price of the output. Some firms use a general price deflator, such as the consumer price index, while others generate their own deflator based on company price change records. Even an intelligent guess at the rate of inflation is better than no adjustment at all if the aim is to measure true productivity.

The same argument applies to the input side of the ratio. Dissimilar inputs can be combined in dollar values (wages plus material costs, for example) if appropriate deflators can be found for each input.

Output weighting

Firms producing dissimilar outputs can sometimes adjust all figures to an equivalent output unit. In a fast-food restaurant, for example, the hamburger may be the basic unit of output. Each cheeseburger could count 1.2 units, a fish sandwich 0.7 units, and so on. Thus, the product mix is converted to a figure that is comparable from one period to the next.

Value added

A popular practice, derived from economic analysis, is to measure output as value added: the sales price minus the cost of raw material and purchased parts. The difference between the sales price and the cost of material inputs is the value added to the product by the company before it reaches the consumer. Again, since dollar values are involved, appropriate deflators should be used to adjust output prices and raw material costs.

Productivity Levels and Trends

A productivity level is usually meaningless in itself. Production of fifteen units per hour must be compared to previous performance, to an engineered standard, to another facility, or to an industry average to make a meaningful assessment of productivity. If the measure was 15.0 in period one and 16.5 in period two, it is apparent that productivity has increased ten percent.

Following a trend over time, or making comparisons to some standard or average, tells a firm if it has become better off or worse.

Quantity, Quality and Timeliness

A frequent misconception about productivity improvement is that it comes at the expense of quality. Rarely is this the case. Improvements in the quality of the output generally lead directly or indirectly to productivity improvement.[3] Low-quality products contain errors, and correcting these errors consumes additional resources that could have been used to produce more products and services.

Output has several dimensions: quantity, quality, timeliness, and service. Unfortunately, but understandably, the focus is generally only on the quantity. But items produced with defects, produced late or delivered without the proper service support should not be counted as equivalent to properly produced units. Although it is difficult to measure the dimensions beyond quantity, it can be done.[4]

MEASUREMENT MISUSES AND PITFALLS

Productivity measures are often misunderstood and misused. The purpose of productivity measures is to feed back information that permits better decision-making about resource utilization. Production measures, like all measures, may reveal that a problem exists, but it is up to management to explore, diagnose, and correct that problem.

Focusing on only one factor of production can lead to sub-optimization and faulty decisions. Labor is important, but so, too, are the other input factors. Productivity is important, but so, too, is the financial management of the operation.

Because productivity measures should be physical units, sometimes measures are developed to count something just because it is countable. A data processing department, for example, may measure its output as the number of reports produced. Maximizing output in this case involves producing unnecessary reports or producing many small reports. The true output is information in the right form, time and place. Cleverly designed measures can more accurately reflect the true output.

"I hope the measurement system does not take more time than the activity it is measuring," said an employee to one of the authors who was developing measures of white-collar operations. The measure should be accurate and reliable, but it should also be efficient. Sometimes a surrogate measure, such as tons of product shipped by a clothing manufacturer, can be sufficiently accurate to determine output levels and more efficient to obtain than a physical count of items.

Perhaps the most serious misuse of measures is the failure to involve employees in the development and selection of the measures by which they will be evaluated. Managers may believe a measure is accurate and reliable, but if employees feel that the measure is unfair, meaningless or not representative of their skill and effort, the measure will fail to properly motivate and control.

FAMILIES OF PARTIAL MEASURES

The confusion about which partial measures to use can be resolved by developing a set or family of measures that complement each other and cover all input factors. A good example of this is the set of measures developed by TRW. (For a description of TRW and its productivity program, see the reading "Productivity Strategies at TRW" in Chapter 19.)

The purpose in developing the measures was to give an indication of resource utilization, so that comparisons could be made over time and across dissimilar divisions in the corporation. TRW wanted to emphasize that labor productivity was most important, but not the only factor. Consequently, their set of partial measures contains three measures for labor, and one each for capital, materials, and energy. The six measures in the family are as follows:

1. Sales per employee (sales are always deflated to constant dollars)
2. Sales divided by total deflated employee compensation costs
3. Value added per employee
4. Sales divided by deflated material cost
5. Sales per unit of energy consumed
6. Sales divided by plant and equipment costs less depreciation

This set of measures is a family, in that all measures are similar in scope (all use deflated sales dollars as the numerator) and cover all factors involved in production.[5]

Some companies try to do too much too soon in productivity measurement. If productivity has not been measured directly in the past, it is best to start with some simple measures and later progress to a more sophisticated system. TRW's family of measures continues to be useful to the company. But TRW is also beginning to implement a system that mathematically separates internal from external factors and plots productivity performance against benchmarks.[6]

AT&T followed a similar pattern by beginning with the volume of business (sales) per employee and the number of telephones served per employee.

> Both of these measures have appeared—in one form or another—in AT&T's annual report for many years. However, even these measures do not encompass all aspects of the company's operations as they focus on only one input, labor, to the exclusion of capital and materials and services from outside suppliers.[7]

Later AT&T implemented a total factor productivity (TFP) measure that compared aggregate output to aggregate inputs (all factors). Eventually the company moved to a net income and productivity analysis (NIPA) system that tied productivity measures directly to capital growth, price changes and other financial factors. Without previous experience with simple measures, however, these organizations would probably have rejected more complex systems as too difficult to understand.

PRODUCTIVITY, PRICE RECOVERY AND PROFITABILITY

Total productivity measurement relies on fundamental relationships involving prices and units. Had more business executives understood these relationships, the productivity decline of the past decade might have been lessened.

Total revenue for any private sector firm is composed of number of units sold times the price per unit, that is:

Revenue = Output Units $\times$ Output Prices

Similarly, all inputs—labor, materials, capital, and energy—must be purchased at a cost determined by the units used and the price paid per unit:

Total Cost = Input Units $\times$ Input Prices

Input units in this case are labor hours, pounds of material, kilowatt hours, and such. Input prices are wage rates, price per pound, cost (price) per kilowatt hour, etc.

The ratio of total revenue to total cost is profitability. Profitability is the proportion of revenue needed to cover costs and, indirectly, the remainder that becomes profit. The following equation expresses these relationships:

$$\frac{\text{Total Revenue}}{\text{Total Cost}} = \frac{\text{Output Units}}{\text{Input Units}} \times \frac{\text{Output Prices}}{\text{Input Prices}}$$

The first ratio, total revenue over total cost, is profitability. Since the second ratio is output to input in physical units, it represents the total productivity of the firm. The third ratio is called price recovery. Thus,

Profitability = Productivity $\times$ Price Recovery

The real value of this framework, however, is in evaluating changes through time. Increased profitability can derive from only two sources: increased productivity or increased price recovery. Better *utilization* of resources (more output per unit of input) will make the firm more profitable even if output and input prices remain the same. If input prices increase, as they usually do, increased productivity can help the firm to remain profitable without passing those cost increases on to the customer in the form of higher prices for products and services. On the other hand, if the firm's productivity is falling, then it must either become less profitable or increase the prices to its customers even faster than input prices are increasing. The inevitable outcome in this case is the failure of the firm as it is displaced by a more productive firm—foreign or domestic.

Most total factor productivity measurement systems begin with this general framework and develop productivity and price recovery ratios that permit the manager to make more intelligent and informed decisions for the operation of the firm.

SUMMARY

Productivity measurement is an essential ingredient in any organized effort to improve productivity. Without measurement, there is no way to evaluate results and monitor progress. Productivity measurements direct employee behavior toward organizational goals by providing feedback. An infinite number of output-to-input ratios can be created; no one productivity measure works for all processes. Within the general framework of measurement theory, the organization's managers must design a set of measures that best fits its situation and its objectives.

SELECTED READINGS OVERVIEW

The Felix and Riggs article, "Productivity Measurement by Objectives," illustrates a useful way to combine a family of measures into a single index number by using a matrix approach. This technique has proven successful in a number of applications where other measurement systems fall short—particularly in measuring white-collar productivity.

   The second reading is an early article by Craig and Harris that explains the theory and practice of total productivity measurement. Developed before energy became as critical as it is today, their model includes labor, capital, material, and other goods and services. The authors use a case study to show how their model can be implemented.

Next Chapter

Productivity measurement gives managers better information on a firm's resource utilization, especially the utilization of labor. Understanding the relationship of productivity to profitability helps managers to make better decisions about work methods, automation and material usage, as well as cost control and wage levels. All of these issues, of course, are of vital concern to the worker, for if productivity is not increased, the firm may fail. But productivity increases cannot derive from worker exploitation. Unions exist to protect the worker's rights and to assure an equitable balance of power in bargaining issues. Unions do not oppose productivity improvement; indeed, they stand to gain as much from it as the firm does. The role of the union in productivity improvement merits explicit discussion. That is the essence of the next chapter.

Review Questions

1. Productivity measurement can be considered a communication tool. Explain how the implementation of new productivity measures, such as output per employee hour or units produced per ton of raw material, could enhance the communication between the supervisor and the worker.

2. According to the framework in the chapter, increased profitability must come from some change in productivity or price recovery. Suppose Exxon wants to improve profitability but is facing a 20% increase in the price of crude from OPEC. Using this framework, explain (with specific examples) what options are available to Exxon managers.

3. Pick any corporate annual report and read it carefully for information on productivity improvement. See if you can take the data in the annual report and develop some productivity information.

4. In the productivity objectives matrix developed by Felix and Riggs, current performance is entered at level 3 on a 10-point scale. If current performance is "average," why is it not entered at level 5? Explain.

5. Most inputs are a "flow"; that is, materials, labor, and services are purchased and used up in the production of goods and services. Capital, however, is usually considered a "level," expressed as the dollar value of machines and equipment on hand. Explain how Craig and Harris treat the capital input in their productivity measurement formula.

GLENN H. FELIX
JAMES L. RIGGS

Productivity Measurement by Objectives

An objectives matrix enables management to combine all important productivity criteria into one easily communicated format.

Productivity measurement can be difficult. Ratios, indexes, percentages, deflators, cost effectiveness, price recovery, guesstimates, and numbers may assault us from all directions, many of them in conflict with others. As a result, accurately determining the net result of improvement efforts can be a dubious and frustrating undertaking for manag-

Glenn H. Felix is associate director of the Oregon Productivity Center, an extension arm of the Engineering School at Oregon State University. He works full-time with Pacific Northwest industries and organizations in their pursuit of productivity. O/P/C publications, employee-involvement, inter-firm comparison, and training, development, and direct assistance in applications of the Objectives Matrix in manufacturing, service, and government settings are his major responsibilities.

James L. Riggs is both director of the Oregon Productivity Center and department head of industrial engineering at Oregon State University. Very active in the productivity field for many years, he was on the steering committee for America's fledgling attempt at a National Productivity Center in 1978, is current president of the World Confederation for Productivity Science, and is the author of more than a dozen books on productivity, industrial engineering, and related topics.

ers and employees alike. For this reason, far too few organizations actively pursue the potential inherent in this information medium.

Nevertheless, somewhere between complex total firm measures and annual profit and loss statements lies a valuable answer to the challenge of meaningful managerial feedback.

At the Oregon Productivity Center, we feel the answer lies in effective use of O/P/C's Objectives Matrix, and this article will explore the manner in which this practical tool can best be used.

The following points will be addressed:

The basics of productivity measurement;

Partial and total productivity measures;

The interrelationship between productivity and quality;

Features of the Objectives Matrix;

Five reasons why the Matrix is especially adaptable to white-collar operations; and

Six steps to Matrix construction

PRODUCTIVITY MEASUREMENT

In its simplest form, productivity is output divided by input.

$$\text{Productivity} = \frac{\text{Output}}{\text{Input}}$$

This is a fraction or ratio. In the case of the productivity ratio, our objective is to regularly increase the quotient or index number, the value that we get when we divide the numerator by the denominator.

As an example, if in July we produced 200 bookshelves and used 50 labor hours to do so, our productivity ratio of 200/50 would yield a productivity index number of 4.

$$\text{Productivity} = \frac{\text{Output}}{\text{Input}} = \frac{200}{50} = 4$$

Our goal in August and beyond is to achieve ever-higher index numbers. This will indicate improvements in productivity. We can do this several ways:

(A) $\dfrac{\text{Increase Output}}{\text{Maintain Input}} = \dfrac{210}{50} = 4.2$

(B) $\dfrac{\text{Maintain Output}}{\text{Decrease Input}} = \dfrac{200}{48} = 4.2$

(C) $\dfrac{\text{Increase Output}}{\text{Increase Input}} = \dfrac{220}{52} = 4.2$

(D) $\dfrac{\text{Decrease Output}}{\text{Decrease Input}} = \dfrac{190}{45} = 4.2$

The first two methods are straightforward. We either (A) increased our output without working any additional hours, or (B) produced the same output in less time.

With (C), we increased both our output and our labor hours (input) but increased our output 10 percent while increasing our input only 4 percent. With (D), we built 5 percent fewer bookshelves but took 10 percent fewer labor hours to do so.

In all cases our index number went from 4 to about 4.2. This resulted in a productivity improvement from July to August of 5 percent.

Percent Productivity = Improvement

$$\frac{4.2 - 4.0}{4.0} \times 100\% = \frac{.2}{4.0} \times 100\% = 5\%$$

As in the above example, our objective in our organization is to increase index numbers as a reflection of increasing productivity. First, however, we have to devise index numbers to increase. We will deal with this problem after exploring productivity measurement a little further.

TOTAL ORGANIZATIONAL PRODUCTIVITY

The output/input example above in which we looked at bookshelves per labor hour is a case of a *partial productivity measure*. It's partial because only a part of the input—labor—is being considered. To measure productivity effectively, it is necessary to consider all other inputs as well. Doing so gives rise to a *total organizational productivity measure*.

Total Organizational = Productivity

$$\frac{\text{Goods} + \text{Services}}{\text{Labor} + \text{Energy} + \text{Materials} + \text{Capital}}$$

Here, everything that is produced, and all the resources necessary to produce it, are accounted for:

OUTPUT =
Goods	—Bookshelves
+	
Services	—Installation and delivery

INPUT =
Labor	—Hours and effort
+	
Energy	—Electricity for shop equipment
+	
Materials	—Wood, glue, nails, etc.
+	
Capital	—The shop and heavy machinery

As in the case of the bookshelves, the goal of every organization is to maximize the goods and services that it provides, while minimizing the resources that are required to produce those goods and services.

As a practical matter, capital (land, buildings, machines, etc.) is not something that managers and employees have daily control over. So, for our purposes in measuring productivity, only the resources of labor, energy, and materials will be considered. "Capital productivity" can be tracked more effectively by evaluation of investments through accepted engineering economics or capital budgeting techniques. This keeps things simple.

PRODUCTIVITY AND QUALITY

It is extremely important to recognize the relationship between productivity and quality before going further.

$$\text{PRODUCTIVITY} = \frac{\text{Goods} + \text{Services}}{\text{Resources}}$$

To improve productivity, organizations increase goods and services and/or decrease resources. However, goods and services can be increased by both their amount *and* by their value. That is, we can produce the same number of bookshelves, but if they are of higher quality (say a hand-rubbed finish), their value rises and, therefore, so does productivity. Likewise, if we are quality conscious when making the shelves, and don't waste lumber, nails, lacquer, energy and time, the amount of resources necessary to produce each bookshelf is less, and productivity rises even further.

Many other concerns have either a direct or an indirect effect on an organization's productivity as well. For example:

Timeliness	Safety
Downtime	Employee Turnover
Attendance	Housekeeping
Yield	Attitudes

Thus, it is not surprising that measuring and improving productivity requires that we consider many, many criteria, and that at times, it can be very, very difficult.

THE VALUE OF AN OBJECTIVES MATRIX

The Objectives Matrix overcomes this problem of complexity by combining all of an operation's important productivity criteria into one interrelated format. This is accomplished by relating various performance levels associated with each criteria to scores from 0 to 10.

For example, in Figure 1, timeliness is defined as the ratio between late orders and total orders. Since the best ratio in this instance would be zero, that performance level receives the highest score, 10. The current performance level (5 percent late orders) is rated at 3. To establish the lowest score, 0, a percent below any likely minimal performance is chosen. For scores 2–9, a series of targeted improvement goals that gradually ascends toward the best score of 10 is selected.

This same procedure can be followed for all productivity-related criteria once the appropriate ratios or other measures are selected.

By establishing a common numerical scoring system, management can select any combination of criteria considered important for its particular productivity mission and combine the scores of all these selected criteria to obtain a single, overall productivity index. Moreover, since all criteria are not likely to be of equal importance, in the matrix format management distributes 100 points among the criteria to give each one a weighted numerical value that reflects its importance in relation to the others. Thus, management can precisely define the productivity mission of each operation. And since these weighted values are used in computing the overall index, that index provides an accurate assessment of how well management's mission objectives are being achieved at each measurement period. A careful reading of Figure 1 should highlight other features of the Matrix.

White-Collar Productivity

Although Figure 1 shows an application of the Matrix in a manufacturing setting, the Matrix is ideally suited to governmental, service, and administrative support type operations as well. This is true for five reasons:

1. *Normalization.* The scores, 0–10, serve to "normalize" the measures used in the matrix by establishing a uniform quantitative rating system. Virtually any type of criteria, from output per hour to subjective attitude surveys, can be incorporated into the Matrix, and by relating

Step 1. Major criteria impacting productivity in a given area are identified, appropriate measures determined for each, and the resultant monitors entered in the boxes slanted across the top.

Step 2. The current level of performance in the area is calculated for each criterion and the ensuing numerical results entered at a level corresponding to a score of 3. (Note the scores listed vertically at the right of the Matrix.)

Step 3. Based on broad organizational goals, productivity objectives are established for all criteria. These quantitative targets are entered at a level corresponding to a score of 10.

Step 4. Step-wise goals, or mini-objectives, are then determined and the squares from score levels 3 to 10 are filled in with these successive "hurdles."

Step 5. At the same time, flexibility to account for tradeoffs or occasional slack periods is recognized, and figures are inserted in the squares below score level 3. Quotients associated with anything less than minimum likely performance correspond to a score of 0.

Step 6. Since some criteria are more important than others, weightings are assigned to each. The sum of these weights equals 100, and can be distributed in any informative fashion (see Weight row). This step defines the productivity mission of the area in question.

Step 7. At the conclusion of every monitoring period, the actual measure for each criterion is calculated and placed in the "performance" boxes on Row A. The level that these achievements represent is then circled in the body of the Matrix and associated with a score of from 0–10. Scores are entered in the appropriate box on Row B at the bottom of the Matrix. Each score is then multiplied by the weight for that same criterion, to obtain a value, listed on Row C. The sum of all values yields a productivity index for the period. Over time, the movement of this single index tracks the net results of productivity efforts in the area of interest.

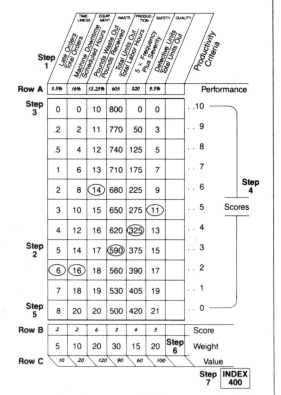

	TIME-LINESS	EQUIPMENT	WASTE	PRODUCTION	SAFETY	QUALITY	
Step 1	Late Orders / Total Orders	Machine Downtime / Scheduled Hours	Pounds Waste Out / Pounds Received	Total Units Out / Total Labor Hours	5 × Frequency Plus Severity	Defective Units / Total Units Out	Productivity Criteria
Row A	5.5%	16%	13.25%	605	320	9.5%	Performance
Step 3	0	0	10	800	0	0	..10
	.2	2	11	770	50	3	.. 9
	.5	4	12	740	125	5	.. 8
	1	6	13	710	175	7	.. 7
	2	8	(14)	680	225	9	.. 6 — Step 4
	3	10	15	650	275	(11)	.. 5 — Scores
	4	12	16	620	(325)	13	.. 4
Step 2	5	14	17	(590)	375	15	.. 3
	(6)	(16)	18	560	390	17	.. 2
	7	18	19	530	405	19	.. 1
Step 5	8	20	20	500	420	21	.. 0
Row B	2	2	6	3	4	5	Score
	5	10	20	30	15	20	Step 6 — Weight
Row C	10	20	120	90	60	100	Value

Step 7 | INDEX 400

Figure 1.   An Objectives Matrix

each such indicator of performance to a 0–10 scale, we can relate all the measures to each other. This is especially valuable for white-collar work, where types of productivity-related criteria are extremely varied.

2. *Flexibility.* With a good mix of criteria identified, many dimensions of performance can be tracked at the same time, thereby giving us a more "global" picture of the operation in question. In effect, through the Matrix, we are able to compare apples and oranges by measuring them on a common scale. We simply call it "fruit."

3. *Results.* In white-collar operations, results are far more important than activities. In fact the classical measure of productivity is best defined in such a fashion:

$$\frac{\text{Output}}{\text{Input}} = \frac{\text{Results}}{\text{Resources}}$$

The Matrix, through the effective identification of criteria and objectives, focuses attention directly on results, and recognizes activities as simply contributing to more important ends.

4. *Sampling.* Many white-collar operations involve literally hundreds of separate tasks that must be accomplished each period. It would be foolish to try to measure each. However, just as 5 or 6 items out of 100 can be randomly sampled to gain some indication of the quality level of an entire "lot," so too can selected criteria be sampled to gain some indication of performance in the entire operation. Weighted outputs can expand the sample base, and what is sacrificed to randomness of selection is somewhat mitigated by the interrelationships that are accounted for in the scoring system.

5. *Trade-offs.* The fact that one index number is generated each period to track the

productivity of an operation makes it possible to assess quantity and quality simultaneously. The effects of trade-offs between the two can be identified with precision. For instance, in the Figure 1 exhibit we might find it necessary to purposely slow the production rate down to 560 units per labor hour in order to improve quality from 9.5 to less than 7 percent defects. The resulting index of 410 indicates that this was a wise productivity decision. In a like fashion, it is extremely important to track trade-offs in white-collar environments, where "improved" productivity can come at the expense of poorer service to internal and external customers.

MATRIX CONSTRUCTION

Construction and implementation of the Matrix is a straightforward process that requires little expertise. The most common method is to form a five-to-ten person task force of first- and second-level managers. With the aid of a knowledgeable coordinator who can detail use of the Matrix, these managers would work through the following six steps to construct a Matrix for each area of interest. Often, and ideally, other employees will be asked to assist.

Determine Criteria

Identify the key performance indicators or criteria for the operations of interest. These are usually related to factors such as timeliness, production, quality, safety, waste, downtime, turnover, attendance, overtime, etc. For each criteria, form a ratio, while, at the same time, ascertaining that the data is obtainable. Typical ratios are oriented to one of three categories, as follows:

Efficiency. How well do we use our resources of labor, energy, capital, and materials?

Good Units/Labor Hours
Transactions/Labor Hours
Waste Out/Good Units
Good Units/BTUs Consumed
Good Units/Gallons Water
Sales Dollars/Expense Dollars

Effectiveness. How well do our results accomplish their stated purpose in an accurate and timely manner?

Late Orders/Total Orders
Rework Units/Good Units
Errors/Items Processed
Customer Complaints/Customer Transactions
Percent Overweight, Badly Mixed, etc.
Average Time to Resolve Customer Inquiries

Inferential. Typically less precise, these measures do not have as direct an impact on productivity performance as do the quantity and quality measures above, but when incorporated into the criteria and properly scaled and weighted, they help account for variables that do affect the major factors.

Safety—Lost Time/Total Work Time
Attendance—Days Out/Days Available
Machine Downtime Hours/Scheduled Hours
Computer Downtime Hours/Scheduled Hours
Overtime Hours/Straight-Time Hours
Housekeeping—Subjective 0–10 Rating
Employee Turnover
Periodic Attitude Survey—Scaled 0–10

Matrices can be installed in virtually any operation of any organization. Where qual-ity circles exist, it is best to have a Matrix for each cohesive work group. In practice, though, separating out the data for specific groups is not often practical. Since departments are generally large enough for more than one team, one departmental Matrix is used as feedback for all circle groups—and for others in the department as well. Additionally, matrices can be introduced on each shift, and at any level of the organization.

Thus, each department could have a Matrix that is keyed to its operations, and the building inhabited by a common group of departments could share a Matrix on housekeeping, attendance, safety, and other inferential measures of importance.

Clarify Data

Having identified the criteria to be included in the Matrix, it is then necessary to define them more precisely. Units, transactions, labor hours, downtime, absent days, errors, defectives—each and every item—needs clarification:

What is a transaction?
Whose hours will be included in labor calculations?
Whose hours will be excluded?
What is an overweight? an underweight?
What constitutes an absent day? What if prior notice is given? How about sick pay?
If a part is out of spec, but functional, is it still defective?

In other words, each and every criteria needs to be thoroughly defined.

Likewise, the sources for each specific measure must be identified. The precise report, person, or other source for each number to be used in matrix computations needs to be specified. In all cases, it is best to leave no doubt as to which number will be used every time matrix results are computed.

Assess Performance

Current performance is usually based upon an average of three months or so of data. In more seasonal types of operations, a longer time frame may be considered, and in some instances of wide fluctuations between periods, a moving average might be appropriate. If criteria are identified for the Matrix that have not been previously tracked, at least two months of information should be garnered before including them.

Current performance is entered at a rating of 3 on the 0–10 scale to allow for greater room for improvement than for declines. It is usually not entered at a lower level so that trade-offs and occasional slack periods can be allowed for.

Target Objectives

While level 3 is where we're at, level 10 is where we want to go. Level 10 is keyed with the objectives we wish to achieve within the next two or three years, and should be accordingly optimistic. Safety, quality, downtime, waste, and many "percentage" efforts should be identified as goals worthy of perfection. This may appear unreasonable over extended time frames, but zero defects, 100 percent on-time deliveries, no accidents, and other such objectives are certainly attainable during an occasional period. In the case of waste or yield figures, perfection may be absolutely unattainable. Then, a more realistic figure should be targeted; but consider the possibility that some three years from now, new technology, revised processes, different raw products, etc., could conceivably help achieve results now considered impossible.

Quantity figures (output versus resources) are a little trickier to objectify. In Figure 1, increasing production from 590 to 800 units per labor hour represents a 35 percent rise. In most manufacturing settings, 20 to 50 per-

cent improvements are reasonable targets. In service operations, even more dramatic gains might be identified. Again, these objectives will probably require much speculation and discussion, but in all cases here, and in moving toward percentage gains, targets are more likely to be hit if they are aimed at.

Define Mini-Objectives

Filling in the remaining score levels of the Matrix is straightforward. Typically, a linear scale is used between current performance and the objective in each category. That is, the numerical distance from each rating step to the next is the same. (Machine downtime in the exhibit is an example of such a distribution.) There is nothing rigid about this requirement, however, and intermediate hurdles on the way to a score of 10 can be progressively less difficult to attain (as in the timeliness category). Movements from a score of 3 to a score of 0 are likewise scaled.

Assign Importance

Next to identifying the important criteria, weighting is the most crucial step, and is accomplished by upper managers, usually a Productivity Council. The Matrix is presented at a meeting of the Council by those who pieced it together. After the criteria, current performance, and objectives are detailed and everyone is satisfied, each council member will subjectively write down his or her choices for distributing the 100 points. Afterwards, these numbers are compared, and one of two approaches is followed: a simple average weight for each of the criteria can be computed and agreed to as the appropriate weighting for the matrix in question, or, preferably, the Council can discuss the various distributions until consensus is reached.

Again, this step defines the productivity mission for the area and should be carried out carefully. A farsighted view is needed. If quality is a particular problem at this point, it's tempting to weight that concern inordinately high, with an eye to perhaps revising emphasis sometime later. Instead, the fit of quality, quantity, timeliness, etc., into overall organizational/departmental goals—down the road as well as now—needs to be considered. With a broad-based Council, this concern should not represent a problem.

Those who construct the Matrix will themselves confidentially weight it before the Council does. Not surprisingly, the two weighting systems are generally within a few percentage points of each other. If not, this exercise is all the more valuable.

IMPLEMENTATION

Once the weighting is accomplished, the Matrix can be implemented. The precise source person for each data input needs to be defined, and the individuals responsible for maintaining the system should be tagged. Next, a meeting should be held with all those who affect, and are affected by, the performance criteria, in order to explain to them their Matrix. One hour should be sufficient.

Ongoing maintenance consists of first gathering data for the period and then determining actual performance for each criterion. That figure is entered at the top of each column. Then, the scoring level corresponding to actual performance is circled in the body of the Matrix. Recall that each box represents a hurdle. If that mini-objective has not been attained, the box below is circled. (For example, in the last criteria column in Figure 1, 9.5 percent defective units is not

yet 9, thus 11 is circled). Any performance worse than the 0 score would still receive a 0 for the period. Every circled box corresponds to a score from 0 to 10, and that number is entered in the appropriate box along Row B. Each score is then multiplied times its weight to yield a value (Row C). The values are summed to yield the index for the period. Computed matrices are then displayed for everyone in the area of interest to view.

Successive index numbers should be tracked on a line graph. After a number of periods, a stringed regression line could also be plotted with each new periodic index. Such a line pictures performance trends more accurately. (Alternately, a three-month moving average index could be graphed.)

If a number of matrices are to be averaged into one overall company productivity indicator, the index of each contributor should be weighted to reflect differing contributions to organizational performance. The most common method of weighting is by head count. The department with 14 percent of the total employees will have its index number multiplied by .14. Every other unit will also "deflate" their index based upon the number of personnel assigned. The sum of these deflated indices yields the weighted-average organizational index for the period.

With matrices in place, each area's primary mission is defined, and specific objectives are established for productivity gains in key criteria. What follows naturally are directed efforts at securing these improvements. Systematic training and involvement contribute to this end and are the next phase toward institutionalizing productivity by objectives.

CHARLES E. CRAIG
The Timken Company

R. CLARK HARRIS
Saginaw Steering Gear Division, General Motors Corporation

Total Productivity Measurement at the Firm Level*

With inflation and wage and price controls now an established fact of life in the United States, a great deal of attention has focused on the determination of a "fair" return to labor and capital. Workers are demanding higher wages, and management desires higher prices. Most experts believe that productivity provides the key to resolving this situation. The authors develop an extremely complete concept of productivity which makes possible a more sophisticated application of productivity measurement at the firm level than was heretofore possible. Managers who adopt this approach to productivity measurement can better understand the trade-offs involved in decisions to increase productivity. Armed with a more thorough understanding of total productivity in their own firm, managers then can bargain more effectively over wages and prices.

INTRODUCTION

Productivity has now become an everyday word. Politicans and economists are concerned with productivity because they feel its movement is integrally related to the nation's general economic health—particularly in relation to inflation control, economic growth, foreign competition, and balance of payments. Corporate managers are concerned with productivity because they feel it is a representative indicator of the overall efficiency of their firms. Recently,

*This paper is based upon the authors' S.M. thesis at the Alfred P. Sloan School of Management, Massachusetts Institute of Technology. The thesis won the Brooks Prize as the best Sloan School S.M. thesis in 1972.

productivity measurement at the firm level has become a factor in government-business relations via the Price Commission, and is expected to play a role in Phase III controls. In 1970 the President of the United States named a high-level commission to formulate national policies designed to increase productivity throughout the economy.

In spite of this activity, productivity remains as one of the most elusive concepts in business and economic literature. It remains elusive because of a lack of definitive theoretical work—mainly at the firm level. There has been very little done to develop measurement and calculation procedures that match the information desired with the intended use of that information. Many firm-level productivity measurement and calculation methods are either extrapolations of methods used to determine national productivity indexes or "rules-of-thumb" developed within a firm. These methods were suitable when only a rough guide for year-to-year performance was needed. However, as productivity indexes enter the pricing decision (via formal or informal governmental controls) and the wage decision (via clauses in labor contracts), the manager needs a suitable measurement scheme. This article describes a theoretical framework for firm-level productivity measurement: a framework particularly suitable for supporting the corporate management decision process.

Productivity is one of those words for which everyone has his own meaning, but often no two meanings agree. A brief overview of general productivity concepts will be useful in the discussion which follows.

Productivity is the efficiency with which outputs are produced—the ratio of output to input. In addition, there are at least two distinct types of productivity ratios, *total* productivity and *partial* productivity.

$$\text{Total Productivity} \quad = \frac{\text{Total Output}}{\text{Total Input}}$$

$$\text{Partial Productivity} = \frac{\text{Total Output}}{\text{Partial Input}}$$

A familiar example of a partial productivity ratio is the output per manhour ratio—the *labor productivity* index.

Another index sometimes cited is the *value added* index. This ratio does not meet the strict definition of a partial productivity ratio just given. It is calculated by beginning with the total productivity ratio and removing the value of raw materials and purchased parts from the numerator and denominator. The value added index, therefore, equals partial output over partial input.

Many other such measures could be listed. The important point is that numerous partial measures exist, but they rarely are defined to the user as such. All partial measures, however, have certain common characteristics.

Fallacies of Partial Productivity Measures

Many of the productivity indexes quoted by economists and businessmen are labor productivity indexes. Their use can lead to serious misunderstandings. A simple example will demonstrate the potential problem. Assume a company procures a higher quality raw material that significantly reduces the man-hours necessary for processing. The output per man-hour index would naturally rise since a worker now can produce more of the same product in less time. However, suppose that the improved raw material is more costly. To simplify the example, assume that the increase in material cost is equal to the savings from reduced processing man-hours. Using the labor productivity index as a guide, labor and stockholders would note an increase in productivity. Either group could take action to distribute this gain. Labor could bargain for increased wages, and stockholders could expect increased dividends or at least a growth in profits. Customers might expect a price reduction. However, there has been no real gain to the corporation. The apparent increase in labor productivity has already been distributed to the raw material supplier; there is nothing available for distribution to labor, stockholders, or customers. Gains indicated by increased labor productivity may not actually be gains at all. *The cost of generating the increased labor productivity must be considered.*

It should be obvious that this type of fallacy is inherent in all partial productivity measures. Therefore, some measure of *total productivity* must be used for most top-level management decisions. Partial productivity measures should not be used as indiscriminately as they usually are.

TOTAL PRODUCTIVITY

Total productivity of the firm can be stated as follows:

$$P_t = \frac{O_t}{L + C + R + Q}$$

where,

P_t = total productivity

L = labor input factor

C = capital input factor

R = raw material and purchased parts input factor

Q = other miscellaneous goods and services input factor

O_t = total output

The output of the firm as well as all inputs must be stated in a common measurement unit. Therefore, to describe the calculation

of total productivity for a firm, a definition in *dollars* of all the above factors is required. Also, to make productivity indexes comparable from period to period, each index must be adjusted to a base period value. This simply means that the output and all inputs for any year after (and including) the base year must be stated in terms of base year dollars. This is often referred to as *deflating* the output and input factors. Deflation is used since prices and wages have typically risen each year.

Up to this point the importance of using all input factors when measuring productivity has been stressed. A proper productivity index for management use, however, is dependent not only on considering all factors, but also on how the factors are defined and used. The contention is that much of the previous work on firm-level productivity measurement has taken too little account of the precise definitions and the resultant consequences of the calculated index. The next section therefore is devoted to a definition of the output and input factors necessary for a total productivity calculation.

THE PROPOSED MODEL OF THE FIRM

The model is described as a service flow model. Physical inputs are converted to dollar equivalents which are remunerations for services provided by those inputs. From the manager's viewpoint, productivity is a measure of the efficiency of the conversion process. The manager converts resources into goods and services which provide returns for all input factors. The model will be expanded below.

Output

The output of a firm is usually expressed in units of physical volume, such as pieces, tons, feet, or number of cars. However, if the output is nonhomogeneous, the different products must be weighted in some manner so that they can be added together. For most purposes, the use of selling price (dollars) is the most suitable weighting unit. Therefore, a definition of output is the summation of all units produced times their selling price. Note that the number of units *produced* is used—not units *sold*. Since productivity is concerned with the efficiency of converting inputs to outputs, units sold cannot be used. Some of the units sold could be from a reduction in finished inventory. Such a condition would yield an overstated output. Conversely, units produced but not sold would not be counted, giving an understated output. In-process inventory must be included in the output calculation as well. In effect, in-process inventory is partial units produced. Adjustment of output will generally take the form of multiplying the in-process units by their selling price and their percentage completion as measured in cost terms.

As discussed previously, it is necessary to calculate productivity indexes in base year terms. This can be most satisfactorily accomplished by using the base year selling price in lieu of the current price. Unfortunately, there are two practical pitfalls to this method: new products and quality changes. New products not produced in the base year obviously have no base year selling price. Product improvements in some sense convert existing products into new products, and thus improved products also have no base year selling prices. For those industries that have frequent product and quality changes (e.g., the auto industry) this is a particularly serious issue.

It is impossible to specify an adjustment technique that is universally applicable. Many firms could use an adjustment method based on the ratios of established costs of new and old products. Such a process can be

accomplished with reasonable accuracy. If the current product line becomes significantly different from that of the base year, a change in base year is suggested.

Perhaps it also is beneficial to point out now the importance of choosing a normal base year. A normal base year is one in which no serious deviations from average production occurred. A year in which the company experienced a strike of some duration would be an unacceptable base year. Likewise, a year in which the company greatly changed its complexion, such as by acquisition or merger, is an unwise choice.

Another component of total output is revenue received from sources other than production. For example, dividends from securities and interest from bonds and other such sources should be included. The reason for this is that a portion of the input factors is being employed to produce these outputs. Both labor and capital (usually current assets) are employed to produce this revenue. To omit this revenue would understate the total output. Granted, the value of labor and capital may not be great in comparison to production output, but they should be included for completeness. These output components also must be adjusted to base year values. An appropriate cost-of-living index could be used. All forms of windfall profits should be excluded on the reasoning that no input was employed to produce them. For example, income derived from the sale of land not purchased for speculation but discovered to contain valuable minerals should not be included as output.

Sometimes it is possible to use a shortcut for deriving the value of output in any year after the base year. This involves beginning with sales revenue, adjusting it for finished and in-process inventory changes, and then deflating (or inflating) the dollars derived by a suitable index to calculate a value for output in base year terms. It is impossible to generalize what one would lose in accuracy by applying this abbreviated method; it simply is another of the many cost-accuracy trade-offs managers must make every day.

Input

The input calculations will be discussed next. Labor input, typically a large part of total input for a firm, is presented first.

Labor. The primary unit of labor input is man-hours worked. The man-hours must be converted into dollars by multiplying total man-hours times an appropriate wage rate ($/hour). Theoretically, each person employed could have a different wage rate. More typically, employees are separated into various job classifications that have more or less identical base wage rates or salaries. In addition to base wages and salaries, fringe benefits must be considered. Therefore, to calculate labor input for the current year in base year dollars, multiply the man-hours worked in each classification by the base year wage rate and/or salary scale for that job classification.

Difficulties similar to those inherent in the output calculation are found in the labor input calculation. Some jobs in the current year will not have been occupied in the base year. Usually, it is not too difficult to estimate what the base year rate for these jobs would have been.

Raw Materials and Purchased Parts. Productive material is quite often a significant input to the production process. The physical units of these inputs are tons, feet, pieces, gallons, etc. Adjustment of material costs to base year prices can be accomplished by multiplying the purchased units (adjusted for inventory changes) times base year material prices. If base year prices are not readily available, an appropriate commodity price index can be used to adjust the current year prices.

Miscellaneous Other Goods and Services. This group of inputs is comprised of all resources except labor, capital, and raw materials/purchased parts. Typical examples would be utilities (heat, light, power), government services (taxes), advertising, and nonproductive materials (office supplies, etc.). Each of these specific inputs must be adjusted to base year terms by using an appropriate price deflator.

It is important to note that interest payments are not considered as an input. Interest on loans is accounted for in the capital input factor calculation. Indirect business taxes, however, should be included. Even though it is impossible to link a government service directly to a tax, it is rational to consider taxes as quasi-license fees. In other words, if a firm wants to produce and sell certain products, the firm is obligated to pay the related business taxes. That some taxes are passed directly to the consumer simply means they appear directly in the output (through the price) and in the input.

Capital. Of all the terms involved in productivity measurement, capital historically has been the most difficult to define. At the same time, capital also is one of the most important resources of any firm. Most previous work in productivity measurement has recommended that capital input be considered as the physical use of the equipment. Depreciation generally is used as the approximation of the capital consumed in the production process. However, there are other ways of viewing capital input.

"At one time it was believed sufficient to measure change in capital input by change in depreciation and other capital consumption changes obtained from accounting records. A later variation of this procedure involved the use of an input-output table to translate the capital consumption charges into labor-input equivalents. Both procedures are deficient, however. It is the *value of the services of capital* that constitutes capital input. This value includes more than capital consumption, and is not necessarily related to capital consumption in any close way . . ."[1]

The deficiency of using a depreciation schedule is caused by the difficulty of representing the actual consumption of an asset. This problem is, of course, not new to accountants.

" . . . This question has a long history of lively controversy for two reasons. First, because factual observation does not determine in any precise way the annual depreciation charge for an asset, considerable variation in the charge is possible. Second, the expenditure or sacrifice by a company in connection with a depreciable asset arises out of the purchase decision and not the depreciation decision. Therefore, in contrast with labor or materials expenses, depreciation expense can never be identified uniquely with any given time period. These characteristics of depreciation would make the consideration of how it should be determined practically meaningless without the careful *examination of the objectives to be served.*"[2]

The authors believe that capital input must be represented by a concept of the service value of capital. The service value concept best fulfills the criteria of the model. Furthermore, a concept of lease value is a better form than other service value concepts. To amplify this point, the model assumes that the firm has a leasing subsidiary to buy the land, buildings, and equipment. The leasing subsidiary also supplies current assets (such as cash) and expects return from them. The capital input term is then the payment made to the leasing subsidiary.

A typical lease is in the form of an annuity. The amount of the annuity depends on three factors: the cost of the asset, the productive life of the asset, and the desired rate of return to the lessor. The cost of the asset is simply the asset's original purchase price plus any capitalized costs necessary to prepare the asset for use. These costs must be stated in base year terms. Adjustments to actual costs can be made by using appropriate capital equipment and building indexes. Productive life (economic life) is the length of time an asset can be expected to be useful prior to either complete physical deterioration or economic obsolescence. This term must be estimated. Time periods currently used for normal accounting practices are probably a good first estimate. The consequences of severely underestimating the life are more serious than those of overestimating.

In this model the lessors are the stockholders and debtors. A proper rate of return for them is derived from the cost of capital theory. The required rate of return is defined as the cost of capital in the base year, where the cost of capital is calculated by a weighted average method. (An example of this is given later.) The cost of capital, of course, varies by firm and industry. Therefore, the capital input factor is defined as the sum of the annuity values calculated for each asset on the basis of its base year cost, productive life, and the firm's cost of capital.

To clarify this important concept, an example is helpful. Assume that $100,000 is supplied for purchasing equipment. The equipment is expected to have a life of five years, and to have no salvage value at the end of that time. A weighted average cost of capital for the firm is calculated from the balance sheet to be 10 percent. The invested $100,000 must earn a 10 percent return on invested capital *and* the entire $100,000 in a five year period to return the proper amount to the investor (the assumed leasing subsidiary). In essence, the manager of this firm must turn over the capital invested *plus* earn a 10 percent return. Therefore, the service cost of using the invested capital is an annual charge that produces this effect. The annual charge can be calculated by using annuity tables. In this case the annual payment (annuity) would be $26,380. Table 1 shows for this example how the investor's (lessor's) money was returned.

Cash, accounts receivable, securities, inventory, and other liquid assets also are part of the capital input factor. The input service cost of these assets is calculated in a manner similar to that just described. The major difference is that liquid assets can be assumed to have an infinite productive life; therefore their costs are calculated on the basis of a perpetuity rather than an annuity. Input costs from these assets are calculated by the general formula $K \times C$, where K is the value of the asset in base year terms and C is the base year cost of capital for the firm. For example, if the firm maintained a cash balance of one million dollars (in base year dollars) and the base year cost of capital were 10 percent, the cash input factor would be one million dollars times 10 percent, or $100,000. Adjusting each of these liquid assets to base year value requires an appropriate deflator for each specific type of asset.

Differences from Prior Productivity Calculations

It is important to note that the method just presented for calculating total productivity is different from some other suggested methods. The main differences can be explained by noting that historical productivity calculations have relied on weighted physical concepts. Output generally is defined strictly as weighted physical output (production of goods and services), i.e., interest earned on investments would not be included as an output of the firm. Interest on capital invested is not what the firm produces (as the argument goes), so it should not be included. Likewise, the capital input is related to the physical consumption of capital assets. Usually this estimate comes from normal accounting definitions of depreciation. Federal, state, and local taxes would be inputs on the basis that they are payments for services rendered by the governments. However, advertising may not be interpreted as contributing to the total output in a physical sense.

As such, numbers derived in the manner just described should not be compared directly with industry figures calculated on a pure physical capital, labor, and raw material (and purchased parts) input basis. However, it is felt that a total productivity approach, as defined here, better suits the manager's needs in that it more accurately describes the efficiency with which *all* inputs are used.

One more point deserves amplification. It could be argued that certain expenditures

Table 1.   Annuity Calculation Example

Year	Net Capital Invested During the Year	Interest on Invested Capital (10%)		Reduction in Invested Capital		Total Annuity Payment
1	$100,000	$10,000	+	$16,380	=	$26,380
2	83,620	8,362	+	18,018	=	26,380
3	65,602	6,560	+	19,820	=	26,380
4	45,782	4,578	+	21,802	=	26,380
5	23,980	2,398	+	23,982	=	26,380

such as research and development and advertising have a lagged effect—they contribute to productivity in the future as well as in the current year. As such, these expenditures could be capitalized according to some appropriate time pattern. One cannot generalize—the individual manager should determine the sensitivity of his productivity measure to these issues. If an argument could be made for any given time pattern, then the manager should adjust his inputs accordingly. Once each individual manager understands the consequences of various actions, he is the best judge of what to use in his firm.

Interpretation of Total Productivity Values

Due to the way the model and calculation are stated, the actual value of the total productivity ratio (and not just its relation to other total productivity ratios) has a special significance. A 1.0, or 100 percent, total productivity ratio indicates that the firm produced *exactly* the correct output necessary to return proper amounts to labor, material, suppliers, outside services, and capital. *Proper in this context, means that base year relationships are maintained in total.*

As it is used here, capital is a measure of the firm's contribution to production input. Workers supply labor, outside dealers provide raw materials, and utilities provide heat and light. The company uses all of these inputs, receiving services from them, to produce output. The input suppliers outside of the firm always will receive their proper return. Workers and suppliers must be paid before the firm computes its profits. The return to capital is the residual left when all other input factors have been paid for their services. Profit, in effect, is the return to capital. If total productivity is 1.0, the firm breaks even. Should total productivity fall below this level, all outside suppliers of input will be paid (i.e., receive their return), but the return to capital for the firm be-

comes negative and the firm goes into the red. A value for total productivity greater than 1.0 means that the company is making a profit and that the return to capital is greater than the cost of capital.

Note that the discussion centers around the return to capital as a *residual* value, i.e., all slack in the total productivity is taken in the capital factor. Using the hypothetical leasing subsidiary once again, a value for total productivity less than 1.0 indicates that the firm could not meet the annuity payment to the leasing subsidiary, and a value greater than 1.0 means that the payment could be met and the firm had some earnings left after making the payment.

TOTAL PRODUCTIVITY MEASUREMENT: A CASE STUDY

The following section describes productivity index calculations for an actual manufacturing company. This case study should help demonstrate the method previously described. It should also point out some of the difficulties in making the actual calculations.

Mid-Region Manufacturing is a relatively large, multi-plant manufacturing company. Its primary products are automobile and truck components, although the company does produce some products for other markets such as mechanical devices for aircraft. All the firm's plants are clustered in and around the city in which the company's headquarters are located. All plants and product lines are grouped together, and productivity calculations are made for the company as a whole. Company accounting records were the primary source of data. The base year chosen was 1968, and productivity indexes were calculated each year for the period 1968 through 1971.

Since the accounting records did not contain all of the specific data required, various estimating processes were used to derive the information. The processes used are described briefly below.

Output

Because complete records of units produced were not available, output was calculated from the annual sales revenue. Total calendar year sales dollars for each year were adjusted by a specifically calculated price index. By using information developed for pricing decisions it was possible to estimate the magnitude of price changes caused by increased input factor costs. The effect of these price changes was subtracted from total sales revenue. Adjustments for price changes due to product configuration changes (quality improvements) were not made because of incomplete data.

After detailing sales revenue with price changes an inventory adjustment was made to convert the sales output to a production output. With the help of the production control department, the total inventory value was subdivided into finished, in-process, and raw materials categories. The finished and in-process categories were then converted into a sales dollar value. Once these calculations were completed the annual inventory change could be added to or subtracted from the deflated sales revenue. This process and the resulting output dollars are summarized in Table 2.

Input

The input calculations will be discussed next. Labor input is first.

Labor. The labor input factor was calculated as follows: Total man-hours worked in the current year by all hourly paid employees was multiplied by the average per hour wage rate in the base year (1968). The average base year wage rate included vacation pay and all fringe benefit costs. As was noted previously, this calculation method does not properly account for skill-mix changes. However, during the four year period studied, the skill-mix had remained relatively unchanged. Thus very little distortion was expected.

A total head count of all salaried employees in the current year was multiplied by the average annual base salary per person. Current year bonus payments, deflated by a cost of living index, were added to total salary dollars. The average base year salary also included fringe benefit costs. This method also is deficient in accounting for skill-mix changes. But, again, it was estimated that significant changes in salary skill-mix had not occurred. The labor input factor is shown in Table 3.

Table 2. Output Calculation

	1968	1969	1970	1971
Total sales revenue	384	394	299	486
Minus price change		−1	−4	−13
Adjusted sales revenue	384	393	295	473
± Inventory change	−7	+22	−5	+5
Output in 1968 terms	377	415	290	478

Table 3. Labor Input Factor

	1968	1969	1970	1971
Hourly paid	76	76	56	76
Salaried	23	25	25	26
Total	99	101	81	102

Capital. The annuity lease concept of capital, as previously described, was used for calculating the capital input factor. The company's accounting records were quite adequate for making this type of calculation. The cost of capital was calculated by the weighted average method as shown in Table 4. Note that this is a cost of capital *after* tax considerations. The common stock and retained earnings costs were obtained by using goals established by management for these inputs.

Current year costs of buildings and equipment were deflated to base year dollars by using appropriate construction and wholesale price indexes.[3] The contribution of other assets was calculated by multiplying the base year value of the asset by the cost of capital. A summary of the capital input factor calculations is given in Table 5.

Raw Material and Purchased Parts. The material input factor was calculated by deflating the current year productive material expense to base year dollars. The adjustment to base year dollars was accomplished by using purchasing department and accounting records that showed price changes. The resulting value of base year material dollars was further adjusted by material inventory changes. This last adjustment converts the material expenses to material consumed in the production process. A summary of these calculations is shown in Table 6.

Miscellaneous Goods and Services. This input factor consists of all other expenses and taxes. Each of these items was deflated to base year dollars. Federal income taxes were deflated by taking the current year

Table 4.   Cost of Capital Calculation

	Percentage of Capital Structure* (1)	Cost (2)	Weighted Cost** (1) × (2)
Capital Structure			
Current liabilities	25	.04	.010
Long term debt	4	.06	.002
Preferred stock	2	.08	.002
Common stock	4	.12	.005
Retained earnings	65	.12	.078
	100		.097

*100 percent = 1.0
**Rounded values. 100 percent = 1.0

Table 5.   Capital Input Factor

	1968	1969	1970	1971
Buildings, land, and equipment	27	30	32	34
Inventory	3	4	4	5
Accounts receivable	4	4	4	3
Cash	2	2	1	2
Total capital input	36	40	41	44

profits, before tax, adjusting them by a cost-of-living index, and then multiplying by the base year tax rate. A summary of these calculations is shown in Table 7.

Total productivity can now be calculated as in Table 8.

Interpretation of Total Productivity Results

Refer first to the actual total productivity figures calculated for Mid-Region Manufacturing in Table 8. Using the *residual* notion of capital return discussed earlier, it can be

Table 6. Material Input Calculation Summary

	1968	1969	1970	1971
Material expenses	139	147	110	184
Minus price increases	—	−4	−7	−12
Base year dollar material expenses	139	143	103	172
± Inventory adjustment	−1	−2	—	—
Material input factor	138	141	103	172

Table 7. Miscellaneous Goods and Services

	1968	1969	1970	1971
Miscellaneous expenses	56	66	60	82
Federal income tax	43	37	19	48
Total	99	103	79	130

Table 8. Total Productivity Calculation Summary

	1968	1969	1970	1971
Output (1)	377	415	290	478
Input				
Capital	36	40	41	44
Material	138	141	103	172
Labor	99	101	81	102
Other	99	103	79	130
Total input (2)	372	385	304	448
Total productivity (1) ÷ (2)	101.3	107.8	95.3	106.7
Total productivity in relation to base year	100.0	106.4	94.1	105.3

seen that only in 1970 was the total productivity ratio less than 100 percent, and thus 1970 was the only year in which Mid-Region failed to earn the required 9.7 percent (after tax) return to capital.

Here it is important to note again that the residual value of capital is used. For example, in 1969 the material cost could have been 131 (instead of 141) and capital 50 (instead of 40) and the same total productivity would result. This is one more reason for analyzing total productivity and partial productivity together.

Note also at this point that one of the more striking observations about the total productivity ratios is their volatility. Relative to the base year, total productivity varied plus or minus roughly six percent. However, total productivity is less volatile than the major partial productivity indexes.

Analysis of Total Productivity Movement

One way to better analyze total productivity movement is to begin by examining the movement of the various partial productivity measures. Partial productivity, as mentioned earlier, is merely the ratio of total output to one or more (but not all) inputs. Figure 1 shows the relationship among total productivity and the various labor productivity (i.e., partial) measures. Figure 2 indicates the relationships among total productivity and the partial productivity of the remaining input factors—capital, material (raw material and purchased parts), and other (miscellaneous goods and services).

In analyzing the movement of total productivity and the various partial productivity ratios it is helpful to consider certain input factors as fixed and others as variable.

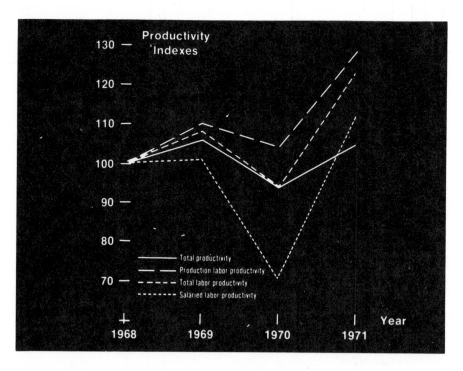

Figure 1.   Total Productivity versus Labor Productivity

Capital, salaried labor, and miscellaneous goods and services tend to be more fixed than the remaining factors. These factors do not vary as significantly with output volume changes as do production labor and raw materials and purchased parts (material).

A further comment is in order relative to the miscellaneous other goods and services input factor. It is inherent in the calculation for total productivity that as output rises, yielding higher profits, the miscellaneous goods and services input factor will rise somewhat disproportionately. This phenomenon is caused by corporate income taxes included in the category. Therefore, this input factor could be considered as a transitional factor between fixed and variable, and is included for the purposes of analysis in the fixed category.

Total Productivity Versus Partial Productivity

In the preceding discussion partial productivity measures were used to help explain the change in total productivity. Such a use of partial productivity indexes obviously is helpful. However, for many types of decisions, only the total productivity index can be used. This point was discussed above but bears repeating.

Suppose that in 1972 Mid-Region raises prices. If *labor* productivity is considered the applicable index, management would be implying that Mid-Region had experienced a 23 percent gain in productivity relative to 1968. If the production labor index were used, the implied gain would be 27 percent. Use of these labor partial productivity mea-

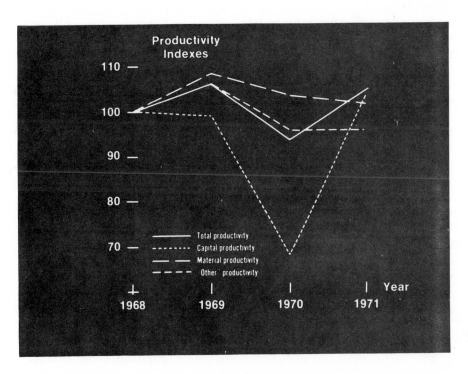

Figure 2.   Total Productivity versus Remaining Partial
Measures

sures would significantly overstate the actual total productivity gain of about five percent. Consequently, either a price increase would not be allowed (under Phase III controls) or the price increase would be substantially less than warranted.

Similarly, if Mid-Region's management were bargaining on wages with its union, equally adverse consequences could arise. If the labor partial productivity indexes were used as the basis for determining reasonable levels of wage increases, the resulting wage settlement could go beyond the company's actual total productivity gain. Increased prices, lower profits, or a combination of both would probably be necessary to accommodate the wage increases.

SUMMARY AND CONCLUSIONS

By far the most important fact for the manager to understand is that for most conditions the total productivity index should be used. Partial productivity measures like labor productivity should be avoided except in the most specific circumstances. Only the total productivity index provides the indication of *real* productivity changes. Therefore, whenever a manager is dealing with productivity, he should insist on a total productivity definition.

As was shown in Mid-Region's case, not all partial productivity measures should show an upward trend. Managers consciously take actions that reduce one partial index (such as material) to increase another (such as production labor). It generally is not even possible to have all partial indexes move upward together. The notion of trade-offs among labor, capital, materials, and "other" almost precludes joint upward movement. Productivity increases and de-

creases are passed from one area of the firm to another through various managerial decisions. Thus the importance of measuring total productivity to determine managerial efficiency cannot be overestimated.

The method of calculating total productivity is also an important consideration. A service flow model has been used to develop a calculation method that is valid for the manager. This method differs from others in its treatment of capital and the use of all inputs and outputs. A lease service concept of capital was used rather than a physical consumption concept. Also, all revenue items were included as outputs and all cost or expense items are inputs.

Proponents of ratio analysis based on earnings statements and balance sheets may argue that nothing new has been presented. However, earnings statements are based primarily on current dollars, but depreciation is not in current dollars. Likewise, balance sheets include many items purchased by the company in prior years at historical costs. Neither earnings statements nor balance sheets measure efficiency. Selling price fluctuations, for example, can cause a good profit picture *this* year, but a more basic loss of efficiency could be developing.

The method for measuring total productivity presented here ties the firm together for the manager. It forces the firm to show a return on invested capital; it forces a meticulous study of trade-offs such as better material for less labor, more current assets for fewer long-term assets, and so on. The analysis of Mid-Region Manufacturing was more complete than an analysis based on earnings statements and balance sheets. Also, the analysis showed to management the result of trade-off decisions regarding labor, materials, and capital.

PART SIX

Organizational Productivity Perspectives

16

Productivity and Unions

*If the QWL process itself is responsible for the development of
mutual respect and is in part responsible for more amicable
relationships in the collective bargaining area, then people
will seek to solve problems instead of creating more problems.*

IRVING BLUESTONE[1]

Managers, workers and union leaders all have a stake in improving productivity. As the organization improves its productivity, it becomes more efficient and more likely to survive competitive and economic hardships. Yet union leaders and managers have developed different perspectives that often block or severely limit the potential for improving productivity through people.[2]

UNION-MANAGEMENT PERSPECTIVES

Union leaders and managers have different perspectives, and this causes them to pursue different objectives. Many managers view unions as an unnecessary restraint on their authority to manage. Simply put, unions are often seen as an intrusion between management and its employees. And if the union has been installed recently, there may be considerable resentment by management that the employees "resorted to a union." As a result, much time, money, and effort is devoted to "policing and maintaining" the union-management relationship. Formal employee complaints, called grievances, and the negotiation of formal contracts between the union and employer can be expensive, time-consuming and an aggravation to management. The result is that in many organizations the union is not treated as a partner in management decisions.[3] Since decisions are made unilaterally by management in most cases, union leaders often remain skeptical about any effort to improve productivity. Too often, productivity is viewed as a "speed up" where people are expected to work faster and harder for the same pay. If the relationship between union and management is already strained or hostile, attempts to improve productivity may be viewed as management's attempt to exploit the workers.

Joint labor-management efforts to improve productivity may be necessary for the survival of the firm or industry. There have been examples of this in such firms as Ford Motor Company, Bethlehem Steel, and other extensively unionized firms.[4] The extension of cooperative labor-management efforts to other firms and industries, however, depends on a better understanding by managers of union objectives and politics.

Union Objectives

Samuel Gompers, the first president of the American Federation of Labor, summarized the objectives of the American labor movement in one word: "More." The century-long history of the AFL substantiates Gompers' view. Excluding depressions and severe recessions, the history of the union movement has been a consistent pattern of gaining more for the members: more wages, more benefits and more rights. That desire for "more" is so ingrained in the union movement and its leaders that even when "more" may not be appropriate, union leaders may still push for a larger piece of the economic pie. An objective analysis of the firm's finances or the industry's competitive posture versus foreign competition may strongly suggest that "more" is a self-destructive strategy: The more the unions get, the weaker the firm or industry becomes and the less able it is to provide more in the future.

What many managers overlook, however, are the political ramifications of "more." First, union leaders are politicians. They are elected to the positions of steward or union president.[5] As politicians, union leaders must meet the perceived needs of their constituents. Second, union leaders who have negotiated with management over the years may be concerned that management's protestations about competition are merely bargaining ploys and not substantive issues. To bolster their claim, they may point to the large salaries and bonuses paid to senior managers, as the United Auto Workers did in the 1984 collective bargaining negotiations with the auto industry. The argument the unions raised is simply this: "If management can afford these large bonuses for itself, then surely it can afford a modest wage increase for the workers." Of course, a 10 percent increase in management salaries may result in only a 1 percent increase in the cost of operations; whereas a 10 percent increase in rank-and-file salaries may be reflected in a 6, 7 or even 8 percent increase in costs in some industries. And although this is contrary to the egalitarian philosophy many unions espouse, capable senior executives are simply worth more because of their leadership skills. They should therefore be paid more (in terms of wages) than unskilled or semi-skilled rank-and-file members.[6]

Closely allied with the concept of "more" is the "room-full-of-cash" theory. Merely walking up to most businesses, you immediately notice land, buildings and (often) company cars. Inside the facility you see expensive equipment, ranging from thousand-dollar word processors to multi-million-dollar pieces of equipment. Many people, particularly those who do not fully grasp the need for a favorable return on investment, would conclude that the company has a lot of money. And compared to the typical workers, most firms are "wealthy." They can afford expensive capital equipment, land, buildings, and other inputs necessary to add value and to produce a product or service. Unfortunately, however, the end result of this industrial opulence sometimes is to create a feeling that the company has a "room-full-of-cash," and that giving a little more to the workers will not seriously deplete this fantastic cache of wealth.[7]

In the final analysis, then, the union's search for "more" is often fueled by executive bonuses and the belief in the "room-full-of-cash" theory. Even when management correctly states that it cannot afford more, its statement may be interpreted as a bargaining strategy or an outright lie. Besides, union leaders believe that there is a safeguard in any contract: Management will never sign a contract that is detrimental to the organization.

Beyond financial gains, another important issue for unions is the availability of work. Workers, union leaders and even managers may resist productivity improvement because they think it means getting more work done with fewer resources, that is, people. Many workers and union leaders view the availability of work on the basis of the "lump-of-work" theory, which states that there is a predetermined, fixed amount of work that needs to be done. When that "lump" is completed, there will be no more work. Therefore, to be more productive is to consume that fixed lump of work sooner, which results in layoffs. In the very short run, the lump-of-work theory is probably accurate. But as workers become more productive, their employer is able to sell more of its product or services, creating additional work. The lag between increased productivity and increased sales is often one of months or even years, however. This makes it difficult to recognize the connection between additional productivity and more jobs.[8] An organization itself can often contribute to belief in the lump-of-work theory. For example, as productivity improvements are implemented, a company may lay off production workers, even though it is seeking to hire clerical workers, technicians and laborers in other skill categories. For the workers in this company, the theory is "proven," and they may act through the union to protect their jobs for the future.

In another organization faced with the same circumstances, workers displaced by productivity enhancement are kept and retrained for other jobs. Employees in this environment are more loyal to the company and more likely to suggest productivity improvements and to cooperate with their implementation. From the union's perspective, of course, the complicating factor in this scenario is that the worker retrained for different responsibilities may cease to be a dues-paying member of the union.

When the search for "more" is considered along with the "room-full-of-cash" and the "lump-of-work" theories, it becomes obvious that these approaches conflict with management's need for improved efficiency and effectiveness. What many managers fail to realize is that efficiency and effectiveness are not the primary goals of unions. Instead, unions are concerned with getting "more" for the employees. These differing perspectives do not preclude union-management cooperation, but as political realities they should always be kept in mind.

Union Politics

Union leaders are very likely to resist any management action that is perceived as a threat to a union leader, union member or the union as an organization. And whenever a threat of this kind is perceived, regardless of management's actual intentions, the union's leadership must react. When it reacts, it may do so in a way that is contrary to management's efficiency and effectiveness goals. The end result is that the union will be seen as uncooperative, or worse.[9]

Consider an example: Suppose a union member is fired for stealing. Suppose further that this worker is actually caught loading company equipment into a private vehicle after hours without authorization, so there is no question about the crime. In most companies, personnel policies allow the employee to be fired immediately by management, on the grounds that stealing from the company is sufficient reason for discharge on the first offense. If management fires the employee, it is almost certain that the union will file a formal complaint called a grievance. In the grievance the union is likely to argue about extenuating circumstances, the employee's past record or other issues it hopes will cause management to reconsider disciplinary action. The untrained manager or observer might conclude that the union "supports stealing," because it works very hard to gain the worker's job back even though the employee is patently a thief. The union's efforts are then likely to be seen as an obstruction to management's search for honest employees. The end result is that management's opinion of the union is likely to decline.

Look at the same example from the eyes of the union leader. First, a loyal, dues-paying member has been fired. *Regardless* of whether that employee should have been fired, the union leader has several considerations that must be weighed. First, how will the rank and file members view the discharge and the union's role in it? If the union does not make some overt move to have the disciplinary discharge rescinded, other rank-and-file members very likely will ask, "What purpose does the union serve?"

What role should the union leader play here? In right-to-work states, employees are not required to remain members of the union in order to keep their jobs. If the union president is not seen as a defender of union members, then the question, "What service does the union provide?" may lead to fewer members paying dues, which are the financial livelihood of the union. For the same reason, any threat to the union as an organization (for example, a plant closing) or to a union leader is likely to evoke a strong response from the union leadership.

Simple actions on the part of management may be seen as attempts to undermine the union leader's position. Suppose management develops a plan for a new productivity improvement effort. The plan is developed without union input, and plant management simply announces the new productivity effort. Workers, who naturally want to know more, are very likely to turn to the local union leadership. If the union leaders were unaware of the plan, they may feel "left out." The plan then becomes something that management is trying to impose on the workers, something that benefits management at the expense of rank-and-file union members. In such a case, the union leaders may strike out at the productivity effort by going "on record" as opposing it. (Keep in mind that the union leaders may oppose the productivity effort without understanding it.) Once on record against it, the union leaders may appear to be "selling out" to management if they reverse their position. From the union leaders' perspective, management was trying to undermine the leaders' credibility and importance by bypassing the union hierarchy and going directly to the employees with an explanation of the new productivity improvement effort. Under these circumstances, union support for the productivity effort is unlikely.[10]

Finally, the Labor-Management Reporting and Disclosure Act of 1959 requires union leaders to exercise their duty to represent the employee's interests diligently. If, for example, a worker was wrongly discharged or disciplined and the union did not attempt to represent the employee's interests, that worker might sue the union leadership for failure of its duty to represent the employee's interests.[11]

As a result of all this, union-management cooperation faces several hurdles. One is their rather different, and at times even divergent, objectives. Although in the long run the interests of both are served if the organization prospers, in the short run their different agendas may cause conflict. The likelihood of conflict is further compounded because the union is a primarily political apparatus within the organization. As a politically oriented organization, it must place the welfare of its members ahead of any "business objectives" that management may be pursuing. The union may have very little reason to consider the company's business objectives; that is why management is there. The union focuses instead on taking care of its membership. Periodically, management fuels the adversary relationship when it politically embarrasses the union leaders by failing to include them in, or at least advise them of, upcoming changes.

Labor Laws

In addition to recognizing the constraints imposed by their differing objectives and by union politics, members of management and the union must also abide by labor laws. Although there are many labor laws designed to regulate aspects of the labor-management relationship, the ones most frequently violated center around the unfair labor practices listed in Figure 16–1. As the list shows, management must treat workers without regard to their union interests. This means that management cannot interfere with or discriminate against an employee who seeks a union or wishes to exercise his or her rights under the National Labor Relations Act. Management also cannot attempt to dominate a union by controlling its leadership; and when the union does represent a majority of the employees, management must negotiate with that union in good faith. Unions are similarly restricted in their rights to use strikes and pickets.[12]

Unilateral and Bilateral Changes

Even though the labor laws require management and unions to negotiate over wages, hours and other terms and conditions of employment, unilateral changes by either party with respect to compensation, hours or other terms or conditions of employment may be a violation of the labor laws. More significantly, such violations may undermine the cooperative efforts between union and management to improve quality of work life and productivity.

MANAGEMENT UNFAIR LABOR PRACTICES

It is a violation of Section 8(a) of the National Labor Relations Act for an employer to:

1. Interfere, coerce or restrain employees who seek to act collectively or refrain from so doing.
2. Interfere or dominate with the formation or administration of a labor organization.
3. Discriminate against anyone in hiring, promotion or any other condition of employment beause of their union activity or lack thereof.
4. Discipline, discharge or otherwise discriminate against employees who exercise their rights under the Act.
5. Refuse to bargain in good faith with employee representatives.

Figure 16–1.   Management Unfair Labor Practices

LABOR-MANAGEMENT COOPERATION

Management, union leaders and union members have a common fate. Their fate rests on the success of the firm. In the 1950s and '60s, when there was little international competition, the time and effort lost on "infighting" may have harmed an organization's profit margin, but generally it did not threaten the life of the business. Today, with severe competition in many industries from Japan and Europe, union-management cooperation is fast becoming a necessity for firms that hope to survive, particularly in the high-tech growth industries. Moreover, this competition is not just between the employer and outside competitors. Competitive pressures also exist within the organization, where senior management typically closes down its non-productive facilities in favor of those that are more productive. The more productive facilities are often located in areas of the country with limited union activity. Although cooperating with management may not be politically advisable for union officials, the survival of the union, the facility and its jobs may depend on it. Otherwise competition or relocation may totally undermine the union's position. Through cooperation, the union and management can find better ways to remove barriers to productivity; and with a cooperative union-management relationship, some of the major restraints on productivity—resistance to change, absenteeism, and work rules—can be removed more effectively.[13]

SUMMARY

Unions exist to represent workers' interests in organizations. Rather than oppose productivity improvement, unions should try to benefit from them as much as the company. Union leaders, employees, and managers must work together toward their common goals.

SELECTED READINGS OVERVIEW

The first article is entitled "Productivity: The Industrial Relations Connection," by Robert B. McKersie and Janice A. Klein, professors at MIT and Harvard, respectively. McKersie and Klein examine the productivity restraints which grow out of union-management relationships. In addition to identifying specific barriers to productivity improvement, they suggest programs and strategies which might increase productivity. The article discusses the issues of productivity, employment security, employee involvement, and incentive pay systems.

This chapter concludes with a *Business Week* editorial entitled "Collective Bargaining is in Danger Without Labor Law Reform." In this essay by John Hoerr, some of the major weaknesses in the collective bargaining arena are explored.

Next Chapter

Unions are not the only special constituencies within organizations. The fastest-growing and perhaps most important constituency is that of white-collar workers. Unlike their largely blue-collar counterparts in unions, white-collar workers include members of management and professional and technical workers. Since their work is often more abstract and intellectual than the physical labor of blue-collar employees, motivating white-collar workers to become more productive presents a special challenge to management.

Review Questions

1. Explain the traditional philosophy of unions since the time of Samuel Gompers.
2. Describe the "lump-of-work" and the "room-full-of-cash" theories.
3. Explain what is meant by the statement, "Unions are political institutions."
4. What problems, if any, do employee involvement approaches to productivity improvement hold for non-union employees?
5. Describe the major union-related barriers to productivity improvement.

ROBERT B. McKERSIE

JANICE A. KLEIN

Productivity: The Industrial Relations Connection

The linkages between U.S. productivity problems and industrial relations arrangements are explored, along with appropriate programs and strategies to increase productivity.

INTRODUCTION

The "labor problem" has been listed as one of the prime culprits behind declining productivity in the U.S. What part have industrial relations practices and procedures played in this arena? This article will address that question by exploring the linkages between productivity and industrial relations arrangements in this country.

The basis for the findings reported here was a study commissioned by the Commit-

tee for Economic Development (CED) to examine the productivity implications of industrial relations, especially institutional arrangements.[1] As a starting point, we surveyed about forty CED member organizations to identify current managerial beliefs and actions concerning work-force and industrial-relations issues.[2] The survey was administered at two levels within each corporation. First, corporate staff personnel were asked to provide a general overview of the corporation's industrial relations policies and practices and a list of productivity programs used within the organization. Second, to better understand the productivity process at the operating level, plant personnel were asked to identify restraints to increased productivity at the work place.

These responses, coupled with field interviews and an extensive review of information from other sources, provided the basis for the following analyses and conclusions.

This article is divided into three major sections that deal with: the problem or restraint side of productivity, positive pro-

Robert R. McKersie is a professor of industrial relations at the Sloan School of Management, Massachusetts Institute of Technology. From 1971–79 he was dean of the New York State School of Industrial and Labor Relations at Cornell University. With Laurence Hunter, he coauthored *Pay, Productivity and Collective Bargaining* (1973).

Janice A. Klein is an assistant professor at the Harvard Business School, where she teaches production and operations management. Previously, she worked for the General Electric Company in various manufacturing and human resource management positions.

Reprinted, with permission of the publisher, from *National Productivity Review* (Winter 1983–84).

grams used by companies for improving productivity, and a discussion of several strategies that tackle the challenging task of increasing productivity on a continuing and comprehensive basis.

PRODUCTIVITY RESTRAINTS

Based on the analysis of sixty-one plant-level questionnaires from the plant survey plus a review of extensive information from other sources about the industrial relations components of the productivity problem, we identified three major productivity restraints: resistance to change, reduced worker motivation, and inhibiting work rules. (See Table 1.)

Resistance to Change

By far the most important and pervasive restraint is resistance to change. The phrase does not apply today so much to outright op-

position to new technology (only 5 percent of the firms surveyed mentioned this as a significant problem) as to resistance to adopting new work arrangements and to aligning the social organization to the requirements of that technology. For example, new technology is being used extensively in the office, but management is finding it difficult to do away with unnecessary labor.

Since resistance to change prevents the organization from using its technical capabilities to the fullest, it represents the biggest drag on productivity. We do not have any precise estimates, but based on the examples that were presented in the survey, we would estimate that the negative impact on labor productivity over a period of several years could be as great as 40 or 50 percent.

Reduced Motivation

This is the least important of the three broad restraints. The labor productivity loss that

Table 1.   Productivity Restraints Identified by 61
Respondents to Plant Survey

	Number of Times Identified As a Restraint		Number of Times Identified As a Restraint
Resistance to Change		Government Regulations	
*worker/supervisor resistance to change	43	*OSHA regulations	25
first-line supervisory		other government regulations	5
resistance	2	Business Conditions	
adapting to change	1	limited resource dollars	8
uncertainty of change	1	volume	2
		lack of sufficient information systems	1
Motivation		product complexity	1
*absenteeism	37	behind in technical	
attitudes	4	improvements or	
work ethic	1	equipment design	3
union-management relationship	1	Training	
		insufficient training programs	5
Work Rules		lack of technical personnel	2
*subcontracting	21		
*crew size	19	Other	
*seniority	30	outdated incentive pay systems	1
contractual restraints/work rules	11	inability to perform time studies	2
		job security	1
Paid Time Off		work stoppages	1
*paid time off	34	overtime	1
		turnover	1
*Listed on the questionnaire.			

occurs when a work force is not well moti-vated might range at any point in time be-tween 15 and 25 percent—the range that wage payment systems or other direct re-ward arrangements seek to eliminate.

One of the problems most frequently men-tioned under the general heading of motiva-tion is that of absenteeism. Plants estimated that this restraint increased work-force lev-els between 2 and 15 percent.

Work-Rule Restraints

This subject was frequently mentioned in survey responses, especially for plants where unions were present. The major type of work rule problem today revolves around the issue of flexibility in the deployment of workers. (The examples often mentioned in the literature, such as crew size problems—what was termed the "featherbedding" issue in the 1960s—and the craft demarcation problem, are apparently not as troublesome today as they were in the past.) We estimate that the work-rule problem may negatively impact labor productivity in the range of 15 to 25 percent.

This conclusion about the negative effect of work rules (and, indirectly, the role of un-ions) needs to be reconciled with academic research which has found that productivity is generally higher in the presence of unions. This finding diverges from the experience of management and from the evidence in our survey.

Our attempt to reconcile research with practice runs as follows:

> When operations are stable and volume is on a large scale, the work rules and the generally higher division of labor found in a unionized plant may enhance produc-tivity. However, with the need to alter the scale and character of operations, work rules become an inhibitor to the redeploy-ment of labor that is required.

Work rules emerge in nonunion as well as union plants. Indeed, the principle of sen-iority often has as much weight as in un-ionized operations. However, management finds it easier to make ex-ceptions and bring into play other consid-erations such as worker qualifications; consequently, the deployment of labor is usually done on a more flexible basis in a nonunion plant.

While work rules can be a limiting factor to the achievement of full productivity, times are changing, and through produc-tivity bargaining and labor-management committees, many of the inhibitors are being revised.

POSITIVE PROGRAMS

Before summarizing the major programs being used by corporations for improving productivity, we should acknowledge some organizational and measurement efforts under way to make productivity a much more central issue within the corporation.

One of the most visible new areas of em-phasis is productivity measurement and control. In the past year or so, many large corporations have established the position of "productivity czar," a person responsible for monitoring overall productivity growth for the corporation and instilling productiv-ity awareness throughout the organization. Usually this new position reports to either the president or vice-president, typically in the functional areas of planning, budgets, or operations—and also, but less frequently, in industrial relations or human resources.

Also involved in this growing interest in productivity is a widespread implementa-tion or revision of corporate productivity measurements. Several corporations are using, or are in the process of developing, multifactor measurements. However, the majority continue to use such traditional forms of labor productivity measurement as man hours/unit, units/employee, or revenue/employee. Whatever measurements are employed, the increased corporate emphasis on them and the extensive associated communication campaigns have led to an enhanced sensitivity toward the subject of productivity in most corporations.

Specific Improvement Approaches

At this point we would like to summarize the variety of programs that are being implemented by corporations, as indicated by the responses to the corporate survey (see Table 2) and other sources.

New Technology.   Perhaps the most effective program for improving productivity has been the introduction of new technology, especially into manufacturing operations. As mentioned previously, many corporations are also automating the office, but this has

not as yet been found to be as effective for improving productivity.

Human Resource Management Techniques. For the growing white-collar area of employment, companies have been resorting to methods of analysis and control such as head-count management and effectiveness scrutiny (wherein staff analysts determine whether a particular function is necessary, and if so how it might be performed more productively). Also in this area would be various programs for controlling absenteeism, although, by and large, companies have not found that traditional "carrot and stick" methods are having much effect.

Over half of the corporate respondents to our survey have experimented with flexible hours, but none placed it in the effective category and about half of those that have used it rated it at the bottom of the list. This suggests that such a program, although perhaps popular with employees, does not help productivity.

Table 2.   Productivity Improvement Programs: Number of Times Specific Programs Were Mentioned (29 respondents to corporate survey)

	Used by Corporation	Falling within Top Three (most effective)	Falling within Bottom Three (least effective)
Management Methods			
Practices/Tools	13	8	1
*Job/Organization Redesign	21	6	3
*Absenteeism Control/Employee Assistance	23	3	11
*Flexible Hours	16	—	8
* Training	28	12	—
Involvement			
*Quality Circles	19	3	3
*Labor-Management Committees	12	3	2
*Opinion Survey	17	1	8
Communications Program	5	1	—
Employee Involvement	6	4	—
Reward Systems			
*Wage Payment System	14	6	2
*Awards/Suggestion Programs	10	3	3
* Productivity Bargaining	8	2	2
Technology			
*Office Automation	25	4	5
*Manufacturing Automation	18	12	—
Other New Systems	7	6	—

*Listed on the questionnaire.

Innovations in shift arrangements, weekend shifts, and the setting up of twelve-hour work patterns have been more advantageous from the corporation's point of view in that they make possible the full utilization of capital and equipment.

By far the most successful positive program in the human resource area, and indeed among all of the positive programs, is training. All but one respondent mentioned it as a key program and twelve placed it in the top three for effectiveness. In addition to traditional, manual-type skills training, many corporations have sponsored short courses to enhance substantive knowledge in such areas as problem-solving approaches and quality awareness.

Employee Involvement. This approach covers a number of important areas and developments. A key mechanism for involvement is that of communication, which aims to place relevant information in the hands of workers on the assumption that, once confronted with the need to improve, change will take place.

The formation of labor-management committees looks promising, even though it is too early to evaluate their effectiveness. As one of the respondents from a major manufacturing company noted: "Labor-management teams are not important yet as compared to reduction in size of the work force or manufacturing automation."

One form of labor-management collaboration is the technology committee, and there are important examples of such groups in the automobile industry. The purpose of these committees is to ensure that the introduction of technology enhances quality of work life and that unions and workers are sufficiently informed about new technology and given a chance to discuss its impact.

Quality circles have become very important. Some large corporations have established hundreds of these circles, and the number across industry is in the tens or perhaps even hundreds of thousands. Typical savings have been estimated to approximate $50,000 per circle. But these figures are quite misleading and ignore the short-term nature of the returns that have been received. Also, the respondents rank them below a number of other productivity programs for effectiveness.

In general, quality-of-work-life programs —which include quality circles, autonomous work groups, and a variety of other methods for tapping the know-how of workers about operations through employee involvement—represent a productivity improvement approach that appears to have gathered full steam.

Some important requirements and consequences of such programs must be understood.

Management will have to relinquish its monopoly on knowledge (which may mean a loss of power and control).

Decisions will take longer to make. This will be a function of both the added time needed to convey necessary information to all decision makers as well as the slower pace of group decision making.

In order to make such programs succeed, considerable training and education will be required at all levels of the organization. This will cost both time and money.

Resistance will most likely develop. This may create a need for special training or the replacement of middle- or lower-level managers who are unable or unwilling to adopt the more participatory supervisory style required.

Wage Payment Systems and Awards for Suggestions. It would appear that there is substantially increased interest in contingency compensation, that is, in relating pay directly to performance.

Corporations are using a variety of ways to focus attention on the benchmark or the standard to be beaten, such as subcontracting prices or costs that exist in similar plants.

A variety of arrangements are being used and developed to bring about a tighter linkage between pay and performance. Gainsharing plans, which are rapidly spreading, appear to increase labor productivity (a one-shot effect) by approximately 17 percent.

Profit sharing possesses the advantage of providing rewards only when the performance of a particular organization is better than its counterparts—a very strong economic argument for this form of wage payment.

Suggestion systems linked to financial awards are used extensively, although their results and management's ranking of them for overall value in our corporate survey is not as high as would be expected. Approximately one-third of the corporate respondents had some type of formal companywide suggestion program. The monetary award ranged from $10 to $100,000 based on the granting of between 10 and 25 percent of the first-year savings. However, only three of the companies listed suggestion systems as an effective productivity program. The modest level of the results is further highlighted by the fact that, for those companies that provided results information, the savings per employee averaged about $50 per employee per year.

A recent study of Japanese suggestion systems indicated that in 1980 they generated 12.8 suggestions per employee.[3] On a very limited comparison base, our survey indicated a yearly rate of approximately 0.1 per employee. However, select success stories in this country can be found that surpass the Japanese rates.

Productivity Bargaining. In unionized plants, productivity bargaining and concession agreements represent attempts to bring

about a realignment of the internal work organization to the requirements of the technology and the market place. A tabulation of the content of concession agreements shows that approximately 30 to 40 percent of these agreements deal with changes in work rules. Generally speaking, in collective bargaining organizations have followed the "buy out" rather than the more open-ended, organizational change approach to improving productivity.

Productivity bargaining should not be utilized unless the gap that can potentially be eliminated through this process is sufficiently important to make a difference for the viability of the enterprise over the foreseeable future. Too often companies have engaged in productivity bargaining, achieved results, and subsequently shut down or cut back their operations—which results in substantial bitterness and dismay, since people "were asked to do their part, made a contribution, and then were let go."

Productivity bargaining works best when the practices to be changed can be clearly pinpointed and removed by agreement of the parties. (Work-rule changes certainly fall into this category.) Therefore, the closer the productivity agreement can be fashioned to the particular operations involved, the better the results. Agreements that state broad principles at the industry level often do not bring about any changes in actual practices. Thus, plant-by-plant agreements are more effective.

Since productivity bargaining often involves concessions, employees need corresponding incentives. In many situations today, the survival of the plant can be a very powerful incentive; nothing else may be needed if management is in a position to say that it will keep a given plant open if it obtains certain kinds of changes. Where survival is not the motive, some financial rewards may be necessary. But given the fact that the changes represent a one-shot adaptation, it can be argued that one-shot rewards are appropriate—that is, some type of bonus paid at the time that the agreement is reached, or better yet at the time the changes are actually implemented (a type of COD arrangement). Given the fact that in many situations wages are already above the competition's, it may not be appropriate to pay further rewards on a continuing basis for the productivity improvements reached through collective bargaining.

Employment Security.   While not a positive program in its own right, the provision of some type of assurance about employment continuity can serve to increase productivity by freeing up workers to think about involving themselves in increasing productivity. The basic proposition and overriding theme is that in the absence of other arrangements for ensuring adequate output (such as machine pacing, close supervision, positive incentives, and disciplinary penalties), the perception of impending unemployment will lower output or productivity.

The key contribution of an assurance about employment continuity is to deal in an affirmative manner with worker expectations. The object is to prevent expectations about future employment from deteriorating. In research work that has been done on the impact of prospective layoffs, it has been shown that labor productivity drops a minimum of 2 percent and in some instances much more.[4] Consequently, if the workforce reduction can be managed through attrition and other devices of human-resource management, such as voluntary separation arrangements, then these productivity slowdowns can be largely avoided.

But not all layoffs can be avoided through good planning by management. In some instances it is necessary to confront the reality of insecurity and to turn it in a positive direction. The latter can be done through a management commitment to see the operation through the difficult period, perhaps

with some new investment. This will encourage employees to accept productivity-enhancing work changes. The result is enhanced job security derived from this linkage of investment and productivity improvements.

STRATEGIC THEMES

At this point we would like to attempt some closure between the problem and program sides by picking up on the notion of strategies or clusters of program ideas. In large part, the need to move up to this overriding level stems from the great mismatch that appears to exist between the basic underlying problems of resistance to change, of work rules, and of motivational difficulties and the "business as usual" programs that do not come to grips with the basic industrial relations problems that are impeding productivity improvement.

Another way to make the point is to use the currently popular term of culture. Too many organizations are characterized by a low-productivity culture. The approach taken to changing the culture is piecemeal, faddish, and superficial. Strategies that grapple with the totality of the culture are needed.

The strategies that we have distilled from our field work begin with the context or the investment arrangement for the enterprise, move to the arrangement of the work organization and the process by which technology and workers are combined, and then, finally, reach the level of the individual workers and the need to intensify the motivation and commitment within the organization.

Creating the Right Context for Productivity Improvement

For the many organizations characterized by a culture of low productivity, the crucial first question is: What are the strategic alternatives for making a sharp break with an existing pattern? The two alternatives that we have isolated involve development of a new organization (usually at a new location) versus realignment and retrofitting of the existing organization. The premise of the first is that "new beginnings" are needed to create a culture of high productivity, whereas the second is based on the premise that any organization can be transformed: if proper ideas and programs are applied, then a high-productivity culture can emerge out of an old culture.

The Greenfield-Site Strategy. For much of the 1960s and 1970s, this strategy represented a common response by corporations, usually in the manufacturing sector, to the problems of a stagnated work culture. By going to a new site (usually in an area of the country where a work force could be recruited from scratch), companies have been able to put in place new technology, appropriate work rules and organizational arrangements, and a brand new work force that tended to be much more adaptable to the technology. Often, the new plants have been established on a sociotechnical basis, making heavy use of teams and other contemporary approaches to changing organizational behavior. Comprehensive personnel policies have been installed that emphasized security, egalitarian arrangements, pay for knowledge, and a host of other ideas that would be characterized as representing the latest thinking in human-resource management for high productivity.

While this strategy has proved popular and successful, it has been eclipsed by others. For one thing, the greenfield-site strategy takes considerable capital, which often is not available today. And while the greenfield-site alternative creates a new beginning, undesirable procedures and rigidities may eventually take root unless other things are done to prevent the development of a routinized pattern. In other words, the establishment of the new plant creates a "step-up" improvement, but the challenge of continuing improvement still remains.

The Retrofit Strategy. An approach that is becoming increasingly important is the reforming of an existing organization in the direction of a high-productivity culture. Often this means scaling down a large manufacturing operation to a smaller, more manageable size, in the range of 500-1,000 workers. The reform of the enterprise is multifaceted. New capital is committed, changes are made in work rules and in the arrangements for workforce deployment, often through the mechanism of productivity bargaining. In this strategy, the work-rule problem is confronted directly, with labor and management finding a way to bring about a realignment of the internal organization. In almost all major U.S. manufacturing industries, examples can be found of how, after a process of change and sorting out, a new type of enterprise has emerged. Capitalizing on the skills and experience of the existing work force and on the close relationship to a particular community and its labor supply, companies with the cooperation of unions have been able to "turn the corner" and to achieve much greater viability for operations that many people would have said were irredeemable.

The Adapting Organization

The basic problem with both the greenfield-site and the retrofit alternatives is that they represent step-up improvements but they do not in and of themselves set in motion forces for continuing adaptation. Ideas from organizational behavior theory that deemphasize status distinctions, as well as the concepts of job enlargement that put in place flexible work assignments, are important for helping an organization adapt on a continuing basis. Several other mechanisms are also vitally important. First is the provision of employment security and the elimination of the downside influence on motivation. Second is communication, which is playing an increasingly important productivity role. One of the reasons that organizations develop a culture of low productivity is that they become parochialized. That is, their operations become more connected to their own past than to the economic realities of the industry or the world market within which the enterprises find themselves. More and more, the function of communication is to provide workers with information about costs and market alternatives so that they can comprehend the need for the changes that must continually take place if jobs are to be secure and if the enterprise is to prosper over the long run.

The best examples of organizations that continue to adapt on a regular basis are to be found in Japan and, to some extent, in West Germany. Interestingly, in both countries trade unions play a dramatically different role at the plant level than they do in the United States. Herein is a challenge for our system of industrial relations. In these two countries, the adversary system does not exist at the plant level (though it may exist to some extent at the central level, where the broad economic parameters are established). At the local level the role of the union is much more supportive and cooperative than is generally the case in the United States. This cooperative stance helps in the adaptation process.

The High-Commitment Strategy

This approach focuses attention on the individual and the small group, and their involvement in improving the labor productivity of the enterprise. Basically, the test of this strategy is the extent to which the human resources of the organization are being used to their fullest capacity. This means much more than eliminating absenteeism or accident costs. It goes to the training and the capability of the human-resource factor in the organization and the maximization of its potential and its value to the organization. Similarly, from the viewpoint of industrial relations, it means much more than the minimization of costs due to grievances, strikes, etc. It seeks maximization of the benefits that can be derived from joint labor-management problem solving and, more broadly, from labor-management cooperation in general.

Businessmen now talk about human-resource management or industrial relations as being a second bottom line. We need to find ways to measure the capability and the performance of the human side of the organization as much as we do for the technology or the physical asset side. When we are able to measure this side of the enterprise, then we will be in a position to know whether it is being totally utilized or whether there is a shortfall.

The Integration of Human Resources and Industrial Relations into Key Business Decisions

Ultimately, the strategy that brings together all of the approaches described in this article is the linkage of the human side of the organization to the key business decisions of the firm. For some organizations, this occurs as a matter of policy or commitment. In such companies, for example, no decision impacting on the work side of the organization (and it is hard to think of a decision that does not) is made without involving the top human-resource people in thinking through the implications of a proposed business decision for their side of the organization. Where such commitment is not present, there is always the danger that management will consider investment decisions and other changes in operations strictly from a financial or technical point of view. To some extent, this is inevitable, given the short-run orientation of many business decisions in the United States. One way to offset this tendency is to develop ways in which workers, either through union representation or other mechanisms, can play a role in the linkage of the human and economic sides of the organization. We do not envision codetermination or any kind of joint decision making, but rather a consideration of employment consequences when investment decisions are made.

Representatives of the "people side" of an organization need to present the perspective that emphasizes the preservation and enhancement of human capital so that decisions which liquidate it precipitously and unfairly are not made. The experience of Japan and Germany offers some dramatically important examples of how job and financial linkage takes place. These examples show how the financial side of the organization is better served by the integration of human-resource considerations into the economics of the businesses, beyond the degree of integration that is usually the case in the United States.

JOHN HOERR

Collective Bargaining is in Danger Without Labor-Law Reform

For nearly 50 years, unions in the U.S. have reverently referred to the National Labor Relations Act as "labor's Magna Carta." But union leaders are now tripping over one another on the way to the podium to demand repeal of the NLRA on grounds that the Reagan Administration is subverting the law and allowing employers to violate it with impunity. This dispute aside, though, there is reason to believe the law should be revised for a more fundamental reason: The NLRA and the industrial relations system that evolved under it are no longer suited to the business environment of the 1980s.

The original NLRA, the Wagner Act of 1935, gave workers the right to form unions and established a national policy of encouraging the use of collective bargaining to resolve labor disputes. The law was right for the times. But many of its provisions, as interpreted by the courts and the National Labor Relations Board (NLRB), have produced a rigid, legalistic system that impedes labor-management collaboration to keep companies competitive. Labor analysts such as Thomas A. Kochan of the Massachusetts Institute of Technology contend that too much energy and money—for legal fees—are wasted defending contractual "rights" and negotiating additional rules to govern relationships between the two sides. Unless the system is changed, Kochan says, "what lies ahead is more polarization and confrontation."

A HEAVY PRICE

Kochan and other labor experts testified about the NLRA at House hearings held in late June. Predictably, the current NLRB, now dominated by President Reagan's appointees, was attacked by union officials—and defended by management lawyers—for recent reversals of decisions made by more liberal boards. More significantly, three union presidents, Richard L. Trumka of the United Mine Workers, William H. Wynn of the United Food & Commercial Workers, and William H. Bywater of the International Union of Electronic Workers, suggested that the NLRA be repealed.

Wynn, for example, said his union can't rely on the NLRB to stop employers from illegally firing union activists to halt organizing campaigns. "We'll make [employers] pay the price—a heavy price, if we can—for denying workers their rights," he warned. AFL-CIO President Lane Kirkland talks of "deregulating" labor law and returning to "the law of the jungle." This may be rhetoric, but it is ominous.

CHILLED

Labor's complaint that the NLRA has no "teeth" to discourage employers from discharging union activists has some merit. It usually takes two to three years of litigation before a worker found to have been fired illegally is reinstated and awarded back pay. Meanwhile, organizing efforts are chilled by the fear of further discharges. Paul Weiler, a Harvard University law professor, notes that in 1980, 10,033 workers were reinstated, either by order of the NLRB or through informal settlements with employers. In the same year, 200,000 workers cast pro-union votes in representation elections. The "odds," as Weiler puts it, were that one in 20 union supporters would be illegally fired. The pattern was the same in 1981.

On collective bargaining issues, the rulings under the NLRA have forced both sides to narrow their focus to the legality, rather than the spirit, of their relationship. The black-and-white distinctions between labor and management of the 1930s have long since become gray. Collaboration requires sharing information and a retreat from authoritarian management by companies. Unions must give management more flexibility in assigning work in return for job security and a larger union role in making decisions.

Instead, says D. Quinn Mills—a labor arbitrator and business professor at Harvard, "all we're doing is importing the legal system into the workplace." For example, employers must negotiate over prices charged by vending machines in a plant but not over pension increases for already retired workers. Increased worker participation is often frustrated by management and labor roles laid down by the NLRA in the 1930s.

Adherence to the old system, says MIT's Kochan, "has kept union leaders from articulating a longer-run, more strategic view" of how best to represent members and at the same time help the employer remain competitive. Unless the NLRA is changed in this and other respects, Weiler says, "free collective bargaining in private-sector employment is on its way to extinction by the turn of the century."

17

Productivity and White-Collar Workers

*Knowledge is perhaps the most expensive of all resources.
Knowledge workers are far more expensive than even their
salaries indicate. . . . And only management can turn the
knowledge worker into a productive resource.*

PETER F. DRUCKER[1]

Sometime, more than a decade ago, the United States became a white-collar economy, with no fanfare or ceremony to mark the event. Once dominated by agricultural workers, then by blue-collar industrial laborers, the U.S. labor force now contains more white-collar workers than all other categories: estimates range around sixty percent today, with predictions as high as ninety percent by the end of the century.[2]

The productivity of white-collar workers, therefore, is of major concern. Little is known about how to define, measure or improve white-collar productivity, but major efforts are underway to study this problem and to build a body of knowledge for the largest—and perhaps most critical—of resources.

DEFINITIONS OF WHITE-COLLAR WORK

A white-collar occupation may be defined as any job not involved in the direct production of manufactured or agricultural goods. The broadest interpretation of this definition includes all employees in the service and government sectors, professionals and their supporting technicians, and all indirect and managerial employees in the manufacturing sector. Most manufacturers report a substantial increase in the ratio of indirect to direct workers as the manufacturing process becomes more efficient and less labor intensive, while the need for support personnel—technicians, analysts, clerks, and others—continues to grow.[3]

Information Workers

Because "white-collar" covers such a great range of jobs, alternative classifications are often used. For example, in one of the preparatory conferences to the White House Conference on Productivity of 1982, the discussion of white-collar workers was changed to a focus on "information workers."[4] Whereas production laborers work with metal, wood or plastic, white-collar workers deal primarily with information—with its creation, organization, processing, storage, and retrieval. Most clerical employees, data-processing workers, accountants, and engineers fit into this category. Some industries, such as insurance, finance and banking, could also be classified as information-processors.

The category of "information workers" is useful for defining and measuring productivity. By viewing information as the intangible product produced by this kind of worker, we can develop more meaningful measures of output, regardless of the format of the information—written report, electronic data bank or any other form.

Knowledge Workers

Another subset of white-collar workers are knowledge workers. The distinction is based on the difference between knowledge (a cognitive ability) and skill (a behavioral ability). A knowledge worker is any worker whose job entails a significant amount of cognitive ability, as opposed to skill-based activities. Knowledge workers do more than just deal with information; they create, design and develop things or ideas. The knowledge worker may plan, schedule, control, direct, supervise, oversee, research, analyze, and make decisions. The knowledge worker's tasks involve exercising judgment within an area of discretion.

Skill-based workers, on the other hand, follow procedures. A skill may take years to master, yet it never involves independent judgment to a great extent. In a skill-based job, there is an ideal method to use and an upper limit to how well the skill can be practiced.

Every job requires some amount of skill and some amount of knowledge, but knowledge is predominant in the knowledge worker's job. Thus, light bulb packer and bricklayer are both skill jobs, even though one requires a great deal more skill than the other. Neither job requires enough thinking and decision-making to be classified as knowledge worker. An assistant buyer for a department store, however, is a knowledge worker, even though this job doesn't entail a fraction of the training or abilities needed by a journeyman bricklayer.

A short-order cook is generally not a knowledge worker. Knowing when to turn the egg to make it "over easy" is a learned skill—there is a correct time at which to turn the egg. The closer the cook comes to the correct time, the better the cook is at this skill. A dietitian, however, is a knowledge worker. The planning of meals and menus requires the exercise of judgment and creativity within the guidelines and general principles of nutrition. Other matched pairs would include the following:

Skill Workers	Knowledge Workers
Clerk Typist	Secretary
Carpenter	Construction Supervisor
Key Punch Operator	Programmer
Bookkeeper	Accountant

Knowledge workers are found in all areas and at all levels of an organization. The CEO is certainly a knowledge worker, but so, too, is a receptionist: Both positions involve exercising judgment, rather than following a procedure. Knowledge workers include bank tellers, travel agents, engineers, managers, supervisors, and most jobs in support areas such as personnel, research and development, data processing, accounting, and purchasing. Most of marketing is also knowledge work. Generally, service firms and government have a higher percentage of knowledge workers than do manufacturing enterprises.

Many positions are impossible to classify on the basis of job title alone. Jobs in maintenance, for example, may be in the knowledge category if the task requires judgment in diagnosis and repair work; but if the position involves doing routine, preventive maintenance according to a predetermined schedule, it is basically a skill position.

A Typology of White-Collar Work

One useful way to subdivide the many and varied forms of white-collar work is with the typology diagrammed in Figure 17-1. One dimension refers to the tangibility of the product or service being produced. In some white-collar work, the output is physical and countable. Reports produced, lines written, policies issued, and people hired are just a few examples. At the low end of this spectrum fall tasks such as medical research or industrial R & D, where a project may consume many work-years before any output becomes apparent.

In between fall many variations. Some services, such as hair styling, gardening and painting, yield physical evidence of the work performed. This evidence can be seen, counted and evaluated after the fact. Other services, such as legal advising, may or may not have a physical output.

The vertical dimension on the graph in Figure 17-1 represents the degree to which a specified procedure exists for the task. In a financial institution, for example, the teller's job is highly specified; a routine set of steps exists for each type of transaction, and every teller follows these same steps.

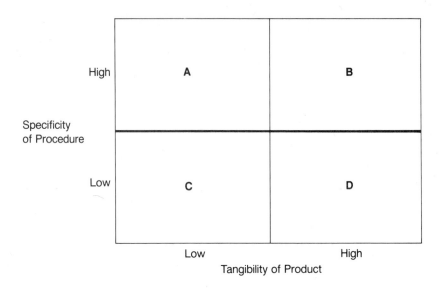

Figure 17–1.   A Typology of White-Collar Work

The loan officer's job is less specified. The loan may be evaluated from a standard form according to a pre-established set of criteria, yet no two loan applications are exactly alike. Discretion and judgment must be exercised.

Finally, the financial advisor's job is even less specified. Whereas transactions performed by two tellers would be *exactly* the same, and decisions by two loan officers would *likely* be the same, recommendations from two financial advisors could be substantially different. The process by which they arrived at their conclusions—if it could be described at all—might also be quite different.

The implications of this typology are clear. Jobs that fall into Quadrant B more closely approximate typical blue-collar work. The vast resources of management and industrial engineering can be applied straightforwardly to measure and improve the productivity of these workers. In contrast, jobs in Quadrant C, where there is neither a specified procedure nor a physical output, present the greatest challenge to productivity management. Jobs in Quadrants A and D offer opportunities and challenges that are more difficult than those in B, but less difficult than those in C.

Using this typology to classify white-collar tasks could lead to better control of the vast part of our work force that is currently grouped together in this category, even though the characteristics of the jobs in question are quite varied.

SPECIAL PROBLEMS IN
THE MANAGEMENT OF
WHITE-COLLAR PRODUCTIVITY

Productivity is a dirty word for many white-collar workers. They associate productivity with machine shops and auto assembly lines, work settings they feel are quite different from their own. Having been "elevated" to the white-collar ranks of the office, they dissociate themselves and their work from work on the factory floor, which is of lower status (albeit often more highly skilled and more highly paid).

Resistance to being measured or managed on the basis of productivity comes from a feeling of "professionalism" in white-collar workers. They often see their jobs as unsuited to measurement and control, and feel degraded if their contribution to the firm is reduced to measured output units. They feel they are being paid (especially if on salary) for the skills, talent and judgment they bring to the job, not necessarily for what they accomplish in any given hour. Often, but not always, their perceptions are accurate. This resistance must be recognized if progress is to be made in improving white-collar productivity. Much more time must be spent in preparing and involving the typical white-collar employee if misconceptions and resistance are to be minimized.

Part of the solution may be as simple as changing terminology. Outputs and inputs may be acceptable terms for the factory floor, but white-collar workers may find them irrelevant or offensive. The authors have encountered much less resistance from white-collar workers to the terms "results" and "resources," words much more palatable to professionals.

Another problem stems from the white-collar workers' conception of the contribution of their jobs to the success of the firm. In one respect, all employees are there to produce the product or service that the firm sells in the marketplace. At one time, the production process may have employed eight blue-collar workers and two white-collar support staff. Today, on the average, four production workers are supported by six staff. In time, one actual production worker may be backed up by nine white-collar employees performing necessary non-production tasks. From the point of view of the firm, though, each scenario requires ten workers to produce a given level of output. Labor productivity has remained constant.

Applying this concept as a measurement logic, however, produces problems. Staff departments such as purchasing, personnel or data processing could be evaluated on the basis of sales per employee. Yet each would claim a foul. Proper staffing of data processing, for example, may or may not be directly correlated with sales. Data processing may lead or lag in sales, and this department may need to expand regardless of sales levels. The manager of the data processing department would prefer to be evaluated on results achieved by the department, not on the overall sales of the firm, which may not be directly influenced by the activities of the data processing department.

This issue cannot be solved here, of course. It is advisable, however, to raise the issue and reach some logical compromise with white-collar workers. The result may be a combination of measures, some involving the total output of the firm relative to the department, and others looking at specific results or activities within the department relative to resources used. In either case, the firm can maintain some control over the growing ranks of white-collar workers while using more specific measures to indicate improvements in the efficiency of the tasks being done.

WHITE-COLLAR MEASUREMENT AND IMPROVEMENT

Productivity measurement is the cornerstone of any program to improve white-collar productivity. Unlike production job descriptions, which are usually written in relation to physical output, white-collar jobs have loosely defined duties, responsibilities and activities. As discussed in Chapter 15, the system of measurement defines the job and directs behavior toward organizational goals. For poorly defined white-collar jobs that lack tangible outputs, it is imperative to develop reasonable productivity measures.

White-Collar Measurement

Many firms use simple partial measures of output to input for white-collar jobs. In one of the readings in this chapter, Ruch gives examples of such measures and how they might be developed.[5]

Some progressive firms have developed special techniques for measuring white-collar productivity. The IBM Common Staffing System[6] and methods used at Westinghouse[7] are notable examples. The IBM system measures headcount against the size of the task to be done, as determined by an indicator of the activity level of the task, such as sales, payroll, amount of material purchased, etc. (For a detailed description of this technique, see the Ruch reading at the end of this chapter.)

Westinghouse has brainstorming sessions to develop performance criteria and performance ratios for white-collar departments. Several ratios are reported regularly, and a composite index for each department is calculated to indicate overall performance.

White-Collar Quality

Quality of white-collar work often is more difficult to isolate; yet, as customers, we easily recognize poor service, errors in bank statements and other forms of poor quality. As was the case with quantity, the lack of a tangible product or a specified procedure presents special challenges for tracking the quality of white-collar work.

Adam, Hershauer and Ruch studied check-processing operations and the personnel departments of several Federal Reserve Banks in order to devise a way to measure the quality of services as a productivity ratio.[8] The result is a series of ratios, comparing the quality of the output to the resources consumed to achieve that quality. Some ratios deal with error prevention while others focus on detection and correction, but all evaluate whether to employ more or fewer resources to achieve certain levels of quality.

Target Segments of White-Collar Work

Researchers and business firms alike are beginning to segment white-collar work into smaller, more homogeneous groups. Each group is then targeted for special study to develop measures, controls and improvement strategies.

Hughes Aircraft conducted an extensive study of corporate R & D activities and published the results in book form.[9] The section on productivity evaluation may be summarized as follows:

1. All work contains a quantitative and a qualitative element; the more complex and unstructured the task, the more reliance must be placed on qualitative assessment.

2. The line manager is in the best position to determine organizational productivity; however, first-line supervision is better able to judge individual productivity.

3. To be effective, any system of productivity evaluation must be easy to understand, simple to implement, easy to administer, and clearly cost-effective. Especially important, it must be endorsed and conscientiously implemented by its users.

4. There is no single measure that clearly indicates the level of productivity. Rather, productivity results from the complex interaction of a number of factors.

5. A universally applicable measurement/assessment system is not feasible. R & D productivity evaluation is unique to each organization and to the specific work involved. Evaluations, therefore, must be tailored to each application.

6. Evaluation techniques considered useful by the Hughes study team include work sampling, analysis of productivity ratios and trends, and assessment of patterns of success and failure in technical, cost and schedule performance.

7. Formal evaluation—especially quantitative measurement of individual output—can easily discourage employees and prove counterproductive.

The Hughes study team developed a number of quantitative and qualitative productivity indicators to monitor the performance of individuals and the organization. General measures (such as profit per employee) and more specific measures (such as engineering drawing releases per clerk per day), enable Hughes to keep track of R & D productivity and to evaluate improvement efforts.

Management productivity was the subject of a study by the consulting firm of Booz-Allen & Hamilton, Inc.[10] Breaking down the time spent by knowledge workers, they found that reading, analyzing and creating documents accounted for less than thirty percent of the day, while the rest was spent in meetings, on the phone or in "less productive activities." They suggest that great benefits are possible through office automation, but only if applied as part of a carefully designed program to improve total productivity. This program must be backed by support from top management.

Office work has been the target of many studies. Based on years of experience in the insurance industry, Val Olsen, author of *White-Collar Waste*, claims that the typical office worker produces four hours of work in an eight-hour day.[11] He suggests that work can be better organized and assigned if scheduling techniques are borrowed from manufacturing technologies.

Government workers were the subject of a study by Shipper and Sniffin.[12] Applying the aforementioned methodology of Adam, Hershauer and Ruch, they found that meaningful measures of productivity and quality could be developed for typical staff functions in the Naval Materiel Command.

Sales and marketing activities have always been subjected to performance measures, but seldom has this been cast in a productivity framework. Carl Thor, vice president of measurement for the American Productivity Center, explains that the sales force's contribution to the firm, in comparison to resources they use, can be calculated with a family of measures.[13] He considers not only gross sales figures, but the composition of those sales, the dollar contribution they make to the firm and their relationship to marketing strategy and sales targets.

Service firms differ from manufacturers in many important respects, not the least of which is the direct contact with the customer in the delivery of the service. A limited (and incorrect) view of productivity in services would emphasize speed at the expense of customer satisfaction. Benjamin Schneider suggests, "It would be useful if the definition of 'productivity'—especially in service industries—were broadened to include at least courtesy and style of performance, particularly because the long-term effectiveness of the organization depends on service."[14] In the direct delivery of services, the customer plays a key role in defining "satisfactory service," so the customer must be considered in the definition and measurement of productivity.

All aspects of white-collar productivity present challenges to management. Some progress has been made, but much remains to be done.

SUMMARY

White-collar work refers to all of the nonproduction work that takes place in manufacturing companies, service firms and government. Depending upon the specific definition used, it may include technical, administrative, clerical, sales, and many other areas not directly involved in producing the firm's output of goods and services. As white-collar work becomes a larger percentage of the economy, the challenges of managing and measuring white-collar productivity become critical. If the white-collar task is repetitive and involves a tangible output, many of the existing principles from blue-collar work can be applied. In non-repetitive, "pure service" jobs, new and creative methods for managing and measuring the work are being developed.

SELECTED READINGS OVERVIEW

Knowledge Worker Productivity is a management briefing by Ira Gregerman, published by the American Management Association. This excerpt from the first chapter, "The Rise of the Knowledge Worker," is an excellent overview of the characteristics of white-collar workers and the factors that influence their productivity.

"The Measurement of White-Collar Productivity," by William Ruch, covers the spectrum of measurement systems, including simple partial measures, specialized techniques and total factor productivity measurement as it applies to white-collar work. Especially useful is the list of guidelines for tailoring white-collar productivity measures to a specific situation.

Next Chapter

Several references to the importance of quality are contained in this chapter. Quality may be more difficult to measure than quantity in any type of process, yet it is imperative that quality be included in productivity equations. Quality is not a trade-off for reduced productivity; indeed, quality is an integral part of productivity. The productivity-quality connection is the subject of the next chapter.

Review Questions

1. Explain why white-collar workers might resist being measured by the same approach that is applied to production workers making metal parts on a machine.
2. The typology of white-collar work contains four cells. Give at least four examples of specific jobs that would fall into each cell. Justify your examples.

3. According to Ira Gregerman, knowledge work is more often group-oriented than individual. Why is this true, and what implications does that have for productivity improvement?

4. Ruch claims that involving people in the development of measures of their work is critically important. Why? What happens if you do? What may happen if you do not?

5. Suppose you are an IBM plant manager using the Common Staffing System (described in the Ruch article), and your plant is above the diagonal line. Does this mean you have high productivity? Explain.

IRA GREGERMAN

The Rise of the Knowledge Worker

CHARACTERISTICS OF KNOWLEDGE WORKERS

Blue collar workers are distinguished from white collar workers by the nature and location of their jobs. Construction laborers and shopworkers are typical blue collar workers, while white collar workers work primarily in offices and have job titles such as clerk, secretary, accountant, engineer, supervisor, and manager. As this group grew larger, so did the need for more precise distinction among its ranks—hence the term *knowledge worker*. Just as the blue collar worker is easily distinguished from the white collar worker, so too is the knowledge worker distinguished from the generic white collar worker. This difference lies in the distinct characteristics of the knowledge worker's job. Falling into eight major categories, these characteristics reflect the knowledge worker's abilities in job planning, creativity, innovation, decision making, and the direct impact on people inside and outside the organization.

1. Nonrepetitive job tasks and unanticipated changes in direction are frequently found in knowledge worker's jobs. The methods used to resolve problems encompass numerous approaches and techniques. For example, it would be virtually impossible to structure the job of an engineer: No method could provide a high level of predictability and repetition for that type of position.

2. The knowledge worker has almost total authority in matching individual work methods to the varying job tasks that he or she faces. For example, it would certainly be ill-advised to preselect research methodology for a research chemist.

3. The output of knowledge workers is at best difficult to quantify. While counting the number of forms a clerk-typist prepares might be a valid performance measurement, it would be meaningless to count the number of drawings a drafter produces or the lines of code a programmer generates.

4. The "production rate" of knowledge workers is dependent upon the complex interactions among intelligence, creativity, and environmental influences. This is in direct contrast with the highly

proceduralized production rates of blue collar workers. The demands on an expeditor working with suppliers are decidedly different from those of a typist or file clerk in the purchasing department.

5. Blue and regular white collar jobs have a relatively short time-span between the job activity and performance or results feedback. Inspectors can quickly notify machine operators of the quality of the products being produced. In comparison, there may be several months—or years—between the design of a computer system and its implementation.

6. The effectiveness of most white and blue collar repetitive jobs is determined through careful design of the process procedures. However, the knowledge worker can be as effective as he or she chooses. How well a job is done frequently depends on how skillfully the knowledge worker applies new technologies and innovations to it.

7. Knowledge worker jobs frequently affect substantial numbers of people both inside and outside the organization. Purchasing agents dealing with suppliers can affect production schedules, quality control engineers can affect the relationships with customers, and personnel managers have an impact on the quality of worklife of the whole organization.

8. Since it is difficult to quantify the output of knowledge workers, it is difficult to measure their productivity with the classic methods. Therefore these traditional techniques (which measure efficiency or productivity of individuals) are gradually being replaced by group techniques that seek to establish productivity measures for knowledge workers.

AT WORK WITH PEERS

It is a rare knowledge worker who functions best alone. In fact, observations lead to the conclusion that most knowledge workers perform best in concert with others. These collaborations range from interactions with peer groups to membership in internal company service organizations to cooperative relationships with external resources such as suppliers, customers, and consultants. In addition to the eight individual characteristics of the knowledge worker previously discussed, there are five primary group characteristics that distinguish the knowledge worker from others.

1. Most knowlege workers adapt easily to group settings and function well in groups. Their higher levels of education and awareness, coupled with the propensity to collaborate with others to accomplish their assigned tasks, are responsible for their group-adaptiveness. Of course, any group activity must be structured to reduce the possibility of threat or the participants will be as uncooperative as any other workers would be in such an environment.

2. Because of better education and greater opportunities to develop problem-solving skills, most knowledge workers are more innovative than other workers. This tendency facilitates productive group activity.

3. In most of their endeavors—from data processing, to engineering, to accounting, to strategic planning—knowledge workers are evaluated on their ability to solve problems. In addition, their formal and informal education is oriented toward the identification and solution of problems. Thus, this third element provides a higher probability of successfully involving knowledge workers in group problem-solving activities.

4. This group also appears to possess a higher level of self-motivation and self-esteem. Therefore group settings that enhance self-motivation and provide an opportunity to contribute to group measures will find a high level of acceptability in knowledge worker groups.

5. In order for most knowledge workers to be task effective, they must have a degree of freedom in choosing the work methods and the environments in which they function. It would be difficult, if not impossible, to provide a highly structured environment that enhances a knowledge worker's method of functioning.

FACTORS THAT INFLUENCE KNOWLEDGE WORKER PRODUCTIVITY

Three primary variables affect productivity of knowledge workers: external influences, internal influences, and peer group influ-ences. Exhibit 2 shows the various components that make up these variables. Each of the items can have either a positive or negative effect on knowledge worker productivity. For example, excessive government regulation controlling the design of automobiles or power plants can force an individual to spend extra time on design elements that do not improve the product. Similarly, poor quality of worklife in an organization will have a negative effect. However, if the opposite is true in these two cases, knowledge worker productivity will flourish.

The Knowledge Worker Productivity Model in Exhibit 3 depicts the relationships among external, internal, and peer group influences as these relate to individual knowledge workers. It demonstrates graphically that the peer group can help overcome negative influences generated by internal or external factors. For example, company policies that may be detrimental to knowledge worker productivity may be smoothed over by the buffering effect of peer group

---

Exhibit 2.   Influences on Knowledge Worker Productivity.

External	*Internal*	*Peer Group*
Goverment regulations	Company benefits	Recognition of technical competence by internal peers
Societal demands	Participative management	Recognition of technical competence by external peers
Community needs	Decision-making involvement	
Professional associations	Quality of worklife	Opportunity to provide assistance to group members
Customer requirements	Two-way communications	
Unionization	Clearly-defined goals	Acceptance by a closed and select group
Economic shifts	Mutual respect	
Competition	Meaningful assignments	A social environment divorced from the general socio-technical environment of the company
Market shifts		
Educational systems		

interactions. In other words, camaraderie among knowledge workers helps to keep productivity high and to deflect hostile influences.

When all three factors—peer group, external environment, and internal environment—function harmoniously together, productivity increases. Look at Exhibit 3 again and imagine that the two lower circles (internal and external environment) are moving upward and inward. The area labeled "productivity" increases, and the need for a buffer zone diminishes. No graphic presentation, of course, can offer an exact replication of reality. But the point remains valid: The more supportive the environment, and the more company policies are aligned to tap into the innate strengths of knowledge workers, the greater their productivity.

Exhibit 3.   The more harmonious the relationship among peer groups, internal environment, and external environment, the more productive the knowledge worker.

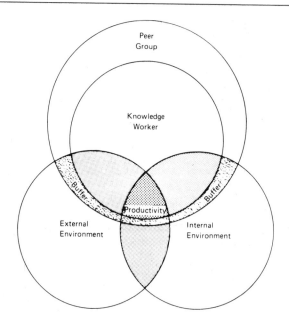

WILLIAM A. RUCH

The Measurement of
White-Collar Productivity

*The author demonstrates how to overcome the obstacles to developing
white-collar productivity measures.*

Productivity is defined as an output to input ratio. It seems simple enough; put the outputs on top and the inputs used to produce those outputs on the bottom, and you have a straightforward measure of resource utilization. Conceptually, the determination of productivity is very easy, but practical applications are difficult when one must deal with multiple products and services, changing prices and costs, redesign of products, services, and processes, quality considerations, and indirect as well as direct inputs.

In the simplest case of a firm manufacturing one tangible product from few resources, productivity measurement is not difficult to handle. But today's complex organizations employ an ever-increasing ratio of white-collar workers, and their output is difficult to define.

Management of the white-collar resource is necessary if the organization is to remain viable, and a prerequisite to effective management of a resource is a reasonably accurate and reliable measurement system. It is

possible to bowl blindfolded, but the bowler would get a much better score if he had some feedback as to which pins remained standing. The measurement system for white-collar workers will be neither as simple nor as concrete as this analogy may suggest, but meaningful feedback on past white-collar effectiveness will lead to better decision making for future allocation and utilization.

In this article, we will first examine the characteristics of white-collar work and indicate how they can lead to difficulties in productivity measurement.

Second, we will examine the basic principles of productivity measurement in general. Many misconceptions are associated with productivity measurement, and if these errors are not resolved, the task of defining and measuring white-collar workers will be even more difficult than it need be. White-collar productivity measurement should not be divorced from other forms of performance measurement for the firm; it

Reprinted, by permission, from *National Productivity Review* (Autumn 1982):416–26.

should be compatible and integrated with the evaluation system for total resource utilization.

Third, the purposes of measuring productivity will be discussed, since these must be established before the measurement system is developed. They apply to all forms of productivity but are especially important to the sensitive area of white-collar workers. This leads directly to the next section, which delineates the special problems of white-collar productivity measurement and how measures of white-collar productivity are unique. Guidelines for developing white-collar measures are then explained and illustrated with several case examples.

WHITE-COLLAR WORKERS

"White collar" is a broad term that has appeared in the literature with a variety of meanings while seldom being explicitly defined. It can refer to anything from clerical workers to engineers and scientists, foremen, salesmen, trainers, material handlers, keypunch operators, or the CEO. Some equate white-collar work with "indirect labor." Others would say that any worker in a service business—insurance, for example—is a white-collar worker.

The crux of the problem is trying to use one category—white collar—to include such a diversity of jobs with vastly different sets of authorities, responsibilities, and duties. Sorely needed is a comprehensive, logical typology of white-collar workers so that subsets with similar characteristics can be dealt with differently than other subsets. Unfortunately, such a scheme is yet to be developed.

It would appear that white collar is not a category but a continuum, and a multidimensional one at that. Therefore, let me pose the beginnings of a classification of white-collar workers by isolating two dimensions that are relevant to this article.

One dimension is the amount of discretion involved in the job—not the amount of skill, but the degree to which there is a specified procedure to follow in the performance of the job. A receptionist, for example, may not be classified at a high-skill level, yet every encounter with the public may require a different response. The receptionist must exercise judgment in handling each inquiry or complaint. Contrast this with the highly skilled task of a dentist. True, not every cavity is the same, but the procedure for filling a cavity is more highly specified than is the procedure for handling customer complaints. It would be easier to measure the number of cavities filled per dentist (and one would expect less variability) than the number of phone inquiries handled per receptionist.

As a basic premise, the less discretion there is in the job, the easier it is to measure.

A second relevant dimension is the degree to which there is a physical product involved in the process. Not only does a cook in a McDonald's hamburger outlet have a specified procedure to follow, but there is a tangible output that can be counted and checked for quality. In the example above, there is a physical manifestation of the dentist's work—it can be examined by others after the work is completed and, if necessary, it can be photographed. This is not true for the receptionist. Once the service is performed, the evidence disappears. It is difficult to count the output or check its quality without being present and observing the process as it takes place.

Combining the two dimensions, we find that some white-collar jobs apply a specified procedure to a physical product, e.g., encoding checks in a bank or processing registrations in a motor-vehicle department. For purposes of analysis, we will call these jobs quasi-manufacturing and measure their productivity as we would any blue-collar, direct manufacturing job: number of units produced per hour. However, if the job contains a high level of discretion and few physical outputs, special measurement problems arise. It is these problems to which the remainder of this article is addressed.

PRODUCTIVITY MEASUREMENT

Measurement of productivity follows directly from its definition: a productivity measurement is any ratio of output to one or more corresponding inputs. The unit of output can be anything—dollars, tons, BTUs, gallons, units of product, customers served, or whatever is meaningful in the context. A true productivity measure, however, is a physical rather than a financial relationship, so if dollars are used to measure either outputs or inputs, some adjustment for price changes should be made to separate inflationary changes from changes in productivity.

When measuring white-collar productivity, defining and counting the output is generally much more difficult than determining the input. A blue-collar worker is generally producing saleable units of product, but a white-collar worker usually supports production by providing an intangible service such as training, data processing, market research, purchasing, or personnel.

Determining the value of these contributions and establishing a meaningful unit of measure is an onerous task, but examination of examples of labor productivity measures indicates that it is not impossible. Although the measure may not be as precise as in the case of blue-collar workers, lawyers can be evaluated in part by the number of briefs filed and engineers by the number of projects completed. Subject to some problems discussed below, the total output of the firm, such as sales or tons shipped, can be used as an output measure in a ratio to, say, the number of employees in the personnel department.

On the input side, a common misconception in all productivity measures is to consider only the labor component. If all of the inputs of the firm are considered, they fall into four categories of resources: labor, capital, materials, and energy. A productivity measure relating outputs to one of these inputs is a partial measure. Obviously, labor productivity could be greatly increased if there were no restrictions on the use or misuse of capital, materials, and energy. Effective management of all resources requires a total productivity measurement system that relates outputs to a combination of all inputs.

An organization can achieve a complete productivity measurement system in one of two ways. First, it can develop a number of measures, at least one for each of the four major input factors. If all are monitored, the effects of the trade-offs can be seen by the relative changes in the different ratios. (Case 1 below is an example of this.)

A second alternative is to implement an integrated productivity measurement sys-

---

**EXAMPLES OF
LABOR PRODUCTIVITY MEASURES**

$$\frac{\text{Units Produced}}{\text{Hour}} \qquad \frac{\text{Value Added}}{\text{Employee}}$$

$$\frac{\text{Briefs Filed}}{\text{Lawyer}} \qquad \frac{\text{Customers Served}}{\text{Full-Time Equivalent Employee}}$$

$$\frac{\text{Billed Hours}}{\text{Actual Hours}} \qquad \frac{\text{Ton-Miles Moved}}{\text{Hour Worked}}$$

$$\frac{\text{Setups Completed}}{\text{Employee}} \qquad \frac{\text{Sales (deflated)}}{\text{Payroll (deflated)}}$$

$$\frac{\text{Tons Shipped}}{\text{Employee}} \qquad \frac{\text{Gallons Produced}}{\text{Total Compensation}}$$

$$\frac{\text{Units Delivered}}{\text{Worker-Day}} \qquad \frac{\text{Jobs Completed}}{\text{Billable Hours}}$$

$$\frac{\text{Student Credit Hours}}{\text{Professor}} \qquad \frac{\text{Keystrokes}}{\text{Hour}}$$

$$\frac{\text{Drawings Accepted}}{\text{Draftsman}} \qquad \frac{\text{Design Projects Completed}}{\text{Engineering Man-Year}}$$

tem that accounts for all four partials and combines them into a total productivity measure for the firm. Although more complex, it is theoretically more sound and provides more feedback for decisions involving trade-offs of one resource for another.

At first it might appear that white-collar measurement is concerned with the labor input only: after all, "white-collar" denotes a type of labor. Such is not the case. Rather than thinking of individual workers, think in terms of a white-collar function, such as secretarial services. In addition to the labor involved, this function consumes capital, materials, and energy to create the services that constitute its output.

Total white-collar productivity measurement should consider not only reports produced per hour worked, but also reports per dollar of capital (typewriters, word processors, files, square feet of floor space, etc.); reports per dollar of material used (paper, correction fluid, file folders, and other office supplies); and reports produced per kilowatt hour of energy consumed. The "office of the future" that receives so much press today generally focuses only on labor savings and increased output. The astute manager will

also consider the effects of office automation on capital requirements, materials usage, and energy consumption to get a complete picture of resource utilization.

Dealing with ratios rather than unitary measures can be a new experience for some managers, especially those in white-collar functions. There is a temptation to think that the only two ways to improve the ratio is to increase the numerator or to decrease the denominator. In fact, five different ways can be identified, and knowledge of all five can often overcome some of the resistance to the implementation of measures.

Another factor to keep in mind when dealing with productivity ratios in general and white-collar measures in particular is the difference between a level and a trend. A productivity level (one ratio of output to input at one point in time) is virtually meaningless unless compared to another ratio. The comparison may be one time period to the next, one plant to another, comparison to a competitor, or comparison to some industry or national average. Knowing that fifteen reports per employee were produced is useless information. Learning that the fifteen in period one changed to sixteen and one-half in period two indicates a 10 percent improvement. It doesn't indicate whether performance is good or bad, but it does show whether performance is getting better or worse.

$$\text{Productivity} = \frac{\text{OUTPUT}}{\text{INPUT}}$$

1. Output increases faster than input; "managed growth."

2. Input decreases more than output (e.g., phasing out an old product, closing an inefficient plant); "managed decline."

3. Producing the same output with fewer inputs; cost reductions and greater efficiency.

4. More outputs from the same inputs; "working smarter."

5. The ideal; maximum increase in the ratio by a combination of the above.

Figure 1. Five Ways to Increase a Ratio

WHY MEASURE PRODUCTIVITY?

There are three major reasons for any type of measure; they apply as well to productivity measures as to financial or other types of measures. The first is evaluation; to answer the question, "How well did we do?" We evaluate for control purposes, to determine the effects of trade-off and allocation decisions made in the past. Problems and opportunities are isolated by measures, particularly when a deviation from the norm occurs or when a trend is noted. Often, the evaluation can lead to a reward—positive or negative—for those responsible for the factor being measured.

A second purpose for measurement is planning: "What should we do now?" The bowling analogy used above is appropriate here. How the second ball is thrown depends upon feedback on the effects of the first ball. Analysis of results of past productivity efforts forms the basis for continuation, discontinuation, or change in future efforts.

A third reason for measurement is often overlooked, yet it is a powerful one: measurements create awareness and direct behavior. The very fact that something is being measured (and something else is not) leads people to work to the measure, even in the absence of an explicit performance/reward relationship. The factor chosen to be measured communicates what is important and, conversely, what is unimportant.

Imagine going to a police squad room and simply posting each day, with no explanation, the name of each patrolman and the number of tickets written in order from highest to lowest. The almost certain result will be that those at the bottom of the list will write more tickets. In one department of an insurance company, post only the number of claims processed each day; in another department, post only the number of errors made. The first department would likely become very quantity conscious and have less regard for quality while the opposite effect would likely occur in the second department.

Determining and communicating the purpose for white-collar productivity measures is critically important. If you are implementing new productivity measures purely for planning purposes, but your employees believe they will be used to determine pay raises, layoffs, and disciplinary actions, the measurement system will not be effective.

Any measurement system can be aborted if it is perceived as a threat.

PROBLEMS IN MEASURING WHITE-COLLAR PRODUCTIVITY[1]

Measuring white-collar productivity is a difficult but not impossible task. The assessment techniques for measuring the contribution of these workers to the goals of the organization simply have not yet been developed and put into widespread use. Obstacles to the development of measures fall into six basic categories.

First, it is difficult to define the output or contribution made by the white-collar worker. At the firm level, output in the productivity equation is the goods or services produced and sold, but seldom is the white-collar worker directly responsible for this output. Generally, she or he contributes to the output through design or improvement of the process or through providing a support service to the production activities. Defining the nature, the value, and the unit of measure of this contribution to output has proven to be a difficult task.

Second, and this difficulty stems from the first, is the tendency of productivity analysts to measure activities rather than results. Countable units of work—such as number of reports created, number of lines of computer programs written, or number of parking tickets issued—are easy to put into a productivity ratio and monitor for control purposes. Yet, the maximization of this ratio may not be in the best interests of the organization and may, in some cases, be counterproductive.

Third, it is difficult to match inputs and outputs within a time frame. The resources currently consumed by the white-collar worker may not show results until several periods later. In many cases, the contribution made in the current period affects the achievable results in all subsequent periods.

Research and development and industrial engineering are prime examples of this problem.

Fourth, quantity and quality are often inseparable. The distinction between quantity and quality is more easily defined in direct manufacturing than in service industries. Thus, in the former, output can be counted as "good units only," or quantification of both output level and quality level can be reported. In most white-collar work, however, the quality of the output is even more difficult to ascertain than is the quantity.

Fifth, the distinction is not always made between efficiency and effectiveness. Efficiency refers to how well the job is done with respect to the consumption of time, materials, capital, or other resources; effectiveness relates to how well the job accomplishes its stated purpose. In white-collar work, the term effectiveness takes on a slightly different meaning: it is often equated with utilization. A computer programmer may be very efficient at developing programs but may be underutilized by not having enough to do, by being required to do too many unrelated activities (such as attending meetings), or by being assigned work that is not within the range of his or her expertise. In order to be productive, the white-collar worker must be both efficient and effective.

Sixth, white-collar workers, unlike production workers, often are not accustomed to being measured. There is often misunderstanding as to why the measures are being implemented and what will be done with the results. They see a measurement system as an infringement on their rights, and they fear the outcome. They firmly believe their contribution to the firm cannot be measured in quantitative terms, and that to attempt to do so reduces their status to that of a blue-collar worker. It is not surprising that there is often a high level of resistance to the implementation of measures. Nor is it surprising that many unsuccessful attempts to measure white-collar workers can be traced back to inadequate preparation and communication with employees or a failure to involve them in the development of the measures.

GUIDELINES FOR DEVELOPING WHITE-COLLAR PRODUCTIVITY MEASURES

Universal measures for white-collar workers do not exist, nor are there magic formulas for developing them. In the absence of easy solutions, however, it is appropriate to summarize the level of knowledge at this time by outlining seven sequential steps to guide efforts toward developing workable measures of white-collar productivity.

1. **Establish the purpose.** Measures should be developed to fit the circumstances and fill the needs of the organization. For example, a high-growth firm wants to plan future staffing requirements; a divisionalized multi-plant operation needs inter-plant comparisons; one company wants to reduce costs; and another is preparing to implement an incentive pay system based upon productivity improvement. The measurement system for each of these purposes may differ slightly in terms of the variables chosen, the unit of measure, the sophistication and precision of the measure, the method of data gathering, and the frequency of calculation and reporting.

   One should begin with the goals of the firm and, with these in mind, work toward a set of measurements that are congruent with these goals. For example, if high quality is a major corporate goal, the productivity measure should contain a quality dimension; pressure for higher output should not be permitted to lower quality.

The acid test for a productivity measure is to think about the five ways that a ratio can be increased (Figure 1). If each of those changes would achieve the goals of the organization, the measure is perfectly congruent.

2. **Involve people.** The people to be evaluated by the measure should be involved in the process as early as possible. It is often said that the worker knows more about the job than anyone else; this is especially true in white-collar work, where the procedure is less rigid and the output often intangible. Discussions on the purpose of the measures and their ultimate use will begin to allay fears and reduce resistance. The use of a brainstorming technique with a representative sample of white-collar workers often yields creative ideas for measurement.

Most important, if people are involved in the development of the measures and understand their purpose, they will be less likely to try to "bust" the measure. Two examples, one positive and one negative, illustrate the point.

Beech Aircraft needed an output measure to adequately combine the many different sizes and types of aircraft produced. Through group consensus, the unit they chose was "tons of aircraft shipped." If the engineers, designers, and others had blindly maximized that measure, the result would obviously have been counterproductive. But these people knew that the weight of an aircraft is only a reasonable surrogate measure for its size, complexity, and cost. They could work effectively with the measure because they understood why it was being used.

Such was not the case in a clerical department, where management decided to attach counters to typewriters and use keystrokes per hour as a basis for an in-

centive pay system for typists. Employees were not consulted in the design of this system, and the incentive pay created strong pressure for high-volume output. Shortly after implementation, one typist was observed during lunch hour eating a sandwich with one hand and holding down a repeating key with the other.

3. **Determine output measures.** Rather than trying to conceive output/input ratios, a more effective strategy is to determine outputs first, then inputs, and finally form ratios by combining the two. The result is a multitude of possible ratios from which the most relevant can be selected.

For white-collar work, most of the problem in measuring output results from an inability to define it. Time spent on determining the boundaries of the area to be measured and defining its output is time well spent; it makes measurement easier and more relevant. For example, the output of the personnel department can be defined as "trained, qualified employees." Closer examination, however, may reveal that the majority of the output is "information" both internally (providing wage classifications to accounting for payroll) and externally (EEO reports to the federal government). Output measures could include number of people screened, hired, trained, and placed, but they should also include number of information requests fulfilled and number of required reports submitted.

Since output measures for white-collar workers often are difficult to determine directly, surrogate measures are often used. Weight or volume can sometimes be used instead of trying to count number of documents. Number of customers or clients served often is used, and this measure can be applied internally by determining, for example, the number of executives served by a typing pool.

If possible, measure results rather than activities. Producing a report is an activity; providing information for decision making is a result. Sometimes the output of a department—in the case of data processing, for example—can be determined best by surveying the users.

Here are some other suggestions for output measures:

a. Include a quality dimension to lessen the quality vs. quantity problem;

b. Include a timeliness dimension to encourage prompt results and penalize delays; and

c. Do not try to measure every aspect of a white-collar job in quantitative terms; some contributions by white-collar workers can be assessed only through judgmental performance evaluation.

4. **Determine input measures.** White-collar labor may be counted as number of employees, number of hours worked, number of hours at work, number of hours paid, total payroll, total compensation, or a wide variety of schemes for combining dissimilar types and levels of workers. The measurement chosen should fit the job being done. For example, a typist may be measured per hour, but a design engineering department may be measured better as number of full-time employees.

Other inputs—capital, materials, and energy—should be included. Often the measures of these inputs can be derived from a departmental budget.

5. **Form ratios.** If a brainstorming session revealed only four output measures and

four input measures, there are then sixteen possible ratios to choose from. Selection of a meaningful set or family of measures may be based on the following factors:

a. Avoid a second measure that gives no additional information;

b. Select measures for which the data is available or easy to gather;

c. Select measures over which workers have some control;

d. Select measures that are easily understood by those being measured; and

e. Select measures that are compatible with other white-collar functions and with corporate measures (see Case 1, below).

6. **Implement the measures.** A good rule of thumb is to start simple, even if the measures are imperfect. Once the simple measures have become familiar, refinements such as a weighting of different inputs and outputs can be added. The less desirable alternative is to spend months developing a complex measure that only a few understand. While theoretically sound, it may have little impact.

Begin with a "dry run" to monitor the measure before actions are taken. This is a break-in period for people to become accustomed to the measure and to test it for accuracy and reliability.

After the trial period, differentiate between the measure and the standard or norm expected. Changes in the measure may be due to differences in location, season of the year, condition of the economy, or many other factors. Try to avoid overreacting to slight changes in the measure, especially in the early stages. The nature of most white-collar work is highly variable. It is best to aggregate the measure over a large group of interdependent employees and to measure over a long time span.

7. **Revise and refine forever.** Implementing a productivity measurement system is not a one-time project. Build into the system periodic reviews and flexibility so the system can be adapted to changes in product or service mix, technology, organizational goals, work processes, etc.

CASE EXAMPLES OF WHITE-COLLAR PRODUCTIVITY MEASUREMENT

Three case examples will illustrate how an organization can accomplish the task of developing white-collar productivity measures. The cases vary in level of complexity and degree of sophistication.

Case 1: Company X

This case represents a simple process for developing white-collar productivity measures using a top-down approach. It is a composite case, drawing on experiences from a number of different companies and amalgamated into a single example called Company X.

After considerable study of the current literature and experiences of other organizations, top management of Company X— a large divisionalized and diversified organization—decided that six measures of productivity could be applied universally across all divisions and would include both production workers and white-collar workers. A top-level committee, chaired by the recently appointed vice-president of productivity, selected one measure each for capital, materials, and energy productivity and three different measures of labor productivity:

1. Sales (deflated) per plant and equipment replacement value less depreciation;
2. Sales (deflated) per material cost (deflated);
3. Sales (deflated) per unit of energy;
4. Sales (deflated) per employee;
5. Sales (deflated) per total compensation (deflated);
6. Value added per employee.

Each of these ratios can be applied to the total corporation, to a division, to a plant, or to the lowest level at which there is a profit center. Even within a profit center, however, the same numerator (sales) can be compared to the denominator for just one department. For example, division sales of $100 million could be placed in ratio to all 5,000 employees or to the 75 employees in the purchasing department.

Although beneficial in many respects, total reliance on this set of measurements causes several problems:

1. Very large ratios (such as 100 million/75) are very sensitive to small changes in inputs.
2. Purchasing people will argue that they do not directly cause sales. Even if they do their job very well, the measure could still go down if sales fall off. The argument is valid.
3. A decline of the measure indicates a potential problem, but it gives the purchasing manager little guidance as to the nature of the problem or appropriate corrective action. Measures more closely related to purchasing activities are needed.

Consultations with purchasing employees led to the acceptance of total dollars purchased as a measure of output for this department. Later, a second set of measures was implemented using number of purchase orders as the output measure. To preserve consistency with corporate measures, each of the two output measures was compared to each of the five different input measures used at the corporate level (corporate measures 4 and 6 use the same denominator). Attempts to isolate energy usage for the purchasing department proved too difficult, so this measure was dropped.

The result was a set of eight measures using as denominators for the two output measures:

1. Employees in the purchasing department;
2. Total compensation for purchasing employees (deflated);
3. Materials (supplies) used by the purchasing department (deflated cost);
4. Plant and equipment—an allocation for space used and computer time used plus the value of all capital equipment "owned" by the purchasing department.

Once employees become used to working with these basic measures, refinements can be developed. For example, different types of purchase orders or purchase contracts can be weighted differently in the output calculation. Types of refinements depend upon discussion with purchasing employees.

Similar measurement systems are being developed for other white-collar areas within the organization.

Case 2: IBM

In 1977, IBM began to study the problem of measuring white-collar workers and came up with a creative solution. Its technique, known as the Common Staffing System, is designed to provide relative measures of white-collar productivity in a multi-plant environment in order to create awareness, identify areas for improvement, support strategic planning, and provide a basis for rewarding productivity improvement.

IBM identified fourteen functions (such as administration) common to all plants and within each function a number of different activities (such as secretarial services). Each activity was then related to a work cause or indicator bearing a direct functional relationship to the size of the task to be done in that activity. For example, secretarial services are seen as a function of the number of exempt employees at the plant; the more exempt employees, the greater the secretarial task to be done. The underlying assumption is that 100 secretaries in a plant with 1,000 exempt employees are just as productive as 50 secretaries in a plant with 500 exempt employees.

Figure 2 indicates graphically how the system works, using as an example the order entry function. Each location (plant) is plotted as to the gross number of orders and full-time equivalent head count in the order entry department. The diagonal is a simple arithmetic average.

Plant C processed 41.5 orders in the time period using 50.6 employees. If it had been operating as productively as the average

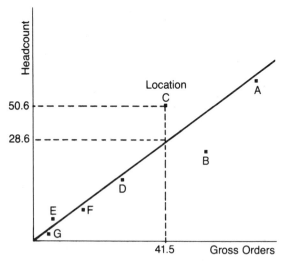

Figure 2.   Order Entry Productivity

IBM plant, only 28.6 employees would have been needed. The excess number of employees represents a potential problem. If it cannot be solved within Plant C, perhaps a visit with the Plant B manager would help, since it is processing more orders with fewer people. It is interesting to note that if Plant C does move downward, the diagonal (average) also shifts downward, and pressure is then applied to those plants now below the line.

An advantage of this system is that in numerical form, activities can be combined to yield relative productivity by fuction, which can be further aggregated to determine the productivity of each plant.

The Common Staffing System works well for IBM, where cross-plant comparisons are possible. IBM counts simplicity and understanding as major advantages of the system. It refrains from using heavy-handed tactics to keep every plant "in line." But properly managed, this measurement system can induce an atmosphere of competition and motivation for improvement.[2]

Case 3: Total Factor Productivity Measurement

The ultimate goal in a productivity measurement system is to combine all four input categories—labor, materials, capital, and energy—into a total firm productivity measurement system that relates productivity to profitability of the firm. The American Productivity Center has developed such a system and implemented it in a number of firms in different industries. As a total system, it includes the measurement of white-collar productivity as well as other human resources and the other factors of production.[3]

The Method. The total factor system uses products or services produced as output compared to each of the four input catego-ries. The basis for the system can be seen in the following equations:

$$\text{Profitability} = \frac{\text{Sales}}{\text{Costs}}$$

$$= \frac{\text{Output Quantities} \times \text{Output Prices}}{\text{Input Quantities} \times \text{Input Prices}}$$

The last term in that equation can be rewritten as two separate ratios:

$$\frac{\text{Output Quantities}}{\text{Input Quantities}} \times \frac{\text{Output Prices}}{\text{Input Prices}}$$

The first ratio is productivity, the physical ratio of output to input. The second ratio is price recovery, the ratio of output prices to the prices the firm pays for various inputs. This leads to the fundamental relationship:

$$\text{Profitability} =$$
$$\text{Productivity} \times \text{Price Recovery}$$

In other words, a firm's profitability derives from productivity—the effective and efficient use of resources—and the ability to pass through input price increases to the customer.

Calculating change ratios between successive periods using price and quantity weighting yields the summary data in Table 1. Note that labor productivity increased by 12 percent (112.0) but apparently wages and salaries increased much more than the prices of the firm's output (price recovery for labor is 81.6). The result of these opposing factors is a downward pressure on profitability. Other resource inputs can be interpreted in the same way, and the totals indicate that overall the firm was more productive but slightly less profitable.

"Labor" in this context includes all human resources. It would be possible, then, to separate this resource into, say, three categories—blue collar, white collar, and managerial (including supervision). The result would be relative productivity, price recovery, and profitability figures for each category.

Table 1.   Total-Firm Performance Measurement

	Value		Performance Indexes		
	Period 1	Period 2	Profit- ability	Produc- tivity	Price Recovery
Output					
Product A	50,000	66,000			
Product B	40,000	33,600			
Total	90,000	99,600			
Input					
Materials	21,200	26,560	88.3	97.8	90.3
Labor	32,000	38,720	91.5	112.0	81.6
Energy	3,000	3,780	87.8	113.6	77.3
Capital	33,800	35,210	106.2	98.1	108.3
Total	90,000	104,270	95.5	103.1	92.7

Productivity of white-collar employees in this system would be defined as a ratio of the total output of the firm (quantities of goods and services produced) to the total hours worked by white-collar employees. Hours would be weighted by wage rates or salaries so that an hour by an employee earning $10 would count the same as two hours by a $5 employee.

If the productivity of white-collar employees were, say, 94 percent, the 6 percent decline would indicate that more white-collar hours were worked per unit of product or service produced. It is then up to the decision makers of the firm to determine if this constitutes a problem. Given different sets of circumstances, any of the following interpretations (or others) is possible:

1. White-collar workers are not doing their job as well as they were.

2. White-collar workers are not being utilized or allocated properly.

3. This is a spurious result; variations within ± 10 percent are normal.

4. This is a business-cycle problem; sales have fallen, but white-collar workers were not laid off in proportion.

5. This is a planned and expected result; the long-term trend is toward a higher proportion of white-collar workers.

6. This is an unfair measure; white-collar workers do not produce the firm's output of goods and services.

7. This is a fair measure; the purpose of this firm is to produce goods and services, and the white-collar workers support that effort.

When this system is used, it can indicate that there is a problem with white-collar workers; but, like other total-firm measures, it provides little guidance for specific corrective action. The next step, therefore, would be to look at specific white-collar measures—such as those described for the purchasing department in Case 1 or the order entry function in Case 2—to isolate the cause of the problem and determine its cure.

Who Should Use the Total Factor System? Not every firm should use a total factor productivity measurement system. It requires reasonably clear definitions of inputs and outputs that can be separated into quantities and prices. It is ideal, therefore, for a large manufacturer, but difficult to apply to a firm doing engineering research on government contracts. It requires a massive amount of calculations, so a computerized and relatively sophisticated cost-accounting system is helpful. Finally, it is a complicated system that is not intuitively obvious at first glance. How quickly employees adjust to this measurement system and understand its nuances depends upon the type of employees and their experience with other sophisticated costing or performance measurement systems.

Firms that have adopted this system find that the new perspective provided by separating productivity from price recovery allows them to manage their resources and costs much more effectively. Many feel that resource management will form the primary basis for survival in the coming decades. For one of the critical resources—the white-collar employee—the effect of this measurement system is just beginning to be felt.

CONCLUSION

Measuring the productivity of white-collar workers is not an easy task, mainly because their output—their contribution to the firm—is difficult to define and count in a meaningful way. The path to white-collar productivity measurement will likely involve first studying the relevant experiences of others[4] and then adopting a strategy and procedure for developing unique measures that reflect the type of work being done and the purpose for which the measures will be used. Successful measurement systems will be developed only by involving the white-collar employees early in the process of developing the measures of their productivity.

18

Productivity and Quality

The aim of any supplier should be to improve quality and to decrease costs to the point where he need not search for customers. Instead, let quality and service be so good that customers plead for his product.
W. EDWARDS DEMING[1]

Our nation is becoming acutely aware of a fundamental problem: The demand for American-made products and services is slipping, partly, if not primarily, because of their relatively low quality. To raise our standard of living, productivity must improve; a critical dimension of productivity is quality. Both managers and employees must place the highest priority on improving the quality of America's products and services, until they are second to none and can meet the needs and expectations of both domestic and foreign customers.

Productivity, as defined earlier, is the amount of products and services produced in relation to the quantity of resources consumed. Seldom is quality included in the definition. Yet, no discussion of productivity can afford to ignore quality, for quantity without quality is meaningless.

Quality is sometimes associated only with manufacturing products. Tools that break, cars that fail to start and appliances that malfunction are all visible evidence of quality problems. Yet quality is an equally important factor in service industries. Errors in bank statements, sloppy paint jobs and incorrect airline reservations are also quality problems. And the costs associated with poor quality can be just as great; consider, for example, the health services industry, where the cost of an error may be a human life. Quality, then, is a critical issue for both goods-producers and service-providers, and in both the private and public sectors.

A DEFINITION OF QUALITY

The term "quality" suffers from some of the same problems as the term "productivity." A "quality" product often means the best—usually the most expensive model in a group of similar products or services. Thus, a Rolls Royce is a "quality" automobile, and the Four Seasons is a "quality" restaurant. For those responsible for the quality of an organization's product or service, however, a much more precise definition is needed. Any number of precise definitions of quality are available. Each reflects different product or service characteristics, measurement techniques and ways of expressing standards.

To be operational, a definition of quality must fall between the everyday understanding of the term and its very specific technical usage. Such a definition must be sufficiently precise to permit measurement, yet sufficiently general to be applied to a wide variety of products and services. The following definition meets these requirements:

> Quality is the degree to which a product or service conforms to a set of predetermined standards related to the characteristics that determine its value in the marketplace and its performance of the function for which it was designed.[2]

This definition of quality meets several key tests. These tests are the various classifications of quality; they are really tests of how generally applicable the definition is.

The first way of classifying quality is to determine whether it is dichotomous or continuous. In statistics, this means determining whether it consists of sampling "attributes" or "variables." Examples of dichotomous characteristics are "good" and "bad," "acceptable" and "unacceptable," "present" and "absent." Continuous characteristics, on the other hand, are those which fall at some point on a scale. For example, a light bulb either works or doesn't work. That characteristic is dichotomous. The intensity of the light from the bulbs that do work, however, is a continuous characteristic, measurable in lumens. Limits on the intensity scale must be set to establish an acceptable range.

The aforementioned definition of quality covers both dichotomous and continuous situations. The degree to which a product or service conforms to a standard may be specified with a yes or no, or with a range of acceptable values.

A second way of classifying quality is to apply it to a specific unit or to a group of units. Our definition covers both applications. In one case, acceptable quality means that a specific unit of product or service meets established criteria. In the other case, a group of units is acceptable if a sufficient percentage of the units pass all quality tests.

Another distinction in quality is between functional and aesthetic attributes. A defect in a functional attribute directly affects the performance of the product or service. A defect in an aesthetic attribute affects such things as appearance, but does not hamper performance of the intended function. For example, a bad valve will affect the function of an automobile, but a bad paint job will not. The definition of quality previously quoted takes both of these factors into account.

A fourth aspect of quality is whether it is measurable or judgmental. Attributes such as size, temperature, voltage, or torque are easily measurable. Standards are therefore set for these measurements and are accurately communicated to the technicians responsible for taking the measurements. Taste, appearance and other subjective characteristics can only be judged by an expert equipped with a personal standard. In a brewery, the brewmaster tastes the beer and makes these judgments. Some characteristics, such as color, are measurable; but a judgmental process may be used to avoid the high cost of precise measurements. In our definition of quality, "standards" and "degree of conformance" may refer to either measurable or judgmental processes.

A final characteristic of quality is the oft-overlooked attribute of timeliness. Work at a construction site, for example, can be stopped by defective material; but it can also be stopped if the material is late in arriving. Frequently, timeliness is associated with services rather than products, but it should be applied to both. A product or service which is not in the right place at the right time is as "defective" as one which is timely but unacceptable. Because time is a continuum, timeliness constitutes another standard for acceptability within this definition of quality.

Each of these quality tests is affected, directly and indirectly, by the motivation and commitment of the organization's human resources.

THE QUALITY-PRODUCTIVITY CONNECTION

Resources of labor, capital, materials, and energy are combined with technical knowledge and managerial know-how to produce products and services for domestic consumption and export. It is a simple economic truth that if we can produce more with the resources we use, we will increase the standard of living, reduce inflation and create the economic strength necessary to ensure sustained high levels of employment. What is not always as evident is that improvements in the quality of products and services can substantially improve productivity and help to reverse the trends that have led to today's weakened economy.

If a process produces substandard products and services, several outcomes are inevitable:

1. Failure to meet customer expectation leads to declining sales, market share, profits, and economies of scale.
2. Defective products must be recalled, returned, replaced, reworked, or scrapped, all of which consume additional resources to meet a cus-

tomer need that should have been met with the original resources used.

3. Poor quality in services leads to many of the same things; loss of sales and market share, as well as the need to find and correct errors, compensate for the inadequate service and perhaps perform the service again in the proper way. Again, the end result is an unnecessary consumption of additional resources.

4. If substandard becomes the norm, the reputation of the organization's products and services is eroded in the minds of the consumer. Whether or not the poor reputation is justified, it is difficult to overcome that negative perception. Far more resources are consumed to reverse a downward trend than to sustain an upward trend.

Each of these results causes resources to be diverted to the detection and correction of poor quality, rather than to the production of additional output that would add to the firm's profits or the nation's wealth. Each of these results is detrimental to productivity. A fundamental principle of all productivity improvement is the simple axiom: "Do it right the first time."

IMPLEMENTING TOTAL QUALITY MANAGEMENT

Quality is a strategic issue. Just as an organization selects strategies in marketing, finance, technology, and other areas, it can choose a quality strategy that permeates all aspects of the business, including the design of products and services, the selection and training of employees, equipment utilization, reward systems, manufacturing processes, and delivery of services. Unfortunately, the quality strategy often is derived indirectly: It is more often determined by a pattern of past operating decisions than by the conscious development of a plan by top management.

Tools and techniques for quality improvement abound: Quality circles, statistical quality control, quality motivation systems, quality measurement techniques, and zero defects are just a few examples. Each can be supported by numerous success stories, yet each has failed in some instances. Perhaps the successes occur because there is so much room for improvement; any attention to quality results in better output. Often, however, the failures happen not because the technique is faulty, but because it is applied on a short-run basis, not as part of an overall strategic approach.

The best American companies do have quality built into their strategic planning. It can be done, it is being done, and it pays substantial dividends to those who are doing it. Ford, TRW, Olin, Westinghouse, B.F. Goodrich, Chrysler, Texas Instruments, American Express, Martin-Marietta, General Dynamics, Fairchild, Motorola, McDonnell Douglas, Armco, and Firestone, as well as government agencies such as NASA and the Department of Defense, are prime cases of organizations that know the importance of quality and systematically build quality into their planning processes, as well as into their products and services.

A PLAN FOR QUALITY IMPROVEMENT

The specifics may differ from one organization to another, and often the details are confidential for competitive reasons. But it is possible to outline a generic plan based on the experiences of these many companies and agencies. The implementation steps would, of course, have to be adapted to the technology, culture and conditions of each organization.

1. Establish quality improvement as a primary business priority, and communicate it to all employees through a carefully worded written policy and set of guidelines.

2. Share information with all employees on the competitive quality position of the company, and on the impact of quality on product acceptance by the customer and the success of the organization.

3. Establish long-term quality goals and objectives that are specific, measurable and consistent with other corporate objectives. Employees should be involved in the development of quality objectives that reflect not only corporate priorities, but customer needs and expectations.

4. Throughout the organization, improve the understanding of advanced quality and productivity techniques, including statistical quality control and other concepts of total quality management.

5. Dedicate the organization to the continuous improvement of quality. Begin with management decisions and actions that communicate by example that quality has a high priority in relation to cost, schedule and short-term pressures that may lead to long-term losses.

6. Conduct regular in-depth quality audits of each of the organization's activities, including products and services, processes, operating systems, plans, and budgets. Audits should generate actions to correct weaknesses, and rewards for superior performance.

A MODEL OF FACTORS AFFECTING QUALITY

To implement the generic plan described above, employees need a general understanding of the factors that affect output quality. The model depicted in Figure 18–1 achieves this purpose.[2] It indicates how human factors interact with the technology of the organization to determine the quality of products and services.

I. **Performance Quality**   II. **Quality Dimensions**   III. **Primary Factors Affecting Quality**

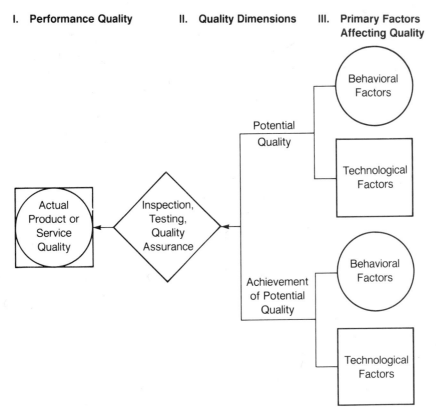

Source: Everett E. Adam, Jr., James C. Hershauer, and William A. Ruch. "Measuring the Quality Dimension of Service Productivity." (Washington, DC: National Science Foundation report number APR76-07140, January, 1978.) © Copyright 1978, Adam, Hershauer, Ruch.

Figure 18–1.   The Behavior/Technology Model of Factors Affecting Quality

Environmental Characteristics and Constraints

Any quality model must fit its environmental context, including important interactions, constraints and limitations, as shown in Figure 18–2. The four basic elements of a business environment—legal/political, economic, technological, and social—have a strong, direct effect on any useful model of quality. The nature of that effect and its relative strength depend upon the particular firm or industry being modeled. For example, quality at a pharmaceutical company like Warner-Lambert may be more constrained by legal than by economic considerations, while at IBM the opposite may be true.

These four environmental characteristic can be further subdivided to provide more clarification. For the quality model presented here, the specific environmental elements and constraints listed in Figure 18–2 are most relevant. These environmental characteristics and constraints must be considered an integral part of the model itself. Attempts to apply the model without due consideration to changing environmental interactions and limitations will severely limit its success.

I. Social Environment
   A. Personal Value Systems
   B. Ethical Considerations
   C. Social Responsibility
   D. Taste and Behavior Patterns
   E. Immediate Community Influence
   F. Greater Community Influence

II. Legal/Political Environment
   A. Regulatory Agencies
   B. National Laws, Local Ordinances and Restrictions
   C. International Considerations
   D. Tax Considerations
   E. Consumer Legislation
   F. Union Agreements

III. Technological Environment
   A. Basic and Applied Research Results
   B. Engineering Knowledge
   C. Management Knowledge
   D. Material/Equipment Innovation
   E. Process Innovation
   F. Product Innovation

IV. Economic Environment
   A. General Economic Conditions
   B. Labor Market Conditions
   C. Vendor Market Conditions
   D. Customer (Competitive) Market Conditions
   E. Inflation

Source: Everett E. Adam, Jr., James C. Hershauer, and William A. Ruch. "Measuring the Quality Dimension of Service Productivity." (Washington, DC: National Science Foundation report number APR76-07140, January, 1978.) © Copyright 1978, Adam, Hershauer, Ruch.

Figure 18–2. Environmental Characteristics and Constraints

Elements of the Model

The Behavior/Technology Model of Factors Affecting Quality begins with a basic dichotomy of quality performance: (1) potential quality, and (2) achievement of that potential (as illustrated in Figure 18–1). Establishing the potential for quality is essentially a design or planning function. It involves making decisions about input factors that affect the capability of the system to produce at a given quality level. In effect, it places an upper limit on the output quality.

Actual quality can be no greater than potential quality, but poor decisions affecting the operation of the system can cause actual quality to fall short of its potential. Quality diagnosis must precede treatment. From a diagnostic point of view, a firm with poor overall quality may be suffering from one of two ills: (1) achievement of a *low* potential, or (2) failure to achieve a *high* potential. Obviously, these ills demand different remedies. If the problem is low potential, the system may need to be redesigned, or perhaps a change in inputs is needed. The problem of failure to achieve a high potential results from a well-designed but improperly managed system. If this is the case, operational policies and decisions should be reviewed and revised.

Between potential and actual quality is the inspection, testing and quality assurance program of the organization. The program's primary function is to monitor the output and pass, reject or screen the product or service to assure conformance to the standard. The responsibilities of diagnosing and correcting quality problems may reside in this unit, at some higher organizational level, or with workers, depending upon the organization's philosophy.

Behavioral factors affecting the potential for quality include the knowledge, skills and attitudes of employees—the potential they bring to the job—which is determined within an organization primarily by its selection, training and reward structures. Technological factors affecting the potential for quality include the product (or service) design, job design, equipment, layout, and raw materials selected by the organization.

Behavioral and technological factors affecting the achievement of potential quality primarily have to do with motivation and organizational procedures—how well the process is managed. Monetary and nonmonetary rewards, communications, and a host of other variables influence the motivation for high-quality performance. And proper adherence to planning, scheduling, control, maintenance, and other policies determines whether the potential is achieved.

Many firms have found that employees can have a significant effect on the potential for quality, and on achieving that potential. Techniques such as quality circles encourage employees to suggest ideas for changing methods or materials in order to improve product and service quality. In total, this model provides a general understanding of quality and traces its origin through the design (potential) and operational (achievement) phases to those behavioral and technological factors which the organization must control to achieve its desired goals.

THE STATUS OF AMERICAN QUALITY

In the 1950s, the phrase "Made in Japan" denoted cheap junk. Today, many of our most sophisticated mechanical and electronic products come from Japan, and these products enjoy a reputation as quality leaders in many industries. By setting national goals for quality improvement and enlisting the help of experts like W. Edwards Deming[3] and J.M. Juran,[4] Japanese firms formed quality circles and employed many other tools and techniques to raise quality to a top priority. Later disciples of the quality doctrine, such as Philip Crosby,[5] had an impact on quality in the United States. It was not until U.S. losses to Japanese products became truly staggering—steel, autos and electronics—that corporate officers became concerned.

At first, many attributed Japanese quality performance to cultural differences, but many examples of a Japanese management system with American workers have arisen to destroy that myth. A truck plant in New Smyrnia, Tennessee, a Honda plant in Marysville, Ohio, and a television plant in Chicago are just a few of the sites where the change to a Japanese management style has produced quality levels equalling or surpassing those in Japan—with the same American workers. Quality is manageable.

Has the quality of U.S. products declined? That question is unanswerable in the absence of universal measures of "quality" that apply to all industries. A few points are clear, however. First, part of the concept of quality is measurable, but another part relates to perceived value, judged by a consumer in relation to an expectation that is impossible to quantify. Second, by any definition many U.S. products have increased in quality. They are more reliable, more durable, and meet standards more consistently than in the past. Third, other U.S. products have actually declined in quality, if one considers the number of failures, warranty and reward costs, product recalls, and the like. Fourth, perhaps the best overall statement is that, in the aggregate, U.S. products have failed to increase in quality as fast as many of our international competitors' products. Finally, even if the statements above are debatable, one thing is clear: There has been a substantial eroding of the quality image of U.S. products in the minds of consumers. However unfair it may seem, if consumers (industrial or household) believe the quality of U.S. products is poor, the actual, verifiable quality level is immaterial. The U.S. will lose sales to foreign competition because of perceived quality differences. The task here is to inform and educate rather than to improve real quality levels.

In 1983, a White House Conference on Productivity was held to solicit expert opinion on how the U.S. should improve productivity.[6] One
input to that conference was a report on quality jointly written by a con-
clave of executives, consultants, government officials, and academics
who had spent months debating quality issues through a computer tele-
conferencing network. An excerpt from that report is relevant here:

> Members of the computer conference discussed many quality
> issues, but among them, three were predominant: awareness,
> corporate leadership, and the relationship of quality to profita-
> bility. Each will be briefly explained.
>
> 1. Quality is a cultural issue. In the role of producer or con-
>   sumer, the shared values concerning quality—sometimes
>   called the "Quality Ethic"—determines the value of quality
>   relative to other characteristics of products and services. In
>   the American consuming public, there is a lack of aware-
>   ness of the seriousness of U.S. quality problems and corpo-
>   rate leadership often subjugates long-term quality improve-
>   ments to the short-term pressures of meeting schedules and
>   reducing costs. Workers read the signals from management
>   and operate accordingly. Significant changes must take
>   place withing the corporation and throughout society to
>   raise the level of awareness, change cultural beliefs, and re-
>   store quality to the priority it deserves.
>
> 2. Corporate leadership in the private sector is the master key
>   to quality improvement. Efforts lacking top management
>   support, commitment, and involvement will be short-lived
>   and of questionable real value. Top-level executives must
>   embrace the concept of total quality management, realizing
>   that every phase of the business affects the quality of the
>   end products. It is insufficient to attempt to control quality
>   at the end of the process; it must be managed from the begin-
>   ning. A long-range commitment to quality incorporated into
>   the strategic planning process of the organization is
>   needed.
>
> 3. Quality and profitability move in the same direction. In
>   most cases, quality can be increased without corresponding
>   decreases in quantity. Thus, quality improvements relate
>   directly to productivity increases. Although quality is not
>   "free," effective expenditures and investments to make
>   quality levels match customer expectations pays dividends
>   in both the short-run and the long-run. These claims can be
>   supported by the experiences of quality leaders in Ameri-
>   can industry.

Managing the quality dimension of an organization is not generally
different from any other aspects of management. It involves the formula-

tion of strategies, setting goals and objectives, developing action plans, implementing plans, and using control systems for monitoring feedback and taking corrective action. If quality is viewed only as a control system, it will never be substantially improved.

SUMMARY

Improvements in quality generally lead to productivity gains. Seldom, if ever, is productivity increased at the expense of quality. Successful firms treat quality as a strategic issue and develop a top-down plan for designing and producing products and services with quality levels that meet the needs and expectations of the market.

SELECTED READINGS OVERVIEW

"Improvement of Quality and Productivity through Action by Management" is by W. Edwards Deming, unquestionably the quality guru of our times. Deming explains his philosophy of the fourteen-point program that has earned him international recognition.

Leonard and Sasser chose the title "The Incline of Quality" (rather than decline) to emphasize the positive outlook they share for quality improvement opportunity in the U.S. They outline their recommendations for managing quality at every stage of the firm, from design of the product to final sale. Managing quality is not easy, they say, but it can be done.

Next Chapter

Quality cuts across many aspects of productivity. For example, measurement systems should include both quantity and quality, as should incentive systems and other motivational techniques. But if *all* aspects of productivity are to be combined in an organization, decision-makers must formulate a strategy, a plan and a program for implementation. Developing a total productivity effort within an organization is the subject of the next chapter.

Review Questions

1. Most quality problems can be traced to a fault in management, rather than to the individual worker. Do you believe this? Why or why not?

2. If the same amount of resources is used to produce the same number of products or services, but the quality of those products or services is higher, is that a productivity improvement?

3. Some people claim that "quality is everybody's job." Do they mean that an office worker can affect, in some way, the quality of the product being produced? What do they mean?

4. Deming focuses on top management's role in improving productivity and quality. In what ways can top management influence quality?

5. We hear so much about the high quality of Japanese products compared to the low quality of American-made goods. According to Leonard and Sasser, how does American quality compare to that of the Japanese?

W. EDWARDS DEMING

Improvement of Quality and Productivity through Action by Management

Management can increase productivity by improving quality.
Dr. Deming's fourteen points show the way.

WHY PRODUCTIVITY INCREASES WITH IMPROVEMENT OF QUALITY

Some simple examples will show how productivity increases with improvement of quality. Other benefits are lower costs, better competitive position, and happier people on the job. It is important to note that a gain in productivity is also a gain in capacity of a production-line.

W. Edwards Deming has been for forty years a consultant in statistical studies, with practice worldwide. He is best known for his work in Japan, which commenced in 1950 and created a revolution in quality and economic production. He is the author of several books on statistical methods and over 150 papers. Dr. Deming is currently working on a book that will elaborate on the fourteen points discussed in this article.

Reprinted, by permission, from *National Productivity Review* (Winter, 1981/82):12–22. All rights reserved.

Best Efforts Are Not Sufficient

"By everyone doing his best."

This is the answer that someone in a meeting volunteered in response to my question, "And how do you go about it to improve quality and productivity?"

It is interesting to note that this answer was wrong—wrong in the sense that best efforts are not sufficient. Best efforts are essential, but unfortunately, best efforts alone will not accomplish the purpose. Everyone is already doing his best. Efforts, to be effective, must move in the right direction. Without guidance, best efforts result in a random walk.

Some Folklore. Folklore has it in America that quality and production are incompatible: that you can not have both. It is either or.

Insist on quality, and you will fall behind in production. Push production and you will find that your quality has suffered.

The fact is that quality is achieved by improvement of the process. Improvement of the process increases uniformity of output of product, reduces mistakes, and reduces waste of manpower, machine-time, and materials.

Reduction of waste transfers man-hours and machine-hours from the manufacture of defectives into the manufacture of additional good product. In effect, the capacity of a production-line is increased. The benefits of better quality through improvement of the process are thus not just better quality, and the long-range improvement of market-position that goes along with it, but greater productivity and much better profit as well. Improved morale of this work force is another gain: they now see that the management is making some effort themselves, and not blaming all faults on the production-workers.

A clear statement of the relationship between quality and productivity comes from my friend Dr. Yoshikasu Tsuda of Rikkyo University in Tokyo, who wrote to me as follows, dated 23 March 1980.

> I have just spent a year in the northern hemisphere, in twenty-three countries, in which I visited many industrial plants, and talked with many industrialists.
>
> In Europe and in America, people are now more interested in cost of quality and in systems of quality-audit. But in Japan, we are keeping very strong interest to improve quality by using statistical methods which you started in your very first visit to Japan. . . . When we improve quality we also improve productivity, just as you told us in 1950 would happen.

A Simple Example. Some simple figures taken from recent experience will illustrate what happens. Defective output of a certain production-line was running along at 11 percent (news to the management). A run-chart of proportion defective day by day over the previous six weeks showed good statistical control of the line as a whole. The main cause of the problem could accordingly only be ascribed to the system. This was also news to the management. The statisticians made the suggestion that possibly the people on the job, and inspectors also, did not understand well enough what kind of work is acceptable and what is not. The manager of the production-line and two supervisors went to work on the matter, and with trial and error came up in seven weeks with better definitions, with examples posted for everyone to see. A new set of data showed the proportion defective to be 5 percent. Cost, zero. Results:

Quality up
Productivity up 6%
Costs down
Profit greatly improved
Capacity of the production line
    increased 6%
Customer happier
Everybody happier

This gain was immediate (seven weeks); cost, zero: same work force, same burden, no investment in new machinery.

This is an example of gain in productivity accomplished by a change in the system, effected by the management, helping people to work smarter, not harder.

Reduction in Cost

Taken from a speech delivered in Rio de Janeiro, March 1981, by William E. Conway, president of the Nashua Corporation.

At Nashua, the first big success took place in March 1980: improvement of quality and reduction of cost in the manufacture of carbonless paper.

Table 1.   Illustrating Gain in Productivity with Improved Quality

Item	Before Improvement 11% Defective	After Improvement 5% Defective
Total cost	100	100
Spent to make good units	89	95
Spent to make defective units	11	5
Average number of good units per unit cost	.89	.95
Proportion of total cost spent to make defectives	.11	.05

Water-based coating that contains various chemicals is applied to a moving web of paper. If the amount of coating is right, the customer will be pleased with a good consistent mark when he uses the paper some months later. The coating-head applied approximately three pounds of dry coating to 3000 square feet of paper at a speed of approximately 1400 linear feet/minute on a web 6-8 feet wide. Technicians took samples of paper and made tests to determine the intensity of the mark. These tests were made on the sample both as it came off the coater and after it was aged in an oven to simulate use by the customer. When test showed the intensity of the mark to be too high or too low, the operator made adjustments that would increase or decrease the amount of coating material. Frequent stops for new settings were a way of life. These stops were costly.

The engineers knew that the average weight of the coating material was too high, but did not know how to lower it without risk of putting on insufficient coating. A new coating-head, to cost $700,000, was under consideration. There would be, besides the cost of $700,000, time lost for installation, and the risk that the new head might not achieve uniformity of coating much better than the equipment in use.

In August 1979, the plant manager decided to utilize the statistical control of quality to study the operation. It was thereby found that the coating-head, if left untouched, was actually in pretty good statistical control at the desired level of 3.0 dry pounds of coating on the paper, plus or minus .4.

Elimination of various special causes, highlighted by points of control, reduced the amount of coating and still maintained good consistent quality.

The coater had by April 1980 settled down to an average of 2.8 pounds per 3000 square feet, varying from 2.4 to 3.2, thereby saving 0.2 pounds per 3000 square feet, or $800,000 per year at present volume and cost levels.

What the operator of the coating-head had been doing, before statistical control was introduced and achieved, was to over-adjust his machine, to put on more coating, or less, reacting to tests of the paper. In doing his best, in accordance with the training and instructions given to him, he was actually doubling the variance of the coating. The control-charts, once in operation, helped him to do a much better job, with less effort. He is happy. His job is easier and more important.

All this was accomplished without making the proposed capital investment of $700,000, which might or might not have improved the process and the quality of the coated paper.

Engineering Innovation.   Statistical control opened the way to engineering innovation. Without statistical control, the process was in unstable chaos, the noise of which would mask the effect of any attempt to bring improvement. Step by step they achieved:

Improvement of the chemical content of the material used for coating, to use less and less coating.

Improvement of the coating-head (without purchase of a new one) to achieve greater and greater uniformity of coating.

Today, only 1.0 pounds of improved coating is used per 3000 square feet of paper. This level is safe, as the variation lies only between .9 and 1.1. Reduction of a tenth of a pound means an annual reduction of $400,000 in the cost of coating.

The reader can do his own arithmetic to compute the annual reduction in cost from the starting point, namely, 3.0 pounds.

Before statistical control was achieved, the engineers had not entertained the thought of improvement of the coating-head. Once statistical control was achieved, it was easy to measure the effect of small changes in the chemistry of the coating and in the coating-head. The next step then became obvious—try to improve the coating and the coating-head, to use less coating with greater and greater uniformity.

Low Quality Means High Cost

A plant was plagued with a huge amount of defective product. "How many people have you on this line for rework of defects made in previous operations?" I asked the manager. He want to the blackboard and put down three people here, four there, etc.—in total, 21 percent of the work force on that line.

Defects are not free. Somebody makes them, and gets paid for making them. On the supposition that it costs as much to correct a defect as to make it in the first place, then 21 percent of his payroll and burden was being spent on rework. In practice, it usually costs more to correct a defect than to make it, so the figure 21 percent is a minimum.

Once the manager saw the magnitude of the problem, and came to the realization that he was paying out good money to make defects as well as to correct them, he found ways to help the people on the line to understand better how to do the job. The cost of rework went down from 21 percent to 9 percent in a space of two months.

Next step: reduce the proportion defective from 9 percent to 0.

From 15 percent to 40 percent of the manufacturer's costs of almost any American product that you buy today is for waste embedded in it—waste of human effort, waste of machine-time, loss of accompanying burden. No wonder that many American products are hard to sell at home or abroad.

American industry (including service-organizations) can no longer tolerate mistakes and defective material at the start nor anywhere along the line, nor equipment out of order.

New Machinery is Not the Answer

Lag in American productivity had been attributed in editorials and in letters in the newspapers to failure to install new machinery and the latest types of automation. Such suggestions make interesting reading and still more interesting writing for people that do not understand problems of production. There is a quicker and surer way, namely, better administration of man and whatever machinery is in use today. Then, after the present problems are conquered, talk about new machinery.

The following paragraph received from a friend in a large manufacturing company will serve as illustration.

This whole program (design and installation of new machines) has led to some unhappy experiences. All these wonderful machines performed their intended functions, on test, but when they were put into operation, they were out of business so much of the time for this and that kind of failure that our overall costs, instead of going down, went up. No one had evaluated the overall probable failure-rates and maintenance. As a result, we were continually caught with stoppages and with not enough spare parts, or with none at all; and with no provision for alternate production-lines.

Comparison between American and Japanese production should take account of some important differences. Japanese manufacturers are already using their machinery to full advantage, not wasting materials, human effort, or machine-time. They have no unemployed people to draw upon for expansion. There are no unemployment agencies in Japan. The Monthly Report on the Labor Force for the United States, in contrast, shows at this writing 7 million unemployed. American industry can expand by drawing upon a supply of labor, a large part of it skilled, experienced, able, and willing to work. The Japanese manufacturer, on the other hand, can expand his production only by use of better machinery or improvement in design. He can not hire more people: there are not any. The fact is that there is only a small amount of automation in Japan. They have been sensible about it.

If I were a banker, I would not lend money for new equipment unless the company that asked for the loan could demonstrate by statistical evidence that they are using their present equipment to full realizable capacity.

Quality Control in Service Industries

Eventually, quality control will assist not only the production of goods and food (the birthplace of modern statistical theory was agriculture) but the service industries as well—hospitals, hotels, transportation, wholesale and retail establishments, perhaps even the U.S. mail. Statistical quality technology has for many years contributed to telecommunications, both in the manufacture of equipment and in service. Statistical quality technology is improving service and lowering costs in the banking business. In fact, one of the most successful applications of statistical methods on a huge scale,

including sample-design and operations, is in the U.S. Census, not only in the decennial Census but in the regular monthly and quarterly surveys of people and of business, an example being the Monthly Report on the Labor Force.

It is interesting to note that some service-industries in Japan have been active in statistical methods from the start, e.g., the Japanese National Railways, Nippon Telegraph and Telephone Corporation, the Tobacco Monopoly of Japan, the Post Office. Department stores have taken up statistical quality control. Takenaka Komuten (architecture and construction) won recognition in 1979 for thoroughgoing improvement of buildings of all types, and for decrease in cost, by studying the needs of the users (in offices, hospitals, factories, hotels) and by reducing the costs of rework in drawings and in the actual construction.

WHAT TOP MANAGEMENT MUST DO

The purpose here is to explain to top management what their job is. No one in management need ask again, "What must we do?" This section serves two purposes: (1) It provides an outline of the obligations of top management; (2) it provides a yardstick by which anyone in the company may measure the performance of the management.

Paper profits, the yardstick by which stockholders and Boards of Directors often measure performance of the president, make no contribution to material living for people anywhere, nor do they improve the competitive position of a company or of American industry. Paper profits do not make bread: improvement of quality and productivity do. They make a contribution to better material living for all people, here and everywhere.

Short-term profits are not an indication of good management. Anybody can pay dividends by deferring maintenance, cutting out research, or acquiring another company.

Ways of doing business with vendors and customers that were good enough in the past must now be revised to meet new requirements of quality and productivity. Drastic revision is required.

What must top management do? As I noted at the beginning of this article, it is not enough for everyone to do his best. Everyone is already doing his best. Efforts, to be effective, must move in the right direction.

It is not enough that top management commit themselves by affirmation for life to quality and productivity. They must know what it is that they are committed to—i.e., what they must do. These obligations can not be delegated. Mere approval is not enough, nor New Year's resolutions. Failure of top management to act on any one of the fourteen points listed ahead will impair efforts on the other thirteen. Quality is everybody's job, but no one else in the company can work effectively on quality and productivity unless it is obvious that the top people are working on their obligations.

"Let me emphasize that where top management does not understand and does not get personally involved, nothing will happen." *(From a speech made by William E. Conway, president of the Nashua Corporation.)*

The 14 Points for Top Management

Here are the obligations of top management. These obligations continue forever: none of them is ever completely fulfilled.

1. *Create constancy of purpose in the company.* The next quarterly dividend is not as important as existence of the company ten, twenty, or thirty years from now.

    a. Innovate. Allocate resources for long-term planning. Plans for the future call for consideration of:

Possible new materials, new service, adaptability, probable cost.

Method of production; possible changes in equipment.

New skills required, and in what number?

Training and retraining of personnel.

Training of supervisors.

Cost of production.

Performance in the hands of the user.

Satisfaction of the user.

One requirement for innovation is faith that there will be a future. Innovation, the foundation of the future, can not thrive unless the top management has declared unshakable policy of quality and productivity. Until this policy can be enthroned as an institution, middle management and everyone in the company will be skeptical about the effectiveness of their best efforts.

The consumer is the most important part of the production-line. Japanese management took on a new turn in 1950 by putting the consumer first.

    b. Put resources into

    research
    education

    c. Put resources into maintenance of equipment, furniture, and fixtures, new aids to production in the office and in the plant.

It is a mistake to suppose that statistical quality technology applied to products and services offered at present can with certainty keep an organization solvent and ahead of competition. It is possible and in fact fairly easy for an organization to go broke making the wrong product or offering the wrong type of service, even though everyone in the organization performs with devotion, employing statistical methods and every other aid that can boost efficiency.

Innovation generates new and improved services. An example is new and different kinds of plans for savings in banks, financial service offered by credit agencies, Meals on Wheels, day care in out-patient clinics. Leasing of automobiles is an example of service that did not exist years ago. Express Mail is a new service of the U.S. post office (equivalent to what a postage stamp would accomplish in Japan or in Europe). Mailgram by Western Union is another. Intercity and intracity messenger service is a growth industry, thriving on the delinquency of the U.S. post office. Services can and do have problems of mistakes, costly correction of mistakes, and consequent impairment of productivity associated with mistakes.

2. *Learn the new philosophy.* We are in a new economic age. We can no longer live with commonly accepted levels of mistakes, defects, material not suited to the job, people on the job that do not know what the job is and are afraid to ask; handling damage; failure of management to understand the problems of the product in use; antiquated methods of training on the job; inadequate and ineffective supervision.

Acceptance of defective materials and poor workmanship as a way of life is one of the most effective roadblocks to better quality and productivity. The Japanese faced it in 1950. Unreliable and nonuniform were kind words for the usual quality of incoming materials. Japanese management took aim at the problem and in time reduced it to a level never before achieved. American industry today faces the same problem. The road that Japanese manufacturers paved would be a good one for American management to copy.

3. *Require statistical evidence of process control along with incoming critical parts.* There is no other way for your supplier nor for you to know the quality that he is delivering, and no other way to achieve best economy and productivity. Purchasing managers must learn the statistical control of quality. They must proceed under the new philosophy: the right quality characteristics must be built in, without dependence on inspection. Statistical control of the process provides the only way for the supplier to build quality in, and the only way to provide to the purchaser evidence of uniform repeatable quality and of cost of production. There is no other way for your supplier to predict his costs.

Most purchasing managers do not know at present which of their suppliers are qualified. One of the first steps for purchasing managers to take is to learn enough about the statistical control of quality to be able to assess the qualifications of a supplier, to talk to him in statistical language. Don't expect him to carry on the conversation in French if you don't know French.

Some suppliers are already qualified and are conforming to this recommendation. Some follow their product through the purchaser's production-lines to learn what problems turn up, and to take action, so far as possible, to avoid problems in the future.

One company may have influence over hundreds of suppliers and over many other purchasers.

Vendors sometimes furnish reams of figures, such as records of adjustment, input of materials (2 kg. chromium added at 1000 h). Figures like these are as worthless to the buyer as they are to the vendor.

The manager of an important plant, which belongs to one of America's largest corporations, lamented to me that he spends most of his time defending good vendors. A typical problem runs like this. A vendor has not for years sent to him a defective item, and his price is right. Some other manufacturer underbids this vendor by a few cents and captures the business. The corporate purchasing department awards the business to him because of price. The plant manager can not take a chance, and must spend many hours and days arguing for the vendor that knows his business.

4. *The requirement of statistical evidence of process control in the purchase of critical parts will mean in most companies drastic reduction in the number of vendors that they deal with.*

Companies will have to consider the cost of having two or more vendors for the same item. A company will be lucky to find one vendor that can supply statistical evidence of quality. A second vendor, if he can not furnish statistical evidence of his quality, will have higher costs than the one that can furnish the evidence, or he will have to chisel on his quality, or go out of business. A man that does not know his costs nor whether he can repeat tomorrow today's distribution of quality is not a good business partner.

We can no longer leave quality and price to the forces of competition—not in today's requirements for uniformity and reliability. Price has no meaning without a measure of the quality being purchased. Without adequate measures of quality, business drifts to the lowest bidder, low quality and high cost being the inevitable result. American industry and the U.S. government are being rooked by rules that award business to the lowest bidder.

The purchasing managers of a company are not at fault for giving business to the lowest bidder, nor for seeking

more bids in the hope of getting a still better price. This is their mandate. Only the top management can change their direction.

Purchasing managers have a new job. It will take five years for them to learn it.

Example. An American manufacturer of automobiles may today have 2500 vendors. A Japanese automobile company may have 380. Rapid and determined reduction of the number of vendors in American manufacturing is already under way.

Made by Company A — 1000 pieces all meet specifications

Made by Company B — 1000 pieces all meet specifications

Problem 1. You wish to purchase 1000 pieces of xbae. You make calls to two companies A and B that offer the product, and you explain the specifications. Each company submits 1000 pieces of xbae—all good, so the companies claim. You satisfy yourself, by your own inspection, that indeed all 2000 pieces meet your specifications. Which lot would you buy? Toss a coin?

Before you make a snap judgment, it might be wise to consider the fact that your specifications may not tell the whole story. There may be characteristics that are important to have in the pieces that you will buy, but not covered in your specifications. There may be other characteristics that you would wish to avoid, and your specifications may not protect you. Company A has been in the business and provides continuing evidence of process control. There may be persuasive arguments in favor of Company A. One must remember that the distribution of the important quality-characteristics of the 1000 parts made by Company A will be more uniform than the distribution of those made by Company B. Uniformity is nearly always important. If the price offered by Company B is the lower of the two, it would be wise to inquire how this could be, as Company A's costs will be lower. Perhaps Company B can offer a bargain. He may have had a cancellation from another customer, and has the material on hand.

Problem 2. Now, we come to a totally different problem. You plan to purchase 1000 pieces of xbae every week. Your requirements in this problem point definitely to selection of Company A. The distribution of the important quality-characteristic of the xbae is predictable. It will be steady week after week. If the distribution falls within your specifications, you can eliminate inspection of incoming parts except for routine observations and comparisons for identification. You will know from the control charts that came along with the product, far better than any amount of inspection can tell you, what the distribution of quality is and what it will be.

If a tail of the distribution falls beyond your specifications, you will require 100 percent inspection.

Another advantage of statistical control is a better price and better quality than Company B can give. If Company B offers you a better price, it is because he knows not what his costs are. He may chisel you on quality, or he may go out of business trying to meet the price that he quoted, and leave you stranded.

You may decide, for protection, to give some of the business to Company B, just to have a second vendor to fall back on in case Company A suffers some hard luck. This is your privilege. You will have to pay the extra cost that Company B must charge you if he stays in business

Company A

X̄-chart for a critical quality-characteristic. If the specifications are at A, A, the output of Company A requires no inspection. Problems will arise (see text) if a specification were at C.

Company B

About Company B we know nothing.

and delivers the quantity that you require, and you will have to inspect the material that comes from him. Whether it is wise to do business with Company B could be questioned, but you now have a rational basis for your decision.

In free enterprise you have a right to make a wrong decision, and to get beat up for it.

A request for bids usually contains a clause to say that quality may be considered along with price. That is, the award will not necessarily be given to the lowest bidder. Such a clause is meaningless without a yardstick by which to measure quality. The buyer and his purchasing manager usually lack such a yardstick. They are candidates for plunder by the lowest bidder.

A flagrant example is a request for professional help, to be awarded to the lowest bidder. Example (actual, from a government agency):

For delivery and evaluation of a course on management for quality control for supervisors...

An order will be issued on the basis of price.

5. *Use statistical methods to find out, in any trouble spot, what are the sources of trouble.* Which are local faults? Which faults belong to the system? Put responsibility where it belongs. Do not rely on judgment. Judgment always gives the wrong answer on the question of where the fault lies. Statistical methods make use of knowledge of the subject matter where it can be effective, but supplant it where it is a hazard.

   Constantly improve the system. This obligation never ceases. Most people in management do not understand that the system (their responsibility) is everything not under the governance of a local group.

6. *Institute modern aids to training on the job.* Training must be totally reconstructed. Statistical methods must be used to learn when training is finished, and when further training would be beneficial. A man once hired and trained, and in statistical control of his own work, whether it be satisfactory or not, can do no better. Further training can not help him. If his work is not satisfactory, move him to another job, and provide better training there.

7. *Improve supervision.* Supervision belongs to the system, and is the responsibility of management.

   Foremen must have more time to help people on the job.

   Statistical methods are vital as aid to the foreman and to the production manager to indicate where fault lies: is it local, or is it in the system?

The usual procedure by which the foreman calls the worker's attention to every defect, or to half of them, may be wrong—is certainly wrong in most organizations—and defeats the purpose of supervision.

Supervision in large segments of American industry is deplorable. For example, a common practice is to look at the production records of people on the job, supervisors, managers, and to deliberately take aim at the lowest 5 percent or the lowest 10 percent. Claims of results from this procedure are nothing but reinvention of the Hawthorne effect. The ultimate result is frustration and demoralization of the organization.

8. *Drive out fear.* Most people on a job, and even people in management positions, do not understand what the job is, nor what is right or wrong. Moreover, it is not clear to them how to find out. Many of them are afraid to ask questions or to report trouble. The economic loss from fear is appalling. It is necessary, for better quality and productivity, that people feel secure. *Se* comes from Latin, meaning without, *cure* means fear or care. Secure means without fear, not afraid to express ideas, not afraid to ask questions, not afraid to ask for further instructions, not afraid to report equipment out of order, nor material that is unsuited to the purpose, poor light, or other working conditions that impair quality and production.

   Another related aspect of fear is inability to serve the best interests of the company through necessity to satisfy specified rules, or to satisfy a production quota, or to cut costs by some specified amount.

   One common result of fear is seen in inspection. An inspector records incorrectly the result of an inspection for fear of overdrawing the quota of allowable defectives of the work force.

9. *Break down barriers between departments.* People in research, design, purchase of materials, sales, receipt of incoming materials, must learn about the problems encountered with various materials and specifications in production and assembly. Otherwise, there will be losses in production from necessity for rework and from attempts to use materials unsuited to the purpose. Why not spend time in the factory, see problems, and hear about them?

I only recently saw a losing game, 40 percent defective output, the basic cause of which was that the sales department and the design department had put their heads together and come through with a style whose tolerances were beyond the economic capability of the process. This lack of coordination helps a plant to become a nonprofit organization.

In another instance, the man in charge of procurement of materials, in attendance at the seminars, declared that he has no problems with procurement, as he accepts only perfect materials. (Chuckled I to myself, "That's the way to do it.") Next day, in one of his plants, a superintendent showed to me two pieces of an item from two different suppliers, same item number, both beautifully made, both met the specifications, yet they were sufficiently different for one to be usable, the other usable only with costly rework, a heavy loss to the plant. The superintendent was charged with 20,000 of each one.

Both pieces satisfied the specifications. Both suppliers had fulfilled their contracts. The explanation lay in specifications that were incomplete and unsuited to the requirements of manufac-

ture, approved by the man that had no problems. There was no provision for a report on material used in desperation. It seems that difficulties like this bring forth solace in such remarks as:

> This is the kind of problem that we see any day in this business.
>
> or
>
> Our competitors are having the same kind of problem.

What would some people do without their competitors? Surely one responsibility of management in production is to provide help in such difficulties, and not leave a plant manager in a state of such utter hopelessness.

Purchasing managers must learn that specifications of incoming materials do not tell the whole story. What problems does the material encounter in production? It is necessary to follow a sample of materials through the whole production process to learn about the problems encountered, and onward to the consumer's problems.

10. *Eliminate numerical goals, slogans, pictures, posters, urging people to increase productivity, sign their work as an autograph, etc., so often plastered everywhere in the plant.* ZERO DEFECTS is an example. Posters and slogans like these never helped anyone to do a better job. Numerical goals even have a negative effect through frustration. These devices are management's lazy way out. They indicate desperation and incompetence of management. There is a better way.

11. *Look carefully at work-standards.* Do they take account of quality, or only numbers? Do they help anyone to do a better job? Work standards are costing the country as much loss as poor materials and mistakes.

Any day in hundreds of factories, men stand around the last hour or two of the day, waiting for the whistle to blow. They have completed their quotas for the day: they may do no more work, and they can not go home. Is this good for the competitive position of American industry? Ask these men. They are unhappy doing nothing. They would rather work.

12. *Institute a massive training program for employees in simple but powerful statistical methods.* Thousands of people must learn rudimentary statistical methods. One in 500 must spend the necessary ten years to become a statistician. This training will be a costly affair.

13. *Institute a vigorous program for retraining people in new skills.* The program should keep up with changes in model, style, materials, methods, and, if advantageous, new machinery.

14. *Create a structure in top management that will push every day on the above thirteen points.* Make maximum use of statistical knowledge and talent in your company. Top management will require guidance from an experienced consultant, but the consultant can not take on obligations that only the management can carry out.

Action Required

The first step is for management to understand what their job is—the fourteen points. The next step is to get into motion on them. Quality and productivity are everybody's job, but top management must lead. Until and unless top management establish constancy of purpose and make it possible for everyone in the company to work without fear for the company and not just to please someone, efforts of other people in the company, however brilliant be the fires that they start, can only be transitory.

How soon? When? A long thorny road lies ahead in American industry—ten to thirty years—to settle down to an accepted competitive position. This position may be second place, maybe fourth. Small gains will be visible within a few weeks after a company mobilizes for quality, but sweeping improvement over the whole company will take a long time, and will continue forever. Unmistakable advances will be obvious within five years, more in ten. Management must learn the new economics: likewise government regulatory agencies, and they may require thirty years. Meanwhile, American industry will continue to suffer under the supposition that competition is the secret to better quality and service, and to lower costs.

Products that have been the backbone of American industry may in time decline to secondary importance. New products and new technology may ascend to top place. Agriculture may move up further in foreign trade.

Tangible results from each of the fourteen points will not all be visible at the same time. Perhaps the best candidate for quickest results is to supplant work-standards (No. 11) with statistical aids to the worker and to supervision. No one knows what productivity can be achieved with statistical methods that help people to accomplish more by working smarter, not harder.

A close second for quick results would be to start to drive out fear (No. 8), to help people to feel secure to find out about the job and about the product, and unafraid to report trouble with equipment and with incoming materials. Once top management takes hold in earnest, this goal might be achieved with 50 percent success, and with powerful economic results, within two or three years. Continuation of effort will bring further success.

A close third, and a winner, would be to break down barriers between departments (No. 9).

Survival of the fittest. Companies that adopt constancy of purpose for quality and productivity, and go about it with intelligence, have a chance to survive. Others have not. Charles Darwin's law of survival of the fittest, and that the unfit do not survive, holds in free enterprise as well as in nature's selections.

FRANK S. LEONARD
W. EARL SASSER

The Incline of Quality

NO LONGER JUST AN AFTERTHOUGHT, THE MANAGEMENT OF PRODUCT QUALITY DETERMINES MARKET SUCCESS

There was a time when engineers designed products, manufacturing people built them, quality personnel inspected them as they came off the line, and marketers sold them. If a problem existed, manufacturing was expected to correct it, to makes things "right." Quality was not an overall approach to doing business but an after-the-fact measurement of production success in statistical terms: so many defects per thousand units, so many deviations from the specs, so high or low a rate of failure in the field. And managing quality was the responsibility of a handful of low-ranking, not very well respected measurement takers in each company. As the authors suggest, because a demonstrated edge in quality has immense strategic value today, that archaic view of things is no longer tolerable. Managing quality well requires attention to the quality-related implications of every decision at every stage of the product development continuum—from design to sales. And it requires careful identification of the most effective levers for improving the quality of each product line. Adopting this changed perspective on what it means to manage quality well is, of course, not easy, but it can be done. In the face of stiff foreign competition, companies that choose not to make the effort are preparing the way for their own demise.

Mr. Leonard is a management educator, consultant, and researcher whose current interests are directed toward the strategic management of manufacturing and quality. At present he is involved in several major projects with large American industrial corporations.

Mr. Sasser is professor of business administration at the Harvard Business School. He specializes in the management of operations, teaches in the Advanced Management Program, and serves as faculty chairman of the summer executive program, Manufacturing in Corporate Strategy.

Reprinted, by permission, from *Harvard Business Review* 60, No. 5 (September-October 1982):163–171. All rights reserved.

Many consumer advocates, government bureaucrats, management consultants, business writers, and even business executives are now convinced that "Made in Japan" has replaced "Made in the USA" as a label guaranteeing qualtiy. In fact, however, this assumption of a decline in the quality of American goods and services is dead wrong. On an absolute scale, their quality has never been higher—witness, for example, the television sets produced by RCA and Zenith, the computers built by Digital Equipment Corporation and IBM, the jeans made by Levi Strauss and Wrangler, and the telephone service provided by AT&T.

Why, then, this widely shared perception of a quality decline? For one thing, the foreign competitors that have taken market share away from domestic producers have largely based their attack not on the poor quality of American goods and services but on the superiority of their own. These competitors, mostly Japanese but also European manufacturers like Volkswagen and Philips, have for 20 years relentlessly pursued quality improvement as an integral part of a national strategy to build an export economy.

In particular, the Japanese determined to sell worldwide products of comparable or higher quality than those of their competitors—and at the same or lower prices. In the past, American companies competed against each other for the U.S. mass market and left the top end open to expensive, high-performance imports (Mercedes cars, Omega and Seiko watches, Nikon and Hasselblad cameras) and the low end to cheap, low-quality imports. Today, however, many American manufacturers see the Japanese as their most serious competitors for both consumer and industrial markets. General Motors and Ford watch Toyota carefully; Caterpillar keeps a close eye on Komatsu; IBM follows Fujitsu's Facom subsidiary with great interest; and RCA monitors Sony's every move.

The success of Japan's export strategy has changed the basis of competition in both American and world markets. Quality has become a major strategic variable in the battle for market share. But this is not the whole story. The perception of a decline in the quality of American goods and services stems not only from Japanese manufacturing successes but also from increased demand for quality products. In our opinion, several crucial developments have effected this change in the nature of demand:

1. Rates of inflation have dramatically increased. Consumers are more attracted by durable products with long useful lives than by disposable items.
2. Energy costs have skyrocketed. Consumers are shifting to energy-efficient goods and services.
3. With rising repair and maintenance costs, consumers are increasingly concerned about warranties and frequency-of-repair records.

Manufacturers in Europe and especially in Japan have adjusted to these conditions faster than U.S. producers and, as a result, have been able to capitalize in the United States on their advantage in product quality. These competitive pressures have, in turn, made themselves felt at each stage of the production chain. As demand for more reliable, durable, and energy-efficient products increases, so does the demand for high-quality components, parts, and materials.

CHANGING NATURE OF QUALITY MANAGEMENT

Given the new strategic importance of quality, American managers must start asking themselves some tough, perhaps embarrassing questions. What are the rules by which the competitive quality game must now be played? Are American managers sensitive to those rules? And to compete more effectively, do they have to change the ways they manage?

To track managers' responses, we conducted extensive field research and interviews in more than 30 corporations and administered a questionnaire on quality to a group of manufacturing executives from many of the *Fortune* "500" companies. The perceived sources of quality problems broke down as follows:

Workmanship/work force	21.5%
Materials/purchases of parts	20.6
Maintenance of process equipment	11.3
Design of process equipment	7.3
Product design	12.2
Control systems	13.9
Management	5.9
Other	7.0
Total	100.0%

(On further discussion, it became clear that most of the executives thought management a much larger cause of the problem than the 6% response indicates; for, as they correctly pointed out, management is responsible for all the other causes listed.)

Even taking these figures as a rough approximation, we can see that the seeds of quality problems are widely distributed and that no simple attention to one or another aspect of a company's operations can nip them all in the bud. Only a determined effort to manage quality throughout an organization promises to be competitively effective, but such an effort requires fundamental changes in the way American executives address the whole quality issue. Happily, we have begun to see two such adjustments take shape.

The first of these, at the general management level, is a shift from an inspection-oriented, manufacturing-focused approach toward a defect-prevention and company-focused strategy. Even at companies like the major pharmaceutical producers, which have traditionally paid close attention to quality, the management of quality is broadening and placing new responsibilities and duties on general managers. *Exhibit I* suggests the implications of this change for organizational structures and management systems and styles.

The second is a change from quality personnel being seen as technically and problem oriented, defensive, powerless, responsible for inspecting and "fixing" failures, and not well respected to their being seen as managerially focused, planning and prevention oriented, assertive, powerful, responsible for preventing failures, and well respected. Quality managers, then, are growing out of their narrow administrator or technician roles and becoming cross-functional.

By no means have both these changes been widely accepted. Few of the 30 companies we studied have taken them beyond the idea stage. We are, however, encountering more and more companies that are willing to experiment with different approaches. But where are these changes leading?

New Direction

To better understand the thrust of these changes, consider an industrial company's product introduction cycle, presented in *Exhibit II*. As new products develop, they generally pass through four separate but overlapping stages: product design, process design, manufacturing-operations, and sales-service. At each stage various kinds of people, possessing varying personalities and technical skills and operating under diverse constraints and priorities, make decisions that cumulatively affect the quality of the final product.

Exhibit I. Changes in American Manufacturers' Views of
Quality for the General Manager

Past:	Present:
General managers are not evaluated on quality.	Quality performance is part of general managers' review.
Manufacturing focus is on product quality.	Organizational focus is on process quality.
Historical dilution and budgeting hunches made on the cost of quality (i.e., scrap, rejects, returns).	Cost of quality measurement made by systems and reporting.
Functional view of quality predominates.	Matrix view of quality predominates.
Quality is quality department's responsibility.	Quality is the management's responsibility.
Quality is predominantly blue-collar related (direct labor).	Quality is predominantly white-collar related (indirect, overt, and staff).
Defects should be hidden.	Defects should be highlighted.
Problems lead to blame, excuses, justifications.	Problems lead to cooperative solutions.

The old way of managing quality occurred almost entirely at the manufacturing-operations stage. Here was where quality problems surfaced—machine maladjustment, operator error, poor training, inadequate supervision, poor sampling techniques, insufficient controls, mechanical malfunctions, and lack of preventive maintenance. And since this was the stage at which assembled products first came together, here was where these problems had to be "solved." Although manufacturing people might complain about "this awful piece of equipment" or be convinced that "this crazy design can't possibly be made," it was their job to "make it right with what you have, now!" Quality people merely culled the output to indicate when it had passed the appropriate tests and was acceptable.

By no means should we paint manufacturing managers as the quality saints, or martyrs, of the industrial era. They not only inherit problems caused elsewhere; they themselves make decisions that influence

Exhibit II. Quality Impact: The Product Design-to-Sales Continuum (Some Types of Decisions that Affect Quality)

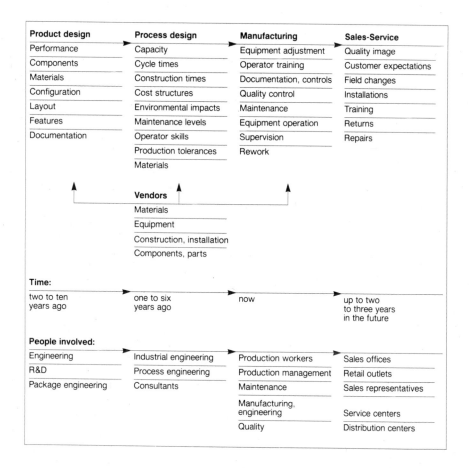

Product design	Process design	Manufacturing	Sales-Service
Performance	Capacity	Equipment adjustment	Quality image
Components	Cycle times	Operator training	Customer expectations
Materials	Construction times	Documentation, controls	Field changes
Configuration	Cost structures	Quality control	Installations
Layout	Environmental impacts	Maintenance	Training
Features	Maintenance levels	Equipment operation	Returns
Documentation	Operator skills	Supervision	Repairs
	Production tolerances	Rework	
	Materials		

Vendors

Materials
Equipment
Construction, installation
Components, parts

Time:

two to ten years ago	one to six years ago	now	up to two to three years in the future

People involved:

Engineering	Industrial engineering	Production workers	Sales offices
R&D	Process engineering	Production management	Retail outlets
Package engineering	Consultants	Maintenance	Sales representatives
		Manufacturing, engineering	Service centers
		Quality	Distribution centers

product quality. In practice, however, they have often had most of the responsibility for—but not much control over—quality, which was often determined by the many actions and decisions taken prior to the manufacturing stage. Even the advances in statistical quality control did not make the placement of responsibility more equitable. These techniques were primarily used to pinpoint what manufacturing could do to solve the problems it was blithely expected to solve.

Under the traditional scheme of product development, product design engineers would first come up with a prototype or model, which of course embodied a number of explicit and implicit decisions on performance, components, materials, configuration, layout, and product features. Process design engineers would then either create a new process from top to bottom or modify the existing process and equipment. Whatever course the designers followed inevitably contained further decisions—about cycle times, capacities, construction times, cost structures (both fixed and variable), environmental impacts, maintenance levels, downtime, necessary operator skills, production tolerance levels, and substitutability of raw materials. At both these stages, there was little understanding of how these decisions affected final product quality.

After the manufacturing department tried its best to make the product as designed on the equipment as designed, sales-service managers would be responsible for selling, installing, and servicing the product. Influenced by such market-related factors as irate customers, commissions and bonuses, competitive market practices, and geographical separation between the manufacturing and design stages, sales-service managers naturally had a lot to do with setting expectations about quality and performance levels, determining product image, and establishing obligations concerning product failure.

Note, again, that responsibility for—but not control over—quality seldom ventured out of the manufacturing stage. The reasons for this are many:

1. Differences in the kind of people who work at the various stages of development.

2. Geographic distances (product R&D is usually located at corporate headquarters, process design at divisional or corporate headquarters, and sales-service at local field offices).

3. Time lags (it often takes years to move a product from design to market).

4. The sheer amount of information needed to trace quality problems in a complex organizational setting.

5. Ways in which managers are trained to solve functional, as opposed to systems, problems.

6. An organization's understanding of who has the power to make inviolable decisions.

Shifting competitive realities and expanding world markets have, however, created increasing pressures for change. Managers are at last recognizing the importance of upstream design decisions and downstream sales-service decisions in establishing product quality. Moreover, many companies are now demanding overall responsibility for quality from their general managers who, along with quality managers at all organizational levels, continually review the entire product-process-operations-service continuum to discover the most significant areas for quality improvement.

In these developments we can see the long-overdue emergence of a systematic approach to quality management. That is, the realization is finally taking hold that the design and production of high-quality goods and services is not just a quality manager's technical problem on the factory floor but a general manager's problem throughout the entire corporation. It leads everywhere and touches everything.

As one executive put it, "Of all our quality problems, about 20% are in manufacturing, 40% are with our vendors, and 40% are in design aspects. I had to start with the 20% in manufacturing, though, to find the others. I had to work backward to solve the problems. Rather than send staff engineers into the plants, I started sending manufacturing people back to the labs."

The companies most successful in changing their approach to quality management use an incremental approach, working backward and forward through the various stages of product development as well as outward to include vendors and customers. Managers are starting to recognize that getting their vendors to provide a consistently reliable supply of parts and materials is of critical importance to their own quality programs. They are also asking customers to participate in various product specification programs.

LEVERS FOR QUALITY

An electronics company specializing in hand-assembled customer-monitoring equipment devoted two-thirds of its design staff to redesigning the product so that it could be assembled and tested more easily. Then it put all its operators and assemblers through a series of training courses tied to the new design.

A specialty chemicals outfit solved a lot of its contamination problems by installing piping that could be easily flushed and cleaned and by changing to a valving system that could not be incorrectly aligned.

A fast-food chain altered its raw material purchases so that all grill items were of the same thickness. As a result, heat settings never had to be changed, which equalized cooking time for all grill items—and thus eliminated overcooking and under-cooking.

A major credit card company, besieged by increasing cost and competitive pressures, redesigned information and process flows to solve customer service problems and curtail processing errors.

As these examples show, a company can improve its product or service quality in many ways. Like most managerial choices, deciding what to do and how to do it depends on many things—for example, the product in question, the relevant process technology, the company's strategy, and its corporate culture. In each instance, the first managerial task is to identify the appropriate quality levers—that is, the exact location, cause, and pattern of distribution of each problem and the best way to resolve it.

The next step—selecting the right quality levers—requires management to evaluate the expected return from different ways of spending its time, effort, and money. Many American managers operate under the mis-taken assumption that improved quality is always costly. Most such managers are detection and rework oriented. "I only add units of inspection and rework," as they would say, "as long as the expected benefits from higher quality are greater than the expected costs of additional inspection and rework. To spend more is foolish." There is nothing wrong with their reasoning; the problem is that they often stop there. The real challenge to management is to discover investments that will yield higher quality at lower unit costs.

Such an investment might, for instance, take the form of adopting a more participative style of management as a way to change workers' attitudes toward quality. Or it might entail the purchase and installation of a numerically controlled milling machine or even a CAD/CAM system. To choose investments with the best return, managers must first ask:

Where on the product-development continuum is the most improvement possible? What are the quality levers?

Do any of these levers require prior action? For example, must operators be trained before new equipment is installed?

What improvements will follow the exercise of each quality lever? How much will quality increase and unit costs decrease?

What is the cost of exercising any one quality lever?

Identifying the different quality levers, understanding their effect on quality and costs, and determining both the investment needed to apply each lever and its overall payback in product quality—these must be the first order of business for all quality-conscious managers.

A Handle on Productivity

When evaluating the various levers on quality, do not overlook the close connection between quality and productivity. Among the examples we have seen or studied:

One company's installation of a new "clean room" reduced the contaminants on the printed circuit boards and boosted output by almost 35%.

Elimination of rework stations at one television factory forced assembly workers to find and solve their own quality mistakes. These adjustments resulted in an increased production rate per hour of direct labor and in the elimination of thousands of dollars of rework costs.

One company using precision assembly equipment designed components that would not fit together unless they were "right." This arrangement raised production rates as well as distribution efficiencies. It also improved the productivity of the sales force since it no longer had to spend time collecting, boxing, and replacing returned components.

Our experience shows that efforts to raise quality almost always result in heightened productivity. We have found that the reverse also holds true: efforts to raise productivity usually pay off in better quality. Traditional wisdom, however, has viewed quality and productivity as being inversely related. For years mangers have believed that, for instance, because it requires more time to do a high-quality job, increases in quality can only come at the expense of productivity. This is simply not true.

Better quality does not automatically mean more machine time, more labor hours, greater skill levels, or higher-cost materials. More often than not, better quality can mean better productivity—but *only* if managers establish a new relationship between quality and cost.

In practice, though, American managers have often taken their product development systems as a given, in which productivity or quality could be improved, but not both.

They have treated the decision before them as an "either/or" choice: either reduce costs or raise quality. What our research suggests—and what Japanese producers have known for the last 20 years—is that the relevant decision is an "and/also" choice: both productivity and quality can be enhanced if managers are willing to make systemic adjustments to their operations and not just to this or that particular detail.

What is needed, then, is a revolution in the way managers think about the continuum of product development activities. By this we do not mean a shift only in their conventional approaches to quality problems but also in their readiness to make the long-term investments in people and equipment necessary to make better products less expensive.

GETTING THERE FROM HERE

None of the dozens of quality programs now being marketed, written up, discussed, debated, and hailed as cure-alls can be universally successful in solving quality problems. These problems and the levers for correcting them differ too much from company to company and even from product to product or location to location. Further, since both problems and solutions are often systemic, any technique that focuses on a single activity or function is suspect. The failure rate of the quality programs that have been sanctimoniously shoved down middle management's throat by well-intentioned or merely desperate executives argues strongly that techniques rarely solve complex organizational problems.

For a quality program to have a real chance of success, it must have:

Top Management's Strategic Support. Top management must be openly and actively committed to improving quality as a strategic necessity. Quality considerations must figure centrally in their strategic planning, in the trade-offs they make among demands for resources, in the risks they are willing to take, in the kinds of corporate performance they find acceptable (off-spec product is off-spec product—whether it is the beginning or the end of the month), and in their evaluation and reward systems for subordinates. In sum, top management should treat quality as an integral part of all corporate review processes.

Organizational Analysis. Managers need to improve their ability to analyze the decisions, work flows, and organizational structures that influence product quality and to anticipate the downstream effects of quality-related decisions. When the analysis is completed, a manager should be able to identify confidently the relevant quality levers for each product in question.

Responsibility. Far too often American companies have treated quality as a functional responsibility when, in fact, it should be an organizational goal. Because most quality problems are caused by managerial action or inaction, the challenge of improving product quality should be the task not only of workers and quality departments but of everyone in an organization, regardless of the person's authority or responsibility.

Open Participation. The successful efforts to improve product quality that we observed shared some form of participative management that cut across traditional organizational boundaries (functional, geographic, social, and temporal). This participation was open and fluid (and thus was not confined to certain times of the week, certain people, certain topics, or certain situations).

Although we do not like the current American addiction to quality circles, we certainly do see that many such programs have made positive contributions. What

works best, however, is not the slickly packaged QC concepts now being peddled by a number of consultants but rather the simple formation of groups of people who share information, interests, skills, resources, and a stake in solving all quality problems. In fact, the most effective groups we encountered acted more like quality "webs" than circles. That is, they did not limit themselves to officially designated quality problems but traced them back to issues in design or whatever. Whether these groups were informal and spontaneous or formal and planned, they accomplished two things: they opened up and helped integrate their parent organizations.

Quality Calculus. Managers should also reexamine the calculus by which they measure, estimate, and account for quality-related decisions. Most of the measurement and performance systems we encountered simply ignored quality issues. Those that did explicitly consider quality were often biased toward short-term measures of performance and thus grossly understated the costs of not getting quality right the first time. Many capital appropriation processes, for example, downplayed the benefits of improved quality as "probabilistic," "subjective," or "qualitative." These benefits are indeed long term and highly uncertain (an increase in market share, say, or customer loyalty; a reduction in warranty costs), but any movement to a lower-cost, higher-quality position requires at some point a leap of faith. What a good quality measurement system should do is provide a diving board.

Quality Assurance and Control. To say that quality is a managerial responsibility does not deny the need for quality professionals. Well-run quality departments—when used as organizational consultants to prevent defects, monitor testing, supervise process checks, and assist line managers in establishing good quality practices and procedures—can provide a valuable perspective. They should not, however, become involved in the direct implementation of activities that fall under line management's discretion.

The tendency to build empires, to waste energy justifying the exercise of professional knowledge, to become mesmerized by intricate and complicated systems, and to confuse corporate with functional goals is a real and present danger. The proper size of the quality function, its place in the organization, the breadth of its mission, and the nature of its role in the strategic process are all issues that a general manager has to confront. The burning question is, "How can the quality area best perform its service role to the line operations?" And the answer, simply put, depends on the situation.

Training and Development.   To produce significant results, efforts to improve quality require an enormous and sustained investment of energy and resources. Ideally, every person in the company should accept responsibility for product quality; employees, suppliers, and even customers require special training to achieve this goal. One of the remarkable things about the Japanese is the amount of training that they have provided for years at all levels of their organizations. Good quality-related training extends far beyond what we normally think of as "quality topics" (statistical methods, sampling techniques, or inspection procedures) and includes equipment operation, advanced milling techniques, preventive maintenance, setups and breakdowns, gauging, computer-aided design, and interpersonal communication.

American managers must think more broadly about this kind of long-term investment in training and encourage it in areas where the leverage on quality is greatest. Of course, as improvements are made, as new people come into the organization and others are promoted, and as product and process technologies change, the nature of the training will itself shift.

Personal Attributes.   As Philip Crosby, author of *Quality Is Free,* (McGraw-Hill, 1979), has argued, improving quality is not a motivational consideration but a matter of managerial style or personal leadership attributes. Quality-oriented managers tend to share a number of characteristics.

The best managers we observed paid attention to detail and were never caught short because of incomplete planning. They always kept track of problems and items that might turn into problems; were conscientious in their striving for quality and had the dignity and integrity to set—and then hold to—high personal standards; never sought personal glory at the expense of product quality; had the personal resolve to keep up their arduous efforts; were modest enough to acknowledge that their achievements were always the work of many; managed with gentleness and finesse—not with a sledgehammer; were trustworthy so that their employees, suppliers, and customers had complete confidence in them.

By no means is this list exhaustive, nor can any of these attributes substitute for deep technical knowledge or administrative ability. We simply mean to suggest that America's difficulties in competing on quality grounds may, to some extent, be a function of the character of its managers. In the battle for industrial survival, managers with good instincts in adversarial situations have usually come out on top. When management battles the worker, suppliers attempt to outwit customers, engineering departments make life miserable for manufacturing departments, and business and government officials distrust every move made by the other, it is these managers who are most in their element. But are their personal characteristics suitable for the competitive environment of the future? We think not—and we hope not.

A FINAL WORD

Most observers of American business would have entitled this article "The Decline of Quality." We have not. Doomsayers have proclaimed that the quality gap between the United States and Japan signals the end of America's dominance of world markets. We have not. Admittedly, many American companies have lost world market share in the last decade, but their vital signs remain strong. The steps we have outlined can make them even stronger.

A number of U.S. companies have already made tremendous progress in improving their competitive positions by discovering that higher quality and lower costs can be achieved through prudent investments in people, product design, and process improvement. The keystone of each of these success stories is that managers understand the systemic nature of quality and make a commitment to improving the quality of their company's products. The more we observe, the more firmly we are convinced that quality improvement is the most fruitful path to higher productivity and competitive success.

WORKMANSHIP*

The instinct of workmanship, on the other hand, occupies the interest with practical expedients, ways and means, devices and contrivances of efficiency and economy, proficiency, creative work and technological mastery of facts. Much of the functional content of the instinct of workmanship is a proclivity for taking pains.

The best or most finished outcome of this disposition is not had under stress of great excitement or under extreme urgency from any of the instinctive propensities with which its work is associated or whose ends it serves.

It shows at its best, both in the individual workman's technological efficiency and in the growth of technological proficiency and insight in the community at large, under circumstances of moderate exigence, where there is work in hand and more of it in sight, since it is initially a disposition to do the next thing and do it as well as may be; whereas when interest falls off unduly through failure of provocation from the instinctive dispositions that afford an end to which to work, the stimulus to workmanship is likely to fail, and the outcome is as likely to be an endless fabrication of meaningless details and much ado about nothing.

On the other hand, in seasons of great stress, when the call to any one or more of the instinctive lines of conduct is urgent beyond measure, there is likely to result a crudity of technique and presently a loss of proficiency and technological mastery. . . .

The sense of workmanship is also peculiarly subject to bias. It does not commonly, or normally, work to an independent, creative end of its own, but is rather concerned with the ways and means whereby instinctively given purposes are to be accomplished. According, therefore, as one or another of the instinctive dispositions is predominant in the community's scheme of life or in the individual's everyday interest, the habitual trend of the sense of workmanship will be bent to one or another line of proficiency and technological mastery.

By cumulative habituation a bias of this character may come to have very substantial consequences for the range and scope of technological knowledge, the state of the industrial arts, and for the rate and direction of growth in workmanlike ideals.

---

*From Thorstein Veblen, *The Instinct of Workmanship and the State of the Industrial Arts*, 1914.

PART SEVEN

Productivity Systems

19

Productivity and Systems Applications

*Being competitive is not just one thing. It involves
productivity, quality of work life, skills training,
compensation, cost reduction, capital investment, marketing,
production, and so on. Granted, each of those things is
important. But industrial competitiveness is, above all, a
package that encompasses everything we do at every
organizational level, from the chairman to the hourly worker.*

RUBEN F. METTLER[1]

Previous chapters have focused on elements of the productivity puzzle, each critically important in its own respect. Yet the operating manager must weave all of these concepts together into a program that is complete, consistent and operational. The program must fit the culture of the company, it must fit the firm's goals and objectives, and it must work—that is, it must increase productivity. This is not an easy task, but the list of companies with successful, ongoing productivity programs continues to grow: TRW, Westinghouse, Ford, General Motors, Control Data, and dozens of others.

Productivity "program" is a misnomer, as most productivity managers are quick to point out. The term "program" implies a concerted effort to solve a specific problem and produce a desired outcome by a specified time. But productivity improvement is a never-ending process. It has always been a goal, explicit or implicit, for all organizations; and there is no upper limit for productivity improvement. The task of the manager, therefore, is to build consciousness of productivity into the very way in which the organization operates.

WHY HAVE A PRODUCTIVITY
IMPROVEMENT EFFORT?

Productivity was defined in Chapter 1 as the effective utilization of resources: labor, capital, materials, and energy. Firms that improve productivity will survive. Those that fail to do so will no longer exist; they will
be replaced by more productive firms. Like the Red Queen in *Alice in
Wonderland*, if they run, they stay in the same place; they must run twice
as fast to get ahead.

Survival means meeting and beating the competition, both domestic
and foreign. Lessons learned in the automobile industry clearly indicate
that potential competitors are always waiting in the wings—sometimes in
the most unlikely places.

Success breeds complacency, and that may be one of the most serious
threats faced by business today. Successful firms tend to lock onto the
strategy that got them there and rigidly adhere to it long after environmental conditions have changed and mounds of evidence exist to show
that the strategy no longer works.

Survival through productivity improvement means different things
to different industries. For automobile firms, it means becoming more responsive to customer needs and more flexible in production processes. In
health care, it means better organization and utilization of resources to
control costs without sacrificing the quality or comprehensiveness of the
service. In electronics, it means trying to keep up with the explosive pace
of technological change while maintaining a cost-effective system. In
steel and other basic industries, it means automating: perhaps replacing
perfectly good but inefficient plants with new processes that can meet
foreign competition. But the common thread among all of these examples
is people. Each system is composed of people who are experts in some aspect of the business. The system designed to improve productivity must
therefore be one that is people-centered, one that not only harnesses energy of people, but elicits ideas that improve the entire process.

Improved productivity, as Chapter 1 explains, forms the basis for
many, if not all, desirable social and economic goals: stable prices, full
employment, high quality of work life, and a rising standard of living.

DEVELOPING A PRODUCTIVE
ORGANIZATION

Begin with the belief that productivity can be managed. The way resources are designed, combined and controlled can be improved so that it
is possible to produce more with less. Then develop a long-range strategic
plan to achieve productivity improvement. According to John Belcher,
staff vice president of the American Productivity Center, the strategy
should begin with a productivity policy statement that gives a sense of direction and addresses issues such as these:

A meaningful definition of productivity;

The importance of productivity performance;

The relationship between productivity and quality of work life;

The role of productivity measurement;

A commitment to human resources strategies to address productivity;

The need to approach productivity as an organizational change effort rather than a "program."[2]

Many companies do precisely what Belcher suggests, but each may take a different approach. TRW, for example, publishes and distributes a statement of company purpose, fundamental objectives and principal goals and strategies. Ruben Mettler, chairman of the board, stated that "it has been our practice periodically to reexamine and reevaluate our established objectives, goals, and strategies. We make modifications where called for, and where we believe our present course is right, we reaffirm it."[3] This document, in turn, gives guidance for the development of more specific plans and programs at operating levels and helps assure a coordinated effort with the same corporate direction. (For more detail, see the article by Ruch and Werther at the end of this chapter.)

Beatrice Foods Company called their program "Uncommon People, Uncommon Goals" and selected the theme "Working smarter...together" to reflect the philosophy that underlies the Beatrice management style. In an effort to increase awareness of productivity, Beatrice published and distributed thousands of booklets explaining why productivity is important to the country as well as to Beatrice, and outlining everyone's role. One booklet says in part:

> Beatrice can say, "We need to improve our productivity." But it's the Beatrice employee who knows how to do it. He's the one who can come up with an idea for using a piece of equipment that could free his hands for a more useful function. She's the one who knows if she can save time by eliminating a hand movement in the assembly of parts. You might already know of a way of organizing the workplace to make the job easier, simpler. Your job. Your program. It's as simple as that.[4]

The productivity policy statement educates employees, raises their level of awareness, and sets the tone for what is to follow: a concerted, coordinated effort to improve productivity through the implementation of one or more approaches and techniques, custom-designed to fit the organization.

If the company is large and diversified, a decentralized effort, with different techniques used in different divisions, would probably be best. One might find quality circles in one plant, a suggestion system in another, heavy reliance on financial incentives in a third, and in a fourth, a number of programs combined under a quality of work life umbrella. In a smaller, less diversified company, however, the effort might more closely reflect the personal philosophy and management style of the owner or CEO.

The nature of the productivity improvement effort is, in some ways, analogous to a personal physical fitness program. First, the goals and objectives must be determined. In physical fitness, the goal of losing weight would lead to a different program than the goal of reducing stress; in productivity improvement, the goal of reducing cost would lead to a different program than the goal of increasing market share.

Second, a number of factors must be combined; no factor can be ignored. In physical fitness, these include diet, exercise and rest. In productivity improvement, they include assets, employee involvement, measurement, and rewards. (See the reading by Belcher at the end of Chapter 3 for a good discussion of the elements involved.)

In both physical fitness and productivity improvement, thousands of specific techniques are available. The set of techniques chosen in each case should be those that accomplish the objectives and match the preferences of those involved.

Finally, the contention could be made that *everyone* is in a physical fitness "program" in the sense that decisions made with respect to diet, exercise and the like will affect physical fitness whether the decisions are made by conscious, informed choice, by habit, or by whim. There is no way to avoid the effect. Some people have an organized, comprehensive physical fitness program based on valid knowledge, and they follow it with enviable self-discipline. Some individuals, on the other hand, are absorbed in one technique with fervor (usually with little benefit), while still others appear to have no conscious program at all.

So it is with companies. All make decisions that affect their rate of productivity, but some are more organized, informed and disciplined than others. In both physical fitness and productivity improvement, those with the better program are more likely to survive.

FACTORS AFFECTING THE SUCCESS OF A PRODUCTIVITY IMPROVEMENT EFFORT

Top Management Commitment

Each organization must design a productivity improvement effort to fit its own people and process, yet some common factors contribute greatly to success or failure across a wide spectrum of companies. Paramount among these is top management commitment. True commitment, in this case, means more than just permission to experiment with new techniques or half-hearted endorsement of plans and procedures. It means that productivity must be a high priority and that top management decisions and actions reflect this. Commitment means backing productivity efforts with sufficient authority and funds to allow them to develop over time and yield visible results. If others in the organization view the productivity effort as a short-lived drive or as the "program of the month," it will have little chance of success. Only when they see that top management is willing to commit time and resources, and make reasonable trade-off decisions with schedules and short-run profit, will they themselves take the productivity effort seriously.

Involve All Employees

All members and all layers of the organization should be involved in the process of productivity improvement as early as possible. If the program is fully designed by a task force and simply announced to the employees as an accomplished fact, it will become "their" program. Involving employees will likely result in a better-designed program; even more important, it will build a sense of commitment to and ownership of the new program. It becomes "our" program (and, therefore, "We will make it work").

Many companies recognize the role that workers play in productivity and so involve them, or their representatives, early in the process of developing a productivity improvement plan. And first-line supervisors, because of the key role they play, are involved in the design and implementation of the plan.

Too often, however, the middle layers of management are forgotten in the planning stages. Failure to involve middle management breeds distrust, fear of loss of responsibility, and other misunderstandings. An essential communication link between top management and the implementation of the program may be lost or considerably distorted.

The union is another vital constituent group that should be involved in the productivity planning process as early as possible. As legal representatives of the workers, the union is responsible for assuring that workers are not exploited, that the labor contract is not violated, and that employees receive fair and equitable treatment as well as compensation. It is natural for union leaders to resist a plan they had no part in developing, and no opportunity to understand. Early participation by the union serves to reduce or remove resistance.

Awareness

Most employees (workers, supervisors and managers) are keenly aware of the importance of controlling costs, schedules and quality, but less aware of the importance of productivity in assuring success for the organization. In fact, there are myriad misconceptions concerning how productivity is improved and the effects of such improvements.

The initial task—often the primary task—in productivity programs is to raise the level of productivity awareness among all employees. This means giving productivity the right perspective and priority in relation to cost, schedule, quality, profit, and other organizational measures. It means dispelling myths and misconceptions. Sometimes education and training can correct false information. Sometimes corporate policy can remove misconceptions, such as the belief that productivity improvement leads to layoffs.

Other Factors

Certainly dozens of other critical factors could be listed: training, reward structures, and measurement systems, to name just a few. The models presented in Chapter 3 demonstrate that productivity is a complex phenomenon influenced by many factors. Any of these factors can be the critical point if it is seriously deficient.

The reasons for the failure of some productivity efforts (sometimes after a remarkably high degree of success in the short run) generally are the same factors that, if properly handled, might have led to success. Goodman, writing for the *National Productivity Review*, lists the following primary reasons for the failure of productivity programs:

1. Commitment: including initial commitment and recommitment.
2. Training process: including initial training, retraining and training new members.
3. Reward process: including types of rewards, linking rewards and behavior, and problems of inequity.
4. Diffusion process: spreading the productivity effort throughout the organization.
5. Feedback and correction: maintaining the productivity improvement effort.[5]

With the multitude of factors that influence productivity and the importance of having an organized effort toward improvement, it is not surprising that many organizations have "put someone in charge" of coordinating the effort.

THE CHIEF PRODUCTIVITY OFFICER

Many organizations, such as Westinghouse, General Motors, Honeywell, TRW, and Bank of America, have implemented formal productivity efforts. These formal efforts often involve considerable change, as well as the creation of one or more new positions with titles such as productivity coordinator, productivity administrator or vice president of productivity. The format of the productivity improvement program differs significantly from one organization to another; hence the duties, responsibilities and hierarchical level of the productivity manager also differ. Textbooks are of little help in prescribing or describing this position. The idea of having a manager whose sole responsibility is to assure that the resources of the organization are combined in a productive way is so new that one must rely on the initial efforts of path-finding companies and learn from their successes and failures.

Generally reporting to the chief executive officer, chief operating officer or executive vice president, this corporate-level position may carry the title of vice president, director or manager. In the future, this position may be called the chief productivity officer (CPO).

The chief productivity officer's job, in a nutshell, is to manage the productivity effort (and it can be managed). Of course, every manager—certainly every line manager—is responsible for controlling the inputs and outputs of the process being managed. It is clear from past records of performance, however, that this objective is not always achieved. Problems of poor measures, ill-focused goals, misunderstandings, and lack of knowledge, among other things, may prevent a manager from guiding his or her unit toward an optimal contribution to the firm's overall productivity.[6]

SUMMARY

Productivity improvement requires a systems approach within the organization, beginning with top management's commitment and involving all employees. Each organization may custom-design its approach to fit its unique circumstances. Many firms have established a chief productivity officer position to coordinate efforts toward long-term productivity improvement.

SELECTED READINGS OVERVIEW

"Productivity Strategies at TRW" is an in-depth look at how a very large, diversified corporation used a productivity strategy to develop an integrated approach for all of its divisions. Ruch and Werther cover the organization, training programs and organizational assessment, then show how it all fits in with their strategic approach.

Next Chapter

The next and final chapter focuses on the information needed to maintain and enhance productivity improvement within the organization. The ceaseless information explosion can be harnessed with advanced technology and creative information systems, such as computer networks and conferencing. Of all resources, information may prove the most critical in the coming decades.

Review Questions

1. Of all the factors affecting the success or failure of the productivity improvement effort, top management commitment is the most critical. Explain why this is true.

2. Why should the union be involved in the early planning and development stages of the productivity improvement effort?

3. The CPO may be the most likely person to be promoted to the presidency of the company in the future. Give several reasons why this may or may not be true.

4. Would you expect productivity programs in different companies to be quite similar or quite different? Explain.

5. Explain why Ruch and Werther claim that the TRW productivity improvement program is strategy-driven.

WILLIAM A. RUCH
WILLIAM B. WERTHER, JR.

Productivity Strategies at TRW

At TRW, productivity improvement efforts are permanently integrated into the management process to secure long-term results.

As TRW enters the 1980s, we face worldwide a rapidly changing and increasingly complex social, economic, technological and political environment. The effects of these changes and complexities on the societies in which we function and their institutions, including business, are and will continue to be profound and pervasive. TRW's success will depend in large part on how well we understand these dynamic forces, influence them in constructive ways and adapt to them in a manner beneficial to the company and its constituents.[1]

This quote from a TRW in-house publication indicates top management's concern about TRW and its future. But TRW has less reason to be concerned about survival than most companies. True, profits were down slightly in 1982, but in a time of severe recession marked by record levels of business failures and massive cutbacks in many primary industries, TRW would be judged highly successful by almost any measure. Why, then, the concern? Why not just continue doing what has been successful in the past?

TRW has operationalized what many simply give lip service to: the principle that present success is a function of past planning. However, what worked in the past is not necessarily what will work in the future. TRW is a well-planned company. Top-level decision makers establish a mission, objectives, goals, strategies, plans, and programs, and these are communicated throughout the company to drive decisions and actions at all levels of a massive and diversified corporation. But, perhaps most importantly, TRW's management recognizes that to merely repeat its past formulas for success will not work in a turbulent environment.

One thrust of the planning process at TRW is productivity improvement. Unlike some companies that seek a quick fix for current lagging productivity or become enamored of one technique for curing all ills, TRW has built productivity into its strategic planning process because it has recognized the pervasive, long-run implications involved. TRW is taking a broad, proactive, and long-term view of productivity improvement.

Reprinted, by permission, from *National Productivity Review* (Spring 1983):109–125.

Often the periodic literature contains thumbnail sketches of productivity efforts in organizations, enough to inform but not enough to guide and direct one who seeks to gain a complete picture of the scope of the effort, the details of the elements involved, the time and timing of phases, and, perhaps most importantly, the positioning of the productivity effort relative to other major strategic issues of the firm. Our purpose in this article is to provide enough detail on each of these aspects of the TRW planning process so that an informed reader can gain an appreciation for the depth and breadth of a fully integrated productivity improvement effort.

In no way is this intended to be an ideal model; in fact, it is a case example of how one company has arrived where it is and the direction it intends to go. Anyone who seeks to duplicate this plan is likely to fail; what works for TRW will not necessarily work for others. Yet there is much to be learned from studying TRW's approach and using it to gain preliminary ideas about the development of a productivity improvement effort customized to fit the culture of one's own organization.

We will first sketch the history of TRW from its birth to its present status as a megacorporation and describe its present structure. Second, since objectives, goals, and strategies are explicitly defined and communicated within TRW, we will outline TRW's plan for the 80s with particular emphasis on how productivity fits in the overall scheme. Next, we will describe how TRW has begun to implement its productivity strategy through a variety of programs, organizational changes, educational efforts, and communications. The five-year plan for 1983-87 provides a picture of the continuation of present efforts. Finally, we will outline the implications of the TRW productivity effort for other organizations in the decade of the 80s and beyond.

TRW IN THE TWENTIETH CENTURY

On January 2, 1901, five men pooled $2,500 to create the Cleveland Cap Screw Company and opened a plant with twenty-nine employees to produce "hexagon and square head cap screws of superior quality, irregular and large heads, a speciality fillister screw, and coupling bolts and studs."[2] Today, on that same site stands a piston manufacturing plant. But it is just a small part of the corporation, which now employs almost 100,000 employees at over 300 locations in twenty-seven countries.

Always a company based on developing new technologies and applying them to new industries, it began making valves for what was then a very young automobile industry. Following further innovations in the design and manufacturing of valves, the company was renamed Thompson Products Company in 1926 and was soon the leading valve producer in the country. Remaining on the leading edge of technology, the company pioneered the development of valves for airplane engines that helped the Allies win World War I. The famous Thompson Trophy races were initiated as proving grounds for new technical ideas that brought faster air speeds and safer transportation. By the end of World War II, sales hit $100 million. At this time, company management saw the need to become an international corporation and began investing in foreign companies.

In the postwar period, it was a natural step for the company to enter the field of military electronics and missiles. The Ramo-Wooldridge Corporation's technical expertise enabled it to win government contracts in 1953 for the early missile development programs, while Thompson provided the financial backing. In 1958, the firms merged to form TRW. The union proved highly successful, and the company whose engine valves once helped Lindbergh cross the Atlantic was now sending spacecraft to the moon, Mars, Jupiter, and Saturn.

Back in the early 1950s, when TRW was a small, growing automotive and aircraft components manufacturer, a dozen or so of its top executives would gather annually at Chairman Fred Crawford's Vermont farm to set long-range goals and strategies.[3] They would review the company's performance, look at factors affecting business, and ask themselves the question: What should TRW be? By 1980 TRW had become a multinational, highly diversified megacorporation. Sales of $5 billion, net earnings of $200 million, assets of $3 billion, nearly 100,000 employees, and subsidiaries in twenty-seven countries qualify it as large by any standard.

The basic structure of TRW is outlined in Figure 1.

The Silverado Conference

Ruben F. Mettler, an aeronautical engineer, became executive vice-president of TRW's Space Technology Laboratory following the 1958 merger. He assumed his present position of chairman of the board and chief executive officer in 1977. Mettler, perhaps more than any single executive, launched TRW into one of the most extensive productivity improvement efforts among major U.S. firms.

Mettler has continued the tradition of face-to-face planning and strategy meetings,

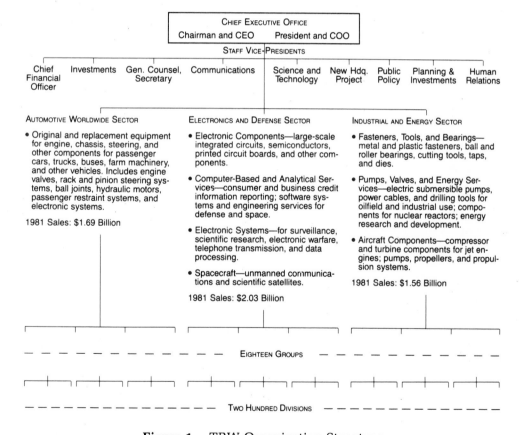

Figure 1. TRW Organization Structure

even though the company has grown twentyfold since its early days. In September 1981, the meeting site was the Silverado conference center in northern California. Attending was a diverse group of TRW professionals: engineers in dozens of disciplines, scientists, marketing and financial experts, lawyers, economists, communications specialists, and production managers seasoned in every aspect of TRW's business from spacecraft, turbine engine blades, and automotive valves to semiconductors, microelectronic chips, oilfield pumps, and information services.

The year prior to the Silverado conference, Mettler's office issued a key guide book, "TRW and the 80s." It outlined corporate purpose, fundamental objectives, and goals and strategies to be pursued during the 1980s. It was distributed to all employees and members of its direct and indirect constituent groups.

Based on the precepts in "TRW and the 80s," the Silverado conference discussed priority projects. Critical to TRW's productivity effort, the conference, according to the vice-president of productivity, "solidified the commitment and helped clarify it through reports of success stories and examples."

The guidebook is a concise statement of top management's consensus about TRW's future and how it expects to get there. It carries with it a top management commitment, but the responsibility for developing specific programs and methods to achieve the objectives outlined in the guidebook are delegated to the lowest level possible.

Three statements from the introduction to "TRW and the 80s" set the tone for the description of objectives, goals, and strategies in the next section.

> In presenting [our] revised financial goals, we want to be certain they are considered in the context of all of our objectives and principal goals, financial and nonfinancial,

quantitative and qualitative. For it is only in the fabric of the integrated whole that they can be viewed meaningfully.

We intend to use this general statement in developing programs designed to help achieve company-wide goals, strategies and programs for operating units and staff functions.

We intend this statement to serve as the basis for the development of additional documents which will be used internally and externally in more detailed communication with our constituent groups. These documents will help explain what we stand for, what we hope to achieve and how we feel about our responsibilities. In the midst of the continuing public discussion of the role of large corporations, our communication of these points will permit public scrutiny of the principles by which we operate. Such communication will also encourage the kind of two-way communication which ...in turn, will help shape our actions and those of our constituents.[4]

OBJECTIVES, GOALS, AND STRATEGIES AT TRW

In TRW's terms a fundamental objective is a statement, often broad and general, that serves as a guide for decisions and actions as well as setting parameters or limits for more specific objectives and goals formulated in operating divisions. Each objective is supported by one or more goals that may be quantitative or qualitative. They serve as controlling standards by which the performance of the total corporation can be judged. Supporting each goal is a set of strategies intended as guides for the development of specific plans and programs designed to fit the culture and technology of the division where they are applied.

The four fundamental objectives set forth in "TRW and the 80s" are shown in Figure 2. Since these objectives are central to understanding TRW's approach to productivity improvement, each will be reviewed.

Figure 2.

TRW's Fundamental Objectives

1. TRW seeks to adhere to the highest standards of conduct in all that it does.

2. TRW seeks to achieve superior performance as an economic unit, with special emphasis on high-quality products and services.

3. TRW seeks to achieve high quality in its internal operations with special focus on its many relationships with employees.

4. TRW seeks to augment its principal social contributions—those resulting from its economic performance and internal operations—by participation in a wide range of community activities and communication programs.

Ethics and Social Responsibilities

One objective states: "TRW seeks to adhere to the highest standards of conduct in all that it does." It is supported by only one goal, which asserts an intention to operate according to the highest legal and ethical standards. The strategies for achieving this emphasize integrity and fairness in dealing with all constituents both in the U.S. and in foreign nations. They also stipulate audits to assure compliance and disciplinary proceedings against individual violators. It is clear that no compromise is possible on this objective; it is, in fact, an attempt to establish one aspect of the corporate culture.

Another objective asserts: "TRW seeks to augment its principal social contributions—those resulting from its economic performance and internal operations—by participation in a wide range of community activities and communication programs." In effect, TRW expects all of its employees to be good citizens who are active in their professions and communities. Unlike many organizations, TRW even encourages participation in political processes. In an era when much lip service is given to corporate social responsibility, TRW seeks to play a constructive role in the community. The fact that senior executives regularly spend 10-15 percent of their time in such activities indicates that this objective is taken seriously at TRW.

Economic Performance and Employee Relations

Two other objectives strike at the heart of financial performance and internal operations. One states: "TRW seeks to achieve superior performance as an economic unit, with special emphasis on high-quality products and services." This objective is supported by seven goals summarized as:

1. Financial performance creating superior relative investment value and steady growth;

2. High-quality products and services at competitive prices;

3. Market strength worldwide;

4. Optimum product, market, and geographic diversification;

5. Effective use of management and technological innovation;

6. Maximum productivity at all levels; and

7. Effective use of resources available from outside the company.

In goal 6, productivity for the first time emerges in the hierarchy of objectives as one of the major thrusts for internal operations. Maximum productivity in this context is defined as the proper use of capital, material, technology, and people. Recognizing that achievement of this goal will play a major part in the achievement of many of the other goals, the following principal productivity strategies were subsumed under goal 6:

a. Keep abreast of developing techniques for measuring and increasing productivity and use new technology and management innovation effectively to improve the efficiency of our operations;

b. Improve our product design, manufacturing engineering and quality control techniques;

c. Make capital expenditures directed toward the most efficient use of our facilities and toward improving our manufacturing and design systems and techniques;

d. Engage in effective cost reduction programs at all levels of the company;

e. Design job assignments and our work environment with an understanding and awareness of the importance of fostering productivity;

f. Promote effective two-way communication between employees at all levels to understand better the problems and concerns that affect productivity;

g. Maintain challenging, achievable and measurable productivity objectives for all employees;

h. Communicate our productivity objectives to employees and make them the subject of regular and meaningful review; and

i. Employ programs that will motivate employees to produce products and provide services more effectively and efficiently.[5]

Included in these strategies are efforts to raise the level of awareness (a and f) and to deal with quality-of-work-life issues (e and i). Some strategies embody a cutback philosophy (such as d) while others encourage expansion (c) where appropriate. The nesting of objectives and goals at different levels of the organization is apparent in strategies which suggest that different productivity objectives are appropriate for different groups and divisions.

A final objective states: "TRW seeks to achieve high quality in its internal operations, with special focus on its many relationships with employees." TRW is saying here that people are its most important resource and should be developed to the maximum. Three goals support this objective:

1. Foster a high-quality human relations environment and to provide our employees at all levels with rewarding work experiences.

2. Achieve a superior level and depth of management talent.

3. Employ management structures, policies, systems and techniques that will contribute to the effective and efficient management of our business.[6]

These last two broad objectives are more than compatible; they are mutually dependent. It would be nearly impossible to accomplish one without accomplishing the other; superior, long-term economic performance requires high-quality employee relations. Together, they provide general guidance for the building of an organization with productivity engrained in the culture. By starting at the top with management commitment and strategy development, TRW is taking a very long-range approach to building productivity consciousness into the daily operations of every manager and every worker. Now we will see specifically how they have done this.

STRATEGY IMPLEMENTATION: THE FIRST TWO YEARS

The importance of productivity had been recognized long before the Silverado conference and the development of objectives for the 1980s. Following the practices of other companies, TRW had established a top-level steering committee and had begun a series of seminars on productivity measurement systems with an outside consultant.

It soon became clear that these efforts were not effective. The steering committee, composed of every top level executive who had a stake in productivity, was far too large to be manageable. It lacked the focus, direction, and coordination necessary to develop a commitment to productivity in all segments of a very diverse organization.

The measurement seminars were a case of too much too soon. The groundwork had not been laid to establish an awareness of the productivity problem and why it was important. Confusion existed as to how to define productivity in different divisions and at different levels. The seminars were encouraging managers to develop measures for something they did not fully understand or consider critical.

A decision was made to "put someone in charge." TRW began a search for a top-level corporate executive with a broad-based knowledge of productivity to coordinate productivity efforts and develop a long-range plan for improving productivity. The person hired would be in a staff capacity, operating with a minimum of support staff, and positioned in the organization's science and technology group on a par with the vice-presidents of technical resources, quality, materiel, manufacturing, and information systems. (See Figure 3.)

In late 1980, Henry P. (Hank) Conn accepted the position of vice-president of productivity. Holding a master of mechanical engineering degree and an MBA, Conn had worked in several engineering positions with the Ford Motor Company and had then joined the Allis Chalmers Corporation as corporate director of manufacturing engineering services. There he was responsible for implementing cost-cutting programs that saved about $100 million.

Conn had a mandate from TRW to build a productivity organization but was faced with a company characterized by decentralization, delegation, and strong autonomous entrepreneurships with less than ideal communication and coordination among them. His specific charge was to "provide leadership to intensify efforts throughout TRW to substantially and continually improve productivity." Some past productivity improvement efforts had been effective, but others may have done more harm than good.

During his first year at TRW, Conn spent most of his time gathering information from inside and outside the company. Visits to over seventy TRW sites and contacts with seventy-five consultants, universities, and

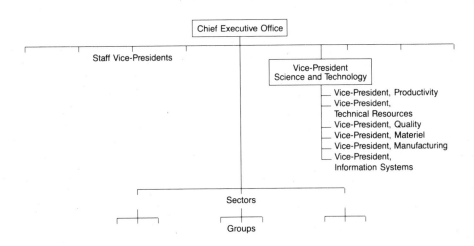

Figure 3. Productivity in the TRW Organization Structure

productivity centers provided the background information necessary for Conn to assess the situation at TRW and begin to focus existing knowledge toward developing the long-range plan.

From the very beginning, Conn said his objective was "to work myself out of a job." His overrriding concern is to build productivity into the framework of the organization and into the thinking of every operating manager so that productivity becomes a line function and staff support is no longer necessary. In short, Conn is aiming to make productivity management an integral part of each manager's job.

The Productivity Network

Conn reorganized and streamlined the steering committee to be just one part of a total network of productivity coordinators throughout the organization. The new steering committee, chaired by Conn, is composed of only four other members representing the three major sectors and the company staff human relations function. It meets four times per year to review and assess the effectiveness of current and planned efforts as well as to maintain two-way communications and a general awareness of productivity improvement efforts.

Below the steering committee is a forty-member productivity council consisting of representatives from corporate staff functions as well as operating managers and general managers from major groups and divisions. Serving as a resource throughout the company, the council may be subdivided into special task forces to aid in setting up new programs such as the development of measurement systems or a value engineering project. The organizational relationship between the steering committee, productivity council, and the remainder of the "productivity organization" is shown in Figure 4.

The next level in the network consists of 400 productivity coordinators, or "receptors" as they are sometimes called, to serve the coordination responsibilities in the operating units. If justified, some of the positions can be full time, but often the responsibilities fall on the shoulders of a plant manager or other operating manager. It is the effectiveness of this critical "grass-roots" level that determines whether the grand objectives and strategies formulated at the top ever find their way into actual improvements in the operations. Conn maintains

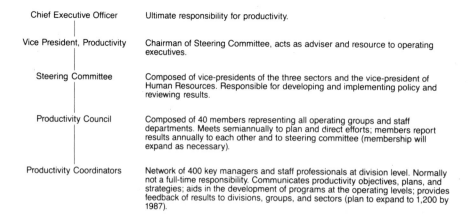

Figure 4. The Productivity Network at TRW

two-way communication with the coordinators. His semimonthly newsletter provides updated published and company information to them while Conn monitors progress and gathers feedback through them. The plan is working, and if it continues to be effective, the number of productivity coordinators will eventually grow to a staggering 1,200, spread among every operating and staff unit of the company.

Results to Date

By some standards, the productivity effort may seem to be moving slowly. Conn has been in his position two years and has spent most of that time learning, designing, developing, reorganizing, and communicating. But that is precisely the point: a long-term program requires an up-front investment in planning and foundation building. Since he is not looking for the quick fix, Conn's accomplishments to date reflect the developmental work necessary to allow productivity improvement to continue after his position "self-destructs."

Conn has initiated a "seed money" program through which corporate funds will support up to 50 percent of the cost of a pilot program in an operating unit that holds promise for applicability across divisions. He has assisted in designing a plant manager's training course to better explain the role of productivity in plant operations. He has held nominal group technique sessions to isolate opportunities for improvement in white-collar and knowledge worker productivity, and he led a task force to design and install two state-of-the-art secretarial work stations for experimentation. He has integrated productivity into the strategic planning process so that written productivity functional plans are now generated each year. And, true to TRW's commitment to social responsibility, Conn shares his productivity expertise with various public and private organizations. He has served on the Executive Committee, Board of Directors, and Advisory Council of the newly formed Northeast Ohio Productivity Center and on the board of directors of the American Productivity Management Association. In addition to working with other government agencies, Conn is currently counseling the City of Cleveland in the start-up of a productivity improvement effort. In a letter to Conn, George Voinovich, Cleveland's mayor said "...you have have provided the necessary leadership and guidance so that the city could get a productivity effort off the ground. Your efforts represent another example of how well the public/private partnership can work."

Two of Conn's most significant accomplishments have been the development of a measurement system and the establishment of a "Productivity College." The measurement system, outlined in Figure 5, establishes guidelines for evaluating productivity on a corporate basis. A system or set of measures was needed to encompass all factors—labor, capital, materials, and energy—but with special emphasis on the human resource. Measures are simple, understand-

Figure 5.

Corporate Productivity Measures

To guide and evaluate the activities of the wide diversity of operations within the corporation, TRW has established the following macro productivity ratios. In each case where a dollar figure is used, figures are converted to constant dollars.

Labor
1. Sales per employee
2. Sales divided by total compensation
3. Value added per employee
   (value added = sales minus direct material cost)
4. Value added divided by total compensation

Materials
5. Sales divided by total materials cost

Capital
6. Sales divided by real net plant, property, and equipment

Energy
7. Sales per unit of energy consumed

able, applicable across all divisions, and, wherever possible, use existing data. These broad "macro" measures are intended to monitor resource utilization apart from the financial measures already in place. Individual operating units may need other measures for closer scrutiny of their processes, but they should be compatible with the corporate measures. Undoubtedly, as results from these measures are used, refinements will be made in the future.

The growing network of productivity coordinators presents an enormous training problem because most are appointed on the basis of their potential, not their knowledge of productivity. To meet this challenge, Conn worked with the American Productivity Center in Houston, Texas, and with outside consultants to develop "TRW's Productivity College." It is a three-day seminar, custom-designed to give participants state-of-the-art knowledge of productivity and

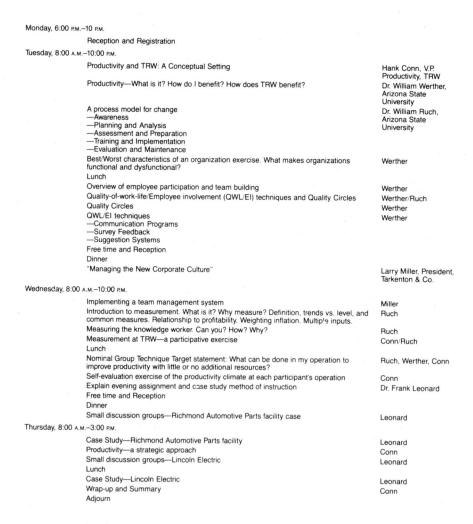

Monday, 6:00 P.M.–10 P.M.

   Reception and Registration

Tuesday, 8:00 A.M.–10:00 P.M.

Productivity and TRW: A Conceptual Setting	Hank Conn, V.P. Productivity, TRW
Productivity—What is it? How do I benefit? How does TRW benefit?	Dr. William Werther, Arizona State University
A process model for change —Awareness —Planning and Analysis —Assessment and Preparation —Training and Implementation —Evaluation and Maintenance	Dr. William Ruch, Arizona State University
Best/Worst characteristics of an organization exercise. What makes organizations functional and dysfunctional?	Werther
Lunch	
Overview of employee participation and team building	Werther
Quality-of-work-life/Employee involvement (QWL/EI) techniques and Quality Circles	Werther/Ruch
Quality Circles	Werther
QWL/EI techniques —Communication Programs —Survey Feedback —Suggestion Systems	Werther
Free time and Reception	
Dinner	
"Managing the New Corporate Culture"	Larry Miller, President, Tarkenton & Co.

Wednesday, 8:00 A.M.–10:00 P.M.

Implementing a team management system	Miller
Introduction to measurement. What is it? Why measure? Definition, trends vs. level, and common measures. Relationship to profitability. Weighting inflation. Multiple inputs.	Ruch
Measuring the knowledge worker. Can you? How? Why?	Ruch
Measurement at TRW—a participative exercise	Conn/Ruch
Lunch	
Nominal Group Technique Target statement: What can be done in my operation to improve productivity with little or no additional resources?	Ruch, Werther, Conn
Self-evaluation exercise of the productivity climate at each participant's operation	Conn
Explain evening assignment and case study method of instruction	Dr. Frank Leonard
Free time and Reception	
Dinner	
Small discussion groups—Richmond Automotive Parts facility case	Leonard

Thursday, 8:00 A.M.–3:00 P.M.

Case Study—Richmond Automotive Parts facility	Leonard
Productivity—a strategic approach	Conn
Small discussion groups—Lincoln Electric	Leonard
Lunch	
Case Study—Lincoln Electric	Leonard
Wrap-up and Summary	Conn
Adjourn	

Figure 6.   An Agenda of the TRW Productivity College

TRW'S strategies and plans. A Productivity College agenda appears in Figure 6 and a list of its objectives is found in Figure 7. Instruction is provided by Conn along with productivity experts from major universities and speakers from organizations involved in productivity improvement. Several sessions have been held, and the program will continue on a bimonthly basis until all productivity coordinators have been trained— 1,200 of them, trained 50 at a time over the next several years.

Productivity and TRW's Culture

Although the process and structure Conn established was right "on paper," productivity improvement was not becoming part of the TRW culture as thoroughly or as quickly as anticipated. In mid-1982, Conn reported the status of TRW's corporate productivity effort to Mettler, as explained in Figure 8.

For this stage of TRW's productivity improvement effort, the responsibility and ca-

Figure 7.

Objectives of TRW's Productivity College

1. Provide some generic productivity philosophies and definitions *and* specific TRW approaches and concepts for meeting "TRW and the 80s" productivity goal.

2. Provide exposure to and training in productivity improvement techniques and measures. These will include tools such as the Nominal Group Technique, Gainsharing, Employee Involvement, TRW Circles, etc.

3. Lead a "hands-on" productivity self-evaluation exercise of each attendee's plant or department to serve as a starting point in establishing a serious improvement effort.

4. Impart some new ideas on strategic productivity planning as opposed to the conventional approach.

5. Utilize the case study method on the final day to introduce real-world situations into the classroom and to put to use some of the tools and concepts developed over the first two days.

pability elements were good and improving. But the commitment throughout the line organization was unacceptable. The issue raised by Conn with Mettler was "What must be done to secure the across-the-board commitment of the division managers to the 'TRW and the 80's' productivity goal?" The answer to this question represented a significant turning point in TRW's productivity effort.

The crux of the problem was uneven commitment by senior operating executives. As a result, the approximately 200 division managers had varying levels of commitment. In divisions that were affiliated with strong productivity councils, enthusiastic productivity coordinators, and a committed group of executives, there were indications that productivity management was becoming part of the corporate culture. But other divisions showed little change.

Mettler responded by seeking more visibility for productivity concerns. Not only was incentive compensation for top executives tied to productivity objectives, but group executives were subsequently required to report to their sector vice-presidents semi-annually about the productivity efforts of the division managers within their group. That is, line managers began reporting to top line managers. Quickly, group executives and their division managers began to show greater interest in and a more explicit commitment toward productivity improvement.

TRW AND THE FUTURE

TRW is in the process of establishing specific goals and strategies for the five-year period 1983-87. Undoubtedly the stress will continue to be on economic performance as a base, but the company has singled out four priority projects for special emphasis: productivity, quality, management development, and management systems—all obvi-

Figure 8. Report on Key Productivity Elements (as of midyear, 1982)

Grade	Element	Explanation
A	Responsibility	Line managers are responsible for productivity improvement, and this responsibility of line managers is widely known throughout TRW and accepted.
B+	Capability	The office of the vice-president of productivity is to establish, in a nonthreatening way, the capabilities for productivity improvement throughout TRW; good but more remains to be done.
C−	Commitment	Although high levels of commitment exist among some managers, the level-by-level commitment to productivity improvement does not exist throughout TRW.

ously interrelated. For each of these, TRW feels it has made a good start, but it still has far to go. Progress in management development and new management systems, according to Mettler, is proceeding at about the right pace; but improvements in productivity and quality, he feels, are coming too slowly. He expects more and will push more aggressively for sector and functional executives to accept more responsibility and exercise more initiative. As far as productivity is concerned, Conn will continue to expand his network of productivity coordinators, develop new plans and programs, begin to log cost savings and resource utilization improvements as programs mature, and continue to try to "work himself out of a job."

As a part of the Productivity College, an evaluation form is used to guide participants in the assessment of productivity efforts in their operating units. The instrument is designed to isolate organizational weaknesses and strengths, thereby allowing the steering committee to concentrate future efforts on the weaknesses. In the detailed version of the questionnaire, each of the ten major factors listed in Figure 9 is subdivided into ten more specific questions for a total of 100 rating scales. Perhaps no company can ever reach a perfect score of 100 points, but TRW is going to see how close it can come by December 1989.

TRW's goal is to move along the productivity improvement continuum toward the strategic end, as shown in Figure 10. Al-

though internal studies reveal TRW is now at the "conventional state," it is making steady progress toward the transitional and ultimately to the strategic state.

CONCLUSION

TRW is a unique company; it has developed and continues to develop a major productivity improvement effort that fits its circumstances, its structure, and its culture. To the extent that a company differs from TRW in size, markets, products, processes, and other key characteristics, the specifics of its productivity improvement effort may differ. There are, however, a number of critically important lessons to be learned from the TRW experience that are applicable to all organizations, large or small, manufacturing or service, public or private.

1. Short-run efforts lead to short-run gains or no gains at all. Long-run results require an initial investment in planning and building foundations so that future efforts provide higher, more lasting yields.

2. Productivity is a strategic issue—it always has been and it always will be. The key question is whether productivity is explicitly woven into the fabric of the organizational purpose, objectives, goals, strategies, plans, and programs in a way that stresses its proper role and guides its accomplishment.

TRW Inc.
Productivity Improvement Program: Evaluations
Operating Unit:
Date: Evaluated by:

1. Top Management Involvement

A successful program needs active participation of top management. Management should be setting and reviewing goals. Its compensation should be linked to productivity improvement. Top management involvement sends a clear, positive message throughout the organization.

Rating

10	9	8	7	6	5	4	3	2	1

Very
involved

Delegating
all
responsibility

2. Proper Organization

For a productivity program to be effective, there needs to be a well-defined organization of the effort. Responsibilities for the ten elements of the program should be clearly defined and understood. The organization should be dealing with long-term objectives and short-term alternatives.

Rating

10	9	8	7	6	5	4	3	2	1

Organization
effectively
deals with all
ten elements of
program

Program not
effective
due to lack of
organization

3. Proper Definition of Productivity

In order to improve productivity, it is important to have the organization define it. The definition should be output/input. The input factors of capital, labor, material and energy should be considered in developing this definition. Definitions of productivity should be established for all organizational functions. These functions should define productivity according to the input factors that they control.

Rating

10	9	8	7	6	5	4	3	2	1

Well defined
and understood

Individuals
unable to define
productivity

4. Measurement System

A system needs to be in place to measure improvement. This will help by making individuals aware of the need for productivity improvement as well as helping to diagnose productivity problems. Profit centers should have a measurement system that takes capital, labor, energy and material into account. This total factor measurement should be complemented with a series of partial factor productivity measures. Organizational functions should measure the productivity of the input factors that they control. Measures should be tied to existing systems and reviewed regularly.

Rating

10	9	8	7	6	5	4	3	2	1

A total factor
system with supporting
partial measures,
regularly reviewed

No measures

5. Training Emphasis

People improve the productivity of material, capital, energy and labor. Therefore it is important to continually review and improve the skills of the organizations and individuals. Training should be used as a tool for solving specific productivity problems as well as increasing overall effectiveness.

Rating

10	9	8	7	6	5	4	3	2	1

Training is an
integral part of
productivity program

No training
program

6. Goal Setting

An effective program will emphasize goals throughout the organization. It is important to be striving to meet clearly-defined objectives. Goal setting helps define responsibilities as well as facilitate effective communications.

Rating

10	9	8	7	6	5	4	3	2	1

Goals are spread
throughout the
organization as
a part of the
productivity program

Goal setting
is nonexistent

Figure 9.   Productivity Evaluation Form

•

7. GOOD COMMUNICATIONS

Communications that are clear, consistent and open are important for a productivity improvement program to be successful. Communications should be frequent and positive. They should go up and down the organization as well as across.

RATING

10   9   8   7   6   5   4   3   2   1
Open, consistent   Communications
communications   not a part of the
flowing both ways   productivity program

8. EMPLOYEE PARTICIPATION

All employees should be active in productivity improvement. It is part of everyone's day-to-day job and they should be responsible for it. As mentioned with reference to training, it is up to people to improve the productivity of capital, material, energy and labor. By actively involving employees, you are using the most powerful tool in effecting productivity improvements.

RATING

10   9   8   7   6   5   4   3   2   1
All employees   Employee
active in and   participation
responsible   not viewed as
for improving   part of productivity
productivity   program

9. PROGRAM EVALUATION

Productivity programs need to be evaluated on a regular basis. The needs of an organization will change as the environment changes. Productivity programs need to adapt to the organization. Evaluations should look at all ten elements necessary for a successful productivity improvement program. The evaluation should consider short term versus long term. The evaluation should be done positively.

RATING

10   9   8   7   6   5   4   3   2   1
Each element   Evaluation
is regularly   is not a part
and objectively   of productivity
evaluated   program

10. INFORMATION RESOURCES

Information resources should be viewed as anything pertaining to productivity that is not presently part of the productivity program. Articles, programs, new techniques, books, seminars, consulting services, educational materials, etc., all need to be integrated into the ten elements of the productivity program. This directly affects training, education, communications and participation. These new ideas and techniques need to be placed in the hands of those people that can use and develop them to the best advantage of the organization.

RATING

10   9   8   7   6   5   4   3   2   1
Information is   No defined
important productivity   information
tool and is an   services
integral part of
productivity program

TOTAL SCORING:

       1. Top management involvement   —
       2. Proper organization   —
       3. Proper definition of productivity   —
       4. Measurement system   —
       5. Training emphasis   —
       6. Goal setting   —
       7. Good communications   —
       8. Employee participation   —
       9. Program evaluation   —
      10. Information resources   —

                                    Total   —

An average score of _____ out of a possible 10 points per element.

Figure 9. Productivity Evaluation Form (continued)

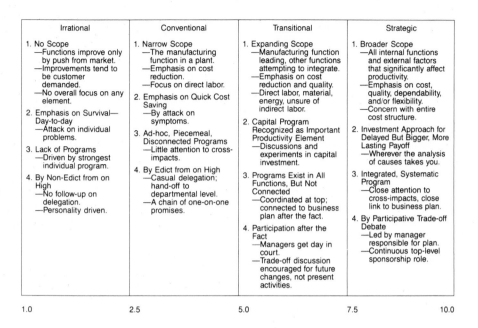

Irrational	Conventional	Transitional	Strategic
1. No Scope —Functions improve only by push from market. —Improvements tend to be customer demanded. —No overall focus on any element. 2. Emphasis on Survival—Day-to-day —Attack on individual problems. 3. Lack of Programs —Driven by strongest individual program. 4. By Non-Edict from on High —No follow-up on delegation. —Personality driven.	1. Narrow Scope —The manufacturing function in a plant. —Emphasis on cost reduction. —Focus on direct labor. 2. Emphasis on Quick Cost Saving —By attack on symptoms. 3. Ad-hoc, Piecemeal, Disconnected Programs —Little attention to cross-impacts. 4. By Edict from on High —Casual delegation; hand-off to departmental level. —A chain of one-on-one promises.	1. Expanding Scope —Manufacturing function leading, other functions attempting to integrate. —Emphasis on cost reduction and quality. —Direct labor, material, energy, unsure of indirect labor. 2. Capital Program Recognized as Important Productivity Element —Discussions and experiments in capital investment. 3. Programs Exist in All Functions, But Not Connected —Coordinated at top; connected to business plan after the fact. 4. Participation after the Fact —Managers get day in court. —Trade-off discussion encouraged for future changes, not present activities.	1. Broader Scope —All internal functions and external factors that significantly affect productivity. —Emphasis on cost, quality, dependability, and/or flexibility. —Concern with entire cost structure. 2. Investment Approach for Delayed But Bigger, More Lasting Payoff —Wherever the analysis of causes takes you. 3. Integrated, Systematic Program —Close attention to cross-impacts, close link to business plan. 4. By Participative Trade-off Debate —Led by manager responsible for plan. —Continuous top-level sponsorship role.

| 1.0 | 2.5 | 5.0 | 7.5 | 10.0 |

Figure 10. Continuum from Irrational to Strategic Productivity Improvement

3. If productivity is infused into the overall planning process, it can become a part of the organization's culture. It is then only necessary to maintain it; it is not necessary to reinstitute it every time there is a crisis or a downturn in the economy.

4. A diversified organization, even one spanning technologies ranging from ancient to leading edge, can be guided under the umbrella of a corporatewide productivity program—provided that it is, in fact, an umbrella and not a smothering blanket.

5. A major part of any productivity improvement effort is raising the level of awareness of all members of the organization. This involves common definitions, common purposes, common goals, and the supplanting of misconceptions with understanding through common knowledge. This invariably presents a formidable education and training task.

And neither awareness nor commitment are likely without the establishment of organizational rewards (and penalties) that are associated with productivity improvement.

6. The further one is in the hierarchy from the actual operation where productivity is to be improved, the more one's role will be "support" rather than "directing." Productivity improvements cannot be mandated across multiple levels of the organization's hierarchy. Top management can establish goals, point directions, and provide resources but must then delegate authority and responsibility to, and reward, those who can make it happen.

7. Communications are at the root of many organizational problems, but nowhere are communications more important than in a productivity improvement effort. Goals and strategies need to be

communicated downward, problems and results communicated upward, and successes, failures, technological advances, and other new information communicated laterally.

8. Productivity improvement is not a staff function; it is a line function. If there is a chief productivity officer in a staff position, the job description is to assist and support the line in improving its own productivity. It is a function that involves gathering and providing information resources, communicating across organizational lines, and coordinating efforts so that productivity improvement in one unit does not come at the expense of another.

9. The principal evaluation of the effectiveness of a chief productivity officer is the number of people he or she can involve in the process. The ultimate goal is to involve absolutely everyone—the top managers in setting productivity goals and strategies, managers in managing the factors affecting productivity, and each worker in the productivity of his or her job. At that point, the chief productivity officer is the only person in the organization who is not productive; it is time for him or her to move on.

10. Productivity can be managed. It is a continuous, iterative, and orderly process. If properly integrated into the management process, productivity improvement can be predicted, planned, organized, and controlled. Management may be defined as getting things done through people. Productivity improvement may be defined as getting people to do more things. Assets and technology are necessary prerequisites, but assets make things possible; people make them happen. Effective management of people is the master key.

The authors wish to express their thanks to Henry P. Conn for his cooperation and help in the research for this article.

20

Productivity and Employee Communications Systems

Why does objective feedback work? There are two reasons: it
both energizes and directs work behavior.
RICHARD E. KOPELMAN[1]

. . . man's main concern is not to gain pleasure or to avoid pain,
but rather to see a meaning in his life.
VIKTOR E. FRANKL[2]

Productivity improvement systems do not just happen. Successful ones, like those discussed in the previous chapter, have several prerequisites. Although top management commitment, clear objectives and a custom-tailored approach are essential, more is needed. Ultimately, the commitment to productivity improvement must permeate the organization's culture and reach each job-holder. For such a productivity improvement system to be created and sustained, it must be supported by a constant flow of information. As the former president of United Airlines observed, "Nothing is worse than a lack of information down in the ranks."[3]

People need feedback about both their own performance and the organization's performance. Feedback about individual performance helps sustain commitment to improve productivity. At the same time, managers need information about enhancing the productivity system they manage. The firm's chief productivity officer (CPO) also needs specialized information about approaches used in other organizations. Since the formal, systematic management of productivity within organizations is a recent development, CPOs have an ongoing need for information about new productivity innovations.[4] A growing web of networks has emerged to provide this information. The remainder of this chapter discusses the relationship between productivity and information systems, from the micro perspective of employee feedback to the macro perspective of the whole productivity system.

THE MICRO PERSPECTIVE: INFORMATION AND EMPLOYEE FEEDBACK

The human commitment to productivity does not emerge in a vacuum. People need to understand the role productivity plays in their lives, as Chapter 1 points out. They also need feedback about their contribution to the organization's productivity effort. Without feedback, progress cannot be measured and reinforcement cannot occur. The effective use of employee feedback demonstrates a manager's understanding of how information influences human behavior.[5] To use feedback effectively, a manager must understand its importance, particularly as it concerns decision-making, employee satisfaction and company objectives.

The Importance of Feedback Loops

Feedback tells a person or system "how it's doing." This information permits corrective action to be taken. Too often, however, feedback about the results attained by an employee's effort fail to reach the employee or to arrive in a timely manner. Even when information does reach the employee, it too seldom includes positive feedback. Good performance is expected. Good performance merely matches expectations, so employees often receive no feedback about it. Since poor performance violates the manager's expectations, negative feedback is more common. Some unenlightened managers formally acknowledge this imbalance by telling employees, "If you don't hear from me, everything is OK." As discussed in Chapter 6, feedback that is primarily negative may actually lower the employee's self-image, which may lead to lower self-expectations and effort. Figure 20–1 suggests that feedback affects the employee just as strongly as the employee's efforts affect results.[6] Although the employee's efforts may depend on many variables, feedback is one of the more critical ones. When feedback is lacking, productivity suffers.

Figure 20–1.   Employee Feedback Loops

Feedback is important because it helps build employee commitment. Managers seek a strong commitment from their employees to the organization's objectives. Many managers argue that it is reasonable to expect commitment in return for compensation and other benefits of employment. However, if commitment were the normal result of an employment relationship, productivity would occur automatically. Instead, managers must earn commitment. It comes only when employees want to give it. As Figure 20–2 suggests, a commitment generally emerges from a sense of "common fate," a sense that employees and management benefit or suffer according to the fortunes of the company. That common fate may emerge out of fear, as employees fear losing their jobs when their employer is no longer competitive. A "common fate" belief also may come from a sense of trust among those in the organization. While fear may result from a sense of disaster (personal or group), trust is likely to emerge from employees when management returns that trust by sharing information.

The process of sharing information with employees about their performance does not necessarily produce trust. Too often, the information being shared tends to be negative. When employees get balanced information, containing both positive and negative feedback, they perceive management as more reasonable. Beyond the process of sharing information, the newly acquired knowledge may allow employees to understand how their efforts affect the organization.[7] Learning about the connection between personal efforts and the organization's success helps implant a positive sense of common fate in employees.

Decision-Making Feedback

When the organization goes beyond merely providing feedback and actually involves the employees in the decision-making process, the quality of information to which they are exposed increases dramatically. Perhaps even more important is the sense of trust that management shows when

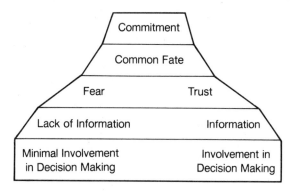

Figure 20–2. The Basis of Commitment

employees share in the decision-making process. Employees tend to return the trust they receive, and that trust may lead to a feeling of common
fate. Of necessity, this process is slow and time-consuming. Only through
time does the underlying organization culture change so that involvement and feedback become the organization norm. A good example
comes from a Westinghouse plant.

Employees in one Westinghouse facility produced components for
large industrial air-conditioning systems. Most of the production work
consisted of machining components. For several years productivity had
remained relatively unchanged, even though the market for such products was extremely competitive. Narrow profit margins and a diminished
order backlog resulted. To improve productivity, a new plant manager instituted a communications program.

One productivity program in the division involved educating blue-
collar workers about productivity and its implications. The educational
process was conducted by the first-line supervisor, and it involved two
concurrent phases. The usual Monday-morning safety meetings held by
the supervisors were expanded to include a discussion of competition
and productivity. These informal sessions were referred to as "stand-up"
meetings, because they were little more than the work team gathering
around the supervisor right on the shop floor. Besides the normal safety-
related information, supervisors covered information about the company's marketing efforts. Newly won or lost contracts were discussed.
Contracts that the company had lost were described to employees. This
information was shared in an attempt to begin the long process of making
businessmen and businesswomen out of the workers. Since this effort
was initiated against the backdrop of multiple plant closings throughout
traditional industries, employees were keenly interested in learning
about how their plant was doing.

The second aspect of the program was to give workers feedback
about their work group's performance. As Figure 20–3 illustrates, employees were told about their weekly productivity. Productivity improvement, in this case, was measured as a ratio of standard hours to actual
hours. Standard hours were the number of hours a particular task was expected to take; actual hours reflected the number of hours the work actually did take. Since Westinghouse already had a "standard hours"
information system in place, use of these measures of productivity was
feasible and required very little change in the organization's internal information system. As actual hours to complete a job were reduced, productivity climbed. The program was started in February. Between
February and the end of the year, productivity climbed by slightly more
than 7%, using the standard/actual hours ratio. A key to this improvement was that each week the supervisor would plot the productivity
changes on a chart that hung in the shop. All week long, employees would
be reminded of their productivity by the feedback provided through the
chart.

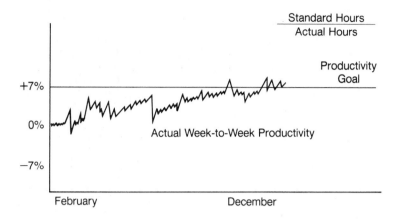

Figure 20–3.   Employee Feedback Chart at Westinghouse

The feedback combined with additional information about Westinghouse's business gradually caused employees to think more and more like businessmen and businesswomen. The blue-collar workers assumed increased responsibility for the weekly productivity trend. Although in some weeks productivity actually declined because of equipment failure or absenteeism, employees realized the need to reattain previous productivity levels and improve upon them.

A greater sense of trust and common fate came from sharing with employees information about Westinghouse's marketing results. When that information also included specific feedback, employees could sense the real connection between their efforts and the organization's results. The outcome of these greater informational inputs was a greater sense of employee commitment to the goals of higher productivity.

Job Satisfaction and QWL

Communication with employees not only enhances their commitment, but it may increase their satisfaction and the quality of their work life. This causes jobs to take on added significance. Even highly specialized tasks seem more meaningful. If employees have enough autonomy to take immediate corrective action, they may feel more pride in their jobs and tasks.

Congruity of Objectives

Even when employees are highly motivated to contribute to the organization, as is often the case among professional and managerial employees, their contribution may be misdirected without appropriate feedback. Feedback is essential if individual precepts are to be molded into a common vision of the organization's objectives.

Most managers can identify the three primary objectives of each employee who directly reports to them. Their direct subordinates also can list the three key objectives they are supposed to fulfill. When the manager and subordinates compare their lists of objectives, however, discrepancies in priorities often appear. Even if agreement exists on two out of three objectives, a serious communications problem is apparent. If only two-thirds of the objectives of any one level are effectively communicated to the next level in the organization's hierarchy, miscommunications are likely to compound as objective-setting meetings cascade through the organization's hierarchy.

Communications Systems

The strength of any organization's communication system rests on several principles. Periodically, management needs to evaluate the organization's communication policies, structure, skills, and efforts.

Policies

Communication policies exist in all organizations. These policies are not reduced to writing nor scrutinized objectively. Instead, individual managers may develop their personal approaches, which are greatly influenced by the organization's culture. For example, a manager who holds a "Theory X" view of workers believes that the employees are unmotivated and not particularly bright. As a result, the communication policies in that department or division may give employees information only on a "need-to-know" basis. General background information about the organization's history, economic health, competition, and overall strategy are seldom, if ever, discussed with employees. It is these informal and unwritten communication policies that spring from a manager's assumptions about employees, and such assumptions are very difficult to analyze and change.

Structure

The structure of the organization also affects the communication system. In traditional functional organizational designs, people work in departments with others who have similar skills (accountants in an accounting department, personnel specialists in a personnel department). People in such circumstances often find that communication within the function to be acceptable or even effective. However, in this type of an organization structure, communications *among* functions, say from accounting to personnel and marketing, may break down. Likewise, communications between geographically remote parts of the organization also tend to be weak.

Skills

Skills influence everyone's ability to communicate. Productivity may be limited by the manager's listening skills, for example. Most managers carefully edit and re-edit their written words. Many have had ample opportunities to make oral presentations and may even have joined Toastmasters and Toastmistresses, or taken speech courses at nearby universities. However, few managers ever take a course in how to listen.[8]

Efforts

The communication system, of course, is affected by the amount of effort made to communicate with employees. Many well-run organizations report that their managers use a "management by wandering around" approach.[9] This means the manager literally wanders around among the employees and strikes up informal conversations to learn about the employee's concerns. Many formal and informal meetings bridge functional barriers or geographic distances. Managers who are effective communicators realize the need to develop new communication approaches from time to time. They realize that traditional communication methods may become little more than background noise that is ignored by the people with whom they are trying to communicate.[10]

THE MACRO PERSPECTIVE: PRODUCTIVITY INFORMATION

Managers of productivity improvement efforts must learn new ways to enhance productivity. This need is difficult to fulfill, because productivity management is a multi-disciplinary effort. It draws on concepts in production management, economics and psychology. Societal attitudes about business organizations affect an organization's productivity and change slowly.[11] Political developments, particularly in the form of new laws and court decisions, may limit or expand the opportunities facing management in the area of productivity improvement. Productivity advancement also comes from technological innovation. Since organizational productivity is shaped by so many diverse forces, it is both difficult and necessary for management to stay informed about a wide range of possible developments.

The need for information on productivity compounds the process of providing employees with performance feedback. Employees need information about their own performance before they can help improve productivity. But they also need information about productivity itself from a variety of sources. On one level, employees need this information to find better approaches to utilizing resources. On another level, employees need information on productivity to stimulate their creativity and increase their awareness of management's continued interest in productivity improvement.[12] Since the formal study of productivity is relatively new, limited sources of information exist. Given the dynamic changes occurring in productivity management and the lack of a common body of knowledge, it is crucial for chief productivity officers and concerned managers to use the information sources that do exist. The remainder of this chapter identifies ways in which interested readers can obtain additional information on an ongoing basis.[13] The article at the end of this chapter entitled "Productivity Information: A Key to Competitiveness" expands upon this presentation.

American Productivity Center

The leading institution involved in providing information on productivity is the American Productivity Center (APC). Founded by C. Jackson Grayson, the APC is a non-profit, non-partisan organization that is supported by a long list of corporate and union organizations. The APC exists as a focal point for the creation of productivity information through traditional research and multi-client studies. In addition, the APC provides hands-on assistance to organizations seeking ways to improve their productivity.

Besides acting as an information center with access to a variety of on-line information services, the APC also conducts a variety of computer conference networks.[14] These innovative approaches to gathering and disseminating information involve a collection of national experts and interested parties connected through a central computer at the New Jersey Institute of Technology, which serves as the data storage and switchboard utility. Users can sign up with the APC, interconnect into any of several ongoing networks, and begin a dialog with other experts on such topics as productivity and human resources, quality, or other emergent issues related to productivity.

In addition to research, consulting, and computer conferences, the American Productivity Center conducts a variety of seminars, holds regional productivity meetings for affiliated productivity professionals and offers a wide range of publications. Through the APC's special publications, a network of affiliated firms receive monthly and quarterly reports on a wide variety of social, technical, political, economic, and managerial topics, related to productivity improvement.

U.S. Department of Commerce

The United States Department of Commerce has a Commerce Productivity Center.[15] The CPC provides organizations with information about productivity, quality and competitiveness. It serves as a clearinghouse for information on productivity-related topics.

Also within the Commerce Department are a variety of other organizations that can help improve productivity. For example, the International Trade Association exists to help U.S. firms improve their competitiveness and develop their export operations. The Bureau of Industrial Economics collects and analyzes data from domestic and international sources on issues related to productivity, such as material requirements, taxation, pricing, financing, marketing, labor, and inventories. The National Technical Information Service is the U.S. government's arm for the distribution of sponsored research and foreign technical reports which the service maintains in its collection. Assistance in the areas of technology, engineering and computer science is available from another Department of Commerce operation, the National Bureau of Standards. And the Office of Business Liaison within the Commerce Department helps match business organizations with appropriate government departments.[16]

Other Productivity Centers and Institutes

A variety of domestic and international centers and institutes address the productivity crisis.[17] Although some of these organizations will do theoretical or applied research, many are information repositories and referral systems. An example of an organization that does multi-client studies is the Manufacturing Productivity Center at the Illinois Institute of Technology. It will, for example, obtain information from a variety of firms within an industry and compile that information into the industry's statistical base. Other organizations, such as the John Gray Institute at Lamar University, focus on narrower topics, such as labor-management cooperation, within their geographical areas. Still others, such as the Arizona State University Productivity Institute, provide information referrals and some local networking among productivity professionals and managers.

Internationally, countries such as Germany, India, Israel, and Japan have government-sponsored productivity institutes and centers. These organizations identify public policy issues that affect productivity. They also provide information referral, database repositories and, in some cases, multi-client applied research.

Associations Related to Productivity

A variety of productivity-related associations also exist. One of the leading associations is the American Productivity Management Association (APMA), which includes some of the nation's leading productivity management practitioners. The APMA seeks to create a cohesive network of chief productivity officers from organizations throughout the United States. Through periodic meetings and plant tours, the APMA and similar organizations are able to provide their members with up-to-date information about productivity innovations. Member Henry Conn, former vice president of productivity of TRW, observed:

Experienced productivity managers with some solid accomplishments under their belts continue to need growth and new ideas. The best way I have found in continuing the process of learning all of this is through boards of directors of organizations that are concerned specifically with productivity—the American Productivity Management Association (APMA), for example, or a group like the Work in Northeast Ohio Council (WNEOC), which is actually a productivity center.[18]

Other Sources of Information

A variety of other sources of information exist to help managers and chief productivity officers stay informed about developments in the field. There are professional associations, such as the American Institute of Industrial Engineers, American Production and Inventory Control Society, or the American Society for Personnel Administrators. In addition, a variety of business-related publications, particularly those put out by the American Productivity Center and the *National Productivity Review*, are excellent sources of information.

SUMMARY

Communication systems are essential for improved productivity. At the micro level, employees within firms need feedback about their performance. At the macro level, organizations must provide information to help managers keep up with new developments in the field of productivity.

SELECTED READINGS OVERVIEW

This chapter concludes with two articles from the *National Productivity Review*. The first is by Professor Richard E. Kopelman, of the City University of New York's Baruch College. In his article entitled "Improving Productivity through Objective Feedback: A Review of the Evidence," he makes a compelling case for the need to give employees feedback about their performance. He illustrates his point by reviewing twenty-seven studies of objective feedback on job performance or work behavior. The compilation of these studies leads to a strong conclusion: Objective feedback can improve productivity.

The second article is by States L. Clawson and Carol Ann Meares, manager and assistant manager, respectively, of the Commerce Productivity Center within the United States Department of Commerce. Their article, "Productivity Information: A Key to Competitiveness," succinctly outlines a variety of sources of productivity information that can be useful to either general managers or productivity professionals. In the article, they describe non-government and government sources and briefly comment on a wide variety of publications.

Review Questions

1. Why is feedback important?

2. From the Kopelman article, cite three examples in which feedback improves productivity.

3. Describe the role of the American Productivity Center and contrast its role with that of the U.S. Department of Commerce's Productivity Center.

4. Besides the APC and government, what other sources of information are available to an organization's chief productivity officer?

RICHARD E. KOPELMAN

Improving Productivity through Objective Feedback: A Review of the Evidence

The author presents evidence indicating that objective feedback does not usually *work—it virtually always works.*

A considerable body of literature provides evidence of the effectiveness of objective feedback as a technology for improving productivity. This article reviews the results of twenty-seven studies that report on the effects of objective feedback on either job performance (eighteen studies) or work behavior (nine studies). More specifically, results are examined in terms of: (a) the magnitude of impact, (b) cost effectiveness, and (c) the reliability and durability of the effect. After reviewing the empirical evidence, the article examines several explanations of why objective feedback is a technique that virtually always works. Finally, suggestions are offered regarding the practical steps an orga-

Richard E. Kopelman, professor of management at Baruch College, is the author of more than forty articles and a forthcoming book, *The Management of Productivity*. Dr. Kopelman has served as a consultant to organizations in both the public and private sectors.

Reprinted, by permission, from *National Productivity Review* (Winter 1982/83):43–55.

nization might take to implement an objective feedback system.

OBJECTIVE FEEDBACK: THE EFFECTIVENESS EVIDENCE

Some indicators of job performance and work behavior are relatively objective, e.g., units of output, attendance, forms completed; others are relatively subjective, e.g., an individual's leadership skills, initiative, sense of responsibility. Importantly, the concept of productivity *requires* that job performance or work behavior be measured in terms of objective indicators. Subjective judgments cannot be incorporated into a ratio of outputs divided by inputs: for instance, it does not make sense to talk about rated leadership "points" per hour worked. Yet the distinction between objective and subjective criteria is one of degree, not kind. Measured output implies judgment about quality; and even attendance implies that the individual is both physically and mentally at work. Nevertheless, it is widely recognized that relatively objective indicators are preferable to relatively subjective ones. They allow computation of productivity ratios, and they provide more accurate information.

In recent years there has been an accelerating increase in research on the impact of objective feedback on job performance and work behavior. Of the twenty-seven studies known to this author, one was published prior to 1975, four between 1975 and 1977, and twenty-two between 1978 and 1980. Of these studies, eighteen focused on such end-result criteria as job performance or productivity (e.g., output per hour or percent defective), and nine focused on intermediate behavioral criteria (e.g., frequency of hand washing by kitchen workers or frequency of smiling at customers by restaurant employees).

Feedback, Job Performance, and Productivity

Table 1 summarizes the results of the eighteen studies that examined the effects of objective feedback on various indicators of job performance or productivity. The sample populations were highly diverse, including such blue-collar workers as truck drivers, sewing machine operators, and auto mechanics and such white-collar workers as payroll clerks, mental health technicians, and salespeople.

Three primary methods of providing feedback were employed: privately communicated individual feedback, publicly communicated individual feedback, and publicly communicated group feedback. Most studies used either (a) public group feedback alone, or (b) private individual and public group feedback combined.

Typically, feedback was used in conjunction with other interventions such as: goal setting, social reinforcers (praise, recognition, encouragement), training, token reinforcers (e.g., pen and pencil sets, coffee and doughnuts), certificates, commendation letters, and preferred task assignments.

The effects of feedback were examined over study periods ranging from eight weeks to four years, the median time period being thirty weeks. In all eighteen studies, objective performance indicators increased after the provision of feedback. Increases ranged from 6 percent to 125 percent; the median result was an increase of 53 percent.

However, the 53 percent figure does not indicate that productivity was on the average increased by 53 percent. This is because some of the objective performance indicators focused only on a component aspect of output, such as truck turnaround time or the incidence of high bobbins. Ten studies did, however, employ comprehensive measures of performance, and in these studies feedback yielded a median productivity increase of 16 percent. This finding closely corresponds to the observation made by Milne and Doyle that feedback interventions alone produce an increase in productivity of 14 percent.

Six of the eighteen studies reported data on annualized dollar savings resulting from the feedback intervention. Savings ranged from $3,500 to $1 million, with the median result being an annual savings of $91,000. In large part, though, the total annualized dollar savings were a function of the number of employees involved in the intervention. Therefore, a more meaningful indicator of the financial impact of objective feedback is the annualized savings per employee involved. On this basis, annualized savings ranged from $500 per employee (at Emery Air Freight, with some 2,000 employees) to $9,533 (6 repair shop workers), the median savings being $3,178.

Table 1.   Effects of Feedback on Job Performance

Year	Sample	Type of Feedback[a]	Other Interventions[b]	Impact on Job Performance	Comments
1973[1]	sales, shipping	Pvt. I G	GS, P, R	150% increase in frequency of time meeting customer service standard; 110% increase in frequency of full use of containers; over 4 years	annualized savings of roughly $1 million
1975[2]	43 die-casting operators	Pvt. I G	P, E	production up 6.1% over 36 weeks	annualized savings of $77,000
1976[3]	4 groups of 113 blue-collar, unionized service workers	Pvt. I	GS, P	7.9% improvement in cost performance; 13.6% improvement in safety; 11.6% increase in service; over 3 months	best results were obtained in the group to which all interventions were applied
1977[4]	8 mental health technicians	Pub. I G		120% increase in group therapy sessions; 150% increase in one-on-one therapy sessions; 70% increase in daily routine activities; over 8 weeks	decrease in both staff complaints and patient complaints
1978[5]	58 plant managers; 92 truck drivers	Pvt. I (to both plant managers and truck drivers)	TR	43.9% decrease in truck turnaround time over 29 weeks	12% increase in total shipping productivity
1978[6]	32 nonunionized industrial workers at PPG Industries	Pvt. I G	P, E	8.7% increase in productivity over 4 months	productivity was higher with both forms of feedback than with G alone

[a]Pvt. I = private individual; Pub. I = public individual; G = public group; Pvt. G = private group.

[b]GS = goal setting; P = praise; R = social recognition; E = encouragement; TR = token reinforcers; PWA = preferred work assignments; T = training; CL = commendation letters.

Table 1.   Effects of Feedback on Job Performance (continued)

Year	Sample	Type of Feedback[a]	Other Interventions[b]	Impact on Job Performance	Comments
1978[7]	doffers in a textile yarn mill	Pvt. I G	GS, P, TR	reduced the incidence of high bobbins (which caused tangles in thread) by 74.6% over 8 weeks	when feedback was discontinued, the incidence of high bobbins increased by 64%
1978[8]	1 draftsman in an engineering firm	Pvt I		72.2% increase in hours worked over 11 weeks	marked improvement in punctuality
1978[9]	4 textile machine operators at PPG Industries	Pvt. I	GS, P	7.8% increase in output over an average period of 32 weeks	annualized savings of $3,500; improved relationships between operators and foreman
1978[10]	195 truck drivers for textile company	Pvt. I Pub. I G	R, TR	5.1% increase in miles per gallon; 56.7% increase in use of company-owned fuel terminals; over 2 years	described as a "very substantial" dollar savings
1978[11]	23 inspectors at Eastman Kodak	Pvt. I G	GS, P	30% increase in productivity over 40 weeks	annualized savings of $105,000; increased contact between workers and supervisor; job seen as more interesting
1978[12]	6 repair shop workers	G	GS	20% increase in productivity over 22 weeks	annualized savings of $57,200
1979[13]	approx. 150 sewing machine operators in a garment factory	G	GS	62% reduction in defective garments ("seconds") over 12 months	pay satisfaction declined

[a]Pvt. I = private individual; Pub. I = public individual; G = public group; Pvt. G = private group.

[b]GS = goal setting; P = praise; R = social recognition; E = encouragement; TR = token reinforcers; PWA = preferred work assignments; T = training; CL = commendation letters.

Table 1.   Effects of Feedback on Job Performance (continued)

Year	Sample	Type of Feedback[a]	Other Interventions[b]	Impact on Job Performance	Comments
1979[14]	approx. 12 workers in a federal agency personnel department	Pvt. I	GS, P, PWA, T, CL	69.7% average improvement in 11 output measures over 7 months	9 of 11 performance indicators improved, 1 was unchanged, and 1 showed a decline
1979[15]	clerical employees in payroll office of a large city personnel department	Pvt. I G		37.6% decrease in average backlog of work over 8 weeks	of 18 categories of work, backlogs decreased in 17 categories, 1 was unchanged
1980[16]	3 sales correspondents in an industrial products company	Pvt. I	more complete sales information from salesmen	67% reduction in price quotation turnaround time over roughly 3 years	contributed to a 45% increase in sales and a 78% increase in profit over 4 years
1980[17]	back-office employees in Marine Midland Bank trust department	Pvt. I G	P, R, and group problem solving	71.9% reduction in outstanding daily accounts receivable (increasing cash flow)	assuming 15% cost of money, the annualized savings were $440,350
1980[18]	all employees in 16 departments of a large state hospital	Pvt. G G		83% increase in staff treatment programs and client hours with private group feedback over 15-23 weeks; 163% increase in the same criteria with public group feedback over 38 weeks	an increase in work-related conversations among all levels of employees

[a]Pvt. I = private individual; Pub. I = public individual; G = public group; Pvt. G = private group.

[b]GS = goal setting; P = praise; R = social recognition; E = encouragement; TR = token reinforcers; PWA = preferred work assignments; T = training; CL = commendation letters.

Feedback and Work Behavior

Table 2 summarizes the results of nine studies that examined the effects of objective feedback on work behavior. The results were uniformly positive and were obtained over treatment periods that ranged in duration from one week to fourteen months, the median time period being eight weeks. Increases in desired work behaviors, or decreases in undesired work behaviors, ranged from 41 percent to 429 percent, the median result being an improvement of 78 percent.

Of course, an improvement in a particular work behavior, e.g., the frequency of hand washing in the preparation of food, typically does not reflect a comparable increase in either job performance or productivity. Work behavior is an antecedent of job performance, which in turn is an antecedent of the ultimate quantity of output produced. Not surprisingly, therefore, there is a diminishing relationship between objective feedback and work behavior, job performance, and productivity, respectively. So while feedback improved work behavior by 78 percent, it raised job performance indicators by 53 percent and productivity by 16 percent, as we have already noted.

Advantages of Feedback

There are six distinct advantages of a feedback intervention. First, a feedback system often can be based on data already being generated. Hence, feedback is unobtrusive, requiring little change in ongoing procedures.

Second, and related to the first advantage, a feedback intervention is relatively simple to implement and requires little investment in time or money. Indeed, the initial outlay associated with the development of a feedback intervention is often less than $1,000; and, as noted previously, the median financial savings has averaged $91,000 per year.

Third, the use of feedback is a natural (although not always welcome) means of control. It does not require use of contrived events, such as a lottery; on the contrary, it typically requires only minor changes in day-to-day routines.

Fourth, the effects of objective feedback are evident rapidly. Indeed, positive results are often achieved within twenty-four hours. In contrast, job redesign and participation interventions typically take 1½ to 3 years to take hold; and substantial changes in managerial practices (e.g., from System 1 to System 4) take 3 to 7 years.

Fifth, objective feedback can be implemented in virtually all work settings, including those where there are few alternative ways to improve productivity. Public agencies and not-for-profit organizations may find it difficult, if not impossible, to employ financial incentives or to redesign jobs. However, the provision of objective feedback should encounter fewer problems than other interventions.

Sixth, the use of feedback generally enhances the effects of other productivity improvement techniques. Describing the use of training alone compared to training combined with feedback, Komaki, Heinzmann, and Lawson[25] have written:

> When employees received training in the form of a slide presentation, verbal explanations, and written rules, performance improved slightly. It was not until feedback was provided along with continued training that performance significantly improved.

Table 2. Effects of Feedback on Work Behavior

Year	Sample	Type of Feedback[a]	Other Interventions[b]	Impact on Job Performance	Comments
1976[19]	30 telephone reservation clerks for Aer Lingus	Pvt. I G	GS	66.5% reduction in undesired verbal behaviors; 84.4% increase in desired verbal behaviors; overall effect was a 77.9% improvement; after 3 months	clerks had a positive reaction to the program
1978[20]	80 employees in a mental health organization	public posting of replies to suggestions offered		222.7% increase in the number of suggestions offered over 32 weeks	98% of employees said the program should be continued
1978[21]	6 therapists at a health service center	Pvt. I G	T, P, R	429% increase in the percentage of graphs (of client behavior) completed over 8½ weeks	individual feedback was superior in impact to group feedback; individual plus group feedback was superior to individual feedback
1978[22]	supervisors and staff at 30 university laboratories	Pvt. G (sent to supervisor)	P	45.4% reduction in observed frequency of hazards over 7 to 14 months	feedback was adopted as a permanent part of a new safety system

[a]Pvt. I = private individual; G = public group

[b]GS = goal setting; T = training; P = praise; R = social recognition

More specifically, they found that training alone yielded an improvement of 24.7 percent, whereas training and feedback yielded an improvement of 41.4 percent.

An even more dramatic illustration of the "enhancement effect" of feedback is provided by the research of Geller, Eason, Phillips, and Pierson.[27] Training alone improved sanitation practices—specifically hand washing behavior—among kitchen workers by 21.7 percent. Training combined with feedback led to an increase in (required) hand washing of 203.1 percent.

Two additional findings concerning feedback might be mentioned. First, it has been found that feedback helps to raise satisfaction and motivation more on nonstimulating jobs than stimulating jobs. Second, there is evidence that individual feedback has a greater impact on performance than does group feedback.

Table 2.   Effects of Feedback on Work Behavior—continued

Year	Sample	Type of Feedback[a]	Other Interventions[b]	Impact on Job Performance	Comments
1979[23]	all salesper-sons in 5 de-partments of a department store	G	T, R	95% increase in the percentage of customers ap-proached by salespeople; serv-ice behavior score rose by 4%; over 5 to 11 weeks	
1979[24]	all workers in a fast-food snack bar	G		94% reduction in employee theft over a 1 to 4 week period	
1980[25]	55 employees in a city's ve-hicle mainte-nance department	G	T, GS	41.4% improve-ment in behav-ioral safety scores over 34 to 36 weeks	83% decrease in the number of lost-time acci-dents; employees had a favorable reaction to the program
1980[26]	11 front-line employees in a fast-food restaurant	Pvt. I	T, P, R	58% increase in friendliness be-havior (smiling) over a 1½ to 10 week period	
1980[27]	9 kitchen workers in a large univer-sity cafeteria	Pvt. I	T	203.7% increase in the frequency of hand washing over 3 weeks	in comparison, training alone in-creased the fre-quency of hand washing by only 21.7%

[a]Pvt. I = private individual; G = public group

[b]GS = goal setting; T = training; P = praise; R = social recognition

WHY FEEDBACK WORKS

There are two primary reasons why feed-back increases productivity: (1) it enhances the desire to perform well, i.e., it functions as a motivator; and (2) it cues learned re-sponses or serves to develop new responses, i.e., functions in an instructional capacity.

How Feedback Motivates

Four explanations have been advanced as to why feedback motivates increased produc-tivity. Although these explanations are actu-ally interrelated, each is discussed sep-arately for the sake of clarity.

1. *Feedback corrects misconceptions.* People often have somewhat distorted perceptions of their own work behaviors. The provision of objective feedback calls attention to these misperceptions and may motivate corrective action.

A dramatic example of this mechanism is provided by the Emery Air Freight intervention conducted by Edward J. Feeney.[1]

Executives at Emery were convinced that containers were being used about 90 percent of the times they could be used. Measurement of the actual usage—a measurement made by the same managers whose guesses had averaged 90 percent—showed that the actual usage was 45 percent, or half the estimate.

Subsequently, Emery Air Freight initiated a motivational program consisting of (a) goal setting, (b) performance measurement and feedback, and (c) positive reinforcement (praise, recognition). The net result was that the container usage rate rose from 45 percent to 95 percent. Also, the motivational program raised customer service so that the standard was met more than 90 percent of the time, compared to the prior level of 30 to 40 percent. Edward J. Feeney, the person responsible for designing and implementing the motivational program at Emery, noted that feedback was the critical variable in explaining the success of the program. In his words, "Most managers genuinely think that operations in their bailiwick are doing well; a performance audit that proves they're not comes as a real and unpleasant surprise."

Another illustration of the effect of objective feedback in eliminating misperceptions is provided by the case of the telephone reservation clerks at Aer Lingus.[19] The clerks were provided with profiles of their verbal behaviors obtained from unobtrusive work samples of twenty telephone calls per clerk. The feedback caused one telephone clerk to comment:

When asked previously whether I used the customer's name I would have said—and believed—'Of course, we were trained to do that.' I was really surprised when I saw objective evidence on how little I was actually doing it.

As a result of the monitoring and feedback program, use of the customer's name by the thirty clerks rose by 87.5 percent. The frequency of interruptions by the telephone clerks dropped by 100 percent.

To the extent that feedback is objective, valid, and hence, incontrovertible, it offers the possibility of informing an individual about his or her false self-perceptions. Certainly, the use of such feedback has been found to motivate improved job performance; presumably, it also has led to more accurate self-perceptions.

2. *Feedback creates internal consequences.* In the absence of performance feedback, it is unlikely that employees will have either positive or negative feelings about themselves as a result of their job performance. The provision of feedback, however, allows employees to experience positive (or negative) feelings about themselves—a psychological state called internal work motivation. Several examples of the motivational impact of performance feedback are to be found in the literature.

After the introduction of objective performance measurement and feedback among cash management clerks at Marine Midland, the average level of cash balances was reduced by 72 percent.[17] Supervisors offered the following comments. "The areas are completely aware of cash flow now; everyone gives 100 percent to the program. There seems to be that extra effort on the part of the people to get more involved in cash flows. . . . People are now trying to solve problems before they occur. People are looking to help out other individuals rather than just saying 'that's not my job.' I can say as a supervisor that it has a big impact on my own feelings toward the people who work for me. I feel a sense of accomplishment. . . ."

One week after the introduction of a performance measurement and feedback system in the emergency room of a large hospital in Manhattan, the proportion of completed reports submitted by emergency-room clerks rose from 67 percent to 95 percent. The casewriter observed that, "The clerks for their part were experiencing increased job satisfaction. As one clerk put it, 'I used to go home evenings wondering what I had done . . . now I look at my feedback report and can see what I have accomplished.'"

In short, objective performance feedback allows the individual employee to be able to "keep score"; improvements or declines in the individual's score may potentially be a source of satisfaction or dissatisfaction. Yet, it should be noted that knowledge of results is a necessary but not sufficient condition for internal work motivation. Other relevant factors include the meaningfulness and responsibility for results that the job incumbent sees in his work and the individual's desire to grow and achieve.

3. *Feedback may entail social consequences.* In situations where objective performance feedback is provided (a) by an employee's supervisor, or (b) by public posting of data, the individual (or work group) will typically experience social consequences, which in turn have been found to increase performance in a wide variety of work settings. For example, among 195 expericed truck drivers, letters of commendation were used to provide private recognition, and the posting at each terminal of the names of drivers who achieved six miles per gallon provided public recognition. These two forms of social reinforcers, plus token tangible rewards, reduced energy consumption substantially for two years and increased drivers' job satisfaction.[10]

In a mental health setting, staff suggestions and comments were publicly posted, and responses (feedback) were posted as well. Although all suggestions or comments were publicly posted, anonymity was assured if desired; participants did not have to sign their names. The net result was that 1.8 suggestions were generated per employee per year, considerably greater than the national average rate of .08 in federal government agencies and .4 in private industry, where sizable cash awards are frequently offered.[20]

The use of recognition in improving performance does not require that performance feedback be uniformly positive. An interesting illustration of this point comes from the world of professional sports. Dave Anderson of the *New York Times* provides the following anecdote concerning Frank Robinson's first year as manager of baseball's Cleveland Indians.

Buddy Bell, now with the Texas Rangers, was the Indians third baseman then. Buddy Bell was even-tempered, quiet, a hard worker, the organizer of the team's Fellowship of Christian Athletes Services. But midway through Frank Robinson's first season,

Buddy Bell confronted him. "You ignore me. You don't pat me on the back when I'm going good. You don't chew me out when I'm going bad...." Apparently...Frank Robinson responded to this criticism. By the end of that season...Buddy Bell confronted Frank Robinson again. "I just want you to know," he said, "that I enjoyed playing for you."

In a more practical vein, it has been found that the feedback of objective performance data can improve both productivity and the supervisor-employee relationship.[2] The supervisors of forty-three machine operators emphasized positive feedback (praise and favorable recognition) and adopted a constructive, problem-solving stance regarding undesirable behavior. Consequently, lines of communication opened up, trust increased, and interpersonal relations improved.

Thus, across such diverse groups as truck drivers, hospital employees, and machine operators, it is evident that recognition via performance feedback is an important motivator of improved work performance.

4. *Feedback creates external consequences.* The process of measuring and feeding back objective performance data tends to generate a heightened sense of evaluation consequences. As a result, individuals strive to "look good" to gain whatever rewards might result from managerial approval and to avoid "looking bad" and the accompanying adverse consequences resulting from managerial disapproval.

In his book, *Feedback and Organization Development*, Nadler has written: "One way in which data collection generates energy is through implied sanctions or rewards. The fact that an activity is measured through data collection sends a message that some po-

tentially powerful individual or group feels that the activity being measured is an important one." Thus, the process of measurement and feedback represents a two-edged sword: there is the threat of punishers or relative deprivation on the one hand and the possibility of rewards on the other.

Reviewing the research literature, there is some evidence indicating that the implied threat/promise of punishment or reward is an important reason for the motivational effect of objective performance feedback.

In the case of the draftsman who monitored the time he spent working, the measurement and feedback intervention led to a 72 percent increase in hours worked.[8] The authors wrote: "The fact that the subject's behavior changed so dramatically with the onset of self-monitoring lends plausibility to the interpretation that the behavior changes were the result of perceived aversive consequences for failure to meet acceptable levels of performance."

As has been suggested by Donald Law of Arthur Young & Company, the absence of performance measurement implies that management finds any level of performance to be acceptable. However, upon the institution of performance measurement and feedback, the implicit message would seem to be that management is interested in how proficient each individual (or work group) is. More specifically, the message that is conveyed by measurement/feedback actions—not merely by words—is that inefficient workers will be treated less favorably than others, possibly penalized or even terminated. Further, because measurement and feedback are absolutely essential to the operation of a merit reward system, these actions raise the possibility that management will be responsive to high levels of proficiency, i.e., that meritorious contributors will in fact be recognized and rewarded.

How Feedback Instructs

The second primary reason why feedback increases productivity is that it serves in an instructional capacity, i.e., it directs or cues behavior. Objective performance feedback can provide information pertinent to (a) the specific kinds of activities that should be performed, (b) the levels of proficiency that should be achieved in each of these activities, and (c) the individual's current level of proficiency in these activities. Interestingly, this information addresses three of the (four) questions that Virgil Rowland, in his book *Evaluating and Improving Managerial Performance*, found managers most wanted to have answered: What are my real job responsiblities?; What standards apply to these areas of responsibility?; and, At what level am I now performing? Clearly, the first two questions directly relate to the instructional role of feedback; the third question relates more to its motivational role.

Lawrence Miller, in his book *Behavior Management*, asserts that feedback will improve job performance to the extent that it pinpoints specific, observable tasks or activities. In his words, "A typical reaction to substandard performance is to assume there is a problem in the employee's motivation.... Often, however, a more fruitful approach is to assume there is a problem in clarity of performance expectations and timely, objective feedback of results to the employee."

Research by Roland Tharp and Ronald Gallimore, in an article in *Psychology Today* (January 1976), is also pertinent to the instructional/correctional capability of feedback. They studied the verbal behaviors of John Wooden, the highly successful UCLA basketball coach, in talking to his team during fifteen practice sessions. Tharp and Gallimore found that at least 75 percent of Wooden's comments contained informational contents. Further, most of his comments were specific statements of what to do or how to do it rather than motivational/positive reinforcing communications. Indeed, Wooden was more than five times as likely to inform than he was to praise or reprimand only.

Not only can feedback inform people about the activities they should be performing, it can also be used to provide information about standards of proficiency. This latter type of information is very important. For example, according to Jewell Westerman, a vice president at Hendrick & Company, a management consulting firm, "people who are measured know what's expected of them." Before going to work for Hendrick & Company, Westerman worked on productivity measurement at Travelers Insurance Company. Westerman found that white-collar workers often had "piles of work in front of them, but they didn't know if they were supposed to get it all out the same day. They needed feedback" and information about work standards. Indeed, insurance companies, such as Travelers, have pioneered in the area of work measurement for white-collar employees.

IMPLEMENTATION OF A PERFORMANCE MEASUREMENT AND FEEDBACK SYSTEM

In a 1980 survey, nearly 46,000 employees of forty large companies responded to questions about their interest in seventeen organization/job-related subjects, including job advancement opportunities and the organization's community involvement. Interest in the issue of productivity improvement ranked second, trailing only the "organization's future plans."

Potential Pitfalls

Apparently, employees today *say* they are very interested in productivity improvement, but to date they have not been particularly eager to adopt performance measurement as a method of improving productivity.

A number of researchers have reported on this reluctance. Lawrence Miller has observed that some employees and managers are apprehensive that work measurement and evaluation will not provide a fair assessment of their work. It has also been reported that white-collar workers frequently are insulted by claims that their work, like that of blue-collar workers, can be measured and graded. Furthermore, Marvin Mundel, a consultant, has found that scientists and engineers argue that since their regular work is constantly interrupted by emergency assignments, time standards cannot be applied to them. (In fact, Mundel observes, estimated time standards pertain to time spent working on a given assignment, not to the time that transpires before an assignment is completed.)

Perhaps the situation is analogous to the case of extrinsic incentives: people work harder if they are paid for performance, but they prefer to be paid for time. Unfortunately, desired outcomes such as increased productivity or higher pay often come at the price of increased effort—in short, there is no free lunch.

Preconditions

Of course, some organizations are more receptive to a measurement program than are others. Irving Siegel, in his *Company Productivity: Measurement for Improvement,* has identified three favorable preconditions for a measurement program: (1) good rapport between labor and management (i.e., high trust); (2) acceptance of analysis and interpretation as necessary complements of measurement; and (3) a prior history of measurement.

But with or without these preconditions, there are a number of concrete steps organizations can take to facilitate the implementation of a performance measurement and feedback system.

Practical Steps

1. *Obtain visible top management support.* Management consultants and practitioners repeatedly stress that a performance measurement system requires effort and committment from top management. In this vein, Gary P. Latham and Kenneth N. Wexley have written in *Increasing Productivity through Performance Appraisal* that "such support is essential as an umbrella under which new norms and expectations can flourish without the constant pressures to revert to the more comfortable and known ways of operating. Active senior management support is necessary for insuring a high level of commitment by middle managers for the system."

2. *Set up mechanisms for insuring middle management/supervisory commitment.* According to Latham and Wexley, "A key reason for the failure of a performance appraisal system/process is lack of middle management support once the system has been implemented. Middle managers can easily sabotage a human resource program. Thus, middle managers must be rewarded for participating in and supporting the various components of the appraisal process." Of course, the same applies to the implementation of objective feedback.

   In addition to using rewards and punishments, another mechanism for increasing support is early training and exposure to the program. There is evidence that when supervisors are trained to use a new system before lower-level personnel, program implementation is better than when supervisors are trained after lower-level personnel.

3. *Encourage a high level of employee participation.* Evidence from various settings supports the finding that the involvement and participation of employees is vital for the successful design and implementation of a measurement program. With professional white-collar employees, it is especially important that participation occur, and early on. Carl Thor, a vice-president at the American Productivity Center, offers the following insight. "One mistake people get into is they adopt a productivity banner, and then dust off their stopwatches and start measuring. But these . . . high level white-collar personnel are college graduates and they aren't going to put up with it." He suggests that employees work with the measurers in determining the correct measures and then in going over the results.

4. *Begin with successes.* The measurement program should be initiated in areas of the organization where there is a good chance of achieving positive results— "winners." With demonstrated successes, the credibility of the program increases, facilitating expansion to more complex and recalcitrant segments of the organization.

5. *Build a critical mass.* Unless a critical mass is attained, the program is unlikely to be sustained. Accordingly, the measurement program must be diffused throughout a significant part of the organization.

6. *Establish a task force.* In order to build a critical mass, the instrument for the design and implementation of the performance measurement system ought to be an ad hoc group of high-level employees. The task force, steering committee, or council should be chartered to represent top management in the development of a system within prescribed guidelines.

7. *Use the communications network.* From the very beginning, the task force should advertise its constructive intent. It should establish communications with a labor union and use in-house media to assure lower management and the operating staff that no revolutionary "new order" lies ahead. Additionally, the task force might designate liaison people throughout the organization, conduct briefings and demonstrations, and send out announcements.

8. *Set up a trial period.* After a "debugging" period, performance measurement should be undertaken on a trial basis. To indicate the trial nature of the first installation, the system should explicitly be labeled as "first generation," suggesting that changes will occur.

9. *Prepare an instruction manual and offer recommendations.* Before the task force is disbanded, an instruction manual should be written for users. The manual should describe (a) the general nature of the system (i.e., the structure, data sources, and purposes), and (b) the measurement process per se (i.e., procedures, periodicity, forms, reports, and staffing). Also, the task force should report on early results and offer recommendations.

10. *Implement review system.* Line managers should be responsible for reporting results of the program periodically. Having line managers do the reporting provides recognition and perhaps a feeling of accomplishment; it may also increase their sense of psychological ownership and commitment. Further, reviews

should be addressed to high-level administrators (e.g., the vice-presidents of operations and human resources).

CONCLUSION

A review of twenty-seven empirical studies indicates that objective feedback does not *usually* work—it virtually *always* works. In all cases, results were positive. On the average: work behaviors improved 78 percent; job performance indicators increased by 53 percent; and overall outputs, i.e., productivity, increased by 16 percent. These uniformly positive results occurred across diverse occupational groups and in various work settings. Moreover, there was little evidence that the effects diminished over time.

Why does objective feedback work? There are two reasons: it both energizes and directs work behavior. What kinds of organizations can profitably apply objective feedback? All kinds. And finally, how can organizations implement such an intervention? The key steps include obtaining managerial support, encouraging employee participation, achieving initial successes, and diffusing the intervention throughout the organization.

STATES L. CLAWSON
CAROL ANN MEARES

Productivity Information: A Key to Competitiveness

The authors present a guide to readily available productivity information and advice on building an information library.

Confronted by intense world competition, American business management is finally realizing the importance of improving productivity. Unprecedented effort is necessary to develop new ideas and refine old techniques.

A key to this effort is using information. But far too many business people are unaware of the vast quantity of productivity information that is readily available in this country. This includes step-by-step instructions on applying improvement tools and problem-solving techniques, descriptions of new technologies and processes, information on new forms of management and organization, and insights into the psychology of people at work.

Productivity-related information can reveal many details on what competitors, both domestic and foreign, are doing to improve operations, including:

States L. Clawson and Carol Ann Meares are manager and assistant manager, respectively, of the Commerce Productivity Center, U.S. Department of Commerce.

Improvement strategies, goals, results, management styles and organizational structuring, operational changes, and plans to upgrade work-force skills. Actual planning documents, evaluative checklists, special forms, and internal guides are sometimes available;

The types of technologies/processes that are in use or planned, and the resulting benefits. Among the details often revealed are those pertaining to what precipitated the decision to adopt innovations, how requirements were determined, selection, costs, implementation, applications, employee attitudes, training, the productivity improvements, cost savings, and expanded capabilities; and

Industry-specific data from special studies that can be used for comparisons, and industrywide surveys of improvement programs.

Some of the numerous and diverse sources of improvement information will be described in this article.

NONGOVERNMENT SOURCES

There are over forty-five productivity centers situated in nearly every region of the U.S. Some centers have special expertise in manufacturing productivity, engineering and technology, quality of work life, or public-sector productivity, and can provide technical assistance on improvement programs or technological applications to companies in their regions. Companies can also take advantage of the literature collections and education and training programs of the productivity centers. The Work in America Institute (Scarsdale, N.Y.) and the American Productivity Center (Houston, Tex.) sponsor peer group forums to stimulate improvement ideas and information exchange among participants. These forums have sponsored site visits in the U.S. and abroad, ongoing "information swapping" networks, computer conferences, and interfirm productivity measurement programs. The productivity centers have courteous, experienced people to assist inquirers.

Information on a particular industry can be obtained from professional associations and societies. Many have specialized libraries. One technical library of interest to improvement managers is the Engineering Societies' Library at 345 East 47th Street, New York, N.Y. 10017, (212) 705-7611. In addition, associations offer a wealth of knowledge in the form of expert opinion and advice from their experienced staffs. Associations also publish specialty periodicals and journals such as *Industrial Engineering* and *Industrial Management*, published by the American Institute of Industrial Engineers (Norcross, Ga.), and *Manufacturing Engineering*, published by the Society of Manufacturing Engineers (Dearborn, Mich.). Associations also sponsor trade shows and equipment expositions such as the Society of Manufacturing Engineers' AUTOFACT Conferences and Expos, which highlight

new manufacturing technologies; the American Institute of Industrial Engineers' Annual Productivity and Engineering Conferences, offering numerous sessions on productivity improvement; and the meetings of the American Productivity Management Association, where managers can hear presentations and discuss their productivity improvement experiences. Associations have participated in joint projects to help individual firms improve productivity. Interfirm productivity measurement programs are being carried out by the American Productivity Center in cooperation with the American Bakers Association and by the Oregon Productivity Center with the Northwest Food Processors Association.

Universities also have some resources for the improvement manager. Engineering and business management schools have libraries with periodicals, basic instructional texts, and handbooks. Companies can take advantage of the continuing education programs, extension services, current research, and expert opinions of professors who have years of experience in research and teaching. Some universities are working with the business community to match curriculum, research, and technological developments to business needs.

U.S. GOVERNMENT SOURCES

The U.S. government is the largest single source of productivity information in the country.

Commerce Department

The Commerce Department's Productivity Center (CPC) provides businesses and other organizations with information on how to improve productivity, quality, and competitiveness. As an information clearinghouse, the CPC can provide publications, articles, reference/referral services, bibliographies, and reading lists on a variety of productivity-related topics. The CPC has access to resources elsewhere in the Department of Commerce, including the Department's library, which contains thousands of specialty periodicals, journals, books, reports, and reference works. The CPC is building a large collection of information on productivity and related topics. As part of the Commerce Department's Office of Productivity, Technology and Innovation, the CPC has access to over thirty-five professionals with expertise in such diverse areas as economic policy, research and development, technology transfer, patent policy, industrial competitiveness, and metric conversion. The CPC is a good place to start when searching for productivity-related information.

The Bureau of Industrial Economics, also located within the Department of Commerce, collects and analyzes domestic and international data on production, pricing, inventories, marketing, labor, financing, taxation, energy consumption, productivity, and materials requirements for individual commodities and industries. The bureau is organized by industry classification and staffed with specialists in each industry category.

Commerce's International Trade Administration (ITA) offers a broad range of services designed to help U.S. firms enhance their competitiveness by developing their full export potential. Assistance includes export counseling sessions for companies, issuance of export licenses, interpretation of U.S. trade regulations, and special help in obtaining major contracts. ITA also collects and analyzes information on export opportunities in specific markets abroad. Additional information on ITA services is provided in its booklet, *USA Exports: Commerce Export Assistance Programs*, available from the U.S. Department of Commerce, International Trade Administration, Washington, D.C. 20230.

The National Technical Information Service, also part of the Commerce Department, is the central source for public sale of U.S. government-sponsored research and development, as well as foreign technical reports. The NTIS information collection has over 1.3 million titles, of which 200,000 contain foreign technology or marketing information.

NTIS publishes twenty-six weekly abstract newsletters, including *Administration and Management, Business and Economics, Government Inventions for Licensing,* and *Industrial and Mechanical Engineering.* These contain summaries of recent reports and research results.

NTIS also offers published searches, which are bibliographies containing between 100-200 document descriptions on the subject areas most frequently requested by NTIS customers. Published search topics include robots, incentive plans, inventory control, job- and industrial-related productivity, organizational planning and design, participative management, research management, computer-aided design of microcircuits, and machine automation and numerical control. At $35.00, the published search is an economical way to review available literature in a shorter time than a library search would require.

Other NTIS services include custom database searches, information on government patents, *Tech Notes* on new federally-developed processes and products considered to have commercial potential, and a standing order service whereby users can regularly receive all new reports on topics selected from one or more of 38 major subject categories and 355 subcategories in microfiche form for $1.10 a report.

More details on NTIS can be obtained from its general catalog of information services, available at National Technical Information Service, 5285 Port Royal Road, Springfield, Virginia 22161.

The National Bureau of Standards provides scientific and technological services for industry and government to aid in increasing productivity and innovation. Expertise and assistance are available in such diverse areas as computer systems engineering, computer programming science and technology, applied mathematics, building technology, chemical engineering, electronics and electrical engineering, manufacturing engineering, analytical chemistry, chemical physics, and materials science. Further information on assistance available from the National Bureau of Standards can be obtained by contacting the Technical Information and Publications Division, National Bureau of Standards, U.S. Department of Commerce, Washington, D.C. 20234, (301) 921-2318.

When assistance is needed in locating the federal agency that can best serve the needs of a particular business firm, the Office of Business Liaison (OBL) within the Commerce Department should be contacted. OBL serves as the focal point for all Department of Commerce agencies' contact with the business community. Through its Roadmap Program, OBL provides assistance to businesses in dealing with the federal government. The *Business Services Directory*, which contains information on all Department of Commerce services, including phone numbers, can be obtained by writing the U.S. Department of Commerce, Office of Business Liaison, Washington, D.C. 20230.

Labor Department

At the U.S. Department of Labor, the Office of Productivity and Technology of the Bureau of Labor Statistics conducts three major research activities. The productivity research program can provide comprehensive statistics for the U.S. economy, its major component sectors, and individual industries. The technological studies program investigates trends in technology and their impact on employment and productivity. The international program compiles and analyzes statistics on productivity and related factors in foreign countries for comparison with similar U.S. statistics. Additional information is contained in the office's Report 671, *BLS Publications on Productivity and Technology*, available at the Office of Productivity and Technology, Bureau of Labor Statistics, U.S. Department of Labor, Washington, D.C. 20212.

The Division of Cooperative Labor-Management Programs at the Labor Department (Washington, D.C. 20210) assists employees and unions in joint efforts to improve productivity and enhance the quality of work life. The division works closely with trade associations, international unions, area labor-management committees, and national, state, and regional productivity/quality-of-work-life centers. In addition, it regularly compiles and disseminates information on labor-management cooperation through publications, conferences, and workshops.

Locating the Appropriate Government Office

To discover which of the hundreds of federal government offices can provide the answer to a particular question, any individual can phone, visit, or write to a local Federal Information Center. The FIC will either answer the question or locate the expert who can. There are centers in forty-one major metropolitan areas, with forty-three other cities connected to the nearest center by toll-free telephone tie lines. Toll-free statewide FIC service is offered in five states.

Another aid in locating federal information sources is *The United States Government Manual*, which comprehensively describes the agencies of the legislative, judicial, and executive branches. A typical agency description includes a list of principal officials, a summary statement of the agency's purpose and role in the government, a brief history of the agency, a description of its programs and activities, and a "Sources of Information" section. The 1983/84 edition of this manual can be purchased for $9.00 from the Superintendent of Documents, U.S. Government Printing Office, Washington, D.C. 20402 (stock no. 022-003-01099-8).

PUBLICATIONS

Published information on productivity improvement can be found in a variety of forms, from brief articles to comprehensive handbooks.

Books, Articles, and Reports

Here are some of the thousands of worthy productivity-related books, articles, and reports.

American Productivity Center Publications Program (Houston, Tex.): *Productivity Briefs*—a four-page briefing on a different productivity-related topic each month; *Pulse Report*—experts comment and advise on a different productivity-related topic bimonthly; *Case Studies*—a six-to-eight-page description of the productivity program of a selected U.S. company each month; *Benchmarks*—a two-page statistical treatment of a productivity topic bimonthly; *Productivity Letter*—productivity news, views, and reports of the American Productivity Center's activities; *Multiple Input Productivity Indexes*—quarterly statistical reporting of U.S. productivity performance and annual industry report; *Productivity Perspectives*—annual analysis of international and national productivity (essential for preparing presentations on U.S. productivity); *Special Reports*—recent reports include *Comparative Productivity Dynamics—Japan and the United States, Productivity Digest* (extensive bibliography on productivity), and *White-Collar Productivity: The National Challenge.*

The Art of Japanese Management: Applications for American Executives, by Richard Pascale and Tony Athos (Simon & Schuster, N.Y.: 1981)—Japanese and American experiences illustrate McKinsey's "Seven S's of Management"—strategy, structure, systems, staff, skills, style, and superordinate goals.

"Building a Program for Productivity Management: A Strategy for IEs," by Scott Sink. *Industrial Engineering* 14(10):42-50, October 1982—a blueprint for a companywide productivity improvement strategy.

Improving Life at Work: Behavioral Science Approaches to Organizational Change, by J. Richard Hackman and J. Lloyd Suttle (Goodyear Publishing Co., Santa Monica, Calif.: 1977)—a basic text on improving quality of work life through career development, work design, reward systems, group and intergroup relations, and managerial practices.

Improving Total Productivity: MBO Strategies for Business, Government, and Not-For-Profit Organizations, by Paul Mali (Wiley-Interscience, N.Y.: 1978)—a step-by-step guide to improved productivity through planning, measuring, evaluating, and motivating.

In Search of Excellence: Lessons from America's Best Run Companies, by Tom Peters and Robert Waterman (Harper & Row, N.Y.: 1982)—a look at organizational excellence in selected U.S. companies.

Introduction to Work Study (third revised edition) (International Labour Office, Washington, D.C. 1979)—over 400 pages of step-by-step instructions and illustrations on work study techniques.

Japanese Manufacturing Techniques: Nine Hidden Lessons in Simplicity, by Richard Schonenberger (The Free Press, N.Y.: 1982)—Japanese management approaches to cost and quality control, inventory, and worker productivity.

"Japan—Where Operations Really Are Strategic," by Steven C. Wheelwright. *Harvard Business Review* 59(4):67-74, July-August 1981—how operational improvements support long-term business strategy.

Managing Productivity, by Joel E. Ross (Reston Publishing Co., Reston, Va.: 1977)—a systematic approach to productivity improvement through management action.

"The New Industrial Relations," *Business Week*, May 11, 1981 (pp.84-98)—a special report on labor-management cooperation.

The One Minute Manager, by Kenneth Blanchard and Spencer Johnson (William Morrow and Co., N.Y.: 1982)—how to develop a management style for effective problem resolution.

People and Productivity, by Robert A. Sutermeister (McGraw-Hill Book Co., N.Y.: 1976) —a text on the people aspect of productivity, including thirty-eight background readings by such leading experts as Maslow, Herzberg, Likert, Drucker, Argyris, and McGregor.

Productivity and the Economy: A Chart Book, U.S. Department of Labor, Bureau of Labor Statistics (U.S. Government Printing Office, Washington, D.C.: 1983)—the chart book of facts on U.S. productivity; very helpful in preparing presentations.

Productivity By Objectives: Results-Oriented Solutions to the Productivity Puzzle, by James L. Riggs and Glenn H. Felix (Prentice-Hall, Inc., Englewood Cliffs, N.J.: 1983)—step-by-step procedures for employee involvement, productivity measurement, productivity skills training, improving managerial performance, quality improvement, and using productivity-enhancing techniques and technologies.

"Productivity Management," by Marta Mooney. *Research Bulletin No. 127* (The Conference Board, N.Y.: 1982)—a report on the productivity management function.

The Productivity Management Process, by John G. Belcher, Jr. (Planning Executives Institute, Oxford, Ohio: 1982)—includes chapters on: the productivity improvement process; commitment and organization; reinforcing, sustaining, and integrating productivity; productivity measurement; quality of work life; and opportunity assessment.

The Productivity Problem: Alternatives for Action, Congressional Budget Office (U.S. Government Printing Office, Washington, D.C.: January 1981)

—"just the facts" on U.S. productivity performance and options for its improvement.

Productivity Sharing Programs: Can They Contribute to Productivity Improvement? (U.S. General Accounting Office, Washington, D.C.: March 3, 1981)—an objective evaluation of productivity sharing programs including the Scanlon, Rucker, and Improshare plans.

Quality is Free, by Philip B. Crosby (paperback, New American Library, N.Y.: 1979)—suggests approaches and provides tools for initiating a successful quality control program.

The Quality of Working Life, Vol. 1: *Problems, Prospects, and the State of the Art;* Vol. 2: *Cases and Commentary*, ed. by Louis E. Davis and Albert B. Cherns (The Free Press, N.Y.: 1975)—thirty-six original articles address quality-of-work-life issues, including enhancement, measurement, change, technology, industrial relations, organization structure, and job design.

Quality, Productivity, and Competitive Position, by W. Edwards Deming (MIT Center for Advanced Engineering Studies, Cambridge, Mass.: 1982)—the father of statistical quality control explains how to improve quality and productivity through a system of statistically-based process control.

"The Reindustrialization of America." *Business Week*, June 30, 1980 (pp. 55-114, 120-142)—a special issue that documents the U.S. industrial decline and its causes, and suggests some specifics for reindustrialization.

R&D Productivity: An Investigation of Ways to Evaluate and Improve Productivity in Technology-Based Organizations (Hughes Aircraft Co., Culver City, Calif.: 1978)—a valuable guide for developing productivity improvement approaches; discusses organizational, managerial, employee, and personal productivity; contains numerous checklists, evaluative work sheets, and an extensive bibliography.

Robotics in Practice: Management and Applications of Industrial Robots, by Joseph F. Engelberger (AMACOM, N.Y.: 1980)—an introduction to robotics, including robot types, selection, applications, costs, benefits, sociological impact, and future systems.

12 Common Sense Steps to Productivity Improvement, by William F. Schleicher (National Productivity Report, Wheaton, Ill.: 1978)— a twenty-two page, step-by-step productivity improvement plan that incorporates many of the elements common to successful programs.

"Why Japanese Factories Work," by Robert H. Hayes. *Harvard Business Review* 59(4):56-66, July-August 1981—shows how close attention to the details of operation is a cornerstone of success in Japanese factories.

Performance measurement guides. Two books offer numerous examples of performance measures for various activities:

How to Measure Managerial Performance, by Richard S. Sloma (Macmillan Publishing Co., Inc., N.Y.: 1980)—sample performance measures are given for managers in marketing, sales, purchasing, production, quality assurance, personnel, EDP/MIS, plant and facilities management, materials handling, accounting, and industrial engineering.

Measuring Productivity in Physical Distribution (National Council of Physical Distribution Management, Chicago, Ill. 1978)—offers suggestions on establishing productivity programs, measurement techniques, and measurement data bases in the physical distribution functions of transportation, warehousing, purchasing, inventory, production management, and administration.

Detailed implementation instruction materials. Handbooks and articles offering detailed instructions are available on many productivity-related topics:

Company Productivity: Measurement for Improvement, by Irving H. Siegel (Upjohn Institute for Employment Research, Kalamazoo, Mich.: 1980).

"Graphic Indicators of Operations," Robert L. Janson, *Harvard Business Review* 58(6):164-170, November-December 1980.

Handbook of Business Adminstration, ed. by H.B. Maynard (McGraw-Hill Book Co., N.Y.: 1967).

Handbook of Industrial Engineering, ed. by Gavriel Salvendy (John Wiley & Sons, Somerset, N.J.: 1982).

Handbook of Modern Manufacturing Management, ed. by H.B. Maynard (McGraw-Hill Book Co., N.Y.: 1970).

Improving Productivity: A Self Audit and Guide for Federal Executives and Managers, National Center for Productivity and Quality of Working Life (U.S. Government Printing Office, Washington, D.C.: Fall 1978).

Improving Productivity in State and Local Government, ed. by George Washnis (Wiley-Interscience, N.Y.: 1980).

Improving Productivity Through Advanced Office Controls, by Robert E. Nolan, et al. (AMACOM, N.Y.: 1980).

Industrial Engineering Handbook, ed. by H.B. Maynard (McGraw-Hill Book Co., N.Y.: 1971).

Measuring Productivity in Accounting and Finance Offices (Joint Financial Management Improvement Program, Washington, D.C.: September 1981).

"Measuring Your Productivity: How To Do It," by George E. Sadler. *Plastics Technology* 28(1):74-81, January 1982.

Production and Inventory Control Handbook, ed. by James H. Greene (McGraw-Hill Book Co., N.Y.: 1970).

Putting Quality Circles to Work, by Ralph Barra (McGraw-Hill Book Co., N.Y.: 1983).

Quality Circles Master Guide: Increasing Productivity With People Power, by Sud Ingle (Prentice-Hall, Inc., Englewood Cliffs, N.J.: 1982).

Quality Control Handbook, by J.M. Juran (McGraw-Hill Book Co., N.Y.: 1974).

Starting a Labor-Management Committee in Your Organization: Some Pointers for Action, National Center for Productivity and Quality of Working Life (U.S. Government Printing Office, Washington, D.C.: Spring 1978).

Implementing a Productivity Program: Points to Consider (Joint Financial Management Improvement Program, Washington, D.C.: 1977).

Techniques of Structured Problem Solving, by Arthur B. VanGundy, Jr. (Van Nostrand Reinhold Co., N.Y.: 1981).

White Collar Productivity, by Robert Lehrer. (McGraw-Hill Book Co., N.Y.: 1982).

Case study volumes. Two recent books offer a variety of productivity improvement experiences:

Productivity Improvement: Case Studies of Proven Practice, ed. by Vernon M. Buehler and Y. Krishna Shetty (AMACOM, N.Y.: 1981)—case studies of Corning Glass Works, Nucor Corp., Kaiser Aluminum and Chemical Corp., Beatrice Foods, Crompton Co., Hughes Aircraft Co., General Foods Co., Continental Group, Burger King Corp., Chicago Title and Trust Co., Detroit Edison, and Tanner Cos.

Quality and Productivity Improvements: U.S. and Foreign Experiences (Utah State University, College of Business, Logan, Utah: 1982)—Japan Steel Works, Nippon Electric Co., Nippon Kokan, Fujitsu Ltd., Toyota, TRW, Matsushita Industrial Co., AT&T, Xerox Corp., American Express Co., and other presentations on European experiences and selected productivity issues.

Bibliographies and directories. Bibliographies can serve as gateways to the vast literature on productivity and related topics. The Work in America Institute (Scarsdale, N.Y.) offers twenty-eight single-subject studies, each containing a review of the literature, abstracted bibliographic citations, and numerous additional references. Topics in this study series include managerial productivity, human-resource accounting, alternative work schedules, occupational stress, job redesign, worker attitudes, productivity measurement, absenteeism, the impact of technology on manufacturing and service industries, white-collar productivity, productivity sharing, productivity in Japan, quality circles, participative management, and labor-management cooperation.

The Department of Labor's Bureau of Labor Statistics has published four bibliographies available from the U.S. Government Printing Office: *Productivity: A Selected, Annotated Bibliography, 1976-78*, BLS Bulletin 2051, April 1980; *Productivity: A Selected, Annotated Bibliography, 1971-75*, BLS Bulletin 1933, 1977; *Productivity: A Selected, Annotated Bibliography, 1965-71*, BLS Bulletin 1776, 1973; and *Productivity: A Bibliography*, BLS Bulletin 1514, July 1966. These bibliographies would be helpful to those seeking documents that provide a historical perspective on macro-productivity.

Two directories useful to those involved with productivity improvement are a directory of professional associations (the subject index will guide the user to the organization that may have the appropriate expertise), and the *Resource Guide to Labor Management Cooperation* (U.S. Government Printing Office, Washington, D.C.: October 1983). The latter contains fact sheets on cooperative programs to improve productivity and quality of work life in U.S. companies and federal, state, and local government agencies. Contact persons' addresses and phone numbers are included for each entry.

Productivity Periodicals

Some of the periodicals dedicated to productivity are:

Executive Productivity (Productivity Newsletter Associates, Boca Raton, Fla.)—eight pages monthly of brief articles containing methods for improving productivity, advice and insights from experts, personal productivity tips, and news items of interest to white-collar workers.

Manufacturing Productivity Frontiers (Manufacturing Productivity Center, Illinois Institute of Technology, Chicago)—over fifty pages each month of feature articles, meeting reviews, brief articles and notes, book reviews, announcements, upcoming meetings, and abstracts of relevant articles.

National Productivity Report (Wheaton, Ill.)—four pages biweekly featuring a case study, improvement technique review, or research findings; also, news items, expert advice, and productivity tips.

National Productivity Review (Executive Enterprises Publications, Co., Inc., N.Y.)—a quarterly journal in which experts write in depth on productivity-related topics; usually nine or ten articles per issue, plus a productivity forum, book reviews, article summaries, a listing of QWL and productivity centers, and a calendar of symposia, conferences, and workshops.

Productivity (Productivity, Inc., Stamford, Conn.) —a twelve-page monthly offering case studies, instructions for applying improvement tools, technology reports, book reviews, interviews, expert advice, and news. White-collar and production improvement information is featured. (NOTE: This organization sponsors two conferences each year featuring keynote addresses and numerous workshop sessions. Cassette tapes of the conference presentations are available).

Productivity Management (Oklahoma Productivity Center, Oklahoma State University Engineering Extension, Stillwater, Okla.)—seven-page quarterly presenting feature-length and brief articles on management of productivity improvement, plus news items.

Productivity Primer (Oregon Productivity Center, Oregon State University, Corvallis, Ore.)—four-page monthly, and occasional eight-page special issues, offering case studies, short articles on improvement techniques, book reviews, brief discussions of national productivity issues, and news items.

Public Productivity Review (National Center for Public Productivity, John Jay College, N.Y.)—a quarterly journal of articles, book reviews, interviews, and case studies on public-sector productivity.

QWL Focus (Ontario Quality of Working Life Center, Ontario Ministry of Labour, Toronto)—over twenty pages quarterly of in-depth examination of QWL topics, case studies, international QWL news, and short abstracts of selected readings.

The Work Life Review (Michigan Quality of Work Life Council, Troy, Mich.)—a quarterly journal on quality-of-work-life and employee involvement theory and practice.

World of Work Report (Work in America Institute, Scarsdale, N.Y.)—an eight-page monthly offering international coverage of new work-place trends, experiments, and developments and other contemporary organizational, industry, and national productivity issues.

Business and Management Periodicals

Of the general business periodicals, the biweekly *Industry Week* (Penton/IPC, Cleveland, Ohio) excels in its coverage of U.S. industrial competitiveness. Its spotlight on contemporary national, industry, and organizational issues is right on target. It highlights timely information for business managers through feature articles, executive commentaries, news analyses, technology reviews, executive profiles, and coverage of business, management, and economic trends.

There are numerous management periodicals to be explored by the productivity professional. Useful information can always be found in *Harvard Business Review* (Woburn, Mass.), *Industrial Management* (American Institute of Industrial Engineers, Norcross, Ga.), *Management Review* (American Management Associations, Saranac Lake, N.Y.— available only to AMA members), *Organizational Dynamics* (AMACOM, N.Y.), *Personnel Administrator* (American Society of Personnel Administration, Berea, Ohio), *Personnel Journal* (Costa Mesa, Calif.), *Research Management* (Lancaster, Pa.), *Sloan Management Review* (Massachusetts Institute of Technology, Cambridge, Mass.), and *Training and Development Journal* (American Society for Training and Development, Washington, D.C.).

Trade, Technical and Specialty Journals

Of the trade, technical, and specialty journals, the American Institute of Industrial

Engineers' *Industrial Engineering* easily qualifies as a productivity publication. This superb monthly has recently devoted entire issues to productivity projects in service/ support industries, improving productivity corporatewide, high-tech projects in manufacturing, work sampling and measurement, incentive systems, the automated factory, and quality control and reliability engineering.

Other specialty journals that provide useful information for improvement managers include *Assembly Engineering* (Hitchcock Publishing, Wheaton, Ill.), *CAD/CAM Technology* (Society of Manufacturing Engineers, Dearborn, Mich.), *Information and Records Management* (PTN Publishing Corp., Woodbury, N.Y.), *Infosystems* (Hitchcock Publishing, Wheaton, Ill.), *Management Technology* (Norwalk, Conn.), *Manufacturing Engineering* (Society of Manufacturing Engineers, Dearborn, Mich.), *Modern Machine Shop* (Gardner Publications, Inc., Cincinnati, Ohio), *Modern Office Technology* (Penton/ IPC, Cleveland, Ohio), *The Office* (Office Publications, Inc., Stamford, Conn.), *Office Administration and Automation* (Geyer-McAllister Publications, N.Y.), *Production* (Bloomfield Hills, Mich.), *Production Engineering* (Penton/IPC, Cleveland, Ohio), *Robotics Today* (Society of Manufacturing Engineers, Dearborn, Mich.), *Today's Office* (Hearst Business Communications, Inc., Garden City, N.Y.), and *Tooling and Production* (Huebner Publications, Inc., Solon, Ohio).

The improvement manager should seek out periodicals appropriate to type of organization (i.e., *Hospitals, Public Administration Review, ABA Banking Journal*), function (i.e., *Graphic Arts Monthly, Equipment Management, Modern Materials Handling, Design News, Sales and Marketing Management*), and product (i.e., *Iron Age, Plastics Technology, Chemical Engineering, Textile World*) and scan them for workable ideas.

National Conference Proceedings

The sponsoring organizations compile informative proceedings of the following national conferences: the American Institute of Industrial Engineers' (Norcross, Ga.) productivity and engineering conferences and expos; the Society of Manufacturing Engineers' (Dearborn, Mich.) AUTOFACT (automated factory) conferences and expos; and the Illinois Institute of Technology Research Institute's (Chicago, Ill.) national conferences on "Improving the Productivity of Technical Resources."

BUILDING AN INTRAFIRM INFORMATION BASE

In many organizations, people keep magazines here and clip articles there. But what's needed is organized information gathering, review, and usage activity wherever productivity improvement is sought. Many companies across the nation are developing their own productivity information collections. Intended for the use of all employees from top management to the assembly line or office employee, these mini-centers are stocked with books, instructional guides and handbooks, periodicals, bibliographies, films, and other information resources.

Those planning a productivity information collection should survey the organization to determine the interests of key managers and the information support needed in work groups. Some of the basic necessities in the mini-productivity collection include instructional guides on productivity measurement, work study, and problem-solving techniques; basic texts on productivity management; basic texts on behavioral science and cooperative approaches to improving productivity and QWL; case studies; information on improving productivity in work functions; and appropriate periodicals. Be sure that some of the information can be understood by people without technical sophistication, because the collection should be of use to everyone in the organization.

Keeping a constant flow of productivity improvement ideas into the organization need not be expensive. Steps for establishing a model productivity information portfolio in an organization that has both production and office functions might include:

Trying to qualify for free subscriptions to *Industry Week*, *Production*, *Production Engineering*, *Tooling and Production*, *The Office*, *Modern Office Technology*, *Today's Office*, and *Information and Records Management*;

Subscribing to *Industrial Engineering* ($35.00 per year), *Industrial Management* ($22.00 per year), *Productivity Management* ($25.00 per year), *Productivity Primer* (free), *Management Review* (available to American Management Association members only); and

Choosing from the following dedicated productivity periodicals those which best meet your organization's needs (request a free sample first to help determine which meet those needs): *Manufacturing Productivity Frontiers* ($100.00 per year), *Executive Productivity* ($72.00 per year), *Productivity* ($126.00 per year), *National Productivity Report* ($66.00 per year); and *National Productivity Review* ($96.00 per year).

The modest investment required can probably be recovered by the adoption of one or two good ideas.

A nonprint source of information is factory tours or visits to other offices. They can provide insights into one's own organization's operations and might reveal new ways to utilize technologies, more effective staffing patterns, or how a competitor maintains a higher level of service. Many U.S. executives have benefited enormously from visits to factories in Japan. They return with a fresh perspective and an eagerness to apply the new ideas stimulated by observing Japanese production and work-force management practices.

Using the Information

Once an organization is committed to using information, the productivity manager or company librarian must devise ways to disseminate it and encourage its use. There are several ways to accomplish this.

Through in-house publications and newsletters, the manager or librarian should advertise that the information is available to all employees, suggest how it might be used, and discuss the benefits of using it. In addition, he or she should distribute personal productivity tips, results of improvement team efforts, facts to illustrate the need for improvements, etc.

Selected information can be sent regularly to key managers and employee groups. The development of "interest profiles" can guide in the selection of information for individuals or groups.

Circulating reading lists of articles on competitiveness issues can encourage employees to broaden their perspectives beyond the scope of their daily activities.

Study guides can be compiled for groups performing particular functions, such as maintenance or word processing. Subject guides can be compiled to complement the improvement approaches being employed, such as quality circles or work simplification.

Productivity information can also be used as a motivational tool. Presentations can be developed to illustrate the competitive nature of today's business environment and the consequences of improvement inaction.

Companies should also regularly monitor information to provide early warning on developments that could affect their competitiveness.

All employees can use information to improve their personal productivity and to contribute to company productivity improvements. Individuals or employee groups can collect information to develop improvement suggestions and to assist in the accomplishment of their daily work in such areas as time management, stress reduction, interpersonal communications, and problem solving. It is interesting to note that a recent survey of 453 Japanese companies showed that the average employee made 39.2 suggestions per year. Armed with the appropriate information and motivation, the U.S. work force could develop this same "power of suggestion."

CONCLUSION

Learning is the first step to improving productivity. Time and money can be saved and mistakes avoided by learning from the experience of others and from the experts who have devoted lifetimes to the study of working smarter. The learning process is continuous and will always reveal new paths for improvement. Any organization not taking advantage of the wealth of good ideas available in improvement information is ignoring a powerful tool for boosting productivity.

Notes and References

CHAPTER 1

REFERENCES

1. C. Jackson Grayson, Jr., "Our Leaders Must Act to Restore Productivity," *Enterprise America Report* (May 1982):4.

2. John J. Hohengarten, "Productivity Management: Planning the Right Opening Moves," *Productivity Brief* 22 (Houston, Texas: American Productivity Center, February 1983):2–7.

3. Robert A. Sutermeister, *People and Productivity*, 3rd ed. (New York: McGraw-Hill Book Company, 1976).

4. Hohengarten, *op. cit.*

5. David M. Miller, "Profitability = Productivity + Price Recovery," *Harvard Business Review* (May/June 1984):145–153.

6. *Workers' Attitudes Toward Productivity* (Washington, D.C.: Chamber of Commerce of the United States of America, 1980); see also *Perspectives on Productivity: A Global View* (Stevens Point, Wisconsin: Sentry Insurance Company, n.p., n.d.).

HOW IT IS MEASURED

1. Ryohei Suzuki, "Worldwide Expansion of U.S. Exports—A Japanese View," *Sloan Management Review*, Spring 1979, p. 1.

2. *Business Week*, February 16, 1976, p. 57.

3. Burton G. Malkiel, "Productivity—The Problem Behind the Headlines," HBR May–June 1979, p. 81.

4. Roger Bennett and Robert Cooper, "Beyond the Marketing Concept," *Business Horizons*, June 1979, p. 76.

5. J. Hugh Davidson, "Why Most New Consumer Brands Fail," HBR March–April 1976, p. 117.

6. *Business Week*, February 16, 1976, p. 57.

7. Eric von Hippel, "The Dominant Role of Users in the Scientific Instrument Innovation Process," MIT Sloan School of Management Working Paper 75-764, January 1975.

8. *Dun's Review*, July 1978, p. 39.

9. *Business Week*, March 3, 1980, p. 76.

CHAPTER 2

REFERENCES

1. "What Can America Do to Solve Its Productivity Crisis?" *World* (Winter 1981):24.

2. Stanley B. Henrici, "How Deadly Is the Productivity Disease?" *Harvard Business Review* (November/December, 1981):123–129.

3. Amitai Etzioni, "Rebuilding Our Economic Foundations," *Business Week* (August 25, 1980):16.

4. Kyonosuke Ibe, "It Took the Japanese to Build Japan," *Business Week* (October 6, 1980):17–18.

5. "How Firms Cut Costs to Battle the Slump," *U. S. News and World Report* (April 5, 1982):73.

6. Lester C. Thurow, "Farms: A Policy Success," *Newsweek* (May 16, 1983):78.

7. Thomas H. Melohn, "How to Build Employee Trust and Productivity," *Harvard Business Review* (January/February 1983):56ff.

8. "What Can America Do to Solve Its Productivity Crisis?", *op. cit.*

9. Herman J. Heinjn, "Automate the Organization... or Organize the Automation," *Productivity Brief* 14 (June 1982):2–8.

10. Thurow, *op. cit.*

11. Carla O'Dell, "Large Majority of Americans Now View Productivity Growth as an Urgent National Issue," *Productivity Brief* 3 (July 1981):2–5.

12. *Ibid.*

CHAPTER 3

REFERENCES

1. Blaise Pascal (1623–1662), *Pensées*, Chapter 1.

2. William A. Ruch and James C. Hershauer, *Factors Affecting Worker Productivity* (Tempe, Arizona: Bureau of Business and Economic Research, 1974).

3. *Ibid.*, 90.

4. For example, see John P. Van Gigch, *Applied General Systems Theory* (New York: Harper & Row, Publishers, 1978).

5. Peter P. Schoderbek, Charles G. Schoderbek, and Asterios G. Kefalas, *Management Systems*, 3d ed. (Plano, Texas: Business Publications, Inc., 1985).

6. David I. Cleland and William R. King, *Systems Analysis and Project Management*, 2d ed. (New York: McGraw-Hill Book Company, 1975), 18.

7. Martin K. Starr, *Systems Management of Operations* (Englewood Cliffs, N.J.: Prentice-Hall, 1971).

8. Excerpted from Everett E. Adam, Jr., James C. Hershauer, and William A. Ruch, *Productivity and Quality: Measurement as a Basis for Improvement*, Copyright Everett E. Adam, Jr., 1984.

9. Peter F. Drucker, "Beyond Efficiency to Effectiveness." Speech given to the Spring Conference of Work Factor Associates of the West, Anaheim, California, May 3, 1974. (Paraphrased, as no text of the speech is available.)

LINCOLN ELECTRIC

1. Ackoff, Russell L. *The Design of Social Research.* Chicago: University of Chicago Press, 1953.

2. *Business Week.* "Productivity, Our Biggest Undeveloped Resource." September 9, 1972.

3. Craig, Charles E. and R. Clark Harris. "Total Productivity Measurement at the Firm Level." *Sloan Management Review.* Spring, 1973.

4. Dunlap, John R. and Vasilii P. Diatchenko. *Labor Productivity.* New York: McGraw-Hill, 1964.

5. Gerstenberg, Richard C. "Productivity: Its Meaning for America." *The Manager's Key*, December, 1973.

6. Greenberg, Leon. *A Practical Guide to Productivity Measurement.* Rockville, Maryland: BNA Books, 1973.

7. Forrester, Jay W. *Industrial Dynamics.* Cambridge, Massachusetts: The M.I.T. Press, 1961.

8. Katzell, R. A. and D. Yankelovich. "Improving Productivity and Job Satisfaction." *Organizational Dynamics*, Summer, 1975.

9. Kendrick, J. W. and D. Creamer. *Measuring Company Productivity.* Studies in Business Economics, No. 89. New York: National Industrial Conference Board, 1965.

10. Kilmann, R. H. and I. I. Mitroff. "Qualitative versus Quantitative Analysis for Management Science: Different Forms for Different Psychological Types." *Interfaces*, Vol. 6, No. 2, February, 1976.

11. Lawler, E. E. III. *Pay and Organizational Effectiveness: A Psychological View.* New York: McGraw-Hill, 1971.

12. Likert, Rensis. *New Patterns of Management.* New York: McGraw-Hill, 1961.

13. National Commission of Productivity, Report of the Commission, *Productivity.* Washington, D.C.: U.S. Government Printing Office, 1972.

14. Roberts, Nancy. "Teaching Dynamic Feedback Systems Thinking: An Elementary View." Paper presented at the National ORSA/TIMS Meeting, Las Vegas, November, 1975.

15. Ruch, W. A. and J. C. Hershauer. "Factors Affecting Worker Productivity." Occasional Paper No. 10, Bureau of Business and Economic Research, Arizona State University, September, 1974.

16. ———— and ————. "A Bibliography on Worker Productivity." Unpublished Report, Arizona State University, October, 1974.

17. ———— and ————. "Increasing Productivity: The Lincoln Electric System and the Donnelly Mirrors System." *The Personnel Administrator*, September, 1975.

18. Smith, Ian G. *The Measurement of Productivity.* 2nd Edition. New York: McGraw-Hill, 1969.

19. Sutermeister, R. A. *People and Productivity.* 3rd Edition. New York: McGraw-Hill, 1976.

20. Taylor, J. C. et al. *The Quality of Working Life: An Annotated Bibliography.* Los Angeles: University of California at Los Angeles, 1973.

21. U.S. Department of Labor, Bureau of Labor Statistics. *Productivity: A Selected Annotated Bibliography* (Bulletin 1776). 1973. Washington, D.C.: Government Printing Office.

22. U.S. Department of Labor, Bureau of Labor Statistics. *The Meaning and Measurement of Productivity.* September, 1971. Washington, D.C.: Government Printing Office.

CHAPTER 4

REFERENCES

1. Maslow, A. H., *The Farther Reaches of Human Nature* (Penguin Books, 1976):227.

2. H. A. Murray, *Exploration in Personality* (Oxford University Press, 1938).

3. A. H. Maslow, "A Theory of Human Motivation," *Psychological Review* 50, no. 4 (July 1943): 370–396.

4. C. P. Alderfer, *Existence, Relatedness and Growth: Human Needs in Organizational Settings* (The Free Press, 1972).

5. M. Wahba and L. Birdwell, "Maslow Reconsidered: A Review of Research on the Need Hierarchy Theory," *Organizational Behavior and Human Performance* 15 (1976):212–240.

6. F. Herzberg, B. Mausner and B. Snyderman, *The Motivation to Work*, 2d ed. (John Wiley and Sons, 1959).

7. V. Vroom, *Work and Motivation* (John Wiley and Sons, 1964).

8. D. Ondrack, "Defense Mechanisms and The Herzberg Theory: An Alternate Test," *Academy of Management Journal* (March, 1974):79–89.

9. D. C. McClelland, "Business Drive and National Achievement," *Harvard Business Review* 40, no. 4 (July–August 1962):99–112.

10. P. R. Lawrence and J. W. Lorsch, *Developing Organizations: Diagnosis and Action* (Addison-Wesley, 1969).

11. M. Patchen, *Participation, Achievement and Involvement on the Job* (Prentice-Hall, 1970).

12. *op. cit.*

13. D. McClelland and D. Burnham, "Power is the Great Motivator," *Harvard Business Review* (March–April, 1976):100–110.

14. *Ibid.*

WHICH COMES FIRST?

1. A. H. Maslow. "A Theory of Human Motivation," *Psychological Review*, 50 (1943), 370–396.

2. Arthur H. Brayfield and Walter H. Crockett. "Employee Attitudes and Employee Performance." *Psychological Bulletin*, 52:5 (1955), 415–422.

3. Karlene Roberts, Raymond E. Miles, and L. Vaughn Blankenship. "Organizational Leadership Satisfaction and Productivity: A Comparative Analysis." *Academy of Management Journal*, 11:4 (December 1968), 401–414.

4. Lyman Porter and Edward E. Lawler. *Managerial Attitudes and Performance* (Homewood, Ill.: Irwin, 1968), p. 167.

5. F. Herzberg et al., *Job Attitudes: Review of Research and Opinion* (Pittsburgh: Psychological Service of Pittsburgh, 1957), p. 103.

6. Melvin Sorcher and Herbert H. Meyer. "Motivating Factory Employees." *Personnel* (Jan.–Feb. 1968), 22–28.

7. Paul Pigors and Charles Myers. *Personnel Administration.* 6th ed. (New York: McGraw-Hill, 1969), pp. 160–161.

8. Robert A. Sutermeister, *People and Productivity*, 2d ed. (New York: McGraw-Hill, 1969), pp. 54–55.

9. Raymond E. Miles, Lyman Porter, and Joseph A. Craft. "Three Models of Leadership Attitudes," in Paul Pigors, Charles Myers, and F.T. Malm. *Management of Human Resources* (New York: McGraw-Hill, 1961), pp. 48–49.

10. Porter and Lawler, p. 165.

11. The terms "climber" and "conserver" are from Anthony Downs. *Inside Bureaucracy* (Boston: Little Brown, 1967), pp. 92 and 96.

12. See Porter and Lawler, "What Job Attitudes Tell About Motivation," *Harvard Business Review* (Jan.–Feb. 1968), 121.

CHAPTER 5

REFERENCES

1. P. Watzlawick, *The Language of Change* (Basic Books, 1978), 119.

2. L. Festinger, "Informal Social Communication," *Psychological Review* 57 (1950):271.

3. W. Kohler, *Gestalt Psychology* (The New American Library, 1947).

4. R. E. Nisbett and T. D. Wilson, *Newsletter* (Institute of Social Research, University of Michigan, Summer 1978).

5. E. Berne, *Beyond Games and Scripts* (Grove Press, 1976).

6. A. A. Harrison, *Individuals and Groups* (Brooks/Cole, 1976), 100–107.

7. L. Festinger, *A Theory of Cognitive Dissonance* (Row-Peterson, 1957).

8. S. J. Adams and P. R. Jacobsen, "Effects of Wage Inequities on Work Quality," *Journal of Abnormal and Social Psychology* 69 (1964):19–25.

9. R. M. Steers and L. W. Porter, "The Role of Task-Goal Attributes in Employee Performance," *Psychological Bulletin* 81 (1974):434–452.

10. A. Bandura, *Social Learning Theory* (Prentice-Hall, 1977).

11. M. Massey, "What You Are is What You Were When" (Magnetic Video Corp., 1976).

PYGMALION

1. See "Jamesville Branch Office (A)," MET003A, and "Jamesville Branch Office (B)," MET003B (Boston, Sterling Institute, 1969).

2. "Jamesville Branch Office (B)," p. 2.

3. "Some Determinants of Early Managerial Success," Alfred P. Sloan School of Management Organization Research Program #81-64 (Cambridge, Massachusetts Institute of Technology, 1964), pp. 13–14.

4. Robert Rosenthal and Lenore Jacobson, *Pygmalion in the Classroom* (New York, Holt, Rinehart, and Winston, Inc., 1968), p. 11.

5. *Ibid.*, Preface, p. vii.

6. *Ibid.*, p. 38.

7. See John W. Atkinson, "Motivational Determinants of Risk-Taking Behavior," *Psychological Review*, Vol. 64, No. 6, 1957, p. 365.

8. David E. Berlew and Douglas T. Hall, "The Socialization of Managers: Effects of Expectations on Performance," *Administrative Science Quarterly*, September 1966, p. 208.

9. See Robert Rosenthal and Lenore Jacobson, op. cit., pp. 3–4.

10. *Ibid.*, pp. 74–81.

11. "Some Determinants of Early Managerial Success," pp. 13–14.

12. "The Socialization of Managers: Effects of Expectations on Performance," p. 219.

13. *Ibid.*, pp. 221–222.

14. Robert T. Davis, "Sales Management in the Field," *HBR* January–February 1958, p. 91.

15. Alfred A. Oberlander, "The Collective Conscience in Recruiting," address to Life Insurance Agency Management Association Annual Meeting, Chicago, Illinois, 1963, p. 5.

16. *Ibid.*, p. 9.

17. "How to Keep the Go-getters," *Nation's Business*, June 1966, p. 74.

18. Robert C. Albrook, "Why It's Harder to Keep Good Executives," *Fortune*, November 1968, p. 137.

CHAPTER 6

REFERENCES

1. B. F. Skinner, *Beyond Freedom and Dignity* (New York: Bantam Books, 1971), 16.

2. See Keith Davis, *Human Behavior at Work: Organizational Behavior* (New York: McGraw-Hill Book Company, 1981), 42–78.

3. A. H. Maslow, "A Theory of Human Motivation," *Psychological Review* 50 (1943):370–396.

4. Clayton P. Alderfer, *Existence, Relatedness, and Growth* (New York: Free Press, 1972).

5. Frederick Herzberg, Bernard Mausner, and Barbara Snyderman, *The Motivation to Work* (New York: John Wiley & Sons, Inc., 1959).

6. Leon Festinger, *A Theory of Cognitive Dissonance* (New York: Harper and Row, 1957).

7. Victor H. Vroom, *Work and Motivation* (New York: John Wiley & Sons, Inc., 1964).

8. Fred Luthans and Robert Kreitners, *Organizational Behavior Modifications* (Glenview, Ill: Scott Foresman and Company, 1975).

9. B. F. Skinner, *Science and Human Behavior* (New York: The Free Press, 1953).

10. B. F. Skinner, *Contingencies of Reinforcement* (New York: Appleton-Century-Crofts, Inc., 1969).

11. "At Emery Air Freight: Positive Reinforcement Boosts Performance," *Organizational Dynamics* (Winter 1973):41–50.

12. Donald B. Fedor and Gerald R. Ferris, "Integrating OB Mod with Cognitive Approaches to Motivation," *Academy of Management Review* (1981):115.

OB MOD

1. We wish to thank Michael K. Moch, Kendrith M. Rowland, and Jeffrey J. Sucec for their comments on earlier drafts of this paper.

References

Adams, E. E. Behavior modification in quality control. *Academy of Management Journal*, 1975, *18*, 662–679.

Adams, J. S. Inequity in social exchange. In L. Berkowitz (Ed.), *Advances in experimental social psychology.* New York: Academic Press, 1965.

Andrasik, F. Organizational behavior modification in business settings: A methodological and content review. *Journal of Organizational Behavior Management*, 1979, *2*, 85–102.

Argyris, C. Beyond freedom and dignity by B. F. Skinner: A review essay. *Harvard Educational Review*, 1971, *41*, 550–567.

At Emery Air Freight: Positive reinforcement boosts performance. *Organizational Dynamics*, 1973, *1*, 41–50.

Bandura, A. *Social learning theory.* Englewood Cliffs, N.J.: Prentice-Hall, 1977.

Barrows, J. C. Worker performance and task complexity as causal determinants of leader behavior style and flexibility. *Journal of Applied Psychology*, 1976, *61*, 443–440.

Campbell, D. T. & Stanley, J. C. *Experimental and quasi-experimental designs for research.* Chicago: Rand-McNally, 1966.

Cummings, T. C. & Molloy, E. S. *Improving productivity and the quality of work life.* New York: Praeger, 1977.

Davis, T. R. V. & Luthans, F. A social learning approach to organizational behavior. *Academy of Management Review*, 1980, *5*, 281–290.

Deci, E. L. *Intrinsic motivation.* New York: Plenum, 1975.

Fry, F. L. Operant conditioning in organizational settings: Of mice or men? *Personnel*, 1974, *51*, 17–24.

Goldstein, A. P. & Sorcher, M. *Changing supervisor behavior.* New York: Pergamon, 1974.

Grey, J. L. The myths of the myths about behavior modification in organizations: A reply to Locke's criticism of behavior modification. *Academy of Management Review*, 1979, *1*, 121–129.

Gupta, N. & Beehr, T. A. Job stress and employee behaviors. *Organizational Behavior & Human Performance*, 1979, *23*, 373–387.

Hackman, J. R. Informal speech given at the Friday Forum, University of Illinois, Urbana-Champaign, September 21, 1979.

Hackman, J. R. & Oldham, G. R. *Work redesign.* Reading, Mass.: Addison-Wesley, 1980.

Hackman, J. R. & Oldham, G. R. Development of the job diagnostic survey. *Journal of Applied Psychology*, 1975, *60*, 159–170.

Haynes, M. G. Developing an appraisal program. In K. M. Rowland, M. London, G. R. Ferris, & J. L. Sherman (Eds.), *Current issues in personnel management.* Boston: Allyn & Bacon, 1980.

Hull, C. L. *Principles of behavior.* New York: Appleton-Century-Crofts, 1943.

Katz, R. Job longevity as a situational factor in job satisfaction. *Administrative Science Quarterly*, 1978, *28*, 204–222.

Kazdin, A. E. Methodological and assessment considerations in evaluating reinforcement programs in applied settings. *Journal of Applied Behavioral Analysis*, 1973, *6*, 517–521.

Kerr, S. On the folly of rewarding A while hoping for B. *Academy of Management Journal*, 1975, *18*, 769–783.

Komaki, J.; Waddell, W. M.; & Pearce, G. M. The applied behavior analysis approach and individual employee: Improving performance in two small businesses. *Organizational Behavior & Human Performance*, 1977, *19*, 337–352.

Latham, G. P. & Saari, L. M. Application of social learning theory to training supervisors through behavioral modeling. *Journal of Applied Psychology*, 1979, *64*, 239–246.

Latham, G. P. & Yukl, G. A. Assigned versus participative goal setting with educated and uneducated woods workers. *Journal of Applied Psychology*, 1975, *60*, 299–302.

Latham, G. P. & Yukl, G. A. Effects of assigned and participative goal setting on performance and job satisfaction. *Journal of Applied Psychology*, 1976, *51*, 166–171.

Lawler, E. E. *Motivation in work organizations*. Monterey, Calif.: Brooks/Cole, 1973.

Locke, E. A. Toward a theory of task motivation and incentives. *Organizational Behavior & Human Performance*, 1968, *3*, 157–189.

Locke, E. A. The nature and causes of job satisfaction. In M. D. Dunnette (Ed.), *Handbook of industrial and organizational psychology*. Chicago: Rand-McNally, 1976.

Locke, E. A. The myths of behavior mod. in organizations. *Academy of Management Review*, 1977, *2*, 543–553.

Locke, E. A. Myths in "The myths of the myths about behavior mod. in organizations." *Academy of Management Review*, 1979, *1*, 131–136.

Lowin, A. & Craig, J. R. The influence of level of performance on managerial style: An experimental object-lesson in the ambiguity of correlational data. *Organizational Behavior & Human Performance*, 1968, *3*, 449–458.

Luthans, F. & Davis, T. R. V. Behavioral self-management: The missing link in managerial effectiveness. *Organizational Dynamics*, Summer 1979, 42–60.

Luthans, F. & Kreitner, R. *Organizational behavior modification*. Glenview, Ill.: Scott, Foresman, 1975.

Maslow, A. H. *Eupsychian management*. Homewood, Ill.: Irwin-Dorsey, 1965.

McCarthy, M. Decreasing the incidence of "high bobbins" in a textile spinning department through a group feedback procedure. *Journal of Organizational Behavior Management*, 1978, *1*, 150–154.

McGregor, D. *The human side of enterprise*. New York: McGraw-Hill, 1960.

Nord, W. R. Beyond the teaching machine: The neglected area of operant conditioning in the theory and practice of management. *Organizational Behavior & Human Performance*, 1969, *5*, 375–401.

Nord, W. R. Improving attendance through rewards. *Personnel Administration*, 1970, *33*, 37–41.

Oldham, G. R.; Hackman, J. R.; & Pearce, J. L. Conditions under which employees respond positively to enriched work. *Journal of Applied Psychology*, 1976, *61*, 395–403.

Parmerlee, M. & Schwenk, C. Radical behaviorism in organizations: Misconceptions in the Locke-Grey debate. *Academy of Management Review*, 1979, *4*, 601–607.

Pedalino, E. & Gamboa, V. V. Behavior modification and absenteeism: Intervention in one industrial setting. *Journal of Applied Psychology*, 1974, *59*, 694–698.

Peters, R. S. *The concept of motivation*. New York: Humanities Press, 1960.

Petrock, F. & Gamboa, V. V. Expectancy theory and operant conditioning: A conceptual comparison. In W.R. Nord (Ed.), *Concepts and controversy in organizational behavior* (2nd ed.). Santa Monica, Calif.: Goodyear, 1976.

Porter, L. W. & Lawler, E. E. *Managerial attitudes and performance*. Homewood, Ill.: Irwin-Dorsey, 1968.

Pritchard, R. D. & Curtis, M. I. The influence of goal setting and financial incentives on task performance. *Organizational Behavior & Human Performance*, 1973, *10*, 175–183.

Reese, E. P. *The analysis of human operant behavior*. Dubuque, Iowa: William C. Brown, 1966.

Runnion, A.; Johnson, T.; & McWhorten, J. The effects of feedback and reinforcement on truck turnaround time in materials transportation. *Journal of Organizational Behavior Management*, 1978, *1*, 100–117.

Runnion, A.; Watson, J. O.; & McWhorten, J. Energy savings in interstate transportation through feedback and reinforcement. *Journal of Organizational Behavior Management*, 1978, *1*, 180–191.

Salancik, G. R. & Pfeffer, J. An examination of the need-satisfaction model of job attitudes. *Administrative Science Quarterly*, 1977, *22*, 427–456.

Sims, H. P.; Szilagyi, R. T.; & Keller, R. T. The measurement of job characteristics. *Academy of Management Journal*, 1976, *19*, 195–224.

Skinner, B. F. *Science and human behavior*. New York: Free Press, 1953.

Skinner, B. F. *Walden two*. New York: MacMillan, 1948.

Terborg, J. R. The motivational components of goal setting. *Journal of Applied Psychology*, 1976, *61*, 613–621.

Tolman, E. C. *Purposive behavior in animals and men*. New York: Century, 1932.

Vroom, V. H. *Work and motivation*. New York: Wiley, 1964.

Walton, R. E. How to counter alienation in the plant. In K. M. Rowland, M. London, G. R. Ferris, & J. L. Sherman (Eds.), *Current Issues in personal management.* Boston: Allyn & Bacon, 1980.

CHAPTER 7

REFERENCES

1. T. J. Peters and R. H. Waterman, Jr., *In Search of Excellence* (Harper and Row, 1982), 261.

2. R. L. Quey, "Functions and Dynamics of Work Groups," *American Psychologist* 26, no. 10 (1971):1081.

3. K. W. Back, "Influence through Social Communication," *Journal of Abnormal and Social Psychology* 46 (1951):9–23.

4. E. Aronson and D. Linder, "Gain and Loss of Self-Esteem as Determinants of Interpersonal Attractiveness," *Journal of Experimental and Social Psychology* 1, no. 2 (1965):156–171.

5. M. Deutsch, "Some Factors Affecting Membership Motivation and Achievement Motivation," *Human Relations* 12 (1959):81–85.

6. E. Aronson, "Who Likes Whom and Why," *Psychology Today* 4, no. 3 (1970):48–50.

7. H. I. Nixon, "Team Orientation, Interpersonal Relations and Team Success," *Research Quarterly* 47, no. 3 (October 1976):429–435.

8. S. Seashore, *Group Cohesiveness in the Industrial Work Group* (Institute for Social Research, 1954).

9. W. N. Morris, "Collective Coping with Stress: Group Reactions to Fear, Anxiety and Ambiguity," *Journal of Personality and Social Psychology* 33, no. 6 (1976):674–679.

10. A. P. Hare, *Handbook of Small Group Research*, 2d ed. (The Free Press, 1976):19–59.

11. S. E. Asch, "Opinions and Social Pressure," *Scientific American* 193, no. 5 (1955):31–35.

12. L. Festinger, "A Theory of Social Comparison Processes," *Human Relations* 7 (1954):117–140.

13. H. B. Gerard, R. A. Wilhelm and E. S. Conolley, "Conformity and Group Size," *Journal of Personality and Social Psychology* 8 (1968):79–82.

14. J. M. Savell, "Prior Agreement and Conformity: An Extension of the Generalization Phenomenon," *Psychonomic Science* 25 (1971):327–328.

15. N. S. Endler, "The Effects of Verbal Reinforcement on Conformity and Social Pressure," *Journal of Social Psychology* 66 (1965):147–154.

16. G. Homans, *Social Behavior: Its Elementary Forms* (Harcourt, Brace, 1961).

17. M. Freeman, "A Conversation with Margaret Singer," *APA Monitor* (July–August, 1979):6–7.

18. S. Milgram, "Behavioral Study of Obedience," *Journal of Abnormal and Social Psychology* 67 (1963):371–378.

19. S. Milgram, "Liberating Effects of Group Pressure," *Journal of Personality and Social Psychology* 1 (1965):127–134.

20. R. Singleton, "Another Look at the Conformity Explanation of Group-Induced Shifts in Choice," *Human Relations* 32, no. 1 (1979):37–56.

21. I. L. Janis, "Group Think," *Psychology Today* 5, no. 6 (1971):43–46, 74–76.

22. K. D. Benne and P. Sheats, "Functional Roles of Group Members," *The Journal of Social Science* (Spring 1948):41–49.

23. S. E. Seashore, *Group Cohesiveness in the Industrial Work Group* (University of Michigan, Institute for Social Research, 1954).

24. K. W. Back, "Influence through Social Communication," *Journal of Abnormal and Social Psychology* 46 (1951):9–23.

25. G. Lippitt, "How to Get Results from a Group." In *Group Development*, ed. L. Bradford (National Training Laboratories, 1961), 34.

CHAPTER 8

REFERENCES

1. Dutch L. Landen, "Beyond QC Circles," *Productivity Brief* 12 (April 1982):6.

2. Max Weber, *The Theory of Social and Economic Organizations*, translated by A.M. Henderson and Talcott Parsons, (New York: The Free Press, 1964); see also Lyndall Urwick, *The Elements of Administration* (New York: Harper & Row, 1943).

3. Tom Burns and G. M. Stalker, *The Management of Innovation* (London: Tavistock Publications Ltd., 1961).

4. Thomas J. Peters and Robert H. Waterman, Jr. *In Search of Excellence* (New York: Harper and Row, 1982).

5. Douglas McGregor, *The Human Side of Enterprise* (New York: McGraw-Hill Book Company, 1960).

6. *Ibid.*

7. Dutch L. Landen, "The Future of Participative Management," *Productivity Brief* 16 (August 1982):1–6.

8. Gary P. Latham, Larry L. Cummings, and Terence R. Mitchell, "Behavioral Strategies to Improve Productivity," *Organizational Dynamics* (Winter 1981):5–23.

9. Robert Tannenbaum and Warren H. Schmidt, "How to Choose a Leadership Pattern," *Harvard Business Review* (May–June 1973):162–180.

10. Latham et al., *op cit.*

11. Edward E. Lawler III, "Strategies for Improving the Quality of Worklife," *American Psychologist* (May 1982):486–493.

PARTICIPATIVE MANAGEMENT

1. Sergiovanni, Thomas and John Corbally, eds., *Administrative Leadership: New Perspectives on Theory and Practice*, Jossey-Bass, 1982.

2. "Work Innovations in the United States," *Harvard Business Review*, July–August 1979, p. 88–98.

3. Gaheille, Kenneth, Harry Katz, Thomas Kochar, *Industrial Relations Performance, Economic Performance and the Effects of QWL Efforts: An Interplant Analysis*, (unpublished study), January 1982.

BEHAVIORAL STRATEGIES

Selected Bibliography

A summary of how managers frequently formulate and identify performance problems can be found in H. Mintzberg's *The Nature of Managerial Work* (Prentice-Hall, 1980).

A review of court cases pertaining to performance appraisal can be found in a book by G. P. Latham and K. N. Wexley, *Increasing Productivity Through Performance Appraisal* (Addison-Wesley, 1981).

A discussion of attribution theory and how it applies to the leadership setting is discussed in S. G. Green and T. R. Mitchell's "Attributional Processes of Leaders in Leader-Member Interactions" (*Organizational Behavior and Human Performance*, Vol. 23, 1979) and in a chapter by T. R. Mitchell, S. G. Green, and R. E. Wood, "An Attributional Model of Leadership and the Poor Performing Subordinate: Development and Validation," in Vol. 3 of L. L. Cummings and B. M. Staw's edited work, *Research in Organizational Behavior* (JAI Press, 1981).

A training program to increase accuracy in appraisal and decrease rating error can be found in the book, *Increasing Productivity Through Performance Appraisal*, (Addison-Wesley, 1981) by G. P. Latham and K. N. Wexley.

A summary of work on goal setting can be found in an earlier issue of *Organizational Dynamics*, "Goal Setting: A Motivational Technique That Works" (*Organizational Dynamics*, Autumn 1979) written by G. P. Latham and E. A. Locke.

Typical workplace offenses and managerial actions in cases of industrial discipline are discussed by H. N. Wheeler in "Punishment Theory and Industrial Discipline" (*Industrial Relations*, May 1976).

Acknowledgments

Professor Latham acknowledges the support of the Office of Naval Research, Contract No. N00014-79-C-0680. Professor Cummings wishes to acknowledge the support of the Office of Naval Research, Contract No. N00014-79-C-0750. In addition, part of the research discussed in this article was supported by the Army Research Institute Contract No. MDA 903-79-C-0543 and The National Science Foundation Grant No. DAR 79-09792 (Terence R. Mitchell and Lee Roy Beach, principal investigators).

CHAPTER 9

REFERENCES

1. A. S. Grove, *High Output Management* (New York: Random House 1983), 47.

2. R. Tannenbaum and W. H. Schmidt, "How to Choose a Leadership Pattern," *Harvard Business Review* (May–June, 1973):162–164, 166–168, 170, 173, 175, 178–180.

3. R. R. Blake and J. S. Mouton, *The Managerial Grid* (Houston: Gulf Publishing, 1964).

4. R. Likert, *New Patterns of Management* (New York: McGraw-Hill Book Co., 1961).

5. F. E. Fiedler, "The Contingency Model—New Directions for Leadership Utilization," *Journal of Contemporary Business* 3, no. 4 (1974):65–79.

6. F. E. Fiedler, "Engineer the Job to Fit the Manager," *Harvard Business Review* 43, no. 5 (September–October, 1965):115–122.

7. J. W. Julian, E. P. Hollander and C. R. Regula, "Endorsement of the Group Spokesman as a Function of His Source of Authority, Competence, and Success," *Journal of Personality and Social Psychology* 11, no. 1 (1969):42–49.

8. R. Albanese, "Criteria for Evaluating Authority Patterns," *Academy of Management Journal* 16, no. 1 (March 1973):102–111.

9. J. MacGinnis, *Heroes* (New York: Viking Press, 1976).

10. T. L. Hudson, ed., *Perspectives on Interpersonal Attraction* (Academic Press, 1973).

11. G. P. Latham and G. A. Yukl, "A Review of Research on the Application of Goal-Setting in Organizations," *Academy of Management Journal* 18 (1975):824–845.

12. L. W. Porter, E. E. Lawler and J. R. Hackman, *Behavior in Organizations* (New York: McGraw-Hill Book Co., 1975).

RELEASING ENERGY

Adams-Webber, J. R., *Personal Construct Theory: Concepts and Application*, Wiley-Interscience, New York, 1979.

Arends, R. I. and Arends, J. H., *System Change Strategies in Educational Settings*, Human Sciences Press, New York, 1977.

Argyris, Chris, *Interpersonal Competence and Organizational Effectiveness*, Dorsey Press, Homewood, Illinois, 1962.

Baldridge, J. V. et al., *Policy Making and Effective Leadership: A National Study of Academic Management*, Jossey-Bass, San Francisco, 1978.

Baldridge, J. V. and Deal, T. S., *Managing Change in Educational Organizations*, McCuthan Publishing Corp., Berkeley, 1975.

Baltes, P. D., *Life-Span Development and Behavior*, Vol. I, Academic Press, New York, 1978.

Barron, F., *Creativity and Psychological Health*, Van Nostrand, Princeton, 1963.

Bell, C. R. and Nadler, L., *The Client-Consultant Handbook* Gulf Publishing Co., Houston, 1979.

Bennis, Warren G., *Changing Organizations*, McGraw-Hill, 1966.

Bennis, W. G., Benne, K. and Chin, R., *The Planning of Change*, Holt, Rinehart & Winston, New York, 1968.

Blake, R. R. and Mouton, J. S., *Consultation*, Addison-Wesley, Reading, Massachusetts, 1976.

Bullmer, K., *The Art of Empathy: A Manual for Improving Interpersonal Perception*, Human Sciences Press, New York, 1975.

Carkhuff, R. R., *Helping and Human Relations: A Primer for Lay and Professional Helpers*, 2 Vols., Holt, Rinehart & Winston, New York, 1969.

Chickering, A. W., *Education and Identify*, Jossey-Bass, San Francisco, 1976.

Coan, R. W., *The Optimal Personality: An Empirical and Theoretical Analysis*, Columbia University Press, New York, 1974.

Combs, A. W. et al., *Helping Relationships: Basic Concepts for the Helping Professions*, 2nd ed., Allyn and Bacon, Rockleigh, New Jersey, 1978.

Combs, A. W. and Snygg, D., *Individual Behavior*, Harper and Row, New York, 1959.

Cross, K. P., *Accent on Learning*, Jossey-Bass, San Francisco, 1976.

Csikszentmihalyi, M., *Beyond Boredom and Anxiety*, Jossey-Bass, San Francisco,1975.

Davis, G. A. and Scott, J. A., *Training Creative Thinking*, Holt, Rinehart & Winston, New York, 1971.

Dykes, A. R., *Faculty Participation in Academic Decision Making*, American Council on Education, Washington DC, 1968.

Erikson, E. H., *Childhood and Society*, W. W. Norton, New York, 1950; *Dimensions of a New Identity*, W. W. Norton, New York, 1974; *Identity and the Life Cycle*, International University Press, New York, 1959; *Insight and Responsibility*, W. W. Norton, New York, 1964.

Etzioni, A., *Complex Organizations*, The Free Press, New York, 1961.

Felker, D. W., *Building Positive Self-Concepts*, Burgess Publishing Co., Minneapolis, 1974.

Gale, R., *The Psychology of Being Yourself*, Englewood Cliffs, Prentice-Hall, New Jersey, 1974.

Gardner, J., *Self-Renewal: The Individual and the Innovative Society*, Harper & Row, New York, 1963.

Getzels, J. W., Lipham, J. M. and Campbell, R. F., *Educational Administration as a Social Process*, Harper & Row, New York, 1968.

Goldstein, K. M. and Blackman, S., *Cognitive Style: Five Approaches and Relevant Research*, Wiley-Interscience, New York, 1978.

Goodlad, J. I., *The Dynamics of Educational Change: Toward Responsive Schools*, McGraw-Hill, New York, 1975.

Goulet, L. R. and Baltes, P., *Life-Span Developmental Psychology*, Academic Press, New York, 1970.

Gowan, J. C. et al., *Creativity: Its Educational Implications*, John Wiley & Sons, New York, 1967.

Greiner, L. E. (Ed.), *Organizational Change and Development*, Richard D. Irwin Inc., Homewood, Illinois, 1971.

Gubrium, J. F. and Buckholdt, D. R., *Toward Maturity: The Social Processing of Human Development*, Jossey-Bass, San Francisco, 1977.

Havighurst, R., *Development Tasks and Education*, 2nd ed., David McKay, New York, 1970.

Hefferlin, J. B. L., *Dynamics of Academic Reform*, Jossey-Bass, San Francisco, 1969.

Herzberg, F. et al., *The Motivation to Work*, John Wiley & Sons, New York, 1959; *Work and the Nature of Man*, World Publishing Co., Cleveland, 1966.

Hornstein, H. A. et al., *Social Intervention: A Behavioral Science Approach*, The Free Press, New York, 1971.

Ingalls, J., *Human Energy*, Addison-Wesley, Reading, Massachusetts, 1976.

Kagan, J. (Ed.), *Creativity and Learning*, Houghton-Mifflin, Boston, 1967.

Kagan, J. and Moss, H. A., *Birth to Maturity: A Study in Psychological Development*, John Wiley & Sons, New York, 1962.

Kelly, G. S., *The Psychology of Personal Constructs*, W. W. Norton, New York, 1955.

Kidd, J. R., *How Adults Learn*, 2nd ed., Association Press/Follett, Chicago, 1973.

Knowles, M. S., *The Adult Learner: A Neglected Species*, 2nd ed., Gulf Publishing Co., Houston, 1978; *The Modern Practice of Adult Education*, 2nd ed., Association Press/Follett, Chicago, 1980; *Self-Directed Learning: A Guide for Learners and Teachers*, Association Press/Follett, Chicago, 1975.

Loughary, J. W. and Ripley, T. M., *Helping Others Help Themselves: A Guide to Counseling Skills*, McGraw-Hill, New York, 1979.

Lefcourt, H. M., *Locus of Control: Current Trends in Theory and Research*, John Wiley & Sons, New York, 1976.

Levinson, H. and Price, C. R. et al., *Men, Management and Mental Health*, Harvard University Press, Cambridge, 1963.

Likert, R., *The Human Organization: Its Management and Value*, McGraw-Hill, New York, 1967.

Lippitt, G., *Organizational Renewal*, Appleton-Century-Crofts, New York, 1969; *Visualizing Change: Model Building and the Change Process*, John Wiley & Sons, Somerset, New Jersey, 1978.

Lippitt, G. and Lippitt, R., *The Consulting Process in Action*, University Associates, La Jolla, California, 1978.

Loevinger, J., *Ego Development: Concepts and Theories*, Jossey-Bass, San Francisco, 1976.

Marrow, A. J., Bowers, D. G. and Seashore, S. E., *Management By Participation*, Harper & Row, New York, 1968.

Martorana, S. V. and Kuhns, E., *Managing Academic Change: Interactive Forces and Leadership in Higher Education*, Jossey-Bass, San Francisco, 1975.

Maslow, A., *The Farther Reaches of Human Nature*, The Viking Press, New York, 1971; *Motivation and Personality*, Van Nostrand, Princeton, New Jersey, 1970.

Mangham, I., *Interactions and Interventions in Organizations: A New Theory That Challenges Traditional Ideas in Organizational Change*, John Wiley & Sons, Somerset, New Jersey, 1978.

McGregor, D., *The Human Side of Enterprise*, McGraw-Hill, New York, 1960; *Leadership and Motivation*, The Massachusetts Institute of Technology Press, Cambridge, Massachusetts, 1967.

McLelland, D. C., *Power: The Inner Experience*, John Wiley & Sons, New York, 1975.

Messick, S. et al., *Individuality in Learning*, Jossey-Bass, San Francisco, 1976.

Millett, J. D., *Decision-Making and Administration in Higher Education*, Kent State University Press, Kent, Ohio, 1968.

Moustakas, C., *Finding Yourself, Finding Others*, Prentice-Hall, Englewood Cliffs, New Jersey, 1974.

Pollack, O., *Human Behavior and the Helping Professions*, John Wiley & Sons, New York, 1976.

Rogers, C. R., *Freedom to Learn*, Charles Merrill, Columbus, Ohio, 1969; *On Becoming a Person*, Houghton Mifflin, Boston, 1961.

Rosenthal, R. and Jacobson, L., *Pygmalion in the Classroom*, Holt, Rinehart & Winston, New York, 1968.

Schon, D. A., *Beyond the Stable State*, W. W. Norton, New York, 1971.

Schein, E., *Process Consultation: Its Role in Organization Development*, Addison-Wesley, Reading, Masachusetts, 1969.

Schein, E. and Bennis, W. G., *Personal and Organizational Change through Group Methods*, John Wiley & Sons, New York, 1965.

Schlossberg, N. K. et al., *Perspective on Counseling Adults: Issues and Skills*, Brooks/Cole Publishing Co., Monterey, California, 1978.

Simon, H. A., *Administrative Behavior*, Macmillan, New York, 1961.

Tedeschi, J. T. (Ed.), *The Social Influence Process*, Aldine-Atherton, Chicago, 1972.

Toffler, A. (Ed.), *Learning for Tomorrow: The Role of the Future in Education*, Random House, New York, 1974.

Tough, A., *The Adult's Learning Projects*. Ontario Institute for Studies in Education, Toronto, 1979; *Learning Without a Teacher*, Ontario Institute for Studies in Education, Toronto, 1967.

Tyler, L., *Individuality: Human Possibilities and Personal Choice in the Psychological Development of Men and Women*, Jossey-Bass, San Francisco, 1978.

Zahn, J. C., *Creativity Research and Its Implications for Adult Education*, Library of Continuing Education, Syracuse University, Syracuse, 1966.

Zander, A., *Groups at Work: Unresolved Issues in the Study of Organizations*, Jossey-Bass, San Francisco, 1977.

Zurcher, L. A., *The Mutable Self: A Self-Concept for Social Change*, Sage Publications, Beverley Hills, California, 1977.

CHAPTER 10

REFERENCES

1. C. Barnard, *The Function of the Executive* (Harvard University Press, 1968), 217.

2. H. J. Erlich, "Affective Style as a Variable in Person Perception," *Journal of Personality* 37 (1969): 522–539.

3. F. Herzberg, "Piecing Together Generations of Values," *Industry Week* (October 1, 1979).

4. M. Massey, "What You Are is Where You Were When" (Magnetic Video Corp., 1976). Videotape.

5. T. J. Peters and R. H. Waterman, Jr., *In Search of Excellence* (Harper and Row, 1982).

6. *Ibid.*

7. W. D. Guth and R. Tagiuri, "Personal Values and Corporate Strategy," *Harvard Business Review* (September–October, 1965).

8. R. L. Katz, *Management of the Total Enterprise* (Prentice-Hall, 1970).

9. W. D. Guth and R. Tagiuri, "Personal Values and Corporate Strategy," *Harvard Business Review* (September–October, 1965).

10. W. B. Werther, "Beyond Job Enrichment to Employment Enrichment," *Personnel Journal* (August 1975):438–442.

11. M. Sinetar, "Management in a New Age: An Exploration of Changing Work Values," *Personnel Journal* (September 1980):749–755.

12. Herzberg, "Piecing together Generations."

CHAPTER 11

REFERENCES

1. A. Toffler, *The Third Wave* (Morrow and Co., 1980), 365.

2. N. Chalofsky and C. I. Lincoln, *Up the HRD Ladder* (Addison-Wesley, 1983).

3. A. Lowen, *The Betrayal of the Body* (MacMillan, 1967).

4. W. L. French, C. H. Bell, Jr. and R. A. Zawacki, *Organization Development—Theory, Practice, Research* (Business Publications, Inc., 1983), 245.

5. T. J. Peters and R. H. Waterman, Jr., *In Search of Excellence* (Harper and Row, 1982), 238–239.

6. R. Tannenbaum and S. A. Davis, "Values, Man and Organization," *Industrial Management Review* 10, no. 8 (Winter, 1969):67–83.

7. R. Ribler, *Training Development Guide* (Reston Publishing Co., 1983).

8. N. Chalofsky and C. I. Lincoln, *Up the HRD Ladder* (Addison-Wesley, 1983).

9. C. Rogers, *Counseling and Psychotherapy* (Houghton-Mifflin, 1942), 113–114.

10. M. Beer, *Organization Change and Development—A Systems View* (Scott, Foresman and Co., 1980), 1.

CHAPTER 12

REFERENCES

1. H. Vaihinger, *The Philosophy of As If* (Routledge and K. Paul, 1935), 11. English version translated by C. K. Ogden.

2. R. Beckhard, "What is Organization Development?" *Organization Development: Strategies and Modes* (Addison-Wesley, 1969), 9–14.

3. W. L. French and C. H. Bell, Jr., "A Bried History of Organization Development," *Journal of Contemporary Business* (Summer 1972):1–8.

4. H. Baumgartel, "Using Employee Questionnaire Results for Improving Organizations: The Survey 'Feedback' Experiment," *Kansas Business Review* (December 1959):2–6.

5. R. Beckard, *op. cit.*

6. W. Burke and H. A. Hornstein, *The Social Technology of Organization Development* (Learning Resources Corp., 1972), xi.

7. W. L. French and C. H. Bell, Jr., "A Definition of Organization Development," *Organization Development: Behavioral Science Interventions for Organization Improvement*, 2d ed. (Prentice-Hall, 1978), 14–19.

8. R. Tannenbaum and S. A. Davis, "Values, Man and Organizations," *Industrial Management Review* 10, no. 2 (Winter 1969):67–83.

9. K. Lewin, "The Field Approach: Culture and Group Life as Quasi-Stationary Processes," *Field Theory in Social Sciences* (Harper & Row, 1951), 172–174.

10. C. Argyris, "Intervention Theory and Method," *Intervention Theory and Methods: A Behavioral Science View* (Addison-Wesley, 1970), 15–20.

11. R. Beckhard, *op. cit.*

12. C. Argyris, *op. cit.*

13. W. L. French, C. H. Bell, Jr. and R. A. Zawacki, *Organization Development: Theory, Practice, and Research* (Business Publications, Inc., 1983), 120

14. *Ibid.*, 121–122.

15. M. Beer, *Organization Change and Development: A Systems View* (Scott, Foresman and Co., 1980), 140.

16. R. Beckhard, "Optimizing Team-Building Efforts," *Journal of Contemporary Business* (Summer 1972) :23–27, 30–32.

17. C. Argyris, *Interpersonal Competence and Organizational Effectiveness* (Dorsey, 1962).

18. D. Katz and R. L. Kahn, *The Social Psychology of Organizations* (Wiley, 1978).

19. E. H. Schein, *Process Consultation: Its Role in Organization Development* (Addison-Wesley, 1966).

20. M. Beer, *op. cit.*, 136.

21. R. R. Blake, J. S. Mouton, L. B. Barnes and L. E. Greiner, "Breakthrough in Organization Development," *Harvard Business Review* 42, no. 6 (1964):133–155.

22. H. J. Leavitt, "Applied Organizational Change in Industry: Structural, Technological and Humanistic Approaches," in J. G. March, ed, *Handbook of Organizations* (Rand McNally, 1965).

23. M. Beer, *op. cit.*, 159.

24. E. E. Lawler, "Reward Systems," in J. R. Hackman and L. S. Suttle, eds., *Improving Life at Work: Behavioral Science Approaches to Organizational Change* (Goodyear, 1977).

25. E. E. Lawler and J. G. Rhode, *Information and Control in Organizations* (Goodyear, 1976).

ORGANIZATIONAL DEVELOPMENT

Beer, M. On gaining influence and power for OD. *Journal of Applied Behavioral Sciences*, 1976, *12*, 45–51.

Benne, K., & Birnbaum, M. Principles of changing. In W. G. Bennis, K. Benne, & R. Chin (Eds.), *The planning of change*. New York: Holt, Rinehart & Winston, 1969.

Bennis, W. G. Unresolved problems facing organization development. *Business Quarterly*, 1969, *34* (4), 80–84.

Burke, W. W. Organization development in transition. *Journal of Applied Behavioral Sciences*, 1976, *12*, 22–43.

Burns, T., & Stalker, G. M. *The management of innovation*. London: Tavistock, 1961.

Cobb, A. T. *Political planning and organizational innovation*. Paper presented at the annual meeting of the Academy of Management, Orlando, Florida, August 1977.

Cyert, R. M., & March, J. G. *A behavioral theory of the firm*. Engelwood Cliffs, N.J.: Prentice-Hall, 1964.

French, W., Bell, C., & Zawacki, R. Mapping the territory. In W. French, C. Bell, & R. Zawacki (Eds.), *Organization development: Theory, practice, and research*. Plano, Tex.: Business Publications, 1978, 5–12.

Friedlander, F. OD reaches adolescence: An exploration of its underlying values. *Journal of Applied Behavioral Science*, 1976, *12*, 7–22.

Friedlander, F., & Brown, L. D. Organization development. In M. Rosenzweig & L. Porter (Eds.), *Annual review of psychology*. Palo Alto, Calif.: Annual Reviews, 1974, 313–41.

Guest, R., Hersey, P., & Blanchard, D. *Organizational change through effective leadership*. Englewood Cliffs, N.J.: Prentice-Hall, 1977.

Harrison, R. When power conflicts trigger team spirit. In W. French, C. Bell, & R. Zawacki (Eds.), 1978, 158–64.

Huse, E. F. *Organization development and change*. New York: West, 1980.

Lawrence, P., & Lorsch, J. *Organization and environment*. Boston: Harvard University Graduate School of Business Administration, 1967.

Leavitt, H. J. Applied organizational change in industry: Structural, technological, and humanistic approaches. In J. C. March (Ed.), *Handbook of organizations*. Skokie, Ill.: Rand McNally, 1965, 1144–1170.

Lewin, K., Lippitt, R., & White, R. Patterns of aggressive behavior in experimentally created "social climates." *Journal of Social Psychology*, 1939, *10*, 271–99.

Likert, R. *New patterns of management*. New York: McGraw-Hill, 1961.

Likert, R. *The human organization: Its management and value*. New York: McGraw-Hill, 1967.

MacCrimmon, K., & Taylor, R. N. Decision making and problem solving. In M. Dunnette (Ed.), *Handbook of industrial and organizational psychology*. Skokie, Ill.: Rand McNally, 1976, 1397–453.

March, J. G. The business firm as a political coalition. *Journal of Politics*, 1962, *24*, 662–78.

March, J. G., & Simon, H. *Organizations*. New York: John Wiley & Sons, 1958.

Margulies, N., & Raia, A. P. *Conceptual foundations of organizational development*. New York: McGraw-Hill, 1978.

Mayes, B. T., & Allen, R. Toward a definition of organizational politics. *Academy of Management Review*, 1977, *2*, 672–78.

McGregor, D. *The human side of enterprise*. New York: McGraw-Hill, 1960.

National Training Laboratories Institute. *1980 programs*. Arlington, Va.: NTL Institute, 1980.

Perrow, C. The short and glorious history of organizational theory. In H. Tosi & W. C. Hamner (Eds.), *Organizational behavior and management*. Chicago: St. Clair, 1977, 8–19.

Pettigrew, A. M. Toward a political theory of organizational intervention. *Human Relations*, 1975, *28*, 191–208.

Schein, E. *Organizational psychology*. Englewood Cliffs, N.J.: Prentice-Hall, 1972.

Schein, V. Political strategies for implementing changes. *Group & Organization Studies*, 1977, *2*, 42–48.

Selznick, P. *TVA and the grass roots*. Berkeley: University of California Press, 1949.

Strauss, G. Some notes on power equalization. In H. J. Leavitt (Ed.), *The social science of organizations*. Englewood Cliffs, N.J.: Prentice-Hall, 1963.

Thompson, J. D. *Organizations in action*. New York: McGraw-Hill, 1967.

CHAPTER 13

REFERENCES

1. Robert A. Sutermeister, *People and Productivity*, 3d ed. (New York: McGraw-Hill Book Company, 1976), 27.

2. J. R. Hackman and E. E. Lawler, III, "Employee Reactions to Job Characteristics" in W. E. Scott and L. L. Cummings, eds. *Readings in Organizational Behavior and Human Performance* (Homewood, Ill.: Richard D. Irwin, Inc., 1973), 231.

3. Keith Davis, "Low Productivity? Try Improving the Social Environment," *Business Horizons* (June 1980):27–29.

4. Glenn H. Matthews, "Run Your Business or Build an Organization?" *Harvard Business Review* (March–April 1984):34ff.

5. Edward E. Lawler, III and Gerald E. Ledford, Jr., "Productivity and the Quality of Work Life," *National Productivity Review* (Winter 1981–82):23–36.

6. William B. Werther, Jr., "Productivity Improvement Through People," *Arizona Business* (February 1981):14–19.

7. Edward E. Lawler, "Strategies for Improving the Quality of Work Life," *American Psychologist* (May 1982):486–493; see also William Fox, "Limits to the Use of Consultative-Participative Management," *California Management Review* (Winter 1977):17–22.

8. Rosabeth Moss Kanter, "Shaping Corporate Change," *Productivity Brief 35* (April 1984):2–8.

9. Daniel Yankelovich, "The New Psychological Contracts at Work," *Psychology Today* (May 1978):46–50.

10. Richard E. Walton and Leonard A. Schlesinger, "Do Supervisors Thrive in Participative Work Systems?" *Organizational Dynamics* (Winter 1979):24–38.

11. Frank Shipper, "Quality Circles Using Small Group Formation," *Training and Development Journal* (May 1983):80ff; see also Ralph Barra, *Putting Quality Circles to Work* (New York: McGraw-Hill Book Company, 1983).

IMPROVEMENT

1. *How to Involve Employees in Productivity Improvement* (Houston: American Productivity Center, 1979), pp. 6/3–6/18, 9/1–9/4, 12/1–12/16.

2. James D. Hodgson, *The Wondrous Working World of Japan* (Washington, D.C.: American Enterprise Institute, 1978).

3. Peter F. Drucker, "The Price of Success: Japan Revisited," *Across the Board*, August, 1978, p. 30.

4. Kyonosuke Ibe, "It Took the Japanese to Build Japan," *Business Week*, October 6, 1980, p. 17.

5. *"How IBM Avoids Layoffs Through Retraining,"* *Business Week*, November 10, 1975, pp. 110, 112.

6. Hiroshi Tanaka, "The Japanese Method of Preparing Today's Graduate to Become Tomorrow's Manager," *Personnel Journal*, February, 1980, pp. 109–112.

7. Thomas J. Peters, "Putting Excellence into Management," *Business Week*, July 21, 1980, pp. 196–197, 200, 205.

8. "Japanese Managers Tell How Their System Works," *Fortune*, November, 1977, p. 127.

9. *Ibid*, p. 130.

CHAPTER 14

REFERENCES

1. Douglas McGregor, "The Scanlon Plan through a Psychologist's Eyes," in *The Scanlon Plan: A Frontier in Labor-Management Cooperation*. Frederick G. Lesieur, ed. (Cambridge, Mass.: The MIT Press, 1958), 98.

2. *Ibid.*, 99.

3. Based on personal interviews by the author with executives in Lincoln Electric Company.

4. Carla O'Dell, "Sharing the Productivity Payoff," *Productivity Brief #24* (Houston, Texas: American Productivity Center). Undated.

5. Adapted from a framework developed by the American Productivity Center of Houston, Texas.

6. Carla O'Dell, *Gainsharing: Involvement, Incentives, and Productivity* (New York, AMACOM, 1981), 17.

7. Stephen Solomon, "How a Whole Company Earned Itself a Roman Holiday," *Fortune* (January 15, 1979):80–83.

8. O'Dell, 1981, 8.

9. "Productivity Sharing Programs: *United States General Accounting Office), Report AFMD–81–22* (March 3, 1981):6–7.

10. Many publications listing statistics and case histories are available from the Profit Sharing Research Foundation, 1718 Sherman Avenue, Evanston, Illinois 60201. Bert Metzger, president.

11. William A. Ruch and James C. Hershauer, *Factors Affecting Worker Productivity* (Tempe, Arizona: Bureau of Business and Economic Research, Arizona State University, 1974).

12. Frederick G. Lesieur, ed., *The Scanlon Plan: A Frontier in Labor Management Cooperation* (Cambridge, Mass.: The MIT Press, 1958).

13. Information on the Rucker Plan is available from the Eddy-Rucker-Nickels Company, 4 Brattle Street, Cambridge, Massachusetts 02138.

CHAPTER 15

REFERENCES

1. Daniel H. Gray, "Organizational Productivity: The Human Dimension." Unpublished paper (Boston, Mass.: Arthur D. Little, Inc.).

2. William A. Ruch, "Your Key to Planning for Profits." *Productivity Brief #6* (Houston, Texas: American Productivity Center, October 1981).

3. Everett E. Adam, Jr., James C. Hershauer, and William A. Ruch, *Productivity and Quality* (Englewood Cliffs, NJ: Prentice-Hall, Inc., 1981).

4. *Ibid.*

5. William A. Ruch and William B. Werther, Jr., "Productivity Strategies at TRW." *National Productivity Review* 2, no. 2 (Spring 1983):117 (included as a reading in Chapter 19).

6. Samir K. Ghose and Thomas R. Paskert, "A Better Way to Measure Productivity" *The TRW Manager* 1, no. 4 (January 1984):20–21.

7. M. Ali Chaudry, "Projecting Productivity to the Bottom Line" *Productivity Brief #18* (Houston, Texas: American Productivity Center, October 1982):2.

MEASUREMENT AT FIRM LEVEL

1. See Fabricant [1], p. 24 (emphasis supplied).

2. See Gordon and Shillinglaw [3], pp. 321–2 (emphasis supplied).

3. If time had permitted, it would have been possible to develop a more accurate set of equipment deflators from company records. Generally, it is believed that specific deflators unique to each company can be calculated.

CHAPTER 16

REFERENCES

1. Irving Bluestone, "QWL Warms Up the Climate for Negotiation," *The Pulse Report* (June 1983):3.

2. John Kirkwood, "Press Demonstrates Lack of Understanding of Cooperative Efforts," *The Pulse Report* (November 1983):4–5.

3. David Lewin, "Collective Bargaining and the Quality of Work Life," *Organizational Dynamics* (Autumn 1981):37–53.

4. Sam Camens, "Steel—An Industry at the Crossroads," *Productivity Brief 17* (September 1982):2–7; see also Jeremy Main, "Anatomy of an Auto-Plant Rescue," *Fortune* (April 4, 1983):108–113.

5. William D. Todor and Dan R. Dalton, "Union Steward: A Little Known Actor with a Very Big Part," *Industrial Management* (September–October 1983):7–11.

6. Lewin, *op. cit.*

7. *Ibid.*

8. John Hoerr, "Why Job Security Is More Important than Income Security," *Business Week* (November 21, 1983):86.

9. Daniel F. Burton, Jr., and Sylvia Ann Hewlett, "Labor-Management Relations and Productivity: A Framework for Success," *National Productivity Review* (Spring 1983):185–194.

10. Robert B. McKersie and Janice A. Klein, "Productivity: The Industrial Relations Connection," *National Productivity Review* (Winter 1983–84):26–35.

11. George W. Bohlander, "Fair Representation: Not Just a Union Problem," *Personnel Administrator* (March 1980):36–40, 82.

12. John Hoerr, "Collective Bargaining Is in Danger without Labor-Law Reform," *Business Week* (July 16, 1984):29; see also "NLRB Rulings That Are Inflaming Labor Relations," *Business Week* (June 11, 1984):122–127, 130.

13. William L. Batt, Jr. and Edgar Weinberg, "Labor-Management Cooperation Today," *Harvard Business Review* (January–February 1978):96–104; see also William B. Werther, Jr., "Reducing Grievances through Effective Contract Administration," *Labor Law Journal* (April, 1984):211–216.

INDUSTRIAL RELATIONS

1. This article is a summary of the total report that is being published as chapter 6 of *Stimulation of U.S. Productivity Growth*. William J. Baumol and Kenneth McLennan, eds. (New York: Oxford University Press, 1984). (Used with the permission of the Committee for Economic Development and Oxford University Press. Copyright © 1984 by Committee for Economic Development.)

2. The majority of the responses are from Fortune 500 companies spread across manufacturing, communications, and service industries. Of the sixty-one plant respondents, forty are unionized and twenty-three are located in the northeast. They range in plant size from 27 to 17,500 employees and in age of facility from 4 to 100 years.

3. See "Quality Control Circle Activities and the Suggestion System," *Japan Labor Bulletin*, January 1, 1982, pp. 5–8.

4. See Leonard Greenhalgh and Robert B. McKersie, "Cost Effectiveness of Alternative Strategies for Cutback Management," *Public Administration Review*, 40(6):575–84. November–December 1980.

CHAPTER 17

REFERENCES

1. Peter F. Drucker, "Managing the Knowledge Worker," *The Wall Street Journal* (November 7, 1975).

2. Steven A. Leth, "White-Collar Productivity," *Productivity Brief #19*(Houston, TX: American Productivity Center, November 1982).

3. John Thackery, "White-Collar Blues," *Management Today* (March 1980): 94–101.

4. *Computer Conferences on Productivity: A Final Report for the White House Conference on Productivity* (Houston, TX: American Productivity Center, 1983.)

5. William A. Ruch, "The Measurement of White-Collar Productivity," *National Productivity Review* (Autumn 1982):416–426. (Included as one of the readings in this chapter.)

6. Kenneth A. Charon and James D. Schlumpf, "How to Measure Productivity of the Indirect Workforce," *Management Review* (August 1981):8–14.

7. David L. Rowe, "How Westinghouse Measures White-Collar Productivity," *Management Review* (November 1981):42–47.

8. Everett E. Adam, Jr., James C. Herschauer, and William A. Ruch, *Productivity and Quality* (Englewood Cliffs, NJ: Prentice-Hall, Inc., 1981).

9. Robert M. Ranftl, ed., *R&D Productivity*, 2d ed. (Culver City, CA: Hughes Aircraft Company, June 1978).

10. *Booz-Allen Multi-Client Study of Managerial/Professional Productivity* (New York: Booz-Allen & Hamilton, Inc., n.d.)

11. Val Olsen, *White-Collar Waste* (Englewood Cliffs, NJ: Prentice-Hall, Inc., 1981).

12. Frank M. Shipper and Robert A. Sniffin, "An Approach to Developing Measures of Staff Productivity," *Defense Management Journal* (Fourth Quarter, 1983): 17–21.

13. Carl G. Thor, "Putting Sales and Marketing on the Charts," *Productivity Brief #34* (Houston, TX: American Productivity Center, March 1984).

14. Benjamin Schneider, "The Service Organization: Climate is Critical," *Organizational Dynamics* (Autumn 1980):52–65. (Quote, p. 53.)

WHITE-COLLAR

1. Parts of this and the following sections are drawn from William A. Ruch, "Measuring Knowledge Worker Productivity," *Dimensions of Productivity Research*, John D. Hogan, ed. (Houston: American Productivity Center, 1980), pp. 339–58.

2. For more information on this system, see Kenneth A. Charon and James D. Schlumpf, "IBM's Common Staffing System: How to Measure Productivity of the Indirect Workforce," *Management Review* 70(8): 8–14, August 1981.

3. Parts of this section are adapted from William A. Ruch, "Total Firm Productivity Measurement," *Productivity Brief #6* (Houston: American Productivity Center, 1981).

4. A good place to start is with the annotated bibliography by William A. Ruch and Judith A. Ruch, "White-Collar Productivity," *Work in America Institute Studies in Productivity #23* (New York: Pergamon Press, 1982).

CHAPTER 18

REFERENCES

1. W. Edwards Deming, MIT Videotape series.

2. Everett E. Adam, Jr., James C. Hershauer, and William A. Ruch, "Measuring the Quality Dimension of Service Productivity" (Washington, D.C., National Science Foundation report number APR76–07140, January 1978).

3. W. Edwards Deming, "Improvement of Quality and Productivity Through Action by Management." *National Productivity Review* 1, no. 1 (Winter 1981–82):12–22.

4. J. M. Juran and F. M. Grynar, *Quality Planning and Analysis*, 2d ed. (New York: McGraw-Hill, 1980).

5. Philip B. Crosby, *Quality Is Free* (New York: McGraw-Hill Book Company, 1979).

6. "Productivity Growth: A Better Life for America." White House Conference on Productivity Report to the President of the United States, April, 1984.

7. "Interim Report of the American Productivity Center Computer Conference on Quality and Productivity for the White House Pre-Conference on Private Sector Initiatives," Pittsburgh, PA, August 2–4, 1983. Available from the American Productivity Center, Houston, TX.

CHAPTER 19

REFERENCES

1. Ruben F. Mettler, "Drawing a Bead on Our Competitiveness," *The TRW Manager* (October 1982):12.

2. John Belcher, "Giving Direction to Company Productivity Efforts," *Productivity Brief* 29 (Houston, Texas: American Productivity Center, 1983):2

3. *TRW and the 80s*, (Copyright TRW, Inc., 1980):1.

4. *Working Smarter . . . Together*. Produced for internal use by Beatrice Foods Co.

5. Paul S. Goodman, "Why Productivity Programs Fail: Reasons and Solutions," *National Productivity Review* (Autumn 1982).

6. William A. Ruch and William B. Werther, Jr., "The Chief Productivity Officer," *National Productivity Review* 4, no. 4 (Autumn 1985):397–410.

STRATEGIES AT TRW

1. "TRW and the 80s." Copyright TRW, Inc. 1980, p. 1.

2. TRW Data Book 1981 (internally published document).

3. Parts of this section are taken from the "Silverado Conference Report," an attachment to the 1981 annual report written by John Berendt, journalist, author, and editor for GEO magazine.

4. "TRW and the 80s," pp. 1–2.

5. *Ibid.*, pp. 15–16.

6. *Ibid.*, pp. 18–20.

Notes

The authors wish to express their thanks to Henry P. Conn for his cooperation and help in the research for this article.

CHAPTER 20

REFERENCES

1. Richard E. Kopelman, "Improving Productivity Through Objective Feedback: A Review of the Evidence," *National Productivity Review* 2, no. 1 (Winter 1982/83):54.

2. Viktor E. Frankl, *Man's Search for Meaning* (New York: Simon & Schuster, 1959, 1963), 179.

3. As quoted in Thomas J. Peters and Robert H. Waterman, Jr., *In Search of Excellence* (New York: Harper & Row, Publishers, 1982), 267.

4. "Associations Offer Information, Support to Productivity/QWL Managers," *The Pulse Report* (December 1982):1.

5. For another perspective, see Douglas McGregor, *The Professional Manager* (New York: McGraw-Hill Book Company, 1967), 151.

6. Kenneth E. Boulding, "General Systems Theory—The Skeleton of Science," *Management Science* (April 1956):197–208; see also James Grier Miller and Jessie Louise Miller, "Systems Science: An Emerging Interdisciplinary Field," *The Center Magazine* (September/October 1981):44–55.

7. Jay Hall, "Communication Revisited," *California Management Review* (May/June 1973):56–67.

8. Ralph G. Nichols, "Listening Is Good Business," *Management of Personnel Quarterly* (Winter 1962):2–9.

9. United Airlines, IBM, Hewlett Packard are examples cited by Peters and Waterman, *op. cit.* 122.

10. Jesse S. Nirenberg, "Communicating for Greater Insight and Persuasiveness," *Advanced Management Journal* (January 1967):82–87.

11. Terrence E. Deal and Allan A. Kennedy, "Rites and Rituals: Culture in Action," *Modern Office Procedures* (January 1983):12–14.

12. Kopelman, *op. cit.*

13. See, for example, "Computer Networks Offer New Potential for Productivity Improvement," *The Productivity Letter* (September 1983):1, 3.

14. Ibid. See also C. Jackson Grayson, "Productivity on Line," *Across the Board* (January 1984):30–35.

15. States L. Clawson and Carol Ann Meares, "Productivity Information: A Key to Competitiveness," *National Productivity Review* (Winter 1983/84):15–25.

16. *Ibid.*

17. "The National Productivity Network," *The Harvest* (February 1984):1–2.

18. Henry P. Conn, "Experienced Managers Need Leading-Edge Ideas," *The Pulse Report* (December 1982):2.

OBJECTIVE FEEDBACK

1. "At Emery Air Freight: Positive Reinforcement Boosts Performance," in Henry L. Tosi and W. Clay Hamner, (eds.), *Organizational Behavior and Management: A Contingency Approach* (Chicago: St. Clair Press, 1974), pp. 113–122. This article originally appeared in *Organizational Dynamics*, Winter 1973.

2. Everett E. Adam, Jr., "Behavior Modification in Quality Control," *Academy of Management Journal* 18(4):662–79, 1975.

3. Jay S. Kim and W. Clay Hamner, "Effect of Performance Feedback and Goal Setting on Productivity and Satisfaction in an Organizational Setting," *Journal of Applied Psychology* 61(1):48–57, 1976.

4. Robert Kreitner, William E. Reif, and Marvin Morris, "Measuring the Impact of Feedback on the Performance of Mental Health Technicians," *Journal of Organizational Behavior Management* 1(1):105–09, 1977.

5. Alex Runnion, Twila Johnson, and John McWhorter, "The Effects of Feedback and Reinforcement on Truck Turnaround Time in Materials Transportation," *Journal of Organizational Behavior Management* 1(2):110–17, 1978.

6. Gerald D. Emmert, "Measuring the Impact of Group Performance Feedback Versus Individual Performance Feedback in an Industrial Setting," *Journal of Organizational Behavior Management* 1(2):134–41, 1978.

7. Michael McCarthy, "Decreasing the Incidence of 'High Bobbins' in a Textile Spinning Department through a Group Feedback Procedure," *Journal of Organizational Behavior Management* 1(2):150–54 1978.

8. P. A. Lamal and A. Benfield, "The Effect of Self Monitoring on Job Tardiness and Percentage o Time Spent Working." *Journal of Organizational Behavior Management* 1(2):142–49, 1978.

9. H. Wayne Dick, "Increasing the Productivity of the Day Relief Textile Machine Operator," *Journal of Organizational Behavior Management* 2(1):45–57, 1978.

10. Alex Runnion, Jesse O. Watson, and John McWhorter, "Energy Savings in Interstate Transportation through Feedback and Reinforcement," *Journal of Organizational Behavior Management* 1(3):180–91, 1978.

11. L. Eldridge, S. Lemasters, and B. Szypot, "A Performance Feedback Intervention to Reduce Waste: Performance Data and Participant Responses," *Journal of Organizational Behavior Management* 1(4): 258–66, 178.

12. Albert Stoerzinger, James M. Johnston, Kim Pisor, and Craig Monroe, "Implementation and Evaluation of a Feedback System for Employees in a Salvage Operation," *Journal of Organizational Behavior Management* 1(4):268–80, 1978.

13. James L. Koch, "Effects of Goal Specificity and Performance Feedback to Work Groups on Peer Leadership, Performance, and Attitudes," *Human Relations* 32(10):819–40, 1979.

14. Craig E. Schneier and Robert Pernick, "Increasing Public Sector Productivity through Organization Behavior Modification: A Successful Application," paper presented at the 39th National Meeting of the Academy of Management (Atlanta), 1979, pp. 1–15.

15. Richard E. Kopelman, unpublished data, 1979.

16. Lucien Rhodes, "It Pays to be on Time," *Inc.*, June 1980, pp. 59–64.

17. John K. Milne and Stephen X. Doyle, "Rx for Ailing Bank Trust Departments," *The Bankers Magazine* 163(1):54–57, January/February 1980.

18. Donald M. Prue, Jon E. Krapfl, James C. Noah, Sherry Cannon, and Roger F. Maley, "Managing the Treatment Activities of State Hospital Staff," *Journal of Organizational Behavior Management* 2(3): 165–81, 1980.

19. Stephen A. Allen, "Aer Lingus—Irish (b)," (Boston: Intercollegiate Case Clearing House, 1976), case #9-477-640, pp. 1–20.

20. O. Robert Quilitch, "Using a Simple Feedback Procedure to Reinforce the Submission of Written Suggestions by Mental Health Employees," *Journal of Organizational Behavior Management* 1(2):155–63, 1978.

21. Gerald L. Shook, C. Merle Johnson, and William F. Uhlman, "The Effect of Response Effort Reduction, Group and Individual Feedback, and Reinforcement on Staff Performance," *Journal of Organizational Behavior Management* 1(3):206–15, 1978.

22. Beth Sulzer-Azaroff, "Behavioral Ecology and Accident Prevention," *Journal of Organizational Behavior Management* 2(1):11–44, 1978.

23. Robert L. Collins, Judi Komaki, and Stephen Temlock, "Behavioral Definition and Improvement of Customer Service in Retail Merchandising," paper presented at the 87th Annual Meeting of the American Psychological Association (New York), 1979, pp. 1–12.

24. Patrick McNees, Sharon W. Gilliam, John F. Schnelle, and Todd Risley, "Controlling Employee Theft through Time and Product Identification," *Journal of Organizational Behavior Management* 2(2):113–19, 1979.

25. Judi Komaki, Arlene T. Heinzmann, and Loralie Lawson, "Effect of Training and Feedback: Component Analysis of a Behavioral Safety Program," *Journal of Applied Psychology* 65(3):261–70, 1980.

26. Judi Komaki, Milton R. Blood, and Donna Holder, "Fostering Friendliness in a Fast Food Franchise," *Journal of Organizational Behavior Management* 2(3):151–64, 1980.

27. E. Scott Geller, Serena L. Eason, Jean A. Phillips, and Merle D. Pierson, "Interventions to Improve Sanitation During Food Preparation," *Journal of Organizational Behavior Management* 2(3):229–40, 1980.

Index

A

Abernathy, W., 177
Absenteeism, 383, 384
Achievement, in needs theory, 83
Acquisitions, impact of on management style, 19–21
Adam, E.E., Jr., 61, 399
Adams, J.S., 98
Adams, E.E., 144
Adams, J.S., 145
Adams-Webber, J.R., 210
Aer Lingus, 502
Affiliation, in needs theory, 83
Affirmative action. See Minorities; Women
Alderfer, C.P., 82, 129
Allen, R., 265
Allen-Bradley, 294
American Express, 296, 304, 305, 423
American Productivity Center, 18, 417–418, 490
American Productivity Management Association (APMA), 491
American Telephone and Telegraph Company, 86, 119, 124, 126, 225, 226, 345, 446
Anderson, D., 503–504
Andrasik, F., 140, 146
Arends, R.I., 212
Arends, J.H., 212
Argyris, C., 140, 210, 244, 246
Arizona State University Productivity Institute, 491
Armco, 423
Arthur Young and Company, 504
Ashcraft, L., 107
Assets, in Productivity Focus Models, 66
Atari, 227
Atkinson, J.W., 122
Atmosphere, in static versus innovative organizations, 213
Attitude surveys, as participation technique, 283
Attribution biases, in evaluations, 187–189, 194
Attribution theory, 187–189
Atwood Vacuum, 334–335
Automobile industry, 17, 37

B

Babcock and Wilcox, 296
Baldridge, J.V., 210, 212

Baltes, P.D., 213
Bandura, A., 99, 139
Bank of America, 464
Barron, F., 212
Barrows, J.C., 140
Baumgartel, H., 243
Beatrice Foods Company, 461
Beckhard, R., 243, 244
Beech Aircraft, 288, 294, 413
Beehr, T.A., 141
Beer, M., 234, 245, 266, 269
Behavior. See also Organizational behavior modification (OB Mod)
    effects of feedback on, 499–501
    measures of, 192–193
Behavioral models. See Models
Behavior observation scales (BOS), 193, 195–196
Belcher, J., 65–68, 460
Bell, C.H., Jr.
Bell, C.R., 214
Bell Labs, 228
Bell System. See American Telephone and Telegraph Company
Bendix, 283, 288
Benne, K., 210, 212, 265, 267
Bennis, W.G., 210, 212, 264, 266, 269–271
Berlew, D.E., 119, 124
Birnbaum, M., 265, 267
Bethlehem Steel, 374
B.F. Goodrich, 423
Bibliographies, 516
Blackman, S., 212
Blake, R.R., 201, 214
Blake-Mouton Managerial Grid, 201
Blanchard, D., 265
Bluestone, I., 175
Bonuses, 326
    basis of as factor in productivity, 208
Booz-Allen and Hamilton, Inc., 400
BOS. See Behavior observation scales (BOS)
Blowers, D.G., 210
Bowmar, 16–17
Brayfield, A.H., 89
Brown, L.D., 266
Buckholdt, D.R., 213